Macroeconomics

A Contemporary Introduction

7|e

William A. McEachern

Professor of Economics
University of Connecticut

THOMSON
SOUTH-WESTERN

Australia · Canada · Mexico · Singapore · Spain · United Kingdom · United States

THOMSON

SOUTH-WESTERN

Macroeconomics: A Contemporary Introduction, 7e

William A. McEachern

VP/Editorial Director:
Jack W. Calhoun

VP/Editor-in-Chief:
Dave Shaut

Sr. Acquisitions Editor:
Michael W. Worls

Sr. Developmental Editor:
Susanna C. Smart

Sr. Marketing Manager:
John Carey

Sr. Production Editor:
Elizabeth A. Shipp

Sr. Technology Project Editor:
Peggy Buskey

Web Coordinator:
Karen L. Schaffer

Sr. Manufacturing Coordinator:
Sandee Milewski

Photography Manager:
John Hill

Photography Researchers:
Sam Marshall & Rose Alcorn

Art Director:
Michelle Kunkler

Internal Designer:
Chris Miller

Cover Designer:
Diane Gliebe/Design Matters
Cincinnati, Ohio

Cover Image:
© Digital Vision, Inc.

Production House:
Pre-Press Company, Inc.

Printer:
CTPS

For permission to use material from
this text or product, contact us by
Tel (800) 730-2214
Fax (800) 730-2215
http://www.thomsonrights.com

For more information
contact South-Western,
5191 Natorp Boulevard,
Mason, Ohio, 45040.
Or you can visit our Internet site at:
http://www.swlearning.com

William A. McEachern began teaching large sections of economic principles when he joined the University of Connecticut in 1973. In 1980, he began offering teaching workshops around the country, and, in 1990, he created *The Teaching Economist*, a newsletter that focuses on making teaching more effective and more fun.

His research in public finance, public policy, and industrial organization has appeared in a variety of journals, including *Economic Inquiry, National Tax Journal, Journal of Industrial Economics, Quarterly Review of Economics and Finance, Southern Economic Journal, Kyklos,* and *Public Choice.* His books and monographs include *Managerial Control and Performance, School Finance Reform,* and *Tax-Exempt Property and Tax Capitalization in Metropolitan Areas.* He has also contributed chapters to edited volumes such as *Rethinking Economic Principles, Federal Trade Commission Vertical Restraint Cases,* and *Issues in Financing Connecticut Governments.*

Professor McEachern has advised federal, state, and local governments on policy matters and directed a bipartisan commission examining Connecticut's finances. He has been quoted in or written for publications such as the *New York Times, London Times, Wall Street Journal, Christian Science Monitor, Boston Globe, USA Today, Challenge Magazine, Connection, CBS MarketWatch.com,* and *Reader's Digest.* He has also appeared on *Now with Bill Moyers,* Voice of America, and National Public Radio.

In 1984, Professor McEachern won the University of Connecticut Alumni Association's Faculty Award for Distinguished Public Service and in 2000 won the Association's Faculty Excellence in Teaching Award. He is the only person in the university's history to receive both awards.

He was born in Portsmouth, N.H., earned an undergraduate degree with honors from College of the Holy Cross, served three years as an Army officer, and earned an M.A. and Ph.D. from the University of Virginia.

To Pat

Brief Contents

PART 1

Introduction to Economics

1	The Art and Science of Economic Analysis	1
2	Some Tools of Economic Analysis	27
3	Economic Decision Makers	46
4	Demand and Supply Analysis	64

PART 2

Fundamentals of Macroeconomics

5	Introduction to Macroeconomics	89
6	Productivity and Growth	109
7	Measuring the Economy and the Circular Flow	131
8	Unemployment and Inflation	153
9	Aggregate Expenditure Components	176
10	Aggregate Expenditure and Aggregate Demand	198
11	Aggregate Supply	220

PART 3

Fiscal and Monetary Policy

12	Fiscal Policy	240
13	Money and the Financial System	261
14	Banking and the Money Supply	284
15	Monetary Theory and Policy	305
16	The Policy Debate: Active or Passive?	325
17	Federal Budgets and Public Policy	348

PART 4

International Macroeconomics

| 18 | International Finance | 367 |

PART 1

Introduction to Economics

1. The Art and Science of Economic Analysis
2. Some Tools of Economic Analysis
3. Economic Decision Makers
4. Demand and Supply Analysis

PART 2

Fundamentals of Macroeconomics

5. Introduction to Macroeconomics ... 109
6. Productivity and Growth ... 139
7. Tracking the Economy and the Circular Flow ... 158
8. Unemployment and Inflation ... 182
9. Aggregate Expenditure Components ... 179
10. Aggregate Expenditure and Aggregate Demand ... 196
11. Aggregate Supply ... 220

PART 3

Fiscal and Monetary Policy

12. Fiscal Policy ... 298
13. Money and the Financial System ... 261
14. Banking and the Money Supply ... 284
15. Monetary Theory and Policy ... 306
16. The Policy Debate: Active or Passive ... 327
17. Federal Finances and Public Policy ... 349

PART 4

International Macroeconomics

18. International Finance

Contents

Part 1

Introduction to Economics

CHAPTER 1

The Art and Science of Economic Analysis 1

**The Economic Problem:
Scarce Resources, Unlimited Wants 2**

Resources 2 | Goods and Services 3 | Economic Decision Makers 4 | A Simple Circular-Flow Model 4 |

The Art of Economic Analysis 6

Rational Self-Interest 6 | Choice Requires Time and Information 6 | Economic Analysis Is Marginal Analysis 7 | Microeconomics and Macroeconomics 7 |

The Science of Economic Analysis 8

The Role of Theory 8 | The Scientific Method 8 | Normative Versus Positive 10 | Economists Tell Stories 10 | *Case Study: A Yen for Vending Machines 11* | Predicting Average Behavior 12 | Some Pitfalls of Faulty Economic Analysis 12 | If Economists Are So Smart, Why Aren't They Rich? 13 | *Case Study: College Major and Career Earnings 13*

Appendix: Understanding Graphs 20

Drawing Graphs 21 | The Slopes of Straight Lines 22 | The Slope, Units of Measurement, and Marginal Analysis 22 | The Slopes of Curved Lines 24 | Line Shifts 25

CHAPTER 2

Some Tools of Economic Analysis 27

Choice and Opportunity Cost 28

Opportunity Cost 28 | *Case Study: The Opportunity Cost of College 28* | Opportunity Cost Is Subjective 29 | Sunk Cost and Choice 30

Comparative Advantage, Specialization, and Exchange 31

The Law of Comparative Advantage 31 | Absolute Advantage Versus Comparative Advantage 31 | Specialization and Exchange 32 | Division of Labor and Gains from Specialization 33 | *Case Study: Specialization Abound 33*

The Economy's Production Possibilities 34

Efficiency and the Production Possibilities Frontier 34 | Inefficient and Unattainable Production 35 | The Shape of the Production Possibilities Frontier 35 | What Can Shift the Production Possibilities Frontier? 36 | What Can We Learn from the PPF? 37 | Three Questions Every Economic System Must Answer 38

Economic Systems 39

Pure Capitalism 39 | Pure Command System 40 | Mixed and Transitional Economies 41 | Economies Based on Custom or Religion 41

CHAPTER 3

Economic Decision Makers 46

The Household 47

The Evolution of the Household 47 | Households Maximize Utility 47 | Households as Resource Suppliers 48 | Households as Demanders of Goods and Services 49

The Firm 49

The Evolution of the Firm 49 | Types of Firms 50 | Nonprofit Institutions 52 | Why Does Household Production Still Exist? 52 | *Case Study: The Electronic Cottage 53*

The Government 53

The Role of Government 54 | Government's Structure and Objectives 55 | The Size and Growth of Government 56 | Sources of Government Revenue 57 | Tax Principles and Tax Incidence 57

The Rest of the World 58

International Trade 59 | Exchange Rates 60 | Trade Restrictions 60 | *Case Study: Wheels of Fortune 60*

CHAPTER 4

Demand and Supply Analysis 64

Demand 65

The Law of Demand 65 | The Demand Schedule and Demand Curve 66 | Shifts of the Demand Curve 68 | Changes in

Consumer Income 68 | Changes in the Prices of Related Goods 68 | Changes in Consumer Expectations 69 | Changes in the Number or Composition of Consumers 70 | Changes in Consumer Tastes 70

Supply 70

The Supply Schedule and Supply Curve 71 | Shifts of the Supply Curve 72 | Changes in Technology 72 | Changes in the Prices of Relevant Resources 72 | Changes in the Prices of Alternative Goods 72 | Changes in Producer Expectations 73 | Changes in the Number of Producers 73 | Demand and Supply Create A Market 74 | Markets 74 | Market Equilibrium 74

Changes lin Equilibrium Price and Quantity 76

Shifts of the Demand Curve 76 | Shifts of the Supply Curve 77 | Simultaneous Shifts of Demand and Supply Curves 79 | *Case Study: The Market for Professional Basketball 80*

Disequilibrium 81

Price Floors 81 | Price Ceilings 81 | *Case Study: The Toy Business Is Not Child's Play 83*

Part 2

Fundamentals of Macroeconomics

CHAPTER 5

Introduction to Macroeconomics 89

The National Economy 90

What's Special About the National Economy? 90 | The Human Body and the U.S. Economy 91 | Knowledge and Performance 91

Economic Fluctuations and Growth 92

U.S. Economic Fluctuations 92 | *Case Study: The Global Economy 94* | Leading Economic Indicators 96

Aggregate Demand and Aggregate Supply 96

Aggregate Output and the Price Level 96 | The Aggregate Demand Curve 97 | The Aggregate Supply Curve 98 | Equilibrium 98

A Short History of the U.S. Economy 99

The Great Depression and Before 99 | The Age of Keynes: After the Great Depression to the Early 1970s 100 | The Great Stagflation: 1973 to 1980 102 | Experience Since 1980 103 | *Case Study: Over Seven Decades of Real GDP and Price Levels 104*

CHAPTER 6

Productivity and Growth 109

Theory of Productivity and Growth 110

Growth and the Production Possibilities Frontier 110 | What Is Productivity? 112 | Labor Productivity 112 | The Per-Worker

Production Function 113 | Technological Change 114 | Rules of the Game 115

Productivity and Growth in Practice 115

Education and Economic Development 116 | U.S. Labor Productivity 117 | Slowdown and Rebound in Productivity Growth 118 | *Case Study: Computers and Productivity Growth 119* | Output per Capita 120 | International Comparisons 120

Other Issues of Technology and Growth 122

Does Technological Change Lead to Unemployment? 123 | Research and Development 123 | Do Economies Converge 125 | Industrial Policy 126 | *Case Study: Picking Technological Winners 126*

CHAPTER 7

Measuring the Economy and the Circular Flow 131

The Product of a Nation 132

National Income Accounts 132 | GDP Based on the Expenditure Approach 133 | GDP Based on the Income Approach 134

The Circular Flow of Income and Expenditure 135

The Income Half of the Circular Flow 135 | The Expenditure Half of the Circular Flow 137 | Leakages Equal Injections 138

Limitations of National Income Accounting 138

Some Production Is Not Included in GDP 138 | Leisure, Quality, and Variety 139 | *Case Study: Tracking a $12 Trillion*

Economy 139 | What's Gross about Gross Domestic Product? 140 | GDP Does Not Reflect All Costs 140 | GDP and Economic Welfare 141

Accounting for Price Changes 141

Price Indexes 141 | Consumer Price Index 142 | Problems with the CPI 143 | The GDP Price Index 144 | Moving from Fixed Weights to Chain Weights 144 | *Case Study: Computer Prices and GDP Estimation 145*

Appendix: National Income Accounts 150

National Income 150 | Personal and Disposable Income 150 | Summary of National Income Accounts 150 | Summary Income Statement of the Economy 151

CHAPTER 8

Unemployment and Inflation 153

Unemployment 154

Measuring Unemployment 154 | Labor Force Participation Rate 156 | Unemployment over Time 156 | Unemployment in Various Groups 156 | Unemployment Varies Across Regions 157 | Sources of Unemployment 160 | The Meaning of Full Employment 161 | Unemployment Compensation 162 | International Comparisons of Unemployment 162 | Problems with Official Unemployment Figures 163

Inflation 163

Case Study: Hyperinflation in Brazil 164 | Two Sources of Inflation 165 | A Historical Look at Inflation and the Price Level 166 | Anticipated Versus Unanticipated Inflation 167 | The Transaction Costs of Variable Inflation 167 | Inflation Obscures Relative Price Changes 168 | Inflation Across Metropolitan Areas 168 | Inflation Across Countries 168 | Inflation and Interest Rates 169 | Why Is Inflation Unpopular? 171 | *Case Study: Poor King Coal 164*

CHAPTER 9

Aggregate Expenditure Components 176

Consumption 177

A First Look at Consumption and Income 177 | The Consumption Function 179 | Marginal Propensities to Consume and to Save 179 | MPC, MPS, and the Slope of the Consumption and Saving Functions 180 | Nonincome Determinants of Consumption 181 | *Case Study: The Life-Cycle Hypothesis 183*

Investment 184

The Demand for Investment 184 | From Micro to Macro 186 | Planned Investment and the Economy's Income 187 |

Nonincome Determinants of Planned Investment 187 | *Case Study: Investment Varies Much More than Consumption 188*

Government 189

Government Purchase Function 190 | Net Taxes 190

Net Exports 190

Net Exports and Income 190 | Nonincome Determinants of Net Exports 191

Composition of Aggregate Expenditure 191

Appendix: Variable Net Exports 196

Net Exports and Income 196 | Shifts of Net Exports 196

CHAPTER 10

Aggregate Expenditure and Aggregate Demand 198

Aggregate Expenditure and Income 199

The Components of Aggregate Expenditure 199 | Real GDP Demanded 201 | What If Planned Spending Exceeds Real GDP? 202 | What If Real GDP Exceeds Planned Spending? 202

The Simple Spending Multiplier 203

An Increase in Planned Spending 203 | Using the Simple Spending Multiplier 205 | *Case Study: Fear of Flying 206*

The Aggregate Demand Curve 207

A Higher Price Level 207 | A Lower Price Level 209 | The Multiplier and Shifts in Aggregate Demand 209 | *Case Study: Falling Consumption Triggers Japan's Recession 211*

Appendix A: Variable Net Exports Revisited 215

Net Exports and the Spending Multiplier 216 | A Change in Autonomous Spending 216

Appendix B: The Algebra of Income and Expenditure 218

The Aggregate Expenditure Line 218 | A More General Form of Income and Expenditure 218 | Varying Net Exports 219

CHAPTER 11

Aggregate Supply 220

Aggregate Supply in the Short Run 221

Labor and Aggregate Supply 221 | Potential Output and the Natural Rate of Unemployment 222 | Actual Price Level

Higher than Expected 222 | Why Costs Rise When Output Exceeds Potential 223 | An Actual Price Level Lower than Expected 224 | The Short-Run Aggregate Supply Curve 224

From the Short Run to the Long Run 225

Closing an Expansionary Gap 225 | Closing a Contractionary Gap 227 | Tracing Potential Output 229 | Wage Flexibility and Employment 229 | *Case Study: U.S. Output Gaps and Wage Flexibility 231*

Changes in Aggregate Supply 232

Increases in Aggregate Supply 232 | Decreases in Aggregate Supply 234 | *Case Study: Why Is Unemployment So High in Europe? 235*

Part **3**

Fiscal and Monetary Policy

CHAPTER 12

Fiscal Policy 240

Theory of Fiscal Policy 241

Fiscal Policy Tools 241 | Changes in Government Purchases 241 | Changes in Net Taxes 242

Including Aggregate Supply 244

Discretionary Fiscal Policy to Close a Contractionary Gap 244 | Discretionary Fiscal Policy to Close an Expansionary Gap 246 | The Multiplier and the Time Horizon 247

The Evolution of Fiscal Policy 247

The Great Depression and World War II 247 | Automatic Stabilizers 248 | From the Golden Age to Stagflation 249 | Fiscal Policy and the Natural Rate of Unemployment 250 | Lags in Fiscal Policy 250 | Discretionary Fiscal Policy and Permanent Income 251 | The Feedback Effects of Fiscal Policy on Aggregate Supply 251 | U.S. Budget Deficits of the 1980s and 1990s 252 | *Case Study: The Supply-Side Experiment 252* | *Case Study: Discretionary Fiscal Policy and Presidential Elections 253* | Balancing the Federal Budget—Temporarily 254

Appendix: The Algebra of Demand-Side Equilibrium 258

Net Tax Multiplier 258 | The Multiplier When Both G and NT Change 258 | The Multiplier with a Proportional Income Tax 258 | Including Variable Net Exports 259

CHAPTER 13

Money and the Financial System 261

The Evolution of Money 262

Barter and the Double Coincidence of Wants 262 | The Earliest Money and Its Functions 262 | Desirable Qualities of Money 264 | Coins 264 | Money and Banking 265 | Paper Money 266 | The Value of Money 267 | When Money Performs Poorly 267 | *Case Study: When Monetary Systems Break Down 268*

Financial Institutions in the United States 269

Commercial Banks and Thrifts 269 | The Birth of the Fed 269 | Powers of the Federal Reserve System 270 | Banking During the Great Depression 271 | Roosevelt's Reforms 272 | Banks Lost Deposits When Inflation Increased 274 | Bank Deregulation 274 | Savings Banks on the Ropes 275 | Commercial Banks Were Also Failing 276 | U.S. Banking Structure 277 | *Case Study: Banking Troubles in Japan 280*

CHAPTER 14

Banking and the Money Supply 284

Money Aggregates 285

The Narrow Definition of Money: M1 285 | *Case Study: Faking It 286* | Broader Money Aggregates 287 | Credit Cards and Debit Cards: What's the Difference? 288

How Banks Work 289

Banks Are Financial Intermediaries 289 | Starting a Bank 290 | Reserve Accounts 291 | Liquidity Versus Profitability 291

How Banks Create Money 292

Creating Money Through Excess Reserves 292 | A Summary of the Rounds 295 | Reserve Requirements and Money Expansion 295 | Limitations on Money Expansion 296 | Multiple Contraction of the Money Supply 296 | *Case Study: Banking on the Net 297*

The Fed's Tools of Monetary Control 298

Open-Market Operations and the Federal Funds Rate 299 | The Discount Rate 299 | Reserve Requirements 300 | The Fed Is a Money Machine 300

CHAPTER 15

Monetary Theory and Policy 305

The Demand and Supply of Money 306

The Demand for Money 306 | Money Demand and Interest
Rates 307 | The Supply of Money and the Equilibrium Interest
Rate 308

**Money and Aggregate Demand in the Short Run
309**

Interest Rates and Planned Investment 309 | Adding Short-Run
Aggregate Supply 310 | *Case Study: Targeting the Federal Funds
Rate 312*

**Money and Aggregate Demand in the Long Run
314**

The Equation of Exchange 314 | The Quantity Theory of
Money 315 | What Determines the Velocity of Money? 316 |
How Stable Is Velocity? 316 | *Case Study: The Money Supply
and Inflation Around the World 318*

Targets for Monetary Policy 319

Contrasting Policies 319 | Targets Before 1982 321 | Targets
After 1982 321

CHAPTER 16

The Policy Debate: Active or Passive? 325

Active Policy Versus Passive Policy 326

Closing a Contractionary Gap 326 | Closing an Expansionary
Gap 328 | Problems with Active Policy 328 | The Problem of
Lags 329 | A Review of Policy Perspectives 331 | *Case Study:
Active Versus Passive Presidential Candidates 331*

The Role of Expectations 332

Monetary Policy and Expectations 333 | Anticipating Monetary
Policy 334 | Policy Credibility 335 | *Case Study: Central Bank
Independence and Price Stability 336*

Policy Rules Versus Discretion 337

Limitations on Discretion 338 | Rules and Rational
Expectations 338

The Phillips Curve 339

The Short-Run Phillips Curve 341 | The Long-Run Phillips
Curve 341 | The Natural Rate Hypothesis 343 | Evidence of
the Phillips Curve 343

CHAPTER 17

Federal Budgets and Public Policy 348

The Federal Budget Process 349

The Presidential and Congressional Roles 350 | Problems with
the Federal Budget Process 350 | Possible Budget Reforms 351

The Fiscal Impact of the Federal Budget 351

The Rationale for Deficits 352 | Budget Philosophies and
Deficits 352 | Federal Deficits Since the Birth of the Nation
353 | Why Have Deficits Persisted? 354 | Deficits, Surpluses,
Crowding Out, and Crowding In 354 | The Twin Deficits 355 |
The Short-Lived Budget Surplus 355 | *Case Study: Reforming
Social Security and Medicare 357* | The Relative Size of the
Public Sector in the United States 358

The National Debt 358

International Perspective on Public Debt 359 | Interest on the
National Debt 360 | Who Bears the Burden of the Debt? 361 |
Crowding Out and Capital Formation 362 | *Case Study: An
Intergenerational View of Deficits and Debt 363*

Part **4**

International Macroeconomics

CHAPTER 18

International Finance 367

Balance of Payments 368

International Economic Transactions 368 | The Merchandise
Trade Balance 368 | The Balance on Goods and Services 370 |

Unilateral Transfers 370 | The Capital Account 371 | Deficits
and Surpluses 371

Foreign Exchange Rates and Markets 373

Foreign Exchange 373 | The Demand for Foreign Exchange
374 | The Supply of Foreign Exchange 374 | Determining the
Exchange Rate 375 | Arbitrageurs and Speculators 375 |

Purchasing Power Parity 377 | *Case Study: The Big Mac Price Index 377* | Flexible Exchange Rates 379 | Fixed Exchange Rates 379

Development of the International Monetary System 379

The Bretton Woods Agreement 380 | The Demise of the Bretton Woods System 380 | The Current System: Managed Float 381 | *Case Study: The Asian Contagion 381*

Glossary 385

Index 393

The Leader in Technology

McEachern's *Economics: A Contemporary Introduction, 7e* has once again raised the bar for Economics resources and builds upon its tradition of innovation by again focusing its newest edition around technological integration. Year after year, this text has consistently been recognized as a leader in technological advances in the Economics classroom by utilizing the most current high-tech resources. Previously, in the Fourth Edition of this text, McEachern integrated the World Wide Web for the very first time, and in the Fifth Edition he introduced multimedia graphing exercises, thus proving the effectiveness and necessity of technology in the classroom. The Sixth Edition took the market by storm, introducing *Xtra!*, a program that assessed students' strengths and provided a unique tutorial system based upon each individual student's needs. Most recently, in the new Seventh Edition, we are proud to introduce the latest innovation in Economics instruction: *Homework Xpress!*, a program that simplifies the process of assigning and grading homework and increases students' comprehension of material through additional review and hands-on learning with practice questions and exercises.

Beyond this, a variety of Economic programs and Web exercises are integrated throughout this updated text, enhancing its effectiveness by engaging today's technologically savvy students with the most up-to-date methods of instruction. This consistent technological integration results in a deeper and richer understanding of the material that comes not just from reading the text, but also from seeing, from hearing, and from doing.

Would you like to be able to assign homework directly from your textbook and have it graded and downloaded to your grade book automatically?

McEachern once again leads the pack in innovation — with this edition he provides a complete homework management solution with **Homework Xpress!**. And, although this beneficial technology is fully integrated into the text, its use is completely optional for those who prefer a more traditional style of instruction.

Homework Management Solution!

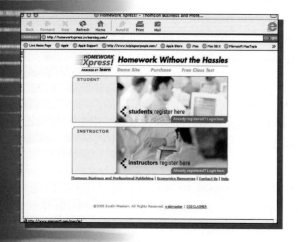

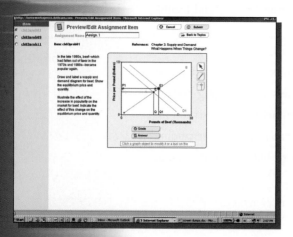

Finally, there is a tool to cut the inefficiencies out of homework—for both instructors and students! Instructors realize the value of assigned homework, but with increasingly demanding schedules, they have little time to grade it—especially frequent assignments. Students, in turn, are also pulling heavy loads and often require concrete incentives like graded assignments to encourage them to invest extra time in studying. **Homework Xpress!** helps both instructors and students make the most efficient use of their time. This easy-to-use, text-specific homework management system allows students to complete end-of-chapter exercises via the Internet. This innovative program alleviates the administrative burden of assigning and grading homework, and makes it simple to give assignments as frequently as you like, while tracking students' results in an integrated grade book. **Homework Xpress!** allows instructors to easily assess whether students have adequately prepared for class, identify potential problem areas to cover in class, and—with students well grounded in the basics—spend more class time covering higher-level or abstract concepts.

Assignment Material

Includes *text-specific* problems and exercises that are derived from and correlate closely with the book's end-of-chapter material. Instructors may pick and choose the assignments they wish to use, and student results are automatically recorded in a grade book.

Concept Practice and Review Activities

Students can access a wide range of practice and review material from a multimedia library of both book-specific and generic elements to build a customized teaching and learning solution. Students can go through a complete review of the material and get feedback on their preparation before they try to do the graded assignments.

Graphing Tools

Homework Xpress! offers graphing problems without the grading hassles through its unique "Sketch It" tool, which gives students freehand graphing problems and checks them automatically. Sketch It problems are provided both as Assignment and as Concept Practice and Review exercises.

Current Events

To help you easily incorporate current events into your classroom without having to devote time to searching for the most relevant and timely articles, links to South-Western's EconNews, EconDebates, and EconData Online features are included in ***Homework Xpress!***.

Customizable

You can tailor ***Homework Xpress!*** to your individualized course needs—pick and choose the assignments you want to give, decide when and for how long to make them available to your students, and use only the features and/or chapters of your choice, or use them all. It's up to you!

Economics in the Movies

Bring economic topics to life in a context that students will really relate to. *Economics in the Movies,* by Professor G. Dirk Mateer of The Pennsylvania State University, is a supplement that consists of clips from recent popular films and classic movies that show economic elements playing a "role" in the story. Students can access these clips on the Internet. A DVD with the clips will be provided to adopting professors.

In addition, a student workbook provides economic background and exercises for each movie clip. The exercises are designed to help students explore the meaning of the economic elements presented and how they might affect people and situations. This is truly an exciting way to showcase economics to a receptive audience!

MarketSim

MarketSim is an online microeconomics simulation designed to help students understand how markets work by allowing them to take on the roles of consumers and producers in a simulated economy. This innovative program helps students master microeconomics concepts by producing and trading with one another in both barter and monetary economies, concurrently having fun and gaining a thorough understanding of real-world concepts such as opportunity cost, price determination, and more.

Instructors value this teaching tool for the way it engages students' interest as classroom instruction alone cannot, and its simple set-up, customizable settings, and user-friendly instruction manuals make it the perfect solution for any section. Perhaps the most valuable aspects of the program, though, are its many benefits for students: Its hands-on method brings abstract economic concepts to life and teaches students to make sound economic decisions through trial-and-error in the simulated environment. Also, its interactive structure allows students to engage in friendly competition with their fellow students and to see the results of their actions almost instantly—and, as a result, they become eager to understand the economic concepts they will need to succeed.

Preface

Economics has a short history but a long past. As a distinct discipline, economics has been studied for only a few hundred years, yet civilizations have confronted the economic problem of scarce resources but unlimited wants for millennia. Economics, the discipline, may be centuries old, but it's renewed every day by fresh evidence that reshapes and extends economic theory. In *Economics: A Contemporary Introduction*, I draw on more than 25 years of teaching and research to convey the vitality, timeliness, and evolving nature of economics.

Leading by Example

Remember the last time you were in unfamiliar parts and had to ask for directions? Along with the directions came the standard comment, "You can't miss it!" So how come you missed it? Because the "landmark," so obvious to locals, was invisible to you, a stranger. Writing a principles textbook is much like giving directions. The author must be familiar with the material, but that very familiarity can cloud the author's ability to see the material through the fresh eyes of a new student. Some authors revert to a tell-all approach, which can overwhelm students who find absorbing so much information like trying to drink from a fire hose. Opting for the minimalist approach, some other authors write abstractly about good x and good y, units of labor and units of capital, or the proverbial widget. But this turns economics into a foreign language.

Good directions rely on landmarks familiar to us all—a stoplight, a fork in the road, a white picket fence. Likewise, a good textbook builds bridges from the familiar to the new. That's what I try to do—*lead by example*. By beginning with examples that draw on common experience, I create graphic images that need little explanation, thereby eliciting from the reader that light of recognition, that "Aha!" I believe that the shortest distance between an economic principle and student comprehension is a lively example. Examples should be self-explanatory to convey the point quickly and directly. Having to explain an example is like having to explain a joke—the point gets lost. Throughout the book, I provide just enough intuition and institutional detail to get the point across without overwhelming students with information. The emphasis is on economic ideas, not economic jargon.

Students show up the first day of class with at least 18 years of experience with economic choices, economic institutions, and economic events. Each grew up in a household—the most important economic institution in a market economy. As consumers, students are familiar with fast-food outlets, cineplexes, car dealerships, online retailers, and scores of stores at the mall. Most students have supplied labor to the job market—more than half held jobs in high school. Students also have ongoing contact with government—they know about taxes, driver's licenses, speed limits, and public education. And students have a growing familiarity with the rest of the world. Thus, students have abundant experience with the stuff of economics. Yet some principles books neglect this rich lode of personal experience and instead try to create for students a new world of economics—a new way of thinking. Such an approach fails to connect economics with what Alfred Marshall called "the ordinary business of life."

Because instructors can cover only a portion of the textbook in class, material should be self-explanatory, thereby providing instructors the flexibility to focus on topics of special interest. This book starts where students are, not where instructors would like them to be. For example, to explain the division of labor, rather than discuss Adam Smith's pin factory, I begin with McDonald's. And to explain resource substitution, rather than rely on abstract units of labor and capital, I begin with washing a car, where the mix can vary from a drive-through car wash (much capital and little labor) to a Saturday morning charity car wash (much labor and little capital). This edition is filled with similar down-to-earth examples that turn the abstract into the concrete to help students learn.

SEVENTH Edition Content and Changes

This edition builds on the success of previous editions to make the material even more student-friendly through additional examples, more questions along the way, and frequent summaries as a chapter unfolds. By making the material both more natural and more personal, I try to draw students into a collaborative discussion. Chapters have been streamlined for a clearer, more intuitive presentation, with fresh examples, new or revised case studies, and added exhibits that crystalize key points.

Introductory Chapters Topics common to both macro- and microeconomics are covered in the first four chapters. Limiting introductory material to four chapters saves precious class time, particularly at institutions where students can take macro and micro courses in either order (and so must cover introductory chapters twice). For this edition, the order of Chapters 3 and 4 have been reversed for a better flow of topics, moving from an introduction to economics in the first three chapters, to an examination of market theory in Chapter 4.

Macroeconomics Rather than focus on the differences among competing schools of thought, I use the aggregate demand and aggregate supply model to underscore the fundamental distinction between the *active approach*, which views the economy as unstable and in need of government intervention when it gets off track, and the *passive approach*, which views the economy as essentially stable and self-correcting.

Wherever possible, I rely on student experience and intuition to help explain the theory behind macroeconomic abstractions such as aggregate demand and aggregate supply. For example, to explain how employment can temporarily exceed its natural rate, I note how students, as the term draws to a close, can temporarily shift into high gear, studying for exams and finishing term papers. And to reinforce the link between income and consumption, I point out how easy it is to figure out the relative income of a neighborhood just by driving through it.

This edition includes added emphasis on the differences between aggregate demand and market demand, more about developing countries, technological change, and cost-of-living adjustment, more on how banks work and how they create money, a new section entitled "Credit Cards and Debit Cards: What's the Difference," updated coverage of the Bush tax cuts and federal deficits for 2003 and 2004, and a discussion of federal deficits since the adoption of the U.S. Constitution rather than just since 1980. There is also more focus on differences in unemployment rates and in inflation rates across U.S. metropolitan areas.

International This edition reflects the growing impact of the world economy on U.S. economic welfare. International issues are introduced early and discussed often. For example, the rest of the world is introduced in Chapter 1 and profiled in Chapter 3. Comparative advantage and the production possibilities frontier are discussed from a global perspective in Chapter 2.

International coverage is woven throughout the text. By comparing the U.S. experience with that of other countries around the world, students gain a better perspective about such topics as unionization trends, antitrust laws, pollution, conservation, environmental laws, tax rates, the distribution of income, economic growth, productivity, unemployment, inflation, central bank independence, and government deficits. Exhibits have been added to show comparisons across countries of various economic measures—everything from the percentage of paper that gets recycled to public outlays relative to GDP. International references are scattered throughout the book, including a number of relevant case studies. This edition reflects additional coverage of international trade and trade barriers—including the Doha Round of WTO negotiations and the Central American Free Trade Agreement (CAFTA), and places more emphasis on the role of technological change in international trade, especially with regard to outsourcing.

Case Studies Some books use case studies as boxed asides to cover material that otherwise doesn't quite fit. I use case studies as real-world applications to reinforce ideas in the chapter and to demonstrate the relevance of economic theory. My case studies are different enough to offer variety in the presentation yet are integrated enough into the flow of the chapter to let students know they should be read. The four categories of case studies in this textbook are as follows: (1) *Bringing Theory to Life* draws on student experience to reinforce economic theory, (2) *Public Policy* highlights trade-offs in the public sector, (3) *The World of Business* offers students a feel for the range of choices confronting business decision makers today, and (4) *The Information Economy* underscores the critical role of information in the economy. All case studies have been either revised or replaced.

In addition, the book features an even tighter integration of text and technology. For example, all case studies include relevant Web addresses and end-of-chapter questions for further analysis. These links plus navigation tips and other information can also be accessed through the McEachern Interactive Study Center at http://mceachern.swlearning.com/.

Clarity by Design

In many principles textbooks, chapters are broken up by boxed material, qualifying footnotes, and other distractions that disrupt the flow of the material. Students aren't sure when or if they should read such segregated elements. But this book has a natural flow. Each chapter opens with a few stimulating questions and then follows with a logical narrative. As noted already, case studies appear in the natural sequence of the chapter, not in separate boxes. Students can thus read each chapter from the opening questions to the conclusion and summary. I also adhere to a "just-in-time" philosophy, introducing material just as it is needed to build an argument. Footnotes are used sparingly and then only to cite sources, not to qualify or extend material in the text.

This edition is more visual than its predecessors, with more exhibits to reinforce key findings. Exhibit titles are also more descriptive to convey the central points, and more exhibits now have summary captions. The idea is to make the exhibits more self-contained. Additional summary paragraphs have been added throughout the chapter, and economics jargon has been cut down. Although the number of terms defined in the margin has increased, definitions have been pared to make them clearer, more concise, and less like entries from a dictionary.

In short, economic principles are now more transparent (a textbook should not be like some giant Easter egg hunt, where it's up to the student to figure out what the author is trying to say). Overall, the seventh edition is a cleaner presentation, a straighter shot into the student's brain. It omits needless words without tightening things too much. Despite the addition of fresh examples, new topics, additional summaries, and new exhibits, this edition contains about 4 percent fewer words of text than the previous one had.

Form Follows Function In most textbooks, the page design—the layout of the page and the use of color—is an afterthought, chosen with little regard for how students learn. No element in the design of this book has been wasted, and all work together for the maximum pedagogical value. By design, all elements of each chapter have been carefully integrated. Every effort has been made to present students with an open, readable page design. The size of the font, the length of the text line, and the amount of white space were all chosen to make learning easier. Graphs are uncluttered and are accompanied by captions explaining the key points. These features are optimal for students encountering college textbooks for the first time.

Color Coordinated Color is used systematically within graphs, charts, and tables to ensure that students can quickly and easily see what's going on. Throughout the book, demand curves are blue and supply curves are red. In each comparative statics example, the curves determining the final equilibrium point are lighter than the initial curves. Color shading distinguishes key areas of many graphs, such as measures of economic profit or loss, tax incidence, consumer and producer surplus, output above or below the economy's potential, and the welfare effects of tariffs and quotas. Graphical areas identifying positive outcomes such as economic profit, consumer surplus, or output exceeding the economy's potential are shaded blue. Areas identifying negative outcomes, such as economic loss, deadweight loss, or output falling below the economy's potential are shaded pink. In short, color is more than mere eye entertainment—it is coordinated consistently and with forethought to help students learn. Students benefit from these visual cues (a dyslexic student has told me that she finds the book's color guide quite helpful).

Net Bookmarks Each chapter includes a Net Bookmark. These margin notes identify interesting Web sites that illustrate real-world examples, giving students a chance to develop their research skills. And these bookmarks are extended at our Web site with additional information on resources as well as step-by-step navigation hints. They can be accessed through the McEachern Interactive Study Center at http://mceachern.swlearning.com/.

Reading It Right Each chapter contains special pedagogical features to facilitate classroom use of *The Wall Street Journal*. "Reading It Right" margin notes ask students to explain the relevance of statements drawn from *The Wall Street Journal*. There are also end-of-chapter questions asking students to read and analyze information from *The Wall Street Journal*.

Experiential Exercises Some end-of-chapter questions encourage students to develop their research and critical-thinking skills. These experiential exercises ask students to apply what they have learned to real-world, hands-on economic analysis. Most of these exercises involve the Internet, *The Wall Street Journal*, or other media resources.

Homework Xpress! Exercises New end-of-chapter exercises tie in to the Homework Xpress! (http://homeworkxpress.swlearning.com) supplement available for packaging with the textbook. The exercises afford additional practice in applying chapter graphing concepts.

THE INTERNET

As mentioned already, we devoted careful attention to capitalizing on the vast array of economic resources and alternative learning technologies the Internet can deliver. I gave much thought to two basic questions: What can this technology do that a textbook cannot do? And how can Web-based enhancements be employed to bring the greatest value to teaching and learning?

It's clear that students learn more when they are involved and engaged. The Internet provides a way to heighten student involvement while keeping the introductory economics course as current as today's news. With these ideas in mind, we have designed the text's supporting Web site to tightly integrate the book and the Internet. We have done this in a way that exploits the comparative advantage of each medium and in a structure that optimizes both teaching and learning experiences. Each chapter opener presents a HomeworkXpress! icon to remind students to check the site for problems, information, videos, news, debates, and graphing that will enhance their understanding of the chapter. In addition, graphs throughout the textbook that are enhanced in HomeworkXpress! Graphing are identified with the HomeworkXpress! icon.

The McEachern Interactive Study Center (http://mceachern.swlearning.com/) The Web site designed to be used with this textbook provides a comprehensive chapter-by-chapter online study guide that includes interactive quizzing, a glossary, updated and extended applications from the textbook, and numerous other features. Some of the highlights include:

> ***Quizzes*** Interactive quizzes help students test their understanding of the chapter's concepts. Multiple-choice questions include detailed feedback for each answer. Students can email the results of a quiz to themselves and/or their instructor.

> ***Key Terms Glossary*** A convenient, online glossary enables students to use the point-and-click flashcard functionality of the glossary to test themselves on key terminology.

> ***Extensions of In-Text Web Features*** To streamline navigation, the Study Center links directly to Web sites discussed in the Internet-enhanced in-text features for each chapter—Net Bookmarks, e-Activities, and end-of-chapter experiential exercises. These applications provide students with opportunities to interact with the material by performing real-world analyses. Their comments and answers to the questions posed in these features can be emailed to the instructor.

McEachern HomeworkXpress! Web Site (http:// homeworkxpress.swlearning.com) This new web-based product allows professors to assign end-of-chapter graphing problems for student completion as well as tests and quizzes. The program grades the assignments and tests and transfers the grades to a gradebook. The students not only get immediate feedback, but can access extensive Review and Tutorial materials. Problems that can be completed using Homework Xpress! Are identified with an icon.

McEachern Xtra! Web Site (http://mceachernxtra.swlearning.com/) Each student has an individual learning style, and different learning styles require different tools. By tapping into today's technology, this textbook can reach out to a variety of students with a variety of learning styles and can help instructors ensure that they address the needs of all students. The McEachern Xtra! available to be packaged with the textbook provides access to a robust set of additional online learning tools. McEachern Xtra! contains these key features:

> ***Master the Learning Objectives*** This element is the central navigational tool for McEachern Xtra! Step-by-step instructions associated with each learning objective systematically guide students through all available textbook and Xtra! multimedia tools to deepen their understanding of that particular concept. Each tool is accompanied by icons that identify the learning styles (print, aural, tactile, haptic, interactive, visual) for which it is most appropriate. Students can thus choose the most appropriate tools to support their own learning styles.

> ***Graphing Workshop*** The Graphing Workshop is a one-stop learning resource for help in mastering the logic of graphs, one of the more difficult aspects of an economics course for many students. It enables students to explore important economic concepts through a unique learning system made up of tutorials, interactive drawing tools, and exercises that teach how to interpret, reproduce, and explain graphs.

CNN Online Video segments from the Cable News Network (CNN) bring the real world right to your desktop. The accompanying exercises illustrate how economics is an important part of daily life and how the material applies to current events.

Ask the InstructorVideo Clips Streaming video explains and illustrates difficult concepts from each chapter. These video clips are extremely helpful review and clarification tools if a student has trouble understanding an in-class lecture or is a visual learner.

Xtra! Quizzing In addition to the open-access chapter-by-chapter quizzes found at the McEachern Product Support Web site (http://mceachern.swlearning.com), McEachern Xtra! offers students the opportunity to practice by taking interactive quizzes.

e-con @pps Economic Applications EconNews Online, EconDebate Online, EconData Online, and EconLinks Online help to deepen students' understanding of theoretical concepts through hands-on exploration and analysis of the latest economic news stories, policy debates, and data.

None of these features requires detailed knowledge of the Internet. Nor are they required for a successful classroom experience if an instructor wants to assign only the materials contained within the textbook. The online enhancements simply offer optional paths for further study and exploration—new ways for students to use their individual learning styles and new ways for instructors to experiment with technology and a wider range of assignment materials.

The Support Package

The teaching and learning support package that accompanies *Economics: A Contemporary Introduction* provides instructors and students with focused, accurate, and innovative supplements to the textbook.

Study Guides Written by John Lunn of Hope College, study guides are available for the full textbook, as well as for the micro and macro "split" versions. Every chapter of each study guide corresponds to a chapter in the textbook and offers (1) an introduction; (2) a chapter outline, with definitions of all terms; (3) a discussion of the chapter's main points; (4) a *lagniappe*, or bonus, which supplements material in the chapter and includes a "Question to Think About"; (5) a list of key terms; (6) a variety of true-false, multiple-choice, and discussion questions; and (7) answers to all the questions. Visit the McEachern Interactive Study Center at http://mceachern.swlearning.com/ for more details.

Instructor's Manual The *Instructor's Manual*, revised by Christy Vineyard of Southwestern Tennessee Community College, is keyed to the text. For each textbook chapter, it includes (1) a detailed lecture outline and brief overview, (2) a summary of main points, (3) pedagogical tips that expand on points raised in the chapter and indicate use of PowerPoint slides, and (4) suggested answers to all end-of-chapter questions and problems. Tina Mosleh of Ohlone College revised each classroom economics experiment to include an abstract, an overview, a clear set of instructions for running the experiment, and forms for recording the results.

Teaching Assistance Manual I have revised the *Teaching Assistance Manual* to provide additional support beyond the *Instructor's Manual*. It is especially useful to new instructors, graduate assistants, and teachers interested in generating more class discussion. This manual offers (1) overviews and outlines of each chapter, (2) chapter objectives and quiz material, (3) material for class discussion, (4) topics warranting special attention, (5) supplementary examples, and (6) "What if?" discussion questions. Appendices provide guidance on (1) presenting material; (2) generating and sustaining class discussion; (3) preparing, administering, and grading quizzes; and (4) coping with the special problems confronting foreign graduate assistants.

Test Banks Thoroughly revised for currency and accuracy by Dennis Hanseman of the University of Cincinnati, the microeconomics and macroeconomics test banks contain over 6,600 questions in multiple-choice and true-false formats. All multiple-choice questions have five possible responses, and each is rated by degree of difficulty.

ExamView—Computerized Testing Software *ExamView* is an easy-to-use test-creation software package available in versions compatible with Microsoft Windows and Apple Macintosh. It contains all the questions in the printed test banks. Instructors can add or edit questions, instructions, and answers; select questions by previewing them on the screen; and then choose them by number or at random. Instructors can also create and administer quizzes online, either over the Internet, through a local area network (LAN), or through a wide area network (WAN).

Microsoft PowerPoint Lecture Slides Lecture slides, created by Dale Bails of Christian Brothers University, contain tables and graphs from the textbook, as well as additional instructional materials, and are intended to enhance lectures and help integrate technology into the classroom.

Microsoft PowerPoint Figure Slides These PowerPoint slides contain key figures from the text. Instructors who prefer to prepare their own lecture slides can use these figures as an alternative to the PowerPoint lecture slides.

Transparency Acetates Many of the key tables and graphs from this textbook are reproduced as full-color transparency acetates.

Economics in the Movies This edition now features a tie-in to Thomson's *Economics in the Movies*. The guide, created by G. Dirk Mateer of The Pennsylvania State University, borrows from feature films in a way that enhances core economics content. Concepts are visualized by utilizing short film scenes, including *Out of Sight, Seabuscuit, Erin Brockovich, Waterworld, Being John Malkovich,* and many others. Icons direct professors to where they can use this guide to tie economic concepts to scenes in popular films.

CNN Economics Video The CNN Economics Video provides a variety of brief video clips, taken from Cable News Network (CNN) programs, that illustrate various aspects of economics.

Market Sim Markets come alive in this new microeconomic simulation product. Students can participate in a barter or a monetary economy while competing with their classmates and learning how markets work with this Web-based program.

Online learning is growing at a rapid pace. Whether instructors are looking to offer courses at a distance or to offer a Web-enhanced classroom, South-Western/Thomson Learning offers them a solution with WebTutor. WebTutor provides instructors with text-specific content that interacts with the two leading systems of higher education course management—WebCT and Blackboard. WebTutor is a turnkey solution for instructors who want to begin using technology like Blackboard or WebCT but do not have Web-ready content available or do not want to be burdened with developing their own content. South-Western offers two levels of WebTutor:

WebTutor Toolbox WebTutor uses the Internet to turn everyone in your class into a front-row student. WebTutor offers interactive study guide features such as quizzes, concept reviews, flashcards, discussion forums, and more. Instructor tools are also provided to facilitate communication between students and faculty. Preloaded with content, *WebTutor ToolBox* pairs all the content of the book's support Web site with all the sophisticated course management functionality of either course management platform.

WebTutor Advantage More than just an interactive study guide, *WebTutor Advantage* delivers innovative learning aids that actively engage students. Benefits include automatic and immediate feedback from quizzes; interactive, multimedia-rich explanations of concepts, such as flash-animated graphing tutorials and graphing exercises that use an online graph-drawing tool; streaming video applications; online exercises; flashcards; and interaction and involvement through online discussion forums. Powerful instructor tools are also provided to facilitate communication and collaboration between students and faculty.

The Teaching Economist For more than a dozen years, I have edited *The Teaching Economist*, a newsletter aimed at making teaching more interesting and more fun. The newsletter discusses imaginative ways to present topics—for example, how to "sensationalize" economic concepts, useful resources on the Internet, economic applications from science fiction, recent research in teaching and learning, and more generally, ways to teach just for the fun of it. A regular feature of *The Teaching Economist*, "The Grapevine," offers teaching ideas suggested by colleagues from across the country.

   The latest issue—and back issues—of *The Teaching Economist* are available online at http://economics.swlearning.com/.

Acknowledgments

Many people contributed to this book's development. I gratefully acknowledge the insightful comments of those who have reviewed the book for this and previous editions. Their suggestions expanded my thinking and improved the book.

Steve Abid
Grand Rapids Community College

Polly Reynolds Allen
University of Connecticut

Hassan Y. Aly
Ohio State University

Ted Amato
University of North Carolina, Charlotte

Donna Anderson
University of Wisconsin, La Crosse

Richard Anderson
Texas A&M University

Kyriacos Aristotelous
Otterbein College

James Aylesworth
Lakeland Community College

Mohsen Bahmani Mohsen Bahmani-Oskooee
University of Wisconsin, Milwaukee

Dale Bails
Christian Brothers College

Benjamin Balak
Rollins College

Andy Barnett
Auburn University

Bharati Basu
Central Michigan University

Klaus Becker
Texas Tech University

Charles Bennett
Gannon University

Trisha L. Bezmen
Old Dominion University

Jay Bhattacharya
Okaloosa Walton Community College

Gerald W. Bialka
University of North Florida

William Bogart
Case Western Reserve University

Kenneth Boyer
Michigan State University

David Brasfield
Murray State University

Jurgen Brauer
Augusta College

Taggert Brooks
University of Wisconsin, La Crosse

Gardner Brown, Jr.
University of Washington

Eric Brunner
Morehead State University

Francine Butler
Grand View College

Judy Butler
Baylor University

Charles Callahan III
SUNY College at Brockport

Giorgio Canarella
California State University, Los Angeles

Shirley Cassing
University of Pittsburgh

Shi-fan Chu
University of Nevada–Reno

Ronald Cipcic
Kalamazoo Valley Community College

Larry Clarke
Brookhaven College

Rebecca Cline
Middle Georgia College

Stephen Cobb
Xavier University

Doug Conway
Mesa Community College

Mary E. Cookingham
Michigan State University

James P. Cover
University of Alabama

James Cox
DeKalb College

Jerry Crawford
Arkansas State University

Thomas Creahan
Morehead State University

Joseph Daniels
Marquette University

Carl Davidson
Michigan State University

Elynor Davis
Georgia Southern University

Susan Davis
SUNY College at Buffalo

A. Edward Day
University of Central Florida

David Dean
University of Richmond

Janet Deans
Chestnut Hill College

Dennis Debrecht
Carroll College

David Denslow
University of Florida

Gary Dymski
University of California–Riverside

John Edgren
Eastern Michigan University

Ron D. Elkins
Central Washington University

Donald Elliott, Jr.
Southern Illinois University

G. Rod Erfani
Transylvania University

Gisela Meyer Escoe
University of Cincinnati

Mark Evans
California State University, Bakersfield

Gregory Falls
Central Michigan University

Eleanor Fapohunda
SUNY College at Farmingdale

Mohsen Fardmanesh
Temple University

Paul Farnham
Georgia State University

Rudy Fichtenbaum
Wright State University

T. Windsor Fields
James Madison University

Rodney Fort
Washington State University

Richard Fowles
University of Utah

Roger Frantz
San Diego State University

Julie Gallaway
Southwest Montana State University

Gary Galles
Pepperdine University

Edward Gamber
Lafayette College

Adam Gifford
California State University, Northridge

J. P. Gilbert
MiraCosta College

Robert Gillette
University of Kentucky

Art Goldsmith
Washington and Lee University

Rae Jean Goodman
U.S. Naval Academy

Robert Gordon
San Diego State University

Fred Graham
American University

Philip Graves
University of Colorado, Boulder

Harpal S. Grewal
Claflin College

Carolyn Grin
Grand Rapids Community College

Daniel Gropper
Auburn University

Simon Hakim
Temple University

Robert Halvorsen
University of Washington

Nathan Eric Hampton
St. Cloud State University

Mehdi Haririan
Bloomsburg University

William Hart
Miami University

Baban Hasnat
SUNY College at Brockport

Julia Heath
University of Memphis

James Heisler
Hope College

James Henderson
Baylor University

James R. Hill
Central Michigan University

Jane Smith Himarios
University of Texas, Arlington

Calvin Hoerneman
Delta College

Tracy Hofer
University of Wisconsin, Stevens Point

George E. Hoffer
Virginia Commonwealth University

Dennis Hoffman
Arizona State University

Bruce Horning
Fordham University

Calvin Hoy
County College of Morris

Jennifer Imazeki
San Diego State University

Beth Ingram
University of Iowa

Paul Isley
Grand Valley State University

Joyce Jacobsen
Wesleyan University

Nancy Jianakoplos
Colorado State University

Claude Michael Jonnard
Fairleigh Dickinson University

Nake Kamrany
University of Southern California

Bryce Kanago
Miami University

John Kane
SUNY College at Oswego

David Kennett
Vassar College

William Kern
Western Michigan University

Robert Kleinhenz
California State University, Fullerton

Faik Koray
Louisiana State University

Joseph Kotaska
Monroe Community College

Barry Kotlove
Edmonds Community College

Marie Kratochvil
Nassau Community College

Joseph Lammert
Raymond Walters College

Christopher Lee
Saint Ambrose University, Davenport

J. Franklin Lee
Pitt Community College

Jim Lee
Fort Hays State University

Dennis Leyden
University of North Carolina, Greensboro

Carl Liedholm
Michigan State University

Hyoung-Seok Lim
Ohio State University

C. Richard Long
Georgia State University

Ken Long
New River Community College

Michael Magura
University of Toledo

Thomas Maloy
Muskegon Community College

Gabriel Manrique
Winona State University

Barbara Marcus
Davenport College

Robert Margo
Vanderbilt University

Nelson Mark
Ohio State University

Richard Martin
Agnes Scott College

Peter Mavrokordatos
Tarrant County College

Wolfgang Mayer
University of Cincinnati

Bruce McCrea
Lansing Community College

John McDowell
Arizona State University

KimMarie McGoldrick
University of Richmond

David McKee
Kent State University

James McLain
University of New Orleans

Mark McNeil
Irvine Valley College

Michael A. McPherson
University of North Texas

Scott Eric Merryman
University of Oregon

Michael Metzger
University of Central Oklahoma

Art Meyer
Lincoln Land Community College

Carrie Meyer
George Mason University

Martin Milkman
Murray State University

Green R. Miller
Morehead State University

Bruce D. Mills
Troy State University, Montgomery

Milton Mitchell
University of Wisconsin, Oshkosh

Shannon Mitchell
Virginia Commonwealth University

Barry Morris
University of North Alabama

Tina Mosleh
Ohlone College

Kathryn Nantz
Fairfield University

Paul Natke
Central Michigan University

Rick Nelson
Lansing Community College

Heather Newsome
Baylor University

Farrokh Nourzad
Marquette University

Maureen O'Brien
University of Minnesota, Duluth

Norman P. Obst
Michigan State University

Jeffrey Phillips
Thomas College

Jeffrey D. Prager
East Central College

Fernando Quijano
Dickinson State University

Jaishankar Raman
Valparaiso University

Reza Ramazani
St. Michael's University

Carol Rankin
Xavier University

Mitch Redlo
Monroe Community College

Kevin Rogers
Mississippi State University

Scanlon Romer
Delta College

Duane Rosa
West Texas A&M University

Robert Rossana
Wayne State University

Mark Rush
University of Florida

Richard Saba
Auburn University

Simran Sahi
University of Minnesota, Twin Cities

Richard Salvucci
Trinity University

Rexford Santerre
University of Connecticut

George D. Santopietro
Radford University

Sue Lynn Sasser
University of Central Oklahoma

Ward Sayre
Kenyon College

Ted Scheinman
Mt. Hood Community College

Peter Schwartz
University of North Carolina, Charlotte

Carol A. Scotese
Virginia Commonwealth University

Shahrokh Shahrokhi
San Diego State University

Roger Sherman
University of Houston

Michael Shields
Central Michigan University

Alden Shiers
California Polytechnic State University

Frederica Shockley
California State University, Chico

William Shughart II
University of Mississippi

Paul Sicilian
Grand Valley State University

Charles Sicotte
Rock Valley College

Calvin Siebert
University of Iowa

Gerald P. W. Simons
Grand Valley State University

Phillip Smith
DeKalb College

V. Kerry Smith
Duke University

David Spencer
Brigham Young University

Jane Speyrer
University of New Orleans

Joanne Spitz
University of Massachusetts

Mark Stegeman
Virginia Polytechnic Institute

Houston Stokes
University of Illinois, Chicago

Robert Stonebreaker
Indiana University of Pennsylvania

Michael Stroup
Stephen Austin State University

William Swift
Pace University

James Swofford
University of South Alabama

Linghui Tang
Drexel University

Donna Thompson
Brookdale Community College

John Tribble
Russell Sage College

Lee J. Van Scyoc
University of Wisconsin, Oshkosh

Percy Vera
Sinclair Community College

Han X. Vo
Winthrop University

Jin Wang
University of Wisconsin, Stevens Point

Richard Winkelman
Arizona State University

Gregory Wassall
Northeastern University

Stephan Woodbury
Michigan State University

William Weber
Eastern Illinois University

Kenneth Woodward
Saddleback College

David Weinberg
Xavier University

Patricia Wyatt
Bossier Parish Community College

Bernard Weinrich
St. Louis Community College

Peter Wyman
Spokane Falls Community College

Donald Wells
University of Arizona

Mesghena Yasin
Morehead State University

Robert Whaples
Wake Forest University

Edward Young
University of Wisconsin, Eau Claire

Mark Wheeler
Western Michigan University

Michael J. Youngblood
Rock Valley College

Michael White
St. Cloud State University

William Zeis
Bucks Community College

To practice what I preach, I relied on the division of labor based on comparative advantage to help put together the most complete teaching package on the market today. John Lunn of Hope College authored the study guides, which have become quite popular. Christy Vineyard of Southwestern Tennessee Community College carefully revised the instructor's manual. Dennis Hanseman of the University of Cincinnati undertook a thorough revision of the test banks. And Dale Bails of Christian Brothers University revised the Power-Point lecture slides. I thank them for their imagination and their discipline.

The talented staff at Thomson Business & Professional Publishing provided invaluable editorial, administrative, and sales support. I owe a special debt to Susan Smart, senior developmental editor, who nurtured the manuscript throughout the revision and production. I also appreciate very much the smooth project coordination by senior production editor Libby Shipp, the exciting design created by Chris Miller, the imaginative photography management of John Hill, the patient production assistance of Jan Turner of Pre-Press Company, and the thoughtful copyediting of Cheryl Hauser. Peggy Buskey, Pam Wallace, and Karen Schaffer have been particularly helpful in developing the McEachern Xtra! and Homework Xpress! Web sites.

In addition, I am most grateful to Jack Calhoun, vice president and editorial director; Dave Shaut, vice president and editor-in-chief; Michael Worls, senior acquisitions editor and problem solver; and John Carey, the senior marketing manager, whose knowledge of the book dates back to the first edition. As good as the book may be, all our efforts would be wasted unless students get to read it. To that end, I greatly appreciate Thomson's dedicated service and sales force, who have contributed in a substantial way to the book's success.

Finally, I owe an abiding debt to my wife, Pat, who provided abundant encouragement and support along the way.

William A. McEachern

The Art and Science of Economic Analysis

"How luscious lies the pea in the pod."
Emily Dickinson

© Julie Dennis/Index Stock Imagery

W hy are comic-strip characters like Hagar the Horrible, Hi and Lois, Cathy, Monty, and FoxTrot missing a finger on each hand? And where is Dilbert's mouth? Why does Japan have twice as many vending machines per capita as the United States? In what way are people who pound on vending machines relying on a theory? What's the big idea with economics? Finally, how can it be said in economics that "what goes around comes around"? These and other questions are answered in this chapter, which introduces the art and science of economic analysis.

You have been reading and hearing about economic issues for years—unemployment, inflation, poverty, federal deficits, college tuition, airfares, stock prices, computer prices, gas prices. When explanations of these issues go into any depth, your eyes may glaze over and you may tune out, the same way you do when a weather

HOMEWORK
Xpress!

Use Homework Xpress! for
economic application,
graphing, videos, and more.

forecaster tries to provide an in-depth analysis of high-pressure fronts colliding with moisture carried in from the coast.

What many people fail to realize is that economics is livelier than the dry accounts offered by the news media. Economics is about making choices, and you make economic choices every day—choices about whether to get a part-time job or focus on your studies, live in a dorm or off campus, take a course in accounting or one in history, pack a lunch or grab a sandwich. You already know much more about economics than you realize. You bring to the subject a rich personal experience, an experience that will be tapped throughout the book to reinforce your understanding of the basic ideas. Topics discussed include:

- The economic problem
- Marginal analysis
- Rational self-interest

- Scientific method
- Normative versus positive analysis
- Pitfalls of economic thinking

The Economic Problem: Scarce Resources, Unlimited Wants

Would you like a new car, a nicer home, better meals, more free time, a more interesting social life, more spending money, more sleep? Who wouldn't? But even if you can satisfy some of these desires, others will pop up. *The problem is that, although your wants, or desires, are virtually unlimited, the resources available to satisfy these wants are scarce.* A resource is *scarce* when it is not freely available—that is, when its price exceeds zero. Because resources are scarce, you must choose from among your many wants and, whenever you choose, you must forgo satisfying some other wants. The problem of scarce resources but unlimited wants exists to a greater or lesser extent for each of the more than 6 billion people around the world. Everybody—taxicab driver, farmer, brain surgeon, shepherd, student, politician—faces the problem.

Economics examines how people use their scarce resources to satisfy their unlimited wants. The taxicab driver uses the cab and other scarce resources, such as knowledge of the city, driving skills, gasoline, and time, to earn income. The income, in turn, buys housing, groceries, clothing, trips to Disney World, and thousands of other goods and services that help satisfy some of the driver's unlimited wants.

Let's pick apart the definition of economics, beginning with resources, then examining goods and services, and finally focusing on the heart of the matter—economic choice, which arises from scarcity.

Resources

Resources are the inputs, or factors of production, used to produce the goods and services that people want. *Goods and services are scarce because resources are scarce.* Resources sort into four broad categories: labor, capital, natural resources, and entrepreneurial ability. **Labor** is human effort, both physical and mental. It includes the effort of the cab driver and the brain surgeon. Labor itself comes from a more fundamental resource: *time.* Without time we can accomplish nothing. We allocate our time to alternative uses: we can *sell* our time as labor, or we can *spend* our time doing other things, like sleeping, eating, studying, playing sports, going online, watching TV, or just relaxing with friends.

Capital includes all human creations used to produce goods and services. Economists often distinguish between physical capital and human capital. *Physical capital* consists of facto-

ECONOMICS

The study of how people use their scarce resources to satisfy their unlimited wants

RESOURCES

The inputs, or factors of production, used to produce the goods and services that people want; resources consist of labor, capital, natural resources, and entrepreneurial ability

LABOR

The physical and mental effort used to produce goods and services

CAPITAL

The buildings, equipment, and human skill used to produce goods and services

ries, machines, tools, buildings, airports, highways, and other human creations employed to produce goods and services. Physical capital includes the taxi driver's cab, the surgeon's scalpel, the farmer's tractor, the interstate highway system, and the building where your economics class meets. *Human capital* consists of the knowledge and skill people acquire to enhance their productivity, such as the taxi driver's knowledge of city streets, the surgeon's knowledge of human biology, and your knowledge of economics.

Natural resources are all so-called *gifts of nature,* including bodies of water, trees, oil reserves, minerals, and even animals. Natural resources can be divided into renewable resources and exhaustible resources. A *renewable resource* can be drawn on indefinitely if used conservatively. Thus, timber is a renewable resource if felled trees are replaced to provide a steady supply. The air and rivers are renewable resources if they are allowed to clean themselves of pollutants. More generally, biological resources like fish, game, livestock, forests, rivers, groundwater, grasslands, and soil are renewable if managed properly. An *exhaustible resource*—such as oil, coal, or copper ore—does not renew itself and so is available in a limited amount. Once burned, each barrel of oil and each ton of coal are gone forever. The world's oil reserves and coal mines are exhaustible.

A special kind of human skill called **entrepreneurial ability** is the talent required to dream up a new product or find a better way to produce an existing one. The *entrepreneur* tries to discover and act on profitable opportunities by hiring resources and assuming the risk of business success or failure. Every large firm in the world today, such as Ford, Microsoft, and Dell, began as an idea in the mind of an entrepreneur.

Resource owners are paid **wages** for their labor, **interest** for the use of their capital, and **rent** for the use of their natural resources. The entrepreneur's effort is rewarded by **profit,** which equals the *revenue* from items sold minus the *cost* of the resources employed to make those items. The entrepreneur claims what's left over after paying other resource suppliers. Sometimes the entrepreneur suffers a loss. Resource earnings are usually based on the *time* these resources are employed. Resource payments therefore have a time dimension, as in a wage of $10 *per hour,* interest of 6 percent *per year,* rent of $600 *per month,* or profit of $10,000 *per year.*

Goods and Services

Resources are combined in a variety of ways to produce goods and services. A farmer, a tractor, 50 acres of land, seeds, and fertilizer combine to grow the good: corn. One hundred musicians, musical instruments, chairs, a conductor, a musical score, and a music hall combine to produce the service: Beethoven's Fifth Symphony. Corn is a **good** because it is something you can see, feel, and touch; it requires scarce resources to produce; and it satisfies human wants. The book you are now holding, the chair you are sitting in, the clothes you are wearing, and your next meal are all goods. The performance of the Fifth Symphony is a **service** because it is intangible, yet it uses scarce resources to satisfy human wants. Lectures, movies, concerts, phone calls, broadband connections, yoga lessons, dry cleaning, and haircuts are all services.

Because goods and services are produced using scarce resources, they are themselves scarce. *A good or service is scarce if the amount people desire exceeds the amount available at a zero price.* Because we cannot have all the goods and services we would like, we must continually choose among them. We must choose among more pleasant living quarters, better meals, nicer clothes, more reliable transportation, faster computers, and so on. Making choices in a world of **scarcity** means we must pass up some goods and services.

A few goods and services seem *free* because the amount available at a zero price exceeds

NATURAL RESOURCES

So-called gifts of nature used to produce goods and services; includes renewable and exhaustible resources

ENTREPRENEURIAL ABILITY

Managerial and organizational skills needed to start a firm, combined with the willingness to take risks

WAGES

Payment to resource owners for their labor

INTEREST

Payment to resource owners for the use of their capital

RENT

Payment to resource owners for the use of their natural resources

PROFIT

The reward for entrepreneurial ability; the revenue from sales minus the cost of resources used by the entrepreneur

GOOD

A tangible item used to satisfy human wants

SERVICE

An activity used to satisfy human wants

SCARCITY

Occurs when the amount people desire exceeds the amount available at a zero price

the amount people want. For example, air and seawater often seem free because we can breathe all the air we want and have all the seawater we can haul away. Yet, despite the old saying "The best things in life are free," most goods and services are scarce, not free, and even those that appear to be free come with strings attached. For example, *clean* air and *clean* seawater have become scarce. *Goods and services that are truly free are not the subject matter of economics. Without scarcity, there would be no economic problem and no need for prices.*

Sometimes we mistakenly think of certain goods as free because they involve no apparent cost to us. Subscription cards that fall out of magazines appear to be free. At least it seems we would have little difficulty rounding up about three thousand if necessary! Producing the cards, however, absorbs scarce resources, resources drawn away from competing uses, such as producing higher-quality magazines. You may have heard the expression "There is no such thing as a free lunch." There is no free lunch because all goods and services involve a cost to someone. The lunch may seem free to us, but it draws scarce resources away from the production of other goods and services, and whoever provides a free lunch often expects something in return. A Russian proverb makes a similar point but with a bit more bite: "The only place you find free cheese is in a mousetrap." And Albert Einstein said, "Sometimes one pays the most for things one gets for nothing."

Economic Decision Makers

There are four types of decision makers, or participants, in the economy: households, firms, governments, and the rest of the world. Their interaction determines how an economy's resources are allocated. *Households* play the leading role. As consumers, households demand the goods and services produced. As resource owners, households supply labor, capital, natural resources, and entrepreneurial ability to firms, governments, and the rest of the world. *Firms, governments,* and *the rest of the world* demand the resources that households supply and then use these resources to supply the goods and services that households demand. The rest of the world includes foreign households, firms, and governments that supply resources and products to U.S. markets and demand resources and products from U.S. markets.

Markets are the means by which buyers and sellers carry out exchange. Bringing together the two sides of exchange, demand and supply, markets determine price and quantity. Markets are often physical places, such as supermarkets, department stores, shopping malls, or flea markets. But markets also include other mechanisms by which buyers and sellers communicate, like classified ads, radio and television ads, telephones, bulletin boards, the Internet, and face-to-face bargaining. These market mechanisms provide information about the quantity, quality, and price of products offered for sale. Goods and services are bought and sold in **product markets.** Resources are bought and sold in **resource markets.** The most important resource market is the labor, or job, market. Think of your own experience looking for a job, and you get some idea of that market.

A Simple Circular-Flow Model

Now that you have learned a bit about economic decision makers, consider how they interact. Such a picture is conveyed by the **circular-flow model,** which describes the flow of resources, products, income, and revenue among economic decision makers. The simple circular-flow model focuses on the primary interaction in a market economy—that between households and firms. Exhibit 1 shows households on the left and firms on the right; please take a look.

Households supply labor, capital, natural resources, and entrepreneurial ability to firms through resource markets, shown in the lower portion of the exhibit. In return, households

---

MARKET

A set of arrangements through which buyers and sellers carry out exchange at mutually agreeable terms

PRODUCT MARKET

A market in which a good or service is bought and sold

RESOURCE MARKET

A market in which a resource is bought and sold

CIRCULAR-FLOW MODEL

A diagram that outlines the flow of resources, products, income, and revenue among economic decision makers

demand goods and services from firms through product markets, shown on the upper portion of the exhibit. Viewed from the business end, firms demand labor, capital, natural resources, and entrepreneurial ability from households through resource markets, and firms supply goods and services to households through product markets.

The flows of resources and products are supported by the flows of income and expenditure—that is, by the flow of money. So let's add money. The demand and supply of resources come together in resource markets to determine resource prices, which flow as *income* to households. The demand and supply of products come together in product markets to determine the prices of goods and services, which flow as *revenue* to firms. Resources and products flow in one direction—in this case, counterclockwise—and the corresponding payments flow in the other direction—clockwise. What goes around comes around. Take a little time now to trace the circular flows.

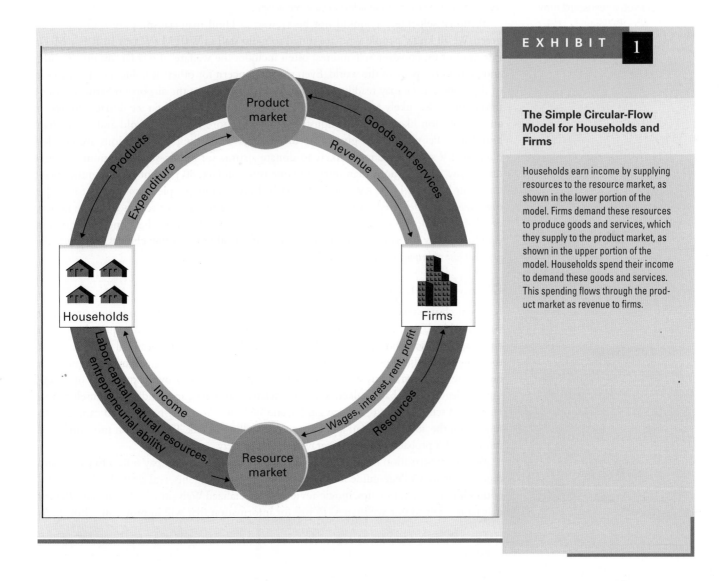

E X H I B I T   **1**

The Simple Circular-Flow Model for Households and Firms

Households earn income by supplying resources to the resource market, as shown in the lower portion of the model. Firms demand these resources to produce goods and services, which they supply to the product market, as shown in the upper portion of the model. Households spend their income to demand these goods and services. This spending flows through the product market as revenue to firms.

The Art of Economic Analysis

An economy results from the choices that millions of individuals make in attempting to satisfy their unlimited wants. Because these choices lie at the very heart of the economic problem—coping with scarce resources but unlimited wants—they deserve a closer look. Learning about the forces that shape economic choice is the first step toward mastering the art of economic analysis.

Rational Self-Interest

A key economic assumption is that individuals, in making choices, rationally select alternatives they perceive to be in their best interests. By *rational*, economists mean simply that people try to make the best choices they can, given the available information. People may not know with certainty which alternative will turn out to be the best. They simply select the alternatives they *expect* will yield the most satisfaction and happiness. *In general, rational self-interest means that individuals try to maximize the expected benefit achieved with a given cost or to minimize the expected cost of achieving a given benefit.*

Rational self-interest should not be viewed as blind materialism, pure selfishness, or greed. We all know people who are tuned to radio station WIIFM (What's In It For Me?). For most of us, however, self-interest often includes the welfare of our family, our friends, and perhaps the poor of the world. Even so, our concern for others is influenced by the cost of that concern. We may readily volunteer to drive a friend to the airport on Saturday afternoon but are less likely to offer if the plane leaves at 6:00 A.M. When we donate clothes to an organization like Goodwill Industries, they are more likely to be old and worn than brand new. People tend to give more to charities when their contributions are tax deductible. TV stations are more likely to donate airtime for public-service announcements during the dead of night than during prime time (in fact, 80 percent of such announcements air between 11:00 P.M. and 7:00 A.M.[1]). In Asia some people burn money to soothe the passage of a departed loved one. But they burn fake money, not real money. The notion of self-interest does not rule out concern for others; it simply means that concern for others is influenced by the same economic forces that affect other economic choices. *The lower the personal cost of helping others, the more help we offer.*

Choice Requires Time and Information

Rational choice takes time and requires information, but time and information are scarce and valuable. If you have any doubts about the time and information required to make choices, talk to someone who recently purchased a home, a car, or a personal computer. Talk to a corporate official deciding whether to introduce a new product, sell over the Internet, build a new factory, or buy another firm. Or think back to your own experience of selecting a college. You probably talked to friends, relatives, teachers, and guidance counselors. You likely used school catalogs, college guides, and Web sites. You may have visited campuses to meet with the admissions staff and anyone else willing to talk. The decision took time and money, and it probably involved aggravation and anxiety.

Because information is costly to acquire, we are often willing to pay others to gather and digest it for us. College guidebooks, stock analysts, travel agents, real estate brokers, career counselors, restaurant critics, movie reviewers, specialized Web sites, and *Consumer Reports* magazine attest to our willingness to pay for information that will improve our choices. As

---

1. Sally Goll Beatty, "Media and Agencies Brawl Over Do-Good Advertising," *Wall Street Journal,* 29 September 1997.

we'll see next, *rational decision makers will continue to acquire information as long as the additional benefit expected from that information exceeds the additional cost of gathering it.*

Economic Analysis Is Marginal Analysis

Economic choice usually involves some adjustment to the existing situation, or status quo. Amazon.com must decide whether to add an additional line of products. The school superintendent must decide whether to hire another teacher. Your favorite jeans are on sale, and you must decide whether to buy another pair. You are wondering whether you should carry an extra course next term. You have just finished dinner at a restaurant and are deciding whether to have dessert.

Economic choice is based on a comparison of the *expected marginal benefit* and the *expected marginal cost* of the action under consideration. **Marginal** means incremental, additional, or extra. Marginal refers to a change in an economic variable, a change in the status quo. *You, as a rational decision maker, will change the status quo as long as your expected marginal benefit from the change exceeds your expected marginal cost.* For example, Amazon.com compares the marginal benefit expected from adding a new line of products (the added sales revenue) with the marginal cost (the added cost of the resources required). Likewise, you compare the marginal benefit you expect from eating dessert (the added pleasure and satisfaction) with its marginal cost (the added money, time, and calories).

Typically, the change under consideration is small, but a marginal choice can involve a major economic adjustment, as in the decision to quit school and get a job. For a firm, a marginal choice might mean building a plant in Mexico or even filing for bankruptcy. By focusing on the effect of a marginal adjustment to the status quo, the economist is able to cut the analysis of economic choice down to a manageable size. Rather than confront a bewildering economic reality head-on, the economist begins with a marginal choice to see how this choice affects a particular market and shapes the economic system as a whole. Incidentally, to the noneconomist, *marginal* usually means relatively inferior, as in "a movie of marginal quality." Forget that meaning for this course and instead think of *marginal* as meaning incremental, additional, or extra.

MARGINAL

Incremental, additional, or extra; used to describe a change in an economic variable

Microeconomics and Macroeconomics

Although you have made thousands of economic choices, you probably have seldom thought about your own economic behavior. For example, why are you reading this book right now rather than doing something else? **Microeconomics** is the study of your economic behavior and the economic behavior of others who make choices about such matters as how much to study and how much to play, how much to borrow and how much to save, what to buy and what to sell. Microeconomics examines the factors that influence individual economic choices and how markets coordinate the choices of various decision makers. Microeconomics explains how price and quantity are determined in individual markets—for breakfast cereal, sports equipment, or used cars, for instance.

You have probably given little thought to what influences your own economic choices. You have likely given even less thought to how your choices link up with those made by millions of others in the U.S. economy to determine economy-wide measures such as total production, employment, and economic growth. **Macroeconomics** studies the performance of the economy as a whole. Whereas microeconomics studies the individual pieces of the economic puzzle, as reflected in particular markets, macroeconomics puts all the pieces together to focus on the big picture.

MICROECONOMICS

The study of the economic behavior in particular markets, such as that for computers or unskilled labor

MACROECONOMICS

The study of the economic behavior of entire economies

To review: The art of economic analysis focuses on how individuals use their scarce resources in an attempt to satisfy their unlimited wants. Rational self-interest guides individual choice. Choice requires time and information, and choice involves a comparison of the marginal cost and marginal benefit of alternative actions. Microeconomics looks at the individual pieces of the economic puzzle; macroeconomics fits the pieces together to shape the big picture.

The Science of Economic Analysis

ECONOMIC THEORY, OR ECONOMIC MODEL

A simplification of reality used to make predictions about cause and effect in the real world

Economists use scientific analysis to develop theories, or models, that help explain economic behavior. An **economic theory,** or **economic model,** is a simplification of economic reality that *is used to make predictions about the real world*. A theory, or model, such as the circular-flow model, captures the important elements of the problem under study; it need not spell out every detail and interrelation. In fact, adding more details may make a theory more unwieldy and less useful. The world is so complex that we must simplify if we want to make sense of things, just as comic strips simplify characters—leaving out fingers or a mouth, for instance. You might think of economic theory as a stripped-down, or streamlined, version of economic reality.

The Role of Theory

Many people don't understand the role of theory. Perhaps you have heard, "Oh, that's fine in theory, but in practice it's another matter." The implication is that the theory provides little aid in practical matters. People who say this fail to realize that they are merely substituting their own theory for a theory they either do not believe or do not understand. They are really saying, "I have my own theory that works better."

All of us employ theories, however poorly defined or understood. Someone who pounds on the Pepsi machine that just ate a quarter has a crude theory about how that machine works and what went wrong. One version of that theory might be "The quarter drops through a series of whatchamacallits, but sometimes it gets stuck. *If* I pound on the machine, *then* I can free up the quarter and send it on its way." Evidently, this theory is pervasive enough that many people continue to pound on machines that fail to perform (a real problem for the vending machine industry and one reason newer machines are fronted with glass). Yet, if you were to ask these mad pounders to explain their "theory" about how the machine operates, they would look at you as if you were crazy.

The Scientific Method

To study economic problems, economists employ a process of theoretical investigation called the *scientific method,* which consists of four steps, as outlined in Exhibit 2.

Step One: Identify the Question and Define Relevant Variables

VARIABLE

A measure, such as price or quantity, that can take on different values

The first step is to identify the economic question and define the variables that are relevant to the solution. For example, the question might be "What is the relationship between the price of Pepsi and the quantity of Pepsi purchased?" In this case, the relevant variables are price and quantity. A **variable** is a measure that can take on different values. The variables of concern become the elements of the theory, so they must be selected with care.

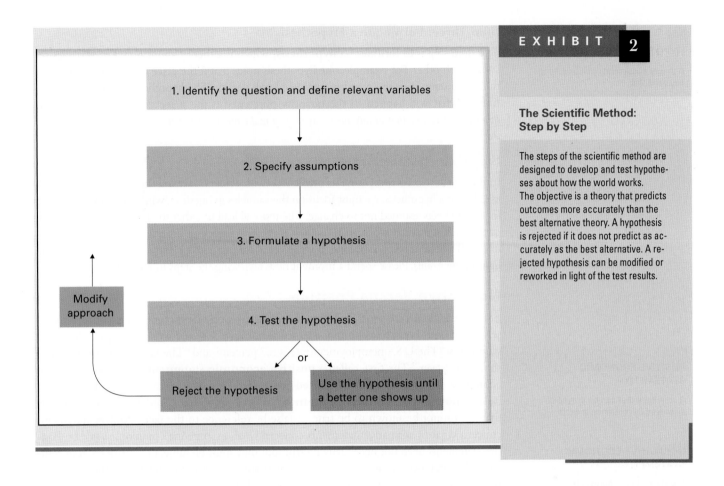

E X H I B I T   2

**The Scientific Method:
Step by Step**

The steps of the scientific method are designed to develop and test hypotheses about how the world works. The objective is a theory that predicts outcomes more accurately than the best alternative theory. A hypothesis is rejected if it does not predict as accurately as the best alternative. A rejected hypothesis can be modified or reworked in light of the test results.

Step Two: Specify Assumptions

The second step is to specify the assumptions under which the theory is to apply. One major category of assumptions is the **other-things-constant assumption**—in Latin, the ceteris paribus assumption. The idea is to identify the variables of interest and then focus exclusively on the relationships among them, assuming that nothing else of importance will change—that other things will remain constant. Again, suppose we are interested in how the price of Pepsi influences the amount purchased. To isolate the relation between these two variables, we assume that there are no changes in other relevant variables such as consumer income, the average temperature, or the price of Coke.

We also make assumptions about how people will behave; these we call **behavioral assumptions.** The primary behavioral assumption is rational self-interest. Earlier we assumed that individual decision makers pursue self-interest rationally and make choices accordingly. Rationality implies that each consumer buys the products expected to maximize his or her level of satisfaction. Rationality also implies that a firm supplies the products expected to maximize profit. These kinds of assumptions are called behavioral assumptions because they specify how we expect economic decision makers to behave—what makes them tick, so to speak.

OTHER-THINGS-CONSTANT ASSUMPTION

The assumption, when focusing on the relation among key economic variables, that other variables remain unchanged

BEHAVIORAL ASSUMPTION

An assumption that describes the expected behavior of economic decision makers, what motivates them

Step Three: Formulate a Hypothesis

The third step is to formulate a **hypothesis,** which is a theory about how key variables relate to each other. For example, one hypothesis holds that if the price of Pepsi goes up, other things constant, then the quantity purchased will decline. The hypothesis becomes a prediction of what will happen to the quantity purchased if the price goes up. *The purpose of this hypothesis, like that of any theory, is to help make predictions about cause and effect in the real world.*

Step Four: Test the Hypothesis

In the fourth step, by comparing its predictions with evidence, we test the validity of a hypothesis. To test a hypothesis, we must focus on the variables in question, while carefully controlling for other effects assumed not to change. The test will lead us either to (1) reject the hypothesis, or theory, if it predicts worse than the best alternative theory or (2) use the hypothesis, or theory, until a better one comes along. If we reject it, we can go back and modify our approach in light of the results. Please spend a moment now reviewing the steps in Exhibit 2.

Normative Versus Positive

Economists usually try to explain how the economy works. Sometimes they concern themselves not with how the economy *does* work but how it *should* work. Compare these two statements: "The U.S. unemployment rate is 5.7 percent" and "The U.S. unemployment rate should be lower." The first, called a **positive economic statement**, is an assertion about economic reality that can be supported or rejected by reference to the facts. The second, called a **normative economic statement,** reflects an opinion. And an opinion is merely that—it cannot be shown to be true or false by reference to the facts. Positive statements concern what *is;* normative statements concern what, in someone's opinion, *should be.* Positive statements need not necessarily be true, but they must be subject to verification or refutation by reference to the facts. Theories are expressed as positive statements such as "If the price of Pepsi increases, then the quantity demanded will decrease."

Most of the disagreement among economists involves normative debates—for example, the appropriate role of government—rather than statements of positive analysis. To be sure, many theoretical issues remain unresolved, but economists generally agree on most fundamental theoretical principles—that is, about positive economic analysis. For example, in a survey of 464 U.S. economists, only 6.5 percent disagreed with the statement "A ceiling on rents reduces the quantity and quality of housing available." This is a positive statement because it can be shown to be consistent or inconsistent with the evidence. In contrast, there was much less agreement on normative statements such as "The distribution of income in the United States should be more equal." Half the economists surveyed "generally agreed," a quarter "generally disagreed," and a quarter "agreed with provisos."[2]

Normative statements, or value judgments, have a place in a policy debate such as the proper role of government, provided that statements of opinion are distinguished from statements of fact. In such policy debates, you are entitled to your own opinion, but you are not entitled to your own facts.

Economists Tell Stories

Despite economists' reliance on the scientific method for developing and evaluating theories, economic analysis is as much art as science. Formulating a question, isolating the key

---

HYPOTHESIS

A theory about relationships among key variables

POSITIVE ECONOMIC STATEMENT

A statement that can be proved or disproved by reference to facts

NORMATIVE ECONOMIC STATEMENT

A statement that represents an opinion, which cannot be proved or disproved

---

2. Richard M. Alston, et al., "Is There a Consensus Among Economists in the 1990s?" *American Economic Review* 82 (May 1992): pp. 203–209, Table 1.

variables, specifying the assumptions, proposing a theory to answer the question, and devising a way to test the predictions all involve more than simply an understanding of economics and the scientific method. Carrying out these steps requires good intuition and the imagination of a storyteller. Economists explain their theories by telling stories about how they think the economy works. To tell a compelling story, an economist relies on case studies, anecdotes, parables, the personal experience of the listener, and supporting data. Throughout this book, you will hear stories that bring you closer to the ideas under consideration. The stories, such as the one about the Pepsi machine, breathe life into economic theory and help you personalize abstract ideas. As another example, here is a case study about the popularity of vending machines in Japan.

A Yen for Vending Machines

© Paul Chesley/Stone/Getty Images

Japan faces a steady drop in the number of working-age people. Here are three reasons why: (1) Japan's birthrate has reached a record low, (2) Japan allows virtually no immigration—only 2 of every 1,000 workers in Japan are foreigners, and (3) Japan's population is aging. As a result, unemployment has usually been lower in Japan than in other countries. Because labor is relatively scarce there, it is relatively costly. To sell products, Japanese retailers rely on capital, particularly vending machines, which obviously eliminate the need for sales clerks.

Japan has more vending machines per capita than any other country on the planet—twice as many as the United States and nearly ten times as many as Europe. And vending machines in Japan sell a wider range of products than elsewhere, including beer, sake, whiskey, rice, eggs, vegetables, pizza, entire meals, fresh flowers, clothes, video games, DVDs, even X-rated comic books. Japan's vending machines are also more sophisticated. The newer models come with video monitors and touch-pad screens. Wireless chips alert vendors when supplies are running low. Machines selling cigarettes or alcohol require a driver's license, which is used to verify the buyer's age (and the machines can spot fake IDs).

Some cold-drink dispensers automatically raise prices in hot weather. Coca-Cola machines allow mobile phone users to pay for drinks by pressing a few buttons on their mobiles. Sanyo makes a giant machine that sells up to 200 different items at three different temperatures. Perhaps the ultimate vending machine is Robo Shop Super 24, a totally automated convenience store in Tokyo. After browsing long display cases, a customer can make selections by punching product numbers on a keyboard. A bucket whirs around the store, collecting the selections.

As noted earlier, it is common practice in the United States to shake down vending machines that malfunction. Such abuse increases the probability the machines will fail again, leading to a cycle of abuse. Vending machines in Japan are less abused, in part because they are more sophisticated and more reliable and in part because the Japanese generally have greater respect for property and, consequently, a lower crime rate (for example, Japan's theft rate is only about half the U.S. rate).

Japanese consumers use vending machines with great frequency. For example, 40 percent of all soft-drink sales in Japan are through vending machines, compared to only 12 percent of

C a s e S t u d y

World of Business

eActivity
Why do Japanese consumers like to buy goods from vending machines? Some of the products offered include music CDs, hot meals, batteries, rice, and toilet paper. Read about vending of these and other products at http://www.japan-guide.com/e/e2010.html.

U.S. sales. Japanese sales per machine are double the U.S. rate. Research shows that most Japanese consumers prefer an anonymous machine to a salesperson (Robo Shop 24's Web site notes, "Grumpy, nervous store clerks have been replaced by the cheery little Robo"). Despite the abundance of vending machines in Japan, more growth is forecast, spurred on by a shrinking labor pool, technological innovations, and wide acceptance of machines there.

Sources: Ginny Parker, "Vending the Rules," *Time,* 25 August 2003; and "In 2001 Japanese Spent $87.5 Billion on Vending Machines," *The Food Industry Report*, 3 March 2003; pictures and descriptions of Robo Shop 24 can be found at http://www.theimageworks.com/Robo/roboftur.htm.

This case study makes two points. First, producers combine resources in a way that conserves, or economizes on, the resource that is more costly—in this case, labor. Second, the customs and conventions of the marketplace can differ across countries, and this variance can result in different types of economic arrangements, such as the more extensive use of vending machines in Japan.

Predicting Average Behavior

The goal of an economic theory is to predict the impact of an economic event on economic choices and, in turn, the effect of these choices on particular markets or on the economy as a whole. Does this mean that economists try predict the behavior of particular consumers or producers? Not necessarily, because a specific individual may behave in an unpredictable way. But the unpredictable actions of numerous individuals tend to cancel one another out, so the *average behavior* of groups can be predicted more accurately. For example, if the federal government cuts personal income taxes, certain households may decide to save the entire tax cut. On average, however, household spending will increase. Likewise, if Burger King cuts the price of Whoppers, the manager can better predict how much sales will increase than how a specific customer will respond. *The random actions of individuals tend to offset one another, so the average behavior of a large group can be predicted more accurately than the behavior of a particular individual.* Consequently, economists tend to focus on the average, or typical, behavior of people in groups—for example, as average taxpayers or average Whopper consumers—rather than on the behavior of a specific individual.

Some Pitfalls of Faulty Economic Analysis

Economic analysis, like other forms of scientific inquiry, is subject to common mistakes in reasoning that can lead to faulty conclusions. We will discuss three possible sources of confusion.

The Fallacy That Association Is Causation

In the last two decades, the number of physicians specializing in cancer treatment increased sharply. At the same time, the incidence of most cancers increased. Can we conclude that physicians cause cancer? No. To assume that event A caused event B simply because the two are associated in time is to commit the **association-is-causation fallacy,** a common error. The fact that one event precedes another or that the two events occur simultaneously does not necessarily mean that one causes the other. Remember: Association is not necessarily causation.

The Fallacy of Composition

Standing up at a football game to get a better view of the action does not work if others stand as well. Arriving early to buy concert tickets does not work if many others have the

ASSOCIATION-IS-CAUSATION FALLACY

The incorrect idea that if two variables are associated in time, one must necessarily cause the other

same idea. These are examples of the **fallacy of composition,** which is an erroneous belief that what is true for the individual, or the part, is also true for the group, or the whole.

The Mistake of Ignoring the Secondary Effects

In many cities, public officials have imposed rent controls on apartments. The primary effect of this policy, the effect on which policy makers focus, is to keep rents from rising. Over time, however, fewer new apartments get built because renting becomes less profitable. Moreover, existing rental units deteriorate because owners have no incentive to pay for maintenance since they have plenty of customers anyway. Thus, the quantity and quality of housing may decline as a result of what appears to be a reasonable measure to keep rents from rising. The mistake was to ignore the **secondary effects,** or the unintended consequences, of the policy. Economic actions have secondary effects that often turn out to be more important than the primary effects. Secondary effects may develop more slowly and may not be obvious, but good economic analysis takes them into account.

If Economists Are So Smart, Why Aren't They Rich?

Why aren't economists rich? Well, some are, earning over $25,000 per appearance on the lecture circuit. Others earn thousands a day as consultants. Economists have been appointed to cabinet positions, such as Secretaries of Commerce, Defense, Labor, State, and Treasury, and to head the Federal Reserve System. Economics is the only social science and the only business discipline for which the prestigious Nobel Prize is awarded, and pronouncements by economists are reported in the media daily. *The Economist,* a widely respected news weekly from London, argues that economic ideas have influenced policy "to a degree that would make other social scientists drool."[3]

The economics profession thrives because its models usually do a better job of making economic sense out of a confusing world than do alternative approaches. But not all economists are wealthy, nor is personal wealth the goal of the discipline. In a similar vein, not all doctors are healthy (some even smoke), not all carpenters live in perfectly built homes, not all marriage counselors are happily married, and not all child psychologists have well-adjusted children. Still, those who study economics do reap financial rewards, as discussed in this closing case study, which looks at the link between earnings and the choice of a college major.

Sidebar

HOMEWORK
Xpress!
Ask the Instructor Video

College Major and Career Earnings

Earlier in the chapter, you learned that economic choice is based on a comparison of expected marginal benefit and expected marginal cost. Surveys show that students go to college because they believe a college diploma is the ticket to better jobs and higher pay. Put another way, for about two-thirds of U.S. high school graduates, the expected marginal benefit of college apparently exceeds the expected marginal cost. The cost of college will be discussed in the next chapter; the focus here is on the benefits of college, particularly expected earnings.

Case Study Sidebar

C a s e **S t u d y**

The Information Economy

eActivity

The Federal Reserve Bank of Minneapolis asked some Nobel Prize winners how they became interested in economics. Their stories can be found at http://woodrow.mpls.frb.fed.us/pubs/region/98-12/quotes.cfm.

3. "The Puzzling Failure of Economics," *The Economist,* 23 August 1997, p. 11.

WALL STREET JOURNAL

Reading It **Right**

What's the relevance of the
following statement from the
Wall Street Journal: "With
economics the most popular
undergraduate major at many top
colleges, demand for economics
professors has led to a bidding
war for the most highly-regarded
candidates."

Among college graduates, all kinds of factors affect earnings, such as general ability, occupation, college attended, college major, and highest degree earned. To isolate the effects of college major on earnings, a National Science Foundation study surveyed people in specific age groups who worked full time and had earned a bachelor's as their highest degree. Exhibit 3 shows the median earnings by major for men and women ages 35 to 44. As a point of reference, the *median* annual earnings for men was $43,199 (half earned more and half earned less). The median earnings for women was $32,155, only 74 percent of the median for men. Among men, the top median pay was the $53,286 earned by engineering majors; that pay was 23 percent above the median for all men surveyed. Among women, the top median pay was the $49,170 earned by economics majors; that pay was 53 percent above the median for all women surveyed.

Incidentally, men who majored in economics earned a median of $49,377, ranking them seventh among 27 majors and 14 percent above the median for all men surveyed. Thus, even though the median pay for all women was only 74 percent of the median pay for all men, women who majored in economics earned about the same as men who majored in economics. We can say that economics majors earned more than most, and they experienced no pay difference based on gender.

Notice that among both men and women, the majors ranked toward the top of the list tend to be more quantitative and analytical. According to the study's author, "Employers may view certain majors as more difficult and may assume that graduates in these fields are more able and hard working, whereupon they offer them higher salaries."[4] The selection of a relatively more challenging major such as economics sends a favorable signal to future employers.

The study also examined the kinds of jobs different majors actually found. Those who majored in economics became mid- and top-level managers, executives, and administrators. They also worked in sales, computer fields, financial analysis, and economic analysis. Remember, the survey was limited to those whose highest degree was the baccalaureate, so it excluded the many economics majors who went on to pursue graduate studies in law, business administration, economics, public administration, journalism, and other fields (a separate study showed that lawyers with undergraduate degrees in economics earned more than other lawyers).

A number of world leaders majored in economics, including three of the last six U.S. presidents, Supreme Court Justice Sandra Day O'Connor, and Philippines President Gloria Macapagal-Arroyo, who earned a Ph.D. in the subject. Other well-known economics majors include eBay President Meg Whitman, Intel President Paul Otellini, Governor Arnold Schwarzenegger, aging rocker Mick Jagger, high-tech guru Esther Dyson, and Scott Adams, creator of Dilbert, the mouthless wonder.

Source: R. Kim Craft and Joe Baker, "Do Economists Make Better Lawyers? Undergraduate Degree Fields and Lawyer Earnings," *Journal of Economic Education,*" Summer 2003; and Daniel E. Hecker, "Earnings of College Graduates, 1993," *Monthly Labor Review,* December 1995. For a survey of employment opportunities, go to the U.S. Labor Department's Occupational Outlook Handbook at http://www.bls.gov/oco/.

4. Daniel E. Hecker, "Earnings of College Graduates, 1993," *Monthly Labor Review* (December 1995): p. 15.

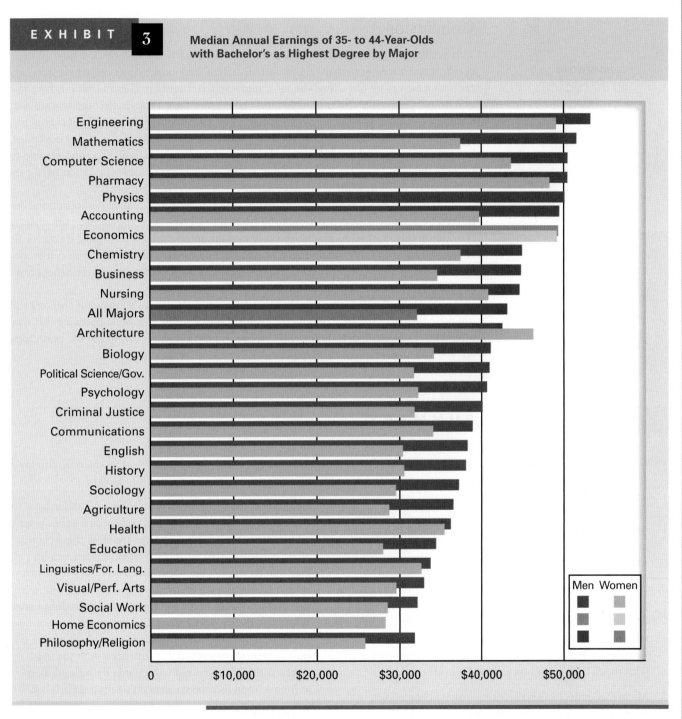

EXHIBIT 3

Median Annual Earnings of 35- to 44-Year-Olds with Bachelor's as Highest Degree by Major

Source: Earnings are for 1993 based on figures reported by Daniel Hecker in "Earnings of College Graduates, 1993," *Monthly Labor Review* (December 1995): 3–17.

Conclusion

This textbook describes how economic factors affect individual choices and how all these choices come together to shape the economic system. Economics is not the whole story, and economic factors are not always the most important. But economic considerations have important and predictable effects on individual choices, and these choices affect the way we live.

Sure, economics is a challenging discipline, but it is also an exciting and rewarding one. The good news is that you already know a lot about economics. To use this knowledge, however, you must cultivate the art and science of economic analysis. You must be able to simplify the world to formulate questions, isolate the relevant variables, and then tell a persuasive story about how these variables relate.

An economic relation can be expressed in words, represented as a table of quantities, described by a mathematical equation, or illustrated as a graph. The appendix to this chapter provides an introduction to graphs. You may find this information unnecessary. If you are already familiar with relations among variables, slopes, tangents, and the like, you can probably just browse. But if you have little recent experience with graphs, you might benefit from a more careful reading with pencil and paper in hand.

The next chapter will introduce key tools of economic analysis. Subsequent chapters will use these ideas to explore economic problems and to explain economic behavior that may otherwise seem puzzling. You must walk before you can run, however, and in the next chapter, you will take your first wobbly steps.

SUMMARY

1. Economics is the study of how people choose to use their scarce resources to produce, exchange, and consume goods and services in an attempt to satisfy unlimited wants. The economic problem arises from the conflict between scarce resources and unlimited wants. If wants were limited or if resources were not scarce, there would be no need to study economics.

2. Economic resources are combined in a variety of ways to produce goods and services. Major categories of resources include labor, capital, natural resources, and entrepreneurial ability. Because economic resources are scarce, only a limited number of goods and services can be produced with them; therefore, choices must be made.

3. Microeconomics focuses on choices made in households, firms, and governments and how these choices affect particular markets, such as the market for used cars. Choice is guided by rational self-interest. Choice typically requires time and information, both of which are scarce and valuable.

4. Whereas microeconomics examines the individual pieces of the puzzle, macroeconomics steps back to look at the big picture—the performance of the economy as a whole

as reflected by such measures as total production, employment, the price level, and economic growth.

5. Economists use theories, or models, to help understand the effects of economic changes, such as changes in price and income, on individual choices and how these choices affect particular markets and the economy as a whole. Economists employ the scientific method to study an economic problem by (a) formulating the question and isolating relevant variables, (b) specifying the assumptions under which the theory operates, (c) developing a theory, or hypothesis, about how the variables relate, and (d) testing that theory by comparing its predictions with the evidence. A theory might not work perfectly, but it is useful as long as it predicts better than competing theories do.

6. Positive economics aims to discover how the economy works. Normative economics is concerned more with how, in someone's opinion, the economy should work. Those who are not careful can fall victim to the fallacy that association is causation, to the fallacy of composition, and to the mistake of ignoring secondary effects.

QUESTIONS FOR REVIEW

1. *(Definition of Economics)* What determines whether or not a resource is scarce? Why is the concept of scarcity important to the definition of economics?

2. *(Resources)* To which category of resources does each of the following belong?

   a. A taxicab
   b. Computer software
   c. One hour of legal counsel
   d. A parking lot
   e. A forest
   f. The Mississippi River
   g. An individual introducing a new way to market products on the Internet

3. *(Goods and Services)* Explain why each of the following would *not* be considered "free" for the economy as a whole:

   a. Food stamps
   b. U.S. aid to developing countries
   c. Corporate charitable contributions
   d. Noncable television programs
   e. Public high school education

4. *(Economic Decision Makers)* Which group of economic decision makers plays the leading role in the economic system? Which groups play supporting roles? In what sense are they supporting actors?

5. *(Micro Versus Macro)* Determine whether each of the following is primarily a microeconomic or a macroeconomic issue:

   a. Determining the price to charge for an automobile
   b. Measuring the impact of tax policies on total consumption spending in the economy
   c. A household's decisions about how to allocate its disposable income among various goods and services
   d. A worker's decision regarding how many hours to work each week
   e. Designing a government policy to affect the level of employment

6. *(Micro Versus Macro)* Some economists believe that to really understand macroeconomics, you must fully understand microeconomics. How does microeconomics relate to macroeconomics?

7. *(Normative Versus Positive Analysis)* Determine whether each of the following statements is normative or positive:

   a. The U.S. unemployment rate was below 6.0 percent in 2003.
   b. The inflation rate in the United States is too high.
   c. The U.S. government should increase the minimum wage.
   d. U.S. trade restrictions cost consumers $20 billion annually.

8. *(Role of Theory)* What good is economic theory if it cannot predict the behavior of a specific individual?

PROBLEMS AND EXERCISES

9. *(Rational Self-Interest)* Discuss the impact of rational self-interest on each of the following decisions:

   a. Whether to attend college full time or enter the workforce full time
   b. Whether to buy a new textbook or a used textbook
   c. Whether to attend a local college or an out-of-town college

10. *(Rational Self-Interest)* If behavior is governed by rational self-interest, why do people make charitable contributions?

11. *(Marginal Analysis)* The owner of a small pizzeria is deciding whether to increase the radius of its delivery area by one mile. What considerations must be taken into account if such a decision is to contribute to profitability?

12. *(Time and Information)* It is often costly to obtain the information necessary to make good decisions. Yet your own interests can be best served by rationally weighing all options available to you. This requires informed decision making. Does this mean that making uninformed decisions is irrational? How do you determine how much information is the right amount?

13. (*C a s e* **S t u d y**: A Yen for Vending Machines) Do vending machines conserve on any resources other than labor? Does your answer offer any additional insight into the widespread use of vending machines in Japan?

14. (*C a s e* **S t u d y**: A Yen for Vending Machines) Suppose you had the choice of purchasing identically priced lunches from a vending machine or at a cafeteria. Which would you choose? Why?

15. *(Pitfalls of Economic Analysis)* Review the discussion of pitfalls in economic thinking in this chapter. Then identify the fallacy or mistake in thinking in each of the following statements:

    a. Raising taxes will always increase government revenues.
    b. Whenever there is a recession, imports decrease. Therefore, to stop a recession, we should increase imports.
    c. Raising the tariff on imported steel will help the U.S. steel industry. Therefore, the entire economy will be helped.
    d. Gold sells for about $400 per ounce. Therefore, the U.S. government could sell all the gold in Fort Knox at $400 per ounce and eliminate the national debt.

16. *(Association Versus Causation)* Suppose I observe that communities with lots of doctors tend to have relatively high rates of illness. I conclude that doctors cause illness. What's wrong with this reasoning?

EXPERIENTIAL EXERCISES

17. *(Micro Versus Macro)* Go to the Bank of Sweden's page on the Nobel Prize in economic science at http://www.nobel.se/economics/. Review the descriptions of some recent awards, and try to determine whether those particular awards were primarily for work in macroeconomics or in microeconomics.

18. (*C a s e* **S t u d y**: College Major and Career Earnings) The Bureau of Labor Statistics maintains online copies of articles from its *Monthly Labor Review*. Go to the site http://stats.bls.gov/opub/mlr/mlrhome.htm, click on "Archives" and find the article by Daniel Hecker entitled "Earnings of College Graduates: Women Compared with Men" (March 1998). What can you learn about the payoff to college education for both women and men? (Note: You will need Adobe Acrobat Reader to get the full text of this article. You can download a copy of Reader at http://www.adobe.com/prodindex/acrobat/readstep.html.

19. *(Wall Street Journal)* Detecting economic fallacies is an important skill. Review the section titled "Some Pitfalls of Faulty Economic Analysis" in this chapter. Then use the *Wall Street Journal* to find at least one example of faulty reasoning. (Hint: Begin with the "Markets Diary" column in the "Money & Investing" section.)

HOMEWORK XPRESS! EXERCISES

These exercises require access to McEachern Homework Xpress! If Homework Xpress! did not come with your book, visit **http://homeworkxpress.swlearning.com** *to purchase.*

1. The price for a basic cheese pizza at Giorgio's is $5. Each additional topping is $1. Sketch a graph to illustrate the relationship between the price of a pizza and the number of toppings for up to 5 toppings.

2. Reproductions of the National Gallery of Art's *Girl with a Watering Can* by Renoir are offered for sale in the gift shop. The manager finds that if she sets the price at $20, no reproductions are sold. For every dollar she reduces the price, 10 additional copies are sold each week. Sketch a graph showing the relationship between the price of a reproduction and the number sold each week.

3. Economists studying consumption of pizza notice that households buy more pizzas per month as income increases, but only up to an income of $3,000 per month. At this income level, the average household consumes 10 pizzas per month. As income increases beyond this level, household consumption of pizzas declines. Sketch a graph showing a curvilinear relationship between household income and the number of pizzas consumed per month.

4. Nicer Pants Inc. found that at a price of $50 per pair, no one bought its product. For every dollar less it charged, it sold an additional 200 pairs of pants per month. Draw a graph to illustrate the relationship between the price of the pants and the quantity purchased per month. Label this as D for consumer demand.

    Due to an economics recession, the firm now finds that it has no sales at prices about $40 per pair. However, for each dollar it reduces the prices, it still sells an additional 200 pairs per month. Sketch a graph to illustrate this new relationship between the price of the pants and the quantity purchased each month. Label this as D1.

Appendix

Understanding Graphs

Take out a pencil and a blank piece of paper. Go ahead. Put a point in the middle of the paper. This is your point of departure, called the **origin.** With your pencil at the origin, draw a straight line off to the right. This line is called the **horizontal axis.** The value of the variable *x* measured along the horizontal axis increases as you move to the right of the origin. Now mark off this line from 0 to 20, in increments of 5 units each. Returning to the origin, draw another line, this one straight up. This line is called the **vertical axis.** The value of the variable *y* measured along the vertical axis increases as you move upward. Mark off this line from 0 to 20, in increments of 5 units each.

Within the space framed by the two axes, you can plot possible combinations of the variables measured along each axis. Each point identifies a value measured along the horizontal, or *x,* axis *and a* value measured along the vertical, or *y,* axis. For example, place point *a* in your graph to reflect the combination where *x* equals 5 units and *y* equals 15 units. Likewise, place point *b* in your graph to reflect 10 units of *x* and 5 units of *y.* Now compare your results with points shown in Exhibit 4.

A **graph** is a picture showing how variables relate, and a picture can be worth a thousand words. Take a look at Exhibit 5, which shows the U.S. annual unemployment rate since 1900. The year is measured along the horizontal axis and the unemployment rate along the vertical axis. Exhibit 5 is a *time-series graph,* which shows the value of a variable, in this case the unemployment rate, over time. If you had to describe the information presented in Exhibit 5 in words, the explanation could take many words. The picture shows not only how one year compares to the next but also how one decade compares to another and how the rate trends over time. The sharply higher unemployment rate during the Great Depression of the 1930s is unmistakable. *Graphs convey information in a compact and efficient way.*

This appendix shows how graphs express a variety of possible relations among variables. Most graphs of interest in this book reflect the relationship between two economic variables, such as the unemployment rate and the year, the price of a product and the quantity demanded, or the price of production and the quantity supplied. Because we focus on just two variables at a time, we usually assume that other relevant variables remain constant.

One variable often depends on another. The time it takes you to drive home depends on your average speed. Your weight depends on how much you eat. The amount of Pepsi people buy depends on its price. A *functional relation* exists between two variables when the value of one variable *depends* on the value of another variable. The value of the **dependent variable** depends on the value of the **independent variable**. The task of the economist is to isolate economic relations and determine the direction of causality, if

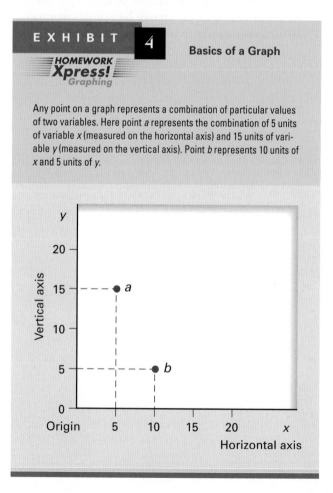

EXHIBIT 4   **Basics of a Graph**

HOMEWORK
Xpress!
Graphing

Any point on a graph represents a combination of particular values of two variables. Here point *a* represents the combination of 5 units of variable *x* (measured on the horizontal axis) and 15 units of variable *y* (measured on the vertical axis). Point *b* represents 10 units of *x* and 5 units of *y.*

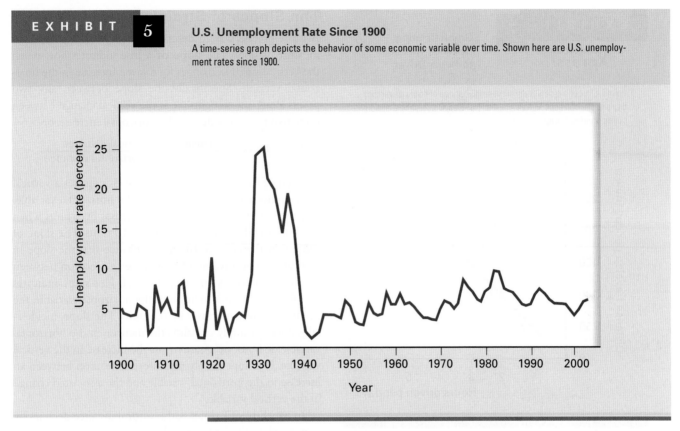

EXHIBIT 5

U.S. Unemployment Rate Since 1900

A time-series graph depicts the behavior of some economic variable over time. Shown here are U.S. unemployment rates since 1900.

Sources: *Historical Statistics of the United States,* 1970, and *Economic Report of the President,* February 2004.

any. Recall that one of the pitfalls of economic thinking is the erroneous belief that association is causation. We cannot conclude that, simply because two events relate in time, one causes the other. There may be no relation between the two events.

Drawing Graphs

Let's begin with a simple relation. Suppose you are planning to drive across country and want to determine how far you will travel each day. You plan to average 50 miles per hour. Possible combinations of driving time and distance traveled appear in Exhibit 6. One column lists the hours driven per day, and the next column lists the number of miles traveled per day, assuming an average speed of 50 miles per hour. The distance traveled, the *dependent* variable, depends on the number of hours driven, the *independent* variable. Combinations of hours driven and distance traveled are shown as *a, b, c, d,* and *e.* Each combination of hours driven and distance

EXHIBIT 6

Schedule Relating Distance Traveled to Hours Driven

	Hours Driven per Day	Distance Traveled per Day (miles)
a	1	50
b	2	100
c	3	150
d	4	200
e	5	250

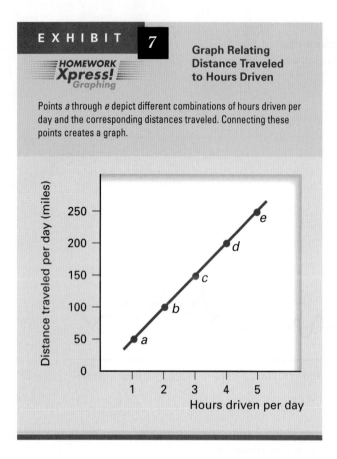

Graph Relating Distance Traveled to Hours Driven

Points *a* through *e* depict different combinations of hours driven per day and the corresponding distances traveled. Connecting these points creates a graph.

traveled is represented by a point in Exhibit 7. For example, point *a* shows that if you drive for 1 hour, you travel 50 miles. Point *b* indicates that if you drive for 2 hours, you travel 100 miles. By connecting the points, or combinations, we create a line running upward and to the right. This makes sense, because the longer you drive, the farther you travel. Assumed constant along this line is your average speed of 50 miles per hour.

Types of relations between variables include the following:

1. As one variable increases, the other increases—as in Exhibit 7; this is called a **positive, or direct, relation** between the variables.

2. As one variable increases, the other decreases; this is called a **negative, or inverse, relation.**

3. As one variable increases, the other remains unchanged; the two variables are said to be *independent,* or *unrelated.* One of the advantages of graphs is that they easily convey the relation between variables. We do not need to examine the particular combinations of numbers; we need only focus on the shape of the curve.

The Slopes of Straight Lines

A more precise way to describe the shape of a curve is to measure its slope. The **slope of a line** indicates how much the vertical variable changes for a given increase in the horizontal variable. Specifically, the slope between any two points along any straight line is the vertical change between these two points divided by the horizontal increase, or

$$\text{Slope} = \frac{\text{Change in the vertical distance}}{\text{Increase in the horizontal distance}}$$

Each of the four panels in Exhibit 8 indicates a vertical change, given a 10-unit increase in the horizontal variable. In panel (a), the vertical distance increases by 5 units when the horizontal distance increases by 10 units. The slope of the line is therefore 5/10, or 0.5. Notice that the slope in this case is a positive number because the relation between the two variables is positive, or direct. This slope indicates that for every 1-unit increase in the horizontal variable, the vertical variable increases by 0.5 units. The slope, incidentally, does not imply causality; the increase in the horizontal variable does not necessarily *cause* the increase in the vertical variable. The slope simply measures the relation between an increase in the horizontal variable and the associated change in the vertical variable.

In panel (b) of Exhibit 8, the vertical distance declines by 7 units when the horizontal distance increases by 10 units, so the slope equals −7/10, or −0.7. The slope in this case is a negative number because the two variables have a negative, or inverse, relation. In panel (c), the vertical variable remains unchanged as the horizontal variable increases by 10, so the slope equals 0/10, or 0. These two variables are unrelated. Finally, in panel (d), the vertical variable can take on any value, although the horizontal variable remains unchanged. Again, the two variables are unrelated. In this case, any change in the vertical measure, for example a 10-unit change, is divided by 0, because the horizontal value does not change. Any change divided by 0 is infinitely large, so we say that the slope of a vertical line is infinite.

The Slope, Units of Measurement, and Marginal Analysis

The mathematical value of the slope depends on the units measured on the graph. For example, suppose copper tubing costs $1 a foot to make. Graphs depicting the relation between output and total cost are shown in Exhibit 9. In panel (a), the total cost of production increases by $1 for each

EXHIBIT **8**

Alternative Slopes for Straight Lines

The slope of a line indicates how much the vertically measured variable changes for a given increase in the variable measured along the horizontal axis. Panel (a) shows a positive relation between two variables; the slope is 0.5, a positive number. Panel (b) depicts a negative, or inverse, relation. When the *x* variable increases, the *y* variable decreases; the slope is –0.7, a negative number. Panels (c) and (d) represent situations in which two variables are unrelated. In panel (c), the *y* variable always takes on the same value; the slope is 0. In panel (d), the *x* variable always takes on the same value; the slope is infinite.

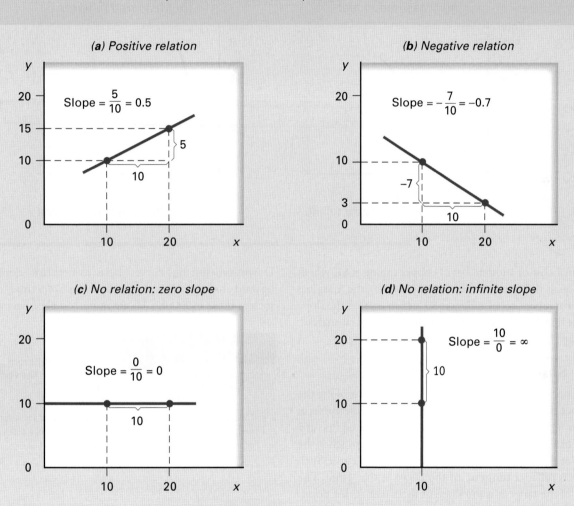

1-foot increase in the amount of tubing produced. Thus, the slope equals 1/1, or 1. If the cost per foot remains the same but the unit of measurement is not *feet* but *yards,* the relation between output and total cost is as depicted in panel (b). Now total cost increases by $3 for each 1-*yard* increase in output, so the slope equals 3/1, or 3. Because different units are used to measure the copper tubing, the two panels reflect different slopes, even though the cost of tubing is $1 per foot

in each panel. Keep in mind that *the slope will depend in part on the units of measurement.*

Economic analysis usually involves *marginal analysis,* such as the marginal cost of producing one more unit of output. The slope is a convenient device for measuring marginal effects because it reflects the change in total cost along the vertical axis for each 1-unit change in output along the horizontal axis. For example, in panel (a) of Exhibit 9, the

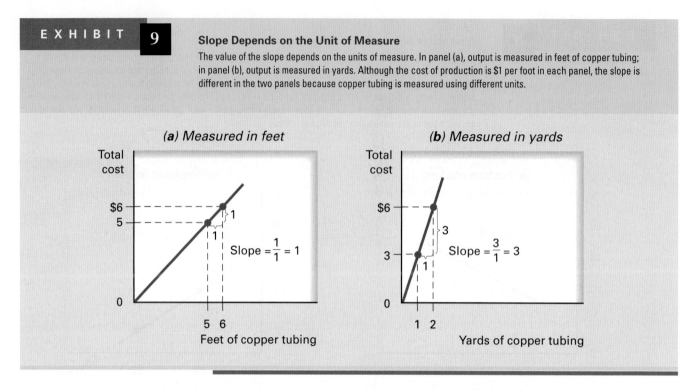

EXHIBIT 9

Slope Depends on the Unit of Measure

The value of the slope depends on the units of measure. In panel (a), output is measured in feet of copper tubing; in panel (b), output is measured in yards. Although the cost of production is $1 per foot in each panel, the slope is different in the two panels because copper tubing is measured using different units.

(a) Measured in feet

$$\text{Slope} = \frac{1}{1} = 1$$

Feet of copper tubing

(b) Measured in yards

$$\text{Slope} = \frac{3}{1} = 3$$

Yards of copper tubing

marginal cost of another *foot* of copper tubing is $1, which also equals the slope of the line. In panel (b), the marginal cost of another *yard* of tubing is $3, which again is the slope of that line. Because of its applicability to marginal analysis, the slope has special relevance in economics.

The Slopes of Curved Lines

The slope of a straight line is the same everywhere along the line, but the slope of a curved line differs along the curve, as shown in Exhibit 10. To find the slope of a curved line at a particular point, draw a straight line that just touches the curve at that point but does not cut or cross the curve. Such a line is called a **tangent** to the curve at that point. The slope of the tangent is the slope of the curve at that point. Look at the line *A*, which is tangent to the curve at point *a*. As the horizontal value increases from 0 to 10, the vertical value drops along *A* from 40 to 0. Thus, the vertical change divided by the horizontal change equals −40/10, or −4, which is the slope of the curve at point *a*. This slope is negative because the curve slopes downward at that point. Line *B*, a line tangent to the curve at point *b*, has the slope −10/30, or −0.33. As you can see, the curve depicted in Exhibit 10 gets flatter as the horizontal variable increases, so the value of its slope approaches zero.

Other curves, of course, will reflect different slopes as well as different changes in the slope along the curve.

Downward-sloping curves have a negative slope, and upward-sloping curves, a positive slope. Sometimes curves, such as those in Exhibit 11, are more complex, having both

EXHIBIT 10

HOMEWORK **Xpress!** *Graphing*

Slope at Different Points on a Curved Line

The slope of a curved line varies from point to point. At a given point, such as *a* or *b*, the slope of the curve is equal to the slope of the straight line that is tangent to the curve at that point.

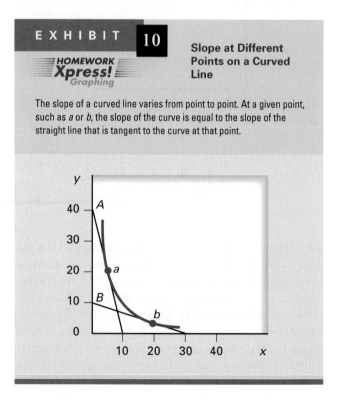

E X H I B I T **11**

Curves with Both Positive and Negative Slopes

Some curves have both positive and negative slopes. The hill-shaped curve has a positive slope to the left of point *a*, a slope of 0 at point *a*, and a negative slope to the right of that point. The U-shaped curve starts off with a negative slope, has a slope of 0 at point *b*, and has a positive slope to the right of that point.

E X H I B I T **12**

Shift in Line Relating Distance Traveled to Hours Driven

Line *T* appeared originally in Exhibit 7 to show the relation between hours driven per day and distance traveled per day, assuming an average speed of 50 miles per hour. If the average speed is only 40 miles per hour, the entire relation shifts to the right to *T'*, indicating that each distance traveled requires more driving time. For example, 200 miles traveled takes 4 hours of driving at 50 miles per hour but 5 hours at 40 miles per hour. This figure shows how a change in assumptions, in this case, the average speed assumed, can shift the entire relationship between two variables.

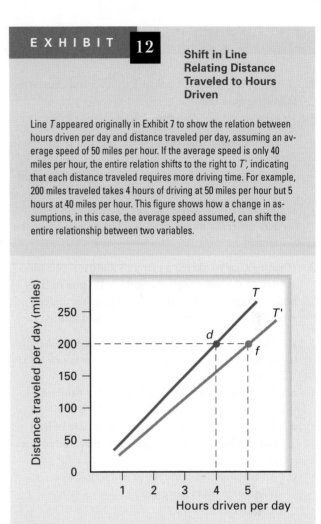

positive and negative ranges. In the hill-shaped curve, for small values of *x*, there is a positive relation between *x* and *y*, so the slope is positive. As the value of *x* increases, however, the slope declines and eventually becomes negative. We can divide the curve into two segments: (1) the segment between the origin and point *a*, where the slope is positive; and (2) the segment of the curve to the right of point *a*, where the slope is negative. The slope of the curve at point *a* is 0. The U-shaped curve in Exhibit 11 represents the opposite relation: *x* and *y* are negatively related until point *b* is reached; thereafter, they are positively related. The slope equals 0 at point *b*.

Line Shifts

Let's go back to the example of your cross-country trip, where we were trying to determine how many miles you traveled per day. Recall that we measured hours driven per day on the horizontal axis and miles traveled per day on the vertical axis, assuming an average speed of 50 miles per hour. That same relation is shown as line *T* in Exhibit 12. What if the average speed is 40 miles per hour? The entire relation

between hours driven and distance traveled would change, as shown by the shift to the right of line *T* to *T'*. With a slower average speed, any distance traveled per day now requires more driving time. For example, 200 miles traveled requires 4 hours of driving when the average speed is 50 miles per hour (as shown by point *d* on curve *T*), but 200 miles takes 5 hours when your speed averages 40 miles per hour (as shown by point *f* on curve *T'*). Thus, *a change in the assumption about average speed changes the relationship between the two variables observed.* This changed relationship is expressed by a shift of the line that shows how the two variables relate.

That ends our once-over of graphs. Return to this appendix when you need a review.

APPENDIX QUESTIONS

1. *(Understanding Graphs)* Look at Exhibit 5 and answer the following questions:

   a. In what year (approximately) was the unemployment rate the highest? In what year was it the lowest?

   b. In what decade, on average, was the unemployment rate highest? In what decade was it lowest?

   c. Between 1950 and 1980, did the unemployment rate generally increase, decrease, or remain about the same?

2. *(Drawing Graphs)* Sketch a graph to illustrate your idea of each of the following relationships. Be sure to label both axes appropriately. In each case, explain under what circumstances, if any, the curve could shift:

   a. The relationship between a person's age and height

   b. Average monthly temperature over the course of a year

   c. A person's income and the number of hamburgers consumed per month

   d. The amount of fertilizer added to an acre of land and the amount of corn grown on that land in one growing season

   e. An automobile's horsepower and its gasoline mileage (in miles per gallon)

3. *(Slope)* Suppose you are given the following data on wage rates and number of hours worked:

Point	Hourly Wage	Hours Worked per Week
a	$0	0
b	5	0
c	10	30
d	15	35
e	20	45
f	25	50

   a. Construct and label a set of axes and plot these six points. Label each point. Which variable do you think should be measured on the vertical axis, and which variable should be measured on the horizontal axis?

   b. Connect the points. Describe the curve you find. Does it make sense to you?

   c. Compute the slope of the curve between points *a* and *b*. Between points *b* and *c*. Between points *c* and *d*. Between points *d* and *e*. Between points *e* and *f*. What happens to the slope as you move from point *a* to point *f*?

Some Tools of Economic Analysis

© Digital Vision/Getty Images

Why are you reading this book right now rather than doing something else? What is college costing you? Why will you eventually major in one subject rather than continue to take courses in different ones? Why is fast food so fast? Why is there no sense crying over spilt milk? These and other questions are addressed in this chapter, which introduces some tools of economics—some tools of the trade.

Chapter 1 introduced the idea that scarcity forces us to make choices, but the chapter said little about how to make economic choices. This chapter develops a framework for evaluating economic alternatives. First, we consider the cost involved in selecting one alternative over others. Next, we develop tools to explore the choices available to individuals and to the economy as a whole. Finally, we examine the questions that different economies must answer—questions about what goods and services to produce, how to produce them, and for whom to produce them. Topics discussed include:

- Opportunity cost
- Division of labor
- Comparative advantage
- Specialization

- Production possibilities frontier
- Three economic questions
- Economic systems

Choice and Opportunity Cost

Think about a decision you just made: the decision to read this chapter right now rather than use your time to study for another course, play sports, watch TV, go online, get some sleep, hang with friends, or do something else. Suppose your best alternative to reading right now is getting some sleep. The cost of reading is passing up the opportunity of sleep. Because of scarcity, whenever you make a choice, you must pass up another opportunity; you must incur an *opportunity cost*.

Opportunity Cost

OPPORTUNITY COST

The value of the best alternative forgone when an item or activity is chosen

Economics in the Movies

What do we mean when we talk about the cost of something? Isn't it what we must give up—must forgo—to get that thing? The **opportunity cost** of the chosen item or activity is *the value of the* best *alternative that is forgone.* You can think of opportunity cost as the *opportunity lost.* Sometimes opportunity cost can be measured in terms of money, although, as we shall see, money is usually only part of opportunity cost.

How many times have you heard people say they did something because they "had nothing better to do"? They actually mean they had no alternatives as attractive as the choice they selected. Yet, according to the idea of opportunity cost, people *always* do what they do because they have nothing better to do. The choice selected seems, at the time, preferable to any other possible choice. You are reading this chapter right now because you have nothing better to do. In fact, you are attending college for the same reason: College appears more attractive than your best alternative, as discussed in the following case study.

The Opportunity Cost of College

What is your opportunity cost of attending college full time this year? What was the best alternative you gave up? If you held a full-time job, you have some idea of the income you gave up to attend college. Suppose you expected to earn $16,000 a year, after taxes, from a full-time job. As a full-time college student, you plan to work part time during the academic year and full time during the summer, earning a total of $7,000 after taxes. Thus, by attending college this year, you gave up after-tax earnings of $9,000 (= $16,000 − $7,000).

There is also the direct cost of college itself. Suppose you are paying $5,000 this year for in-state tuition, fees, and books at a public college (paying out-of-state rates would add another $5,000 to that, and attending a private college would add about $13,000). The opportunity cost of paying for tuition, fees, and books is what you and your family could otherwise have purchased with that money.

How about room and board? Expenses for room and board are not necessarily an opportunity cost because, even if you were not attending college, you would still need to live somewhere and eat something, though these could cost more in college. Likewise, whether or not you attended college, you would still buy items such as DVDs, CDs, clothes, toiletries, and laundry. These items are not an opportunity cost of attending college; they are personal upkeep costs that arise regardless of what you do. So for simplicity, assume that room, board, and personal expenses are the same whether or not you attend college. The forgone earnings of $9,000 plus the $5,000 for tuition, fees, and books yield an opportunity cost of $14,000 this year for a student paying in-state rates at a public college. Opportunity cost jumps to about $19,000 for students paying out-of-state rates and to about $27,000 for those at private colleges. Scholarships, but not loans, would reduce your opportunity cost (why not loans?).

This analysis assumes that other things remain constant. But if, in your view, attending college is more of a pain than you expected your next best alternative to be, then the opportunity cost of attending college is even higher. In other words, if you are one of those people who find college difficult, often boring, and in most ways more unpleasant than a full-time job, then the cost in money terms understates your opportunity cost. Not only are you incurring the expense of college, but you are also forgoing a more pleasant quality of life. If, on the other hand, you believe the wild and crazy life of a college student is more enjoyable than a full-time job would be, then the above figures overstate your opportunity cost, because the next best alternative involves a less satisfying quality of life.

Apparently, you view college as a wise investment in your future, even though it's costly and maybe even painful. College graduates on average earn about twice as much per year as high school graduates, a difference that exceeds $1 million over a lifetime. These pay gains from college encourage a growing fraction of college students to pile up debts to finance their education.

Still, college is not for everyone. Some find the opportunity cost too high. For example, Tiger Woods, once an economics major at Stanford, dropped out after two years to earn a fortune in professional golf. Some high school seniors who believe they are ready for professional basketball skip college altogether, as do most pro tennis players and many singers and actors. Some would-be actors even drop out of high school to pursue their careers, including Drew Barrymore, Tom Cruise, Cameron Diaz, Matt Dillon, Nicole Kidman, Demi Moore, Keanu Reeves, Kiefer Sutherland, and Catherine Zeta-Jones.

Sources: "College Tuition 101," *Wall Street Journal*, 15 September 2003; and Mary Beth Marklein, "College Braces for Bigger Classes and Less Bang for More Buck," *USA Today*, 27 August 2003; Greg Winter and Jennifer Medina, "More Students Line Up at Financial Aid Office," *New York Times*, 10 March 2003; and "2002–2003 College Costs," http://www.collegeboard.com/.

Opportunity Cost Is Subjective

Like beauty, opportunity cost is in the eye of the beholder. It is subjective. Only the individual making the choice can identify the most attractive alternative. But the chooser seldom knows the actual value of the best alternative forgone, because that alternative is "the road not taken." If you give up an evening of pizza and conversation with friends to work on a term paper, you will never know the exact value of what you gave up. You know only what you *expected*. Evidently, you expected the value of working on that paper to exceed the value of the best alternative. (Incidentally, focusing on the best alternative forgone makes all other alternatives irrelevant.)

Calculating Opportunity Cost Requires Time and Information

Economists assume that people rationally choose the most valued alternative. The idea of choosing rationally does not mean people exhaustively calculate the value of all possibilities. Because acquiring information about alternatives is costly and time consuming, people usually make choices based on limited or even incorrect information. Indeed, some choices may turn out to be poor ones (you went for a picnic but it rained; the DVD you rented stunk; your new shoes pinch; the exercise equipment you bought gets no exercise). Regret about lost opportunities is captured in the common expression "coulda, woulda, shoulda." At the time you made the choice, however, you thought you were making the best use of all your scarce resources, including the time required to gather and evaluate information about your alternatives.

Time Is the Ultimate Constraint

The sultan of Brunei is among the world's richest people, with wealth estimated at over $10 billion based on huge oil revenues that flow into his tiny country. He has two palaces, one for each wife (though he divorced one in 2003). The larger palace has 1,788 rooms, with walls of fine Italian marble and a throne room the size of a football field. The royal family owns hundreds of cars, including dozens of Rolls-Royces. Supported by such wealth, the sultan appears to have overcome the economic problem caused by scarcity. But though he can buy just about whatever he wants, he lacks the time to enjoy his stuff. If he pursues one activity, he cannot at the same time do something else, so each activity he undertakes has an opportunity cost. Consequently, the sultan must choose from among the competing uses of his scarcest resource, time. Although your alternatives are less exotic, you too face time constraints, especially toward the end of the college term.

Opportunity Cost May Vary with Circumstance

Opportunity cost depends on the value of your alternatives. This is why you are more likely to study on a Tuesday night than on a Saturday night. On a Tuesday night, the opportunity cost of studying is lower because your alternatives are less attractive than on a Saturday night, when more is happening. Suppose you go to a movie on Saturday night. Your opportunity cost is the value of your best alternative forgone, which might be attending a college game. For some of you, studying on Saturday night may be well down the list of alternatives—perhaps ahead of reorganizing your closet but behind doing your laundry.

Opportunity cost is subjective, but in some cases, money paid for goods and services is a reasonable approximation. For example, the opportunity cost of the new DVD player you bought is the value of spending that $100 on the best forgone alternative. The money measure may leave out some important elements, however, particularly the value of the time involved. For example, renting a movie costs you not just the $4 rental fee but the time and travel required to get it, watch it, and return it.

Sunk Cost and Choice

Suppose you have just finished shopping for groceries and are wheeling your grocery cart toward the checkout counters. How do you decide which line to join? You pick the shortest one. Suppose, after waiting 10 minutes in a line that barely moves, you notice that a cashier has opened another cash register and invites you to check out. Do you switch to the open line, or do you think, "Since I've already spent 10 minutes in this line, I'm staying put"? The 10 minutes you waited represents a **sunk cost,** which is a cost that has already been incurred and cannot be recovered, regardless of what you do now. You should ignore sunk cost in making economic choices. Hence, you should switch to the newly opened register. *Economic decision makers should consider only those costs that are affected by the choice. Sunk costs have already been incurred and are not affected by the choice, so they are irrelevant.* Likewise, you should walk out on a bad movie, even if it cost you $10 to get in. That $10 is gone and sitting through that stinker only makes you worse off. The irrelevance of sunk costs is underscored by the proverb "There's no sense crying over spilt milk." The milk has already spilled, so whatever you do now cannot change that.

Now that you have some idea about opportunity cost, you are ready to consider applying this idea to how best to use scarce resources to help satisfy unlimited wants.

SUNK COST

A cost that has already been incurred in the past, cannot be recovered, and thus is irrelevant for present and future economic decisions

Comparative Advantage, Specialization, and Exchange

Suppose you live in a dormitory. You and your roommate have such tight schedules that you each can spare only about an hour a week for mundane tasks like ironing shirts and typing papers (granted, in reality you may not iron shirts or type papers, but this example will help you understand some important points). Each of you must turn in a typed three-page paper every week, and you each prefer to have your shirts ironed when you have the time. Let's say it takes you a half hour to type your handwritten paper. Your roommate is from the hunt-and-peck school and takes about an hour to type a handwritten paper. But your roommate is a talented ironer and can iron a shirt in 5 minutes flat (or should that be, iron it flat in 5 minutes?). You take twice as long, or 10 minutes, to iron a shirt.

During the hour set aside each week for typing and ironing, typing takes priority. If you each do your own typing and ironing, you type your paper in a half hour and iron three shirts in the remaining half hour. Your roommate takes the entire hour typing the paper, leaving no time for ironing. Thus, if you each do your own, the combined output is two typed papers and three ironed shirts.

The Law of Comparative Advantage

Before long, you each realize that total output would increase if you did all the typing and your roommate did all the ironing. In the hour available for these tasks, you type both papers and your roommate irons 12 shirts. As a result of specialization, total output increases by 9 shirts! You strike a deal to exchange your typing for your roommate's ironing, so you each end up with a typed paper and 6 ironed shirts. Thus, *each of you is better off as a result of specialization and exchange.* By specializing in the task that you each do best, you are using the **law of comparative advantage,** which states that the individual with the lowest opportunity cost of producing a particular output should specialize in producing that output. You face a lower opportunity cost of typing than does your roommate, because in the time it takes to type a paper, you could iron 3 shirts whereas your roommate could iron 12 shirts. And if you face a lower opportunity cost of typing, your roommate must face a lower opportunity cost of ironing (try working that out).

LAW OF COMPARATIVE ADVANTAGE

The individual, firm, region, or country with the lowest opportunity cost of producing a particular good should specialize in that good

Absolute Advantage Versus Comparative Advantage

The gains from specialization and exchange so far are obvious. A more interesting case is if you are faster at both tasks. Suppose the example changes in one way: your roommate takes

12 minutes to iron a shirt compared with your 10 minutes. You now have an *absolute advantage* in both tasks, meaning each task takes you less time than it does your roommate. More generally, having an **absolute advantage** means making something using fewer resources than other producers require.

Does your absolute advantage in both activities mean specialization is no longer a good idea? Recall that the law of comparative advantage states that the individual with *the lower opportunity cost* of producing a particular good should specialize in that good. You still take 30 minutes to type a paper and 10 minutes to iron a shirt, so your opportunity cost of typing the paper remains at three ironed shirts. Your roommate takes an hour to type a paper and 12 minutes to iron a shirt, so your roommate could iron five shirts in the time it takes to type a paper. Your opportunity cost of typing a paper is ironing three shirts; for your roommate it's ironing five shirts. *Because your opportunity cost of typing is lower than your roommate's, you still have a comparative advantage in typing.* Consequently, your roommate must have a comparative advantage in ironing (again, try working this out to your satisfaction). Therefore, you should do all the typing and your roommate, all the ironing. Although you have an absolute advantage in both tasks, your **comparative advantage** calls for specializing in the task for which you have the lower opportunity cost—in this case, typing.

If neither of you specialized, you could type one paper and iron three shirts. Your roommate could still type just the one paper. Your combined output would be two papers and three shirts. If you each specialized according to comparative advantage, in an hour you could type both papers and your roommate could iron five shirts. Thus, specialization increases total output by two ironed shirts. Even though you are better at both tasks than your roommate, you are comparatively better at typing. Put another way, your roommate, although worse at both tasks, is not quite as bad at ironing as at typing.

Don't think that this is simply common sense. Common sense would lead you to do your own ironing and typing, because you are better at both. *Absolute advantage focuses on who uses the fewest resources, but comparative advantage focuses on what else those resources could have produced—that is, on the opportunity cost of those resources.* Comparative advantage is the better guide to who should do what.

The law of comparative advantage applies not only to individuals but also to firms, regions of a country, and entire nations. Individuals, firms, regions, or countries with the lowest opportunity cost of producing a particular good should specialize in producing that good. Because of such factors as climate, workforce skills, natural resources, and capital stock, certain parts of the country and certain parts of the world have a comparative advantage in producing particular goods. From Washington State apples to Florida oranges, from software in India to hardware in Taiwan—*resources are allocated most efficiently across the country and around the world when production and trade conform to the law of comparative advantage.*

Specialization and Exchange

In the previous example, you and your roommate specialized and then exchanged output. No money was involved. In other words, you engaged in **barter,** where products are traded directly for other products. Barter works best in simple economies with little specialization and few traded goods. But for economies with greater specialization, *money* facilitates exchange. Money—coins, bills, and checks—is a *medium of exchange* because it is the one thing that everyone accepts in return for goods and services.

Because of specialization and comparative advantage, most people consume little of what they produce and produce little of what they consume. Each individual specializes then exchanges that product for money, which in turn is exchanged for goods and services. Did you

ABSOLUTE ADVANTAGE

The ability to produce something using fewer resources than other producers use

COMPARATIVE ADVANTAGE

The ability to produce something at a lower opportunity cost than other producers face

BARTER

The direct exchange of one good for another without using money

make anything you are wearing? Probably not. Think about the degree of specialization that went into your cotton shirt. A farmer in a warm climate grew the cotton and sold it to someone who spun it into thread, who sold it to someone who wove it into fabric, who sold it to someone who sewed the shirt, who sold it to a wholesaler, who sold it to a retailer, who sold it to you. Your shirt was produced by many specialists.

Division of Labor and Gains from Specialization

Picture a visit to McDonald's: "Let's see, I'll have a Big Mac, an order of fries, and a choco-late shake." Less than a minute later your order is ready. It would take you much longer to make a homemade version of this meal. Why is the McDonald's meal faster, cheaper, and—for some people—tastier than one you could make yourself? Why is fast food so fast? Mc-Donald's takes advantage of the gains resulting from the **division of labor.** Each worker, rather than preparing an entire meal, specializes in separate tasks. This division of labor al-lows the group to produce much more.

DIVISION OF LABOR

Organizing production of a good into its separate tasks

How is this increase in productivity possible? First, the manager can assign tasks according to *individual preferences and abilities*—that is, according to the law of comparative advantage. The worker with the toothy smile and pleasant personality can handle the cus-tomers up front; the one with the strong back but few social graces can handle the heavy lifting out back. Second, a worker who performs the same task again and again gets better at it (experience is a good teacher). The worker filling orders at the drive-through, for exam-ple, learns to deal with special problems that arise. Third, no time is lost in moving from one task to another. Finally, and perhaps most importantly, the **specialization of labor** allows for the introduction of more sophisticated production techniques—techniques that would not make sense on a smaller scale. For example, McDonald's large shake machine would be impractical in the home. Specialized machines make workers more productive.

SPECIALIZATION OF LABOR

Focusing work effort on a particu-lar product or a single task

To review: The specialization of labor takes advantage of individual preferences and nat-ural abilities, allows workers to develop more experience at a particular task, reduces the time required to shift between different tasks, and permits the introduction of laborsaving machinery. Specialization and the division of labor occur not only among individuals but also among firms, regions, and indeed entire countries. The cotton shirt mentioned earlier might involve growing cotton in one country, turning it into cloth in another, making the shirt in a third, and selling it in a fourth.

We should also acknowledge the downside of specialization. Doing the same thing all day can become tedious. Consider, for example, the assembly-line worker whose sole task is to tighten a particular bolt. Such a job could drive that worker bonkers or lead to repetitive motion injury. Thus, the gains from dividing production into individual tasks must be weighed against the problems caused by assigning workers to repetitive and tedious jobs.

Specialization is discussed in the following case study.

Specialization Abounds

Evidence of specialization is all around us. Look at the extent of specialization in higher ed-ucation. A large university may house a dozen or more schools and colleges—agriculture, architecture, business, drama, education, engineering, law, fine arts, liberal arts and sciences, medicine, music, nursing, pharmacy, social work, and more. Some of these include a dozen or more departments. And each department may offer courses in a dozen or more special-ties. Economics, for example, offers courses in micro, macro, development, econometrics, economic history, health, industrial organization, international finance, international trade, labor, law and economics, money and banking, poverty, public finance, regulation, urban and

C a s e **Study**

Bringing Theory to Life

eActivity

Economics is a subject that has bene-fited from specialization and the divi-sion of labor. To get a feel for the many

34

different subjects that economists investigate, take a look at the *Journal of Economic Literature*'s classification system at http://www.aeaweb.org/journal/jel_class_system.html.

regional, and more. Altogether, a university may offer courses in thousands of specialized fields.

How about a trip to the mall? Specialty shops range from luggage to lingerie. Restaurants can be quite specialized—from subs to sushi. Or let your fingers do the walking through the *Yellow Pages,* where you find thousands of specializations. Under "Physicians" alone, you uncover dozens of medical specialties. With-

© Robert Holmes/Corbis

out moving a muscle, you can witness the division of labor within a single industry as the credits roll at the end of a movie. There you will see scores of specialists—from gaffer (lighting electrician) to assistant location scout. TV is no different. An episode of *The Sopranos,* for example, requires contributions from about three hundred people.

Magazines also offer fine degrees of specialization, with tens of thousands to choose from. Fans of the Chevy Corvette, for example, can subscribe to *Corvette Enthusiast, Corvette Fever,* or *Vette.* The extent of specialization is perhaps most obvious on the Web, where the pool of potential customers is so vast that individual sites become sharply focused. For example, you can find sites for each of the following: miniature furniture, paper airplanes, musical bowls, prosthetic noses, tongue studs, toe rings, brass knuckles, mouth harps, ferret toys, cat bandannas, juggling equipment, and bug visors (for motorcycle helmets)—just to name a few of the hundreds of thousands of specialty sites. You won't find such specialists at the mall, but they can find their niche in the virtual world. Adam Smith said the degree of specialization is limited by the extent of the market. Sellers on the Web face the broadest customer base in the world.

Source: You can find online versions of the *Yellow Pages* at http://www.yellowpages.com/ and http://www.superpages.com/. Any search engine will turn up the specialty sites reported above.

The Economy's Production Possibilities

The focus to this point has been on how individuals choose to use their scarce resources to satisfy their unlimited wants or, more specifically, how they specialize based on comparative advantage. This emphasis on the individual has been appropriate because the economy is shaped by the choices of individual decision makers, whether they are consumers, producers, or public officials. Just as resources are scarce for the individual, they are also scarce for the economy as a whole (no fallacy of composition here). An economy has millions of different resources that can be combined in all kinds of ways to produce millions of different goods and services. This section steps back from the immense complexity of the real economy to develop our second model, which explores the economy's production options.

Efficiency and the Production Possibilities Frontier

Let's develop a model to get some idea of how much an economy can produce with the resources available. What are the economy's production capabilities? Here are the model's simplifying assumptions:

1. To simplify matters, output is limited to just two broad classes of products: consumer goods, such as pizzas and haircuts, and capital goods—physical capital, such as a pizza ovens, and human capital, such as higher education.

2. The focus is on production during a given period—in this case, a year.

3. The economy's resources are fixed in both quantity and quality during that period.

4. Society's knowledge about how these resources combine to produce output—that is, the available *technology*—does not change during the year.

The point of these assumptions is to freeze the economy's resources and technology in time so we can focus on the economy's production alternatives.

Given the resources and the technology available in the economy, the **production possibilities frontier,** or **PPF,** identifies possible combinations of the two types of goods that can be produced when all available resources are employed fully and efficiently. *Resources are employed fully and efficiently when there is no change that could increase the production of one good without decreasing the production of the other good.* **Efficiency** involves getting the maximum possible output from available resources.

The economy's PPF for consumer goods and capital goods is shown by the curve *AF* in Exhibit 1. Point *A* identifies the amount of consumer goods produced per year if all the economy's resources are used efficiently to produce consumer goods. Point *F* identifies the amount of capital goods produced per year if all the economy's resources are used efficiently to produce capital goods. Points along the curve between *A* and *F* identify possible combinations of the two goods that can be produced when *all* the economy's resources *are used efficiently*.

Inefficient and Unattainable Production

Points inside the PPF, such as *I* in Exhibit 1, represent combinations that do not employ resources fully, employ them inefficiently, or both. Note that point *C* yields more consumer goods and no fewer capital goods than *I*. And point *E* yields more capital goods and no fewer consumer goods than *I*. Indeed, any point along the PPF between *C* and *E,* such as point *D,* yields both more consumer goods and more capital goods than *I*. Hence, point *I* is *inefficient*. By using resources more efficiently or by using previously idle resources, the economy can produce more of at least one good without reducing the production of the other good. Points outside the PPF, such as *U* in Exhibit 1, represent *unattainable* combinations, given the resources and the technology available. Thus, *the PPF not only shows efficient combinations of production but also serves as the boundary between inefficient combinations inside the frontier and unattainable combinations outside the frontier.*

The Shape of the Production Possibilities Frontier

Focus again on point *A* in Exhibit 1. Any movement along the PPF involves giving up some of one good to get more of the other. Movement down along the curve indicates that the opportunity cost of more capital goods is fewer consumer goods. For example, moving from point *A* to point *B increases* the amount of capital goods produced from none to 10 million units but *reduces* production of consumer goods from 50 million to 48 million units. Increasing production of capital goods to 10 million units reduces consumer goods only a little. Capital production initially employs resources (such as heavy machinery used to build factories) that add little to production of consumer goods but are quite productive in making capital goods.

As shown by the dashed lines in Exhibit 1, each additional 10 million units of capital goods reduces consumer goods by successively larger amounts. As more capital goods are produced, the resources drawn away from consumer goods are those that are increasingly better suited to producing consumer goods. *Opportunity cost increases as the economy produces*

PRODUCTION POSSIBILITIES FRONTIER (PPF)

A curve showing alternative combinations of goods that can be produced when available resources are used fully and efficiently; a boundary between inefficient and unattainable combinations

EFFICIENCY

The condition that exists when there is no way resources can be reallocated to increase the production of one good without decreasing the production of another

EXHIBIT **1**

The Economy's Production Possibilities Frontier

If the economy uses its available resources and technology fully and efficiently in producing consumer goods and capital goods, that economy is on its production possibilities frontier, *AF.* The PPF is bowed out to illustrate the law of increasing opportunity cost: additional units of capital goods require the economy to sacrifice more and more units of consumer goods. Note that more consumer goods must be given up in moving from *E* to *F* than in moving from *A* to *B,* although in each case the gain in capital goods is 10 million units. Points inside the PPF, such as *I,* represent inefficient use of resources. Points outside the PPF, such as *U,* represent unattainable combinations.

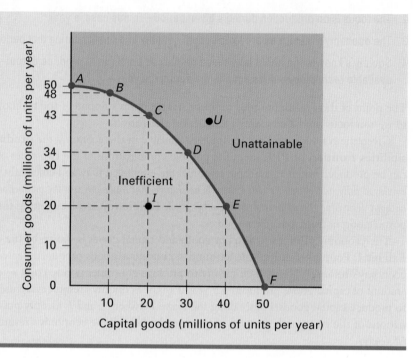

LAW OF INCREASING OPPORTUNITY COST

To produce each additional increment of a good, a successively larger increment of an alternative good must be sacrificed if the economy's resources are already being used efficiently

ECONOMIC GROWTH

An increase in the economy's ability to produce goods and services; an outward shift of the production possibilities frontier

more capital goods, because the resources in the economy are not all perfectly adaptable to the production of both types of goods. The shape of the production possibilities frontier reflects the **law of increasing opportunity cost.** If the economy uses all resources efficiently, the law of increasing opportunity cost states that each additional increment of one good requires the economy to sacrifice successively larger and larger increments of the other good.

The PPF derives its bowed-out shape from the law of increasing opportunity cost. For example, whereas the first 10 million units of capital goods have an opportunity cost of only 2 million units of consumer goods, the final 10 million—that is, the increase from point *E* to point *F*—have an opportunity cost of 20 million units of consumer goods. Notice that the slope of the PPF shows the opportunity cost of an increment of capital. As the economy moves down the curve, the curve becomes steeper, reflecting the higher opportunity cost of capital goods in terms of forgone consumer goods. The law of increasing opportunity cost also applies when moving from the production of capital goods to the production of consumer goods. If resources were perfectly adaptable to alternative uses, the PPF would be a straight line, reflecting a constant opportunity cost along the PPF.

What Can Shift the Production Possibilities Frontier?

Any production possibilities frontier assumes the economy's resources and technology are fixed. Over time, however, the PPF may shift if resources or technology change. **Economic growth** is an expansion in the economy's production possibilities and is reflected by an outward shift of the PPF.

Changes in Resource Availability

If people decide to work longer hours, the PPF shifts outward, as shown in panel (a) of Exhibit 2. An increase in the size or health of the labor force, an increase in the skills of the labor force, or an increase in the availability of other resources, such as new oil discoveries, also shifts the PPF outward. In contrast, a decrease in the availability or quality of resources shifts the PPF inward, as depicted in panel (b). For example, in 1990 Iraq invaded Kuwait, setting oil fields ablaze and destroying much of Kuwait's physical capital, thereby shifting Kuwait's PPF inward. In West Africa, the encroaching sands of the Sahara cover and destroy thousands of square miles of productive farmland each year, shifting the PPF of that economy inward.

The new PPFs in panels (a) and (b) appear to be parallel to the original ones, indicating that the resources that changed could produce both capital goods and consumer goods. For example, an increase in electrical power can enhance the production of both. If a resource such as farmland benefits just consumer goods, then increased availability or productivity of that resource shifts the PPF more along the consumer goods axis, as shown in panel (c). Panel (d) shows the effect of an increase in a resource such as construction equipment that is suited only to capital goods.

Increases in the Capital Stock

An economy's PPF depends in part on the stock of human and physical capital. The more capital an economy produces during one period, the more output can be produced in the next period. Thus, producing more capital goods this period (for example, more machines in the case of physical capital or better education in the case of human capital) shifts the economy's PPF outward the next period. The choice between consumer goods and capital goods is really the choice between present consumption and future production. Again, the more capital goods produced this period, the greater the economy's production possibilities next period.

Technological Change

A technological discovery that employs resources more efficiently could shift the economy's PPF outward. Some discoveries enhance the production of both capital goods and consumer goods, as shown in panel (a) of Exhibit 2. For example, the Internet has increased each firm's ability to identify available resources. A technological discovery that benefits consumer goods only, such as more disease resistant seeds, is reflected by a rotation outward of the PPF along the consumer goods axis, as shown in panel (c). Note that point F remains unchanged because the technological breakthrough does not affect the production of capital goods. Panel (d) shows a technological advance in the production of capital goods, such as improved software for designing heavy machinery.

What Can We Learn from the PPF?

The PPF demonstrates several ideas introduced so far. The first is *efficiency:* The PPF describes the efficient combinations of outputs, given the economy's resources and technology. The second idea is *scarcity:* Given the stock of resources and technology, the economy can produce only so much. The PPF slopes downward, indicating that, as the economy produces more of one good, it must produce less of the other good, thus demonstrating *opportunity cost.* The PPF's bowed-out shape reflects the *law of increasing opportunity cost,* which arises because some resources are not perfectly adaptable to the production of each good. And a shift outward in the PPF reflects *economic growth.*

Finally, because society must somehow select a specific combination of output—a single point—along the PPF, the PPF also underscores the need for *choice.* Selecting a particular combination determines not only current consumption but also the capital stock available next period. One thing the PPF does not tell us is which combination to choose. The PPF tells us only about the costs, not the benefits, of the two goods. To make a selection, we need

EXHIBIT   2

Shifts in the Economy's Production Possibilities Frontier

When the resources available to an economy change, the PPF shifts. If more resources become available or if technology improves, the PPF shifts outward, as in panel (a), indicating that more output can be produced. A decrease in available resources causes the PPF to shift inward, as in panel (b). Panel (c) shows a change affecting consumer goods production. More consumer goods can now be produced at any given level of capital goods. Panel (d) shows a change affecting capital goods production.

(a) *Increase in available resources*

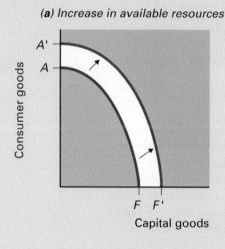

(b) *Decrease in available resources*

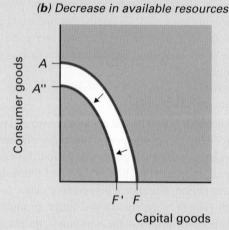

(c) *Increase in resources or technological advance that benefits consumer goods*

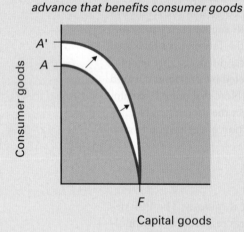

(d) *Increase in resources or technological advance that benefits capital goods*

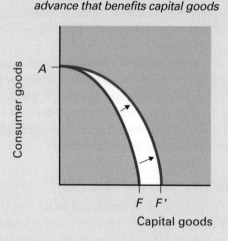

information on both costs *and* benefits. How society goes about choosing a particular combination depends on the nature of the economic system, as you will see shortly.

Three Questions Every Economic System Must Answer

Each point along the economy's production possibilities frontier is an efficient combination of outputs. Whether the economy produces efficiently and how the economy selects the most preferred combination depends on the decision-making rules employed. Regardless of how decisions are made, each economy must answer three fundamental questions: What goods and services are to be produced? How are they to be produced? And for whom are they to be produced? An **economic system** is the set of mechanisms and institutions that resolve the *what, how,* and *for whom* questions. Some criteria used to distinguish among economic systems are (1) who owns the resources, (2) what decision-making process is used to allocate resources and products, and (3) what types of incentives guide economic decision makers.

What Goods and Services Will Be Produced?

Most of us take for granted the incredible number of choices that go into deciding what gets produced—everything from which new kitchen appliances are introduced and to which roads get built and which movies get made (for example, movie studios pay for about 10,000 scripts a year but make only about 500 movies[1]). Although different economies resolve these and millions of other questions using different decision-making rules and mechanisms, all economies must somehow make such choices.

How Will Goods and Services Be Produced?

The economic system must determine how output gets produced. Which resources should be used, and how should they be combined to produce each product? How much labor should be used and at what skill levels? What kinds of machines should be used? What new technology should be incorporated into the latest video games? Should the factory be built in the city or closer to the interstate highway? Millions of individual decisions determine which resources are employed and how these resources are combined.

For Whom Will Goods and Services Be Produced?

Who will actually consume the goods and services produced? The economic system must determine how to allocate the fruits of production among the population. Should everyone receive equal shares? Should the weak and the sick get more? Should those willing to wait in line get more? Should goods be allocated according to height? Weight? Religion? Age? Gender? Race? Looks? Strength? Political connections? The value of resources supplied? The question "For whom will goods and services be produced?" is often referred to as the distribution question.

Economic Systems

Although the three economic questions were discussed separately, they are closely interwoven. The answer to one depends very much on the answers to the others. For example, an economy that distributes goods and services uniformly to all will, no doubt, answer the what-will-be-produced question differently than an economy that somehow allows personal choice. Laws about resource ownership and the role of government determine the "rules of the game"—the set of conditions that shape individual incentives and constraints. Along a spectrum ranging from the freest to the most regimented types of economic systems, *capitalism* would be at one end and the *command system* at the other.

Pure Capitalism

Under **pure capitalism,** the rules of the game include the private ownership of resources and the market allocation of products. Owners have *property rights* to the use of their resources and are therefore free to supply those resources to the highest bidder. **Private property rights** allow individuals to use resources or to charge others for their use. Any

1. As reported in Ian Parker, "The Real McKee," *New Yorker*, 20 October 2003.

ECONOMIC SYSTEM

The set of mechanisms and institutions that resolve the what, how, and for whom questions

WALL STREET JOURNAL

Reading It **Right**

What's the relevance of the following statement from the Wall Street Journal*: "Capitalism is supposed to be the one economic system that puts consumers at the center."*

PURE CAPITALISM

An economic system characterized by the private ownership of resources and the use of prices to coordinate economic activity in unregulated markets

PRIVATE PROPERTY RIGHTS

An owner's right to use, rent, or sell resources or property

*Net***Bookmark**

The Center for International Comparisons at the University of Pennsylvania at http://pwt.econ.upenn.edu/ is a good source of information on the performance of economies around the world.

income derived from supplying labor, capital, natural resources, or entrepreneurial ability goes to the individual resources owners. Producers are free to make and sell whatever they think will be profitable. Consumers are free to buy whatever goods they can afford. All this voluntary buying and selling is coordinated by unrestricted markets, where buyers and sellers make their intentions known. Market prices guide resources to their most productive use and channel goods and services to the consumers who value them the most.

Under pure capitalism, markets answer the what, how, and for whom questions. That's why capitalism is also referred to as *market system.* Markets transmit information about relative scarcity, provide individual incentives, and distribute income among resource suppliers. No individual or small group coordinates these activities. Rather, it is the voluntary choices of many buyers and sellers responding only to their individual incentives and constraints that direct resources and products to those who value them the most. According to Adam Smith (1723–1790), market forces allocate resources as if by an "invisible hand"—an unseen force that harnesses the pursuit of self-interest to direct resources where they earn the greatest payoff. According to Smith, *although each individual pursues his or her self-interest, the "invisible hand" of markets promotes the general welfare.* Capitalism is sometimes called *laissez-faire;* translated from the French, this phrase means "to let do," or to let people do as they choose without government intervention. Thus, under capitalism, voluntary choices based on rational self-interest are made in unrestricted markets to answer the questions what, how, and for whom.

As we will see in later chapters, pure capitalism has its flaws. The most notable market failures are:

1. No central authority protects property rights, enforces contracts, and otherwise ensures that the rules of the game are followed.

2. People with no resources to sell could starve.

3. Some producers may try to monopolize markets by eliminating the competition.

4. The production or consumption of some goods involves harmful side effects, such as pollution, that affect people not involved in the market transaction.

5. Private firms have no incentive to produce so-called *public goods,* such as national defense, because private firms cannot prevent nonpayers from enjoying the benefits of public goods.

Because of these limitations, countries have modified pure capitalism to allow a role for government. Even Adam Smith believed government should play a role. The United States is one of the most market-oriented economies in the world today.

Pure Command System

PURE COMMAND SYSTEM

An economic system characterized by the public ownership of resources and centralized planning

In a **pure command system,** resources are directed and production is coordinated not by market forces but by the "command," or central plan, of government. In theory at least, instead of private property, there is public, or communal, ownership of property. That's why central planning is sometimes called *communism.* Government planners, as representatives of all the people, answer such questions through *central plans* spelling out how much steel, how many cars, and how many homes to produce. They also decide how to produce these goods and who gets them.

In theory, the pure command system incorporates individual choices into collective choices, which, in turn, are reflected in central plans. In practice, the pure command system also has flaws, most notably:

1. Running an economy is so complicated that some resources are used inefficiently.

2. Because nobody in particular owns resources, people have less incentive to employ them in their highest-valued use, so some resources are wasted.

3. Central plans may reflect more the preferences of central planners than those of society.

4. Because government is responsible for all production, the variety of products tends to be more limited than in a capitalist economy.

5. Each individual has less personal freedom in making economic choices.

Because of these limitations, countries have modified the pure command system to allow a role for markets. North Korea is perhaps the most centrally planned economy in the world today.

Mixed and Transitional Economies

No country on earth exemplifies either type of economic system in its pure form. Economic systems have grown more alike over time, with the role of government increasing in capitalist economies and the role of markets increasing in command economies. The United States represents a **mixed system,** with government directly accounting for about one-third of all economic activity. What's more, government regulates the private sector in a variety of ways. For example, local zoning boards determine lot sizes, home sizes, and the types of industries allowed. Federal bodies regulate workplace safety, environmental quality, competitive fairness, food and drug quality, and many other activities.

Although both ends of the spectrum have moved toward the center, capitalism has gained more converts in recent decades. Perhaps the benefits of markets are no better illustrated than where countries were divided by ideology into capitalist economies and command economies, such as Taiwan and China or South Korea and North Korea. In each case, the economies began with similar human and physical resources, but income per capita diverged sharply, with the capitalist economies outperforming the command economies. For example, Taiwan's production per capita in 2003 was 4 times that of China's, and South Korea's production per capita was 13 times that of North Korea's.

Recognizing the incentive power of markets, some of the most die-hard central planners now reluctantly accept some free-market activity. For example, about 20 percent of the world's population lives in China, which grows more market oriented each day, even going so far as to give private property constitutional protection. More than a decade ago, the former Soviet Union dissolved into 15 independent republics; most are trying to convert state-owned enterprises into private firms. From Hungary to Mongolia, the transition to mixed economies now under way in former command economies will shape economies of this new century.

Economies Based on Custom or Religion

Finally, some economic systems are molded largely by custom or religion. For example, caste systems in India and elsewhere restrict occupational choice. Family relations also play significant roles in organizing and coordinating economic activity. Even in the United States, some occupations are still dominated by women, others by men, largely because of tradition. Your own pattern of consumption and choice of occupation may be influenced by some of these factors.

MIXED SYSTEM

An economic system characterized by the private ownership of some resources and the public ownership of other resources; some markets are unregulated and others are regulated

Conclusion

Although economies can answer the three economic questions in a variety of ways, this book will focus primarily on the mixed market system, such as exists in the United States. This type of economy blends *private choice,* guided by the price system in competitive markets, with *public choice,* guided by democracy in political markets. The study of mixed market systems grows more relevant as former command economies try to develop markets. The next chapter focuses on the economic actors in a mixed economy and explains why government gets into the act.

SUMMARY

1. Resources are scarce, but human wants are unlimited. Because you cannot satisfy all your wants, you must choose, and choice involves an opportunity cost. The opportunity cost of the selected option is the value of the best alternative forgone.

2. The law of comparative advantage says that the individual, firm, region, or country with the lowest opportunity cost of producing a particular good should specialize in that good. Specialization according to the law of comparative advantage promotes the most efficient use of resources.

3. The specialization of labor increases efficiency by (a) taking advantage of individual preferences and natural abilities, (b) allowing each worker to develop expertise and experience at a particular task, (c) reducing the time required to move between different tasks, and (d) allowing for the introduction of more specialized capital and large-scale production techniques.

4. The production possibilities frontier, or PPF, shows the productive capabilities of an economy when all resources are used fully and efficiently. The frontier's bowed-out shape reflects the law of increasing opportunity cost, which arises because some resources are not perfectly adaptable to the production of different goods. Over time, the frontier can shift in or out as a result of changes in the availability of resources and in technology. The frontier demonstrates several economic concepts, including efficiency, scarcity, opportunity cost, the law of increasing opportunity cost, economic growth, and the need for choice.

5. All economic systems, regardless of their decision-making processes, must answer three fundamental questions: What will be produced? How will it be produced? And for whom will it be produced? Economies answer the questions differently, depending on who owns the resources and how economic activity is coordinated. Economies can be directed by market forces, by the central plans of government, or by a mix of the two.

QUESTIONS FOR REVIEW

1. *(Opportunity Cost)* Discuss the ways in which the following conditions might affect the opportunity cost of going to a movie tonight:

   a. You have a final exam tomorrow.
   b. School will be out for one month starting tomorrow.
   c. The same movie will be on TV next week.

2. *(Opportunity Cost)* Determine whether each of the following statements is true, false, or uncertain. Explain your answers:

   a. The opportunity cost of an activity is the total value of all the alternatives passed up.
   b. Opportunity cost is an objective measure of cost.

c. When making choices, people gather all available information about the costs and benefits of alternative choices.

d. A decision maker seldom knows the actual value of a forgone alternative and must base decisions on expected values.

3. *(Comparative Advantage)* "You should never buy precooked frozen foods because you are paying for the labor costs of preparing food." Is this conclusion always valid, or can it be invalidated by the law of comparative advantage?

4. *(Specialization and Exchange)* Explain how the specialization of labor can lead to increased productivity.

5. *(Production Possibilities)* Under what conditions is it possible to increase production of one good without decreasing production of another good?

6. *(Production Possibilities)* Under what conditions would an economy be operating inside its PPF? Outside its PPF?

7. *(Shifting Production Possibilities)* In response to an influx of illegal aliens, Congress made it a federal offense to hire

them. How do you think this measure affected the U.S. production possibilities frontier? Do you think all industries were affected equally?

8. *(Production Possibilities)* "If society decides to use its resources fully and efficiently (that is, to produce *on* its production possibilities frontier), then future generations will be worse off because they will not be able to use these resources." If this assertion is true, full employment of resources may not be a good thing. Comment on the validity of this assertion.

9. *(Economic Questions)* What basic economic questions must be answered in a barter economy? In a primitive economy? In a pure capitalist economy? In a command economy?

10. *(Economic Systems)* What are the major differences between a pure capitalist system and a pure command system? Is the United States more like a pure capitalist system or more like a pure command system?

PROBLEMS AND EXERCISES

11. (*C a s e* **S t u d y :** The Opportunity Cost of College) During the Vietnam War, colleges and universities were overflowing with students. Was this bumper crop of students caused by a greater expected return on a college education or by a change in the opportunity cost of attending college? Explain.

12. *(Sunk Cost and Choice)* You go to a restaurant and buy an expensive meal. Halfway through, despite feeling quite full, you decide to clean your plate. After all, you think, you paid for the meal, so you are going to eat all of it. What's wrong with this thinking?

13. *(Opportunity Cost)* You can either spend spring break working at home for $80 per day or go to Florida for the week. If you stay home, your expenses will total about $100. If you go to Florida, the airfare, hotel, food, and miscellaneous expenses will total about $700. What's your opportunity cost of going to Florida?

14. *(Absolute and Comparative Advantage)* You have the following information concerning the production of wheat and cloth in the United States and the United Kingdom:

Labor Hours Required to Produce One Unit

	United Kingdom	United States
Wheat	2	1
Cloth	6	5

a. What is the opportunity cost of producing a unit of wheat in the United Kingdom? In the United States?

b. Which country has an absolute advantage in producing wheat? In producing cloth?

c. Which country has a comparative advantage in producing wheat? In producing cloth?

d. Which country should specialize in producing wheat? In producing cloth?

15. (*C a s e* **S t u d y :** Specialization Abounds) Provide some examples of specialized markets or retail outlets. What makes the Web conducive to specialization?

16. *(Shape of the PPF)* Suppose a production possibilities frontier includes the following combinations:

Cars	Washing Machines
0	1,000
100	600
200	0

a. Graph the PPF, assuming that it has no curved segments.

b. What is the cost of producing an additional car when 50 cars are being produced?

c. What is the cost of producing an additional car when 150 cars are being produced?

d. What is the cost of producing an additional washing machine when 50 cars are being produced? When 150 cars are being produced?

e. What do your answers tell you about opportunity costs?

17. *(Production Possibilities)* Suppose an economy uses two resources (labor and capital) to produce two goods (wheat and cloth). Capital is relatively more useful in producing cloth, and labor is relatively more useful in producing wheat. If the supply of capital falls by 10 percent and the supply of labor increases by 10 percent, how will the PPF for wheat and cloth change?

18. *(Production Possibilities)* There's no reason why a production possibilities frontier could not be used to represent the situation facing an individual. Imagine your own PPF. Right now—today—you have certain resources—your time,

your skills, perhaps some capital. And you can produce various outputs. Suppose you can produce combinations of two outputs, call them studying and partying.

a. Draw your PPF for studying and partying. Be sure to label the axes of the diagram appropriately. Label the points where the PPF intersects the axes, as well as several other points along the frontier.

b. Explain what it would mean for you to move upward and to the left along your personal PPF. What kinds of adjustments would you have to make in your life to make such a movement along the frontier?

c. Under what circumstances would your personal PPF shift outward? Do you think the shift would be a "parallel" one? Why, or why not?

19. *(Shifting Production Possibilities)* Determine whether each of the following would cause the economy's PPF to shift inward, outward, or not at all:

a. An increase in average length of annual vacations

b. An increase in immigration

c. A decrease in the average retirement age

d. The migration of skilled workers to other countries

20. *(Economic Systems)* The United States is best described as having a mixed economic system. What are some elements of command in the U.S. economy? What are some elements of tradition?

EXPERIENTIAL EXERCISES

21. *(Production Possibilities Frontier)* Here are some data on the U.S. economy taken from the *Economic Report of the President* at http://www.access.gpo.gov/eop/.

Year	Unemployment Rate	Real Government Spending (billions)	Real Civilian Spending (billions)
1982	9.7%	$ 947.7	$3,672.6
1983	9.6	960.1	3,843.6
1996	5.4	1,257.9	5,670.5
1997	4.9	1,270.6	5,920.8

a. Sketch a production possibilities frontier for the years 1982 and 1983, showing the trade-off between public-sector (government) and private-sector (civilian) spending. Assume that resource availability and technology were the

same in both years, but notice that the unemployment rate was relatively high.

b. Sketch a PPF for the years 1996 and 1997. Assume that resource availability and technology were the same in both years but higher than in 1982 and 1983. Note that the unemployment rate in the late 1990s was much lower than in the early 1980s.

c. What lessons did you learn about the U.S. economy of the past 20 years?

22. *(Economic Systems)* The transitional economies of Eastern Europe are frequently in the news because they provide testing grounds for the transition from socialist central

planning to freer, more market-oriented economies. Take a look at the World Bank's Transition Newsletter at http://www.worldbank.org/html/prddr/trans/recent.htm. Click on "Recent Issues," open an issue, and choose a particular country. Try to determine how smoothly the transition is proceeding. What problems is that nation encountering?

23. *(Wall Street Journal)* The ability to measure the true (opportunity) cost of a choice is a skill that will pay you great dividends. Use any issue of the *Wall Street Journal,* and find an article that discusses a decision some firm has made. (Try the "Business Bulletin" column on the front page of Thursday's issue.) Then review this chapter's section titled "Choice and Opportunity Cost." Finally, make a list of the kinds of opportunity costs involved in the firm's decision.

HOMEWORK XPRESS! EXERCISES

These exercises require access to McEachern Homework Xpress! If Homework Xpress! did not come with your book, visit **http://homeworkxpress.swlearning.com** *to purchase.*

An economy producing only two goods—silver and potatoes—faces a bowed-out production possibility frontier. Draw one in the diagram and label it.

1. Suppose plant biologists develop a new type of potato that increases the quantity of potatoes produced without any additional resources. Show how the new production possibilities curve would differ from the original.

2. Suppose mining engineers find a new technique that results in extracting more silver from the mines than previously without using additional resources. Show how the new production possibilities curve differs from the original.

3. Suppose that immigrants arrive seeking work in both potato production and silver mining. Show how the new production possibilities curve will differ from the original.

Economic Decision Makers

I
f we live in the age of specialization, then why haven't specialists taken over all production? For example, why do most of us still do our own laundry and perform dozens of other tasks for ourselves? In what sense has production moved from the household to the firm and then back to the household? If the "invisible hand" of competitive markets is so efficient, why does government get into the act? Answers to these and other questions are addressed in this chapter, which examines the four economic decision makers: households, firms, governments, and the rest of the world.

To develop a better feel for how the economy works, you must get more acquainted with these key players. You already know more about them than you may realize. You grew up in a household. You have dealt with firms all your life, from

HOMEWORK
Xpress!

Use Homework Xpress! for economic application, graphing, videos, and more.

Sony to Subway. You know a lot about governments, from taxes to public schools. And you have a growing awareness of the rest of the world, from international Web sites to foreign travel. This chapter will draw on your abundant personal experience with economic decision makers to consider their makeup and objectives. Topics discussed include:

- Evolution of the household
- Evolution of the firm
- Types of firms
- Market failures and government remedies
- Taxing and public spending
- International trade and finance

HOMEWORK
Xpress!
Pre-test

The Household

Households play the starring role in a market economy. Their demand for goods and services determines what gets produced. And their supplies of labor, capital, natural resources, and entrepreneurial ability produce that output. As demanders of goods and services and suppliers of resources, households make all kinds of choices, such as what to buy, how much to save, where to live, and where to work. Although a household usually consists of several individuals, we will view each household as acting like a single decision maker.

The Evolution of the Household

In earlier times, when the economy was primarily agricultural, a farm household was largely self-sufficient. Each family member specialized in a specific farm task—cooking, making clothes, tending livestock, planting crops, and so on. These early households produced what they consumed and consumed what they produced. With the introduction of new seed varieties, better fertilizers, and laborsaving machinery, farm productivity increased sharply. Fewer farmers were needed to grow enough food to feed a nation. Simultaneously, the growth of urban factories increased the demand for factory labor. As a result, many people moved from farms to cities, where they became more specialized but less self-sufficient.

Households evolved in other ways. For example, in 1950, only about 15 percent of married women with young children were in the labor force. Since then, higher levels of education among married women and a growing demand for labor increased women's earnings, thus raising their opportunity cost of working in the home. This higher opportunity cost contributed to their growing labor force participation. Today more than half of married women with young children are in the labor force.

The rise of two-earner households has affected the family as an economic unit. Households produce less for themselves and demand more from the market. For example, child-care services and fast-food restaurants have displaced some household production. Most people eat at least one meal a day away from home. The rise in two-earner families has reduced specialization within the household—a central feature of the farm family. Nonetheless, some production still occurs in the home, as we'll explore later.

Households Maximize Utility

There are more than 110 million U.S. households. All those who live under one roof are considered part of the same household. What exactly do households attempt to accomplish in making decisions? Economists assume that people attempt to maximize their level of satisfaction, sense of well-being, or overall welfare. In short, households attempt to maximize **utility.** Households, like other economic decision makers, are viewed as rational, meaning that they try to act in their best interests and do not deliberately make themselves worse off. Utility maximization depends on each household's subjective goals, not on some objective

UTILITY

The satisfaction or sense of well-being received from consumption

standard. For example, some households maintain neat homes with well-groomed lawns; others pay little attention to their homes and use their lawns as junkyards.

Households as Resource Suppliers

Households use their limited resources—labor, capital, natural resources, and entrepreneurial ability—in an attempt to satisfy their unlimited wants. They can use these resources to produce goods and services in their homes. For example, they can prepare meals, mow the lawn, and fix a leaky faucet. They can also sell these resources in the resource market and use the income to buy goods and services in the product market. The most valuable resource sold by most households is labor.

Panel (a) of Exhibit 1 shows the sources of personal income received by U.S. households in 2003, when personal income totaled $9.2 trillion. As you can see, 63 percent of personal income came from wages, salaries, and other labor income. A distant second was transfer payments (to be discussed shortly), at 13 percent of personal income, followed by personal interest at 10 percent, and proprietors' income at 8 percent each. *Proprietors* are people who work for themselves rather than for employers; farmers, plumbers, and doctors are often self-employed. Proprietors' income could also be considered a form of labor income. *Over two-thirds of personal income in the United States comes from labor earnings rather than from the ownership of other resources such as capital or natural resources.*

HOMEWORK
Xpress!
econ-apps news

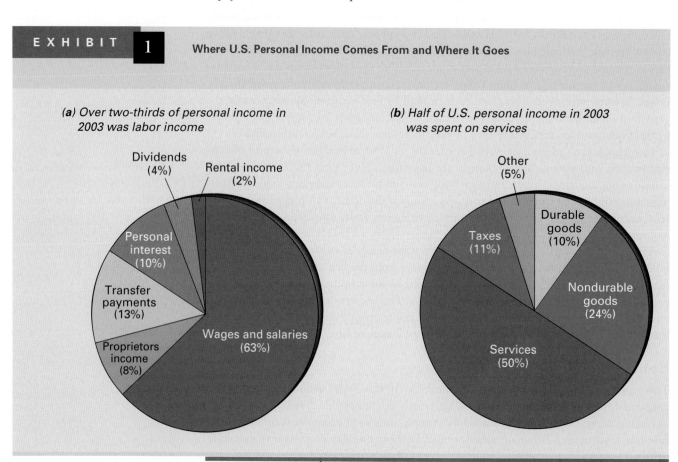

| EXHIBIT | 1 | Where U.S. Personal Income Comes From and Where It Goes |

(a) *Over two-thirds of personal income in 2003 was labor income*

Dividends (4%)
Rental income (2%)
Personal interest (10%)
Transfer payments (13%)
Proprietors income (8%)
Wages and salaries (63%)

(b) *Half of U.S. personal income in 2003 was spent on services*

Other (5%)
Durable goods (10%)
Taxes (11%)
Nondurable goods (24%)
Services (50%)

Source: Based on figures from *Survey of Current Business*, Bureau of Economic Analysis, April 2004, Table B-1. For the latest figures, go to http://www.bea.doc.gov/bea/pubs.htm.

Because of a poor education, disability, discrimination, time demands of caring for small children, or bad luck, some households have few resources that are valued in the market. Society has made the political decision that individuals in such circumstances should receive short-term public assistance. Consequently, the government gives some households **transfer payments,** which are outright grants. *Cash transfers* are monetary payments, such as welfare benefits, Social Security, unemployment compensation, and disability benefits. *In-kind* transfers provide for specific goods and services, such food stamps, health care, and housing.

TRANSFER PAYMENTS

Cash or in-kind benefits given to individuals as outright grants from the government

Households as Demanders of Goods and Services

What happens to personal income once it comes into the household? Most goes to personal consumption, which sorts into three broad spending categories: (1) *durable goods*—that is, goods expected to last three or more years—such as an automobile or a refrigerator; (2) *nondurable goods,* such as food, clothing, and gasoline; and (3) *services,* such as haircuts, plane trips, and medical care. As you can see from panel (b) of Exhibit 1, durable goods in 2003 claimed 10 percent of U.S. personal income; nondurables, 24 percent; and services, 50 percent. Taxes claimed 11 percent, and all other categories, including savings, claimed just 5 percent. So half of all personal income went for services—the fastest growing sector, since many services, such as child care, are shifting from home production to market production.

The Firm

Households members once built their own homes, made their own clothes and furniture, grew their own food, and amused themselves with books, games, and hobbies. Over time, however, the efficiency arising from comparative advantage resulted in a greater specialization among resource suppliers. This section takes a look at firms, beginning with their evolution.

The Evolution of the Firm

Specialization and comparative advantage explain why households are no longer self-sufficient. But why is a firm the natural result? For example, rather than make a woolen sweater from scratch, couldn't a consumer take advantage of specialization by negotiating with someone who produced the wool, another who spun the wool into yarn, and a third who knit the yarn into a sweater? Here's the problem with that model: If the consumer had to visit each of these specialists and strike an agreement, the resulting *transaction costs* could easily erase the gains from specialization. Instead of visiting and bargaining with each specialist, the consumer can pay someone to do the bargaining—an entrepreneur, who hires all the resources necessary to make the sweater. *An entrepreneur, by contracting for many sweaters rather than just one, is able to reduce the transaction costs per sweater.*

For about two hundred years, profit-seeking entrepreneurs relied on "putting out" raw material, like wool and cotton, to rural households that turned it into finished products, like woolen goods made from yarn. The system developed in the British Isles, where workers' cottages served as tiny factories. This approach, which came to be known as the *cottage industry system,* still exists in some parts of the world. You might think of this system as halfway between household self-sufficiency and the modern firm.

As the British economy expanded in the 18th century, entrepreneurs began organizing the stages of production under one roof. Technological developments, such as waterpower and later steam power, increased the productivity of each worker and contributed to the shift of employment from rural areas to urban factories. *Work, therefore, became organized in large, centrally powered factories that (1) promoted a more efficient division of labor, (2) allowed for the*

INDUSTRIAL REVOLUTION

Development of large-scale factory production that began in Great Britain around 1750 and spread to the rest of Europe, North America, and Australia

FIRMS

Economic units formed by profit-seeking entrepreneurs who use resources to produce goods and services for sale

direct supervision of production, (3) reduced transportation costs, and (4) facilitated the use of machines far bigger than anything used in the home. The development of large-scale factory production, known as the **Industrial Revolution,** began in Great Britain around 1750 and spread to the rest of Europe, North America, and Australia.

Production, then, evolved from self-sufficient rural households to the cottage industry system, where specialized production occurred in the household, to the current system of production in a firm. Today, entrepreneurs combine resources in firms such as factories, mills, offices, stores, and restaurants. **Firms** are economic units formed by profit-seeking entrepreneurs who combine labor, capital, and natural resources to produce goods and services. Just as we assume that households try to maximize utility, we assume that firms try to *maximize profit.* Profit, the entrepreneur's reward, equals sales revenue minus the cost of production.

Types of Firms

There are about 25 million for-profit businesses in the United States. Two-thirds are small retail businesses, small service operations, part-time home-based businesses, and small farms. Each year more than a million new businesses start up and almost as many fail. Entrepreneurs organize a firm in one of three ways: as a sole proprietorship, as a partnership, or as a corporation.

Sole Proprietorships

SOLE PROPRIETORSHIP

A firm with a single owner who has the right to all profits and who bears unlimited liability for the firm's debts

The simplest form of business organization is the **sole proprietorship,** a single-owner firm. Examples are self-employed plumbers, farmers, and dentists. Most sole proprietorships consist of just the self-employed proprietor—there are no hired employees. To organize a sole proprietorship, the proprietor simply opens for business by, for example, taking out a classified ad announcing availability for plumbing, or whatever. The owner is in complete control. But he or she faces unlimited liability and could lose everything, including a home and other assets, as a result of debts or claims against the business. Also, since the sole proprietor has no partners or other financial backers, raising enough money to get the business going can be challenging. One final disadvantage is that a sole proprietorship usually goes out of business when the proprietor dies. Still, a sole proprietorship is the most common type of business, accounting most recently for 72 percent of all U.S. businesses. Nonetheless, because this type of firm is typically small, proprietorships generate just a tiny portion of all U.S. business sales—only 4 percent.

Partnerships

PARTNERSHIP

A firm with multiple owners who share the firm's profits and bear unlimited liability for the firm's debts

A more complicated form of business is the **partnership,** which involves two or more individuals who agree to contribute resources to the business in return for a share of the profit or loss. Law, accounting, and medical partnerships typify this business form. Partners have strength in numbers and often find it easier than sole proprietors to raise sufficient funds to get the business going. But partners may not always agree. Also, each partner usually faces unlimited liability for any debts or claims against the partnership, so one partner could lose everything because of another's mistake. Finally, the death or departure of one partner can disrupt the firm's continuity and prompt a complete reorganization. The partnership is the least common form of U.S. business, making up only 8 percent of all firms and 10 percent of all business sales.

Corporations

CORPORATION

A legal entity owned by stockholders whose liability is limited to the value of their stock

By far the most influential form of business is the corporation. A **corporation** is a legal entity established through articles of incorporation. Shares of stock confer corporate ownership, thereby entitling stockholders to a claim on any profit. A major advantage of the corporate form is that many investors—hundreds, thousands, even millions—can pool their funds, so incorporating represents the easiest way to amass large sums of money to finance the business. Also, stockholder liability for any loss is limited to the value of their stock, meaning stockholders enjoy limited liability. A final advantage of this form of organization is that the corporation has a life apart from its owners. The corporation survives even if ownership changes hands, and it can be taxed and sued as if it were a person.

The corporate form has some disadvantages as well. A stockholder's ability to influence corporate policy is limited to voting for a board of directors, which oversees the operation of the firm. Each share of stock usually carries with it one vote. The typical stockholder of a large corporation owns only a tiny fraction of the shares and thus has little say. Whereas the income from sole proprietorships and partnerships is taxed only once, corporate income gets whacked twice—first as corporate profits and second as stockholder income, either as corporate dividends or as realized capital gains. A *realized capital gain* is any increase in the market value of a share that occurs between the time the share is purchased and the time it is sold.

A hybrid type of corporation has evolved to take advantage of the limited liability feature of the corporate structure while reducing the impact of double taxation. The *S corporation* provides owners with limited liability, but profits are taxed only once—as income on each shareholder's personal income tax return. To qualify as an S corporation, a firm must have no more than 75 stockholders and must have no foreign or corporate stockholders.

Corporations make up only 20 percent of all U.S. businesses, but because they tend to be much larger than the other two business forms, they account for 86 percent of all business sales. Exhibit 2 shows, by business type, the percentage of U.S. firms and the percentage of U.S. sales. *The sole proprietorship is the most important form in the sheer number of firms, but the corporation is the most important in terms of total sales.*

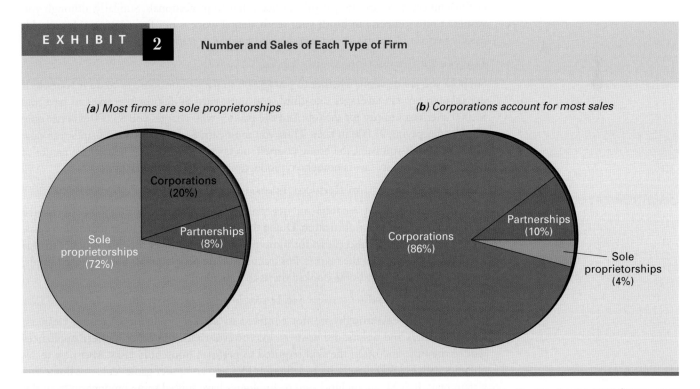

EXHIBIT 2   **Number and Sales of Each Type of Firm**

(a) Most firms are sole proprietorships

Corporations (20%)
Sole proprietorships (72%)
Partnerships (8%)

(b) Corporations account for most sales

Corporations (86%)
Partnerships (10%)
Sole proprietorships (4%)

Source: U.S. Census Bureau, *Statistical Abstract of the United States: 2003*, U.S. Bureau of the Census, Table No. 731. For the latest figures, go to http://www.census.gov/statab/www/.

Nonprofit Institutions

To this point we have considered firms that maximize profit. Some institutions, such as museums, ballet companies, nonprofit hospitals, the Red Cross, the Salvation Army, churches, synagogues, mosques, and perhaps the college you attend, are private organizations that do not have profit as an explicit goal. Yet even nonprofit institutions must somehow pay the bills. Revenue sources typically include some combination of voluntary contributions and service charges, such as college tuition and hospital bills. According to the U.S. Internal Revenue Service, there were 1.6 million tax-exempt organizations in the United States in 2001 and they controlled assets totaling $2.4 trillion. So the average tax-exempt organization controlled assets worth $1.5 million. Although the nonprofit sector is important, the *firms* discussed in this book will have profit as their goal.

Why Does Household Production Still Exist?

If firms are so great at reducing transaction and production costs, why don't they make everything? Why do households still perform some tasks, such as cooking and cleaning? *If a household's opportunity cost of performing a task is below the market price, then the household usually performs that task.* People with a lower opportunity cost of time will do more for themselves. For example, janitors are more likely to mow their lawns than are physicians. Let's look at some reasons for household production.

No Skills or Special Resources Are Required

Some activities require so few skills or special resources that householders find it cheaper to do the jobs themselves. Sweeping the floor requires only a broom and some time so it's usually performed by household members. Sanding a wooden floor, however, involves special machinery and expertise, so this service is left to professionals. Similarly, although you wouldn't hire someone to brush your teeth, dental work is not for amateurs. Households usually perform domestic chores that demand neither expertise nor special machinery.

Household Production Avoids Taxes

Suppose you are deciding whether to pay $3,000 to paint your house or to do it yourself. If the income tax rate averages one-third, you must earn $4,500 before taxes to have the $3,000 after taxes to pay for the job. And the painter who charges you $3,000 will net only $2,000 after paying $1,000 in taxes. Thus, you must earn $4,500 so that the painter can take home $2,000. If you paint the house yourself, no taxes are collected. The tax-free nature of do-it-yourself activity favors household production over market transactions.

Household Production Reduces Transaction Costs

Getting estimates, hiring a contractor, negotiating terms, and monitoring job performance all take time and require information. Doing the job yourself reduces these transaction costs. Household production also allows for more personal control over the final product than is usually available through the market. For example, some people prefer home-cooked meals, because they can season home-cooked meals to individual tastes.

Technological Advances Increase Household Productivity

Technological breakthroughs are not confined to market production. Vacuum cleaners, clothes washers and dryers, dishwashers, microwave ovens, and other modern appliances reduce the time and often the skill required to perform household tasks. Also, new technologies such as DVD players, high-definition TVs, and computer games enhance home entertainment. Indeed, microchip-based technologies have shifted some production from the firm back to the household, as discussed in the following case study.

The Electronic Cottage

The Industrial Revolution shifted production from rural cottages to large urban factories. But the **Information Revolution** spawned by the microchip and the Internet is decentralizing the acquisition, analysis, and transmission of information. These days, someone who claims to work at a home office is usually referring not to a corporate headquarters but to a spare bedroom. According to one recent survey, in the last decade the number of telecommuters more than doubled. Worsening traffic in major cities and wider access to broadband is pushing the trend. Nearly half the white-collar employees at AT&T work at home at least part of the time.

From home, people can write a document with coworkers scattered throughout the world, then discuss the project online in real time or have a videoconference (McDonald's saves millions in travel costs by videoconferencing). Software allows thousands of employees to share electronic files. When Accenture moved its headquarters from Boston to a suburb, the company replaced 120 tons of paper records with a huge online database accessible anytime from anywhere in the world.

To support those who work at home, an entire industry has sprung up, with magazines, newsletters, Web sites, and national conferences. In fact, an office need not even be in a specific place. Some people now work in *virtual offices,* which have no permanent locations. With mobile phones and other handhelds, people can conduct business on the road—literally, "deals on wheels." Accountants at Ernst & Young spend most of their time in the field. When returning to company headquarters, they call a few hours ahead to reserve an office. IBM is developing "Butler in a Dashboard" to help people work on the road. Speech recognition software allows the driver to dictate and send emails as well as send and receive voicemails. If traffic is too noisy, a tiny camera mounted on the visor reads the driver's lips. This Butler also provides directions and weather conditions, and warns of traffic tie-ups and flight delays. The model is expected to reach the market in 2005.

Chip technology is decentralizing production, shifting work from a central place either back to the household or to no place in particular. More generally, the Internet has reduced the transaction costs, whether it's a market report authored jointly by researchers from around the world or a new computer system assembled from parts ordered over the Internet. Easier communication has even increased contact among distant research scholars. For example, economists living in distant cities were four times more likely to collaborate on research during the 1990s than during the 1970s.

Sources: "IBM Envisions Butler in a Dashboard," *USA Today*, 25 June 2003; Jonathan Glater, "Telecommuting's Big Experiment," *New York Times*, 9 May 2001; and Daniel Hamermesh and Sharon Oster, "Tools or Toys? The Impact of High Technology on Scholarly Productivity," *Economic Inquiry*, October 2002. For a discussion of the virtual office, go to http://www.office.com/.

The Government

You might think that production by households and firms could satisfy all consumer wants. Why must yet another economic decision maker get into the act?

The Role of Government

Sometimes the unrestrained operation of markets yields undesirable results. Too many of some goods and too few of other goods get produced. This section discusses the sources of **market failure** and how society's overall welfare may be improved through government intervention.

Establishing and Enforcing the Rules of the Game

Market efficiency depends on people like you using your resources to maximize your utility. But what if you were repeatedly robbed of your paycheck on your way home from work? Or what if, after you worked two weeks in a new job, your boss called you a sucker and said you wouldn't get paid? Why bother working? The system of private markets would break down if you could not safeguard your private property or if you could not enforce contracts. Governments safeguard private property through police protection and enforce contracts through a judicial system. More generally, governments try to make sure that market participants abide by the "rules of the game." These rules are established through laws and through the customs and conventions of the marketplace.

Promoting Competition

Although the "invisible hand" of competition usually promotes an efficient allocation of resources, some firms try to avoid competition through collusion, which is an agreement among firms to divide the market and fix the price. Or an individual firm may try to eliminate the competition by using unfair business practices. For example, to drive out local competitors, a large firm may temporarily sell at a price below cost. Government antitrust laws try to promote competition by prohibiting collusion and other anticompetitive practices.

Regulating Natural Monopolies

Competition usually keeps the product price below what it would be without competition—that is below the price charged by a **monopoly,** a sole supplier to the market. In rare instances, however, a monopoly can produce and sell the product for less than could competing firms. For example, electricity is delivered more efficiently by a single firm that wires the community than by competing firms each stringing its own wires. When it is cheaper for one firm to serve the market than for two or more firms to do so, that one firm is called a **natural monopoly.** Since a natural monopoly faces no competition, it maximizes profit by charging a higher price than would be optimal from society's point of view. Therefore, the government usually regulates the natural monopoly, forcing it to lower its price.

Providing Public Goods

So far this book has been talking about private goods, which have two important features. First, private goods are *rival* in consumption, meaning that the amount consumed by one person is unavailable for others to consume. For example, when you and some friends share a pizza, each slice they eat is one less available for you. Second, the supplier of a private good can easily exclude those who fail to pay. Only paying customers get pizza. Thus, private goods are said to be *exclusive*. So **private goods** are both rival in consumption and exclusive, such as pizza. In contrast, **public goods,** such as reducing terrorism, providing national defense, and administering a system of justice, are *nonrival* in consumption. One person's benefit from the good does not diminish the amount available to others. Your family's benefit from a safer neighborhood does not reduce your neighbor's benefit. What's more, once produced, public goods are available to all. Suppliers cannot easily prevent consumption by those who fail to pay. For example, reducing terrorism is *nonexclusive*. It benefits all in the community, regardless of who pays for it and who doesn't. Because public goods are *nonrival* and *nonexclusive*, private firms cannot sell them profitably. The government, however, has the authority to collect taxes for public goods.

Dealing with Externalities

Market prices reflect the private costs and private benefits of producers and consumers. But sometimes production or consumption imposes costs or benefits on third parties—on those who are neither suppliers nor demanders in a market transaction. For example, a paper mill fouls the air breathed by nearby residents, but the market price of paper fails to reflect such costs. Because these pollution costs are outside, or external to, the market, they are called externalities. An **externality** is a cost or a benefit that falls on a third party. A negative externality imposes an external cost, such as factory pollution or auto emissions. A positive externality confers an external benefit, such as driving carefully or beautifying your property. Because market prices do not reflect externalities, governments often use taxes, subsidies, and regulations to discourage negative externalities and encourage positive externalities. For example, because education generates positive externalities (educated people can read road signs and have better paying options other than crime as sources of income), governments try to encourage education with free public schools, subsidized higher education, and keeping people in school until their 16th birthdays.

EXTERNALITY

A cost or a benefit that falls on a third party and is therefore ignored by the two parties to the market transaction

A More Equal Distribution of Income

As mentioned earlier, some people, because of poor education, mental or physical disabilities, or perhaps the need to care for small children, are unable to support themselves and their families. Because resource markets do not guarantee even a minimum level of income, transfer payments reflect society's attempt to provide a basic standard of living to all households. Nearly all citizens agree that government should redistribute income to the poor (note the normative nature of this statement). Opinions differ about how much should be redistributed, what form it should take, who should receive benefits, and how long benefits should last.

Full Employment, Price Stability, and Economic Growth

Perhaps the most important responsibility of government is fostering a healthy economy, which benefits just about everyone. The government—through its ability to tax, to spend, and to control the money supply—attempts to promote full employment, price stability, and economic growth. Pursuing these objectives by taxing and spending is called **fiscal policy.** Pursuing them by regulating the money supply is called **monetary policy.** Macroeconomics examines both policies.

Government's Structure and Objectives

The United States has a *federal system* of government, meaning that responsibilities are shared across levels of government. State governments grant some powers to local governments and surrender some powers to the national, or federal, government. As the system has evolved, the federal government has assumed primary responsibility for national security, economic stability, and market competition. State governments fund public higher education, prisons, and—with aid from the federal government—highways and welfare. Local governments provide primary and secondary education with aid from the state, plus police and fire protection. Here are some distinguishing features of government.

Difficulty in Defining Government Objectives

We assume that households try to maximize utility and firms try to maximize profit, but what about governments—or, more specifically, what about government decision makers?

Net **Bookmark**

The annual Economic Report of the President is an invaluable source of information on current economic policy. It also contains many useful data tables. You can find it online at http://w3.access.gpo.gov/eop/index.html.

FISCAL POLICY

The use of government purchases, transfer payments, taxes, and borrowing to influence economy-wide activity such as inflation, employment, and economic growth

MONETARY POLICY

Regulation of the money supply to influence economy-wide activity such as inflation, employment, and economic growth

What do they try to maximize? One problem is that our federal system consists of not one but many governments—more than 87,000 separate jurisdictions in all. What's more, because the federal government relies on offsetting, or countervailing, powers across the executive, legislative, and judicial branches, government does not act as a single, consistent decision maker. Even within the federal executive branch, there are so many agencies and bureaus that at times they seem to work at cross-purposes. For example, at the same time as the U.S. Surgeon General requires health warnings on cigarettes, the U.S. Department of Agriculture pursues policies to benefit tobacco growers. Given this thicket of jurisdictions, branches, and bureaus, one useful theory of government behavior is that elected officials try to maximize the number of votes they receive in the next election. So let's assume that elected officials try to maximize votes. In this theory, vote maximization guides the decisions of elected officials who, in turn, control government employees.

Voluntary Exchange Versus Coercion

Market exchange relies on the voluntary behavior of buyers and sellers. Don't like tofu? No problem—don't buy any. But in political markets, the situation is different. Any voting rule except unanimous consent must involve some government coercion. Public choices are enforced by the police power of the state. Those who fail to pay their taxes could go to jail, even though they may object to some programs those taxes support.

No Market Prices

Another distinguishing feature of governments is that the selling price of public output is usually either zero or below the cost. If you are now paying in-state tuition at a public college or university, your tuition probably covers only about half the state's cost of providing your education. Because the revenue side of the government budget is usually separate from the expenditure side, there is no necessary link between the cost and the benefit of a public program. In the private sector, the expected marginal benefit is at least as great as marginal cost; otherwise, market exchange would not occur.

The Size and Growth of Government

One way to track the impact of government over time is by measuring government outlays relative to the U.S. *gross domestic product,* or *GDP,* which is the total value of all final goods and services produced in the United States. In 1929, the year the Great Depression began, government outlays, mostly by state and local governments, totaled about 10 percent of GDP. At the time, the federal government played a minor role. In fact, during the nation's first 150 years, federal outlays, except during wars, never exceeded 3 percent relative to GDP.

The Great Depression, World War II, and a change in macroeconomic thinking boosted the share of government outlays to 36 percent of GDP in 2004, with about two-thirds of that by the federal government. In comparison, government outlays relative to GDP were 38 percent in Japan, 40 percent in Canada, 43 percent in the United Kingdom, 48 percent in Germany and Italy, and 54 percent in France. Government outlays by the 24 largest industrial economies averaged 40 percent of GDP in 2004.[1] Thus, government outlays in the United States represent a relatively small share of GDP compared to other advanced economies.

Let's look briefly at the composition of federal outlays. Since 1960, defense spending has declined from over half of federal outlays to one-fifth by 2004, as shown in Exhibit 3.

HOMEWORK
Xpress!
Ask the Instructor
Video

1. The Organization of Economic Cooperation and Development, *OECD Economic Outlook* (June 2004), Annex Table 26.

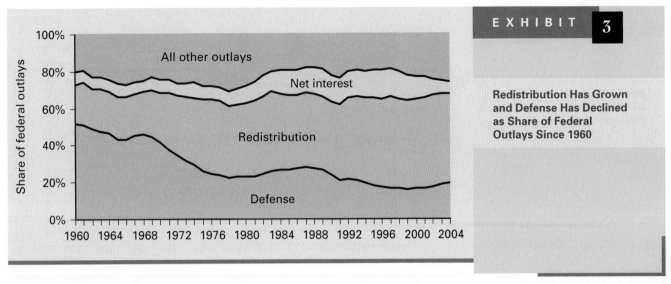

Redistribution Has Grown and Defense Has Declined as Share of Federal Outlays Since 1960

Source: Computed based on figures from the *Economic Report of the President*, February 2004, Table B-80. For the latest figures, go to http://w3.access.gpo.gov/eop.

Redistribution—Social Security, Medicare, and welfare programs—is the mirror image of defense spending, jumping from only about one-fifth of federal outlays in 1960 to nearly half by 2004.

Sources of Government Revenue

Taxes provide the bulk of revenue at all levels of government. The federal government relies primarily on the individual income tax, state governments rely on income and sales taxes, and local governments rely on the property tax. In addition to taxes, other revenue sources include user charges, such as highway tolls, and borrowing. To make money, some states monopolize certain markets, such as for lottery tickets and liquor.

Exhibit 4 focuses on the composition of federal revenue since 1960. The share made up by the individual income tax has remained relatively constant, ranging from a low of 42 percent in the mid-1960s to a high of 50 percent in 2000. The share from payroll taxes more than doubled from 15 percent in 1960 to 40 percent in 2004. *Payroll taxes* are deducted from paychecks to support Social Security and Medicare, which funds medical care for the elderly. Corporate taxes and revenue from other sources, such as excise (sales) taxes and user charges, have declined as a share of the total since 1960.

Tax Principles and Tax Incidence

The structure of a tax is often justified on the basis of one of two general principles. First, a tax could relate to the individual's ability to pay, so those with a greater ability pay more taxes. Income or property taxes often rely on this **ability-to-pay tax principle.** Alternatively, the **benefits-received tax principle** relates taxes to the benefits taxpayers receive from the government activity funded by the tax. For example, the tax on gasoline funds highway construction and maintenance, thereby linking tax payment to road use, since the more people drive, the more gas tax they pay.

Tax incidence indicates who actually bears the burden of the tax. One way to evaluate tax incidence is by measuring the tax as a percentage of income. Under **proportional taxation,** taxpayers at all income levels pay the same percentage of their income in taxes. A

ABILITY-TO-PAY TAX PRINCIPLE

Those with a greater ability to pay, such as those with a higher income or those who own more property, should pay more taxes

BENEFITS-RECEIVED TAX PRINCIPLE

Those who receive more benefits from the government program funded by a tax should pay more taxes

TAX INCIDENCE

The distribution of tax burden among taxpayers; who ultimately pays the tax

PROPORTIONAL TAXATION

The tax as a percentage of income remains constant as income increases; also called a flat tax

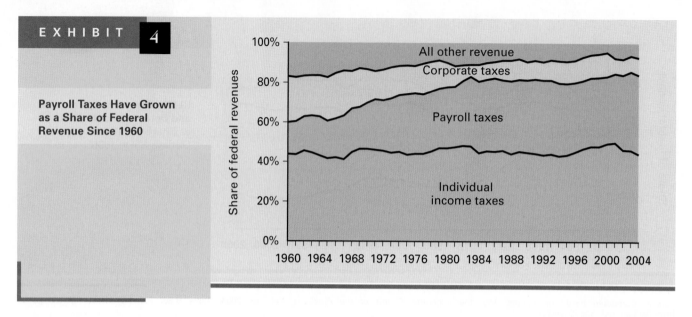

EXHIBIT 4

Payroll Taxes Have Grown as a Share of Federal Revenue Since 1960

Source: Computed based on figures from the *Economic Report of the President*, February 2004, Tables B-81 and B-84. For the latest figures, go to http://w3.access.gpo.gov/eop.

PROGRESSIVE TAXATION

The tax as a percentage of income increases as income increases

MARGINAL TAX RATE

The percentage of each additional dollar of income that goes to the tax

REGRESSIVE TAXATION

The tax as a percentage of income decreases as income increases

proportional income tax is also called a flat tax, since the tax as a percentage of income remains constant, or flat, as income increases. Under **progressive taxation,** the percentage of income paid in taxes increases as income increases.

The **marginal tax rate** indicates the percentage of each additional dollar of income that goes to taxes. Because high marginal rates reduce the after-tax return from working or investing, they can reduce people's incentives to work and invest. As of 2004, the six marginal rates range from 10 to 35 percent, down from a range of 15 to 39.6 percent in 2000. The top marginal tax bracket each year during the history of the personal income tax is shown by Exhibit 5. Although the top marginal rate in 2004 was lower than it was during most other years, high income households still pay most of the federal income tax collected. For example, the top 1 percent of tax filers, based on income, pay about 33 percent of all income taxes collected. The bottom 50 percent pay less than 5 percent of all income taxes collected. So the U.S. income tax is progressive, and high-income filers pay the overwhelming share of the total.

Finally, under **regressive taxation,** the percentage of income paid in taxes decreases as income increases, so the marginal tax rate declines as income increases. Most U.S. *payroll taxes* are regressive, because they impose a flat rate up to a certain level of income, above which the marginal rate drops to zero. For example, Social Security taxes were levied on the first $87,900 of workers' pay in 2004. Half the 12.4 percent tax is paid by employers and half by employees (the self-employed pay the entire amount).

This discussion of revenue sources brings to a close, for now, our examination of the role of government in the U.S. economy. Government has a pervasive influence on the economy, and its role is discussed throughout the book.

The Rest of the World

So far, the focus has been on institutions within the United States—that is, on *domestic* households, firms, and governments. This focus is appropriate because our primary objective

HOMEWORK Xpress!
Ask the Instructor Video

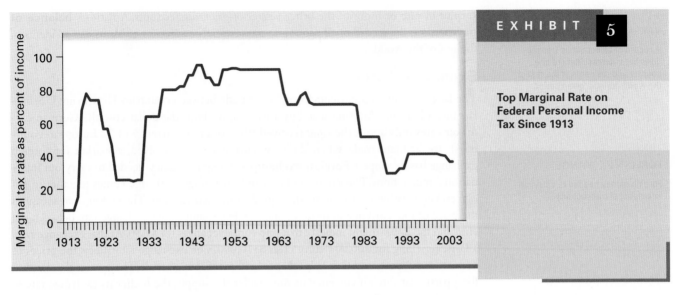

EXHIBIT 5

Top Marginal Rate on Federal Personal Income Tax Since 1913

Source: U.S. Internal Revenue Service. For the latest figures on the personal income tax go to http://www.irs.gov/individuals/index.html.

is to understand the workings of the U.S. economy, by far the largest in the world. But the rest of the world affects what U.S. households consume and what U.S. firms produce. For example, Japan and China supply U.S. markets with all kinds of manufactured goods, thereby affecting U.S. prices, wages, and profits. Likewise, political events in the Persian Gulf can affect what Americans pay for oil. Foreign decision makers, therefore, have a significant effect on the U.S. economy—on what we consume and what we produce. The *rest of the world* consists of the households, firms, and governments in the two hundred or so sovereign nations throughout the world.

International Trade

In the previous chapter, you learned about comparative advantage and the gains from specialization. These gains explain why householders stopped doing everything for themselves and began to specialize. International trade arises for the same reasons. *International trade occurs because the opportunity cost of producing specific goods differs across countries.* Americans import raw materials like crude oil, diamonds, and coffee beans and finished goods like cameras, DVD players, and automobiles. U.S. producers export sophisticated products like computer hardware and software, aircraft, and movies, as well as agricultural products like wheat and corn.

International trade between the United States and the rest of the world has increased in recent decades. In 1970, U.S. exports of goods and services amounted to only 6 percent of the gross domestic product. That percentage has since nearly doubled. Chief destinations for U.S. exports in order of importance are Canada, Japan, Mexico, the United Kingdom Germany, France, South Korea, and Taiwan.

The **merchandise trade balance** equals the value of exported goods minus the value of imported goods. Goods in this case are distinguished from services, which show up in another trade account. For the last two decades, the United States has imported more goods than it has exported, so there has been a merchandise trade deficit. Just as a household must pay for its spending, so too must a nation. The merchandise trade deficit must be offset by a

MERCHANDISE TRADE BALANCE

The value of a country's exported goods minus the value of its imported goods during a given period

surplus in one or more of the other *balance-of-payments* accounts. A nation's **balance of payments** is the record of all economic transactions between its residents and residents of the rest of the world.

Exchange Rates

The lack of a common currency complicates trade between countries. How many U.S. dollars buy a Porsche? An American buyer cares only about the dollar cost; the German carmaker cares only about the *euros* received (the common currency of 12 European countries). To facilitate trade when different currencies are involved, a market for foreign exchange has developed. **Foreign exchange** is foreign currency needed to carry out international transactions. The supply and demand for foreign exchange comes together in *foreign exchange markets* to determine the equilibrium exchange rate. The *exchange rate* measures the price of one currency in terms of another. For example, the exchange rate between the euro and the dollar might indicate that one euro exchanges for $1.10. At that exchange rate, a Porsche selling for 100,000 euros costs $110,000. The exchange rate affects the prices of imports and exports and thus helps shape the flow of foreign trade. The greater the demand for a particular foreign currency or the smaller the supply, the higher its exchange rate—that is, the more dollars it costs.

Trade Restrictions

Although there are clear gains from international specialization and exchange, nearly all nations restrict trade to some extent. These restrictions can take the form of (1) **tariffs,** which are taxes on imports; (2) **quotas,** which are limits on the quantity of a particular good that can be imported from a country; and (3) other trade restrictions. If specialization according to comparative advantage is so beneficial, why do most countries restrict trade? Restrictions benefit certain domestic producers that lobby their governments for these benefits. For example, U.S. textile manufacturers have benefited from legislation restricting textile imports, thereby raising U.S. textile prices. These higher prices hurt domestic consumers, but consumers are usually unaware of this harm. Trade restrictions interfere with the free flow of products across borders and tend to hurt the overall economy. International trade in the auto industry is discussed in the following case study.

Wheels of Fortune

The U.S. auto industry is huge, with annual sales of about $300 billion a year, an amount exceeding the gross domestic product of 90 percent of the world's economies. There are over 200 million motor vehicles in the United States alone, about two for every three people. In the decade following World War II, imports accounted for just 0.4 percent of U.S. auto sales. In 1973, however, the suddenly powerful Organization of Petroleum Exporting Countries (OPEC) more than tripled

oil prices. In response, Americans scrambled for more fuel-efficient cars, which at the time were primarily by foreign makers. As a result, imports jumped to 21 percent of U.S. auto sales by 1980.

BALANCE OF PAYMENTS
A record of all economic transactions between residents of one country and residents of the rest of the world during a given period

FOREIGN EXCHANGE
Foreign money needed to carry out international transactions

TARIFF
A tax on imports

QUOTA
A legal limit on the quantity of a particular product that can be imported or exported

C a s e S t u d y

World of Business

eActivity
The International Motor Vehicle Program at MIT maintains a Web site rich with links and other useful information about automobile production worldwide. You can find it at http://web.mit.edu/ctpid/www/impv.html.

In the early 1980s, at the urging of the so-called Big Three automakers (General Motors, Ford, and, at the time, Chrysler), the Reagan administration persuaded Japanese producers to adopt "voluntary" quotas limiting the number of automobiles they exported to the United States. The quotas, or supply restrictions, drove up the price of Japanese imports. U.S. automakers used this as an opportunity to raise their own prices. Experts estimate that reduced foreign competition cost U.S. consumers over $15 billion.

The quotas had two effects on Japanese producers. First, faced with a strict limit on the number of cars they could export to the United States, they began shipping more upscale models instead of subcompacts. Second, Japanese firms built factories in the United States. Making autos here also reduced complications caused by fluctuations in yen-dollar exchange rates. Japanese-owned auto plants in the United States now account for more than one-quarter of auto production in the United States. Imports still make up about one-quarter of U.S. car sales, with Japan accounting for most of that. Imports include cars produced abroad by foreign firms but sold under the names of U.S. firms. U.S. automakers also produce around the world. In fact, Ford is the largest automaker in Australia, the United Kingdom, Mexico, and Argentina.

In China, India, and Latin America, the potential car market is enormous. Here's something to consider: There are more people in China under age of 26 than the combined population of the United States, Japan, Germany, the United Kingdom, and Canada. For years private car ownership was banned in China by Chairman Mao. Now car ownership there is on a roll. Passenger car sales grew from 0.5 million in 1998 to 1.2 million in 2002, for an average annual growth of 24 percent. Because of high tariffs in China, less than 10 percent of cars sold are imports. As a condition for entry into the World Trade Organization, a group that streamlines world trade, China has agreed to reduce tariffs. So China's auto market should gradually open up.

Sources: "Ford to Triple China Production," *South China Morning Post,* 24 September 2003; "China Goes Car Crazy," *Fortune,* 8 September 2003; Micheline Maynard, "Foreign Automakers Unleash a New Wave of Luxury," *New York Times,* 27 September 2003; and Walter Adams and James Brock, "Automobiles," in *The Structure of American Industry,* 9th ed. (New York: Prentice-Hall, 1995), 65–92. For the latest in the auto industry, go to http://www.autocentral.com/.

Conclusion

This chapter examined the four economic decision makers: households, firms, governments, and the rest of the world. Domestic households are by far the most important, for they, along with foreign households, supply the resources and demand the goods and services produced. In recent years, the U.S. economy has come to depend more on the rest of the world as a market for U.S. goods and as a source of products.

If you were to stop reading right now, you would already know more economics than most people. But to understand market economies, you must learn how markets work. The next chapter introduces demand and supply.

SUMMARY

1. Most household income arises from the sale of labor, and most household income is spent on personal consumption, primarily services.

2. Household members once built their own homes, made their own clothes and furniture, grew their own food, and

supplied their own entertainment. Over time, however, the efficiency arising from comparative advantage resulted in a greater specialization among resource suppliers.

3. Firms bring together specialized resources and reduce the transaction costs of bargaining with all these resource

providers. Firms can be organized in three different ways: as sole proprietorships, partnerships, or corporations. Because corporations are typically large, they account for the bulk of sales.

4. When private markets yield undesirable results, government may intervene to address these market failures. Government programs are designed to (a) protect private property and enforce contracts; (b) promote competition; (c) regulate natural monopolies; (d) provide public goods; (e) discourage negative externalities and encourage positive externalities; (f) promote equality in the distribution of income; and (g) promote full employment, price stability, and economic growth.

5. In the United States, the federal government has primary responsibility for providing national defense, ensuring market competition, and promoting stability of the economy. State governments fund public higher education, prisons, and—with aid from the federal government—

highways and welfare. And local governments fund police and fire protection, and, with aid from the state, provide primary and secondary education.

6. The federal government relies primarily on the personal income tax, states rely on income and sales taxes, and localities rely on the property tax. A tax is often justified based on (a) the individual's ability to pay or (b) the benefits the taxpayer receives from the activities financed by the tax.

7. The rest of the world is also populated by households, firms, and governments. International trade creates gains that arise from comparative advantage. The balance of payments summarizes transactions between the residents of one country and the residents of the rest of the world. Despite the benefits from comparative advantage, nearly all countries impose trade restrictions to protect specific domestic industries.

QUESTIONS FOR REVIEW

1. *(Households as Demanders of Goods and Services)* Classify each of the following as a durable good, a nondurable good, or a service:

   a.   A gallon of milk
   b.   A lawn mower
   c.   A DVD player
   d.   A manicure
   e.   A pair of shoes
   f.   An eye exam
   g.   A personal computer
   h.   A neighborhood teenager mowing a lawn

2. (*Case* **Study**: The Electronic Cottage) How has the development of personal computer hardware and software reversed some of the trends brought on by the Industrial Revolution?

3. *(Evolution of the Firm)* Explain how production after the Industrial Revolution differed from production under the cottage industry system.

4. *(Household Production)* What factors does a householder consider when deciding whether to produce a good or service at home or buy it in the marketplace?

5. *(Corporations)* Why did the institution of the firm appear after the advent of the Industrial Revolution? What type of business organization existed before this?

6. *(Sole Proprietorships)* What are the disadvantages of the sole proprietorship form of business?

7. *(Government)* Often it is said that government is necessary when private markets fail to work effectively and fairly. Based on your reading of the text, discuss how private markets might break down.

8. *(Externalities)* Suppose there is an external cost associated with production of a certain good. What's wrong with letting the market determine how much of this good will be produced?

9. *(Government Revenue)* What are the sources of government revenue in the United States? Which types of taxes are most important at each level of government? Which two taxes provide the most revenue to the federal government?

10. *(Objectives of the Economic Decision Makers)* In economic analysis, what are the assumed objectives of households, firms, and the government?

11. *(International Trade)* Why does international trade occur? What does it mean to run a deficit in the merchandise trade balance?

12. *(International Trade)* Distinguish between a tariff and a quota. Who benefits from and who is harmed by such restrictions on imports?

13. (*Case* **Study**: Wheel of Fortune) What factors led Japanese auto producers to build factories in the United States?

PROBLEMS AND EXERCISES

14. *(Evolution of the Household)* Determine whether each of the following would increase or decrease the opportunity costs for mothers who choose not to work outside the home. Explain your answers.

    a. Higher levels of education for women
    b. Higher unemployment rates for women
    c. Higher average pay levels for women
    d. Lower demand for labor in industries that traditionally employ large numbers of women

15. *(Household Production)* Many households supplement their food budget by cultivating small vegetable gardens. Explain how each of the following might influence this kind of household production:

    a. Both husband and wife are professionals who earn high salaries.
    b. The household is located in a city rather than in a rural area.
    c. The household is located in a region where there is a high sales tax on food.
    d. The household is located in a region that has a high property tax rate.

16. *(Government)* Complete each of the following sentences:
    a. When the private operation of a market leads to over-production or underproduction of some good, this is known as a(n) _____.
    b. Goods that are nonrival and nonexcludable are known as _____.
    c. _____ are cash or in-kind benefits given to individuals as outright grants from the government.
    d. A(n) _____ confers an external benefit on third parties that are not directly involved in a market transaction.
    e. _____ refers to the government's pursuit of full employment and price stability through variations in taxes and government spending.

17. *(Tax Rates)* Suppose taxes are related to income level as follows:

Income	Taxes
$1,000	$200
$2,000	$350
$3,000	$450

    a. What percentage of income is paid in taxes at each level?
    b. Is the tax rate progressive, proportional, or regressive?
    c. What is the marginal tax rate on the first $1,000 of income? The second $1,000? The third $1,000?

EXPERIENTIAL EXERCISES

18. *(The Evolution of the Firm)* Get a library copy of *The Wealth and Poverty of Nations,* by David Landes, and read pages 207–210. How would you interpret Landes's story about mechanization using the ideas developed in this chapter?

19. *(The Evolution of the Firm)* The Contracting and Organizations Research Institute at the University of Missouri maintains lots of interesting information about the evolution of the firm. Visit the institute's Web site at http://cori.missouri.edu/index.htm to familiarize yourself with the kinds of issues economists are studying.

20. *(International Trade)* Visit McEachern Xtra! at http://mceachernxtra.swlearning.com and go to Econ-Debate Online. Review the materials on "Does the U.S. economy benefit from foreign trade?" in the "International Trade" section. What are some of the benefits of international trade—not just to the United States, but to all nations?

21. *(Wall Street Journal)* The household is the most important decision-making unit in our economy. Look through the rotating columns (e.g., "Work and Family" and "Personal Technology") in the *Wall Street Journal* this week. Find a description of some technological change that might affect household production. Explain how production would be affected.

Demand and Supply Analysis

© Connie Coleman/Stone/Getty Images

W hy do roses cost more on Valentine's Day than during the rest of the year?

Why do TV ads cost more during the Super Bowl ($2.3 million for 30 sec-

onds in 2004) than during *Nick at Nite* reruns? Why do hotel rooms in Phoenix cost

more in February than in August? Why do surgeons earn more than butchers? Why

do pro basketball players earn more than pro hockey players? Why do economics

majors earn more than most other majors? Answers to these and most economic

questions boil down to the workings of demand and supply—the subject of this

chapter.

This chapter introduces demand and supply and shows how they interact in com-

petitive markets. *Demand and supply are the most fundamental and the most powerful of all

economic tools*—important enough to warrant their own chapter. Indeed, some believe that if you program a computer to answer "demand and supply" to every economic question, you could put many economists out of work. An understanding of the two ideas will take you far in mastering the art and science of economic analysis. This chapter uses graphs, so you may need to review the Chapter 1 appendix as a refresher. Topics discussed include:

- Demand and quantity demanded
- Movement along a demand curve
- Shift of a demand curve
- Supply and quantity supplied
- Movement along a supply curve
- Shift of a supply curve
- Markets and equilibrium
- Disequilibrium

Demand

How many six packs of Pepsi will people buy each month if the price is $3? What if the price is $2? What if it's $4? The answers reveal the relationship between the price of Pepsi and the quantity purchased. Such a relationship is called the *demand* for Pepsi. **Demand** indicates how much of a good consumers are both *willing* and *able* to buy at each possible price during a given period, other things remaining constant. Because demand pertains to a specific period—a day, a week, a month—think of demand as the *planned rate of purchase per period* at each possible price. Also, notice the emphasis on *willing* and *able*. You may be *able* to buy a new Harley-Davidson for $5,000 because you can afford one, but you may not be *willing* to buy one if motorcycles don't interest you.

The Law of Demand

In 1962, Sam Walton opened his first store in Rogers, Arkansas, with a sign that read: "Wal-Mart Discount City. We sell for less." Wal-Mart now sells more than any other retailer in the world because its prices are among the lowest around. As a consumer, you understand why people buy more at a lower price. Sell for less, and the world will beat a path to your door. Wal-Mart, for example, sells on average over 20,000 pairs of shoes *an hour*. This relation between the price and the quantity demanded is an economic law. The **law of demand** says that quantity demanded varies inversely with price, other things constant. Thus, the higher the price, the smaller the quantity demanded; the lower the price, the greater the quantity demanded.

Demand, Wants, and Needs

Consumer demand and consumer wants are not the same. As we have seen, wants are unlimited. You may want a new Mercedes SL600 convertible, but the $130,000 price tag is likely beyond your budget (that is, the quantity you demand at that price is zero). Nor is demand the same as need. You may need a new muffler for your car, but if the price is $200, you decide, "I am not going to pay a lot for this muffler." Apparently, you have better uses for your money. If, however, the price drops enough—say, to $100—then you become both willing and able to buy one.

The Substitution Effect of a Price Change

What explains the law of demand? Why, for example, is more demanded when the price is lower? The explanation begins with unlimited wants confronting scarce resources. Many goods and services could satisfy particular wants. For example, you can satisfy your hunger

DEMAND

A relation between the price of a good and the quantity that consumers are willing and able to buy during a given period, other things constant

LAW OF DEMAND

The quantity of a good demanded during a given period relates inversely to its price, other things constant

with pizza, tacos, burgers, chicken, or hundreds of other goodies. Similarly, you can satisfy your desire for warmth in the winter with warm clothing, a home-heating system, a trip to Hawaii, or in many other ways. Clearly, some alternatives have more appeal than others (a trip to Hawaii is more fun than warm clothing). In a world without scarcity, everything would be free, so you would always choose the most attractive alternative. Scarcity, however, is a reality, and the degree of scarcity of one good relative to another helps determine each good's relative price.

Notice that the definition of *demand* includes the other-things-constant assumption. Among the "other things" assumed to remain constant are the prices of other goods. For example, if the price of pizza declines while other prices remain constant, pizza becomes relatively cheaper. Some consumers are more *willing* to purchase pizza when its relative price falls; they substitute pizza for other goods. This principle is called the **substitution effect of a price change**. On the other hand, an increase in the price of pizza, other things constant, causes some consumers to substitute other goods for the now higher-priced pizza, thus reducing their quantity of pizza demanded. Remember that *it is the change in the relative price—the price of one good relative to the prices of other goods—that causes the substitution effect*. If all prices changed by the same percentage, there would be no change in relative prices and no substitution effect.

The Income Effect of a Price Change

A fall in the price of a product increases the quantity demanded for a second reason. Suppose you clear $30 a week from a part-time job, so that's your money income. **Money income** is simply the number of dollars received per period, in this case, $30 per week. Suppose you spend all your income on pizza, buying three a week at $10 each. What if the price drops to $6? At the lower price you can now afford five pizzas a week. Your money income remains at $30 per week, but the decrease in the price has increased your **real income**—that is, your income measured in terms of what it can buy. The price reduction, other things constant, increases the purchasing power of your income, thereby increasing your ability to buy pizza. The quantity of pizza you demand will likely increase because of this **income effect of a price change.** You may not increase your quantity demanded to five pizzas, but you could. If you decide to purchase four pizzas a week when the price drops to $6, you have $6 remaining to buy other goods.

Thus, the income effect of a lower price increases your real income and thereby increases your ability to purchase all goods. Because of the income effect of a price decrease, other things constant, consumers typically increase their quantity demanded. Conversely, an increase in the price of a good, other things constant, reduces real income, thereby reducing the *ability* to purchase all goods. Because of the income effect of a price increase, consumers typically reduce their quantity demanded as price increases. Again, note that money income, not real income, is assumed to remain constant along a demand curve.

The Demand Schedule and Demand Curve

Demand can be expressed as a *demand schedule* or as a *demand curve*. Panel (a) of Exhibit 1 shows a hypothetical demand schedule for pizza. In describing demand, we must specify the units measured and the period considered. In our example, the unit is a 12-inch regular pizza and the period is a week. The schedule lists possible prices, along with the quantity demanded at each price. At a price of $15, for example, consumers demand 8 million pizzas per week. As you can see, the lower the price, other things constant, the greater the quantity demanded. Consumers substitute pizza for other foods. And as the price falls, real income

SUBSTITUTION EFFECT OF A PRICE CHANGE

When the price of a good falls, consumers substitute that good for other goods, which become relatively more expensive

MONEY INCOME

The number of dollars a person receives per period, such as $400 per week

REAL INCOME

Income measured in terms of the goods and services it can buy

INCOME EFFECT OF A PRICE CHANGE

A fall in the price of a good increases consumers' real income, making consumers more able to purchase goods; for a normal good, the quantity demanded increases

increases, causing consumers to increase the quantity of pizza they demand. If the price drops as low as $3, consumers demand 32 million per week.

The demand schedule in panel (a) appears as a **demand curve** in panel (b), with price on the vertical axis and the quantity demanded per week on the horizontal axis. Each price-quantity combination listed in the demand schedule in the left panel becomes a point in the right panel. Point *a,* for example, indicates that if the price is $15, consumers demand 8 million pizzas per week. These points connect to form the demand curve for pizza, labeled *D*. (By the way, some demand curves are straight lines, some are curved lines, and some are even jagged lines, but all are called demand *curves*.)

The demand curve slopes downward, reflecting the *law of demand:* Price and quantity demanded are inversely related, other things constant. Assumed constant along the demand curve are the prices of other goods. Thus, along the demand curve for pizza, the price of pizza changes *relative to the prices of other goods*. The demand curve shows the effect of a change in the *relative price* of pizza—that is, relative to other prices, which do not change.

Take care to distinguish between *demand* and *quantity demanded*. The *demand* for pizza is not a specific amount, but rather the *entire relationship* between price and quantity demanded—represented by the demand schedule or the demand curve. An individual point on the demand curve indicates the **quantity demanded** at a particular price. For example, at a price of $12, the quantity demanded is 14 million pizzas per week. If the price drops to, say, $9, this drop is shown in Exhibit 1 by *a movement along the demand curve*—in this case from point *b* to point *c*. Any movement along a demand curve reflects a *change in quantity demanded*, not a change in demand.

DEMAND CURVE

A curve showing the relation between the price of a good and the quantity demanded during a given period, other things constant

QUANTITY DEMANDED

The amount demanded at a particular price, as reflected by a point on a given demand curve

---

EXHIBIT   1

The Demand Schedule and Demand Curve for Pizza

The market demand curve *D* shows the quantity of pizza demanded, at various prices, by all consumers. Price and quantity demanded are inversely related.

(a) Demand schedule

	Price per Pizza	Quantity Demanded per Week (millions)
a	$15	8
b	12	14
c	9	20
d	6	26
e	3	32

(b) Demand curve

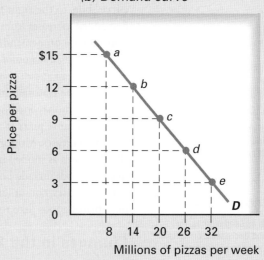

The law of demand applies to the millions of products sold in grocery stores, department stores, clothing stores, drugstores, music stores, bookstores, travel agencies, and restaurants, as well as through mail-order catalogs, the *Yellow Pages,* classified ads, Internet sites, stock markets, real estate markets, job markets, flea markets, and all other markets. The law of demand applies even to choices that seem more personal than economic, such as whether or not to own a pet. For example, after New York City passed an anti-dog-litter law, owners had to follow their dogs around the city with scoopers, plastic bags—whatever would do the job. Because the law raised the personal cost of owning a dog, the quantity demanded decreased. Some owners simply abandoned their dogs, raising the number of strays in the city. The number of dogs left at animal shelters doubled. The law of demand predicts this inverse relation between cost, or price, and quantity demanded.

It is useful to distinguish between **individual demand,** which is the demand of an individual consumer, and **market demand,** which is the sum of the individual demands of all consumers in the market. In most markets, there are many consumers, sometimes millions. Unless otherwise noted, when we talk about demand, we are referring to market demand, as in Exhibit 1.

Shifts of the Demand Curve

A demand curve isolates the relation between prices of a good and quantities demanded when other factors that could affect demand remain unchanged. What are those other factors, and how do changes in them affect demand? Variables that can affect market demand are (1) the money income of consumers, (2) prices of related goods, (3) consumer expectations, (4) the number or composition of consumers in the market, and (5) consumer tastes. How do changes in each affect demand?

Changes in Consumer Income

Exhibit 2 shows the market demand curve *D* for pizza. This demand curve assumes a given level of money income. Suppose consumer income increases. Some consumers will then be willing and able to buy more pizza at each price, so market demand increases. The demand curve shifts to the right from *D* to *D'*. For example, at a price of $12, the amount of pizza demanded increases from 14 million to 20 million per week, as indicated by the movement from point *b* on demand curve *D* to point *f* on demand curve *D'*. In short, *an increase in demand—that is, a rightward shift of the demand curve—means that consumers are willing and able to buy more pizza at each price.*

Goods are classified into two broad categories, depending on how demand responds to changes in money income. The demand for a **normal good** increases as money income increases. Because pizza is a normal good, its demand curve shifts rightward when consumer income increases. Most goods are normal. In contrast, demand for an **inferior good** actually decreases as money income increases, so the demand curve shifts leftward. Examples of inferior goods include bologna sandwiches, used furniture, and used clothing. As money income increases, consumers tend to switch from consuming these inferior goods to consuming normal goods (like roast beef sandwiches, new furniture, and new clothing).

Changes in the Prices of Related Goods

Again, the prices of other goods are assumed to remain constant along a given demand curve. Now let's bring these other prices into the picture. There are various ways of addressing any particular want. Consumers choose among substitutes based on relative prices. For example,

INDIVIDUAL DEMAND
The demand of an individual consumer

MARKET DEMAND
Sum of the individual demands of all consumers in the market

NORMAL GOOD
A good, such as new clothes, for which demand increases, or shifts rightward, as consumer incomes rise

INFERIOR GOOD
A good, such as used clothes, for which demand decreases, or shifts leftward, as consumer incomes rise

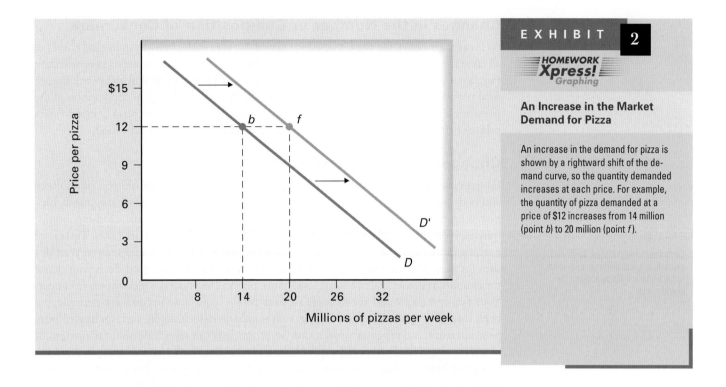

E X H I B I T **2**

HOMEWORK
Xpress!
Graphing

An Increase in the Market Demand for Pizza

An increase in the demand for pizza is shown by a rightward shift of the demand curve, so the quantity demanded increases at each price. For example, the quantity of pizza demanded at a price of $12 increases from 14 million (point *b*) to 20 million (point *f*).

pizza and tacos are substitutes, though not perfect ones. An increase in the price of tacos, other things constant, reduces the quantity of tacos demanded along a given taco demand curve. An increase in the price of tacos also shifts the demand curve for pizza to the right. Two goods are considered **substitutes** if a price increase of one shifts the demand for the other rightward and, conversely, if a price decrease of one shifts demand for the other leftward.

Two goods used in combination are called *complements*. Examples include Coke and pizza, milk and cookies, computer software and hardware, and airline tickets and rental cars. Two goods are considered **complements** if a price increase of one shifts the demand for the other leftward. For example, an increase in the price of pizza shifts the demand curve for Coke leftward. But most pairs of goods selected at random are *unrelated*—for example, pizza and socks, or milk and gasoline.

Changes in Consumer Expectations

Another factor assumed constant along a given demand curve is consumer expectations about factors that influence demand, such as income or prices. A change in consumers' *income expectations* can shift the demand curve. For example, a consumer who learns about a pay raise might increase demand well before the raise takes effect. A college senior who lands that first real job may buy a new car even before graduation. Likewise, a change in consumers' *price expectations* can shift the demand curve. For example, if you expect the price of pizza to jump next week, you may buy an extra one today for the freezer, shifting this week's demand for pizza rightward. Or if consumers come to believe that home prices will climb next month, some will increase their demand for housing now, shifting this month's demand for housing rightward. On the other hand, if housing prices are expected to fall next month, some consumers will postpone purchases, thereby shifting this month's housing demand leftward.

SUBSTITUTES

Goods, such as Coke and Pepsi, that are related in such a way that an increase in the price of one shifts the demand for the other rightward

COMPLEMENTS

Goods, such as milk and cookies, that are related in such a way that an increase in the price of one shifts the demand for the other leftward

Changes in the Number or Composition of Consumers

As mentioned earlier, the market demand curve is the sum of the individual demand curves of all consumers in the market. If the number of consumers changes, the demand curve will shift. For example, if the population grows, the demand curve for pizza will shift rightward. Even if total population remains unchanged, demand could shift with a change in composition of the population. For example, a bulge in the teenage population could shift pizza demand rightward. A baby boom would shift rightward the demand for car seats and baby food.

Changes in Consumer Tastes

Do you like anchovies on your pizza or sauerkraut on your hot dog? Are you into tattoos and body piercings? Is music to your ears more likely to be rock, country, heavy metal, hip-hop, reggae, jazz, new age, or classical? Choices in food, body art, music, clothing, books, movies, TV—indeed, all consumer choices—are influenced by consumer tastes. **Tastes** are nothing more than your likes and dislikes as a consumer. What determines tastes? Your desires for food when hungry and drink when thirsty are largely biological. So is your desire for comfort, rest, shelter, friendship, love, status, personal safety, and a pleasant environment. Your family background affects some of your tastes—your taste in food, for example, has been shaped by years of home cooking. Other influences include the surrounding culture, peer influence, and religious convictions. So economists can say a little about the origin of tastes, but they claim no special expertise in understanding how tastes develop. Economists recognize, however, that tastes have an important impact on demand. For example, although pizza is popular, some people just don't like it and those who are lactose intolerant can't stomach the cheese topping. Thus, some people like pizza and some don't.

In our analysis of consumer demand, *we will assume that tastes are given and are relatively stable.* Tastes are assumed to remain constant along a demand curve. A change in the tastes for a particular good shifts the demand curve. For example, a discovery that the tomato sauce and cheese combination on pizza promotes overall health could change consumer tastes, shifting the demand curve for pizza to the right. But because a change in tastes is so difficult to isolate from other economic changes, we should be reluctant to attribute a shift of the demand curve to a change in tastes.

That wraps up our look at changes in demand. Before we turn to supply, you should remember the distinction between a **movement along a given demand curve** and a **shift of a demand curve.** A change in *price,* other things constant, causes a *movement along a demand curve,* changing the quantity demanded. A change in one of the determinants of demand other than price causes a *shift of a demand curve,* changing demand.

Supply

Just as demand is a relation between price and quantity demanded, supply is a relation between price and quantity supplied. **Supply** indicates how much producers are *willing* and *able* to offer for sale per period at each possible price, other things constant. The **law of supply** states that the quantity supplied is usually directly related to its price, other things constant. Thus, the lower the price, the smaller the quantity supplied; the higher the price, the greater the quantity supplied.

TASTES

Consumer preferences; likes and dislikes in consumption; assumed to be constant along a given demand curve

MOVEMENT ALONG A DEMAND CURVE

Change in quantity demanded resulting from a change in the price of the good, other things constant

SHIFT OF A DEMAND CURVE

Movement of a demand curve right or left resulting from a change in one of the determinants of demand other than the price of the good

SUPPLY

A relation between the price of a good and the quantity that producers are willing and able to sell during a given period, other things constant

LAW OF SUPPLY

The quantity of a good supplied during a given period is usually directly related to its price, other things constant

The Supply Schedule and Supply Curve

Exhibit 3 presents the market *supply schedule* and market **supply curve** *S* for pizza. Both show the quantities of pizza supplied per week at various possible prices by the thousands of pizza makers in the economy. As you can see, price and quantity supplied are directly, or positively, related. Producers offer more at a higher price than at a lower price, so the supply curve slopes upward.

There are two reasons producers offer more for sale when the price rises. First, as the price increases, other things constant, a producer becomes more *willing* to supply the good. Prices act as signals to existing and potential suppliers about the rewards for producing various goods. An increase in the price of pizza, with other prices constant, provides suppliers a profit incentive to shift some resources from producing other goods, for which the price is now relatively lower, and into pizza, for which the price is now relatively higher. *A higher pizza price attracts resources from lower-valued uses.*

Higher prices also increase the producer's *ability* to supply the good. The law of increasing opportunity cost, as noted in Chapter 2, states that the opportunity cost of producing more of a particular good rises as output increases—that is, the *marginal cost* of production increases as output increases. Because producers face a higher marginal cost for additional output, they must receive a higher price for that output to be *able* to increase the quantity supplied. *A higher price makes producers more able to increase quantity supplied.* As a case in point, a higher price for gasoline increases oil companies' ability to drill deeper and to explore in

SUPPLY CURVE

A curve showing the relation between price of a good and the quantity supplied during a given period, other things constant

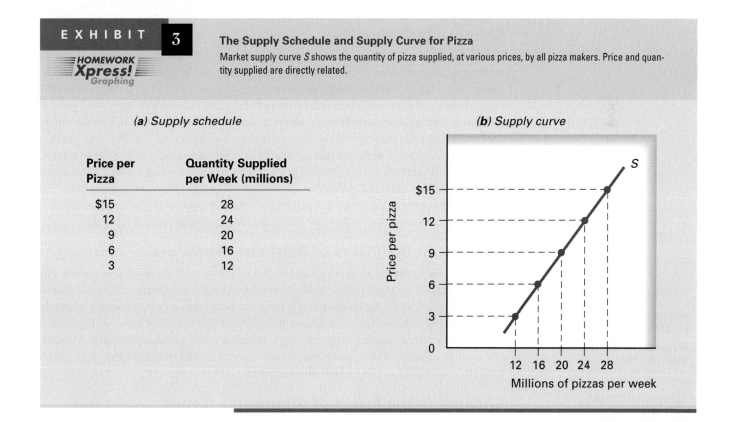

EXHIBIT 3

HOMEWORK Xpress! *Graphing*

The Supply Schedule and Supply Curve for Pizza

Market supply curve *S* shows the quantity of pizza supplied, at various prices, by all pizza makers. Price and quantity supplied are directly related.

(a) Supply schedule

Price per Pizza	Quantity Supplied per Week (millions)
$15	28
12	24
9	20
6	16
3	12

(b) Supply curve

less accessible areas, such as the remote jungles of the Amazon, the stormy waters of the North Sea, and the frozen tundra above the Arctic Circle. On the other hand, the price of gold today is only half what it was decades ago so miners are less able to prospect for gold or to refine ore with lower gold content.

Thus, a higher price makes producers more *willing* and more *able* to increase quantity supplied. Producers are more *willing* because production becomes more profitable than the alternative uses of the resources involved. The higher price also *enables* producers to cover the higher marginal cost that typically results from a greater rate of output.

As with demand, we distinguish between *supply* and **quantity supplied.** *Supply* is the entire relationship between prices and quantities supplied, as reflected by the supply schedule or supply curve. *Quantity supplied* refers to a particular amount offered for sale at a particular price, as reflected by a point on a given supply curve. We also distinguish between **individual supply,** the supply of an individual producer, and **market supply,** the sum of individual supplies of all producers in the market. Unless otherwise noted the term supply refers to market supply.

Shifts of the Supply Curve

The supply curve isolates the relation between the price of a good and the quantity supplied, other things constant. Assumed constant along a supply curve are the determinants of supply other than the price of the good, including (1) the state of technology, (2) the prices of relevant resources, (3) the prices of alternative goods, (4) producer expectations, and (5) the number of producers in the market. Let's see how a change in each affects the supply curve.

Changes in Technology

Recall from Chapter 2 that the state of technology represents the economy's stock of knowledge about how to combine resources efficiently. Along a given supply curve, technology is assumed to remain unchanged. If a more efficient technology is discovered, production costs will fall; so suppliers will be more willing and more able to supply the good at each price. Consequently, supply will increase, as reflected by a rightward shift of the supply curve. For example, suppose a new high-tech oven bakes pizza in half the time. Such a breakthrough would shift the market supply curve rightward, as from S to S' in Exhibit 4, where more is supplied at each possible price. For example, if the price is $12, the amount supplied increases from 24 million to 28 million pizzas, as shown in Exhibit 4 by the movement from point *g* to point *h*. In short, *an increase in supply—that is, a rightward shift of the supply curve—means that producers are willing and able to sell more pizza at each price.*

Changes in the Prices of Relevant Resources

Relevant resources are those employed in the production of the good in question. For example, suppose the price of mozzarella cheese falls. This price decrease reduces the cost of pizza production, so producers are more willing and better able to supply pizza. The supply curve for pizza shifts rightward, as shown in Exhibit 4. On the other hand, an increase in the price of a relevant resource reduces supply, meaning a shift of the supply curve leftward. For example, a higher cheese price increases the cost of making pizzas. Higher production costs decrease supply, so pizza supply shifts leftward.

Changes in the Prices of Alternative Goods

Nearly all resources have alternative uses. The labor, building, machinery, ingredients, and knowledge needed to run a pizza business could produce other baked goods. **Alternative**

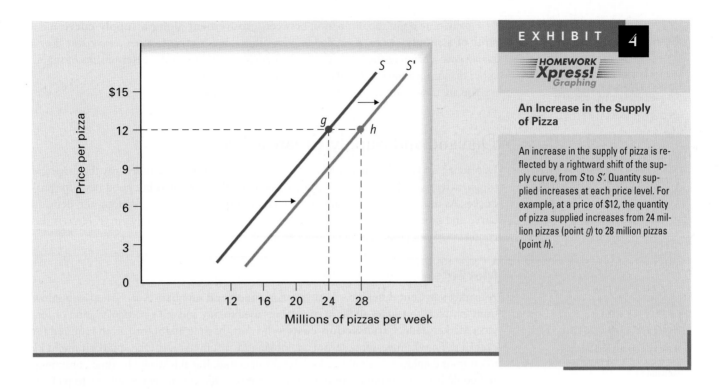

EXHIBIT 4

HOMEWORK
Xpress!
Graphing

An Increase in the Supply of Pizza

An increase in the supply of pizza is reflected by a rightward shift of the supply curve, from *S* to *S'*. Quantity supplied increases at each price level. For example, at a price of $12, the quantity of pizza supplied increases from 24 million pizzas (point *g*) to 28 million pizzas (point *h*).

goods are those that use some of the same resources employed to produce the good under consideration. For example, a decrease in the price of Italian bread reduces the opportunity cost of making pizza. As a result, some bread makers become pizza makers so the supply of pizza increases, shifting the supply curve rightward as in Exhibit 3. On the other hand, if the price of an alternative good, such as Italian bread, increases, supplying pizza becomes relatively less attractive compared to supplying Italian bread. As resources shift into bread making, the supply of pizza decreases, or shifts to the left.

Changes in Producer Expectations

Changes in producer expectations can shift the supply curve. For example, a pizza maker expecting higher pizza prices in the future may expand his or her pizzeria now, thereby shifting the supply of pizza rightward. When a good can be easily stored (crude oil, for example, can be left in the ground), expecting higher prices in the future might prompt some producers to *reduce* their current supply while awaiting the higher price. Thus, an expectation of higher prices in the future could either increase or decrease current supply, depending on the good. More generally, any change expected to affect future profitability, such as a change in business taxes, could shift the supply curve now.

Changes in the Number of Producers

Because market supply sums the amounts supplied at each price by all producers, market supply depends on the number of producers in the market. If that number increases, supply will increase, shifting supply to the right. If the number of producers decreases, supply will decrease, shifting supply to the left. As an example of increased supply, the number of gourmet coffee bars more than quadrupled in the United States during the last decade (think Starbucks), shifting the supply curve of gourmet coffee to the right.

MOVEMENT ALONG A SUPPLY CURVE

Change in quantity supplied resulting from a change in the price of the good, other things constant

SHIFT OF A SUPPLY CURVE

Movement of a supply curve left or right resulting from a change in one of the determinants of supply other than the price of the good

TRANSACTION COSTS

The costs of time and information required to carry out market exchange

SURPLUS

At a given price, the amount by which quantity supplied exceeds quantity demanded; a surplus usually forces the price down

SHORTAGE

At a given price, the amount by which quantity demanded exceeds quantity supplied; a shortage usually forces the price up

Finally, note again the distinction between a **movement along a supply curve** and a **shift of a supply curve.** A change in *price,* other things constant, causes *a movement along a supply curve,* changing the quantity supplied. A change in one of the determinants of supply other than price causes a *shift of a supply curve,* changing supply.

You are now ready to put demand and supply together.

Demand and Supply Create a Market

Demanders and suppliers have different views of price, because demanders pay the price and suppliers receive it. Thus, a higher price is bad news for consumers but good news for producers. As the price rises, consumers reduce their quantity demanded along the demand curve and producers increase their quantity supplied along the supply curve. How is this conflict between producers and consumers resolved?

Markets

A market sorts out differences between demanders and suppliers. A *market,* as you know from Chapter 1, includes all the arrangements used to buy and sell a particular good or service. Markets reduce **transaction costs**—the costs of time and information required for exchange. For example, suppose you are looking for a summer job. One approach might be to go from employer to employer looking for openings. But this would be time consuming and could have you running around for days. A more efficient strategy would be to pick up a copy of the local newspaper and read through the help-wanted ads or go online and look for openings. Classified ads and Web sites, which are elements of the job market, reduce the transaction costs of bringing workers and employers together.

The coordination that occurs through markets takes place not because of some central plan but because of Adam Smith's "invisible hand." For example, the auto dealers in your community tend to locate together, usually on the outskirts of town, where land is cheaper. The dealers congregate not because someone told them to or because they like one another's company but because together they become a more attractive destination for car buyers. Similarly, stores group together so that more shoppers will be drawn by the call of the mall. From Orlando theme parks to Broadway theaters to Las Vegas casinos, suppliers congregate to attract demanders. Some gatherings of suppliers can be quite specialized. For example, shops selling dress mannequins cluster along Austin Road in Hong Kong.

Market Equilibrium

To see how a market works, let's bring together market demand and supply. Exhibit 5 shows the market for pizza, using schedules in panel (a) and curves in panel (b). Suppose the price initially is $12. At that price, producers supply 24 million pizzas per week, but consumers demand only 14 million, resulting in an *excess quantity supplied,* or a **surplus,** of 10 million pizzas per week. Producers' desire to eliminate this surplus puts downward pressure on the price, as shown by the arrow pointing down in the graph. As the price falls, producers reduce their quantity supplied and consumers increase their quantity demanded. The price continues to fall as long as quantity supplied exceeds quantity demanded.

Alternatively, suppose the price initially is $6 per pizza. You can see from Exhibit 5 that at that price, consumers demand 26 million pizzas but producers supply only 16 million, resulting in an *excess quantity demanded,* or a **shortage,** of 10 million pizzas per week. Producers quickly notice that their quantity supplied has sold out and those customers still demanding pizzas are grumbling. Profit-maximizing producers and frustrated consumers create market pressure for a higher price, as shown by the arrow pointing up in the graph. As the price rises, producers increase their quantity supplied and consumers reduce their quantity demanded. The price continues to rise as long as quantity demanded exceeds quantity supplied.

Thus, *a surplus creates downward pressure on the price, and a shortage creates upward pressure.* As long as quantity demanded differs from quantity supplied, this difference forces a price change. Note that a shortage or a surplus depends on the price. There is no such thing as a general shortage or a general surplus.

A market reaches equilibrium when the quantity demanded equals quantity supplied. In **equilibrium,** the independent plans of both buyers and sellers exactly match, so market forces exert no pressure to change price or quantity. In Exhibit 5, the demand and supply curves intersect at the *equilibrium point,* identified as point *c.* The *equilibrium price* is $9 per pizza, and the *equilibrium quantity* is 20 million per week. At that price and quantity,

EQUILIBRIUM

The condition that exists in a market when the plans of buyers match those of sellers, so quantity demanded equals quantity supplied and the market clears

---

EXHIBIT 5

HOMEWORK
Xpress!
Graphing

Equilibrium in the Pizza Market

Market equilibrium occurs at the price where quantity demanded equals quantity supplied. This is shown at point *c.* Above the equilibrium price, quantity supplied exceeds quantity demanded. This creates a surplus, which puts downward pressure on the price. Below the equilibrium price, quantity demanded exceeds quantity supplied. The resulting shortage puts upward pressure on the price.

(a) Market schedules

Millions of Pizzas per Week

Price per Pizza	Quantity Demanded	Quantity Supplied	Surplus or Shortage	Effect on Price
$15	8	28	Surplus of 20	Falls
12	14	24	Surplus of 10	Falls
9	20	20	Equilibrium	Remains the same
6	26	16	Shortage of 10	Rises
3	32	12	Shortage of 20	Rises

(b) Market curves

the market *clears*. Because there is no shortage or surplus, there is no pressure for a price change.

A market finds equilibrium through the independent actions of thousands, or even millions, of buyers and sellers. In one sense, the market is personal because each consumer and each producer makes a personal decision regarding how much to buy or sell at a given price. In another sense, the market is impersonal because it requires no conscious coordination among consumers or producers. *Impersonal market forces synchronize the personal and independent decisions of many individual buyers and sellers to achieve equilibrium price and quantity.*

Changes in Equilibrium Price and Quantity

Equilibrium is the combination of price and quantity at which the intentions of demanders and suppliers exactly match. Once a market reaches equilibrium, that price and quantity will prevail until one of the determinants of demand or supply changes. A change in any one of these determinants usually changes equilibrium price and quantity in a predictable way, as you'll see.

Shifts of the Demand Curve

In Exhibit 6, demand curve *D* and supply curve *S* intersect at point *c* to yield the initial equilibrium price of $9 and the initial equilibrium quantity of 20 million 12-inch regular pizzas per week. Now suppose that one of the determinants of demand changes in a way that increases demand, shifting the demand curve to the right from *D* to *D'*. Any of the following could shift the demand for pizza rightward: (1) an increase in the money income of consumers (because pizza is a normal good); (2) an increase in the price of a substitute, such as tacos, or a decrease in the price of a complement, such as Coke; (3) a change in consumer

**Effects of an
Increase in Demand**

An increase in demand is shown by a shift of the demand curve rightward from *D* to *D'*. Quantity demanded exceeds quantity supplied at the original price of $9 per pizza, putting upward pressure on the price. As the price rises, quantity supplied increases along supply curve *S*, and quantity demanded decreases along demand curve *D'*. When the new equilibrium price of $12 is reached at point *g*, quantity demanded once again equals quantity supplied. Both price and quantity are higher following the rightward shift of the demand curve.

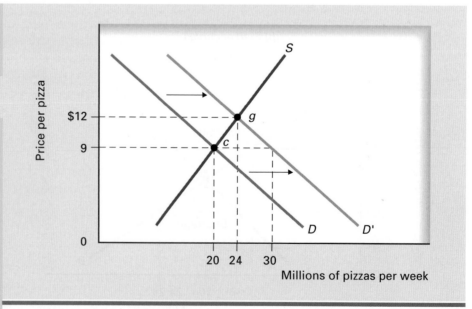

expectations that encourages them to demand more pizzas now; (4) a growth in the number of pizza consumers; or (5) a change in consumer tastes—based, for example, on a discovery that the tomato sauce on pizza has antioxidant properties that improve overall health.

After the demand curve shifts rightward to *D'* in Exhibit 6, the amount demanded at the initial price of $9 is 30 million pizzas, which exceeds the amount supplied of 20 million by 10 million pizzas. This shortage puts upward pressure on the price. As the price increases, the quantity demanded decreases along the new demand curve *D'*, and the quantity supplied increases along the existing supply curve *S* until the two quantities are equal once again at equilibrium point *g*. The new equilibrium price is $12, and the new equilibrium quantity is 24 million pizzas per week. Thus, given an upward-sloping supply curve, an increase in demand, meaning a rightward shift of the demand curve, increases both equilibrium price and quantity. A decrease in demand, meaning a leftward shift of the demand curve, would lower both equilibrium price and quantity. These results can be summarized as follows: *Given an upward-sloping supply curve, a rightward shift of the demand curve increases both equilibrium price and quantity and a leftward shift of the demand curve decreases both equilibrium price and quantity.*

Shifts of the Supply Curve

Let's consider shifts of the supply curve. In Exhibit 7, as before, we begin with demand curve *D* and supply curve *S* intersecting at point *c* to yield an equilibrium price of $9 and an equilibrium quantity of 20 million pizzas per week. Suppose one of the determinants of supply changes, increasing supply from *S* to *S'*. Changes that could shift the supply curve rightward include (1) a technological breakthrough in pizza ovens; (2) a reduction in the price of a relevant resource, such as mozzarella cheese; (3) a decline in the price of an alternative good,

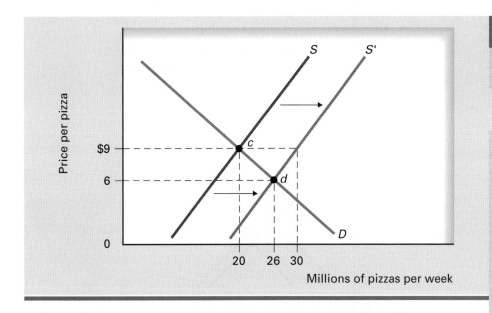

EXHIBIT 7

HOMEWORK **Xpress!** *Graphing*

Effects of an Increase in Supply

An increase in supply is shown by a shift of the supply curve rightward, from *S* to *S'*. Quantity supplied exceeds quantity demanded at the original price of $9 per pizza, putting downward pressure on the price. As the price falls, quantity supplied decreases along supply curve *S'*, and quantity demanded increases along demand curve *D*. When the new equilibrium price of $6 is reached at point *d*, quantity demanded once again equals quantity supplied. At the new equilibrium, quantity is greater and the price is lower than before the increase in supply.

such as Italian bread; (4) a change in expectations that encourages pizza makers to expand production now; or (5) an increase in the number of pizzerias.

After the supply curve shifts rightward in Exhibit 7, the amount supplied at the initial price of $9 increases from 20 million to 30 million, so producers now supply 10 million more pizzas than consumers demand. This surplus forces the price down. As the price falls, the quantity supplied declines along the new supply curve and the quantity demanded increases along the existing demand curve until a new equilibrium point *d* is established. The new equilibrium price is $6, and the new equilibrium quantity is 26 million pizzas per week. In short, an increase in supply reduces the price and increases the quantity. On the other hand, a decrease in supply increases the price but decreases the quantity. Thus, *given a downward-sloping demand curve, a rightward shift of the supply curve decreases price but increases quantity, and a leftward shift increases price but decreases quantity.*

EXHIBIT   8

Indeterminate Effect of an Increase in Both Demand and Supply

When both demand and supply increase, the equilibrium quantity also increases. The effect on price depends on which curve shifts more. In panel (a), the demand curve shifts more, so the price rises. In panel (b), the supply curve shifts more, so the price falls.

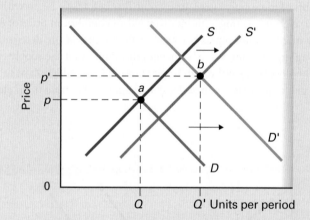

(a) Shift of demand dominates

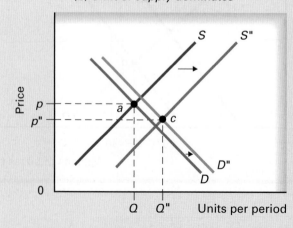

(b) Shift of supply dominates

Simultaneous Shifts of Demand and Supply Curves

As long as only one curve shifts, we can say for sure how equilibrium price and quantity will change. If both curves shift, however, the outcome is less obvious. For example, suppose both demand and supply increase, or shift rightward, as in Exhibit 8. Note that in panel (a), demand shifts more than supply, and in panel (b), supply shifts more than demand. In both panels, equilibrium quantity increases. The change in equilibrium price, however, depends on which curve shifts more. If demand shifts more, as in panel (a), equilibrium price increases. For example, in the last decade, the demand for housing has increased more than the supply, so both price and quantity have increased. But if supply shifts more, as in panel (b), equilibrium price decreases. For example, in the last decade, the supply of personal computers has increased more than the demand, so price has decreased and quantity increased.

Conversely, if both demand and supply decrease, or shift leftward, equilibrium quantity decreases. But, again, we cannot say what will happen to equilibrium price unless we examine relative shifts. (You can use Exhibit 8 to consider decreases in demand and supply by viewing *D'* and *S'* as the initial curves.) If demand shifts more, the price will fall. If supply shifts more, the price will rise.

If demand and supply shift in opposite directions, we can say what will happen to equilibrium price. Equilibrium price will increase if demand increases and supply decreases. Equilibrium price will decrease if demand decreases and supply increases. Without reference to particular shifts, however, we cannot say what will happen to equilibrium quantity.

These results are no doubt confusing, but Exhibit 9 summarizes the four possible combinations of changes. Using Exhibit 9 as a reference, please take the time right now to work through some changes in demand and supply to develop an intuitive understanding of the results. Then, in the following case study, evaluate changes in the market for professional basketball.

WALL STREET JOURNAL
Reading It **Right**

What's the relevance of the following statement from the Wall Street Journal: *"California officials attribute generally lower electricity prices to relatively mild weather in recent days, conservation efforts in the state, and the return of some power plants to full operation."*

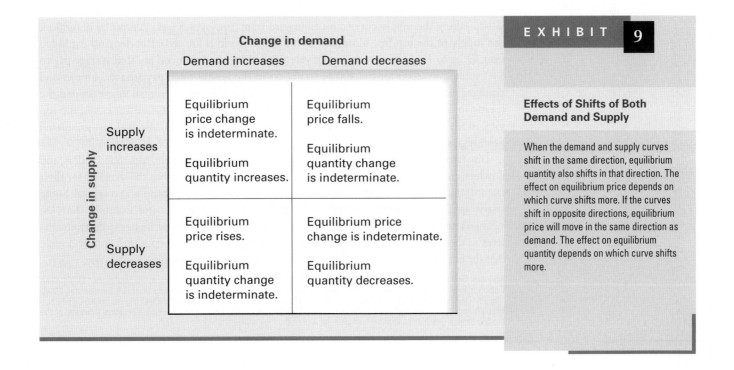

Change in demand

		Demand increases	Demand decreases
Change in supply	**Supply increases**	Equilibrium price change is indeterminate. Equilibrium quantity increases.	Equilibrium price falls. Equilibrium quantity change is indeterminate.
	Supply decreases	Equilibrium price rises. Equilibrium quantity change is indeterminate.	Equilibrium price change is indeterminate. Equilibrium quantity decreases.

EXHIBIT 9

Effects of Shifts of Both Demand and Supply

When the demand and supply curves shift in the same direction, equilibrium quantity also shifts in that direction. The effect on equilibrium price depends on which curve shifts more. If the curves shift in opposite directions, equilibrium price will move in the same direction as demand. The effect on equilibrium quantity depends on which curve shifts more.

Case **Study**

World of Business

eActivity

InsideHoops hosts a current salary list for top NBA players at http://www.insidehoops.com/nbasalaries.shtml.

The Market for Professional Basketball

Toward the end of the 1970s, the National Basketball Association (NBA) seemed on the verge of collapse. Attendance had sunk to little more than half capacity. Some teams were nearly bankrupt. Championship games didn't even get prime-time television coverage. But in the 1980s, three superstars turned things around. Michael Jordan, Larry Bird, and Magic Johnson attracted millions of new fans and breathed new life into the sagging league. Now a generation of new stars, including Allen Iverson, Tracy McGrady, and LeBron James, continue to fuel interest.

© Mike Cassese/Reuters/Corbis

Since 1980, game attendance has doubled, and the league expanded from 22 to 29 teams. New franchises sold for record amounts. More importantly, league revenue from broadcast rights jumped more than *40-fold* from $19 million per year during the 1978–1982 contract to $785 million per year during the 2002–2008 contract. Popularity also increased around the world as international players, such as Yao Ming, joined the league (basketball is now the most widely played team sport among young people in China). NBA rosters in 2003 included 80 international players from 36 countries. The NBA formed marketing alliances with global companies such as Coca-Cola and McDonald's, and league playoffs are now televised around the world.

What's the key resource in the production of NBA games? Talented players. Exhibit 10 shows the market for NBA players, with demand and supply in 1980 as D_{1980} and S_{1980}. The intersection of these two curves generated an average pay in 1980 of $170,000, or $0.17 million, for the 300 or so players in the league. Since 1980, the talent pool expanded somewhat, shifting the supply curve a bit rightward from S_{1980} to S_{2003} (almost by definition, the supply of the top few hundred players in the world is limited). But demand exploded from D_{1980} to D_{2003}. With supply relatively fixed, the greater demand boosted average pay to $4.1 million by 2003 for the 400 or so players in the league. Such pay attracts younger and younger players. For example, Kevin Garnett, whose $28 million annual salary topped the league in 2003, entered the NBA in 1995 right out of high school. LeBron James, the top pick in the 2003 NBA draft, and heir apparent to Michael Jordan, also had just graduated from high school.

But rare talent alone does not command high pay. For example, top rodeo riders, top bowlers, and top women basketball players also possess rare talent, but the demand for their talent is not enough to support pay anywhere near NBA levels. Demand is also critical. Some sports aren't even popular enough to support professional leagues (for example, the U.S. women's pro soccer league folded in 2003). NBA players are now the highest-paid team athletes in the world—earning 60 percent more than pro baseball's average and at least double that for pro football and pro hockey. Both demand *and* supply determine average pay.

Sources: Brian Straus, "Women's Pro Soccer League Forced to Fold," *Washington Post,* 16 September 2003; Allen Cheng, "Basketball Shoots to Top Sport for Young Chinese," *South China Morning Post,* 25 September 2003; "Salary Cap for 2003–04 Set at $43.8 million," http://www.nba.com/; "NBA TV Deal Moves to ABC, ESPN," http://espn.go.com/nba/news/2002/0122/1315389.html; and U.S. Census Bureau, *Statistical Abstract of the United States: 2003,* http://www.census.gov/prod/www/statistical-abstract-02.html.

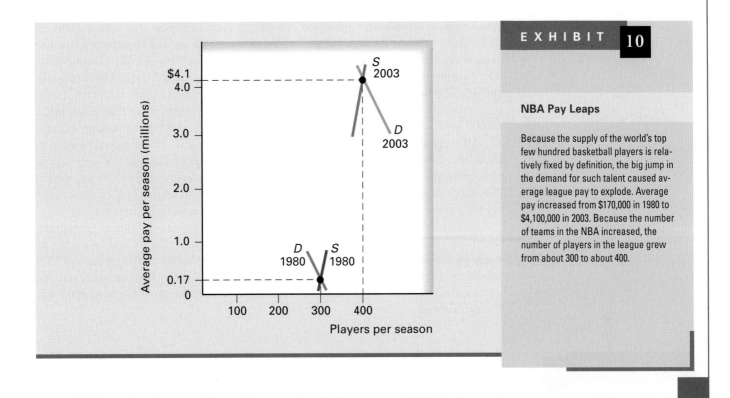

NBA Pay Leaps

Because the supply of the world's top few hundred basketball players is relatively fixed by definition, the big jump in the demand for such talent caused average league pay to explode. Average pay increased from $170,000 in 1980 to $4,100,000 in 2003. Because the number of teams in the NBA increased, the number of players in the league grew from about 300 to about 400.

Disequilibrium

A surplus exerts downward pressure on the price, and a shortage exerts upward pressure. Markets, however, do not always reach equilibrium quickly. During the time required to adjust, the market is said to be in disequilibrium. **Disequilibrium** is usually temporary as the market gropes for equilibrium. But sometimes, often as a result of government intervention, disequilibrium can last a while, as we will see next.

Price Floors

Sometimes public officials set prices above their equilibrium levels. For example, the federal government regulates some agriculture prices in an attempt to ensure farmers a higher and more stable income than they would otherwise earn. To achieve higher prices, the federal government sets a **price floor,** or a *minimum* selling price that is above the equilibrium price. Panel (a) of Exhibit 11 shows the effect of a $2.50 per gallon price floor for milk. At that price, farmers supply 24 million gallons per week, but consumers demand only 14 million gallons, yielding a surplus of 10 million gallons. This surplus milk will pile up on store shelves, eventually souring. To take it off the market, the government usually agrees to buy the surplus milk. The federal government, in fact, spends billions buying and storing surplus agricultural products. Note, to have an impact, a price floor must be set above the equilibrium price. A floor set below the equilibrium price would be irrelevant (how come?).

Price Ceilings

Sometimes public officials try to keep prices below their equilibrium levels by establishing a **price ceiling,** or a *maximum* selling price. For example, concern about the rising cost of

DISEQUILIBRIUM

The condition that exists in a market when the plans of buyers do not match those of sellers; a temporary mismatch between quantity supplied and quantity demanded as the market seeks equilibrium

PRICE FLOOR

A minimum legal price below which a good or service cannot be sold; to have an impact, a price floor must be set above the equilibrium price

PRICE CEILING

A maximum legal price above which a good or service cannot be sold; to have an impact, a price ceiling must be set below the equilibrium price

rental housing in some cities prompted city officials there to impose rent ceilings. Panel (b) of Exhibit 11 depicts the demand and supply of rental housing in a hypothetical city. The vertical axis shows monthly rent, and the horizontal axis shows the quantity of rental units. The equilibrium, or market-clearing, rent is $1,000 per month, and the equilibrium quantity is 50,000 housing units.

Suppose the government sets a maximum rent of $600 per month. At that ceiling price, 60,000 rental units are demanded, but only 40,000 supplied, resulting in a housing shortage of 20,000 units. Because of the price ceiling, the rental price no longer rations housing to those who value it the most. Other devices emerge to ration housing, such as long waiting lists, personal connections, and the willingness to make under-the-table payments, such as "key fees," "finder's fees," high security deposits, and the like. To have an impact, a price ceiling must be set below the equilibrium price. Price floors and ceilings distort markets.

Government intervention is not the only source of market disequilibrium. Sometimes, when new products are introduced or when demand suddenly changes, it takes a while to reach equilibrium. For example, popular toys, best-selling books, and chart-busting CDs sometimes sell out. On the other hand, some new products attract few customers and pile up unsold on store shelves, awaiting a "clearance sale." Disequilibrium is discussed in the following case study.

HOMEWORK
Xpress!
Ask the Instructor Video

EXHIBIT 11

HOMEWORK
Xpress!
Graphing

Price Floors and Price Ceilings

A price floor set above the equilibrium price results in a surplus, as shown in panel (a). A price floor set at or below equilibrium price has no effect. A price ceiling set below the equilibrium price results in a shortage, as shown [in p]anel (b). A price ceiling set at or above the equilibrium price has no effect.

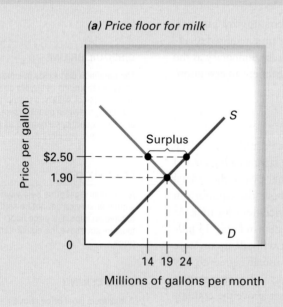

(a) Price floor for milk

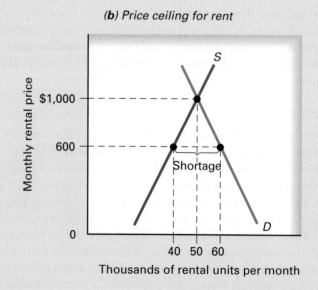

(b) Price ceiling for rent

The Toy Business Is Not Child's Play

U.S. toy sales exceeded $25 billion a year in 2003, but the business is not much fun for toy makers. Most toys don't make it from one season to the next, turning out to be costly duds. A few have staying power, like G.I. Joe, who could retire after 40 years of military service; Barbie, who is now over 40; and the Wiffle Ball, still a hit after 50 years. Because toy factories, which are mostly in China, need time to gear up, most retailers must order in February for Christmas delivery. Can you imagine the

© Photodisc/Getty Images

uncertainty of this market? Who, for example, could have anticipated the success of Chicken Dance Elmo, Beanie Babies, Teletubbies, FurReal Friends, or Yu-Gi-Oh trading cards?

A few years ago, the Mighty Morphin Power Rangers were the rage. Within a year, the manufacturer increased production 10-fold, with 11 new factories churning out nearly $1 billion in Rangers. Still, at $13 each, quantity demanded exceeded quantity supplied. Why don't toy makers simply let the price find its equilibrium level? Suppose, for example, that the market-clearing price for Power Rangers was $26, twice the actual price. First, it's hard for toymakers to anticipate demand well enough to boost the price before supplies run out. Second, suppliers who hope to retain customers over the long haul may want to avoid appearing greedy. That may be why Home Depot doesn't raise the price of snow shovels after the first winter storm, why Wal-Mart doesn't boost air conditioner prices during the dog days of summer, and why DaimlerChrysler preferred long waiting lists to raising prices still higher for its Mercedes SUV.

To sum up, uncertainty abounds in the market for new products. Suppliers can only guess what the demand will be, so they must feel their way in deciding what price to charge and how much to produce. Eventually, markets do achieve equilibrium. For example, Daimler-Chrysler doubled production of its SUV, eventually erasing the shortage. Because finding the market-clearing price takes time, some markets are temporarily in disequilibrium. But even when hot toys are sold out at retailers, they are usually available on the Internet at a higher price. For example, just before one recent Christmas, the hot toy that year, Spider-Man Web Blaster, was sold out most everywhere. But the toy was still available on eBay for $135, or nine times its $15 retail price.

Sources: Alexander Coolidge, "Hot Toys Are Hard to Come By for Those Who Wait," *Sarasota Herald Tribune,* 21 December 2002; "Hot Toys," *BusinessWeek,* 9 December 2002; Raymond Gorman and James Kehr, "Fairness as a Constraint on Profit Seeking," *American Economic Review,* March 1992; the Official Yu-Gi-Oh site at http://www.yugiohkingofgames.com; and the Toy Industry Association site at http://www.toy-tia.org/.

Conclusion

Demand and supply are the building blocks of a market economy. Although a market usually involves the interaction of many buyers and sellers, few markets are consciously designed. Just as the law of gravity works whether or not we understand Newton's principles, market forces operate whether or not participants understand demand and supply. These forces arise naturally, much the way car dealers cluster on the outskirts of town.

Markets have their critics. Some observers may be troubled, for example, that NBA star Kevin Garnett's annual salary could fund a thousand new schoolteachers, or that U.S. consumers spend billions each year on pet food when some people lack enough to eat. On your next trip to the supermarket, notice how much shelf space goes to pet products—often an entire aisle. Petsmart, a chain store, sells over 12,000 pet items. Veterinarians offer cancer treatment, cataract removal, and root canals for pets. Kidney dialysis for a pet can cost $55,000 per year.

SUMMARY

1. Demand is a relationship between the price and the quantity consumers are willing and able to buy per period, other things constant. According to the law of demand, quantity demanded varies inversely with its price, so the demand curve slopes downward.

2. A demand curve slopes downward for two reasons. A price decrease makes consumers (a) more *willing* to substitute this good for other goods and (b) more *able* to buy the good because the lower price increases real income.

3. Assumed to be constant along a demand curve are (a) money income, (b) prices of related goods, (c) consumer expectations, (d) the number and composition of consumers in the market, and (e) consumer tastes. A change in any one of these will shift the demand curve.

4. Supply is a relationship between the price of a good and the quantity producers are willing and able to sell per period, other things constant. According to the law of supply, price and quantity supplied are usually directly related, so the supply curve typically slopes upward. The supply curve slopes upward because higher prices make producers (a) more *willing* to supply this good rather than supply other goods that use the same resources and (b) more *able* to cover the higher marginal cost associated with greater output rates.

5. Assumed to be constant along a supply curve are (a) the state of technology; (b) the prices of resources used to produce the good; (c) the prices of other goods that could be produced with these resources; (d) supplier expectations; and (e) the number of producers in this market. A change in any one of these will shift the supply curve.

6. Demand and supply come together in the market for the good. Markets provide information about the price, quantity, and quality of the good. In doing so, markets reduce the transaction costs of exchange—the costs of time and information required for buyers and sellers to make a deal. The interaction of demand and supply guides resources and products to their highest-valued use.

7. Impersonal market forces reconcile the personal and independent intentions of buyers and sellers. Market equilibrium, once established, will continue unless there is a change in factor that shapes demand or supply. Disequilibrium is usually temporary while markets seek equilibrium, but sometimes disequilibrium lasts a while, such as when government regulates the price or when new products are introduced.

8. A price floor is the minimum legal price below which a particular good or service cannot be sold. The federal government imposes price floors on some agricultural products to help farmers achieve a higher and more stable income than would be possible with freer markets. If the floor price is set above the market clearing price, quantity supplied exceeds quantity demanded. Policy makers must figure out some way to prevent this surplus from pushing the price down.

9. A price ceiling is a maximum legal price above which a particular good or service cannot be sold. Governments impose price ceilings to reduce the price of some consumer goods such as rental housing. If the ceiling price is below the market clearing price, quantity demanded exceeds the quantity supplied, creating a shortage. Because the price system is not allowed to clear the market, other mechanisms arise to ration the product among demanders.

QUESTIONS FOR REVIEW

1. *(Law of Demand)* What is the law of demand? Give two examples of how you have observed the law of demand at work in the "real world." How is the law of demand related to the demand curve?

2. *(Changes in Demand)* What variables influence the demand for a normal good? Explain why a reduction in the price of a normal good does not increase the demand for that good.

3. *(Substitution and Income Effects)* Distinguish between the substitution effect and income effect of a price change. If a good's price increases, does each effect have a positive or a negative impact on the quantity demanded?

4. *(Demand)* Explain the effect of an increase in consumer income on the demand for a good.

5. *(Income Effects)* When moving along the demand curve, income must be assumed constant. Yet one factor that can cause a change in the quantity demanded is the "income effect." Reconcile these seemingly contradictory facts.

6. *(Demand)* If chocolate is found to have positive health benefits, would this lead to a shift of the demand curve or a movement along the demand curve?

7. *(Supply)* What is the law of supply? Give an example of how you have observed the law of supply at work. What is the relationship between the law of supply and the supply curve?

8. *(Changes in Supply)* What kinds of changes in underlying conditions can cause the supply curve to shift? Give some examples and explain the direction in which the curve shifts.

9. *(Supply)* If a severe frost destroys some of Florida's citrus crop, would this lead to a shift of the supply curve or a movement along the supply curve?

10. *(Markets)* How do markets coordinate the independent decisions of buyers and sellers?

11. (*C a s e* **S t u d y**: The Market for Professional Basketball) In what sense can we speak of a market for professional basketball? Who are the demanders and who are the suppliers? What are some examples of how changes in supply or demand conditions have affected this market?

PROBLEMS AND EXERCISES

12. *(Shifting Demand)* Using demand and supply curves, show the effect of each of the following on the market for cigarettes:

   a. A cure for lung cancer is found.
   b. The price of cigars increases.
   c. Wages increase substantially in states that grow tobacco.
   d. A fertilizer that increases the yield per acre of tobacco is discovered.
   e. There is a sharp increase in the price of matches, lighters, and lighter fluid.
   f. More states pass laws restricting smoking in public places.

13. *(Substitutes and Complements)* For each of the following pair of goods, determine whether the goods are substitutes, complements, or unrelated:

   a. Peanut butter and jelly
   b. Private and public transportation
   c. Coke and Pepsi
   d. Alarm clocks and automobiles
   e. Golf clubs and golf balls

14. *(Equilibrium)* "If a price is not an equilibrium price, there is a tendency for it to move to its equilibrium value. Regardless of whether the price is too high or too low to begin with, the adjustment process will increase the quantity of the good purchased." Explain, using a demand and supply diagram.

15. *(Market Equilibrium)* Determine whether each of the following statements is true, false, or uncertain. Then briefly explain each answer.

    a. In equilibrium, all sellers can find buyers.
    b. In equilibrium, there is no pressure on the market to produce or consume more than is being sold.
    c. At prices above equilibrium, the quantity exchanged exceeds the quantity demanded.
    d. At prices below equilibrium, the quantity exchanged is equal to the quantity supplied.

16. *(Equilibrium)* Assume the market for corn is depicted as in the table that appears below.
    a. Complete the table.
    b. What market pressure occurs when quantity demanded exceeds quantity supplied? Explain.
    c. What market pressure occurs when quantity supplied exceeds quantity demanded? Explain.
    d. What is the equilibrium price?
    e. What could change the equilibrium price?
    f. At each price in the first column of Exhibit 12, how much is sold?

17. *(Demand and Supply)* How do you think each of the following affected the world price of oil? (Use basic demand and supply analysis.)

    a. Tax credits were offered for expenditures on home insulation.
    b. The Alaskan oil pipeline was completed.
    c. The ceiling on the price of oil was removed.
    d. Oil was discovered in the North Sea.
    e. Sport utility vehicles and minivans became popular.
    f. The use of nuclear power decreased.

18. *(Demand and Supply)* What happens to the equilibrium price and quantity of ice cream in response to each of the following? Explain your answers.

    a. The price of dairy cow fodder increases.
    b. The price of beef decreases.
    c. Concerns arise about the fat content of ice cream. Simultaneously, the price of sugar (used to produce ice cream) increases.

19. *(Equilibrium)* Consider the following graph in which demand and supply are initially *D* and *S*, respectively. What are the equilibrium price and quantity? If demand increases to *D'*, what are the new equilibrium price and quantity? What happens if the government does not allow the price to change when demand increases?

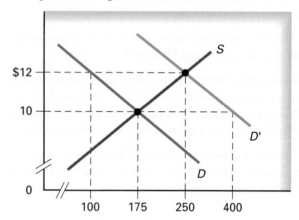

20. *(Changes in Equilibrium)* What are the effects on the equilibrium price and quantity of steel if the wages of steelworkers rise and, simultaneously, the price of aluminum rises?

Price per Bushel	Quantity Demanded (millions of bushels)	Quantity Supplied (millions of bushels)	Surplus/ Shortage	Will Price Rise or Fall?
$1.80	320	200	_____	_____
2.00	300	230	_____	_____
2.20	270	270	_____	_____
2.40	230	300	_____	_____
2.60	200	330	_____	_____
2.80	180	350	_____	_____

21. *(Price Floor)* There is considerable interest in whether the minimum wage rate contributes to teenage unemployment. Draw a demand and supply diagram for the unskilled labor market, and discuss the effects of a minimum wage. Who is helped and who is hurt by the minimum wage?

22. *(Price Ceilings)* Suppose the demand and supply curves for rental housing units have the typical shapes and that the rental housing market is in equilibrium. Then, government establishes a rent ceiling below the equilibrium level.

a. What happens to the quantity of housing consumed?
b. Who benefits from rent control?
c. Who loses from rent control?

23. (*C a s e* **S t u d y :** The Toy Business Is Not Child's Play) Use a demand and supply graph to describe developments in the market for Mighty Morphin Power Rangers toys. Keep in mind the shortage at the $13 selling price, the development of new factories, and the continued shortage.

E X P E R I E N T I A L   E X E R C I S E S

24. *(Market Demand)* With some other students in your class, determine your market demand for gasoline. Make up a chart listing a variety of prices per gallon of gasoline—$1.00, $1.25, $1.50, $1.75, $2.00, $2.25. Ask each student—and yourself—how many gallons per week they would purchase at each possible price. Then:

a. Plot each student's demand curve. Check to see whether each student's responses are consistent with the law of demand.
b. Derive the "market" demand curve by adding the quantities demanded by all students at each possible price.
c. What do you think will happen to that market demand curve after your class graduates and your incomes rise?

25. *(Price Floors)* The minimum wage is a price floor in a market for labor. The government sets a minimum price per

hour of labor in certain markets, and no employer is permitted to pay a wage lower than that. Go to the Department of Labor's minimum wage Web page to learn more about the mechanics of the program: http://www.dol.gov/esa/whd/flsa. Then use a demand and supply diagram to illustrate the effect of imposing an above-equilibrium minimum wage on a particular labor market. What happens to quantity demanded and quantity supplied as a result of the minimum wage?

26. *(Wall Street Journal)* After reading this chapter, you have a basic understanding of how demand and supply determine market price and quantity. Find an article in the "first section" of today's *Wall Street Journal* and interpret the article, using a demand and supply diagram. Explain at least one case in which a curve shifts. What caused the shift, and how did it affect price and quantity?

HOMEWORK XPRESS! EXERCISES

These exercises require access to McEachern Homework Xpress! If Homework Xpress! did not come with your book, visit **http://homeworkxpress.swlearning.com** *to purchase.*

1. Ice cream sellers recognize that demand for ice cream is seasonal: high in the summer, lower in the winter. Draw a demand curve for ice cream in the winter months. Draw a demand curve for ice cream in the summer months.

2. The major ingredients in ice cream are dairy products derived from milk. This summer the price of milk is expected to rise significantly. Draw a supply curve for ice cream before the price increase in milk is known. Draw a supply curve for ice cream in the summer months following the increase in the price of milk.

3. The increasing popularity of sports utility vehicles, SUVs, has led auto dealers to keep a large quantity of them in stock. With the increase in the price of gasoline, however, demand has been falling. Draw demand and supply curves in the diagram for SUVs before the increase in the price of gasoline. Show the equilibrium price and quantity. Illustrate the effect of the increase in the price of gasoline in the market for SUVs. Indicate the effect of this on equilibrium price and quantity.

4. Innovations in materials engineering allow automakers to substitute lower cost materials in their production of sports utility vehicles, SUVs, without reducing the safety of the vehicles. Draw demand and supply curves in the diagram for SUVs before the innovations in materials and show the equilibrium price and quantity. Illustrate the effect of the cost reducing innovations in the market for SUVs. Indicate the effect of this on equilibrium price and quantity.

Introduction to Macroeconomics

© M. SAT Editions SARL/Corbis Sygma

W hat's the big idea with macroeconomics? Why is its focus the national economy? How do we measure the economy's performance over time? Which has more impact on your standard of living, the economy's ups and downs or its long-term growth? Answers to these and related questions are provided in this chapter, which introduces macroeconomics. Macroeconomics looks at the big picture—not the demand for Dunkin' Donuts but the demand for everything produced in the economy; not the price of gasoline but the average price of all goods and services produced in the economy; not consumption by the Martinez household but consumption by all households; not investment by the Disney Corporation but investment by all firms in the economy.

Macroeconomists develop and test theories about how the economy as a whole works—theories that can help predict the consequences of economic policies and events. Macroeconomists are concerned not only with what determines such big-picture indicators as production, employment, and the price level but also with understanding how and why these measures change over time. Macroeconomists are especially interested in what makes an economy grow, because a growing economy creates more jobs and more goods and services—in short, faster growth means a higher standard of living. What determines the economy's ability to use resources productively, to adapt, to grow? This chapter begins exploring such questions. Topics discussed include:

- The national economy
- Economic fluctuations
- Aggregate demand
- Aggregate supply

- Equilibrium level of price and aggregate output
- Short history of the U.S. economy
- Demand-side economics
- Supply-side economics

The National Economy

ECONOMY

The structure of economic activity in a community, a region, a country, a group of countries, or the world

Macroeconomics concerns the overall performance of the *economy*. The term **economy** describes the structure of economic life, or economic activity, in a community, a region, a country, a group of countries, or the world. We could talk about the Chicago economy, the Illinois economy, the Midwest economy, the U.S. economy, the North American economy, or the world economy. We measure an economy's size in different ways, such as the amount produced, the number of people working, or their total income. The most common yardstick is *gross product,* which measures the market value of final goods and services produced in a particular geographical region during a given period, usually one year.

GROSS DOMESTIC PRODUCT (GDP)

The market value of all final goods and services produced in the nation during a particular period, usually a year

If the focus is the Illinois economy, we consider the *gross state product*. If the focus is the U.S. economy, we consider the **gross domestic product,** or **GDP,** which measures the market value of all final goods and services produced in the United States during a given period, usually a year. GDP adds up production of the economy's incredible variety of goods and services, from trail bikes to pedicures. We can use the gross domestic product to compare different economies at the same time or to track the same economy over time.

What's Special About the National Economy?

The national economy deserves special attention. Here's why. If you were to drive west on Interstate 10 in Texas, you would hardly notice crossing the state line into New Mexico. But if you took the Juarez exit south into Mexico, you would be stopped at the border, asked for identification, and possibly searched. You would become quite aware of crossing an international border. Like most countries, the United States and Mexico usually allow people and goods to move more freely *within* their borders than *across* their borders.

The differences between the United States and Mexico are far greater than the differences between Texas and New Mexico. For example, each country has its own standard of living and currency, its own culture and language, its own communication and transportation system, its own system of government, and its own "rules of the game"—that is, its own laws, regulations, customs, and conventions for conducting economic activity both within and across its borders.

Macroeconomics typically focuses on the performance of the national economy, including how the national economy interacts with other economies around the world. The U.S. economy is the largest and most complex in the world, with about 110 million households, 24 million businesses, and 87,400 separate government jurisdictions. The world economy includes about 200 sovereign nations, ranging from tiny Liechtenstein, with only 33,000 residents, to China, with 1.3 billion people. These numbers offer snapshots, but the economy is a moving picture, a work in progress—too complex to capture in snapshots. This is why we use theoretical models to focus on key relationships. To help you get your mind around the economy, let's begin with a simple analogy.

The Human Body and the U.S. Economy

Consider the similarities and differences between the human body and the economy. The body consists of millions of cells, each performing particular functions yet each linked to the entire body. Similarly, the U.S. economy is composed of millions of decision makers, each acting with some independence yet each connected with the economy as a whole. The economy, like the body, is continually renewing itself, with new households, new businesses, a changing group of public officials, and new foreign competitors and customers. Blood circulates throughout the body, facilitating the exchange of oxygen and vital nutrients among cells. Similarly, *money* circulates throughout the economy, facilitating the exchange of resources and products among individual economic units. In fact, blood and money are each called a *medium of exchange.* In Chapter 1 we saw that the movement of money, products, and resources throughout the economy follows a *circular flow,* as does the movement of blood, oxygen, and nutrients, throughout the body.

Flow and Stock Variables

Just as the same blood recirculates as a medium of exchange in the body, the same dollars recirculate as a medium of exchange in the economy to finance transactions. The dollars you spend on croissants are spent by the baker on butter and then spent by the dairy farmer on work boots. Dollars *flow* through the economy. To measure a flow, we use a **flow variable,** which is an amount per unit of time, such as your average spending per week or your heartbeats per minute. In contrast, a **stock variable** is an amount measured at a particular point in time, such as the amount of money you have with you right now or your weight this morning.

Testing New Theories

Physicians and other natural scientists test their theories using controlled experiments. Macroeconomists, however, have no laboratories and little ability to run economy-wide experiments. Granted, they can study different economies around the world, but each economy is unique, so comparisons are tricky. Controlled experiments also provide natural scientists with something seldom available to macroeconomists—the chance, or serendipitous, discovery (such as penicillin). Macroeconomists studying the U.S. economy have only one patient, so they can't introduce particular policies in a variety of alternative settings. Cries of "Eureka!" are seldom heard from macroeconomists.

Knowledge and Performance

Throughout history, little was known about the human body, yet many people still enjoyed good health. For example, the fact that blood circulates in our bodies was not discovered until 1638; it took scientists another 150 years to figure out why. Similarly, over the millennia, various complex economies developed and flourished, although there was little known about how these economies worked.

The economy is much like the body: As long as it functions smoothly, policy makers need not understand how it works. But if a problem develops—severe unemployment, high inflation, or sluggish growth, for example—we must know how a healthy economy works before we can consider if and how the problem can be corrected. We need not know every

FLOW VARIABLE

A variable that measures something over an interval of time, such as your income per week

STOCK VARIABLE

A variable that measures something at a particular point in time, such as the amount of money you have with you right now

detail of the economy, just as we need not know every detail of the body. But we must understand essential relationships among key variables. For example, does the economy work well on its own, or does it often perform poorly? If it performs poorly, what remedies are available? Can we be sure that the proposed remedy would not do more harm than good? When doctors didn't understand how the human body worked, their attempted "cures" were often worse than the diseases. Much of the history of medicine describes misguided efforts to deal with maladies. Even today, medical care is based on less scientific evidence than you might think. According to one study, only one in seven medical interventions is supported by reliable scientific evidence.[1]

Likewise, policy makers may adopt the wrong prescription because of a flawed theory about how the economy works. At one time, for example, a nation's economic vitality was thought to spring from the stock of precious metals accumulated in the public treasury. This theory spawned a policy called **mercantilism,** which held that, as a way of accumulating gold and silver, a nation should try to export more than it imports. To achieve this, nations restricted imports by such barriers as tariffs and quotas. But these restrictions led to retaliations by other countries, reducing international trade and the gains from specialization. Another flawed economic theory prompted President Herbert Hoover to introduce a major tax *increase* during the Great Depression. Economists have since learned that such a policy does more harm than good.

We turn now to the performance of the U.S. economy.

Economic Fluctuations and Growth

The U.S. economy and other industrial market economies historically have experienced alternating periods of expansion and contraction in economic activity. **Economic fluctuations** are the rise and fall of economic activity relative to the long-term growth trend of the economy. These fluctuations, or *business cycles,* vary in length and intensity, yet some features appear common to all. The ups and downs usually involve the entire nation and often the world and they affect nearly all dimensions of economic activity, not just production and employment.

U.S. Economic Fluctuations

Perhaps the easiest way to understand economic fluctuations is to examine their components. During the 1920s and 1930s, Wesley C. Mitchell, director of the National Bureau of Economic Research (NBER), analyzed economic fluctuations, noting that the economy has two phases: periods of *expansion* and periods of *contraction.* Prior to World War II, a contraction might be so severe as to be called a **depression,** which is a sharp reduction in the nation's total production lasting more than a year and accompanied by high unemployment. A milder contraction is called a **recession,** which is a decline in total output lasting at least two consecutive quarters, or at least six months. The U.S. economy experienced both recessions and depressions before World War II. Since then, there have been recessions but no depressions, so things have improved.

Despite these ups and downs, the U.S. economy has grown dramatically over the long run. The economy produced about 12 times more output in 2004 than it did in 1929. Output is measured by real GDP, the value of final goods and services after stripping away changes due to **inflation,** which is an increase in the economy's price level. Production increased because

MERCANTILISM

The incorrect theory that a nation's economic goal should be to accumulate precious metals in the public treasury; this theory prompted trade barriers to reduce imports, but other countries retaliated, reducing trade and the gains from specialization

ECONOMIC FLUCTUATIONS

The rise and fall of economic activity relative to the long-term growth trend of the economy; also called business cycles

DEPRESSION

A sharp reduction in an economy's total output accompanied by high unemployment lasting more than a year; a severe economic contraction

RECESSION

A decline in the economy's total output lasting at least two consecutive quarters, or six months; an economic contraction

INFLATION

An increase in the economy's average price level

---

1. As reported by Sherwin Nuland, "Medical Fads: Bran, Midwives and Leeches," *New York Times,* 25 January 1995.

of (1) increases in the amount and quality of resources, especially labor and capital; (2) better technology; and (3) improvements in the *rules of the game* that facilitate production and exchange, such as property rights, patent laws, the legal system, and market practices.

Exhibit 1 shows such a long-term growth trend in real GDP as an upward-sloping straight line. Economic fluctuations reflect movements around this growth trend. A contraction begins after the previous expansion has reached its *peak,* or high point, and continues until the economy reaches a *trough,* or low point. The period between a peak and trough is a *contraction,* and the period between a trough and subsequent peak is an **expansion.** Note that expansions last longer than contractions, but the length of the full cycle varies.

Analysts at NBER have tracked the U.S. economy back to 1854. Since then, the nation has experienced 32 peak-to-trough-to-peak cycles. No two have been exactly alike. The longest contraction lasted five and a half years from 1873 to 1879. The longest expansion lasted nearly 10 years, beginning in the spring of 1991. Year-to-year changes in output since 1929 appear in Exhibit 2, which shows the annual percentage change in real GDP. Years of declining real GDP are shown as red bars and years of increasing real GDP as blue bars. The big decline during the Great Depression of the early 1930s and the sharp jump during World War II stand in stark contrast. Growth averaged 3.4 percent a year for the entire period. Since 1948, the economy has experienced 10 full cycles, with expansions averaging just under five years and recessions just under one year. Notice that since 1948 the annual declines have been less frequent and less negative.

The intensity of U.S. economic fluctuations varies across regions. A recession hits hardest those regions that produce capital goods, such as heavy machinery, and durable goods, such as appliances, furniture, and automobiles. The demand for these goods falls more during hard times than does the demand for other goods and services. Because of seasonal fluctuations

EXPANSION

A phase of economic activity during which the economy's output increases

N e t **B o o k m a r k**

Read the Economic Review articles for the third quarter of 2003 at http://www.kc.frb.org/publicat/ econrev/er03q3.htm. Some of the articles focus on urban growth, travel and tourism, and entrepreneurship, all of which are aspects of expansion. How long do economic expansions last? Why do they end? Read some of the Chicago Fed National Activity Index reports, from most recent to those in 2001 or 2002, at http://www.chicagofed.org. How do the numbers and tone of the reports compare? What do they say about economic expansion?

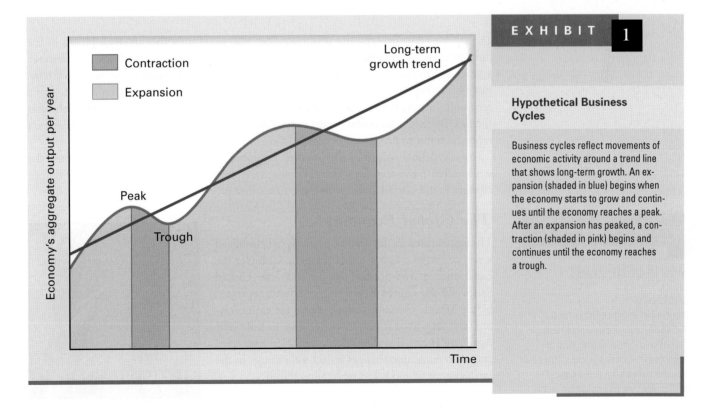

E X H I B I T   **1**

Hypothetical Business Cycles

Business cycles reflect movements of economic activity around a trend line that shows long-term growth. An expansion (shaded in blue) begins when the economy starts to grow and continues until the economy reaches a peak. After an expansion has peaked, a contraction (shaded in pink) begins and continues until the economy reaches a trough.

EXHIBIT **2**

Annual Percentage Change in U.S. Real GDP from 1929 to 2003

Years of declining real GDP are shown as red bars and years of growth as blue bars. Note that the year-to-year swings in output became less pronounced after World War II.

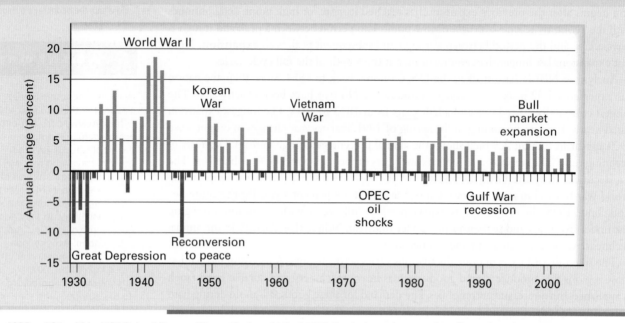

Source: "GDP and Other Major NIPA Series," *Survey of Current Business* 84 (April 2004). For the latest data, go to http://www.bea.doc.gov.

and random disturbances, the economy does not move smoothly through phases of the business cycle. Economists can't always distinguish between temporary setbacks in economic activity and the beginning of a downturn. A drop in production may result from such temporary interruptions as a snowstorm or a poor harvest rather than marking the onset of a recession. Turning points—peaks and troughs—are thus identified by the NBER only after the fact. Because a recession means output declines for at least two consecutive quarters, a recession is not so designated until at least six months after it begins.

As noted, fluctuations usually involve the entire nation. Indeed, economies around the world often move together. The following case study compares the year-to-year output changes in the United States with those in another major economy, the United Kingdom.

Case **Study**

World of Business

*e*Activity

Standard-of-living statistics for the United Kingdom are available from the Office of National Statistics at http://www.statistics.gov.uk/. This site includes data on the percentage of households owning appliances, autos,

The Global Economy

Though business cycles are not perfectly synchronized across countries, a link is often apparent. Consider the experience of two leading economies—the United States and the United Kingdom, economies separated by the Atlantic Ocean. Exhibit 3 shows for each economy the year-to-year percentage change in real GDP. Again, *real* means that the effects of inflation have been erased, so remaining changes reflect *real* changes in the total amount of goods and services produced.

If you spend a little time following the annual changes in each economy, you will see the similarities. For example, both economies went into recession in the early 1980s, grew well for the rest of the decade, entered another recession in 1991, recovered for the rest of the decade, then slowed down in 2001. And both economies picked up steam in 2004.

One problem with the linkage across economies is that a slump in other major economies could worsen a recession in the United States, and vice versa. For example, the terrorist attacks on the United States in September 2001 affected economies around the world, reducing airline travel and lowering stock market prices. At the time people feared difficulties in the top two economies in the world, the United States and Japan, would feed into each other, dragging other economies down with them.

Sources: Edmund Andrews, "America's Economic Cloud Extends to Europe," *New York Times*, 28 September 2001; Michael Williams et al., "Japan Must Finish Its Stalled Reform," *Wall Street Journal*, 16 March 2001; *Economic Report of the President*, February 2004; *OECD Economic Outlook* 75 (June 2004); and the Bureau of Economic Analysis Web site at http://www.bea.gov/.

etc. Compare the availability of cars and telephones in the United Kingdom to the United States by viewing the U.S. Census reports at http://www.census.gov/apsd/www/cqc.html.

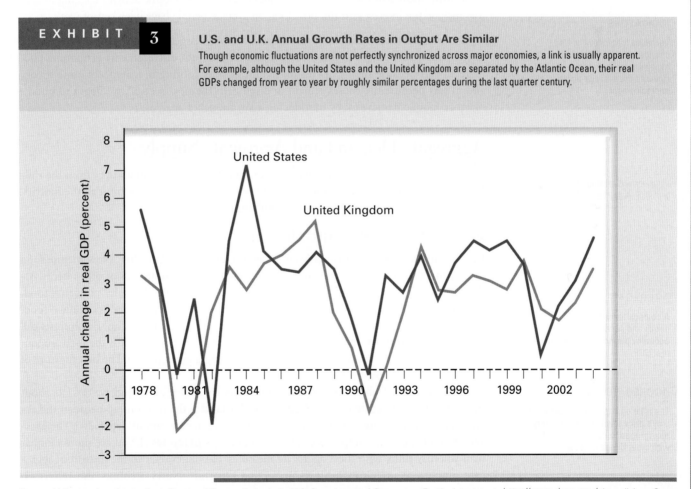

E X H I B I T   3

U.S. and U.K. Annual Growth Rates in Output Are Similar
Though economic fluctuations are not perfectly synchronized across major economies, a link is usually apparent. For example, although the United States and the United Kingdom are separated by the Atlantic Ocean, their real GDPs changed from year to year by roughly similar percentages during the last quarter century.

Source: U.S. growth estimates from Bureau of Economic Analysis, U.S. Department of Commerce. For the latest, go to http://www.bea.gov/ then click on Gross Domestic Product. U.K. growth estimates from *OECD Economic Outlook* 75 (June 2004).

Leading Economic Indicators

Certain events foreshadow a turning point in economic activity. Months before a recession is fully under way, changes in leading economic indicators point to the coming storm. In the early stages of a recession, business slows down, orders for machinery and computers slip, and the stock market, anticipating lower profits, turns down. Consumer confidence in the economy also begins to sag, so households spend less, especially on big-ticket items like automobiles and homes. Unsold goods start piling up. All these signs are called **leading economic indicators** because they usually predict, or *lead to,* a downturn. Upturns in leading indicators point to an economic recovery. But leading indicators cannot predict precisely *when* a turning point will occur, or even whether one will occur. Sometimes leading indicators sound a false alarm, and sometimes the economy slows down but does not contract.

Some economic indicators measure what's going on in the economy right now. **Coincident economic indicators** are those measures that reflect peaks and troughs as they occur. Coincident indicators include total employment, personal income, and industrial production. And some economic indicators measure what has already happened. **Lagging economic indicators** follow, or trail, changes in overall economic activity. Lagging indicators include the interest rate and how long on average people have been out of work.

Our introduction to economic fluctuations has been largely mechanical, focusing on the history and measurement of these fluctuations. We have not discussed why economies fluctuate, in part because such a discussion requires firmer footing in macroeconomic theory and in part because the causes remain in dispute. In the next section, we begin to build a macroeconomic framework by introducing a key model of analysis.

Aggregate Demand and Aggregate Supply

The economy is so complex that we need to simplify matters, or to abstract from the millions of relationships to isolate the important ones. We must step back from all the individual economic transactions to survey the resulting mosaic.

Aggregate Output and the Price Level

Let's begin with something you already know. Picture a pizza. Got that? Now picture food more generally. Food, of course, includes not just pizza but thousands of other items. Although food is more general than pizza, you probably have no difficulty picturing food. Now make the leap from food to all goods and services produced in the economy—food, housing, clothing, entertainment, transportation, medical care, and so on. Economists call this **aggregate output.** Because *aggregate* means total, aggregate output is the total amount of goods and services produced in the economy during a given period. The best measure of aggregate output is *real GDP.*

Just as we can talk about the demand for pizza, or the demand for food, we can talk about the demand for aggregate output. **Aggregate demand** is the relationship between the average price of aggregate output and the quantity of aggregate output demanded. The average price of aggregate output is called the economy's **price level.** You are more familiar than you may think with these aggregate measures. Headlines refer to the growth of aggregate output—as in "Growth Slows in Second Quarter." News accounts also report on changes in the "cost of living," reflecting movements in the economy's price level—as in "Prices Jump in June."

In a later chapter, you will learn how the economy's price level is computed. All you need to know now is that the price level in any year is an *index number,* or a reference number, comparing average prices that year to average prices in some base, or reference, year. If we say that the price level is higher, we mean compared with where it was. In Chapter 4, we talked about the price of a particular product, such as pizza, *relative to the prices of other products.* Now we talk about the *average price* of all goods and services produced in the economy *relative to the price level in some base year.*

The price level in the *base year* is standardized to a benchmark value of 100, and price levels in other years are expressed relative to the base-year price level. For example, in 2003, the U.S. price level, or price index, was 106, indicating that the price level that year was 6 percent higher than its value of 100 in the base year of 2000. The price level, or price index, is used not only to make comparisons in prices across time but also to make accurate comparisons of real aggregate output over time. Economists use the *price index* to eliminate any year-to-year change in GDP due solely to a change in the price level. What's left is the change in real output—the change in the amount of goods and services produced. After adjusting GDP for price level changes, we end up with what is called the **real gross domestic product,** or **real GDP.** So the price index (1) shows how the economy's price level changes over time and (2) can be used to figure out real GDP each year. You will get a better idea of these two roles as we discuss the U.S. economy.

REAL GROSS DOMESTIC PRODUCT (REAL GDP)

The economy's aggregate output measured in dollars of constant purchasing power

The Aggregate Demand Curve

In Chapter 4, you learned about the demand for a particular product. Now let's talk about the demand for our composite measure of output—aggregate output, or real GDP. The **aggregate demand curve** shows the relationship between the price level in the economy and real GDP demanded, other things constant. Exhibit 4 shows a hypothetical aggregate demand curve, *AD.* The vertical axis measures an index of the economy's price level relative to a 2000 base-year price level of 100. The horizontal axis shows real GDP, which measures output in dollars of constant purchasing power (here we use 2000 prices).

AGGREGATE DEMAND CURVE

A curve representing the relationship between the economy's price level and real GDP demanded per period, with other things constant

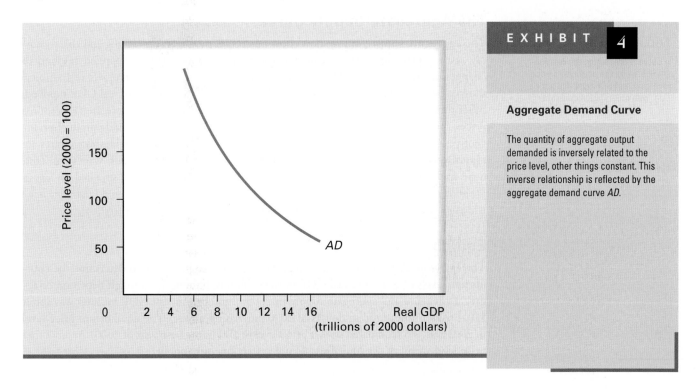

EXHIBIT 4

Aggregate Demand Curve

The quantity of aggregate output demanded is inversely related to the price level, other things constant. This inverse relationship is reflected by the aggregate demand curve *AD.*

The aggregate demand curve in Exhibit 4 reflects an inverse relationship between the price level in the economy and real GDP demanded. Aggregate demand sums demands of the four economic decision makers: households, firms, governments, and the rest of the world. As the price level increases, other things constant, households demand less housing and furniture, firms demand fewer trucks and tools, governments demand less computer software and military hardware, and the rest of the world demands less U.S. grain and U.S. aircraft.

The reasons behind this inverse relationship will be examined more closely in later chapters, but here's a quick summary. Real GDP demanded depends in part on household *wealth*. Some wealth is typically held in bank accounts and currency. An increase in the price level, other things constant, decreases the purchasing power of bank accounts and currency. Households are therefore poorer when the price level increases, so the quantity of real GDP they demand decreases. Conversely, a reduction in the price level increases the purchasing power of bank accounts and currency. Because households are richer as the price level decreases, the quantity of real GDP demanded increases.

Among the factors held constant along a given aggregate demand curve are the price levels in other countries as well as the exchange rates between the U.S. dollar and foreign currencies. When the U.S. price level increases, U.S. products become more expensive relative to foreign products. Consequently, households, firms, and governments both here and abroad decrease the quantity of U.S. real GDP demanded. On the other hand, a lower U.S. price level makes U.S. products cheaper relative to foreign products, so the quantity of U.S. real GDP demanded increases.

Consider the demand for a particular product versus aggregate demand. If the price of a particular product, such as pizza, increases, quantity demanded declines in part because pizza becomes more costly compared to substitutes. If the economy's price level increases, the quantity of U.S. real GDP demanded declines in part because U.S. products become more costly compared to foreign products.

The Aggregate Supply Curve

AGGREGATE SUPPLY CURVE

A curve representing the relationship between the economy's price level and real GDP supplied per period, with other things constant

The **aggregate supply curve** shows how much U.S. producers are willing and able to supply at each price level, other things constant. How does quantity supplied respond to changes in the price level? The upward-sloping aggregate supply curve, *AS*, in Exhibit 5 shows a positive relationship between the price level and the quantity of real GDP supplied, other things constant. Assumed constant along an aggregate supply curve are (1) resource prices, (2) the state of technology, and (3) the rules of the game that provide production incentives, such as patent and copyright laws. With regard to resource prices, wage rates are typically assumed to be constant along the aggregate supply curve. With wages constant, firms find a higher price level more profitable, so they increase real GDP supplied. *As long as the prices firms receive for their products rise faster than their cost of production, firms find it profitable to expand output, so real GDP supplied varies directly with the economy's price level.*

Equilibrium

The aggregate demand curve intersects the aggregate supply curve to determine the equilibrium levels of price and real GDP in the economy. Exhibit 5 is a rough depiction of aggregate demand and aggregate supply in 2003. Equilibrium real GDP in 2003 was about $10.4 trillion (measured in dollars of 2000 purchasing power). The equilibrium price level in 2003 was 106 (compared with a price level of 100 in the base year of 2000). At any other price level, quantity demanded would not match quantity supplied.

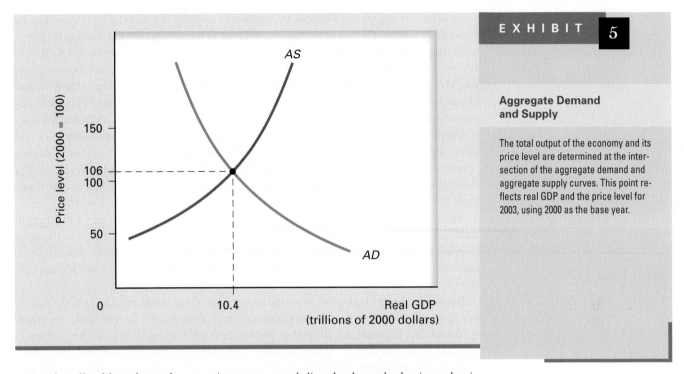

EXHIBIT 5

Aggregate Demand and Supply

The total output of the economy and its price level are determined at the intersection of the aggregate demand and aggregate supply curves. This point reflects real GDP and the price level for 2003, using 2000 as the base year.

Incidentally, although employment is not measured directly along the horizontal axis, firms usually must hire more workers to produce more output. So higher levels of real GDP can be beneficial because (1) more goods and services become available in the economy, and (2) more people are usually employed. Perhaps the best way to understand aggregate demand and aggregate supply is to apply these tools to the U.S. economy. The following section simplifies U.S. economic history to review changes in the price and output levels over time.

A Short History of the U.S. Economy

The history of the U.S. economy can be divided roughly into four economic eras: (1) before and during the Great Depression, (2) after the Great Depression to the early 1970s, (3) from the early 1970s to the early 1980s, and (4) since the early 1980s. The first era was marked by recessions and depressions, culminating in the Great Depression of the 1930s. These depressions were often accompanied by a falling price level. The second era was one of generally strong economic growth, with only moderate increases in the price level. The third era saw both high unemployment and high inflation at the same time. And the fourth era was more like the second, with good economic growth on average and only moderate increases in the price level.

The Great Depression and Before

Before World War II, the U.S. economy alternated between hard times and prosperity. As noted earlier, the longest contraction on record occurred between 1873 and 1879, when 80 railroads went bankrupt and most of the steel industry was shut down. During the depression of the 1890s the unemployment rate topped 18 percent. In October 1929, the stock market crash began what was to become the deepest, though not the longest, economic contraction in our nation's history, the Great Depression of the 1930s.

In terms of aggregate demand and aggregate supply, the Great Depression can be viewed as a shift to the left of the aggregate demand curve, as shown in Exhibit 6. AD_{1929} is the aggregate demand curve in 1929, before the onset of the depression. Real GDP in 1929 was $865 billion (measured in dollars of 2000 purchasing power), and the price level was 11.9 (relative to a 2000 base-year price level of 100). By 1933, aggregate demand had shifted leftward, decreasing to AD_{1933}. Why did aggregate demand decline? Though economists still debate the causes, most agree that the stock market crash of 1929 was the trigger. From there, grim business expectations cut investment, consumer spending fell, banks failed, the nation's money supply dropped, and world trade was severely restricted. All this contributed to a big decline in aggregate demand. The aggregate supply curve probably also shifted somewhat during this period, but the drop in aggregate demand was the dominant factor.

Because of the decline in aggregate demand, both the price level and real GDP dropped. Real GDP fell 27 percent, from $865 billion in 1929 to $636 billion in 1933, and the price level fell 25 percent, from 11.9 to 8.9. As real GDP declined, unemployment soared, climbing from only 3 percent of the labor force in 1929 to 25 percent in 1933, the highest U.S. rate ever recorded.

Before the Great Depression, macroeconomic policy was based primarily on the *laissez-faire* philosophy of Adam Smith. Smith, you may recall, argued in his famous book, *The Wealth of Nations*, that if people are allowed to pursue their self-interest in free markets, resources would be guided as if by an "invisible hand" to produce the most efficient and most valued level of aggregate output. Although the U.S. economy had suffered many sharp contractions since the beginning of the 19th century, most economists of the day viewed these as a natural phase of the economy—unfortunate but ultimately therapeutic and essentially *self-correcting.*

The Age of Keynes: After the Great Depression to the Early 1970s

The Great Depression was so severe that it stimulated new thinking about how the economy worked (or didn't work). In 1936, John Maynard Keynes (1883–1946) published *The*

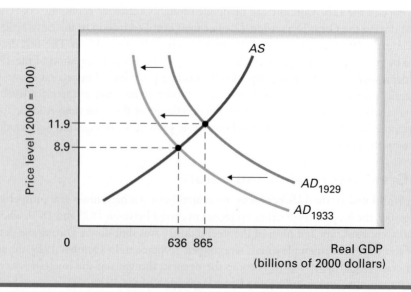

EXHIBIT   6

The Decrease in Aggregate Demand from 1929 to 1933

The Great Depression of the 1930s can be represented by a shift to the left of the aggregate demand curve, from AD_{1929} to AD_{1933}. In the resulting depression, real GDP fell from $865 billion to $636 billion, and the price level dropped from 11.9 to 8.9, measured relative to a price level of 100 in the base year 2000.

General Theory of Employment, Interest, and Money, the most famous economics book of the 20th century. In it, Keynes argued that aggregate demand was inherently unstable, in part because investment decisions were often guided by the unpredictable "animal spirits" of business expectations. If businesses grew pessimistic about the economy, they would invest less, which would reduce aggregate demand, output, and employment. For example, investment dropped more than 80 percent between 1929 and 1933. Keynes saw no natural market forces operating to ensure that the economy, even if allowed a reasonable time to adjust, would get output and employment back on the right track.

Keynes proposed that the government jolt the economy out of its depression by increasing aggregate demand. He recommended an expansionary fiscal policy to offset contractions. The government could achieve this stimulus either directly by increasing its own spending, or indirectly by cutting taxes to stimulate consumption and investment. But either action could create a federal budget deficit. A **federal budget deficit** is a flow variable that measures, for a particular period, the amount by which federal outlays exceed federal revenues.

To understand what Keynes had in mind, imagine federal budget policies that would increase aggregate demand in Exhibit 6, shifting the aggregate demand curve to the right, back to its original position. Such a shift would raise real GDP, which would increase employment. According to the Keynesian prescription, the miracle drug of fiscal policy—changes in government spending and taxes—could compensate for what he viewed as the instability of private spending, especially investment. If demand in the private sector declined, Keynes said the government should pick up the slack. We can think of the Keynesian approach as **demand-side economics** because it focused on how changes in aggregate demand could promote full employment. Keynes argued that government stimulus could shock the economy out of its depression. Once investment returned to normal levels, the government's shock treatment would no longer be necessary.

The U.S. economy bounced back some during the second half of the 1930s (see Exhibit 2). Then World War II broke out, boosting war-related demand for tanks, ships, aircraft, and the like. Government spending increased more than sixfold between 1940 and 1944. The explosion of output and sharp drop in the unemployment seemed to confirm the powerful role government spending could play in the economy. The increase in government spending, with no significant increase in tax rates, created federal deficits during the war.

Immediately after the war, memories of the Great Depression were still vivid. Trying to avoid another depression, Congress approved the *Employment Act of 1946,* which imposed a clear responsibility on the federal government to promote "maximum employment, production, and purchasing power." The act also required the president to appoint a *Council of Economic Advisers,* a three-member team of economists to provide economic advice and report annually on the economy.

The economy seemed to prosper during the 1950s largely without the added stimulus of fiscal policy. The 1960s, however, proved to be the *golden age of Keynesian economics,* a period when fiscal policy makers thought they could "fine-tune" the economy for top performance—just as a mechanic fine-tunes a racecar. During the early 1960s, nearly all advanced economies around the world enjoyed low unemployment and healthy growth with only modest inflation. In short, the world economy was booming, and the U.S. economy was on top of the world.

The economy was on such a roll that toward the end of the 1960s some economists believed the business cycle was history. As a sign of the times, the name of a federal publication, *Business Cycle Developments,* was changed to *Business Conditions Digest.* In the early 1970s, however, fluctuations returned with a fury. Worse yet, the problems of recession were compounded by inflation, which increased during the recessions of 1974–1975 and of

FEDERAL BUDGET

A plan for federal government outlays and revenues for a specific period, usually a year

FEDERAL BUDGET DEFICIT

A flow variable that measures the amount by which federal government outlays exceed federal government revenues in a particular period, usually a year

DEMAND-SIDE ECONOMICS

Macroeconomic policy that focuses on shifting the aggregate demand curve as a way of promoting full employment and price stability

1979–1980. Until then, inflation was limited primarily to periods of expansion. Confidence in demand-side policies was shaken, and the expression "fine-tuning" dropped from the economic vocabulary. What ended the golden age of Keynesian economics?

The Great Stagflation: 1973 to 1980

HOMEWORK
Xpress!
Ask the Instructor
Video

STAGFLATION

A contraction, or *stagnation*, of a nation's output accompanied by *inflation* in the price level

During the late 1960s, federal spending increased on both the war in Vietnam and social programs at home. This combined stimulus increased aggregate demand enough that in 1968 the *inflation rate,* the annual percentage increase in the price level, rose to 4.4 percent, after averaging only 2.0 percent during the previous decade. Inflation climbed to 4.7 percent in 1969 and to 5.3 percent in 1970. These rates were so alarming that in 1971, President Richard Nixon imposed ceilings on prices and wages. Those ceilings were eliminated in 1973, about the time that crop failures around the world caused grain prices to soar. To compound these problems, the Organization of Petroleum Exporting Countries (OPEC) cut its supply of oil, so oil prices jumped. Crop failures around the world plus the OPEC action reduced aggregate supply, shown in Exhibit 7 by the leftward shift of the aggregate supply curve from AS_{1973} to AS_{1975}. This resulted in **stagflation,** meaning a *stag*nation, or a contraction, in the economy's aggregate output and in*flation,* or increase, in the economy's price level. Real GDP declined by about $30 billion between 1973 and 1975, and unemployment climbed from 4.9 percent to 8.5 percent. During the same period, the price level jumped 19 percent.

Stagflation hit again five years later, fueled again by OPEC cutbacks. Between 1979 and 1980, real GDP declined but the price level increased by 9.1 percent. Macroeconomics has not been the same since. Because stagflation was on the supply side, not on the demand side, the demand-management prescriptions of Keynes seemed ineffective. Increasing aggregate demand might reduce unemployment but would worsen inflation.

EXHIBIT **7**

Stagflation from 1973 to 1975

The stagflation of the mid-1970s can be represented as a leftward shift of the aggregate supply curve from AS_{1973} to AS_{1975}. Aggregate output fell from $4.34 trillion in 1973 to $4.31 trillion in 1975, for a decline of about $30 billion (*stagnation*). The price level rose from 31.9 to 38.0, for a growth of 19 percent (*inflation*).

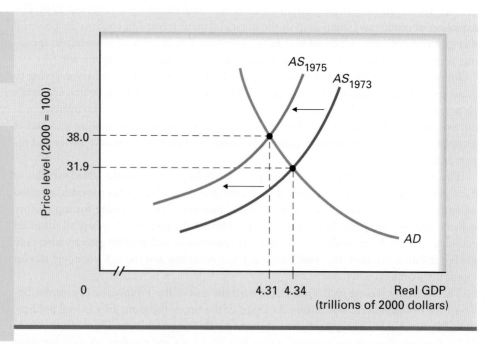

Experience Since 1980

Increasing aggregate supply seemed an appropriate way to combat stagflation, for such a move would both lower the price level and increase output and employment. Attention therefore turned from aggregate demand to aggregate supply. A key idea behind **supply-side economics** was that the federal government, by lowering tax rates, would increase after-tax wages, which would provide incentives to increase the supply of labor and other resources. According to advocates of the supply-side approach, the resulting increase in aggregate supply would achieve the happy result of expanding real GDP and reducing the price level. But this was easier said than done.

In 1981, to provide economic incentives to increase aggregate supply, President Ronald Reagan and Congress cut personal income tax rates by an average of 23 percent to be phased in over three years. Their hope was that aggregate supply would increase output and employment enough to increase tax revenue. Put another way, they believed the tax cuts would stimulate economic growth enough that the government's smaller share of a bigger pie would exceed what had been its larger share of a smaller pie.

But before the tax cut took effect, recession hit in 1981, contracting output and pushing the unemployment rate to 10 percent by 1982. Once the recession ended, the economy began what at the time was to be the longest peacetime expansion on record. For the rest of the decade, output grew, unemployment fell, and inflation settled down. But the growth in federal spending exceeded the growth in federal tax revenues during this period, so federal budget deficits swelled.

Deficits worsened with the onset of a recession in 1990. Even though that recession officially ended in March 1991, the deficit climbed, topping $290 billion in 1992. Annual deficits accumulated as a huge federal debt. **Government debt** is a stock variable that measures the net accumulation of prior deficits. To reduce federal deficits, President George H. W. Bush increased taxes in 1990, President William Clinton in 1993 increased tax rates for those in the highest tax bracket, and in 1995 a newly elected Republican Congress put the brakes on federal spending. Higher tax rates and a slower growth in federal spending combined with an improving economy to cut federal deficits. By 1998, the federal budget had turned into a surplus. By late 2000, the U.S. economic expansion became the longest on record, a stretch during which 22 million jobs were added, the unemployment rate dropped from 7.5 percent to 4.2 percent, and inflation remained tame. But after achieving this record, the economy slipped into recession by early 2001 and stretched into November of that year, aggravated by the terrorist attacks of September 2001. The recovery was slow and uneven and the unemployment continued to rise, peaking at 6.3 percent in June 2003. President Bush pushed through tax cuts "to get the economy moving again." Output was growing even though employment was not because those working had become more productive. But the tax cuts and spending programs increased the federal budget deficit, which exceeded $400 billion in 2004. Despite uncertainty created by the war in Iraq and higher oil prices, the U.S. economy started adding jobs in 2004.

Focusing on the ups and downs of the economy can miss the point that the U.S. economy over the long run has been an incredible creator of jobs and output—the most productive economy in the world. To underscore that point, we close with a case study that shows U.S. economic growth since 1929.

SUPPLY-SIDE ECONOMICS

Macroeconomic policy that focuses on a rightward shift of the aggregate supply curve through tax cuts or other changes that increase production incentives

GOVERNMENT DEBT

A stock variable that measures the net accumulation of annual budget deficits

WALL STREET JOURNAL

Reading It **Right**

What's the relevance of the following statement from the Wall Street Journal: *"Federal Reserve Chairman Alan Greenspan painted a grim picture of short-run economic weakness in the aftermath of last week's terrorist attacks, echoing widespread concerns about weak corporate earnings and rising layoffs that sent markets tumbling again."*

Public Policy

*e*Activity
Are you interested in learning more about the economic history of the past century? J. Bradford De Long's brief article, "Slouching Toward Utopia," provides one economist's evaluation of key developments. You can read it at http://www.bos.frb.org/economic/nerr/rr1998/q3/delo98_3.htm.

Over Seven Decades of Real GDP and Price Levels

Exhibit 8 traces the U.S. real GDP and price level for each year since 1929. Aggregate demand and aggregate supply curves are shown for 2003, but all points in the series reflect such intersections. Years of growing GDP are indicated as blue points and years of declining GDP as red ones. Despite the Great Depression of the 1930s and the 10 recessions since World War II, the long-term growth in output is unmistakable. Real GDP, measured along the horizontal axis in 2000 constant dollars, grew from $0.9 trillion in 1929 to $10.4 trillion in 2003—a twelvefold increase and an average annual growth rate of 3.4 percent. The price level also rose, but not quite as much, rising from 11.9 in 1929 to 105.7 in 2003—nearly a ninefold increase and an average inflation rate of 3.0 percent per year.

© Dave G. Houser/Corbis

Because the U.S. population is growing, the economy must create new jobs just to employ the additional people looking for work. For example, the U.S. population grew from 122 million in 1929 to 291 million in 2003, a rise of 139 percent. Fortunately, employment grew even faster, from 47 million in 1929 to 138 million in 2003, for a growth of 194 percent. So, since 1929, employment grew more than enough to keep up with a growing population. The United States has been an impressive job machine.

EXHIBIT 8

Tracking U.S. Real GDP and Price Level Since 1929

As you can see, both real GDP and the price level trended higher since 1929. Blue points indicate years of growing real GDP, and red points are years of declining real GDP. Real GDP in 2003 was 12 times greater than in 1929, and the price level was nearly nine times greater.

[Graph: Price level (2000 = 100) on vertical axis, Real GDP (trillions of 2000 dollars) on horizontal axis. Data points labeled: 1929, 1933, 1940, 1950, 1960, 1970, 1974, 1975, 1980, 1982, 1991, 2003. Curves labeled AS_{2003}, AD_{2003}, and 2003 at intersection.]

Source: Developed from data in *Survey of Current Business* 84 (February 2004). For the latest data, go to http://www.bea.gov.

Not only did the number of workers more than double, their average education increased as well. Other resources, especially capital, also rose sharply. What's more, the level of technology improved steadily, thanks to breakthroughs like the computer chip and the Internet. The availability of more and higher-quality human capital and physical capital increased the productivity of each worker, contributing to the twelvefold jump in real GDP since 1929.

Real GDP is important, but the best measure of the average standard of living is an economy's **real GDP per capita,** which tells us how much an economy produces on average per resident. Because real GDP grew much faster than the population, real GDP *per capita* jumped fivefold from $6,740 in 1929 to about $35,700 in 2003. The United States is the largest economy in the world and a leader in output per capita. We will examine U.S. productivity and growth more closely in the next chapter.

REAL GDP PER CAPITA

Real GDP divided by the population; the best measure of an economy's standard of living

Sources: "National Income and Product Account Tables," *Survey of Current Business* 84 (February 2004); *Economic Report of the President*, February 2004; *Economic Report of the President*, January 1980; and *OECD Economic Outlook* 75 (June 2004). For the latest real GDP and price level data, go to http://www.bea.doc.gov.

Conclusion

Because macroeconomists have no test subjects and cannot rely on luck, they hone their craft by developing models of the economy and then searching for evidence to support or reject these models. In this sense, macroeconomics is retrospective, always looking at recent developments for hints about which model works best. The macroeconomist is like a traveler who can see only the road behind and must find the way using a collection of poorly drawn maps. The traveler must continually check each map (or model) against the landmarks to see whether one map is more consistent with the terrain than the others. Each new batch of information about the economy causes macroeconomists to shuffle through their "maps" to check their models. Macroeconomics often emphasizes what can go wrong with the economy. Sagging output, high unemployment, and rising inflation capture much of the attention. But perhaps the most important performance measure is economic growth, which is examined in the next chapter. In a later chapter, we discuss two potential problems confronting the economy: unemployment and inflation.

SUMMARY

1. Macroeconomics focuses on the national economy. A standard measure of performance is the growth of real gross domestic product, or real GDP, the value of final goods and services produced in the nation during the year.

2. The economy has two phases: periods of expansion and periods of contraction. No two business cycles are the same; since 1948 peacetime expansions averaged just under five years and contractions averaged just less than one year. Before World War II, expansions were shorter and contractions longer. Despite these ups and downs, the economy has grown twelvefold since 1929 and jobs have grown faster than the population.

3. The aggregate demand curve slopes downward, reflecting a negative, or inverse, relationship between the price level and real GDP demanded. The aggregate supply curve slopes upward, reflecting a positive, or direct, relationship between the price level and real GDP supplied. The intersection of the two curves determines the economy's real GDP and price level.

4. The Great Depression and earlier depressions prompted John Maynard Keynes to argue that the economy is inherently unstable, largely because the components of private spending, particularly business investment, are erratic. Keynes did not believe that depressions were self-correcting, as

most economists before him believed. He argued that whenever aggregate demand sagged, the federal government should spend more or tax less to stimulate aggregate demand. His demand-side policies dominated macroeconomic thinking between World War II and the late 1960s.

5. During the 1970s, higher oil prices and global crop failures reduced aggregate supply. The result was stagflation, the troublesome combination of declining real GDP and rising inflation. Demand-side policies appeared less effective in an economy suffering from a reduction in aggregate supply, because stimulating aggregate demand would worsen inflation.

6. Supply-side tax cuts in the early 1980s were supposed to increase aggregate supply, thereby increasing output while dampening inflation. But federal spending increased faster than federal revenue, resulting in big budget deficits, which grew into the early 1990s. Tax increases, a slower growth in government spending, and an expanding economy all helped erase budget deficits by 1998, creating a federal budget surplus. But after the longest expansion on record, the economy suffered a recession. The recession ended in November 2001, but unemployment continued to rise into 2003. Tax cuts and a sluggish recovery boosted the federal deficit. Jobs began growing once again in 2004.

QUESTIONS FOR REVIEW

1. *(The National Economy)* Why do economists pay more attention to national economies (for example, the U.S. or Canadian economies) than to state or provincial economies (such as California or Ontario)?

2. *(The Human Body and the U.S. Economy)* Based on your own experiences, extend the list of analogies between the human body and the economy as outlined in this chapter. Then, determine which variables in your list are stocks and which are flows.

3. *(Stocks and Flows)* Differentiate between stock and flow variables. Give an example of each.

4. *(Economic Fluctuations)* Describe the various components of fluctuations in economy activity over time. Because the economic activity fluctuates, how is long-term growth possible?

5. *(Economic Fluctuations)* Why doesn't the National Bureau of Economic Research identify the turning points in economic activity until months after they occur?

6. (*C a s e* **S t u d y** : The Global Economy) How are economic fluctuations linked among national economies? Could a recession in the United States trigger a recession abroad?

7. *(Leading Economic Indicators)* Define *leading economic indicators* and give some examples. You may wish to take a look

at The Conference Board's index of leading economic indictors at http://www.conference-board.org/economics/indicators.cfm.

8. *(Aggregate Demand and Aggregate Supply)* Why does a decrease in aggregate demand result in a lower level of employment, given an aggregate supply curve?

9. *(Aggregate Demand and Aggregate Supply)* Is it possible for the price level to fall while production and employment both rise? If it is possible, how could this happen? If it is not possible, explain why not.

10. *(Aggregate Demand Curve)* Describe the relationship illustrated by the aggregate demand curve. Why does this relationship exist?

11. *(Demand-Side Economics)* What is the relationship between demand-side economics and the federal budget deficit?

12. *(Stagflation)* What were some of the causes of the stagflations of 1973 and 1979? In what ways were these episodes of stagflation different from the Great Depression of the 1930s?

13. (*C a s e* **S t u d y** : Over Seven Decades of Real GDP and Price Levels) The price level grew faster than real GDP between 1947 and 2003. Does this mean that the rising price level masked an actual decline in output? Why or why not?

PROBLEMS AND EXERCISES

14. *(Aggregate Demand and Supply)* Review the information on demand and supply curves in Chapter 4. How do the aggregate demand and aggregate supply curves presented in this chapter differ from the market curves of Chapter 4?

15. *(Aggregate Demand and Supply)* Determine whether each of the following would cause a shift of the aggregate demand curve, the aggregate supply curve, neither, or both. Which curve shifts, and in which direction? What happens to aggregate output and the price level in each case?

   a. The price level changes
   b. Consumer confidence declines
   c. The supply of resources increases
   d. The wage rate increases

16. *(Supply-Side Economics)* One supply-side measure introduced by the Reagan administration was a cut in income tax rates. Use an aggregate demand-supply diagram to show what effect was intended. What might happen if such a tax cut also generated a change in aggregate demand?

EXPERIENTIAL EXERCISES

17. *(Economic Fluctuation)* The National Bureau of Economic Research maintains a Web page devoted to business cycle expansions and contractions at http://www.nber.org/cycles.html. Take a look at this page and see if you can determine how the business cycle has been changing in recent decades. Has the overall length of cycles been changing? Have recessions been getting longer or shorter?

18. *(Experience Since 1980)* Review the Summary of Commentary on Current Economic Conditions by Federal Reserve District (Beige Book), available through the Federal Reserve System at http://www.federalreserve.gov/FOMC/BeigeBook/2004/default.htm.

   a. Summarize the national economic conditions for the most recent period covered in the report. Overall, is the economy healthy? If not, what problems is it experiencing?

   b. Go to the summary applicable to your district. Summarize the economic conditions for the last reporting period. Is the economy in your district healthy? If not, what problems is it experiencing?

19. *(Wall Street Journal)* This chapter introduced the tools of aggregate demand and supply. Can you use them? Test your understanding by finding an article in today's *Wall Street Journal* describing an event that may affect the U.S. price level and real GDP. Look under "Economy" or "International" in the First Section of the newspaper. Draw an initial set of *AD* and *AS* curves and then determine which curve will be affected and in which direction it will shift. What do you predict will happen to the price level and real GDP?

HOMEWORK XPRESS! EXERCISES

*These exercises require access to McEachern Homework Xpress! If Homework Xpress! did not come with your book, visit **http://homeworkxpress.swlearning.com** to purchase.*

1. In the diagram, sketch an aggregate demand curve for the year 2000 when real GDP was $9.8 trillion.

2. In the diagram, the aggregate demand curve is for the year 2002. Sketch an aggregate supply curve that shows the economy at an equilibrium real GDP of $10.1 trillion. Identify the price level.

3. In the diagram, the aggregate supply curve is for the year 2000. Sketch an aggregate demand curve that shows the economy at an equilibrium real GDP of $9.8 trillion. Il-lustrate how a shift of aggregate demand could decrease the equilibrium level of real GDP to $9.5 trillion. Identify the price level for this new equilibrium.

4. In the diagram, the aggregate demand curve is for the year 1995. Sketch in an aggregate supply curve that shows the economy at an equilibrium real GDP of $8 trillion. Identify the price level. Illustrate how a shift of aggregate supply could decrease the equilibrium level of GDP to $7.5 trillion. Identify the price level for this new equilibrium.

Productivity and Growth

© Ralf-Finn Hestoft/Index Stock Imagery

Why is the standard of living so much higher in some countries than in others? How does an economy increase its living standard? Why is the long-term growth rate more important than short-term fluctuations in economic activity? What's labor productivity and why has it picked up in recent years? What's the impact of the recent surge in labor productivity on your living standard? Answers to these and other questions are addressed in this chapter, which focuses on arguably the most important criteria for judging an economy's performance—productivity and growth.

The single most important determinant of a nation's standard of living in the long run is the productivity of its resources. Even seemingly low growth in productivity, if sustained for years, can have a substantial effect on the average living standard—that is, on the average availability of goods and services per capita. Growing productivity is therefore critical to a rising standard of living and has kept the U.S. economy a world leader.

Economic growth is a complicated process, one that even experts do not yet fully understand. Since before Adam Smith inquired into the *Wealth of Nations,* economists have puzzled over what makes some economies prosper while others founder. Because a market economy is not the product of conscious design, it does not reveal its secrets readily, nor can it be easily manipulated in pursuit of growth. We can't simply push here and pull there to achieve the desired result. Changing the economy is not like remodeling a home by knocking out a wall to expand the kitchen. Because we have no clear blueprint of the economy, we cannot make changes to specifications.

Still, there is much economists do know. In this chapter, we first develop a few simple models to examine productivity and growth. Then, we use these models to help explain why some nations are rich and some poor. U.S. performance gets special attention, particularly compared with other major economies around the world. We close with some current issues of technology and growth. Topics include:

- Labor productivity
- The production function
- U.S. productivity and growth
- Technological change and unemployment
- Research and development
- Convergence

Theory of Productivity and Growth

Two centuries ago, 90 percent of the American workforce was in agriculture, where the hours were long and rewards unpredictable. Other workers had it no better, toiling from sunrise to sunset for a wage that bought just the bare necessities. People had little intellectual stimulation and little contact with the outside world. A skilled worker's home in 1800 was described as follows: "Sand sprinkled on the floor did duty as a carpet. . . . What a stove was he did not know. Coal he had never seen. Matches he had never heard of. . . . He rarely tasted fresh meat. . . . If the food of a [skilled worker] would now be thought coarse, his clothes would be thought abominable."[1]

Over the last two centuries, there has been an incredible increase in the U.S. *standard of living* as measured by the amount of goods and services available on average per person. An economy's standard of living grows over the long run because of (1) increases in the amount and quality of resources, especially labor and capital, (2) better technology, and (3) improvements in the *rules of the game* that facilitate production and exchange, such as tax laws, property rights, patent laws, the legal system, and customs of the market. Perhaps the easiest way to introduce economic growth is by beginning with something you have already read about, the production possibilities frontier.

Growth and the Production Possibilities Frontier

The *production possibilities frontier,* or *PPF,* first introduced in Chapter 2, shows what the economy can produce if available resources are used efficiently. Let's briefly review the assumptions made in developing the frontier shown in Exhibit 1. During the period under consideration, usually a year, the quantity of resources in the economy and the level of technology are assumed to be fixed. Although not mentioned in Chapter 2, also assumed fixed during the period are the rules of the game that facilitate production and exchange. We clas-

1. E. L. Bogart, *The Economic History of the United States* (New York: Longmans, Green, and Co., 1912), pp. 157–158.

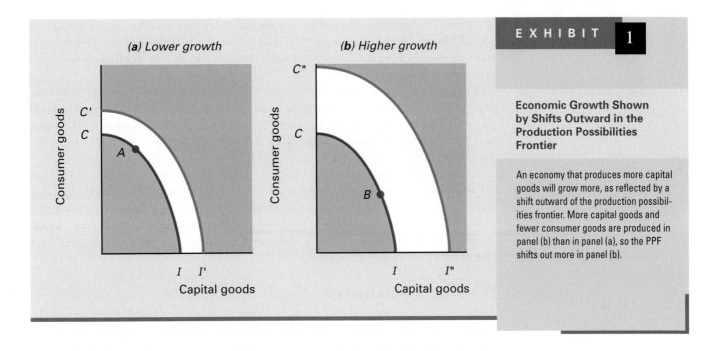

EXHIBIT 1

Economic Growth Shown by Shifts Outward in the Production Possibilities Frontier

An economy that produces more capital goods will grow more, as reflected by a shift outward of the production possibilities frontier. More capital goods and fewer consumer goods are produced in panel (b) than in panel (a), so the PPF shifts out more in panel (b).

sify all production into two broad categories—in this case, consumer goods and capital goods. Capital goods are used to produce other goods. For example, the economy can make pizzas and pizza ovens. Pizzas are consumer goods and ovens are capital goods.

When resources are employed efficiently, the production possibilities frontier *CI* in each panel of Exhibit 1 shows the possible combinations of consumer goods and capital goods that can be produced in a given year. Point *C* depicts the quantity of consumer goods produced if all the economy's resources are employed efficiently to produce them. Point *I* depicts the same for capital goods. Points inside the frontier show inefficient combinations, and points outside the frontier show unattainable combinations, given the resources, technology, and rules of the game. The production possibilities frontier is bowed out because resources are not perfectly adaptable to the production of both goods; some resources are specialized.

Economic growth is an outward shift of the production possibilities frontier, as shown in each panel of Exhibit 1. What can cause growth? An increase in resources, such as a growth in the labor supply or in the capital stock, shifts the frontier outward. Labor supply can increase either because of population growth or because the existing population is willing to work more. The capital stock expands if the economy produces more capital this year. The more capital produced this year, the more the economy grows, as reflected by an outward shift of the production frontier.

Breakthroughs in technology also expand the frontier by making more efficient use of existing resources. Technological change often improves the quality of capital, but it can enhance the productivity of any resource. Technological change often can free up resources for other uses. For example, the development of synthetic dyes in the 19th century freed up millions of acres of agricultural land that had been devoted to dye crops such as madder (red) and indigo (blue). The development of fiber-optic cable and cellular technology freed up the world's largest stock of copper in the form of existing telephone wires strung on poles across the nation.

Finally, any improvement in the rules of the game that nurtures production and exchange promotes growth and expands the frontier. For example, the economy can grow as a result of a patent laws that encourages more inventions[2] or legal reforms that reduce transaction costs. Thus, *the economy grows because of a greater availability of resources, an improvement in the quality of resources, technological change that makes better use of resources, or improvements in the rules of the game that enhance production.*

The amount of capital produced this year will affect the location of the PPF next year. For example, in panel (a) of Exhibit 1, the economy has chosen point *A* from possible points along *CI*. The capital produced this year shifts the PPF from *CI* this year out to *C'I'* next year. But if more capital goods are produced this year, as reflected by point *B* in panel (b), the PPF will shift outward farther next year, to *C"I"*.

An economy that produces more capital this year is said to *invest* more in capital. As you can see, to invest more, people must give up some consumer goods. Thus, the opportunity cost of more capital goods is having fewer consumer goods. More generally, we can say that people must *save* more now—that is, forgo some current consumption—to invest in capital. *Investment cannot occur without saving.* Economies that save more can invest more, as we'll see later. But let's get back to production.

What Is Productivity?

Production is a process that transforms resources into products. Resources coupled with technology produce output. Productivity measures how efficiently resources are employed. In simplest terms, the greater the productivity, the more goods and services can be produced from a given amount of resources, and the farther out will be the production possibilities frontier. Economies that use resources more efficiently create a higher standard of living, meaning that more goods and services are produced per capita.

Productivity is defined as the ratio of total output to a specific measure of input. It usually reflects an average, expressing total output divided by the amount of a particular kind of resource employed. For example, **labor productivity** is the output per unit of labor and measures total output divided by the hours of labor employed to produce that output.

We can talk about the productivity of any resource, such as labor, capital, or natural resources. When agriculture accounted for most output in the economy, land productivity, or bushels of grain per acre, was a key measure of economic welfare. Where soil was rocky and barren, people were poorer than where soil was fertile and fruitful. Even today, soil productivity determines the standard of living in some economies. Industrialization and trade, however, have liberated many from dependence on soil fertility. Today, some of the world's most productive economies have little land or have land of poor fertility. For example, Japan has a high living standard even though its population, which is nearly half that of the United States, lives on a land area only one twenty-fifth the U.S. land area.

Labor Productivity

Labor is the resource most commonly used to measure productivity. Why labor? First, labor accounts for most production cost—about 70 percent on average. Second, labor is more easily measured than other inputs, whether we speak of hours per week or full-time workers per year. Statistics about employment and hours worked are more readily available and more reliable than those about other resources used.

But the resource most responsible for increasing labor productivity is capital. As introduced in Chapter 1, the two broad categories are human capital and physical capital. *Human*

PRODUCTIVITY

The ratio of a specific measure of output, such as real GDP, to a specific measure of input, such as labor; in this case productivity measures real GDP per hour of labor

LABOR PRODUCTIVITY

Output per unit of labor; measured as real GDP divided by the hours of labor employed to produce that output

---

2. For evidence how the greater protection of intellectual property stimulates technological change, see Sunil Kanwar and Robert Evenson, "Does Intellectual Property Protection Spur Technological Change?" *Oxford Economic Papers* 55 (April 2003): 235–264.

capital is the accumulated knowledge, skill, and experience of the labor force. As workers acquire more human capital, their productivity and their incomes grow. That's why surgeons earn more than butchers and accountants earn more than file clerks. You are reading this book right now to enhance your human capital. *Physical capital* includes the machines, buildings, roads, airports, communication networks, and other manufactured creations used to produce goods and services. Think about digging a ditch with bare hands versus using a shovel. Now switch the shovel for a backhoe. More physical capital obviously makes diggers more productive. Or consider picking oranges with bare hands versus using a picking machine that combs the trees with steel bristles. In less than 15 minutes the machine can pick 18 tons of oranges from 100 trees, catch the fruit, and drop it into storage carts. Without the machine, that would take four workers all day.[3]

In poorer countries labor is cheap and capital dear, so producers substitute labor for capital. For example, in India a beverage truck will make its rounds festooned with workers, as many as 10, so as to minimize the time the truck, the valuable resource, spends at each stop. In the United States, where labor is more costly (compared to capital), the truck will make its rounds with just the driver. As another example, in Haiti, the poorest country in the Western Hemisphere, a ferry service could not afford to build a dock, so it hired workers to carry passengers through the water to and from the ferry on their shoulders.[4]

As an economy accumulates more capital per worker, labor productivity increases and the standard of living grows. The most productive combination of all is human capital combined with physical capital. For example, one certified public accountant with a computer and specialized software can sort out a company's finances more quickly and more accurately than can a thousand high-school-educated file clerks with pencils and paper.

The Per-Worker Production Function

We can express the relationship between the amount of capital per worker and the output per worker as an economy's **per-worker production function.** Exhibit 2 shows the relationship between the amount of capital per worker, measured along the horizontal axis, and average output per worker, or labor productivity, measured along the vertical axis, other things constant—including the level of technology and rules of the game. Any point on the production function, *PF,* shows how much output can be produced per worker for each amount of capital per worker. For example, when there are k units of capital per worker, average output per worker in the economy is y. The curve slopes upward from left to right because an increase in capital per worker helps each worker produce more output. For example, a bigger truck makes the driver more productive.

As the quantity of capital per worker increases, output per worker increases but at a diminishing rate, as reflected by the shape of the per-worker production function. The diminishing slope of this curve reflects the *law of diminishing marginal returns from capital,* which says that beyond some level of capital per worker, increases in capital add less and less to output per worker. For example, adding to the size and number of trucks at a shipping company initially increases the productivity of drivers. Once all drivers have big trucks, however, more trucks add little to total output. Thus, given the supply of other resources, the level of technology, and the rules of the game, additional gains from more capital per worker eventually diminish. An increase in the amount of capital per worker is called **capital deepening** and is one source of rising productivity. *Capital deepening contributes to labor productivity and economic growth.*

PER-WORKER PRODUCTION FUNCTION

The relationship between the amount of capital per worker in the economy and average output per worker

CAPITAL DEEPENING

An increase in the amount of capital per worker; one source of rising labor productivity

3. Eduardo Porter, "In Florida Groves, Cheap Labor Means Machines," *New York Times,* 22 March 2004.
4. This example was noted by Tyler Cowen, "The Ricardo Effect in Haiti," 23 February 2004, http://www.marginalrevolution.com.

Per-Worker Production Function

The per-worker production function, *PF*, shows a direct relationship between the amount of capital per worker, *k*, and the output per worker, *y*. The bowed shape of *PF* reflects the law of diminishing marginal returns from capital, which holds that as more capital is added to a given number of workers, gains in output diminish.

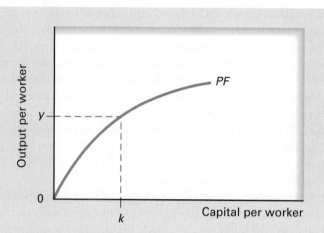

Technological Change

Held constant along a per-worker production function is the level of technology in the economy. Technological change usually improves the *quality* of capital and represents another source of increased productivity. For example, a tractor is more productive than a horse-drawn plow, a word processor more productive than a typewriter, and an Excel spreadsheet more productive than pencil and paper. Better technology is reflected in Exhibit 3 by an upward rotation in the per-worker production function from *PF* to *PF'*. As a result of a technological breakthrough, more is produced at each level of capital per worker. For example, if there are *k* units of capital per worker, a major breakthrough in technology increases the output per worker in the economy from *y* to *y'*.

Simon Kuznets, who won a Nobel Prize in part for his analysis of economic growth, claimed that technological change and the ability to apply such breakthroughs to all aspects of production were the driving forces behind economic growth in market economies.

HOMEWORK
Xpress!
Ask the Instructor
Video

Impact of a Technological Breakthrough on the Per-Worker Production Function

A technological breakthrough increases output per worker at each level of capital per worker. Better technology makes workers more productive. This is shown by a rotation upward in the per-worker production function from *PF* to *PF'*. An improvement in the rules of the game would have a similar effect.

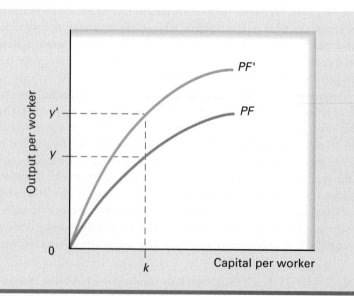

Kuznets argued that changes in the *quantities* of labor and capital account for only one-tenth of the increase in economic growth. Nine-tenths came from improvements in the *quality* of inputs. As technological breakthroughs become *embodied* in new capital, resources are combined more efficiently, increasing total output. *From the wheel to the assembly-line robot, capital embodies the fruits of discovery and drives economic growth.*

Thus, two kinds of changes in capital improve worker productivity: (1) an increase in the *quantity* of capital per worker, as reflected by a movement along the per-worker production function, and (2) an improvement in the *quality* of capital per worker, as reflected by technological change that rotates the curve upward. More capital per worker and better capital per worker result in more output per worker, which, over time, translates into more output per capita, meaning a higher standard of living.

Rules of the Game

Perhaps the most elusive ingredients for productivity and growth are the **rules of the game,** the formal and informal institutions that promote economic activity: the laws, customs, conventions, and other institutional elements that encourage people to undertake productive activity. A stable political environment and system of well-defined property rights are important. Less investment will occur if potential investors believe their capital could be appropriated by government, stolen by thieves, destroyed by civil unrest, or blown up by terrorists. Improvements in the rules of the game could result in more output for each level of capital per worker, thus reflected in a rotation up in the per-worker production function. Simply put, a more stable political climate could have a similar beneficial effect on productivity as a technological improvement. Conversely, events that foster instability can harm an economy's productivity and rotate the per-worker production function downward. The terrorist attack of the World Trade Center and Pentagon was such a destabilizing event. According to Albert Abadie, a Harvard economist, the attack affected "the spinal cord of any favorable business environment"—the ability of business and workers "to meet and communicate effectively without incurring risks."[5] For example, airport security has clearly added to the cost of flying. Shops in countries plagued by suicide bombers must hire guards to deter such horror, and this adds to the cost of doing business.

Now that you have some idea about the theory of productivity and growth, let's look at them in practice, beginning with the vast difference in performance among economies around the world. Then we turn to the United States.

Productivity and Growth in Practice

Economics in the Movies

Differences in the standard of living among countries are profound. To give you some idea, per capita output in the United States, the world leader, is about 50 times that of the world's poorest countries. With only one-twentieth of the world's population, the United States produces more than all the nations comprising the bottom half of the world's population put together. At the risk of appearing simplistic, we might say that poor countries are poor because they experience low labor productivity. We can sort the world's economies into two broad groups. **Industrial market countries,** or *developed countries,* make up about 20 percent of the world's population. They consist of the economically advanced capitalist countries of Western Europe, North America, Australia, New Zealand, and Japan, plus the newly

5. As quoted in Greg Ip and John McKinnon, "Economy Likely Won't See Gain from War Against Terrorism," *Wall Street Journal,* 25 September 2001.

RULES OF THE GAME

The formal and informal institutions that promote economic activity; the laws, customs, conventions, and other institutional elements that determine transaction costs and thereby affect people's incentive to undertake production and exchange

WALL STREET JOURNAL
Reading It Right

What's the relevance of the following statement from the Wall Street Journal: *"Some economists say productivity growth will take an additional and longer-lasting hit in the terrorist attack's aftermath."*

INDUSTRIAL MARKET COUNTRIES

Economically advanced capitalist countries of Western Europe, North America, Australia, New Zealand, and Japan, plus the newly industrized Asian economies of Taiwan, South Korea, Hong Kong, and Singapore

DEVELOPING COUNTRIES

Countries with a low living standard because of little human and physical capital per worker

industrialized Asian countries of Taiwan, South Korea, Hong Kong, and Singapore. Industrial market countries were usually the first to experience long-term economic growth during the 19th century, and today have the world's highest standard of living based on abundant human and physical capital. The rest of the world, the remaining 80 percent of the world's population, consists of **developing countries,** which have a lower standard of living because they have less human and physical capital. Most workers in developing countries are farmers. Because farming methods there are primitive, labor productivity is low and most people barely subsist, much like Americans two centuries ago.

Education and Economic Development

Another important source of productivity is human capital—the skill, experience, and education of workers. If knowledge is lacking, other resources may not be used efficiently. For example, a country may be endowed with fertile land, but farmers may lack knowledge of irrigation and fertilization techniques. What exactly is the role of education in economic development? *Education makes workers aware of the latest production techniques and more receptive to new ideas and methods.* Countries today with the most advanced educational systems were also the first to develop. For example, America led the world in education during the last century and is today the world's premier economy.

Exhibit 4 shows the average years of schooling of the working-age population in the United States and six other industrial market economies (together called the *Group of Seven,* or *G-7*). In 1970, the U.S. working population averaged 11.6 years of schooling, the highest in the world. Among other advanced economies, education ranged from a low of 6.6 years in Italy to 11.3 years in Canada. The U.S. average grew to 12.7 years by 1998, but other countries became even more educated, so Americans ranked third behind Germany, at 13.6 years, and Canada, at 12.9 years.

EXHIBIT   4

Average Years of Education of Working-Age Populations in 1970 and 1998

In 1970 the United States led major economies in average education of the working-age population. By 1998 education increased more in Germany and Canada than in the United States, ranking America third.

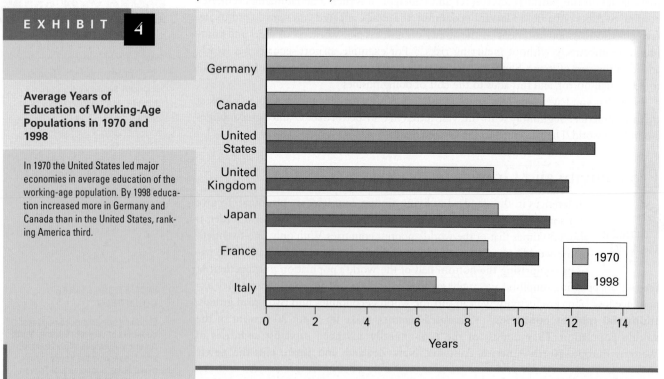

Source: Based on estimates developed in *OECD Economic Outlook* 68 (December 2000), Figure IV.1.

Not shown in Exhibit 4 are developing countries, which have far lower levels of education. For example, while the literacy rate exceeds 95 percent in industrial market economies, more than half the adults in the world's poorest countries can't read or write.

U.S. Labor Productivity

What has been the record of labor productivity in the United States? Exhibit 5 offers a long-run perspective, showing growth in real output per work hour. Annual productivity growth is averaged by decade. The huge dip during the Great Depression and the strong rebound during World War II are unmistakable. Growth slowed during the 1970s and 1980s but recovered since 1990. Labor productivity has grown an average of 2.1 percent per year since 1870. This may not impress you, but because of the power of compounding, output per hour has jumped over 1,500 percent during the period. To put this in perspective, if a roofer in 1870 could shingle one roof in a day, today's roofer could shingle 16 roofs in a day.

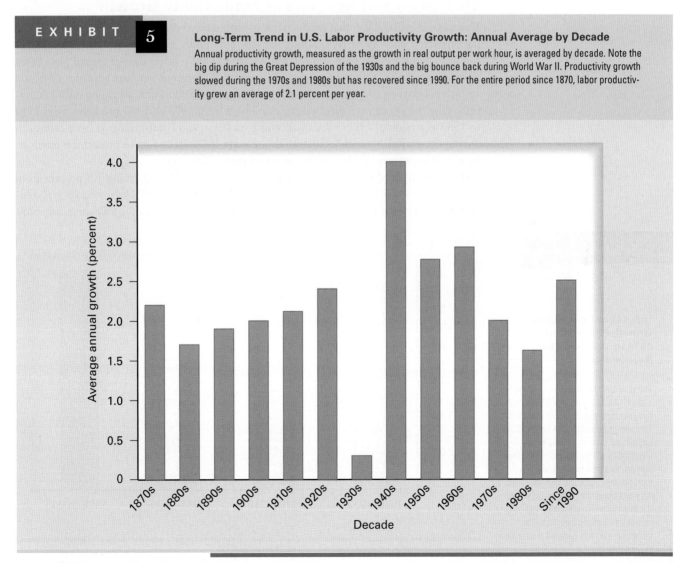

E X H I B I T   5

Long-Term Trend in U.S. Labor Productivity Growth: Annual Average by Decade

Annual productivity growth, measured as the growth in real output per work hour, is averaged by decade. Note the big dip during the Great Depression of the 1930s and the big bounce back during World War II. Productivity growth slowed during the 1970s and 1980s but has recovered since 1990. For the entire period since 1870, labor productivity grew an average of 2.1 percent per year.

Sources: Angus Maddison, *Phases of Capitalist Development* (New York: Oxford University Press, 1982) and U.S. Bureau of Labor Statistics. "Since 1990" goes through 2003. For the latest data, go to http://www.bls.gov/lpc/.

Over long periods, small differences in productivity can make huge differences on the economy's ability to produce and therefore on the standard of living. For example, if productivity grew only 1.1 percent per year instead of 2.1 percent, output per work hour since 1870 would have increased by only 333 percent, not 1,520 percent. On the other hand, if productivity grew 3.1 percent per year, output per work hour since 1870 would have jumped 5,880 percent! The wheels of progress seem to grind slowly but they grind very fine, and the cumulative effect is powerful.

So far, we have averaged productivity growth for all workers. Productivity has grown more in some industries than in others. In ocean shipping, for example, cargo carried per worker hour is now about 80 times greater than it was in 1900, for an average annual growth of 4.3 percent. On the other hand, those making wooden office furniture are only three times more productive today than in 1900, for an average annual growth in productivity of only 1.1 percent.

Slowdown and Rebound in Productivity Growth

You can see in Exhibit 5 that productivity growth slowed during the 1970s and 1980s and has recovered since 1990. By breaking the data down into intervals other than decades, we can get a better feel for years since World War II. Exhibit 6 offers average annual growth for four periods. Labor productivity growth averaged 2.9 percent per year between 1948 and 1973, but, between 1974 and 1982, fell to only about a third of that, averaging only 1.0 percent. Why the slowdown? First, oil prices jumped from 1973 to 1974 and again from 1979 to 1980 as a result of OPEC actions, boosting inflation and contributing to three recessions during the period. Second, legislation in the early 1970s necessary to protect the environment and improve workplace safety increased production costs.

Fortunately, productivity rebounded off the 1974–1982 low, growing 1.8 percent from 1983 to 1995 and 3.1 percent from 1996 to 2003. Why the rebound? The information revolution powered by the computer chip started paying off, as discussed in the following case study.

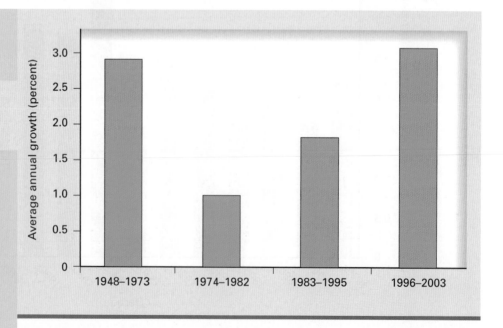

EXHIBIT 6

U.S. Labor Productivity Growth Slowed During 1974 to 1982 and Then Rebounded

The growth in labor productivity declined from an average of 2.9 percent per year between 1948 and 1973 to only 1.0 percent between 1974 and 1982. A jump in the price of oil helped contribute to three recessions during that stretch, and new environmental and workplace regulations, though necessary and beneficial, slowed down productivity growth temporarily. The information revolution powered by the computer chip has boosted productivity in recent years.

Source: Averages based on annual estimates from the U.S. Bureau of Labor Statistics. For the latest data go to http://www.bls.gov/lpc/home.htm.

Computers and Productivity Growth

The first microprocessor, the Intel 4004, could execute about 400 computations per second when it hit the market in 1971. IBM's first personal computer, introduced a decade later, could execute 330,000 computations per second. Today a $500 PC can handle over 2 billion computations per second, or *5 million* times what the 1971 Intel 4004 could handle. Such advances in computing power have fueled a boom in computer use. There are over 65 PCs per 100 persons in the United States, the world leader. There are now more computers in the United States than automobiles. U.S. companies and universities are well ahead of other countries in high-technology applications, ranging from software to biotechnology.

© Photodisc/Getty Images

PCs are moving beyond word processing and spreadsheet analysis to help people work together. For example, design engineers in California can use the Internet to test new ideas with marketers in New York, cutting development time in half. Sales representatives on the road can use laptops or other wireless devices to log orders and serve customers. U.S. insurance companies can coordinate data entry done as far away as India to handle claims more efficiently. An operator of multiple restaurants can use the Internet to track sales up to the minute, check the temperatures of freezers, refrigerators, and fryers, and observe each restaurant through a live video feed. A new generation of machines monitors itself and sends messages to a service center, detailing any problems as they arise. For example, General Electric uses the Internet to keep tabs on factory equipment thousands of miles away. Some home appliances, such as refrigerators, are also Internet compatible. Computers not only improve the quality and safety in many industries, including automobiles and airlines, but they increase the versatility of machines, which can be reprogrammed for different tasks.

A study by economists from the Federal Reserve System notes that computers boost productivity through two channels: (1) efficiency gains in the production of computers and semiconductors and (2) greater computer use by industry. These two channels accounted for much of the gain in productivity growth since 1996. Although computer hardware manufacturers make up only a small fraction of the U.S. economy, their pace of innovation quickened enough since 1996 to boost overall U.S. productivity growth. For example, Intel's 1.7-gigahertz Pentium 4 processor sold for $342 when introduced, much less than the $990 for the 1.1-gigahertz Pentium 3 it replaced. What's more, the efficiency in semiconductor production and the price declines since 1996 advanced IT use by business more generally, which also enhanced labor productivity. America invested more and earlier in IT than did other big economies, so economic benefits should show up here first. In fact, labor productivity grew an impressive 4.9 percent in 2002, 4.5 percent in 2003, and 3.1 percent in the first half of 2004. This growth was the fastest pace of consecutive years in more than 50 years. What's also impressive is that since 1996 productivity growth in services has exceeded that in manufacturing.

Sources: Kevin Kliesen, "Was Y2K Behind the Business Investment Boom and Bust?" *Federal Reserve Bank of St. Louis Review*, (January–February 2003): 31–42; Hal Varian, "Information Technology May Cure Low Productivity," *New York Times*, 12 February 2004; and Stephen Oliner and Daniel Sichel, "Information Technology and Productivity," *Economic Review*, Federal Reserve Bank of Atlanta (Third Quarter 2002): 15–44. The federal government's labor productivity home page is http://www.bls.gov/lpc/home.htm.

The Information Economy

*e*Activity

The application of computing technologies by U.S. firms has grown drastically, but until recently the connection between computer use and business productivity growth has been unclear. Read "Computer Use and Productivity Growth" in *National Economic Trends* from the Federal Reserve Bank of St. Louis, at http://research.stlouisfed.org/publications/net/20031201/cover.pdf.

Higher labor productivity growth can easily make up for output lost during recessions. For example, if over the next 10 years the U.S. labor productivity grew an average of 3.1 percent per year (the average from 1996 to 2003) instead of 1.8 percent (the average from 1982 to 1995), that higher growth would add nearly $2 trillion to GDP in the 10th year—more than enough to make up for the output lost during three typical recessions. *This cumulative power of productivity growth is why economists now pay less attention to short-term fluctuations in output and more to long-term growth.*

Output per Capita

So far, we have focused on rising labor productivity as an engine of economic growth—that is, growth achieved by getting more output from each hour worked. But even if labor productivity did not increase, total output would grow if the quantity of labor increased. After all, because labor productivity equals real GDP divided by the quantity of labor, then real GDP equals labor productivity times the quantity of labor. Therefore, total output can grow as a result of higher labor productivity, more labor, or both.

As noted earlier, the best measure of an economy's standard of living is output per capita. *Output per capita,* or real GDP divided by the population, indicates how much an economy produces on average per resident. Let's relate output per capita to labor productivity by using an example. Suppose labor productivity in the economy averages $70,000 per worker per year. If there is one worker for every two people in the economy, then *output per capita* equals output per worker divided by two, which is $70,000/2, or $35,000.

Even if labor productivity does not change over time, output per capita would grow if the number of workers grows faster than the population—that is, if the worker–population ratio increases. More generally, output per capita increases if (1) labor productivity increases for a given worker–population ratio, (2) the worker–population ratio increases for given labor productivity, or (3) labor productivity and the worker–population ratio both increase. In fact, output per capita would increase as long an increase in one of the variables more than offsets any decrease in the other one. For example, if labor productivity increases 2.3 percent but the worker–population ratio declines 2.0 percent, output per capita would increase. Before you move on, please take a minute now to reread this paragraph and give it some thought.

Exhibit 7 presents real GDP per capita for the United States since 1959. Notice the general upward trend, interrupted by seven recessions, indicated by the pink-shaded bars. Real GDP per capita nearly tripled (in 2000 dollars) from about $13,700 in 1959 to $35,700 in 2003, for an average annual growth rate of 2.2 percent. Incidentally, since 1959, labor productivity grew an average of 2.1 percent. Output per capita grew faster than did labor productivity because the number of workers grew faster than did the population, so the worker–population ratio increased.

International Comparisons

How does U.S. output per capita compare with that of other industrial countries? Exhibit 8 compares GDP per capita in 2002 for the United States and the six other leading industrial nations. The United States stands alone at the top, with a per capita income 18 percent above second-ranked Canada and about 40 percent above the rest. Thus, the United States produced more per capita than any other major economy.

Exhibit 8 looks at the level of output per capita. What about the growth in output per capita? Exhibit 9 shows growth in real GDP per capita from 1982 to 2002. With an average growth of 2.2 percent per year, the United States ranked second among the seven major economies. The United Kingdom ranked first, thanks in part to Prime Minister Margaret

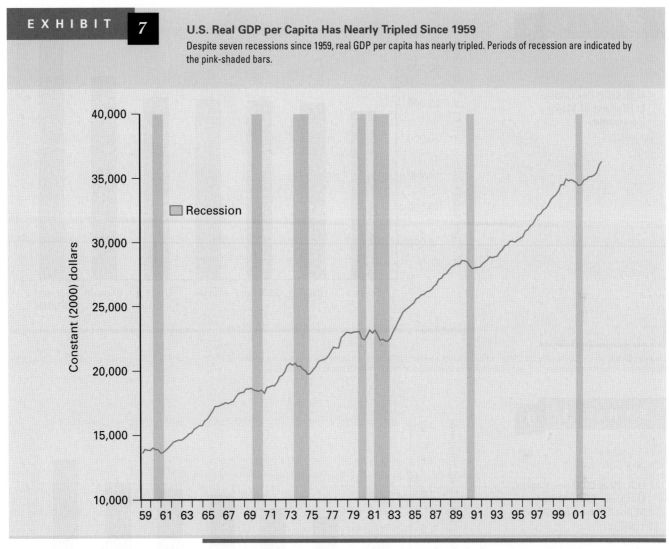

EXHIBIT 7

U.S. Real GDP per Capita Has Nearly Tripled Since 1959

Despite seven recessions since 1959, real GDP per capita has nearly tripled. Periods of recession are indicated by the pink-shaded bars.

Source: *Survey of Current Business* 84 (April 2004). For the latest data, go to http://www.bea.doc.gov/bea/pubs.htm. Select the most recent month, go to the "National Data" section toward the end of the page, and then select "Charts."

Thatcher, who converted crusty government enterprises into dynamic for-profit firms. Industries she *privatized* during the 1980s include coal, iron and steel, gas, electricity, railways, trucking, airlines, telecommunications, and the water supply. She also reduced income tax rates.

To review, over the last 130 years, U.S. labor productivity has grown an average of 2.1 percent per year. Output per hour of work is now 16 times its 1870 level. Growth slowed between 1974 and 1982, because of spikes in energy prices and implementation of necessary but costly new environmental and workplace regulations. Since 1982 labor productivity growth has picked up, especially since 1996, due primarily to breakthroughs in information technology. Among the seven major economies, the United States experienced the second fastest growth in per capita income from 1982 to 2002, and in 2002 boasted the highest GDP per capita among major economies.

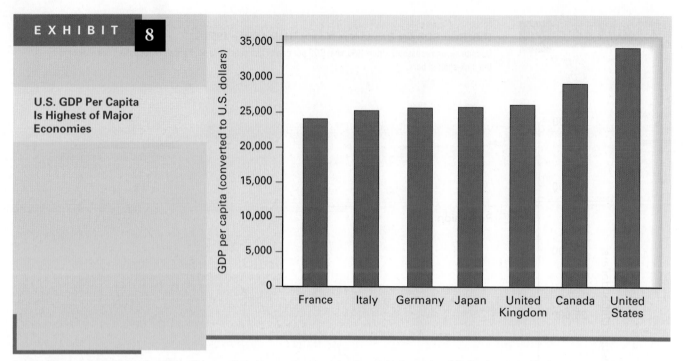

EXHIBIT 8

U.S. GDP Per Capita Is Highest of Major Economies

Source: Based on OECD figures for 2002, which are adjusted across countries using the purchasing power of the local currency. For the latest data, go to the Organization for Economic Cooperation and Development Web page at http://www.oecd.org/home/.

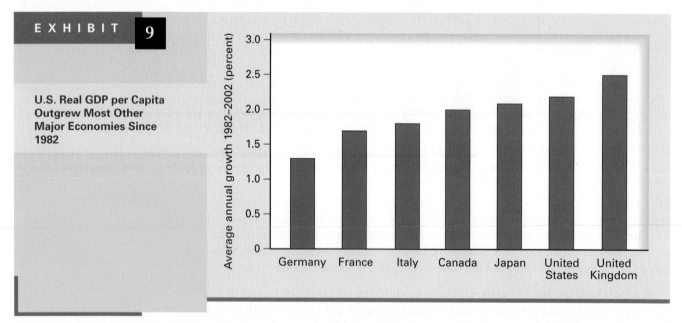

EXHIBIT 9

U.S. Real GDP per Capita Outgrew Most Other Major Economies Since 1982

Source: Based on annual figures from 1982 through 2002 from the U.S. Bureau of Labor Statistics at http://www.stats.bls.gov/fls/flsgdp.pdf. Figures were converted into U.S. dollars based on the purchasing power of local currency. For the latest data, go to http://www.stats.bls.gov/fls/.

Other Issues of Technology and Growth

In this section we consider some other issues of technology and growth, beginning with the question of whether technological change creates unemployment.

Does Technological Change Lead to Unemployment?

Because technological change can reduce the labor needed to produce a given amount of output, some observers fear technological change will increase unemployment. True, technological change can create dislocations as displaced workers try to find jobs elsewhere. But technological change can also make products more affordable. For example, the introduction of the assembly line cut the cost of automobiles, making them more affordable for the average household. This change increased the quantity demanded, boosting production and employment in the auto industry. The same happened with personal computers. Even in industries where machines displace some workers, those who keep their jobs are more productive, so they earn more. And *because human wants are unlimited, displaced workers will usually find jobs producing other goods and services demanded in a growing economy.*

Although data from the 19th century are sketchy, there is no evidence that the unemployment rate is any higher today than it was in 1870. Since then, worker productivity has increased over 1,500 percent, and the length of the average workweek has been cut nearly in half. Although technological change may displace some workers in the short run, long-run benefits include higher real incomes and more leisure—in short, a higher standard of living.

If technological change caused unemployment, then the recent spurt in productivity growth should have increased unemployment compared to the slow-growth years from 1974 to 1982. But the unemployment rate, the percentage of the workforce looking for jobs, averaged 7.2 percent during 1974 to 1982, compared to only 4.9 percent since 1996. And if technological change causes unemployment, then unemployment rates should be lower in economies where the latest technology has not yet been adopted, such as in developing countries. But unemployment rates are much higher there, and those who do find work earn little because they are not very productive.

Again, there is no question that technological change sometimes creates job dislocations and hardships in the short run, as workers scramble to adjust to a changing world. Some workers with specialized skills made obsolete by technology may be unable to find jobs that pay as well as the ones they lost. These temporary dislocations are one price of progress. Over time, however, most displaced workers find other jobs, often in new industries created by technological change. In a typical year, the U.S. economy eliminates about 10 million jobs but creates nearly 12 million new ones. Out with the old, in with the new.

Research and Development

As noted several times already, a major contributor to productivity growth has been an improvement in the quality of human and physical capital. In terms of human capital, this improvement results from more education and more job training. In terms of physical capital, this improvement springs from better technology embodied in this capital. For example, because of extensive investments in cellular transmission, new satellites, and fiber-optic technology, labor productivity in the telecommunications industry has increased by an average of 5.5 percent per year during the past three decades.

Improvements in technology arise from scientific discovery, which is the fruit of research. We can distinguish between basic research and applied research. **Basic research,** the search for knowledge without regard to how that knowledge will be used, is a first step toward technological advancement. In terms of economic growth, however, scientific discoveries are meaningless until they are implemented, which requires applied research. **Applied research** seeks to answer particular questions or to apply scientific discoveries to the development of specific products. Because technological breakthroughs may or may not have commercial possibilities, the payoff is less immediate with basic research than with applied research. *Yet basic research yields a higher return to society as a whole than does applied research.*

BASIC RESEARCH

The search for knowledge without regard to how that knowledge will be used

APPLIED RESEARCH

Research that seeks answers to particular questions or to apply scientific discoveries to develop specific products

Because technological change is the fruit of research and development (R&D), investment in R&D aims to improve productivity through technological discovery. One way to track R&D spending is to measure it relative to gross domestic product, or GDP. Exhibit 10 shows R&D spending as a share of GDP for the United States and the six other major economies for the 1980s and 1990s. Overall R&D spending in the United States averaged 2.7 percent of GDP in both the 1980s and the 1990s. During the 1990s, R&D as a share of GDP ranked the United States second among the major economies, slightly behind Japan, at 2.9 percent, but well ahead of last placed Italy, at only 1.1 percent.

Bar segments in the chart distinguish between R&D by businesses and R&D by governments and nonprofit institutions. Business R&D is more likely to target applied research and

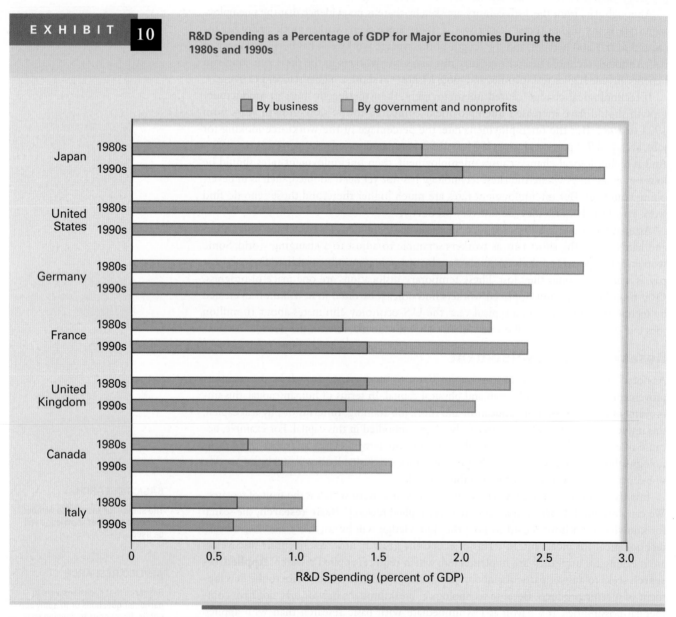

EXHIBIT **10**   **R&D Spending as a Percentage of GDP for Major Economies During the 1980s and 1990s**

Source: Based on estimates developed in *OECD Economic Outlook 68* (December 2000). Figure IV.2.

innovations. R&D spending by governments and nonprofits, such as universities, may generate basic knowledge that has applications in the long run (for example, the Internet sprang from R&D spending on national defense). R&D by U.S. businesses averaged 1.9 percent of GDP in the 1990s, the same as in the 1980s. Three of the six other major countries experienced an increase in business R&D between the 1980s and 1990s, and three saw a decrease. Again, only Japan had higher business R&D than the United States in the 1990s, at 2.0 percent of GDP. Italy had the lowest at 0.6 percent.

In short, the United States devotes more resources to R&D than most other advanced economies, and this should help America maintain a higher standard of living.

Do Economies Converge?

If given enough time, will poor countries eventually catch up with rich ones? The **convergence** theory argues that developing countries can grow faster than advanced ones and should eventually close the gap. Here's why: It is easier to copy new technology once it is developed than to develop that technology in the first place. Countries that are technologically backward can grow faster by copying existing technology. But economies that already use the latest technology can boost productivity only with a steady stream of new breakthroughs.

Advanced countries, such as the United States, will find their growth limited by the rate of creation of new knowledge and improved technology. But follower countries can grow more quickly by, for example, adding computers where they previously had none. Until 1995, the United States, which makes up just 5 percent of the world's population, accounted for most of the world's computer purchases by households. But by 2000, most computers were bought by non-U.S. households.

What's the evidence on convergence? Some poor countries have begun to catch up with richer ones. For example, the newly industrialized Asian economies of Hong Kong, Singapore, South Korea, and Taiwan have invested heavily in technology acquisition and human resources and are closing the gap with the world leaders, moving from the ranks of developing nations to the ranks of industrial market economies. For example, real output per capita in South Korea has grown three times faster than the average for the seven major economies. But these so-called *Asian Tigers* are the exceptions. Among the nations that comprise the poorest third of the world's population, consumption per capita has grown only about 1.0 percent per year over the last two decades compared with a 2.5 percent growth in the rest of the world,[6] so the standard of living in the poorest third of the world has grown somewhat in absolute terms but has fallen further behind in relative terms.

One reason per capita consumption has grown so slowly in the poorest economies is that birthrates there are double those in richer countries, so poor economies must produce still more just to keep up with a growing population. Another reason why convergence has not begun, particularly for the poorest third of the world, is the vast difference in the quality of human capital across countries. Whereas technology is indeed portable, the knowledge, skill, and training needed to take advantage of that technology are not. Countries with a high level of human capital can make up for other shortcomings. For example, much of the capital stock in Japan and Germany was destroyed during World War II. But the two countries retained enough of their well-educated and highly skilled labor force to rejoin elite industrial market economies in little more than a generation. But some countries, such as those in Africa, simply lack the human capital needed to identify and absorb new technology. As noted already, such poor economies tend to have low education levels and low literacy rates.

CONVERGENCE

A theory predicting that the standard of living in economies around the world will grow more similar over time, with poorer countries eventually catching up with richer ones

---

6. Based on figures developed by the World Bank in *World Development Report 2002/2003* (New York: Oxford University Press, 2003), Tables 1 and 2.

What's more, some countries lack the stable macroeconomic environment and the established institutions needed to nurture economic growth. Many developing countries have serious deficiencies in their infrastructures, lacking, for example, the reliable source of electricity to power new technologies. For example, in Northern Nigeria, near the Sahara, 90 percent of the villages have no electricity. Some of the poorest nations have been ravaged by civil war for years. And simply communicating can be challenging in some developing countries. In Nigeria, for example, more than 400 languages are spoken by 250 distinct ethnic groups.

Industrial Policy

Policy makers have debated whether government should become more involved in shaping an economy's technological future. One concern is that technologies of the future will require huge sums to develop, sums that an individual firm cannot easily raise and put at risk. Another concern is that some technological breakthroughs spill over to other firms and other industries, but the firm that develops the breakthrough may not be in a position to reap benefits from these spillover effects, so individual firms may underinvest in such research. One possible solution is more government involvement.

Industrial policy is the idea that government, using taxes, subsidies, regulations, and coordination of the private sector, could help nurture the industries and technologies of the future to give domestic industries an advantage over foreign competition. The idea is to secure a leading global role for domestic industry. One example of European industrial policy is Airbus Industrie, a four-nation aircraft consortium. With an estimated $20 billion in government aid, the aircraft maker has become Boeing's main rival. When Airbus seeks aircraft orders around the world, it can draw on government backing to promise favorable terms, such as landing rights at key European airports and an easing of regulatory constraints. U.S. producers get less government backing. Industrial policy is discussed in the following case study.

INDUSTRIAL POLICY

The view that government—using taxes, subsidies, and regulations—should nurture the industries and technologies of the future, thereby giving these domestic industries an advantage over foreign competition

Public Policy

eActivity

State and local governments sometimes engage in industrial policies of their own. For examples and arguments against such policies, read Melvin L. Burstein and Arthur J. Rolnick's "Congress Should End the Economic War Among the States" at http://minneapolisfed.org/pubs/ar/ar1994.cfm. Also read a prize-winning essay on this subject by a high school student, "The Economic War Among the States Subsidizes Inefficiency" found also at the Minneapolis Fed Web site, http://minneapolisfed.org/econed/essay/results/1-97.cfm. What guarantees come with government subsidies for industrial development? For more examples of how a state tries to attract business, visit Virginia is for Business

Picking Technological Winners

U.S. industrial policy over the years was aimed at creating the world's most advanced military production capacity. With the demise of the Soviet Union, however, defense technologies became less important. Some argue that U.S. industrial policy should shift from a military to a civilian focus. Former President Clinton once talked about establishing a powerful agency to help finance and coordinate R&D for what he called "cutting-edge products and technologies." He also proposed bringing together businesses, universities, and laboratories to carry out R&D in civilian technologies.

© Gerald French/Corbis

Many state governments are also trying to identify what industries to support. Economists have long recognized that firms in some industries gain a performance advantage by *clustering*—that is, by locating in a region already thick with firms in the same industry or in related industries. Clusters such as Hollywood entertainers, Wall Street brokers, Broadway theaters, Las Vegas casinos, and Silicon Valley software makers facilitate communication and promote healthy competition among cluster members. The flow of information and cooperation between firms, as well as the competition among firms in close proximity, stimulates regional innovation and propels growth. By locating in a region already settled with similar firms, a firm can also tap into established local markets for specialized labor and for other inputs.

But skeptics wonder whether the government should be trusted to identify emerging technologies and to pick the industry clusters that will lead the way. Critics of industrial policy believe that markets allocate scarce resources better than governments do. For example, European governments' costly attempt to develop the supersonic transport Concorde did not work. As another example, in the early 1980s, the U.S. government spent $1 billion to help military contractors develop a high-speed computer circuit. But Intel, a company getting no federal aid, was the first to develop the circuit. Japan has had the most aggressive support for favored industries, an approach that includes discouraging competition and encouraging joint research. But those Japanese industries getting the most government help, like chemicals and aircraft manufacturing, simply became uncompetitive in the world market. Meanwhile, industries with little government backing, like automobiles, cameras, and video games, turned out to be innovative world leaders.

There is also concern that an industrial policy would evolve into a government giveaway program. Rather than going to the most promising technologies, the money and the competitive advantages would go to the politically connected. Critics also wonder how wise it is to sponsor corporate research when beneficiaries may share their expertise with foreign companies and may build factories abroad. Most economists would prefer to let Microsoft, General Electric, or some start-up bet on the important technologies of the future.

Sources: "The Complications of Clustering," *Economist*, 2 January 1999; Michael Porter, "Japan: What Went Wrong," *Wall Street Journal*, 21 March 2001; and Ron Martin, "The New 'Geographical' Turn in Economics," *Cambridge Journal of Economics*, January 1999. The Web site for a firm advising governments about clustering can be found at http://www.sri.com/policy/csted/economics/clustering.html.

at http://www.yesvirginia.org/ or use a search engine such as Google to find a similar Web site for your state.

Conclusion

Productivity and growth depend on the supply and quality of resources, the level of technology, and the rules of the game that nurture production and exchange. These elements tend to be correlated with one another. An economy with an unskilled and poorly educated workforce will usually be deficient in physical capital, in technology, and in the institutional support that promotes production and exchange. Similarly, an economy with a high-quality workforce will likely excel in the other sources of productivity and growth.

We should distinguish between an economy's standard of living, as measured by output per capita, and improvements in that standard of living, as measured by the growth in output per capita. Growth in output per capita can occur when labor productivity increases or when the number of workers in the economy grows faster than the population. *In the long run, productivity growth and the growth in workers relative to the growth in population will determine whether or not the United States continues to enjoy the world's highest standard of living.*

In the next chapter, you will learn how to measure output in the economy and how to adjust for changes in the price level. In later chapters, you will develop aggregate demand and aggregate supply curves to build a model of the economy. Once you have an idea how a healthy economy works, you can consider the policy options in the face of high unemployment, high inflation, or both.

SUMMARY

1. If the population is continually increasing, an economy must produce more goods and services simply to maintain its standard of living, as measured by output per capita. If output grows faster than the population, the standard of living will rise.

2. An economy's standard of living grows over the long run because of (a) increases in the amount and quality of resources, especially labor and capital, (b) better technology, and (c) improvements in the rules of the game that facilitate production and exchange, such as tax laws, property

rights, patent laws, the legal system, and customs of the market.

3. The per-worker production function shows the relationship between the amount of capital per worker in the economy and the output per worker. As capital per worker increases, so does output per worker but at a decreasing rate. Technological change and improvements in the rules of the game shift the per-worker production function upward, so more is produced for each ratio of capital per worker.

4. Since 1870, U.S. labor productivity growth has averaged 2.1 percent per year. Output per work hour has grown sixteen-fold. The *quality* of labor and capital is much more important than the *quantity* of these resources. Labor productivity growth slowed between 1974 and 1982, in part because of spikes in energy prices and implementation of costly but necessary environmental and workplace regulations. Since 1983 productivity growth has picked up, especially since 1996, due primarily to information technology.

5. Among the seven major industrial market economies, the United States has the highest standard of living as measured by real GDP per capita.

6. Technological change sometimes creates job dislocations and hardships in the short run, as workers scramble to adjust to a changing world. Over time, however, most displaced workers find other jobs, sometimes in new industries created by technological change. There is no evidence that, in the long run, technological change increases unemployment in the economy.

7. Convergence is a theory predicting that economies around the world will grow more alike, as poorer countries catch up with richer ones. Some Asian countries that had been poor are catching up with the leaders, but most poor countries around the world have failed to close the gap.

8. Some governments use industrial policy in an effort to nurture the industries and technologies of the future, giving domestic industries an advantage over foreign competitors. But critics are wary of the government's ability to pick the winning technologies of the future.

QUESTIONS FOR REVIEW

1. *(Productivity)* As discussed in the text, per capita GDP in many developing countries depends on the productivity of land there. However, many richer economies have little land or land of poor quality. How can a country with little land or unproductive land become rich?

2. *(Labor Productivity)* What two kinds of changes in the capital stock can improve labor productivity? How can each type be illustrated with a per-worker production function? What determines the slope of the per-worker production function?

3. *(Slowdown in Labor Productivity Growth)* What contributed to the slower rate of growth in labor productivity during the 1974–1982 period?

4. *(Output per Capita)* Explain how output per capita can grow faster than labor productivity. Is it possible for labor productivity to grow faster than output per capita?

5. *(Technology and Productivity)* What measures can government take to promote the development of practical technologies?

6. *(Basic and Applied Research)* What is the difference between basic research and applied research? Relate this to the human genome project—research aimed at developing a complete map of human chromosomes, showing the location of every gene.

7. *(Rules of the Game)* How do "rules of the game" affect productivity and growth? What types of "rules" should a government set to encourage growth?

8. (*Case* **Study**: Computers and Productivity Growth) How has the increased use of computers affected U.S. productivity in the last few years? Is the contribution of computers expected to increase or decrease in the near future? Explain.

9. *(International Productivity Comparisons)* How does output per capita in the United States compare with output per capita in other industrial economies? How has this comparison changed over time?

10. *(Industrial Policy)* Define industrial policy. What are some arguments in favor of industrial policy?

11. (*C a s e* **S t u d y**: Picking Technological Winners) What was the central focus of U.S. industrial policy in the past? Is the same focus appropriate today? What are the arguments against an active U.S. industrial policy?

12. *(Technological Change and Unemployment)* Explain how technological change can lead to unemployment in certain industries. How can it lead to increased employment?

13. *(Convergence)* Explain the convergence theory. Under what circumstances is convergence unlikely to occur?

14. *(Productivity)* What factors might contribute to a low *level* of productivity in an economy? Regardless of the level of labor productivity, what impact does slow *growth* in labor productivity have on the economy's standard of living?

PROBLEMS AND EXERCISES

15. *(Growth and the PPF)* Use the production possibilities frontier (PPF) to demonstrate economic growth.

    a. With consumption goods on one axis and capital goods on the other, show how the combination of goods selected this period affects the PPF in the next period.
    b. Extend this comparison by choosing a different point on this period's PPF and determining whether that combination leads to more or less growth over the next period.

16. *(Long-Term Productivity Growth)* Suppose that two nations start out in 2004 with identical levels of output per work hour—say, $100 per hour. In the first nation, labor productivity grows by 1 percent per year. In the second, it grows by 2 percent per year. Use a calculator or a spreadsheet to determine how much output per hour each nation will be producing 20 years later, assuming that labor

productivity growth rates do not change. Then, determine how much each will be producing per hour 100 years later. What do your results tell you about the effects of small differences in growth rates?

17. *(Technological Change and Unemployment)* What are some examples, other than those given in the chapter, of technological change that has caused unemployment? And what are some examples of new technologies that have created jobs? How do you think you might measure the net impact of technological change on overall employment and GDP in the United States?

18. *(Shifts in the PPF)* Terrorist attacks foster instability and may affect productivity over the short and long term. Do you think the September 11, 2001, terrorist attacks on the World Trade Center and the Pentagon affected short and/or long-term productivity in the United States? Explain your response and show any movements in the PPF.

EXPERIENTIAL EXERCISES

19. *(Labor Productivity)* Go to the Bureau of Labor Statistics (BLS) page on Quarterly Labor Productivity at http://www.bls.gov/lpc/ and get the latest news release on productivity and costs. Rank the various sectors of the U.S. economy from highest to lowest according to their most recent productivity growth rates. Does what you found make sense to you? Why or why not?

20. *(International Productivity Comparisons)* The BLS also compiles international data on manufacturing productivity at http://stats.bls.gov/news.release/prod4.toc.htm. For the most recent period, which nations have enjoyed the most rapid growth in manufacturing productivity? Which nations have experienced the slowest growth? Has productivity actually declined anywhere? How could this be related to the convergence theory explained in this chapter?

21. *(Wall Street Journal)* Technological change is an important driver of economic growth. Refer to the "Technology" column in the Marketplace section of a recent *Wall Street Journal*. Find a story about a technological innovation that seems interesting to you. How will this innovation affect the U.S. production possibilities frontier? Does it seem likely to affect employment as well? If so, which types of workers will be harmed, and which types will benefit?

HOMEWORK XPRESS! EXERCISES

These exercises require access to McEachern Homework Xpress! If Homework Xpress! did not come with your book, visit **http://homeworkxpress.swlearning.com** *to purchase.*

1. Two economies, the United States and country G, currently have identical production possibilities frontiers, *CI*, but have chosen differing combinations of capital and consumer goods as indicated. Illustrate how these choices will affect economic growth by adding a PPF for the United States ten years into the future, and then one for country G ten years from now.

2. Sketch a per-worker production function in the diagram that illustrates the law of diminishing marginal returns. Identify the level of output per worker produced given k capital per worker.

3. Sketch a per-worker production function in the diagram that illustrates the law of diminishing marginal returns.

Identify the level of output per worker produced given k capital per worker. Illustrate the impact of technological changes that increase productivity. Identify the new level of output per worker that can be produced given k capital per worker.

4. A per-worker production function is shown in the diagram for an economy currently producing with k units of capital per worker. Illustrate how the economy can increase output per worker to y_1 by increasing capital per worker. Then illustrate how y_1 could be achieved by improving technology instead of increasing capital.

Measuring the Economy and the Circular Flow

© Leslie Harris/Index Stock Imagery

Ｈow do we keep track of the most complex economy in world history? What's gross about the gross domestic product? What's domestic about it? If you make yourself a tuna sandwich, how much does your effort add to the gross domestic product? Because prices change over time, how can we compare the economy's production in one year with that in other years? Answers to these and other questions are addressed in this chapter, which introduces an economic scorecard for a $12 trillion economy. That scorecard is the national income accounting system, which reduces a huge network of economic activity to a few aggregate measures.

As you will see, aggregate output can be measured either by the spending on that output or by the income derived from producing it. We examine each approach and see why they are equivalent. The major components and important equalities built into the national income accounts are offered here as another way of understanding how the economy works—not as a foreign language to be mastered before the next exam. The emphasis is more on economic intuition than on accounting precision. The body of the chapter provides the background you will need for later chapters. More details about the national income accounts are offered in the appendix. Topics discussed in this chapter include:

- National income accounts
- Expenditure approach to GDP
- Income approach to GDP
- Circular flow of income and expenditure

- Leakages and injections
- Limitations of national income accounting
- Consumer price index
- GDP price index

The Product of a Nation

How do we measure the economy's performance? During much of the 17th and 18th centuries, when the dominant economic policy was mercantilism, many thought that economic prosperity was best measured by the *stock* of precious metals a nation accumulated in the public treasury. Mercantilism led to restrictions on international trade, but this restriction had the unintended consequence of limiting the gains from comparative advantage. In the latter half of the 18th century, François Quesnay became the first to measure economic activity as a *flow*. In 1758 he published his *Tableau Économique,* which described the *circular flow* of output and income through different sectors of the economy. His insight was likely inspired by his knowledge of blood's circular flow in the body—Quesnay was court physician to King Louis XV of France.

Rough measures of national income were developed in England two centuries ago, but detailed calculations built up from microeconomic data were refined in the United States during the Great Depression. The resulting *national income accounting system* organizes huge quantities of data collected from a variety of sources across America. These data were summarized, assembled into a coherent framework, and reported by the federal government. The conception and implementation of these accounts has been hailed as one of the greatest achievements of the 20th century. The U.S. national income accounts are the most widely copied and most highly regarded in the world and earned their developer, Simon Kuznets, the Nobel Prize in 1971 for "giving quantitative precision to economic entities."

National Income Accounts

How do the national income accounts keep track of the economy's incredible variety of goods and services, from hiking boots to guitar lessons? The *gross domestic product,* or GDP, measures the market value of all final goods and services produced during a year by resources located in the United States, regardless of who owns the resources. For example, GDP includes production in the United States by foreign firms, such as a Japanese auto plant in Kentucky, but excludes foreign production by U.S. firms, such as a General Motors plant in Mexico. Incidentally, until 1992, the federal government's yardstick was gross *national* product, or GNP, which measures the market value of all goods and services produced by resources supplied by U.S. residents and firms, regardless of the location of the resources.

The national income accounts are based on the simple fact that *one person's spending is another person's income.* GDP can be measured either by total spending on U.S. production or by total income received from that production. The **expenditure approach** adds the spending on all final goods and services produced during the year. The **income approach** adds the earnings during the year by those who produce that output. In the *double-entry bookkeeping sys-*

EXPENDITURE APPROACH TO GDP

A method of calculating GDP by adding spending on all final goods and services produced in the nation during the year

INCOME APPROACH TO GDP

A method of calculating GDP by adding all payments for resources used to produce output in the nation during the year

tem used to track the economy, spending on aggregate output is recorded on one side of the ledger and income from producing that aggregate output is recorded on the other side.

Gross domestic product includes only **final goods and services,** which are goods and services sold to the final, or end, user. A toothbrush, a pair of contact lenses, and a bus ride are examples of final goods and services. Whether a sale is to the final user depends on who buys the product. Your purchase of chicken from a grocer is reflected in GDP. When KFC buys chicken, however, this is not counted in GDP because KFC is not the final consumer. Only after the chicken is cooked and sold by KFC is the transaction counted in GDP.

Intermediate goods and services are those purchased for additional processing and resale, like KFC's chicken. This change may be imperceptible, as when a grocer buys canned goods to stock the shelves. Or the intermediate goods can be dramatically altered, as when a painter transforms a $100 canvas and $30 in oils into a work of art that sells for $5,000. Sales of intermediate goods and services are excluded from GDP to avoid the problem of **double counting,** which is counting an item's value more than once. For example, suppose the grocer buys a can of tuna for $0.60 and sells it for $1.00. If GDP counted both the intermediate transaction of $0.60 and the final transaction of $1.00, the recorded value of $1.60 would exceed its final value by $0.60. Hence, GDP counts only the final value. GDP also ignores most of the secondhand value of used goods, such as existing homes, used cars, and used textbooks. These goods were counted in GDP when they were produced. But just as the services provided by the grocer are included in GDP, so are the services provided by real estate agents, used-car dealers, and used-book sellers.

GDP Based on the Expenditure Approach

As noted already, one way to measure GDP is to add spending on all final goods and services produced in the economy during the year. The easiest way to understand the spending approach is to divide aggregate expenditure into its components: consumption, investment, government purchases, and net exports. **Consumption,** or more specifically, *personal consumption expenditures,* consists of purchases of final goods and services by households during the year. Consumption is the largest spending category, averaging about two-thirds of U.S. GDP during the last decade. Along with *services* like dry cleaning, haircuts, and air travel, consumption includes *nondurable goods,* like soap and soup, and *durable goods,* like furniture and major appliances. Durable goods are expected to last at least three years.

Investment, or more specifically, *gross private domestic investment,* consists of spending on new capital goods and on net additions to inventories. The most important investment is **physical capital,** such as new buildings and new machinery. Investment also includes new **residential construction.** Although it fluctuates from year to year, investment averaged about one-sixth of U.S. GDP during the last decade. More generally, investment consists of spending on current production that is not used for current consumption. A net increase to inventories also counts as investment because it represents current production not used for current consumption. **Inventories** are stocks of goods in process, such as computer parts, and stocks of finished goods, such as new computers awaiting sale. Inventories help manufacturers cope with unexpected changes in the supply of their resources or in the demand for their products.

Although investment includes purchasing a new residence, it excludes purchases of *existing* buildings and machines and purchases of financial assets, such as stocks and bonds. Existing buildings and machines were counted in GDP when they were produced. Stocks and bonds are not investments themselves but simply indications of ownership.

Government purchases, or more specifically, *government consumption and gross investment,* include government spending for goods and services—from clearing snowy roads to clearing court dockets, from library books to the librarian's pay. Government purchases

---

FINAL GOODS AND SERVICES

Goods and services sold to final, or end, users

INTERMEDIATE GOODS AND SERVICES

Goods and services purchased by firms for further reprocessing and resale

DOUBLE COUNTING

The mistake of including the value of intermediate goods plus the value of final goods in gross domestic product; counting the same good more than once

CONSUMPTION

Household purchases of final goods and services, except for new residences, which count as investments

INVESTMENT

The purchase of new plants, new equipment, new buildings, and new residences, plus net additions to inventories

PHYSICAL CAPITAL

Manufactured items used to produce goods and services; includes new plants and new equipment

RESIDENTIAL CONSTRUCTION

Building new homes or dwelling places

INVENTORIES

Producers' stocks of finished and in-process goods

GOVERNMENT PURCHASES

Spending for goods and services by all levels of government; government outlays minus transfer payments

averaged a bit less than one-fifth of U.S. GDP during the last decade. Government purchases, and therefore GDP, exclude transfer payments, such as Social Security, welfare benefits, and unemployment insurance. Such payments are not true purchases by the government or true earnings by the recipients.

The final spending component, net exports, reflects international trade in goods and services. Goods, or *merchandise* traded, include physical items such as bananas and DVD players (stuff you can drop on your toes). Services, or so-called *invisibles,* include intangible items, such as European tours and online customer service from India. Foreign purchases of U.S. goods and services are counted as part of U.S. GDP. But U.S. purchases of foreign goods and services are subtracted from U.S. GDP. **Net exports** equal the value of U.S. exports of goods and services minus the value of U.S. imports of goods and services. U.S. imports have exceeded U.S. exports nearly every year since the 1960s, meaning U.S. net exports have been negative. During the last decade, net exports averaged a negative 2 percent of GDP, but this has increased to a negative 4 or 5 percent of GDP in recent years.

With the expenditure approach, the nation's **aggregate expenditure** equals the sum of consumption, *C,* investment, *I,* government purchases, *G,* and net exports, which is the value of exports, *X,* minus the value of imports, *M,* or $(X - M)$. Summing these yields aggregate expenditure, or GDP:

$$C + I + G + (X - M) = \text{Aggregate expenditure} = \text{GDP}$$

GDP Based on the Income Approach

The expenditure approach sums, or aggregates, spending on production. The income approach sums, or aggregates, income arising from that production. Again, double-entry bookkeeping ensures that the value of aggregate output equals the aggregate income paid for resources used to produce that output: the wages, interest, rent, and profit arising from production. The price of a Hershey Bar reflects the income of resource suppliers along the way. **Aggregate income** equals the sum of all the income earned by resource suppliers in the economy. Thus, we can say that

$$\text{Aggregate expenditure} = \text{GDP} = \text{Aggregate income}$$

A product usually goes through stages involving several firms on its way to the consumer. A wooden desk, for example, starts as raw timber, which is typically cut by one firm, milled by another, made into a desk by a third, and retailed by a fourth. We avoid double counting either by including only the market value of the desk when it is sold to the final user or by *calculating the value added at each stage of production.* The **value added** by each firm equals that firm's selling price minus payments for inputs from other firms. The value added at each stage is the income earned by resource suppliers at that stage. *The value added at all stages sums to the market value of the final good, and the value added for all final goods sums to GDP based on the income approach.* For example, suppose you buy a wooden desk for $200. This final market value gets added directly into GDP. Consider the history of that desk. Suppose the tree that gave its life for your studies was cut into a log and sold to a miller for $20. That log was milled into lumber and sold for $50 to a manufacturer, who built your desk and sold it for $120 to a retailer, who sold it to you for $200.

Column (1) of Exhibit 1 lists the selling price at each stage of production. If all these transactions were added up, the total of $390 would exceed the $200 market value of the desk. To avoid double counting, we include only the value added at each stage, listed in column (3) as the difference between the purchase price and the selling price at that stage. Again, *the value added at each stage equals the income earned by those who supplied their resources at*

NET EXPORTS
The value of a country's exports minus the value of its imports

AGGREGATE EXPENDITURE
Total spending on final goods and services during a given period, usually a year

AGGREGATE INCOME
The sum of all income earned by resource suppliers in an economy during a given period

VALUE ADDED
The difference at each stage of production between the selling price of a product and the cost of intermediate goods purchased from other firms

Stage of Production	(1) Sale Value	(2) Cost of Intermediate Goods	(3) Value Added
Logger	$ 20	——	$ 20
Miller	50	$ 20	30
Manufacturer	120	50	70
Retailer	200	120	80
		Market value of final good	**$200**

Computation of Value Added for a New Desk

The value added at each stage of production is the sale price at that stage minus the cost of intermediate goods, or column (1) minus column (2). The values added at each stage sum to the market value of the final good, shown at the bottom of column (3).

that stage. For example, the $80 in value added by the retailer consists of income to resource suppliers at that stage, from the salesperson to the janitor who cleans the showroom to the trucker who provides "free delivery" of your desk. The value added at all stages totals $200, which is both the final market value of the desk and the total income earned by all resource suppliers along the way.

To reinforce your understanding of the equality of income and spending, let's return to something introduced in the first chapter, the circular-flow model.

The Circular Flow of Income and Expenditure

The model in Exhibit 2 outlines the circular flow of income and spending in the economy for not only households and firms, as was the case in Chapter 1, but governments and the rest of the world too. The main stream flows clockwise around the circle, first as income from firms to households (in the lower half of the circle), and then as spending from households back to firms (in the upper half of the circle). For each flow of money, there is an equal and opposite flow of products or resources. Here we follow the money.

The Income Half of the Circular Flow

In the process of developing a circular flow of income and spending, we must make some simplifying assumptions. Specifically, by assuming that physical capital does not wear out (i.e., no capital depreciation) and that firms pay out all profits to firm owners (i.e., firms retain no earnings), we can say that *GDP equals aggregate income.* The circular flow is a continuous process, but the logic of the model is clearest if we begin at juncture (1) in Exhibit 2, where U.S. firms make production decisions. After all, production must occur before output can be sold and income earned. As Henry Ford explained, "It is not the employer who pays the wages—the employer only handles the money. It is the product that pays wages." Households supply their labor, capital, natural resources, and entrepreneurial ability to make products that sell to pay wages, interest, rent, and profit. Production of aggregate output, or GDP, gives rise to an equal amount of aggregate income.

Thus, at juncture (1), aggregate output equals aggregate income. But not all that income is available to spend. At juncture (2), governments collect taxes. Some of these tax dollars return as transfer payments to the income stream at juncture (3). By subtracting taxes and adding transfers, we transform aggregate income into **disposable income, *DI,*** which flows to households at juncture (4). Disposable income is take-home pay, which households can spend or save.

DISPOSABLE INCOME (DI)

The income households have available to spend or to save after paying taxes and receiving transfer payments

E X H I B I T   **2**

Circular Flow of Income and Expenditure

The circular-flow model captures important relationships in the economy. The bottom half depicts the income arising from production. At juncture (1), GDP equals aggregate income. Taxes leak from the flow at (2), but transfer payments enter the flow at (3). Taxes minus transfers equals net taxes, *NT*. Aggregate income minus net taxes equals disposable income, *DI*, which flows to households at juncture (4). The top half of the model shows the flow of expenditure. At (5), households either spend disposable income or save it. Consumption enters the spending flow directly. Saving leaks from the spending flow into financial markets, where it is channeled to borrowers. At (6), investment enters the spending flow. At (7), government purchases enter the spending flow. At (8), imports leak from the spending flow, and at (9), exports enter the spending flow. Consumption plus investment plus government purchases plus net exports add up to the aggregate expenditure on GDP received by firms at (10).

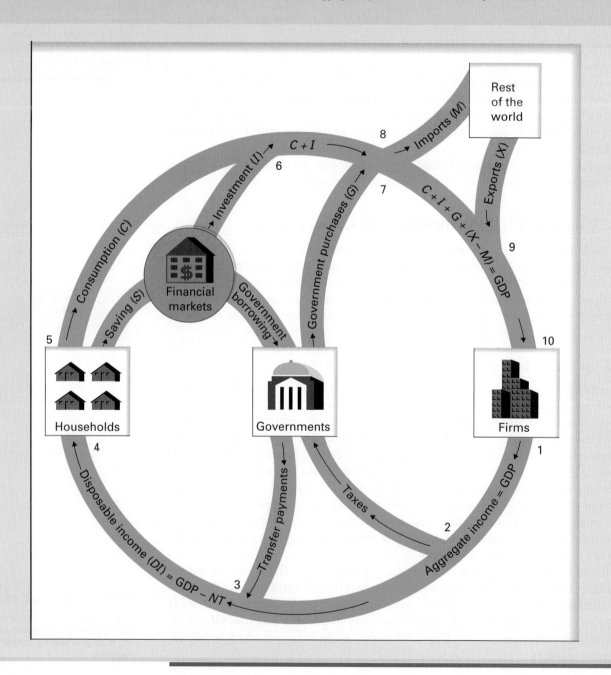

The bottom half of this circular flow is the *income half* because it focuses on the income arising from production. Aggregate income is the total income from producing GDP, and disposable income is the income remaining after taxes are subtracted and transfers added. To simplify the discussion, we define **net taxes, *NT,*** as taxes minus transfer payments. So *disposable income equals GDP minus net taxes.* Put another way, we can say that aggregate income equals disposable income plus net taxes:

$$GDP = \text{Aggregate income} = DI + NT$$

NET TAXES (NT)

Taxes minus transfer payments

At juncture (4), firms have produced output and have paid resource suppliers; governments have collected taxes and made transfer payments. With the resulting disposable income in hand, households must now decide how much to spend and how much to save. Because firms have already produced the output and have paid resource suppliers, firms wait to see how much consumers want to spend. Any unsold production gets added to firm inventories.

The Expenditure Half of the Circular Flow

Disposable income splits at juncture (5). Part goes for consumption, *C,* and the rest is saved, *S.* Thus,

$$DI = C + S$$

Spending on consumption remains in the circular flow and is the biggest aggregate expenditure, about two-thirds of the total. Household saving flows to **financial markets,** which consist of banks and other financial institutions that link savers to borrowers. For simplicity, Exhibit 2 shows households as the only savers, though governments, firms, and the rest of the world could save as well. The primary borrowers are firms and governments, but households borrow too, particularly for new homes, and the rest of the world also borrows. In reality, financial markets should be connected to all four economic decision makers, but we have simplified the flows to keep the model from looking like a plate of spaghetti.

FINANCIAL MARKETS

Banks and other financial institutions that facilitate the flow of funds from savers to borrowers

In our simplified model, firms pay resource suppliers an amount equal to the entire value of output. With nothing left for investment, firms must borrow to finance purchases of physical capital plus any increases in their inventories. Households also borrow to purchase new homes. Therefore, investment, *I,* consists of spending on new capital by firms, including inventory changes, plus spending on residential construction. Investment enters the circular flow at juncture (6), so aggregate spending at that point totals *C + I.*

Governments must also borrow whenever they incur deficits, that is, whenever their total *outlays*—transfer payments plus purchases of goods and services—exceed their revenues. Government purchases of goods and services, represented by *G,* enter the spending stream in the upper half of the circular flow at juncture (7). Remember that *G excludes* transfer payments, which already entered the stream as income at juncture (3).

Some spending by households, firms, and governments goes for imports. Because spending on imports flows to foreign producers, spending on imports, *M,* leaks from the circular flow at juncture (8). But the rest of the world buys U.S. products, so foreign spending on U.S. exports, *X,* enters the spending flow at juncture (9). Net exports, the impact of the *rest of the world* on aggregate expenditure, equal exports minus imports, *X − M,* which can be positive, negative, or zero.

The upper half of the circular flow, the *expenditure half,* tracks components of aggregate expenditure: consumption, *C,* investment, *I,* government purchases, *G,* and net exports, *X − M.* Aggregate expenditure flows into firms at juncture (10). Aggregate expenditure equals the market value of aggregate output, or GDP. In other words,

$$C + I + G + (X - M) = \text{Aggregate expenditure} = GDP$$

Leakages Equal Injections

Let's step back now to see the big picture. In the lower half of the circular flow, aggregate income equals disposable income plus net taxes. In the upper half, aggregate expenditure equals the total spending on U.S. output. *The aggregate income arising from production equals the aggregate expenditure on that production.* This is the first accounting identity. Thus, aggregate income (disposable income plus net taxes) equals aggregate expenditure (spending by each sector), or

$$DI + NT = C + I + G + (X - M)$$

Because disposable income equals consumption plus saving, we can substitute $C + S$ for DI in the above equation to yield

$$C + S + NT = C + I + G + (X - M)$$

After subtracting C from both sides and adding M to both sides, the equation reduces to

$$S + NT + M = I + G + X$$

Note that at various points around the circular flow, some of the flow leaks from the main stream. Saving, S, net taxes, NT, and imports, M, are **leakages** from the circular flow. **Injections** into the main stream also occur at various points around the circular flow. Investment, I, government purchases, G, and exports, X, are *injections* of spending into the circular flow. As you can see from the preceding equation, *leakages from the circular flow equal injections into that flow.* This leakages-injections equation demonstrates a second accounting identity based on double-entry bookkeeping.

Limitations of National Income Accounting

Imagine the difficulty of developing an accounting system that must capture the subtleties of such a complex and dynamic economy. In the interest of clarity and simplicity, certain features get neglected. In this section, we examine some limitations of the national income accounting system, beginning with productive activity not captured by GDP.

Some Production Is Not Included in GDP

With some minor exceptions, GDP includes only those products that are sold in markets, thereby neglecting all do-it-yourself household production—child care, meal preparation, house cleaning, home maintenance and repair. Thus, an economy in which householders are largely self-sufficient will have a lower GDP than will an otherwise similar economy in which households specialize and sell products to one another. During the 1950s, more than 80 percent of American mothers with small children remained at home caring for the family, but all this care added not one cent to GDP. Today most mothers with small children are in the workforce, where their labor gets counted in GDP. Meals, child care, and the like are now often purchased in markets and thus get reflected in GDP. In less developed economies, more economic activity is do-it-yourself.

GDP also ignores off-the-books production. The term **underground economy** describes market activity that goes unreported because either it's illegal or people want to evade taxes on otherwise legal activity. Although there is no official measure of the underground economy, most economists agree that it is substantial. A federal study suggests the equivalent of 7.5 percent of GDP is underground production; this would have amounted to about $800 billion in 2004.

LEAKAGE

Any diversion of income from the domestic spending stream; includes saving, taxes, and imports

INJECTION

Any spending other than by households or any income other than from resource earnings; includes investment, government purchases, exports, and transfer payments

WALL STREET JOURNAL

Reading It **Right**

What's the relevance of the following statement from the Wall Street Journal: *"The economic package approved by the Italian Parliament includes measures to encourage firms operating in the underground economy to come out in the open."*

UNDERGROUND ECONOMY

Market exchange that goes unreported either because it is illegal or because those involved want to evade taxes

For some economic activity, income must be *imputed*, or assigned, because market exchange does not occur. For example, included in GDP is an *imputed rental income* that homeowners receive from home ownership, even though no rent is actually paid or received. Also included in GDP is an imputed dollar amount for (1) wages paid *in kind,* such as employers' payments for employees' medical insurance, and (2) food produced by farm families for their own consumption. *GDP therefore includes some economic production that does not involve market exchange.*

Leisure, Quality, and Variety

The average U.S. workweek is much shorter now than it was a century ago, so people work less to produce today's output. People also retire earlier and live longer after retirement. Over the years, there has been an increase in the amount of leisure available. But leisure is not reflected in GDP because it is not directly bought and sold in a market. The quality and variety of products sold have also improved on average over the years because of technological advances and greater competition. Yet most of these improvements are not reflected in GDP. Recording systems, computers, tires, running shoes, and hundreds of other products have gotten better over the years. Also, new products are being introduced all the time, such as high-definition television and MP3 players. *The gross domestic product fails to capture changes in the availability of leisure time and often fails to reflect changes in the quality of products and the availability of new products.* The special problem of measuring production in an economy shaped by changing technology is discussed in the following case study.

Tracking a $12 Trillion Economy

Ever since Article I of the U.S. Constitution required a decennial population census, the federal government has been gathering data. The three data-gathering agencies are the Census Bureau, the Commerce Department's Bureau of Economic Analysis, and the Bureau of Labor Statistics. Since 1980, real GDP has more than doubled, employment has increased more than 40 million, and real foreign trade has more than tripled. Yet the federal budget for these agencies has declined in real terms. Only 0.2 percent of the federal budget goes toward keeping track of the nation and its economy.

© Photodisc/Getty Images

The Information Economy

eActivity
How does the Bureau of Economic Analysis go about incorporating changes to industry into national income statistics? Visit the site of National Income and Product Accounts for 2003 at http://www.bea.gov/bea/dn/2003benchmarck/CR2003content.htm, and click on "Highlights" to see the kinds of changes and the issues involved, and then select FAQs to learn more about this process. If you select "Interactive NIPA Tables," you can view some of the statistics.

Budget cuts have eliminated some data collection and have slowed down others. For example, computations of monthly international trade statistics have become so overwhelming that as many as half the imports counted for a particular month reflect a "carryover" from previous months. Some agencies must do more with the same staff. For example, in 1980, the Bureau of Labor Statistics had 18 analysts to monitor productivity in 95 different industries. The number of industries now tracked has quadrupled, but the number of analysts has changed little. The Census Bureau proposed collecting data on the Internet economy, but Congress said no.

Ways of monitoring economic activity were developed in the 1930s and 1940s, when manufacturing dominated. Because manufacturing is tangible, such as automobiles and toasters, output is easy to measure. But services are intangible, such as medical care and on-line services, and are harder to measure. Yet services now make up most of the GDP. Even where services would appear to be easily measured, government does not yet collect such data. For example, although there are thousands of nail salons in the country, nobody knows exactly how many and nobody keeps track of manicures and pedicures.

Because services are intangible, measures for the service sector tend to be less reliable than those for the manufacturing sector. Measures of service output often fail to reflect improvements in the speed or quality of services. For example, some trucking firms use on-board computers to map the most efficient route and remap the route should priorities change. The increased efficiency has reduced the number of ton-miles (tonnage times miles) carried per month. Yet, according to federal statisticians, these more efficient drivers appear to be producing less because output in this industry is measured by ton-miles.

Because of technological advances in health care, diagnosis is now more accurate, treatments are less invasive and less painful, and people recover faster, so hospital stays are shorter. These improvements suggest big cost savings and greater convenience for patients. But because output in health care is usually measured by inputs, such as the doctor's time and hospital-bed days, these measures miss the improved quality. Federal statisticians are working on getting better measures of services, but they still have difficulty measuring output in a wide range of industries, including medicine, banking, education, software, legal services, wholesale trade, and communications. Researchers have found that, after 1995, labor productivity in the service sector grew faster than in the goods sector.

Sources: "The U.S. Statistical System and a Rapidly Changing Economy," *Brookings Policy Brief*, No. 63 (July 2000): 2–8; Barry Bosworth and Jack Triplett, "Productivity in Services Industries: Trends and Measurement Issues," 17 November 2003, Brookings Institution, http://www.brookings.edu; and *Economic Report of the President*, February 2004. For the latest labor productivity data, go to http://www.bls.gov/lpc/home.htm.

What's Gross about Gross Domestic Product?

In the course of producing GDP, some capital wears out, such as the delivery truck that finally dies, and some capital becomes obsolete, such as an aging computer that can't run the latest software. A new truck that logs 100,000 miles its first year has been subject to wear and tear, and therefore has a diminished value as a resource. A truer picture of the *net* production that actually occurs during a year is found by subtracting this capital *depreciation* from GDP. **Depreciation** measures the value of the capital stock that is used up or becomes obsolete in the production process. Gross domestic product is called "gross" because it fails to take into account this depreciation. **Net domestic product** equals gross domestic product minus depreciation, the capital stock used up in the production process.

We can now have two measures of investment. *Gross investment* is the value of all investment during a year, and is used in computing GDP. *Net investment* equals gross investment less depreciation. The economy's production possibilities depend on what happens to net investment. If net investment is negative—that is, if depreciation exceeds gross investment—the economy's capital stock declines, so its contribution to output will decline as well. If net investment is zero, the capital stock remains constant, as does its contribution to output. And if net investment is positive, the capital stock grows, as does its contribution to output.

As the names imply, *gross* domestic product reflects gross investment and *net* domestic product reflects net investment. But estimating depreciation involves much guesswork. For example, what is the appropriate measure of depreciation for the roller coasters at Busch Gardens, the metal display shelves at Wal-Mart, or the parking lots at Disney World?

GDP Does Not Reflect All Costs

Some production and consumption degrades the quality of our environment. Trucks and automobiles pump pollution into the atmosphere. Housing displaces forests. Paper mills foul

DEPRECIATION

The value of capital stock used up to produce GDP or that becomes obsolete during a year

NET DOMESTIC PRODUCT

Gross domestic product minus depreciation

the lungs and burn the eyes. These negative externalities—costs that fall on those not directly involved in the transactions—are mostly ignored in GDP accounting, even though they diminish the quality of life and may limit future production. To the extent that growth in GDP also involves growth in negative externalities, a rising GDP may not be as attractive as it would first appear.

Although the national income accounts reflect the depreciation of buildings, machinery, vehicles, and other manufactured capital, this accounting ignores the depletion of natural resources, such as standing timber, fish stocks, and soil fertility. So national income accounts reflect depreciation of the manufactured capital stock but not the natural capital stock. For example, intensive farming may raise productivity temporarily and boost GDP, but this depletes soil fertility. Worse still, some economic development may cause the extinction of certain plants and animals. The U.S. Commerce Department is now in the process of developing so-called *green accounting*, or *green GDP*, to reflect the impact of production on air pollution, water pollution, soil depletion, and the loss of other natural resources.

GDP and Economic Welfare

In computing GDP, the market price of output is the measure of its value. Therefore, each dollar spent on handguns or cigarettes is counted in GDP the same as each dollar spent on baby formula or fitness programs. Positive economic analysis tries to avoid making value judgments about how people spend their money. Because the level of GDP provides no information about its composition, some economists question whether GDP is a good measure of the nation's economic welfare.

Despite the limitations of official GDP estimates, the trend of GDP offers a good snapshot of the U.S. economy. Inflation, however, clouds comparability over time. In the next section, we discuss how to adjust GDP for changes in the economy's price level.

Accounting for Price Changes

As noted earlier, the national income accounts are based on the market values of final goods and services produced in a particular year. Initially, gross domestic product measures the value of output in *current dollars*—that is, in the dollar values at the time production occurs. When GDP is based on current dollars, the national income accounts measure the *nominal value* of national output. Thus, the current-dollar GDP, or **nominal GDP,** is based on the prices prevailing when production takes place.

National income accounts based on current, or nominal, dollars allow for comparisons among income or expenditure components in a particular year. Because the economy's average price level changes over time, however, current-dollar comparisons across years can be misleading. For example, between 1979 and 1980, nominal GDP increased by about 9 percent. That sounds impressive, but the economy's average price level rose more than 9 percent. So the growth in nominal GDP resulted entirely from inflation. Real GDP, or GDP measured in terms of the goods and services produced, in fact declined. If nominal GDP increases in a given year, part of this increase may simply reflect inflation—pure hot air. To make meaningful comparisons of GDP across years, we must take out the hot air, or *deflate* nominal GDP. We focus on *real* changes in production by eliminating changes due solely to inflation.

NOMINAL GDP

GDP based on prices prevailing at the time of the transaction; current-dollar GDP

Price Indexes

To compare the price level over time, let's first establish a point of reference, a base year to which prices in other years can be compared. An *index number* compares the value of some

BASE YEAR

The year with which other years are compared when constructing an index; the index equals 100 in the base year

variable in a particular year to its value in a base year, or reference year. Think about the simplest of index numbers. Suppose bread is the only good produced in an economy. As a reference point, let's look at its price in some specific year. The year selected is called the **base year;** prices in other years are expressed relative to the base-year price.

Suppose the base year is 2003, when a loaf of bread in our simple economy sold for $1.25. Let's say the price of bread increased to $1.30 in 2004 and to $1.40 in 2005. We construct a **price index** by dividing each year's price by the price in the base year and then multiplying by 100, as shown in Exhibit 3. For 2003, the base year, we divide the base price of bread by itself, $1.25/$1.25, which equals 1, so the price index in 2003 equals $1 \times 100 = 100$. *The price index in the base year is always 100.* The price index in 2004 is $1.30/$1.25, which equals 1.04, which when multiplied by 100 equals 104. In 2005, the index is $1.40/$1.25, or 1.12, which when multiplied by 100 equals 112. Thus, the index is 4 percent higher in 2004 than in the base year and 12 percent higher in 2005. The price index permits comparisons across years. For example, what if you were provided the indexes for 2004 and 2005 and asked what happened to the price level between the two years? By dividing the 2005 price index by the 2004 price index, 112/104, you find that the price level rose 7.7 percent.

PRICE INDEX

A number that shows the average price of goods; changes in a price index over time show changes in the economy's average price level

This section has shown how to develop a price index assuming we already know the price level each year. Determining the price level is a bit more involved, as we'll now see.

Consumer Price Index

The price index most familiar to you is the **consumer price index,** or **CPI,** which measures changes over time in the cost of buying a "market basket" of goods and services purchased by a typical family. For simplicity, suppose a typical family's market basket for the year includes 365 packages of Twinkies, 500 gallons of heating oil, and 12 months of cable TV. Prices in the base year are listed in column (2) of Exhibit 4. The total cost of each product in the base year is found by multiplying price by quantity, as shown in column (3). The cost of the market basket in the base year is shown at the bottom of column (3) to be $1,184.85.

CONSUMER PRICE INDEX, OR CPI

A measure of inflation based on the cost of a fixed market basket of goods and services

Prices in the current year are listed in column (4). Notice that not all prices changed by the same percentage since the base year. The price of fuel oil increased by 50 percent, but the price of Twinkies declined. The cost of purchasing that same basket in the current year increased to $1,398.35, shown as the sum of column (5). To compute the consumer price index for the current year, we simply divide the cost in the current year by the cost of that same basket in the base year, $1,398.35/$1,184.85, and then multiply by 100. This yields a price index of 118. We could say that between the base period and the current year, the "cost of living" increased by 18 percent, although not all prices increased by the same percentage.

EXHIBIT 3	Year	(1) Price of Bread in Current Year	(2) Price of Bread in Base Year	(3) Price Index (3) = (1)/(2) x 100
	2003	$1.25	$1.25	100
Hypothetical Example of a Price Index (base year = 2003)	2004	1.30	1.25	104
	2005	1.40	1.25	112
The price index equals the price in the current year divided by the price in the base year, all multiplied by 100.				

	(1) Quantity in Market Basket	(2) Prices in Base Year	(3) Cost of Basket in Base Year (3) = (1) x (2)	(4) Prices in Current Year	(5) Cost of Basket in Current Year (5) = (1) x (4)
Product					
Twinkies	365 packages	$ 0.89/package	$ 324.85	$ 0.79	$ 288.35
Fuel Oil	500 gallons	1.00/gallon	500.00	1.50	750.00
Cable TV	12 months	30.00/month	360.00	30.00	360.00
			$1,184.85		$1,398.35

EXHIBIT 4

Hypothetical Market Basket Used to Develop the Consumer Price Index
The cost of a market basket in the current year, shown at the bottom of column (5), sums the quantities of each item in the basket, shown in column (1), times the price of each item in the current year, shown in column (4).

The federal government uses the 36 months of 1982, 1983, and 1984 as the base period for calculating the CPI for a market basket consisting of hundreds of goods and services. The CPI is reported monthly based on prices collected from about 23,000 sellers across the country in 87 metropolitan areas. In reality, each household consumes a unique market basket, so we could theoretically develop about 110 million CPIs—one for each household.

Problems with the CPI

Economics in
the Movies

There is no perfect way to measure changes in the price level. As we have already seen, the quality and variety of some products are improving all the time, so some price increases may be as much a reflection of improved quality as of inflation. Thus, there is a *quality bias* in the CPI, because it assumes that the quality of the market basket remains relatively constant over time. *As a result of ignoring quality improvements, the CPI overstates the true extent of inflation.*

The CPI tends to overstate inflation for another reason. Recall that the CPI holds constant over time the kind and amount of goods and services in the typical market basket. Because not all items in the market basket experience the same rate of price change, relative prices change over time. A household would respond to changes in relative prices by purchasing less of the more expensive products and more of the cheaper products. But, because the CPI holds the market basket constant for long periods, the CPI is slow to incorporate consumer responses to changes in relative prices. *The CPI calculations, by not allowing households to shift away from goods that have become more costly, overestimates the true extent of inflation experienced by the typical household.*

The CPI has also failed to keep up with the consumer shift toward discount stores such as Wal-Mart, Target, and Home Depot. Government statisticians consider goods sold by discounters as different from goods sold by regular retailers. Hence, the discounter's lower price does not translate into a reduction in the cost of living.

Experts conclude the CPI has overestimated inflation by about 1 percent per year. This problem is of more than academic concern because changes in the CPI determines changes in tax brackets and in an array of payments, including wage agreements that include a cost-of-living adjustment, Social Security benefits, and welfare benefits. In fact, about 30 percent

N e t Bookmark

Possible biases in the CPI are discussed in detail by Brian Motley in his "Bias in the CPI: Roughly Right or Precisely Wrong?" available from Federal Reserve Bank of San Francisco at http://www.frbsf.org/ econrsrch/wklyltr/el97-16.html.

of federal outlays are tied to changes in the CPI. A 1 percent correction in the upward bias of the CPI would save the federal budget nearly $200 billion annually by 2010.

Overstating the CPI also distorts other measures, such as wages, that use the CPI to adjust for inflation. For example, based on the official CPI, the average real wage in the U.S. economy fell by a total of about 2 percent in the last two decades. But if the CPI overstated inflation by 1 percent per year, as researchers believe, then the average real wage, instead of dropping by 2 percent, actually increased by about 20 percent. The Bureau of Labor Statistics, the group that estimates the CPI, is now working on these problems and has introduced an experimental version of the CPI that would reduce measured inflation. One experiment uses scanner data at supermarkets to find out how consumers respond, for example, to a rise in the price of romaine lettuce relative to iceberg lettuce, two products assumed to be reasonable substitutes.

The GDP Price Index

GDP PRICE INDEX

A comprehensive price index of all goods and services included in the gross domestic product

Price indexes are weighted sums of various prices. Whereas the CPI focuses on just a sample of consumer purchases, a more complex and more comprehensive price index, the **GDP price index,** measures the average price of all goods and services produced in the economy. To calculate the GDP price index, we use the formula

$$\text{GDP price index} = \frac{\text{Nominal GDP} \times 100}{\text{Real GDP}}$$

where nominal GDP is the dollar value of GDP measured in current-year prices, and real GDP is the dollar value of GDP measured in base-year prices. If we know both nominal GDP and real GDP, then finding the GDP price index is easy. Nominal GDP is simply current-dollar GDP. The challenge is finding real GDP. Any measure of real GDP is constructed as the weighted sum of thousands of different goods and services produced in the economy. The question is what weights, or prices, to use. Between World War II and 1995, the Bureau of Economic Analysis (BEA) used prices for a particular base year (most recently 1987) to estimate real GDP. In this case, the quantity of each output in a particular year was valued by using the 1987 price of each output. So real GDP in, say, 1994 was the sum of 1994 output valued at 1987 prices.

Moving from Fixed Weights to Chain Weights

CHAIN-WEIGHTED SYSTEM

An index that adjusts the weights from year to year in calculating a price index, thereby getting rid of much of the bias caused by a fixed-price weighting system

Estimating real GDP by using prices from a base year yields an accurate measure of real GDP as long as the year in question is close to the base year. But BEA used prices that prevailed in 1987 to value production from 1929 to 1995. In early 1996, BEA switched from a fixed-price weighting system to a **chain-weighted system,** using a complicated process that changes price weights from year to year. All you need to know is that the chain-weighted real GDP adjusts the weights more or less continuously from year to year, reducing the bias caused by a fixed-price weighting system.

Even though the chain-type index adjusts the weights from year to year, any index, by definition, must still use some year as an anchor, or reference point—that is, any index must answer the question, "Compared to what?" To provide such a reference point, BEA measures U.S. real GDP and its components in *chained (2000) dollars.* Exhibit 5 presents current-dollar estimates of GDP as well as chained (2000) dollar estimates of real GDP. The blue line indicates current-dollar GDP, or nominal GDP, since 1959. The red line indicates real GDP since 1959, or GDP measured in chained (2000) dollars. The two lines intersect in 2000, because that's when real GDP equaled nominal GDP. Nominal, or current-dollar, GDP is be-

EXHIBIT 5

U.S. Gross Domestic Product in Current Dollars and Chained (2000) Dollars

Real GDP, the red line, shows the value of output measured in chained (2000) dollars. The blue line measures GDP in current dollars, or nominal dollars, of each year shown. The two lines intersect in 2000, when real GDP equaled nominal GDP. Year-to-year changes in current-dollar GDP reflect changes in real GDP and in the price level. Year-to-year changes in chained-dollar GDP reflect changes in real GDP only. Current-dollar GDP grows faster than chained-dollar GDP. Prior to 2000, current-dollar prices are less than chained-dollar prices, so current-dollar GDP is less than chained-dollar GDP.

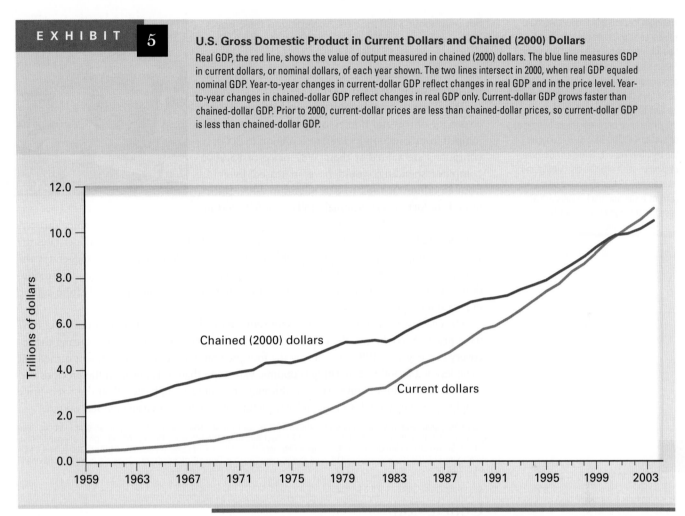

Source: Based on annual estimates from the Bureau of Economic Analysis, U.S. Department of Commerce. For the latest data, go to http://www.bea.doc.gov/bea/pubs.htm.

low real GDP in years prior to 2000 because real GDP is based on chained (2000) prices, which on average are higher than prices prior to 2000. Current-dollar GDP reflects growth in real GDP and in the price level. Chained-dollar GDP reflects growth only in real GDP. So current-dollar GDP grows faster than chained-dollar GDP. An example of the bias resulting from a fixed-price weighting system involves computers, as discussed in this closing case study.

Computer Prices and GDP Estimation

As noted already, until 1996, federal statisticians based their real GDP estimates on 1987 prices. Relying on such estimates, economists believed that the recovery that began in the spring of 1991 was spurred by investment spending, especially spending on new computers. In this case study, we reconsider the role of computer production as an economic stimulus to that recovery.

Computer prices have fallen by an average of about 13 percent per year since 1982. Based on this rate of decline, a computer that cost, say, $10,000 in 1982 cost about $5,000 in 1987

C a s e S t u d y

Public Policy

eActivity
The Bureau of Economic Analysis is charged with estimating GDP and its components. You can find selected

National Income and Product Account tables at http://www.bea.doc.gov/ bea/dn/nipaweb/index.asp. Summary Table S1 tells you by how much each component has grown. Summary Table S2 shows the contribution of each component to GDP growth. Can you explain the difference between these two types of statistics? The BEA also produces the monthly report, *Survey of Current Business,* with articles describing and interpreting national income data. The current issue and back issues are accessible through http://www.bea.doc. gov/bea/pubs.htm.

but only about $450 in 2004. According to these prices, that computer cost about the same in 1982 as a Chrysler minivan; in 2004, you could buy about 50 computers for the cost of a minivan. So the price of computers fell sharply between 1982 and 2004.

The sharp decline in computer prices spurred purchases for offices and homes. Suppose computer sales jumped from 1 million in 1982 to 5 million in 2004. If computers are valued at their 1987 price of $5,000, computer spending would have increased fivefold, from $5 billion in 1982 to $25 billion in 2004. But if priced in current, or nominal, dollars, of $10,000 in 1982 and $450 in 2004, computer spending would have declined more than three quarters from $10 billion in 1982 to only $2.2 billion in 2004. Using the 1987 price understates the value of computer production in 1982, overstates it in 2004, and thus exaggerates the growth between 1982 and 2004. It was this exaggeration in the value of computer production in 1991 that led to the incorrect belief that the recovery resulted primarily from a jump in investment spending.

The chain-weighted measure adjusts for some of the distortion that comes from using 1987 fixed prices. According to the chain-weighted measure, investment grew less during the recovery that began in 1991 than during the four previous recoveries, so investment turned out to be less of a factor in stimulating economic expansion than it had been in the previous two decades. The chain-weighted system, although it is more complicated than the fixed-price weighting system, provides a more reliable picture of year-to-year changes in real output.

Sources: "Dell Says That Revenues Are Ahead of Plan, But Profits Trail," *Wall Street Journal,* 9 April 2004; "Improved Estimates of the National Income and Product Accounts for 1959–95: Results of the Comprehensive Revision," *Survey of Current Business* 76 (January/February 1996); *Survey of Current Business* 84 (April 2004); and Dell's Web site at http://www.dell.com/. The home page for the Bureau of Economic Analysis is at http://www. bea.doc.gov/.

Conclusion

This chapter examined how GDP is measured and how it's adjusted for changes in the price level over time. The national income accounts have limitations, but they offer a reasonably accurate picture of year-to-year movements in the economy. The national income accounts are published in much greater detail than this chapter suggests. The appendix provides some flavor of the additional detail available. Subsequent chapters will refer to the distinction between real and nominal values.

SUMMARY

1. The gross domestic product, or GDP, measures the market value of all final goods and services produced during the year by resources located in the United States, regardless of who owns those resources.

2. The expenditure approach to GDP adds the market value of all final goods and services produced in the economy

during the year. The income approach to GDP adds all the income generated as a result of that production.

3. The circular-flow model summarizes the flow of income and spending through the economy. Saving, net taxes, and imports are leakages from the circular flow. These leakages equal the injections into the circular flow from investment, government purchases, and exports.

4. GDP reflects market production. Most household production and the underground economy are not captured by GDP. Improvements in the quality and variety of goods also are often missed in GDP. In other ways GDP may overstate production. GDP fails to subtract for the depreciation of the capital stock or for the depletion of natural resources and fails to account for negative externalities arising from production.

5. Nominal GDP in a particular year values output based on market prices prevailing at the time production occurs. To determine real GDP, nominal GDP must be adjusted for price changes. The consumer price index, or CPI, tracks prices for a basket of goods and services over time. The GDP price index tracks price changes for all output. No adjustment for price changes is perfect, but current approaches offer a reasonable estimate of real GDP over time.

QUESTIONS FOR REVIEW

1. *(National Income Accounting)* Identify the component of aggregate expenditure to which each of the following belongs:

   a. A U.S. resident's purchase of a new automobile manufactured in Japan
   b. A household's purchase of one hour of legal advice
   c. Construction of a new house
   d. An increase in semiconductor inventories over last year's level
   e. A city government's acquisition of 10 new police cars

2. *(National Income Accounting)* Define *gross domestic product*. Determine whether each of the following would be included in the 2004 U.S. gross domestic product:

   a. Profits earned by Ford Motor Company in 2004 on automobile production in Ireland
   b. Automobile parts manufactured in the United States in 2004 but not used until 2005
   c. Social Security benefits paid by the U.S. government in 2004
   d. Ground beef purchased and used by McDonald's in 2004
   e. Ground beef purchased and consumed by a private U.S. household in 2004
   f. Goods and services purchased in the United States in 2004 by a Canadian tourist

3. *(National Income Accounting)* Explain why intermediate goods and services generally are not included directly in GDP. Are there any circumstances under which they would be included directly?

4. *(Leakages and Injections)* What are the leakages from and injections into the circular flow? How are leakages and injections related to the circular flow?

5. *(Investment)* In national income accounting, one component of investment is net changes in inventories. Last year's inventories are subtracted from this year's inventories to obtain a net change. Explain why net inventory increases are counted as part of GDP. Also, discuss why it is not sufficient to measure the level of inventories only for the current year. (Remember the difference between stocks and flows.)

6. *(Limitations of National Income Accounting)* Explain why each of the following should be taken into account when GDP data are used to compare the "level of well-being" in different countries:

   a. Population levels
   b. The distribution of income
   c. The amount of production that takes place outside of markets
   d. The length of the average work week
   e. The level of environmental pollution

7. (*Case* **Study:** Tracking a $12 Trillion Economy) Why has it become increasingly difficult for the federal government to monitor economic activity in the United States?

8. *(Nominal GDP)* Which of the following is a necessary condition—something that must occur—for nominal GDP to rise? Explain your answers.

   a. Actual production must increase.
   b. The price level must increase.
   c. Real GDP must increase.
   d. Both the price level and actual production must increase.
   e. Either the price level or real GDP must increase.

9. *(Price Indexes)* Home computers and DVD players have not been part of the U.S. economy for very long. Both goods have been decreasing in price and improving in quality. What problems does this pose for people responsible for calculating a price index?

10. *(GDP and Depreciation)* What is gross about gross domestic product? Could an economy enjoy a constant—or growing—GDP while not replacing worn-out capital?

11. *(Consumer Price Index)* One form of the CPI that has been advocated by lobbying groups is a "CPI for the elderly." The Bureau of Labor Statistics currently produces only indexes for "all urban households" and "urban wage earners and clerical workers." Should the BLS produce such an index for the elderly?

12. *(GDP Price Index)* The health expenditure component of the GDP price index has been rising steadily. How might this index be biased by quality and substitution effects? Are there any substitutes for health care?

13. *(Case Study: Computer Prices and GDP Estimation)* Compared to the fixed-price weighting system, how does the chain-weighted system better account for the economic incentives provided by price changes?

PROBLEMS AND EXERCISES

14. *(Income Approach to GDP)* How does the income approach to measuring GDP differ from the expenditure approach? Explain the meaning of *value added* and its importance in the income approach. Consider the following data for the selling price at each stage in the production of a 5-pound bag of flour sold by your local grocer. Calculate the final market value of the flour.

Stage of Production	Sale Price
Farmer	$0.30
Miller	0.50
Wholesaler	1.00
Grocer	1.50

15. *(Expenditure Approach to GDP)* Given the following annual information about a hypothetical country, answer questions a through d.

	Billions of Dollars
Personal consumption expenditures	$200
Personal taxes	50
Exports	30
Depreciation	10
Government purchases	50
Gross private domestic investment	40
Imports	40
Government transfer payments	20

a. What is the value of GDP?
b. What is the value of net domestic product?
c. What is the value of net investment?
d. What is the value of net exports?

16. *(Investment)* Given the following data, answer questions a through c.

	Billions of Dollars
New residential construction	$500
Purchases of existing homes	250
Sales value of newly issued stocks and bonds	600
New physical capital	800
Depreciation	200
Household purchases of new furniture	50
Net change in firms' inventories	100
Production of new intermediate goods	700

a. What is the value of gross private domestic investment?
b. What is the value of net investment?
c. Are any intermediate goods counted in gross investment?

17. *(Consumer Price Index)* Calculate a new consumer price index for the data in Exhibit 4 in this chapter. Assume that current-year prices of Twinkies, fuel oil, and cable TV are $0.95/package, $1.25/gallon, and $15.00/month, respec-

tively. Calculate the current year's cost of the market basket and the value of the current year's price index. What is this year's percentage change in the price level compared to the base year?

18. *(Consumer Price Index)* Given the following data, what was the value of the consumer price index in the base year?

Calculate the annual rate of consumer price inflation in 2004 in each of the following situations:

a. The CPI equals 200 in 2003 and 240 in 2004.
b. The CPI equals 150 in 2003 and 175 in 2004.
c. The CPI equals 325 in 2003 and 340 in 2004.
d. The CPI equals 325 in 2003 and 315 in 2004.

EXPERIENTIAL EXERCISES

19. *(Limitations of National Income Accounting)* One often-heard criticism of the U.S. national income accounts is that they ignore the effect of environmental pollution. The World Bank's group on Environmental Economics and Indicators has been investigating ways of assessing environmental degradation. Take a look at their work on "green accounting" at http://lnweb18.worldbank.org/ESSD/envext.nsf/44ByDocName/GreenAccounting. What kinds of problems have they identified, and what proposals have they made to deal with those problems?

20. *(Problems with the CPI)* The importance of the bias in the U.S. consumer price index is reviewed in an article in the June 1997 issue of *Finance and Development* from the International Monetary Fund at http://www.imf.org/external/pubs/ft/fandd/1997/06/pdf/armknech.pdf. Tao Wu of the Federal Reserve Bank of San Francisco discusses current issues with the calculation of the consumer price index at

http://www.frbsf.org/publications/economics/letter/2003/el2003-24.html. What are the criticisms of the CPI as it is now calculated?

21. *(Wall Street Journal)* Data on the consumer price index are released near the middle of each month. Data on GDP are released on the last Friday of each month (in preliminary, revised, and then final form). Analysis of these data releases appears in the first section of the following weekday's *Wall Street Journal*. Look in the Economy section to find the story. What do the latest available data tell you about the current rate of inflation and the current rate of GDP growth? Is the economy in a recession or an expansion?

22. *(Wall Street Journal)* New economic data are regularly reported in the *Wall Street Journal*. Look in section C of the paper (the Money and Investing section) the day after a major piece of economic information was released to see how the stock market reacted to the news.

National Income Accounts

This chapter has focused on the gross domestic product, or GDP, the measure of output that will be of most interest in subsequent chapters. Other economic aggregates also convey useful information and receive media attention. One of these, *net domestic product,* has already been introduced. Exhibit 6 shows that net domestic product equals gross domestic product minus depreciation. In this appendix we examine other aggregate measures.

National Income

So far, we have been talking about the value of production from resources located in the United States, regardless of who owns them. Sometimes we want to know how much American resource suppliers earn for their labor, capital, natural resources, and entrepreneurial ability. **National income** captures all income earned by American-owned resources, whether located in the United States or abroad. To get the net value of production from American-owned resources, we add income earned by American resources abroad and subtract income earned by resources in the United States owned by those outside the country.

National income therefore equals net domestic product plus net earnings from American resources abroad. Exhibit 6

shows how to go from net domestic product to national income. We have now moved from gross domestic product to net domestic product to national income. Next we peel back another layer from the onion to arrive at personal income, the income people actually receive.

Personal and Disposable Income

Some of the income received this year was not earned this year, and some of the income earned this year was not received this year by those who earned it. By adding to national income the income received but not earned and subtracting the income earned but not received, we move from national income to the income *received* by individuals, which is called **personal income,** a widely reported measure of economic welfare. The federal government computes and reports personal income monthly.

The adjustment from national income to personal income is shown in Exhibit 7. Income *earned but not received* in the current period includes the employer's share of Social Security taxes, taxes on production (e.g., sales and property taxes) net of to subsidies, corporate income taxes, and undistributed corporate profits, which are profits the firm retains rather than pays out as dividends. Income *received but not earned* in the current period includes government transfer payments, receipts from private pension plans, and interest paid by government and by consumers.

Although business taxes have been considered so far, we have not yet discussed personal taxes, which consist mainly of federal, state, and local personal income taxes and the employee's share of the Social Security tax. Subtracting personal taxes and other government charges from personal income yields *disposable income,* which is the amount available for spending or saving—the amount that can be "disposed of" by the household. Think of disposable income as take-home pay. Exhibit 7 shows that personal income minus personal taxes and other government charges yields disposable income.

Summary of National Income Accounts

Let's summarize the income side of national income accounts. We begin with *gross domestic product,* or *GDP,* the

EXHIBIT 6	Deriving Net Domestic Product and National Income (in trillions of dollars)
Gross domestic product (GDP)	$11.00
Minus depreciation	−1.35
Net domestic product	9.65
Plus net earnings of American resources abroad	0.03
National income	$9.68

Source: Figures are current, or nominal, estimates for 2003 from the Bureau of Economic Analysis, U.S. Department of Commerce. For the latest figures, go to http://www.bea.doc.gov/bea/dn/nipaweb/populartables.asp.

EXHIBIT 7	Deriving Personal Income and Disposable Income (in trillions of dollars)

National income	$9.68
Minus income earned but not received (Social Security taxes, net taxes on production, corporate income taxes, undistributed corporate profits)	−3.18
Plus income received but not earned (government and business transfers, net personal interest income)	2.66
Personal income	9.16
Minus personal taxes and nontax charges	−1.00
Disposable income	$8.16

Source: Figures are current, or nominal, estimates for 2003 from the Bureau of Economic Analysis, U.S. Department of Commerce. For the latest figures, go to http://www.bea.doc.gov/bea/dn/nipaweb/populartables.asp.

market value of all final goods and services produced during the year by resources located in the United States. We subtract depreciation from GDP to yield the *net domestic product*. To net domestic product we add net earnings from American resources abroad to yield *national income*. We obtain *personal income* by subtracting from national income all income earned this year but not received this year (for example, undistributed corporate profits) and by adding all income received this year but not earned this year (for example, transfer payments). By subtracting personal taxes and other government charges from personal income, we arrive at the bottom line: *disposable income,* the amount people are actually free either to spend or to save.

Summary Income Statement of the Economy

Exhibit 8 presents an annual income statement for the entire economy. The upper portion lists aggregate expenditure, which consists of consumption, gross investment, government purchases, and net exports. Because imports exceeded exports, net exports are negative. The aggregate income from this expenditure is allocated as shown in the lower portion of Exhibit 8. Some spending goes to cover depreciation

and net taxes on production, and so is not received as income by anyone. What remains are five income sources: employee compensation, proprietors' income, corporate profits, net interest, and rental income of persons. *Employee compensation,* by far the largest income source, includes both money wages and employer contributions to cover Social Security taxes, medical insurance, and other fringe benefits. *Proprietors' income* includes the earnings of unincorporated businesses. *Corporate profits* are the net revenues received by incorporated businesses but before subtracting corporate income taxes. *Net interest* is the interest received by individuals, excluding interest paid by consumers to businesses and interest paid by government.

Each family that owns a home is viewed as a tiny firm that rents that home to itself. Because homeowners do not, in fact, rent homes to themselves, an imputed rental value is estimated based on what the market rent would be. *Rental*

EXHIBIT 8	Expenditure and Income Statement for the U.S. Economy (in trillions of dollars)

Aggregate Expenditure	
Consumption (C)	$7.76
Gross investment (I)	1.67
Government purchases (G)	2.07
Net exports (X − M)	−0.50
GDP	$11.00

Aggregate Income	
Depreciation	$1.35
Net taxes on production	0.75
Compensation of employees	6.29
Proprietors' income	0.83
Corporate profits	1.02
Net interest	0.60
Rental income of persons	0.16
GDP	$11.00

Source: Figures are current, or nominal, estimates for 2003 from the Bureau of Economic Analysis, U.S. Department of Commerce. For the latest figures, go to http://www.bea.doc.gov/bea/dn/nipaweb/populartables.asp.

income of persons consists primarily of the imputed rental value of owner-occupied housing minus the cost of owning that property (such as property taxes, insurance, depreciation, and interest paid on the mortgage). From the totals in Exhibit 8, you can see that *aggregate spending in the economy equals the income generated by that spending*, thus satisfying the accounting identity.

APPENDIX QUESTIONS

1. *(National Income Accounting)* Use the following data to answer the questions below:

	Billions of Dollars
Net investment	$110
Depreciation	30
Exports	50
Imports	30
Government purchases	150
Consumption	400
Indirect business taxes (net of subsidies)	35
Income earned but not received	60
Income received but not earned	70
Personal income taxes	50
Employee compensation	455
Corporate profits	60
Rental income	20
Net interest	30
Proprietor's income	40
Net earnings of U.S. resources abroad	40

a. Calculate GDP using the income and the expenditure methods.

b. Calculate gross investment.

c. Calculate net domestic product, national income, personal income, and disposable income.

2. *(National Income Accounting)* According to Exhibit 8 in this chapter, GDP can be calculated either by adding expenditures on final goods or by adding the allocations of these expenditures to the resources used to produce these goods. Why do you suppose the portion of final goods expenditures that goes to pay for intermediate goods or raw materials is excluded from the income method of calculation?

Unemployment and Inflation

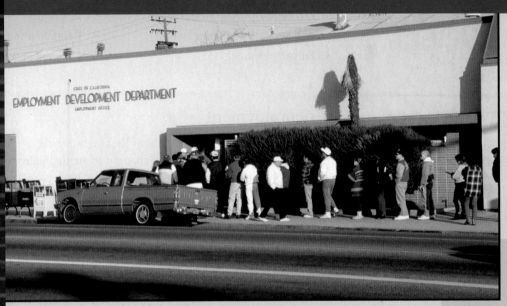

W ho among the following would be counted as unemployed: a college student who is not working, a bank teller displaced by an automatic teller machine, Kirsten Dunst between movies, or baseball slugger Barry Bonds in the off-season? What type of unemployment might be healthy for the economy? What's so bad about inflation? Why is unanticipated inflation worse than anticipated inflation? These and other questions are answered in this chapter, where we explore two macroeconomic problems: unemployment and inflation.

To be sure, unemployment and inflation are not the only problems an economy could face. Sluggish growth and widespread poverty are other possibilities. But low unemployment and low inflation go a long way toward reducing other economic problems. Although unemployment and inflation are often related, each initially will be described separately. The causes of each and the relationship between the two will become clearer as you learn more about how the economy works.

This chapter shows that not all unemployment or all inflation harms the economy. Even in a healthy economy, a certain amount of unemployment reflects the voluntary choices of workers and employers seeking their best options. And inflation that is fully anticipated creates fewer distortions than does unanticipated inflation. Topics discussed include:

- Measuring unemployment
- Frictional, structural, seasonal, and cyclical unemployment
- Full employment

- Sources and consequences of inflation
- Relative price changes
- Nominal and real interest rates

Unemployment

Economics in the Movies

"They scampered about looking for work. . . . They swarmed on the highways. The movement changed them; the highways, the camps along the road, the fear of hunger and the hunger itself, changed them. The children without dinner changed them, the endless moving changed them."[1] There is no question, as John Steinbeck writes in *The Grapes of Wrath,* that a long stretch of unemployment profoundly affects the individual and the family. The most obvious loss is a steady paycheck, but the unemployed often lose self-esteem and part of their identity as well. According to psychologists, in terms of stressful events, the loss of a good job ranks only slightly below the death of a loved one or a divorce. Moreover, unemployment appears to be linked to a greater incidence of crime and to a variety of afflictions, including heart disease, suicide, and mental illness.[2] No matter how much people complain about their jobs, they rely on those same jobs not only for income but also for their personal identity. When strangers meet, one of the first questions asked is "what do you do?"

In addition to these personal costs, unemployment imposes a cost on the economy as a whole because fewer goods and services are produced. When those who are willing and able to work can't find jobs, that unemployed labor is lost forever. *This lost output coupled with the economic and psychological cost of unemployment on the individual and the family are the true costs of unemployment.* As we begin our analysis, keep in mind that the national unemployment rate reflects millions of individuals with their own stories. As President Harry Truman remarked, "It's a recession when your neighbor loses his job; it's a depression when you lose your own." For some lucky people, unemployment is a brief vacation between jobs. For others, a long stretch can have a lasting effect on family stability, economic welfare, self-esteem, and personal identity.

Measuring Unemployment

The unemployment rate is the most widely reported measure of the nation's economic health. What does the unemployment rate measure? What are the sources of unemployment? How has unemployment changed over time? These are some of the questions explored in this section. Let's first see how to measure unemployment.

---

1. John Steinbeck, *The Grapes of Wrath* (New York: Viking Press, 1939), p. 392.
2. For a study linking a higher incidence of suicides to recessions, see Christopher Ruhm, "Are Recessions Good for Your Health," *Quarterly Journal of Economics* 115 (May 2000): 617–650.

We begin with the U.S. *civilian noninstitutional adult population,* which consists of all civilians 16 years of age and older, except those in prison or in mental hospitals. The adjective *civilian* means the definition excludes those in the military. In this chapter, when we refer to the *adult population,* we mean the civilian noninstitutional adult population. The **labor force** consists of the people in the adult population who are either working or looking for work. *Those who want a job but can't find one are unemployed.* The Bureau of Labor Statistics interviews 55,000 households monthly and counts people as unemployed if they have no job but want one and have looked for work at least once during the preceding four weeks. Thus, the college student, the displaced bank teller, Kirsten Dunst, and Barry Bonds would all be counted as unemployed if they want a job and looked for work in the previous month. The unemployment rate measures the percentage of those in the labor force who are unemployed. Hence, the **unemployment rate,** which is reported monthly, equals the number unemployed—that is, people without jobs who are looking for work—divided by the number in the labor force.

Only a fraction of adults who are not working are considered unemployed. The others may have retired, are students, are caring for children at home, or simply don't want to work. Others may be unable to work because of long-term illness or disability. Some may have become so discouraged by a long, unfruitful job search that they have given up in frustration. These **discouraged workers** have, in effect, dropped out of the labor force, so they are not counted as unemployed. Finally, about one-third of those working part time would prefer to work full time, yet all part-timers are counted as employed. Because the official unemployment rate does not include discouraged workers and counts all part-time workers as employed, it may underestimate the true extent of unemployment in the economy. Later we will consider some factors that work in the opposite direction.

These definitions are illustrated in Exhibit 1, where circles represent the various groups, and the number (in millions) of individuals in each category and subcategory is shown in

LABOR FORCE

Those 16 years of age and older who are either working or looking for work

UNEMPLOYMENT RATE

The number unemployed as a percentage of the labor force

DISCOURAGED WORKERS

Those who drop out of the labor force in frustration because they can't find work

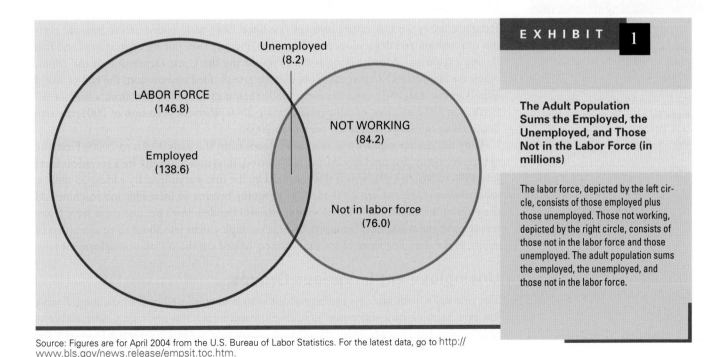

E X H I B I T   1

The Adult Population Sums the Employed, the Unemployed, and Those Not in the Labor Force (in millions)

The labor force, depicted by the left circle, consists of those employed plus those unemployed. Those not working, depicted by the right circle, consists of those not in the labor force and those unemployed. The adult population sums the employed, the unemployed, and those not in the labor force.

Unemployed (8.2)

LABOR FORCE (146.8)

Employed (138.6)

NOT WORKING (84.2)

Not in labor force (76.0)

Source: Figures are for April 2004 from the U.S. Bureau of Labor Statistics. For the latest data, go to http://www.bls.gov/news.release/empsit.toc.htm.

parentheses. The circle on the left depicts the entire U.S. labor force, including both employed and unemployed people. The circle on the right represents members of the adult population who, for whatever reason, are not working. These two circles combined show the entire adult population. The overlapping area identifies the number of *unemployed* workers—that is, people in the labor force who are not working. The unemployment rate is found by dividing the number unemployed by the number in the labor force. In April 2004, 8.2 million people were unemployed in a labor force of 146.8 million, yielding an unemployment rate of 5.6 percent.

Labor Force Participation Rate

The productive capability of any economy depends in part on the proportion of adults in the labor force, measured as the *labor force participation rate*. In Exhibit 1, the U.S. adult population equals those in the labor force (146.8 million) plus those not in the labor force (76.0 million)—a total of 222.8 million. The **labor force participation rate** therefore equals the number in the labor force divided by the adult population, or 65.9 percent ($=146.8/222.8$). So, on average, two out of three adults are in the labor force. The labor force participation rate increased from about 60 percent in 1970 to about 67 percent in 1990, and has remained relatively steady since then.

One striking development since World War II has been the convergence in the labor force participation rates of men and women. In 1950, only 34 percent of adult women were in the labor force. Today 60 percent are, with the greatest increase among younger women. The labor force participation rate among men has declined from 86 percent in 1950 to about 75 percent today, primarily because of earlier retirement. The participation rate is slightly higher among white males than black males but higher among black females than white females. Finally, the participation rate increases with education—from 44.2 percent for those without a high school diploma to 77.6 percent among those with a college degree.

Unemployment over Time

Exhibit 2 shows the U.S. unemployment rate since 1900, with shaded bars to indicate periods of recession and depression. As you can see, the rate rises during contractions and falls during expansions. Most striking is the jump during the Great Depression of the 1930s, when the rate reached 25 percent. Note that the rate trended upward from the end of World War II in the mid-1940s until the early 1980s; then it came back down, from a high of 9.7 percent in 1982 to a low of 3.9 percent in late 2000. With the recession of 2001, the rate began rising until it peaked at 6.0 percent in 2003.

Why did the unemployment rate trend down from the early 1980s to 2000? First, the overall economy was on a roll during that period, interrupted briefly by a recession from July 1990 to March 1991, which was triggered by the first war in Iraq. By adding 35 million jobs between 1982 and late 2000, the U.S. economy became an incredible job machine and the envy of the world. The unemployment rate also trended down because there were fewer teenagers in the workforce. Teenagers have an unemployment rate about three times that of adults, so the declining share of teenage workers helped cut the overall unemployment rate.

Unemployment in Various Groups

The unemployment rate says nothing about who is unemployed or for how long. Even a low rate can mask wide differences in unemployment rates across age, race, gender, and geographic area. For example, when the unemployment rate in April 2004 was 5.6 percent, the

Net **Bookmark**

The Bureau of Labor Statistics provides abundant data on labor market conditions, including unemployment rates, labor force estimates, and earnings data. Go to their Web site at http://stats.bls.gov. Go to the section, U.S. Economy at a Glance, at http://stats.bls.gov/eag/eag.us.htm for easy access to the latest data.

**HOMEWORK
Xpress!**
*Ask the Instructor
Video*

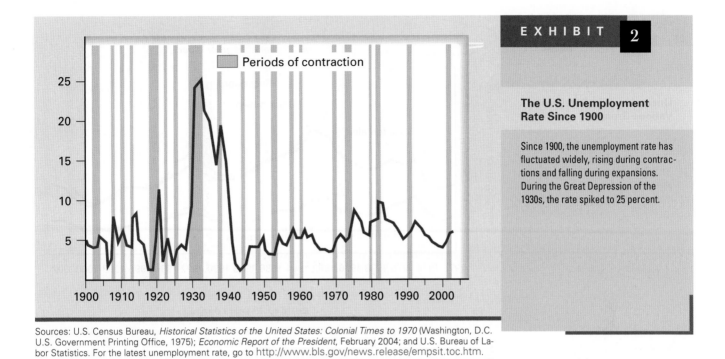

EXHIBIT 2

The U.S. Unemployment Rate Since 1900

Since 1900, the unemployment rate has fluctuated widely, rising during contractions and falling during expansions. During the Great Depression of the 1930s, the rate spiked to 25 percent.

Sources: U.S. Census Bureau, *Historical Statistics of the United States: Colonial Times to 1970* (Washington, D.C. U.S. Government Printing Office, 1975); *Economic Report of the President*, February 2004; and U.S. Bureau of Labor Statistics. For the latest unemployment rate, go to http://www.bls.gov/news.release/empsit.toc.htm.

rate was 16.9 percent among teenagers, 9.7 percent among black workers, and 7.2 percent among people of Hispanic ethnicity. Why are unemployment rates among teenagers so much higher than among older workers? Because young workers enter the job market with little training, they take unskilled jobs, and they are the first to be fired if demand softens. Young workers also move in and out of the job market more frequently during the year as they juggle school demands. Even those who have left school often shop around more than older workers, quitting one job in search of a better one.

Unemployment rates for different groups appear in Exhibit 3. Each panel shows the rate by race and by gender since 1972 (historical data are not available for those of Hispanic ethnicity). Panel (a) shows the rates for people 20 and older, and panel (b) the rates for 16 to 19 year olds. Years of recession are shaded pink. As you can see, rates are higher among black workers than among white, and rates are higher among teenagers than among those 20 and older. During recessions, the rates climbed for all groups. Rates peaked during the recession of 1982 and then trended down. After the recession of the early 1990s, unemployment rates continued downward, with the rate among black people falling in 2000 to the lowest on record. Rates rose again beginning with the recession of 2001.

Unemployment also varies by occupation. Professional and technical workers experience lower unemployment rates than blue-collar workers. Construction workers face high unemployment because that business is both seasonal and subject to wide swings over the business cycle.

Unemployment Varies Across Regions

The unemployment rate varies across the country. For example, in 2004, unemployment rates in Alaska, Michigan, and South Carolina were double those in North Dakota, South

EXHIBIT 3

Unemployment Rates for Various Groups

Different groups face different unemployment rates. The unemployment rate is higher for black workers than for white and higher for teenagers than for those 20 and older.

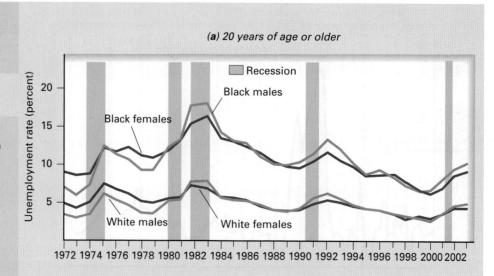

(a) 20 years of age or older

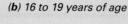

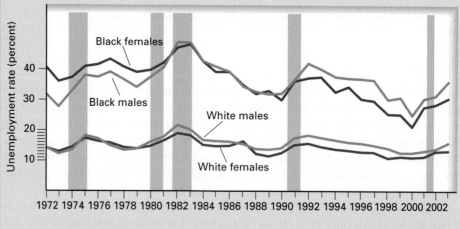

(b) 16 to 19 years of age

Source: *Economic Report of the President*, February 2004; U.S. Bureau of Labor Statistics. For the latest data, go to http://www.bls.gov/news.release/empsit.toc.htm.

Dakota, and Virginia. Even within states, unemployment varies widely. For example, in Virginia, the unemployment rate in Danville was triple that of Charlottesville. Exhibit 4 shows unemployment rates in 2004 for 26 U.S. metropolitan areas. As you can see, the unemployment in New York City, which was slow to recover from the 2001 recession and the terrorist attacks that year, was more than double the rate in Honolulu. The point is that the national unemployment rate masks wide differences across the country and even across an individual state. The following case study examines the plight of one troubled county in West Virginia.

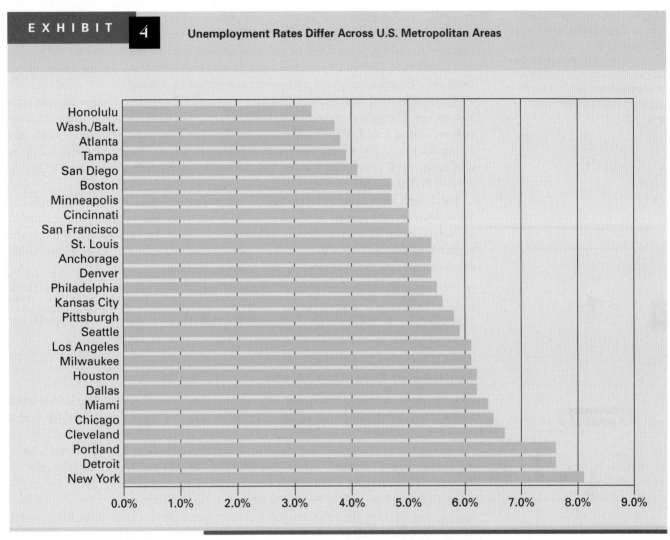

EXHIBIT 4   **Unemployment Rates Differ Across U.S. Metropolitan Areas**

Source: Based on figures for March 2004 from the U.S. Bureau of Labor Statistics. For the latest figures, go to http://www.bls.gov/lau/home.htm.

Poor King Coal

For decades McDowell County, West Virginia, prospered by supplying the coal that fired the nation's steel mills. In 1980 mining jobs were abundant, accounting for half of all jobs in the county. And mining wages were attractive, with average pay exceeding $80,000 in today's dollars. Many young people quit school to become miners (more than half of those over age 25 in 1980 were high school dropouts). Mining companies dominated the county, owning most of the property and paying a chunk of local taxes.

But two developments in the early 1980s hurt McDowell County's coal industry. First, the value of the dollar rose relative to foreign

© Omni Photo Communications/Index Stock Imagery

Case **Study**

World of Business

eActivity

Carolyn Sherwood-Call of the Federal Reserve Bank of San Francisco has written "The 1980s Divergence in State per Capita Incomes: What Does It Tell Us?" Access her article at http://www. frbsf.org/econrsrch/econrev/96-1/ 14-25.pdf to learn more about the shifting fortunes of various U.S. regions during the 1980s—your own included. Go to the Bureau of Labor Statistics at http://www.bls.gov/schedule/archives/laus_nr.htm and read some of the more recent regional and state employment and unemployment reports to see if things have changed, and in what ways.

currencies, so American steel became more expensive overseas and foreign steel became cheaper here. Steel imports rose substantially, reducing the demand for U.S. steel and the coal used to make it. Second, tighter pollution controls reduced the demand for the kind of coal mined in McDowell County. As a result, many mines shut down, putting miners out of work. By 1983, the county's unemployment rate topped 40 percent.

The county tried to attract new industry—even a nuclear-waste dump—but met with little success. The poor roads and bridges, the mountainous terrain, and a labor force trained only for mining scared off potential employers. Between 1980 and 2000, mining jobs in the county fell from 7,200 to only 700 while all private-sector jobs dropped more than half. As jobs disappeared, people left. County population dropped nearly in half from 49,550 in 1980 to 27,329 in 2000.

For decades, the county put all its eggs in one basket—mining—but that basket fell. The unemployment rate in early 2004 exceeded 11 percent; double the state and the national averages. County officials are hoping that two highways under construction through the rugged West Virginia hills will open the region to new opportunities. Another promising development is the use of abandoned coal mines as fish farms.

Sources: Walter Adams, "Steel," in *The Structure of American Industry*, edited by Walter Adams and James Brock (Englewood Cliffs, N.J.: Prentice Hall, 1995), pp. 93–118; and Beth Gorczyca, "Past Woes, Future Hope," *Herald Dispatch*, 18 September 2000. Information about McDowell County can be found at http://www.wv.gov/county.aspx?regID=3&cID=16. For the latest unemployment rate in the county, go to http://www.state.wv.us/bep/lmi/datarel/drcntyem.htm.

Sources of Unemployment

Pick up any metropolitan newspaper and thumb through the classifieds. The help-wanted section may include thousands of jobs, from accountants to X-ray technicians. Job search sites such as Monster.com list hundreds of thousands of openings. Why, when millions are unemployed, are so many jobs available? To understand this, we must take a closer look at the reasons behind unemployment. Think about all the ways people become unemployed. They may be looking for a first job, or they may be reentering the labor force after an absence. They may have quit or been fired from their last job. Fifty-five percent of those unemployed in 2003 lost their previous job, 9 percent quit, 8 percent entered the labor market for the first time, and 28 percent reentered the labor market. *Thus, 45 percent were unemployed either because they quit jobs or because they were just joining or rejoining the labor force.*

There are four sources of unemployment: frictional, seasonal, structural, and cyclical.

Frictional Unemployment

Just as employers do not always hire the first applicant who comes through the door, job seekers do not always accept the first offer. Both employers and job seekers need time to explore the job market. Employers need time to learn about the talent available, and job seekers need time to learn about employment opportunities. The time required to bring together employers and job seekers causes **frictional unemployment.** Although unemployment often creates economic and psychological hardships, not all unemployment is necessarily bad. Frictional unemployment does not usually last long and it results in a better match between workers and jobs, so the entire economy becomes more efficient. Policy makers are not that concerned with frictional unemployment.

Seasonal Unemployment

Unemployment caused by seasonal changes in labor demand during the year is called **seasonal unemployment**. During cold winter months, demand for farm hands, lifeguards,

FRICTIONAL UNEMPLOYMENT

Unemployment that occurs because job seekers and employers need time to find each other

SEASONAL UNEMPLOYMENT

Unemployment caused by seasonal changes in the demand for certain kinds of labor

landscapers, and construction workers shrinks, as it does for dozens of other seasonal occupations. Likewise, tourism in places such as Miami and Phoenix melts in the summer heat. The Christmas season increases the demand for sales clerks, postal workers, and Santa Clauses. Those holding seasonal jobs know those jobs will disappear in the off-season. Some even choose such jobs to complement their lifestyles or academic schedules. To eliminate seasonal unemployment, we would have to outlaw winter and abolish Christmas. Monthly employment statistics are "seasonally adjusted" to smooth out the bulges that result from seasonal factors. Policy makers are not that concerned with seasonal unemployment.

Structural Unemployment

A third reason why job vacancies and unemployment coexist is that unemployed workers often do not have the skills demanded by employers or do not live where their skills are demanded. For example, the Lincoln Electric Company in Euclid, Ohio, could not fill 200 openings because few among the thousands who applied could operate computer-controlled machines. Unemployment arising from a mismatch of skills or geographic location is called **structural unemployment.** *Structural unemployment occurs because changes in tastes, technology, taxes, and competition reduce the demand for certain skills and increase the demand for other skills.* In our dynamic economy, some workers, such as the coal miners in West Virginia, are stuck with skills no longer demanded. Likewise, golf carts replaced caddies, ATMs replaced bank tellers, and office technology is replacing clerical staff. For example, because of email, voice mail, PCs, PDAs, and other wireless devices, the number of secretaries, typists, and administrative assistants in the United States has fallen by half since 1987.

Whereas most frictional unemployment is short-term and voluntary, structural unemployment poses more of a problem because workers must develop the skills demanded in the local job market or look elsewhere. For example, unemployed coal miners and bank tellers must seek work in other industries or in other regions. But moving where the jobs are is easier said than done. Most prefer to remain near friends and relatives. Those laid off from good jobs hang around in hopes of getting rehired. Married couples with one spouse still employed may not want to give up one job to seek two jobs elsewhere. Finally, available jobs may be in regions where the living cost is much higher. So those structurally unemployed often stay put. Federal retraining programs aim to reduce structural unemployment.

Cyclical Unemployment

As output declines during recessions, firms reduce their demand for inputs, including labor. **Cyclical unemployment** increases during recessions and decreases during expansions. Between 1932 and 1934, when unemployment averaged about 24 percent, there was clearly much cyclical unemployment. Between 1942 and 1945, when unemployment averaged less than 2 percent, there was no cyclical unemployment. Cyclical unemployment means the economy is operating inside its production possibilities frontier. Government policies that stimulate aggregate demand during recessions aim to reduce cyclical unemployment.

The Meaning of Full Employment

In a dynamic economy such as ours, changes in product demand and in technology continually alter the supply and demand for particular types of labor. Thus, even in a healthy economy, there will be some frictional, structural, and seasonal unemployment. The economy is viewed as operating at *full employment* if there is no cyclical unemployment. When economists talk about "full employment," they do not mean zero unemployment but low unemployment, with estimates ranging from 4 to 6 percent. Even when the economy is at **full employment,** there will be some frictional, structural, and seasonal unemployment. After

STRUCTURAL UNEMPLOYMENT

Unemployment because (1) the skills in demand do not match those of the unemployed, or (2) the unemployed do not live where the jobs are

CYCLICAL UNEMPLOYMENT

Unemployment that fluctuates with the business cycle, increasing during contractions and decreasing during expansions

FULL EMPLOYMENT

Employment level when there is no cyclical unemployment

WALL STREET JOURNAL

Reading It **Right**

What's the relevance of the following statement from the Wall Street Journal: *"Initial jobless claims jumped to a nine-year high last week, boosted partly by layoffs following the September 11 terrorist attack."*

UNEMPLOYMENT BENEFITS

Cash transfers for those who lose their jobs and actively seek employment

all, nearly half of those unemployed have quit their last job or are new entrants or reentrants into the labor force. We can't expect people to find jobs overnight. Many in this group would be considered frictionally unemployed.

Unemployment Compensation

As noted at the outset, unemployment often imposes an economic and psychological hardship. For a variety of reasons, however, the burden of unemployment on the individual and the family may not be as severe today as it was during the Great Depression. Today, many households have two workers in the labor force, so if one loses a job, another is likely to still have one—a job that may provide health insurance and other benefits. Having more than one family member in the labor force cushions the shock of unemployment.

Moreover, unlike the experience during the Great Depression, most who lose their jobs now collect unemployment benefits. In response to the Great Depression, Congress passed the Social Security Act of 1935, which provided unemployment insurance financed by a tax on employers. Unemployed workers who meet certain qualifications can receive **unemployment benefits** for up to six months, provided they actively seek work. During recessions, benefits often extend beyond six months in states with especially high unemployment. Benefits go mainly to people who have lost jobs. Those just entering or reentering the labor force are not covered, nor are those who quit their last job or those fired for just cause, such as excessive absenteeism or theft. Because of these restrictions, about half those unemployed receive benefits.

Unemployment benefits replace on average about 40 percent of a person's take-home pay, with a higher share for those whose jobs paid less. Benefits averaged about $260 per week in 2003. Because these benefits reduce the opportunity cost of remaining unemployed, they may reduce the incentives to find work. For example, if faced with a choice of washing dishes for $240 per week or collecting $200 per week in unemployment benefits, which would you choose? Evidence suggests that those collecting unemployment benefits remain out of work weeks longer than those without benefits. So although unemployment insurance provides a safety net, it may reduce the urgency of finding work, thereby increasing unemployment. On the plus side, because beneficiaries need not take the first job that comes along, unemployment insurance allows for a higher quality search. As a result of a higher quality job search, there is a better match between job skills and job requirements, and this promotes economic efficiency.

International Comparisons of Unemployment

How do U.S. unemployment rates compare with those around the world? Exhibit 5 shows rates since 1982 for the United States, Japan, and the average of four major Western European economies. Over the last two decades, unemployment trended down in the United States, trended up in Japan, and remained high in Western Europe. At the beginning of the period, the United States had the highest rates among the three economies. More recently, the U.S. rate was well below Western Europe's and only slightly above Japan's.

Why are rates so high in Western Europe? The ratio of unemployment benefits to average pay is higher in Western Europe than in the United States, and unemployment benefits last longer there, sometimes years. So those collecting unemployment benefits have less incentive to find work. What's more, government regulations make European employers more reluctant to hire new workers because firing them is difficult. For example, Germany imposes penalties on firms for "socially unjustified" layoffs.

Historically, unemployment has been low in Japan because many firms there offered job security for life. Thus, some employees there who do little or no work are still carried on

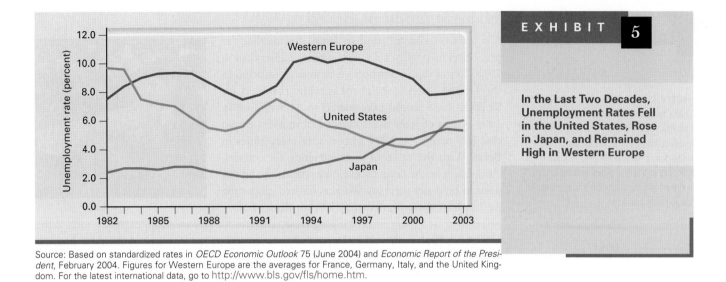

Source: Based on standardized rates in *OECD Economic Outlook* 75 (June 2004) and *Economic Report of the President*, February 2004. Figures for Western Europe are the averages for France, Germany, Italy, and the United Kingdom. For the latest international data, go to http://www.bls.gov/fls/home.htm.

company payrolls. Both labor laws and social norms limit layoffs in Japan. Unemployment has increased there in the last decade because firms went bankrupt.

Problems with Official Unemployment Figures

Official unemployment statistics are not without their problems. As we saw earlier, not counting discouraged workers as unemployed understates unemployment. Official employment data also ignore the problem of **underemployment,** which arises because people are counted as employed even if they can find only part-time work or are vastly overqualified for their job, as when someone with a Ph.D. in literature can find only a clerk's position. Counting overqualified and part-time workers as employed tends to understate the actual amount of unemployment.

On the other hand, because unemployment benefits and most welfare programs require recipients to seek employment, some people may go through the motions of looking for work just to qualify for benefits. If they do not in fact want a job, counting them as unemployed overstates actual unemployment. Likewise, some people who would prefer to work part time can find only full-time jobs, and some forced to work overtime and weekends would prefer to work less. To the extent that people must work more than they want to, the official unemployment rate overstates the actual rate. Finally, people in the underground economy may not admit they have jobs because they are breaking the law. *On net, however, because discouraged workers aren't counted as unemployed and because underemployed workers are counted as employed, most experts believe that official U.S. unemployment figures tend to underestimate unemployment.* Still, the size of this underestimation may not be large. For example, counting discouraged workers as unemployed would have raised the unemployment rate in April 2004 from 5.6 percent to 5.9 percent.

Despite these qualifications and limitations, the unemployment rate is a useful measure of trends over time. We turn next to another major problem: inflation.

Inflation

As noted already, *inflation* is a sustained increase in the economy's average price level. Let's begin with a case study that underscores the cost of high inflation.

UNDEREMPLOYMENT

Workers are overqualified for their jobs or work fewer hours than they would prefer

Case **Study**

Bringing Theory to Life

eActivity

What's happening in Brazil? Look at the Economic Bulletin from the Brazilian Development Bank at http://www.bndes.gov.br/english/bndes/synop.pdf to access the latest news and reports on the economic situation and current stabilization policies.

Hyperinflation in Brazil

Six years of wild inflation in Brazil meant that the price level in 1994 was *3.6 million* times higher than in 1988! To put this in perspective, with such inflation in the United States, a gallon of gasoline that sold for $1.25 in 1988 would have soared to $4.5 million in 1994. A pair of jeans that sold for $25 in 1988 would cost $90 million in 1994. Those were crazy times in Brazil. With the value of their currency, the *cruzeiro,* cheapening by the hour, people understandably did not want to hold any currency. Workers insisted on getting paid at least daily, immediately buying things before prices increased more or exchanging their cruzeiros for a more stable currency, such as the U.S. dollar. With such wild inflation, everyone, including merchants, had difficulty keeping up with prices. Different price increases among sellers of the same product encouraged buyers to shop around more.

The exploding price level meant even the simplest transactions required mountains of cash. Think again in terms of dollars. As a consequence of such inflation, dinner for two would cost more than $120 million. Such a stack of $100 bills would weigh more than a ton, literally. Because carrying enough money for even modest purchases became physically impossible, currency was issued in ever larger denominations. Between the mid-1980s and 1994, new denominations were issued five times, each a huge multiple of the previous one. For example, the new *cruzeiro real* issued in 1994 exchanged for 2,750 of the cruzeiro it replaced. Larger denominations facilitated purchases. Still, lugging money around, searching for the lowest price, and generally obsessing about money sucked up time and energy and, in the process, reduced productivity. This focus on money was rational for each individual but wasteful for the economy as a whole.

Since 1994 inflation in Brazil has dropped to single digits (the rate in 2004 was down to 6 percent). Fernando Henrique Cardoso, the finance minister in 1994, became a national hero for taming inflation. He was elected president in1994 and reelected in 1998. Although Brazil ended its inflation nightmare, hyperinflation is usually a problem somewhere in the world. The latest casualty was Zimbabwe, where the price level quadrupled in 2003.

Sources: "Battle Begins for Cardoso's Successor," *Economist,* 6 January 2001; "Emerging Market Indicators," *Economist,* 14 May 2004; and "Brazil," *Britannica Book of the Year* (Chicago: Encyclopedia Britannica, 1995). For more on the Brazilian economy, go to http://www.latin-focus.com/latinfocus/countries/brazil/brazil.htm.

HYPERINFLATION

A very high rate of inflation

DEFLATION

A sustained decrease in the price level

DISINFLATION

A reduction in the rate of inflation

We have already discussed inflation in different contexts. If the price level bounces around—moving up one month, falling back the next month—any particular increase in the price level would not necessarily be called inflation in a meaningful sense. We typically measure inflation on an annual basis. The annual *inflation rate* is the percentage increase in the average price level from one year to the next. For example, between January 2003 and January 2004, the U.S. *consumer price index* increased 1.8 percent. Extremely high inflation, as in Brazil, is called **hyperinflation.** A sustained *decrease* in the average price level is called **deflation,** as occurred in the United States during the Great Depression and most recently in Japan, Hong Kong, and Israel. And a reduction in the rate of inflation is called **disinflation**, as occurred in the United States during the first half of the 1980s and first half of the 1990s.

In this section, we first consider two sources of inflation. Then, we examine the extent and consequences of inflation in the United States and around the world.

Two Sources of Inflation

Inflation is a sustained increase in the economy's price level; it results from an increase in aggregate demand, a decrease in aggregate supply, or both. Panel (a) of Exhibit 6 shows that an increase in aggregate demand raises the economy's price level from *P* to *P'*. In such cases, a shift to the right of the aggregate demand curve *pulls up* the price level. Inflation resulting from increases in aggregate demand is called **demand-pull inflation.** To generate continuous demand-pull inflation, the aggregate demand curve would have to keep shifting out along a given aggregate supply curve. Rising U.S. inflation during the late 1960s resulted from demand-pull inflation, when federal spending for the Vietnam War and expanded social programs boosted aggregate demand.

Alternatively, inflation can arise from reductions in aggregate supply, as shown in panel (b) of Exhibit 6, where a leftward shift of the aggregate supply curve raises the price level. For example, crop failures and OPEC price hikes reduced aggregate supply during 1974 and 1975, thereby raising the price level. Inflation stemming from decreases in aggregate supply is called **cost-push inflation,** suggesting that increases in the cost of production *push up* the price level. Prices increase and real GDP decreases, a combination identified earlier as *stagflation.* Again, to generate sustained and continuous cost-push inflation, the aggregate supply curve would have to keep shifting left along a given aggregate demand curve.

DEMAND-PULL INFLATION

A sustained rise in the price level caused by a rightward shift of the aggregate demand curve

COST-PUSH INFLATION

A sustained rise in the price level caused by a leftward shift of the aggregate supply curve

---

EXHIBIT 6

Inflation Caused by Shifts of Aggregate Demand and Aggregate Supply Curves

Panel (a) illustrates demand-pull inflation. An outward shift of the aggregate demand to *AD'* "pulls" the price level up from *P* to *P'*. Panel (b) shows cost-push inflation. A decrease of aggregate supply to *AS'* "pushes" the price level up from *P* to *P'*.

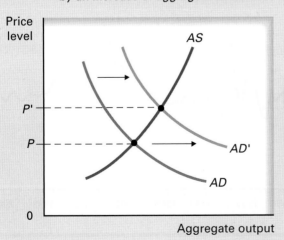

(a) *Demand-pull inflation: inflation induced by an increase of aggregate demand*

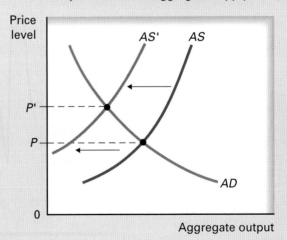

(b) *Cost-push inflation: inflation induced by a decrease of aggregate supply*

A Historical Look at Inflation and the Price Level

Economics in the Movies

The consumer price index is the price measure you most often encounter, so it gets attention here. As you learned in the previous chapter, the *consumer price index*, or *CPI*, measures the cost of a market basket of consumer goods and services over time. Exhibit 7 shows prices in the United States since 1913, using the consumer price index. Panel (a) shows the price *level*, measured by an

---

EXHIBIT   **7**

Consumer Price Index Since 1913

Panel (a) shows that, despite fluctuations, the price level, as measured by the consumer price index, was lower in 1940 than in 1920. Since 1940, the price level has risen nearly every year. Panel (b) shows the annual rate of change in the price level. Since 1948, the inflation rate has averaged 3.9 percent annually.

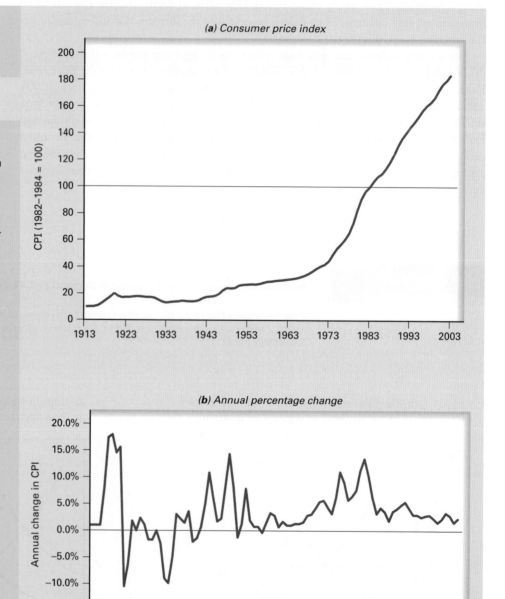

(a) Consumer price index

(b) Annual percentage change

Source: The CPI home page of the U.S. Bureau of Labor Statistics is at http://www.bls.gov/cpi/home.htm. Go there for the latest figures.

index relative to the base period of 1982 to 1984. As you can see, the price level was lower in 1940 than in 1920. Since 1940, however, it has risen steadily, especially during the 1970s.

People are concerned less about the price level and more about year-to-year changes in that level. The lower panel shows the annual *rate of change* in the CPI, or the annual rate of *inflation* or *deflation*. The decade of the 1970s was not the only period of high inflation. Inflation exceeded 10 percent from 1916 to 1919 and in 1947—periods associated with world wars. Prior to the 1950s, high inflation was war related and was usually followed by deflation. Such an inflation-deflation cycle stretches back over the last two centuries. In fact, between the Revolutionary War and World War II, the price level fell in about as many years as it rose. At the end of World War II, the price level was about where it stood at the end of the Civil War.

So fluctuations in the price level are nothing new. But prior to World War II, years of inflation and deflation balanced out over the long run. Therefore, people had good reason to believe the dollar would retain its purchasing power over the long term. Since the end of World War II, however, the CPI has increased by an average of 3.9 percent per year. That may not sound like much, but it translates into an *eightfold* increase in the consumer price index since 1947. *Inflation erodes confidence in the value of the dollar over the long term.*

Anticipated Versus Unanticipated Inflation

What is the effect of inflation on the economy? *Unanticipated inflation* creates more problems than *anticipated inflation*. To the extent that inflation is higher or lower than anticipated, it arbitrarily creates winners and losers. If inflation is higher than expected, the winners are buyers who agreed to a price that anticipated lower inflation. The losers are those who agreed to sell at that price. If inflation is lower than expected, the situation is reversed: The winners are sellers who agreed to a price that anticipated higher inflation, and the losers are buyers who agreed to that price.

Suppose inflation is expected to be 3 percent next year, and you agree to a 4 percent increase in your nominal, or money, wage. You expect your *real* wage—that is, your wage measured in dollars of constant purchasing power—to increase by 1 percent. If inflation turns out to be 3 percent, you and your employer will both be satisfied with your nominal wage increase of 4 percent. If inflation turns out to be 5 percent, your real wage will fall by 1 percent, so you will be a loser and your employer a winner. If inflation turns out to be only 1 percent, your real wage will increase by 3 percent, so you will be a winner and your employer a loser. *The arbitrary gains and losses arising from unanticipated inflation is one reason inflation is so unpopular.* Inflation just doesn't seem fair.

The Transaction Costs of Variable Inflation

During long periods of price stability, people correctly believe that they can predict future prices and can therefore plan accordingly. If inflation changes unexpectedly, however, the future is cloudier, so planning gets harder. Uncertainty about inflation undermines money's ability to link the present with the future. Firms dealing with the rest of the world face an added burden. They must not only plan for U.S. inflation, they must also anticipate how the value of the dollar might change relative to foreign currencies. Inflation uncertainty and the resulting exchange-rate uncertainty complicate international transactions. In this more uncertain environment, managers must shift their attention from production decisions to anticipating the effects of inflation and exchange-rate changes on the firm's finances. Market transactions, particularly long-term contracts, become more complicated as inflation becomes more unpredictable. Some economists believe that the high and variable U.S. inflation during the 1970s and early 1980s cut economic growth during those periods.

Inflation Obscures Relative Price Changes

Even with no inflation, some prices would increase and some would decrease, reflecting normal market activity. For example, since 1980 the U.S. price level doubled, yet the prices of color televisions, computers, phone service and many other products fell sharply. Because the prices of various goods change by different amounts, *relative prices* change. Consider price changes over a longer period. In the last hundred years, consumer prices overall increased about 2,000 percent, but the price of a hotel room in New York City jumped 7,500 percent, while the price of a three-minute phone call from New York to Chicago dropped 99 percent. Whereas the economy's price level describes the exchange rate between a market basket and *money,* relative prices describe the exchange rate between goods—that is, how much one good costs compared to another.

Inflation does not necessarily cause a change in relative prices, but it can obscure that change. During periods of volatile inflation, there is greater uncertainty about the price of one good relative to another—that is, about relative prices. But relative price changes are important for allocating the economy's resources efficiently. If all prices moved together, suppliers could link the selling prices of their goods to the overall inflation rate. Because prices usually do not move in unison, however, tying a particular product's price to the overall inflation rate may result in a price that is too high or too low based on market conditions. The same is true of agreements to link wages with inflation. If the price of an employer's product grows more slowly than the rate of inflation in the economy, the employer may be hard-pressed to increase wages by the rate of inflation. Consider the problem confronting oil refiners who signed labor contracts agreeing to pay their workers cost-of-living wage increases. In some years, those employers had to provide pay increases at a time when the price of oil was falling like a rock.

Inflation Across Metropolitan Areas

Inflation rates differ across regions mostly because of differences in housing prices, which grow faster in some places than in others. But most prices, such as for automobiles, refrigerators, or jeans, do not differ that much across regions. The federal government tracks separate CPIs for each of 26 metropolitan areas. Based on these CPIs from 1994 to 2004, the average annual inflation rate is presented in Exhibit 8. Average annual inflation during the decade ranged from a low of 1.4 percent in Honolulu to a high of 3.2 percent in Denver. Most cities averaged between 2.0 percent and 3.0 percent per year. The median city averaged 2.4 percent per year, which was also the U.S. average annual inflation rate during the 10-year period.

Inflation Across Countries

Exhibit 9 shows annual inflation based on the CPI for the past two decades in the United States, Japan, and the Western European economy, represented here as the average of four major nations. All three economies show a similar trend, with declining inflation, or disinflation, during the first half of the 1980s, rising inflation during the second half of the 1980s to a peak in the early 1990s, and then another trend lower. The overall trend during the two decades was toward lower inflation. Inflation rates in Western Europe were similar to those in the United States. Rates in Japan were consistently lower, even dipping into deflation in recent years. Inflation since 1980 averaged 4.2 percent in Western Europe, 3.6 percent in the United States, and 1.2 percent in Japan.

The quantity and quality of data going into the price index varies across countries. Governments in less-developed countries sample fewer products and measure prices only in the

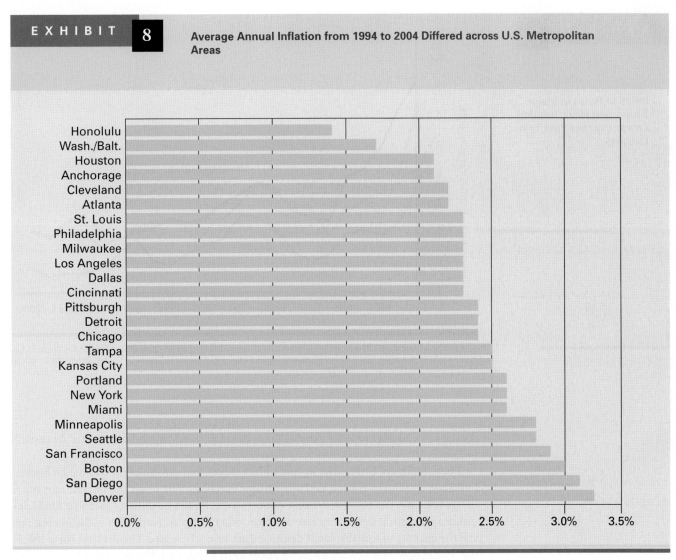

EXHIBIT **8**

Average Annual Inflation from 1994 to 2004 Differed across U.S. Metropolitan Areas

Source: Annual averages for 1994 to 2004 based on CPI estimates from the U.S. Bureau of Labor Statistics. For the latest figures go to http://www.bls.gov/cpi/home.htm and find "Regional Resources."

capital city. Whereas hundreds of items are sampled to determine the U.S. consumer price index, as few as 30 might be sampled in some developing countries.

Inflation and Interest Rates

No discussion of inflation would be complete without some mention of the interest rate. **Interest** is the dollar amount paid by borrowers to lenders. Lenders must be rewarded for forgoing present consumption, and borrowers are willing to pay a premium to spend now. The **interest rate** is the amount paid per year as a percentage of the amount borrowed. For example, an interest rate of 5 percent means $5 per year on a $100 loan. The greater the interest rate, other things constant, the greater the reward for lending money. The amount of money people are willing to lend, called *loanable funds,* increases as the interest rate rises, other things

INTEREST

The dollar amount paid by borrowers to lenders

INTEREST RATE

Interest per year as a percentage of the amount loaned

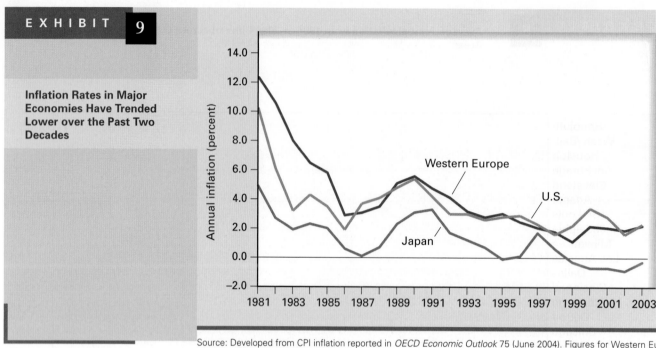

EXHIBIT 9

Inflation Rates in Major Economies Have Trended Lower over the Past Two Decades

Source: Developed from CPI inflation reported in *OECD Economic Outlook* 75 (June 2004). Figures for Western Europe are the averages for France, Germany, Italy, and the United Kingdom. For the latest data, go to http://www.bls.gov/fls/home.htm.

constant. The supply curve for loanable funds therefore slopes upward, as indicated by curve *S* in Exhibit 10.

These funds are demanded by households, firms, and governments to finance homes, buildings, machinery, college, and other major purchases. The lower the interest rate, other things constant, the cheaper the cost of borrowing. So the quantity of loanable funds demanded increases as the interest rate decreases, other things constant. That is, the interest rate and the quantity of loanable funds demanded are inversely related. The demand curve therefore slopes downward, as indicated by curve *D* in Exhibit 10. The downward-sloping demand curve and the upward-sloping supply curve intersect to yield the equilibrium nominal rate of interest, *i*.

NOMINAL INTEREST RATE

The interest rate expressed in current dollars as a percentage of the amount loaned; the interest rate on the loan agreement

REAL INTEREST RATE

The interest rate expressed in dollars of constant purchasing power as a percentage of the amount loaned; the nominal interest rate minus the inflation rate

The **nominal interest rate** measures interest in terms of the current dollars paid. The nominal rate is the one that appears on the loan agreement; it is the rate discussed in the news media and is often of political significance. The **real interest rate** equals the nominal rate minus the inflation rate:

$$\text{Real interest rate} = \text{Nominal interest rate} - \text{Inflation rate}$$

For example, if the nominal interest rate is 5 percent and the inflation rate is 3 percent, the real interest rate is 2 percent. With no inflation, the nominal rate and the real rate would be identical. But with inflation, the nominal rate exceeds the real rate. If inflation is unexpectedly high—higher, for example, than the nominal rate—then the real interest rate would be negative. In this case, the nominal interest earned for lending money would not even cover the loss in spending power caused by inflation. Lenders would lose purchasing power. This is why lenders and borrowers are concerned more about the real rate than the nominal rate. The real interest rate, however, is known only after the fact—that is, only after inflation actually occurs.

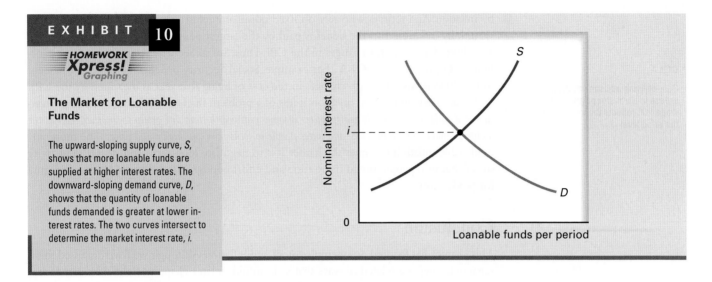

EXHIBIT **10**

HOMEWORK **Xpress!** *Graphing*

The Market for Loanable Funds

The upward-sloping supply curve, *S*, shows that more loanable funds are supplied at higher interest rates. The downward-sloping demand curve, *D*, shows that the quantity of loanable funds demanded is greater at lower interest rates. The two curves intersect to determine the market interest rate, *i*.

Because the future is uncertain, lenders and borrowers must form expectations about inflation, and they base their willingness to lend and borrow on these expectations. The higher the *expected* inflation, the higher the nominal rate of interest that lenders require and that borrowers are willing to pay. Lenders and borrowers base their decisions on the *expected* real interest rate, which equals the nominal rate minus the expected inflation rate.

Although the discussion has implied that there is only one market rate of interest, there are many rates. Rates differ depending on such factors as the duration of the loan, and tax treatment of interest, and the risk the loan will not be repaid.

Why Is Inflation Unpopular?

Whenever the price level increases, spending increases just to buy the same amount of goods and services. If you think of inflation only in terms of spending, you consider only the problem of paying those higher prices. But if you think of inflation in terms of the higher money income that result, you see that higher prices mean higher receipts for resource suppliers, including higher wages for workers. When viewed from the income side, inflation is not so bad.

If every higher price is received by some resource supplier, why are people so troubled by inflation? People view their higher incomes as well-deserved rewards for their labor, but they see inflation as a penalty that unjustly robs them of purchasing power. Most people do not stop to realize that unless their labor productivity increases, higher wages *must* result in higher prices. Prices and wages are simply two sides of the same coin. To the extent that nominal wages on average keep up with inflation, workers retain their purchasing power.

Presidents Ford and Carter could not control inflation and were turned out of office. Inflation slowed significantly during President Reagan's first term, and he won reelection easily, even though the unemployment rate was higher during his first term than during President Carter's tenure. During the 1988 election, George H. W. Bush won in part by reminding voters what inflation was in 1980, the last time a Democrat was president. But he lost his bid at reelection in part because inflation spiked to 6.0 percent in 1990, the highest in a decade. Inflation remained under 3.0 percent during President Clinton's first term, and he was reelected easily. In the elections of 2000 and 2004, inflation was low enough as not to be an issue in either presidential election.

Although inflation affects everyone to some extent, it hits hardest those whose incomes are fixed in nominal terms. For example, pensions are often fixed amounts and are eroded

COLA

Cost-of-living adjustment; the increase in a transfer payment or wage that reflects the increase in the price level

by inflation. And retirees who rely on fixed nominal interest income also see their incomes shrunk by inflation. But the benefits paid by the largest pension program, Social Security, are adjusted annually for changes in the CPI. Thus, Social Security recipients get a cost-of-living adjustment, or a **COLA.** For example, Social Security benefits increased 2.1 percent in late 2003 to keep up with changes in the cost of living that year as measured by the CPI.

In summary, anticipated inflation is less of a problem than unanticipated inflation. *Unanticipated inflation arbitrarily redistributes income and wealth from one group to another, reduces the ability to make long-term plans, and forces people to focus more on money and prices.* The more unpredictable inflation becomes the harder it is to negotiate long-term contracts. Productivity suffers because people spend more time and effort coping with inflation, leaving less time for production.

Conclusion

This chapter has focused on unemployment and inflation. Although we have discussed them separately, they are related in ways that will unfold in later chapters. Politicians sometimes add the unemployment rate to the inflation rate to come up with what they refer to as the "misery index." In 1980, for example, an unemployment rate of 7.1 percent combined with a CPI increase of 13.6 percent to yield a misery index of 20.7—a number that helps explain why President Carter was not reelected. By 1984 the misery index had dropped to 11.8, and by 1988 to 9.6; Republicans retained the White House in both elections. In 1992, the index climbed slightly to 10.4 percent, spelling trouble for President George H. W. Bush. And in 1996, the index fell back to 8.4 percent, assuring President Clinton's reelection. During the election of 2000, the misery index was down to 7.7, which should have helped Al Gore, the candidate of the incumbent party. But during the campaign, Gore distanced himself from President Clinton and thus was not able to capitalize on the strong economy. And in the 2004 election the misery index remained about the same as in 2000, which helps explains why challenger John Kerry had difficulty making an issue of the economy.

SUMMARY

1. The unemployment rate is the number of people looking for work divided by the number in the labor force. The unemployment rate masks differences among particular groups and across regions. The rate is lowest among white adults and highest among black teenagers.

2. There are four sources of unemployment. Frictional unemployment arises because employers and qualified job seekers need time to find one another. Seasonal unemployment stems from the effects of weather and the seasons on certain industries, such as construction and agriculture. Structural unemployment arises because changes in tastes, technology, taxes, and competition reduce the demand for certain skills and increase the demand for other skills. And cyclical unemployment results from fluctuations in employment caused by the business cycle. Pol-

icy makers are less concerned with frictional and seasonal unemployment. Full employment occurs when cyclical unemployment is zero.

3. Unemployment often creates both an economic and a psychological hardship. For some, this burden is reduced by an employed spouse and by unemployment insurance. Unemployment insurance provides a safety net for some, but it may also reduce incentives to find work.

4. Inflation is a sustained rise in the average price level. An increase in aggregate demand can cause demand-pull inflation. A decrease in aggregate supply can cause cost-push inflation. Until World War II, both inflation and deflation were common, but since then the price level has increased virtually every year.

5. Anticipated inflation causes fewer distortions in the economy than unanticipated inflation. Unanticipated inflation arbitrarily creates winners and losers, and forces people to spend more time and energy coping with the effects of inflation. The negative effects of high and variable inflation on productivity can be observed in countries that have experienced hyperinflation, such as Brazil.

6. Because not all prices change by the same amount during inflationary periods, people have trouble keeping track of changes in relative prices. Unexpected inflation makes long-term planning more difficult and more risky.

7. The intersection of the demand and supply curves for loanable funds yields the market interest rate. The real interest rate is the nominal interest rate minus the inflation rate. Borrowers and lenders base decisions on the expected real interest rate.

QUESTIONS FOR REVIEW

1. *(Labor Force)* Refer to Exhibit 1 in the chapter to determine whether each of the following statements is true or false.

   a. Some people who are officially unemployed are not in the labor force.
   b. Some people in the labor force are not working.
   c. Everyone who is not unemployed is in the labor force.
   d. Some people who are not working are not unemployed.

2. *(Unemployment in Various Groups)* Does the overall unemployment rate provide an accurate picture of the impact of unemployment on all U.S. population groups?

3. (*C a s e* **S t u d y** : Poor King Coal) Was the high unemployment in McDowell County primarily frictional, seasonal, structural, or cyclical? Explain your answer, using the text definitions for these categories of unemployment.

4. *(The Meaning of Full Employment)* When the economy is at full employment, is the unemployment rate at 0 percent? Why or why not? How would a more generous unemployment insurance system affect the full employment figure?

5. *(International Comparisons of Unemployment)* In recent years how has the U.S. unemployment rate compared with rates in other major economies? Why should we be careful in comparing unemployment across countries?

6. *(Official Unemployment Figures)* Explain why most experts believe that official U.S. data underestimate the actual rate of unemployment. What factors could make the official rate overstate the actual unemployment rate?

7. (*C a s e* **S t u d y** : Hyperinflation in Brazil) In countries such as Brazil and Russia, which had problems with high inflation, the increased use of another country's currency (such as the U.S. dollar) became common. Why do you suppose this occurred?

8. *(Sources of Inflation)* What are the two sources of inflation? How would you illustrate them graphically?

9. *(Anticipated Versus Unanticipated Inflation)* If actual inflation exceeds anticipated inflation, who will lose purchasing power and who will gain?

10. *(Inflation and Relative Price Changes)* What does the consumer price index measure? Does the index measure changes in relative prices? Why, or why not?

11. *(Inflation and Interest Rates)* Explain as carefully as you can why borrowers would be willing to pay a higher interest rate if they expected the inflation rate to increase in the future.

12. *(Inflation)* Why is a relatively constant and predictable inflation rate less harmful to an economy than a rate that fluctuates unpredictably?

13. *(Inflation)* Why do people dislike inflation?

PROBLEMS AND EXERCISES

14. *(Measuring Unemployment)* Determine the impact on each of the following if 2 million formerly unemployed workers decide to return to school full time and stop looking for work:

    a. The labor force participation rate
    b. The size of the labor force
    c. The unemployment rate

15. *(Measuring Unemployment)* Suppose that the U.S. noninstitutional adult population is 230 million and the labor force participation rate is 67 percent.

    a. What is the size of the U.S. labor force?
    b. If 85 million adults are not working, what is the unemployment rate?

16. *(Types of Unemployment)* Determine whether each of the following would be considered frictional, structural, seasonal, or cyclical unemployment:

    a. A UPS employee who was hired for the Christmas season is laid off after Christmas.
    b. A worker is laid off due to reduced aggregate demand in the economy.
    c. A worker in a video rental stores becomes unemployed as video-on-demand cable service becomes more popular.
    d. A new college graduate is looking for employment.

17. *(Inflation)* Here are some recent data on the U.S. consumer price index:

Year	CPI	Year	CPI	Year	CPI
1988	118.3	1994	148.2	1999	166.6
1989	124.0	1995	152.4	2000	172.2
1990	130.7	1996	156.9	2001	177.1
1991	136.2	1997	160.5	2002	179.9
1992	140.3	1998	163.0	2003	184.0
1993	144.5				

Compute the inflation rate for each year 1989–2003 and determine which were years of inflation. In which years did deflation occur? In which years did disinflation occur? Was there hyperinflation in any year?

18. *(Sources of Inflation)* Using the concepts of aggregate supply and aggregate demand, explain why inflation usually increases during wartime.

19. *(Inflation and Interest Rates)* Using a demand-supply diagram for loanable funds (like Exhibit 10), show what happens to the nominal interest rate and the equilibrium quantity of loans when both borrowers and lenders increase their estimates of the expected inflation rate from 5 percent to 10 percent.

EXPERIENTIAL EXERCISES

20. *(Measuring Unemployment)* The chapter explains the definitions the government employs in measuring unemployment. Interview 10 members of your class to determine their labor market status—employed, unemployed, or not in the labor force. Include yourself, and then compute the unemployment rate and the labor force participation rate for these 11 people.

21. *(International Comparisons of Inflation)* In recent years, how has the U.S. inflation rate compared with rates in other industrial economies? Why should we be careful in comparing inflation rates across countries? The Federal Reserve Bank of St. Louis maintains a Web page devoted to

international economic trends: http://www.stls.frb.org/publications/iet/. Choose two countries and compare their recent inflation experiences. (If you have Adobe Acrobat Reader, you can look at bar charts of the data.)

22. *(Wall Street Journal)* Scan the Economy page in the First Section of today's *Wall Street Journal*. You are almost sure to find a discussion of a policy proposal that will affect unemployment, inflation, or both. Use the aggregate demand and supply model to describe the effect of the proposal—if enacted—on the U.S. unemployment and inflation rates.

23. In January 1997, the U.S. Treasury began issuing inflation-indexed bonds. The bonds pay a fixed rate of interest and

the par value of the bond is increased each year by the rate of inflation, as measured by the CPI. Look in the Money & Investing section of the *Wall Street Journal* on the page where U.S. Treasury bond information is provided and compare the rates on these inflation indexed bonds with nonindexed U.S. Treasury bonds.

HOMEWORK XPRESS! EXERCISES

*These exercises require access to McEachern Homework Xpress! If Homework Xpress! did not come with your book, visit **http://homeworkxpress.swlearning.com** to purchase.*

In the diagram for this exercise, use aggregate demand and aggregate supply curves to show an economy initially at equilibrium and identify the price level as P.

1. Illustrate how demand-pull inflation arises.

2. Illustrate how cost-push inflation arises.

3. Illustrate how a change in aggregate demand would cause deflation.

4. Illustrate how a change in aggregate supply would cause deflation.

Aggregate Expenditure Components

© Wendell Metzen/Index Stock Imagery

When driving through a neighborhood new to you, how can you figure out the income of the residents? How would your spending change if you won the lottery? What's the most predictable and useful relationship in macroeconomics? Why are consumer confidence and business confidence in the economy so important? Answers to these and other questions are addressed in this chapter, which focuses on the makeup of aggregate expenditure. Consumption is the most important, accounting for about two-thirds of all spending. But in this short chapter, we also examine investment, government purchases, and net exports. We will discuss how each relates to income in the economy.

Let's see where this leads. In the next chapter, we combine these spending components to derive the aggregate demand curve. After that, we derive the aggregate supply curve and see how it interacts with the aggregate demand curve to determine the economy's equilibrium levels of price and output. Topics in the current chapter include:

- Consumption and income
- Marginal propensities to consume and to save
- Changes in consumption and in saving

- Investment
- Government purchases
- Net exports
- Composition of spending

Consumption

What if a new college friend invites you home for the weekend? On your first visit, you would get some idea of the family's standard of living. Is their house a mansion, a dump, or in between? Do they drive a new BMW or take the bus? The simple fact is that consumption tends to reflect income. Although some households can temporarily live beyond their means and others still have the first nickel they ever earned, in general consumption depends on income. *The positive and stable relationship between consumption and income, both for the household and for the economy as a whole, is the main point of this chapter.* Got it?

A key decision in the circular-flow model developed two chapters back was how much households spent and how much they saved. Consumption depends primarily on income. Although this relationship seems obvious, the link between consumption and income is fundamental to understanding how the economy works. Let's look at this link in the U.S. economy over time.

A First Look at Consumption and Income

Exhibit 1 shows consumer spending, or consumption, in the United States since 1959 as the red line and *disposable income* as the blue line. Disposable income, remember, is the income actually available for consumption and saving. Data have been adjusted for inflation so that dollars are of constant purchasing power—in this case, 2000 dollars. Notice that consumer spending and disposable income move together over time. Both increased nearly every year, and the relationship between the two appears stable. Specifically, consumer spending has averaged about 90 percent of disposable income. Disposable income minus consumption equals saving. In Exhibit 1, saving is measured by the vertical distance between the two lines. Saving has averaged about 10 percent of disposable income.

Another way to graph the relationship between consumption and income over time is shown in Exhibit 2, where consumption is measured along the vertical axis and disposable income along the horizontal axis. Notice that each axis measures the same units: trillions of 2000 dollars. Each year is depicted by a point that reflects two values: disposable income and consumption. For example, the combination for 1985, identified by the red point, shows that when disposable income (measured along the horizontal axis) was $4.6 trillion, consumption (measured along the vertical axis) was $4.1 trillion.

As you can see, there is a clear and direct relationship between consumption and disposable income, a relationship that should come as no surprise after Exhibit 1. You need little imagination to see that by connecting the dots in Exhibit 2, you could trace a line relating consumption to income. That relationship has special significance in macroeconomics.

EXHIBIT 1

Disposable Income, Consumption, and Saving in the United States

There is a clear and direct relationship between consumption, shown by the red line, and disposable income, shown by the blue line. Disposable income minus consumption equals saving, shown by the vertical distance between disposable income and consumption.

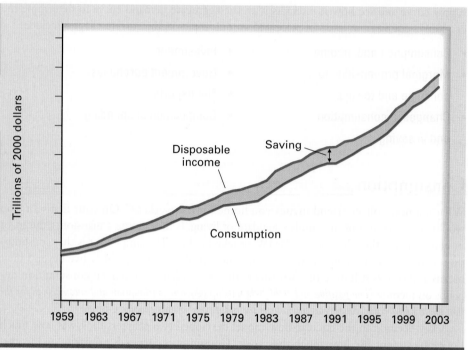

Source: Based on annual estimates from the Bureau of Economic Analysis, U.S. Department of Commerce. For the latest data, go to http://www.bea.doc.gov/bea/pubs.htm.

EXHIBIT 2

U.S. Consumption Depends on Disposable Income

Consumption is on the vertical axis and disposable income on the horizontal axis. Notice that each axis measures trillions of 2000 dollars. For example, in 1985, identified by the red point, consumption was $4.1 trillion and disposable income $4.6 trillion. There is a clear and direct relationship over time between disposable income and consumption. As disposable income increases, so does consumption.

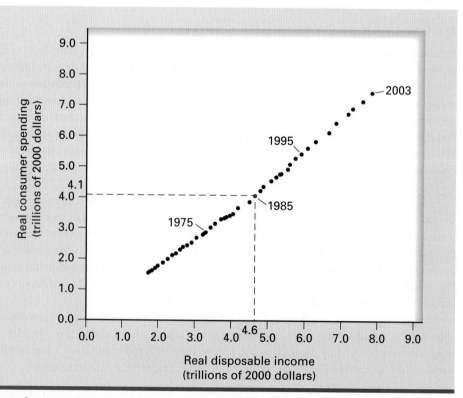

Source: Based on estimates from the Bureau of Economic Analysis, U.S. Department of Commerce. For the latest data, go to http://www.bea.doc.gov/bea/pubs.htm.

The Consumption Function

After examining the link between consumption and income, we found it to be quite stable. Based on their disposable income, households decide how much to consume and how much to save. So consumption depends on disposable income. *Consumption is the dependent variable and disposable income, the independent variable.* Because consumption depends on income, we say that consumption is a *function* of income. Exhibit 3 presents for the economy a hypothetical **consumption function,** which shows that consumption increases with disposable income, assuming other determinants of consumption remain constant. Again, both consumption and disposable income are in real terms, or in inflation-adjusted dollars. Notice that this hypothetical consumption function reflects the historical relationship between consumption and income shown in Exhibit 2.

Marginal Propensities to Consume and to Save

In Chapter 1, you learned that economic analysis focuses on activity at the margin. For example, what happens to consumption if income changes by a certain amount? Suppose U.S. households receive another billion dollars in disposable income. Some of it will be spent on consumption, and the rest will be saved. The fraction of the additional income that is spent is called the marginal propensity to consume. More precisely, the **marginal propensity to consume,** or **MPC,** equals the change in consumption divided by the change in income. Likewise, the fraction of that additional income that is saved is called the marginal propensity to save. More precisely, the **marginal propensity to save,** or **MPS,** equals the change in saving divided by the change in income.

For example, if U.S. income increases from $12.0 trillion to $12.5 trillion, consumption increases by $0.4 trillion and saving by $0.1 trillion. The marginal propensity to consume

CONSUMPTION FUNCTION

The relationship between consumption and income, other things constant

MARGINAL PROPENSITY TO CONSUME (MPC)

The fraction of a change in income that is spent on consumption; the change in consumption divided by the change in income that caused it

MARGINAL PROPENSITY TO SAVE (MPS)

The fraction of a change in income that is saved; the change in saving divided by the change in income that caused it

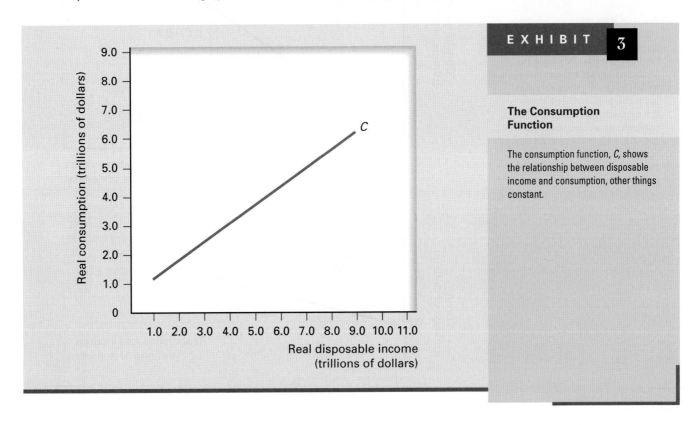

E X H I B I T   3

The Consumption Function

The consumption function, *C,* shows the relationship between disposable income and consumption, other things constant.

equals the change in consumption divided by the change in income. In this case, the change in consumption is \$0.4 trillion and the change in income is \$0.5 trillion, so the marginal propensity to consume is 0.4/0.5, or 4/5. Income not spent is saved. Saving increases by \$0.1 trillion as a result of the \$0.5 trillion increase in income, so the marginal propensity to save equals 0.1/0.5, or 1/5. Because disposable income is either spent or saved, the marginal propensity to consume plus the marginal propensity to save must sum to 1. In our example, $4/5 + 1/5 = 1$. We can say more generally that $MPC + MPS = 1$.

MPC, MPS, and the Slope of the Consumption and Saving Functions

You may recall from the appendix to Chapter 1 that the slope of a straight line is the vertical distance between any two points divided by the horizontal distance between those same two points. Consider, for example, the slope between points *a* and *b* on the consumption function in panel (a) of Exhibit 4, where Δ means "change in." The horizontal distance between these points shows the change in disposable income, denoted as ΔDI—in this case, \$0.5 trillion. The vertical distance shows the change in consumption, denoted as ΔC—in

---

EXHIBIT 4

Marginal Propensities to Consume and to Save

The slope of the consumption function equals the marginal propensity to consume. For the straight-line consumption function in panel (a), the slope is the same at all levels of income and is given by the change in consumption divided by the change in disposable income that causes it. Thus, the marginal propensity to consume equals $\Delta C/\Delta DI$, or 0.4/0.5 = 4/5. The slope of the saving function in panel (b) equals the marginal propensity to save, $\Delta S/\Delta DI$, or 0.1/0.5 = 1/5.

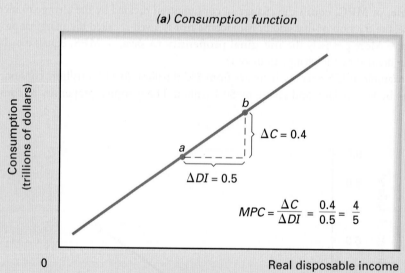

(a) Consumption function

$$MPC = \frac{\Delta C}{\Delta DI} = \frac{0.4}{0.5} = \frac{4}{5}$$

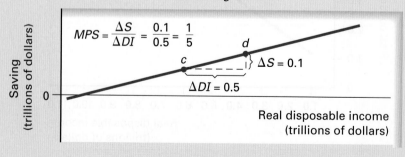

(b) Saving function

$$MPS = \frac{\Delta S}{\Delta DI} = \frac{0.1}{0.5} = \frac{1}{5}$$

this case, $0.4 trillion. The slope equals the vertical distance divided by the horizontal distance, or 0.4/0.5, which equals the marginal propensity to consume of 4/5.

Thus, *the marginal propensity to consume is measured graphically by the slope of the consumption function.* After all, the slope is nothing more than the increase in consumption divided by the increase in income. *Because the slope of any straight line is constant everywhere along the line, the MPC for any linear, or straight-line, consumption function is constant at all incomes.* We assume for convenience that the consumption function is a straight line, though it need not be.

Panel (b) of Exhibit 4 presents the **saving function,** *S,* which relates saving to income. The slope between any two points on the saving function measures the change in saving divided by the change in income. For example, between points *c* and *d* in panel (b) of Exhibit 4, the change in income is $0.5 trillion and the resulting change in saving is $0.1 trillion. The slope between these two points therefore equals 0.1/0.5, or 1/5, which by definition equals the marginal propensity to save. Because the marginal propensity to consume and the marginal propensity to save are simply different sides of the same coin, from here on we focus more on the marginal propensity to consume.

Nonincome Determinants of Consumption

Along a given consumption function, consumer spending depends on disposable income in the economy, other things constant. Now let's see what factors are held constant and how changes in them could cause the entire consumption function to shift.

Net Wealth and Consumption

Given the economy's income, an important influence on consumption is each household's **net wealth**—that is, the value of all assets that each household owns minus any liabilities, or debts. Your family's assets may include a home, furnishings, automobiles, bank accounts, cash, and the value of stocks, bonds, and pensions. Your family's liabilities, or debts, may include a mortgage, car loans, student loans, credit card balances, and the like. According to the Federal Reserve, the net wealth of U.S. households totaled $44.3 trillion at the end of 2003, the highest on record.[1] Net wealth increased in 2003 because of rising house prices and a recovery in stock market prices. Net wealth is a stock variable. Consumption and income are flow variables. Net wealth is assumed to be constant along a given consumption function.

A decrease in net wealth would make consumers less inclined to spend and more inclined to save at each income level. To see why, suppose prices fall sharply on the stock market. Stockholders are poorer than they were, so they spend less. For example, following the stock market crash of October 1987, consumption declined and saving increased. Household saving as a percentage of disposable income increased from 3.9 percent in the quarter before the crash to 5.7 percent in the quarter following the crash. Spending on new homes and cars fell. As another example, stock market declines in 2000, 2001, and 2002 cut into the purchases of luxury goods. Our original consumption function is depicted as line *C* in Exhibit 5. If net wealth declines, the consumption function shifts from *C* down to *C',* because households now spend less and save more at every income level.

Conversely, suppose stock prices increase sharply. This increase in net wealth increases the desire to spend. For example, stock prices surged in 1999, increasing stockholders' net wealth. Consumers spent 94 percent of disposable income that year compared with an average of about 90 percent during the first half of the 1990s. Purchases of homes and cars

SAVING FUNCTION

The relationship between saving and income, other things constant

NET WEALTH

The value of a assets minus liabilities

1. James Hagerty and Deborah Lagomarsino, "U.S. Household Wealth Hits Record," *Wall Street Journal*, 5 March 2004.

EXHIBIT   5

Shifts of the Consumption Function

A downward shift of the consumption function, such as from *C* to *C'*, can be caused by a decrease in wealth, an increase in the price level, an unfavorable change in consumer expectations, or an increase in the interest rate. An upward shift, such as from *C* to *C"*, can be caused by an increase in wealth, a decrease in the price level, a favorable change in expectations, or a decrease in the interest rate.

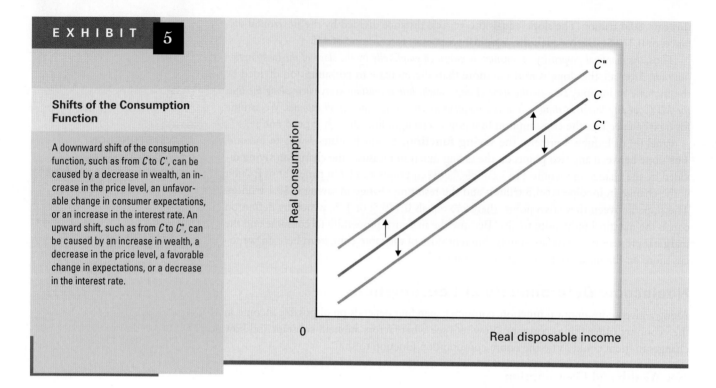

soared. Because of an increase in net wealth, the consumption function shifts from *C* up to *C"*, reflecting households' desire to spend more at each income level. Research by the Federal Reserve indicates that consumer spending eventually rises or falls between three to five cents for every dollar rise or fall in the value of stock market holdings.

Again, *it is a change in net wealth, not a change in disposable income, that shifts the consumption function. A change in disposable income, other things constant, means a movement along a given consumption function, not a shift of that function.* Be mindful of the difference between a movement along the consumption function, which results from a change in income, and a shift of the consumption function, which results from a change in one of the nonincome determinants of consumption, such as net wealth.

The Price Level

Another variable that can affect the consumption function is the price level prevailing in the economy. As we have seen, net wealth is an important determinant of consumption. The greater the net wealth, other things constant, the greater consumption will be at each income level. Some household wealth is held as money, such as cash and bank accounts. When the price level changes, so does the real value of cash and bank accounts.

For example, suppose your wealth consists of a $20,000 bank account. If the economy's price level increases by 5 percent, your bank account will buy about 5 percent less in real terms. You feel poorer because you are poorer. To rebuild the real value of your money holdings to some desired comfort level, you decide to spend less and save more. *An increase in the price level reduces the purchasing power of money holdings, causing households to consume less and save more at each income level.* So the consumption function would shift downward from *C* to *C'*, as shown in Exhibit 5.

Conversely, should the price level ever fall, as it did frequently before World War II and recently in Japan and Hong Kong, the real value money holdings increases. Households would be wealthier, so they decide to consume more and save less at each income level. For example, if the price level declined by 5 percent, your $20,000 bank account would then buy about 5 percent more in real terms. A drop in the price level would shift the consumption function from C up to C''. *At each income, a change in the price level influences consumption by affecting the real value of money holdings.*

The Interest Rate

Interest is the reward savers earn for deferring consumption and the cost borrowers pay for current spending power. When graphing the consumption function, we assume a given interest rate in the economy. If the interest rate increases, other things constant, savers or lenders are rewarded more, and borrowers are charged more. The higher the interest rate, the less is spent on those items typically purchased on credit, such as cars. Thus, at a higher interest rate, households save more, borrow less, and spend less. Greater saving at each income level means less consumption. Simply put, *a higher interest rate, other things constant, shifts the consumption function downward.* Conversely, *a lower interest rate, other things constant, shifts the consumption function upward.*

Expectations

Expectations influence economic behavior in a variety of ways. For example, suppose as a college senior, you land a good job that starts after graduation. Your consumption will probably jump long before the job actually begins because you expect an increase in your income; you might buy a car, for example. Conversely, a worker who gets a layoff notice to take effect at the end of the year will likely reduce consumption immediately, well before the actual date of the layoff. More generally, if people grow concerned about their job security, they will reduce the amount they consume at each income level.

Changing expectations about price levels and interest rates also affect consumption. For example, a change that leads householders to expect higher car prices or higher interest rates in the future will prompt some to buy new cars now. On the other hand, a change leading householders to expect lower prices or lower interest rates in the future will cause some to defer car purchases. Thus, expectations affect spending at each income, and a change in expectations can shift the consumption function. This is why economic forecasters monitor consumer confidence so closely.

Keep in mind the distinction between *movements along a given consumption function,* which result from a change in income, and *shifts in the consumption function,* which result from a change in one of the factors assumed to remain constant along a given consumption function. We conclude our introduction to consumption with the following case study, which discusses consumption and saving patterns over a lifetime.

The Life-Cycle Hypothesis

Do people with high incomes save a larger fraction of their incomes than those with low income? Both theory and evidence suggest they do. The easier it is to make ends meet, the more income is left over for saving. Does it follow from this that richer economies save more than poorer ones—that economies save a larger fraction of total disposable income as they grow? In his famous book, *The General Theory of Employment, Interest, and Money,* published in 1936, John Maynard Keynes drew that conclusion. But as later economists studied the

© EPA/AKIO SUG/AP Photo

C a s e S t u d y

Bringing Theory to Life

eActivity
Until quite recently, the Japanese government had been trying various changes in government spending and tax policies to encourage more consumer spending. However, the

Japanese public often would just put any extra income into savings. How could they be persuaded to spend more? An innovative policy was to issue purchase vouchers. The Japanese Information Network reports on these at http://web-japan.org/trends98/hon-bun/ntj981201.html. To whom did the government intend to distribute these coupons? Why? Would receiving 20,000 yen in vouchers ensure that spending would increase by that amount?

LIFE-CYCLE MODEL OF CONSUMPTION AND SAVING

Young people borrow, middle agers pay off debts and save, and older people draw down their savings; on average net savings over a lifetime is small

data—such as that presented in Exhibit 2—it became clear that Keynes was wrong. *The fraction of disposable income saved in an economy seems to stay constant as the economy grows.*

So how can it be that richer people save more than poorer people, yet richer countries do not necessarily save more than poorer ones? Several answers have been proposed. One of the most important is the **life-cycle model of consumption and saving.** According to this model, young people tend to borrow to finance education and home purchases. In middle age, people pay off debts and save more. In old age, they draw down their savings, or dissave. Some still have substantial wealth at death, because they are not sure when death will occur and because some parents want to bequeath wealth to their children. And some people die in debt. But on average net savings over a person's lifetime tend to be small. The life-cycle hypothesis suggests that the saving rate for an economy as a whole depends on, among other things, the relative number of savers and dissavers in the population.

Other factors that influence the saving rate across countries include the tax treatment of interest, the convenience and reliability of saving institutions, national customs, and the relative cost of a household's major purchase—housing. In Japan, for example, about 24,000 post offices nationwide offer convenient savings accounts. Japan's postal savings system holds over $2 trillion in savings deposits, more than one-third of Japan's total. Also, a home buyer in Japan must come up with a substantial down payment, one that represents a large fraction of the home's purchase price, and housing there is more expensive than in the United States. Finally, borrowing is considered by some Japanese to be shameful, so households save to avoid having to borrow. Because saving in Japan is necessary, convenient, and consistent with an aversion to borrowing, the country has one of the highest saving rates in the world. In a recent year, for example, Japanese households saved 13 percent of their disposable income compared with a saving rate of only about 4 percent in the United States.

Sources: "Leviathan Unbound," *The Economist,* 27 May 2003; Martin Browning and Thomas Crossley, "The Life-Cycle Model of Consumption and Saving," *Journal of Economic Perspective* 15 (Summer 2001): 3–22; *OECD Economic Outlook* 75 (June 2004); and "Overview of the Postal Savings Operation" at http://www.yu-cho.japanpost.jp/e_index.htm.

We turn next to the second component of aggregate expenditure—investment. Keep in mind that our initial goal is to understand the relationship between total spending and income.

Investment

The second component of aggregate expenditure is investment, or, more precisely, *gross private domestic investment.* Again, by *investment* we do not mean buying stocks, bonds, or other financial assets. Investment consists of spending on (1) new factories, office buildings, malls, and new equipment, such as computers; (2) new housing; and (3) net increases to inventories. Firms invest now in the expectation of a future return. Because the return is in the future, a would-be investor must estimate how much a particular investment will yield this year, next year, the year after, and in all years during the productive life of the investment. *Firms buy new capital goods only if they expect this investment to yield a higher return than other possible uses of their funds.*

The Demand for Investment

To understand the investment decision, let's consider a simple example. The operators of the Hacker Haven Golf Course are thinking about buying some solar-powered golf carts. The model under consideration, called the Weekend Warrior, sells for $2,000, requires no maintenance or operating expenses, and is expected to last indefinitely. *The expected rate of return of each cart equals the expected annual earnings divided by the cart's purchase price.* The first cart is expected to generate rental income of $400 per year. This income, divided by the cost of the cart, yields an expected rate of return on the investment of $400/$2,000, or 20 percent per year. Additional carts will be used less. A second is expected to generate $300 per year in rental income, yielding a rate of return of $300/$2,000, or 15 percent; a third cart, $200 per year, or 10 percent; and a fourth cart, $100 per year, or 5 percent. They don't expect a fifth cart will get rented at all, so it has a zero expected rate of return.

Should the operators of Hacker Haven invest in golf carts, and if so, how many? Suppose they plan to borrow the money to buy the carts. The number of carts they purchase will depend on the interest rate they must pay for borrowing. If the market interest rate exceeds 20 percent, the cost of borrowing would exceed the expected rate of return for even the first cart, so the club would buy no carts. What if the operators have enough cash on hand to buy the carts? The market interest rate also reflects what club owners could earn on savings. If the interest rate paid on savings exceeded 20 percent, course owners would earn more saving their money than buying golf carts. *The market interest rate is the opportunity cost of investing in capital.*

Suppose the market rate is 8 percent per year. At that rate, the first three carts, all with expected returns exceeding 8 percent, would each yield more than the market rate. A fourth cart would lose money, because its expected rate of return is only 5 percent. Exhibit 6 measures the nominal interest rate along the vertical axis and the amount invested in golf carts along the horizontal axis. The step-like relationship shows the expected rate of return earned on additional dollars invested in golf carts. This relationship also indicates the amount invested in golf carts at each interest rate, so you can view this step-like relationship as Hacker Haven's demand curve for this type of investment. For example, the first cart costs $2,000 and earns a rate of return of 20 percent. A firm should reject any investment with an expected rate of return that falls below the market rate of interest.

The horizontal line at 8 percent indicates the market interest rate, which is Hacker Haven's opportunity cost of investing. The course operators' objective is to choose an investment strategy that maximizes profit. Profit is maximized when $6,000 is invested in the

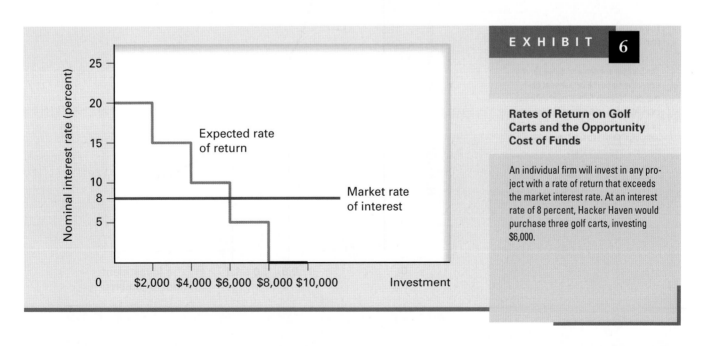

EXHIBIT 6

Rates of Return on Golf Carts and the Opportunity Cost of Funds

An individual firm will invest in any project with a rate of return that exceeds the market interest rate. At an interest rate of 8 percent, Hacker Haven would purchase three golf carts, investing $6,000.

carts—that is, when three carts are purchased. The expected return from a fourth cart is 5 percent, which is below the opportunity cost of funds. Therefore, investing in four or more carts would lower total profit.

From Micro to Macro

So far, we have looked at the investment decision for a single golf course, but there are over 13,000 golf courses in the United States. The industry demand for golf carts shows the relationship between the amount all courses invest and the expected rate of return. Like the step-like relationship in Exhibit 6, the investment demand curve for the golf industry slopes downward.

Let's move beyond golf carts and consider the invest decisions of all industries: publishing, hog farming, fast food, software, and thousands more. Individual industries have downward-sloping demand curves for investment. More is invested when the opportunity cost of borrowing is lower, other things constant. A downward-sloping investment demand curve for the entire economy can be derived, with some qualifications, from a horizontal summation of all industries' downward-sloping investment demand curves. The economy's *investment demand curve* is represented as *D* in Exhibit 7, which shows the inverse relationship between the quantity of investment demanded and the market interest rate, other things—including business expectations—held constant. For example, in Exhibit 7, when the market rate is 8 percent, the quantity of investment demanded is $1.0 trillion. If the interest rate rises to 10 percent, investment declines to $0.9 trillion, and if the rate falls to 6 percent, investment increases to $1.1 trillion. Assumed constant along the investment demand curve are business expectations about the economy. If firms grow more optimistic

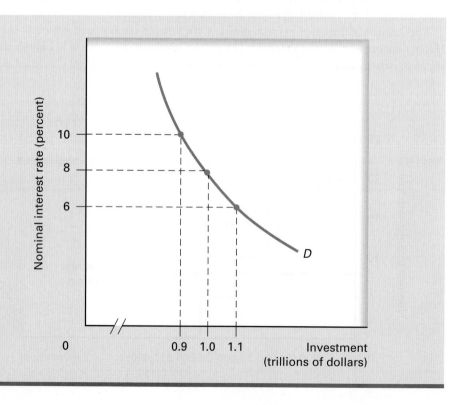

EXHIBIT 7

Investment Demand Curve for the Economy

The investment demand curve for the economy sums the investment demanded by each firm at each interest rate. At lower interest rates, more investment projects become profitable for individual firms, so total investment in the economy increases.

about profit prospects, the demand for investment increases, so the investment demand curve shifts to the right.

Planned Investment and the Economy's Income

To integrate the discussion of investment with our earlier analysis of consumption, we need to know if and how investment varies with income in the economy. Whereas we were able to present evidence relating consumption to income over time, the link between investment and income is weaker. Investment in a particular year shows little relation to income that year. *Investment depends more on interest rates and on business expectations than on the prevailing income.* One reason investment is less related to income is that some investments, such as a new power plant, take years to build. And investment, once in place, is expected to last for years, sometimes decades. The investment decision is thus said to be *forward looking*, based more on expected profit than on current income.

So how does the amount firms plan to invest relate to income? The simplest **investment function** assumes that *planned investment* is unrelated to disposable income. Planned investment is assumed to be **autonomous** with respect to disposable income. For example, suppose that, given current business expectations and an interest rate of 8 percent, firms plan to invest $1.0 trillion per year, regardless of the economy's income level. Exhibit 8 measures disposable income on the horizontal axis and planned investment on the vertical axis. Planned investment of $1.0 trillion is shown by the flat investment function, *I.* As you can see, along *I,* planned investment does not vary even though real disposable income does.

Nonincome Determinants of Planned Investment

The investment function isolates the relationship between income in the economy and *planned investment*—the amount firms would like to invest, other things constant. We have already mentioned two determinants that are assumed constant: the interest rate and business expectations. Now let's look at how changes in these factors affect investment.

Net **Bookmark**

For a personal view on Keynes and his work, read "Cairncross on Keynes," an obituary written by one of his students, Sir Alec Cairncross. It originally appeared in the *Economist* and is now available online at a site maintained by Professor Brad DeLong at http://econ161. berkeley.edu/Economists/ cairncrossonkeynes.html.

INVESTMENT FUNCTION

The relationship between the amount businesses plan to invest and the economy's income, other things constant

AUTONOMOUS

A term that means "independent"; for example, autonomous investment is independent of income

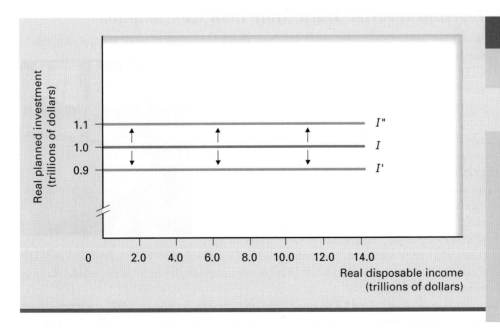

EXHIBIT 8

Planned Investment Function

Planned investment is assumed to be independent of income, as shown by the horizontal lines. Thus, planned investment is assumed to be autonomous. An increase in the interest rate or less favorable business expectations would decrease investment at every level of income, as shown by the downward shift from *I* to *I'*. A decrease in the interest rate or more upbeat business expectations would increase investment at every level of income, as shown by the upward shift from *I* to *I"*.

Market Interest Rate

Exhibit 7 shows that if the interest rate is 8 percent, planned investment is $1.0 trillion. This investment is also shown as *I* in Exhibit 8. If the interest rate increases because of, say, a change in the nation's monetary policy (as happened in 2004), the cost of borrowing increases, which increases the opportunity cost of investment. For example, if the interest rate increases from 8 percent to 10 percent, planned investment drops from $1.0 trillion to $0.9 trillion. This decrease is reflected in Exhibit 8 by a shift of the investment function from *I* down to *I'*. Conversely, if the interest rate decreases because of, say, a change in the nation's monetary policy (as happened in 2001 and 2002), the cost of borrowing decreases, which reduces the opportunity cost of investment. For example, a drop in the rate of interest from 8 percent to 6 percent, other things remaining constant, will reduce the cost of borrowing and increase planned investment from $1.0 trillion to $1.1 trillion, as reflected by the upward shift of the investment function from *I* to *I''*. Notice that the shifts in Exhibit 8 match interest rate movements along the investment demand curve in Exhibit 7.

Business Expectations

Investment depends primarily on business expectations, or on what Keynes called the "animal spirits" of business. Suppose planned investment initially is $1.0 trillion, as depicted by *I* in Exhibit 8. If firms now become more pessimistic about their profit prospects, perhaps expecting the worst, as in 2001 when terrorists leveled the World Trade Center, planned investment will decrease at every income, as reflected in Exhibit 8 by a shift of the investment function from *I* down to *I'*. On the other hand, if profit expectations become rosier, as they did in 2003, firms become more willing to invest, thereby increasing the investment function from *I* up to *I''*. *Examples of factors that could affect business expectations, and thus investment plans, include wars, technological change, tax changes, and destabilizing events such as terrorist attacks.* Changes in business expectations also shift the investment demand curve in Exhibit 7.

Now that we have examined consumption and investment individually, let's take a look at their year-to-year variability in the following case study.

Investment Varies Much More than Consumption

We already know that consumption makes up about two-thirds of GDP and that investment varies from year to year, averaging about one-sixth of GDP over the last decade. Now let's compare their year-to-year variability. Exhibit 9 shows the annual percentage changes in GDP, consumption, and investment, all measured in real terms. Two points are obvious. First, investment fluctuates much more than either consumption or GDP. For example, in the recession year of 1982, GDP declined 1.9 percent but investment crashed 14.0 percent; consumption actually increased 1.4 percent. In 1984, GDP increased 7.2 percent, consumption rose 5.3 percent, but investment soared 29.5 percent. Second, fluctuations in consumption and in GDP appear to be entwined, although consumption varies a bit less than GDP. Consumption varies less than GDP because consumption depends on disposable income, which varies less than GDP.

© Peter Morgan/Reuters/Corbis

During years of falling GDP since 1959, the average decline in GDP was 0.6 percent, but investment dropped an average of 11.7 percent. Consumption actually increased 0.6

EXHIBIT   9

Annual Percentage Change in U.S. Real GDP, Consumption, and Investment
Investment varies much more year-to-year than consumption does and accounts for nearly all the variability in real GDP. This is why economic forecasters pay special attention to the business outlook and investment plans.

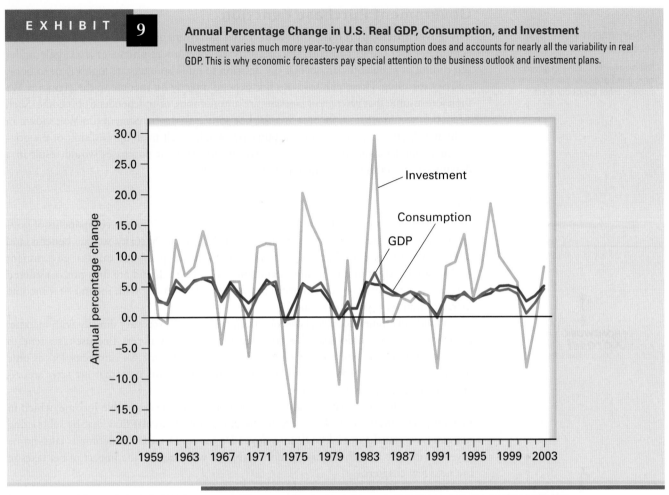

Source: Bureau of Economic Analysis, U.S. Department of Commerce. For the latest data, go to http://www.bea.doc.gov/bea/pubs.htm.

percent. So *while consumption is the largest spending component, investment varies much more than consumption and accounts for nearly all the year-to-year variability in real GDP.* Note that GDP does not always fall during years in which a recession occurs. For example, in the 2001 recession, GDP managed a tiny gain for the year of 0.5 percent and consumption increased 2.5 percent. It was the 8.3 percent fall in investment that caused the recession. This is why economic forecasters pay special attention to business expectations and investment plans.

that the types of consumption and investment spending cited in the text will change and affect real GDP?

Sources: *Economic Report of the President*, February 2004; U.S. Department of Commerce, *Survey of Current Business* 84, various months for 2004; and *OECD Economic Outlook* 75 (June 2004). For data and articles about economic aggregates, go to the Bureau of Economic Analysis site at http://www.bea.doc.gov/.

Government

The third component of aggregate expenditure is government purchases of goods and services. Federal, state, and local governments purchase thousands of goods and services, ranging from weapon systems to road signs. During the last decade, government purchases in the United States accounted for a little less than one-fifth of GDP, most of that by state and local governments.

Government Purchase Function

The **government purchase function** relates government purchases to income in the economy, other things constant. Decisions about government purchases are largely under the control of public officials, such as the decision to build an interstate highway or to boost military spending. These purchases do not depend directly on income in the economy. We therefore assume that *government purchases* are autonomous, or independent of income. Such a function would relate to income as a flat line similar to the investment function shown in Exhibit 8. An increase in government purchases would result in an upward shift of the government purchase function. And a decrease in government purchases would result in a downward shift of the government purchase function.

Net Taxes

As noted earlier, government purchases represent only one of the two components of government outlays; the other is *transfer payments,* such as Social Security, welfare benefits, and unemployment benefits. Transfer payments, which make up about a third of government outlays, are outright grants from governments to households and are thus not considered part of aggregate expenditure. Transfer payments vary inversely with income—as income increases, transfer payments decline.

To fund government outlays, governments impose taxes. Taxes vary directly with income; as income increases, so do taxes. *Net taxes* equal taxes minus transfers. Because taxes tend to increase with income but transfers tend to decrease with income, for simplicity, let's assume that net taxes do not vary with income. Thus, we assume for now that *net taxes* are *autonomous,* or independent of income.

Net taxes affect aggregate spending indirectly by changing disposable income, which in turn changes consumption. We saw from the discussion of circular flow that by subtracting net taxes, we transform real GDP into *disposable income.* Disposable income is take-home pay—the income households can spend or save. We will examine the impact of net taxes in the next few chapters.

Net Exports

The rest of the world affects aggregate expenditure through imports and exports and has a growing influence on the U.S. economy. The United States, with only one-twentieth of the world's population, accounts for about one-sixth of the world's imports and one-ninth of the world's exports.

Net Exports and Income

How do imports and exports relate to the economy's income? When incomes rise, Americans spend more on all normal goods, including imports. Higher incomes lead to more spending on Persian rugs, French wine, Korean DVD players, German cars, Chinese toys, European vacations, African safaris, and thousands of other foreign goods and services.

How do U.S. exports relate to the economy's income? U.S. exports depend on the income of foreigners, not on U.S. income. U.S. disposable income does not affect French purchases of U.S. computers or Saudi Arabian purchases of U.S. military hardware. The **net export function** shows the relationship between net exports and U.S. income, other things constant. Because our exports are insensitive to U.S. income but our imports tend to increase with income, *net exports,* which equal the value of exports minus the value of imports, tend to decline as U.S. incomes increase. Such an inverse relationship is developed

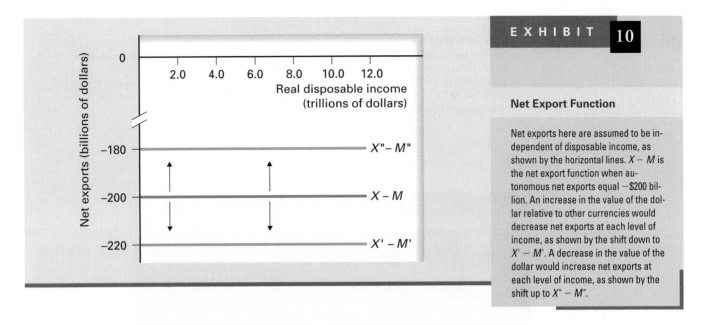

Net Export Function

Net exports here are assumed to be in-dependent of disposable income, as shown by the horizontal lines. $X - M$ is the net export function when au-tonomous net exports equal −$200 bil-lion. An increase in the value of the dol-lar relative to other currencies would decrease net exports at each level of income, as shown by the shift down to $X' - M'$. A decrease in the value of the dollar would increase net exports at each level of income, as shown by the shift up to $X'' - M''$.

graphically in the appendix to this chapter. For now, we assume that net exports are *au-tonomous,* or independent of income.

If exports exceed imports, net exports are positive; if imports exceed exports, net exports are negative; and if exports equal imports, net exports are zero. U.S. net exports have been negative nearly every year during the past three decades, so let's suppose net exports are au-tonomous and equal to −$0.2 trillion, or −$200 billion, as shown by the net export func-tion $X - M$ in Exhibit 10.

Nonincome Determinants of Net Exports

Factors assumed constant along the net export function include the U.S. price level, price levels in other countries, interest rates here and abroad, foreign income levels, and the ex-change rate between the dollar and foreign currencies. Consider the effects of a change in one of these factors. Suppose the value of the dollar increases relative to foreign currencies such as those of Asia, as happened in 1998. With the dollar worth more on world markets, foreign products become cheaper for Americans, and U.S. products become more costly for foreigners. A rise in the dollar's exchange value will increase imports and decrease exports, thus reducing net exports, shown in Exhibit 10 by a parallel drop in the net export line from $X - M$ down to $X' - M'$, a decline from −$200 billion to −$220 billion.

A decline in the value of the dollar, as occurred in 2003, will have the opposite effect, in-creasing exports and decreasing imports. An increase in autonomous net exports is shown in our example by a parallel increase in the net export function, from $X - M$ up to $X'' - M''$, reflecting an increase in autonomous net exports from −$200 billion to −$180 billion. A country sometimes tries to devalue its currency in an attempt to increase its net exports and thereby increase employment. The effect of changes in net exports on aggregate spending will be taken up in the next chapter.

Composition of Aggregate Expenditure

Now that we have examined each component of aggregate spending, let's get a better idea of spending over time. Exhibit 11 shows the composition of spending in the United States

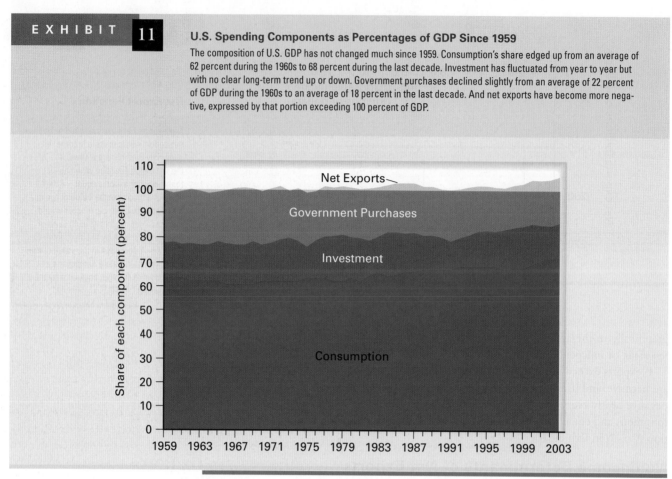

EXHIBIT 11

U.S. Spending Components as Percentages of GDP Since 1959

The composition of U.S. GDP has not changed much since 1959. Consumption's share edged up from an average of 62 percent during the 1960s to 68 percent during the last decade. Investment has fluctuated from year to year but with no clear long-term trend up or down. Government purchases declined slightly from an average of 22 percent of GDP during the 1960s to an average of 18 percent in the last decade. And net exports have become more negative, expressed by that portion exceeding 100 percent of GDP.

Source: Computed from annual estimates in *Survey of Current Business* 84 (February 2004). For the latest data, go to http://www.bea.doc.gov/bea/pubs.htm.

since 1959. As you can see, consumption's share of GDP appears stable from year to year, but the long-term trend shows an increase from an average of 62 percent during the 1960s to 68 percent during the last decade. Investment fluctuates more from year to year but with no long-term trend up or down.

Government purchases declined from an average of 22 percent of GDP during the 1960s to an average of 18 percent during the last decade, due primarily to decreases in defense spending. (But defense spending has picked up lately with the war on terrorism.) Net exports averaged 0.3 percent of GDP in the 1960s but were negative nearly every year since then, averaging a minus 2.5 percent of GDP during the last decade. Negative net exports mean that the sum of spending on consumption, investment, and government purchases exceeds GDP, the amount produced in the U.S. economy. Americans are spending more than they make, and they are covering the difference by borrowing from abroad. U.S. spending exceeds U.S. GDP by the amount shown as negative net exports. Because the spending components must sum to GDP, *negative* net exports are expressed in Exhibit 11 by that portion of spending that exceeds 100 percent of GDP.

In summary: During the last four decades, consumption's share of total spending increased and government purchases decreased. Investment's share bounced around and net exports' share turned negative, meaning that imports exceeded exports.

Conclusion

This chapter has focused on the relationship between spending and income. We considered the four components of aggregate expenditure: consumption, investment, government purchases, and net exports. Consumption increases with income. Investment relates more to interest rates and business expectations than it does to income. Government purchases also tend to be autonomous, or independent of income. And net exports are assumed, for now, to be affected more by such factors as the exchange rate than by U.S. income. The appendix to this chapter develops a more realistic but also more complicated picture by showing how net exports decline as income increases. In the next chapter, we will see how aggregate spending depends on income and how this link helps shape the aggregate demand curve.

SUMMARY

1. The most predictable and most useful relationship in macroeconomics is between consumption and income. The more people have to spend, the more they spend on consumption, other things constant.

2. The consumption function shows the link between consumption and income in the economy. The slope of the consumption function reflects the marginal propensity to consume, which equals the change in consumption divided by the change in income. The slope of the saving function reflects the marginal propensity to save, which equals the change in saving divided by the change in income.

3. Certain factors can cause consumers to change the amount they want to spend at each income level. An increase in net wealth reduces the need to save, thus increasing consumption at every income. A higher price level reduces the value of money holdings, thereby reducing net wealth, which in turn reduces consumption. An increase in the interest rate makes saving more rewarding and borrowing more costly, thus increasing saving and decreasing consumption at each income. Expectations about future incomes, prices, and interest rates also influence consumption.

4. Planned investment depends on the market interest rate and on business expectations. Investment fluctuates from year to year but averaged about one-sixth of GDP during the last decade. We assume for now that investment in the economy is unrelated to income.

5. Government purchases of goods and services averaged a little less than one-fifth of GDP during the last decade. Government purchases are based on the public choices of elected officials and are assumed to be autonomous, or independent of the economy's income level. Net taxes, or taxes minus transfer payments, are also assumed for now to be unrelated to income.

6. Net exports equal the value of exports minus the value of imports. U.S. exports depend on foreign income, not on U.S. income. Imports increase with U.S. income. So net exports decline as income increases. For simplicity, however, we initially assume that net exports are autonomous, or unrelated to domestic income.

QUESTIONS FOR REVIEW

1. *(Consumption Function)* How would an increase in each of the following affect the consumption function? How would it affect the saving function?

   a. Autonomous net taxes
   b. The interest rate
   c. Consumer optimism, or confidence
   d. The price level
   e. Consumers' net wealth
   f. Disposable income

2. *(Consumption Function)* A number of factors can cause the consumption function to shift. What, if anything, happens to the saving function when the consumption function shifts? Explain.

3. *(C a s e* **S t u d y :** The Life-Cycle Hypothesis) According to the life-cycle hypothesis, what is the typical pattern of saving for an individual over his or her lifetime? What impact does this behavior have on an individual's lifetime consumption pattern? What impact does the behavior have on the saving rate in the overall economy?

4. *(Investment)* What are the components of gross private domestic investment? What is the difference between the investment curve shown in Exhibit 6 and the one shown in Exhibit 7?

5. *(Investment)* Why would the following investment expenditures increase as the interest rate declines?

   a. Purchases of a new plant and equipment
   b. Construction of new housing
   c. Accumulation of planned inventories

6. *(Nonincome Determinants of Investment)* What are some factors assumed to be constant along the autonomous planned investment function? What kinds of changes in each factor could cause investment spending to increase at each level of real disposable income?

7. *(C a s e* **S t u d y :** Investment Varies Much More Than Consumption) Why do economic forecasters pay special attention to investment plans? Take a look at the Conference Board's index of leading economic indictors at http://www.conferenceboard.org. Which of those indicators might affect investment?

8. *(Government Spending)* How do changes in disposable income affect government purchases and the government purchase function? How do changes in net taxes affect the consumption function?

9. *(Net Exports)* What factors are assumed constant along the net export function? What would be the impact on net exports of a change in real disposable income?

PROBLEMS AND EXERCISES

10. *(Consumption)* Use the following data to answer the questions below:

Real Disposable Income (billions)	Consumption Expenditures (billions)	Saving (billions)
$100	$150	$_____
200	200	_____
300	250	_____
400	300	_____

   a. Graph the consumption function, with consumption spending on the vertical axis and disposable income on the horizontal axis.
   b. If the consumption function is a straight line, what is its slope?
   c. Fill in the saving column at each level of income. If the saving function is a straight line, what is its slope?

11. *(MPC and MPS)* If consumption increases by $12 billion when disposable income increases by $15 billion, what is the value of the MPC? What is the relationship between the MPC and the MPS? If the MPC increases, what must happen to the MPS? How is the MPC related to the consumption function? How is the MPS related to the saving function?

12. *(Consumption and Saving)* Suppose that consumption equals $500 billion when disposable income is $0 and that each increase of $100 billion in disposable income causes consumption to increase by $70 billion. Draw a graph of the saving function using this information.

13. *(Investment Spending)* Review Exhibit 6 in this chapter. If the operators of the golf course revised their revenue estimates so that each cart is expected to earn $100 less, how many carts would they buy at an interest rate of 8 percent? How many would they buy if the interest rate is 3 percent?

EXPERIENTIAL EXERCISES

14. *(Marginal Propensity to Consume)* Find some recent data on U.S. real disposable income and real consumption spending. (One possible source is the *Economic Report of the President* at http://w3.access.gpo.gov/eop/, but there are many others.) Use the data to compute the marginal propensity to consume for each year, 1991 to 2004. Has the MPC been relatively constant?

15. *(Variability of Consumption and Investment)* Expectations and consumer confidence are important in determining fluctuations in aggregate spending. What is the present status of consumer confidence as measured by the Conference

Board's index? You can find the data, with interpretation, at The Conference Board at http://www.conference-board.org/economics/consumerConfidence.cfm.

16. *(Wall Street Journal)* Business investment spending is an important component of aggregate expenditure. Review the "Business Bulletin" column on the front page of Thursday's *Wall Street Journal*. What are some recent trends in investment spending? Are they likely to increase or decrease aggregate expenditure? (Remember that purchases of stocks and bonds are not investment, in the sense described in this chapter!)

HOMEWORK XPRESS! EXERCISES

These exercises require access to McEachern Homework Xpress! If Homework Xpress! did not come with your book, visit **http://homeworkxpress.swlearning.com** *to purchase.*

1. In the diagram for this exercise, plot the consumption function line for the data in the table below. Calculate savings at each level of real disposable income and plot the savings function.

Real Disposable Income (trillions)	Consumption (trillions)
$2.00	$2.50
3.00	3.25
4.00	4.00
5.00	4.75
6.00	5.50
7.00	6.25
8.00	7.00

2. In the diagram draw a linear consumption function. Illustrate the effect on the consumption function of an in-

crease in net wealth. Then illustrate the effect on the consumption function of an increase in the price level.

3. In the diagram sketch an investment demand curve illustrating the relationship between the quantity of investment undertaken and the interest rate.

4. In the diagram sketch an autonomous investment function showing the level of investment as $1 trillion at the current market interest rate. Illustrate the effect on the function of an inprovement in business expectations. Then illustrate the effect of an increase in the interest rate.

5. In the diagram, sketch an autonomous net export function showing the U.S. economy with a trade balance of $−50 billion. Illustrate how a decrease in the value of the U.S. dollar could lead to a positive trade balance. Then illustrate the effect of a decrease in the value of the currency of a major trading partner.

Variable Net Exports

In this appendix, we examine the relationship between net exports and U.S. income. We first look at exports and imports separately and then consider exports minus imports, or net exports.

Net Exports and Income

As noted earlier in the chapter, the amount of U.S. output purchased by foreigners depends not on U.S. income but on income in foreign countries. We therefore assume that U.S. exports do not vary with U.S. income. Specifically, suppose the rest of the world spends $0.9 trillion, of $900 billion, per year on U.S. exports of goods and services. The export function, X, is as shown in panel (a) of Exhibit 12. But when income increases, Americans spend more on all goods and services, including imports. Thus, the relationship between imports and income is positive, as expressed by the upward-sloping import function, M, in panel (b) of Exhibit 12. If Americans spend 10 percent of their disposable income on imports, when disposable income is $9.0 trillion, imports are $0.9 trillion.

So far, we have considered imports and exports as separate functions of income. What matters in terms of total spending on U.S. products are exports, X, minus imports, M, or net exports, $X - M$. Because money spent on imports goes to foreign producers, not U.S. producers, imports get subtracted from the circular flow of spending. By subtracting the import function depicted in panel (b) from the export function in panel (a), we derive the *net export function*, depicted as $X - M$ in panel (c) of Exhibit 12.

Because exports in panel (a) equal $0.9 trillion at all levels of income, net exports equal zero when U.S. disposable income is $9.0 trillion. At incomes less than $9.0 trillion, net exports are positive because exports exceed imports. At incomes greater than $9.0 trillion, net exports are negative because imports exceed exports. As a case in point, recessions in 1991 and 2001 reduced the trade deficits those years as imports declined. As the economy recovered, the trade deficit increased, reaching a record to that point in 2004.

Shifts of Net Exports

The net export function, $X - M$, shows the relationship between net exports and disposable income, other things constant. Suppose the value of the dollar increases relative to for-

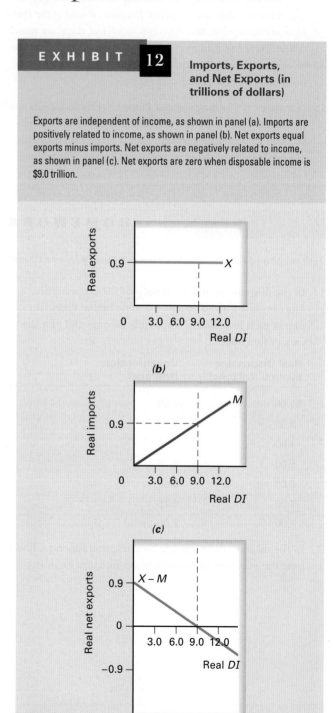

EXHIBIT **12**

Imports, Exports, and Net Exports (in trillions of dollars)

Exports are independent of income, as shown in panel (a). Imports are positively related to income, as shown in panel (b). Net exports equal exports minus imports. Net exports are negatively related to income, as shown in panel (c). Net exports are zero when disposable income is $9.0 trillion.

eign currencies, as happened in 1999. With the dollar worth more, foreign products become cheaper for Americans, and U.S. products become more expensive for foreigners. The impact of a rising dollar is to decrease exports but increase imports at each income level, thus decreasing net exports. This relationship is shown in Exhibit 13 by the shift from $X - M$ down to $X' - M'$. A decline in the dollar's value, as occurred in 2003, has the opposite effect, increasing exports and de-

creasing imports, as reflected in Exhibit 13 by an upward shift of the net export function from $X - M$ to $X'' - M''$.

In summary, in this appendix we assumed that imports relate positively to income, whereas exports are independent of domestic income. Therefore, net exports, which equal exports minus imports, vary inversely with income. The net export function shifts downward if the value of the dollar rises and shifts upward if the value of the dollar falls.

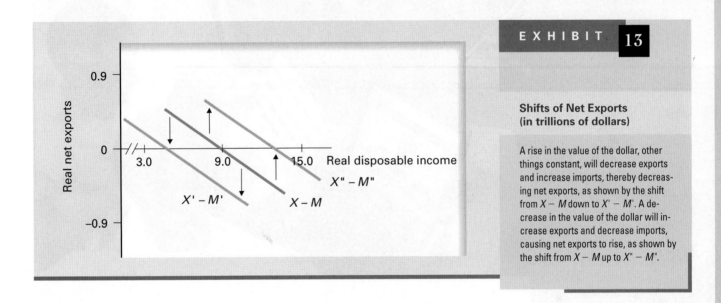

EXHIBIT 13

Shifts of Net Exports (in trillions of dollars)

A rise in the value of the dollar, other things constant, will decrease exports and increase imports, thereby decreasing net exports, as shown by the shift from $X - M$ down to $X' - M'$. A decrease in the value of the dollar will increase exports and decrease imports, causing net exports to rise, as shown by the shift from $X - M$ up to $X'' - M''$.

APPENDIX QUESTION

1. *(Rest of the World)* Using a graph of net exports $(X - M)$ against disposable income, show the effects of the following. Explain each of your answers.

   a. An increase in foreign disposable income
   b. An increase in U.S. disposable income

   c. An increase in the U.S. interest rate
   d. An increase in the value of the dollar against foreign currencies

Aggregate Expenditure and Aggregate Demand

© Jon Riley/Index Stock Imagery

N ow that we have considered consumption, investment, government purchases, and net exports, how do we combine them to get aggregate expenditure for the economy? How is aggregate expenditure linked to income? How does a change in spending ripple through the economy, magnifying the impact? For example, how did the fear of flying after the terrorist attacks of September 11 affect the economy as a whole? What happens to spending if the economy's price level changes? Answers to these and other questions are covered in this chapter, which develops the aggregate demand curve.

Your economic success depends in part on the overall performance of the economy. When the economy grows, job opportunities expand, so your chances of finding a good job increase. When the economy contracts, job opportunities shrink, and so do your job prospects. Thus, you have a personal stake in the economy's success.

The previous chapter showed how each spending component relates to income in the economy. In this chapter, these components are added to learn how total spending, or aggregate expenditure, relates to income. We then see how a change in the economy's price level affects aggregate expenditure. All this is aimed at getting to the economy's aggregate demand curve. Aggregate supply will be developed in the next chapter. The effects of government spending and taxing will be explored in the chapter after that. Topics discussed include:

- Aggregate expenditure line
- Real GDP demanded
- Changes in aggregate expenditure

- Simple spending multiplier
- Changes in the price level
- Aggregate demand curve

Aggregate Expenditure and Income

In the previous chapter, the big idea was the link between consumption and income, a link that is the most stable in all of macroeconomics. In this section, we build on that connection to uncover the link between total spending in the economy and income. If we try to confront the economy head-on, it soon becomes a bewildering maze, which is why we make progress by beginning with simple models. We continue to assume, as we did in developing the circular-flow model, that there is no capital depreciation and no business saving. Thus, we can say that *each dollar of spending translates directly into a dollar of aggregate income.* Therefore, gross domestic product, or GDP, equals aggregate income. We also continue to assume that investment, government purchases, and net exports are *autonomous,* or independent of the income. Appendix A shows what happens when imports increase with income, and Appendix B develops the algebra behind all this.

The Components of Aggregate Expenditure

Let's begin developing the aggregate demand curve by asking how much aggregate output would be demanded at a given price level. By finding the quantity demanded at a given price level, we'll identify a single point on the aggregate demand curve. We begin by considering the relationship between aggregate spending in the economy and aggregate income. To get us started, suppose the price level in the economy is 130, or 30 percent higher than in the base year. We want to find out how much will be spent at various levels of real income, or real GDP. By *real* GDP, we mean GDP measured in terms of real goods and services produced. Exhibit 1 puts into tabular form relationships introduced in the previous chapter—consumption, saving, planned investment, government purchases, net taxes, and net exports. Although the entries are hypothetical, they bear some relation to levels observed in the U.S. economy. For example, real GDP in the U.S. economy is nearly $12 trillion a year.

Column (1) lists possible real GDP levels in the economy, symbolized by Y. Remember, real GDP also means real income in the economy. Column (2) shows *net taxes,* or *NT,* assumed here to be $1.0 trillion at each real GDP level. Subtracting net taxes from real GDP yields *disposable income,* listed in column (3) as $Y - NT$. Note that at each real GDP level, disposable income equals real GDP minus net taxes of $1.0 trillion. Because net taxes do not vary with income, each time real GDP increases by $0.5 trillion, disposable income also increases by $0.5 trillion.

Households have only two possible uses for disposable income: consumption and saving. Columns (4) and (5) show that the levels of *consumption, C,* and *saving, S,* increase with disposable income. Each time real GDP and disposable income increase by $0.5 trillion, con-

EXHIBIT 1		**Real GDP with Net Taxes and Government Purchases (trillions of dollars)**							
(1) Real GDP (Y)	(2) Net Taxes (NT)	(3) Disposable Income (Y − NT) (3) =(1) − (2)	(4) Consumption (C)	(5) Saving (S)	(6) Planned Investment (I)	(7) Government Purchases (G)	(8) Net Exports (X − M)	(9) Planned Aggregate Expenditure (AE)	(10) Unplanned Inventory Adjustment (Y − AE) (10) = (1) − (9)
11.0	1.0	10.0	9.4	0.6	1.0	1.0	−0.2	11.2	−0.2
11.5	1.0	10.5	9.8	0.7	1.0	1.0	−0.2	11.6	−0.1
12.0	**1.0**	**11.0**	**10.2**	**0.8**	**1.0**	**1.0**	**−0.2**	**12.0**	**0.0**
12.5	1.0	11.5	10.6	0.9	1.0	1.0	−0.2	12.4	+0.1
13.0	1.0	12.0	11.0	1.0	1.0	1.0	−0.2	12.8	+0.2

sumption increases by $0.4 trillion and saving increases by $0.1 trillion. Thus, as in the previous chapter, the marginal propensity to consume is 4/5, or 0.8, and the marginal propensity to save is 1/5, or 0.2.

Columns (6), (7), and (8) list three now-familiar injections of spending into the circular flow: *planned investment* of $1.0 trillion, *government purchases* of $1.0 trillion, and *net exports* of −$0.2 trillion. In the table, government purchases equal net taxes, so the government budget is balanced. We first want to see how a balanced budget works before we consider the effects of budget deficits or surpluses, which will be discussed in the chapter after next. *The sum of consumption, C, planned investment, I, government purchases, G, and net exports, X − M, is listed in column (9) as planned aggregate expenditure, AE, which shows how much households, firms, governments, and the rest of the world plan to spend on U.S. output at each level of real GDP, or real income.* Note that the only spending component that varies with real GDP is consumption. As real GDP increases, so does disposable income, which increases consumption.

The final column in Exhibit 1 lists any unplanned adjustment to inventories, which equal real GDP minus planned aggregate expenditure, or *Y* − *AE*. For example, when real GDP is $11.0 trillion, planned aggregate expenditure is $11.2 trillion. Because planned spending exceeds the amount produced by $0.2 trillion, firms must rely on inventories to make up the shortfall in output. So when real GDP is $11.0 trillion, the unplanned inventory adjustment in the final column is −$0.2 trillion. Because firms cannot reduce inventories indefinitely, they respond to shortfalls in output by increasing production, and they continue to do so until they produce the amount people want to buy—that is, until real GDP equals planned aggregate expenditure.

If the amount produced exceeds planned spending, firms get stuck with unsold goods, which become unplanned increases in inventories. For example, if real GDP is $13.0 trillion, planned aggregate expenditure is only $12.8 trillion, so $0.2 trillion in output remains unsold. Thus, inventories increase by $0.2 trillion. Firms respond by reducing output and do so until they produce the amount people want to buy.

Note the distinction here between **planned investment,** the amount firms plan to invest, and **actual investment,** which includes both planned investment and any unplanned

PLANNED INVESTMENT

The amount of investment that firms plan to undertake during a year

ACTUAL INVESTMENT

The amount of investment actually undertaken; equals planned investment plus unplanned changes in inventories

changes in inventories. Unplanned increases in inventories cause firms to smarten up and decrease their production next time around so as not to get stuck with more unsold goods. When the amount people plan to spend equals the amount produced, there are no unplanned inventory adjustments. And when there are no unplanned adjustments in inventories, planned investment equals actual investment. More precisely, *at a given price level, the quantity of real GDP demanded occurs where spending plans match the amount produced.* In Exhibit 1, this occurs where both planned aggregate expenditure and real GDP equal $12.0 trillion.

Real GDP Demanded

Using a table, we have seen how firms adjust output until production just equals desired spending. You may find graphs easier. Graphs are more general than tables and can show relationships between variables without focusing on specific numbers. The tabular relationship between real GDP and planned aggregate expenditure in Exhibit 1 can be expressed as an **aggregate expenditure line** in Exhibit 2. Like the planned aggregate expenditure amounts shown in column (9) of Exhibit 1, the aggregate expenditure line in Exhibit 2 reflects the sum of consumption, planned investment, government purchases, and net exports, or $C + I + G + (X - M)$. Aggregate expenditure is measured on the vertical axis.

Real GDP, measured along the horizontal axis in Exhibit 2, can be viewed in two ways—as the value of *aggregate output* and as the *aggregate income* generated by that output. Because real GDP, or aggregate income, is measured on the horizontal axis and aggregate expenditure is measured on the vertical axis, this graph is often called the **income-expenditure model.** To gain perspective on the relationship between income and expenditure, we use a handy analytical tool: the 45-degree ray from the origin. The special feature of this line is that any point along it is the same distance from each axis. Thus, the 45-degree line

AGGREGATE EXPENDITURE LINE

A relationship showing, for a given price level, planned spending at each income, or real GDP; the total of $C + I + G + (X - M)$ at each income, or real GDP

INCOME-EXPENDITURE MODEL

A relationship between aggregate income and aggregate spending that determines, for a given price level, where the amount people plan to spend equals the amount produced

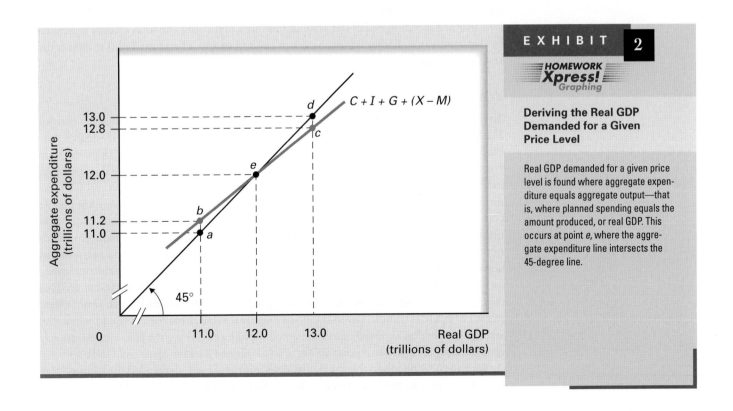

EXHIBIT 2

HOMEWORK **Xpress!** *Graphing*

Deriving the Real GDP Demanded for a Given Price Level

Real GDP demanded for a given price level is found where aggregate expenditure equals aggregate output—that is, where planned spending equals the amount produced, or real GDP. This occurs at point *e*, where the aggregate expenditure line intersects the 45-degree line.

identifies all points where planned expenditure equals real GDP. *Aggregate output demanded at a given price level occurs where planned aggregate expenditure, measured along the vertical axis, equals real GDP, measured along the horizontal axis.* In Exhibit 2, this occurs at point *e,* where the aggregate expenditure line intersects the 45-degree line. At point *e,* the amount people plan to spend equals the amount produced. We conclude that, at the given price level of 130, the quantity of real GDP demanded equals $12.0 trillion.

What If Planned Spending Exceeds Real GDP?

To find the real GDP demanded at the given price level, consider what happens when real GDP is initially less than $12.0 trillion. As you can see from Exhibit 2, when real GDP is less than $12.0 trillion, the aggregate expenditure line is above the 45-degree line, indicating that planned spending exceeds the amount produced (give this a little thought). For example, if real GDP is $11.0 trillion, planned spending is $11.2 trillion, as indicated by point *b* on the aggregate expenditure line, so planned spending exceeds output by $0.2 trillion. When the amount people plan to spend exceeds the amount produced, something has to give. Ordinarily what gives is the price, but remember that we are seeking the real GDP demanded for a given price level, so the price level is assumed to remain constant, at least for now. What gives in this model are *inventories.* Unplanned reductions in inventories make up the $0.2 trillion shortfall in output. Because firms can't draw down inventories indefinitely, *unplanned inventory reductions* prompt firms to produce more. That increases employment and consumer income, leading to more spending. As long as planned spending exceeds output, firms increase production to make up the difference. This process of more output, more income, and more spending will continue until planned spending equals real GDP, an equality achieved at point *e* in Exhibit 2.

When output reaches $12.0 trillion, planned spending exactly matches output, so no unintended inventory adjustments occur. More importantly, when output reaches $12.0 trillion, planned spending equals the amount produced and equals the total income generated by that production. Earlier we assumed a price level of 130. Therefore, $12.0 trillion is the real GDP demanded at that price level.

What If Real GDP Exceeds Planned Spending?

To reinforce the logic of the model, consider what happens when real GDP initially exceeds $12.0 trillion—that is, when the aggregate expenditure line is below the 45-degree line. Notice in Exhibit 2 that, to the right of point *e,* planned spending falls short of production. For example, if the amount produced in the economy is $13.0 trillion, planned spending, as indicated by point *c* on the aggregate expenditure line, is $0.2 trillion less than real GDP, indicated by point *d* on the 45-degree line. Because real GDP exceeds the amount people plan to buy, unsold goods accumulate. This swells inventories by $0.2 trillion more than firms planned. Rather than allow inventories to pile up indefinitely, firms reduce production, which reduces employment and income. As an example of such behavior, a recent news account read, "General Motors will idle two assembly plants in a move to trim inventories in the wake of slowing sales." *Unplanned inventory buildups* cause firms to cut production until the amount they produce equals aggregate spending, which occurs, again, where real GDP is $12.0 trillion. Given the price level, real GDP demanded is found where the amount people plan to spend equals the amount produced. *For a given price level, there is only one point along the aggregate expenditure line at which planned spending equals real GDP.*

We have now discussed the forces that determine real GDP demanded for a given price level. In the next section, we examine changes that can shift planned spending.

The Simple Spending Multiplier

In the previous section, we used the aggregate expenditure line to find real GDP demanded for a particular price level. In this section, we continue to assume that the price level remains unchanged as we trace the effects of changes in planned spending. Like a stone thrown into a still pond, the effect of any shift of planned spending ripples through the economy, generating changes in aggregate output that exceed the initial change in spending.

An Increase in Planned Spending

We begin at point *e* in Exhibit 3, where planned spending equals real GDP at $12.0 trillion. Now let's consider the effect of an increase in one of the components of spending. Suppose that firms become more optimistic about future profits and decide to increase their investment from $1.0 trillion to $1.1 trillion per year. Exhibit 3 reflects this change by a shift upward of the aggregate expenditure line by $0.1 trillion, from $C + I + G + (X - M)$ to $C + I' + G + (X - M)$.

What happens to real GDP demanded? An instinctive response is to say that real GDP demanded increases by $0.1 trillion. In this case, however, instinct is a poor guide. As you can see, the new spending line intersects the 45-degree line at point *e'*, where real GDP demanded is $12.5 trillion. How can a $0.1 trillion increase in planned spending increase real GDP demanded by $0.5 trillion? What's going on?

The idea of the circular flow is central to an understanding of the adjustment process. As noted earlier, real GDP can be thought of as both the value of production and the income arising from that production. Recall that production yields income, which generates spending. We can think of each trip around the circular flow as a "round" of income and spending.

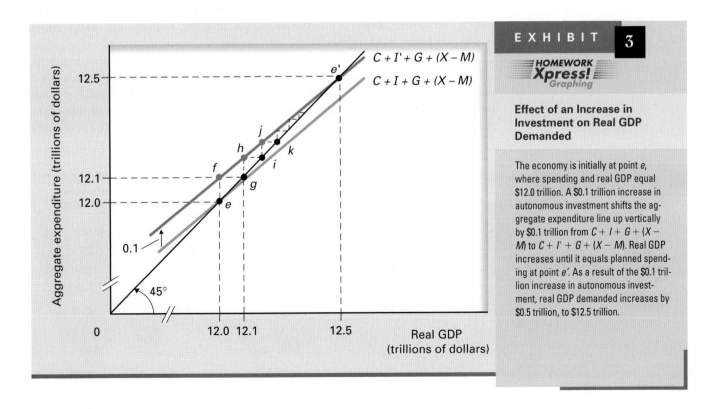

EXHIBIT 3

Effect of an Increase in Investment on Real GDP Demanded

The economy is initially at point *e*, where spending and real GDP equal $12.0 trillion. A $0.1 trillion increase in autonomous investment shifts the aggregate expenditure line up vertically by $0.1 trillion from $C + I + G + (X - M)$ to $C + I' + G + (X - M)$. Real GDP increases until it equals planned spending at point *e'*. As a result of the $0.1 trillion increase in autonomous investment, real GDP demanded increases by $0.5 trillion, to $12.5 trillion.

Round One

An upward shift of the aggregate expenditure line means that, at the initial real GDP of $12.0 trillion, planned spending now exceeds output by $0.1 trillion, or $100 billion. This is shown in Exhibit 3 by the distance between point *e* and point *f*. Initially, firms match this increased spending by an unplanned reduction in inventories. But reduced inventories prompt firms to expand production by $100 billion, as shown by the movement from point *f* to point *g*. This generates $100 billion more income. The movement from *e* to *g* shows the first round in the multiplier process. The income-generating process does not stop there, however, because those who earn this additional income spend some of it and save the rest, leading to round two of spending and income.

Round Two

Given a marginal propensity to consume of 0.8, those who earn the additional $100 billion will spend $80 billion on toasters, backpacks, gasoline, restaurant meals, and thousands of other goods and services. They save the other $20 billion. The move from point *g* to point *h* in Exhibit 3 shows this $80 billion spending increase. Firms respond by increasing their output by $80 billion, shown by the movement from point *h* to point *i*. Thus, the initial $100 billion in new income increases real GDP by $80 billion during round two.

Round Three and Beyond

We know that four-fifths of the $80 billion earned during round two will get spent during round three and one-fifth will get saved. Thus, $64 billion is spent during round three on still more goods and services, as reflected by the movement from point *i* to point *j*. The remaining $16 billion gets saved. The added spending causes firms to increase output by $64 billion, as shown by the movement from point *j* to point *k*. Round three's additional production generated $64 billion more income, which sets up subsequent rounds of spending, output, and income. *As long as planned spending exceeds output, production will increase, thereby creating more income, which will generate still more spending.*

Exhibit 4 summarizes the multiplier process, showing the first three rounds, round 10, and the cumulative effect of all rounds. The new spending each round is shown in the second column and the accumulation of new spending appears in the third column. For example, the new spending accumulated as of the third round is $244 billion—the sum of the first three rounds of spending ($100 billion + $80 billion + $64 billion). The new saving

---

EXHIBIT   4

Tracking the Rounds of Spending Following a $100 Billion Increase in Investment (billions of dollars)

Round	New Spending This Round	Cumulative New Spending	New Saving This Round	Cumulative New Saving
1	100	100	—	—
2	80	180	20	20
3	64	244	16	36
⋮	⋮	⋮	⋮	⋮
10	13.4	446.3	3.35	86.6
⋮	⋮	⋮	⋮	⋮
∞	0	500	0	100

from each round appears in the fourth column, and the accumulation of new saving appears in the final column.

Using the Simple Spending Multiplier

In our model, consumers spend four-fifths of their income each round, with each new round equal to spending from the previous round times the marginal propensity to consume, or the MPC. This goes on round after round, leaving less and less to fuel more spending and income. At some point, the new rounds of income and spending become so small that they disappear and the process stops. The question is, by how much does total spending increase? We can get some idea of the total by working through a limited number of rounds. For example, as shown in Exhibit 4, total new spending after 10 rounds sums to $446.3 billion. But calculating the exact total for all rounds would require us to work through an infinite number of rounds—an impossible task.

Fortunately, we can borrow a shortcut from mathematicians, who have found that the sum of an infinite number of rounds, each of which is MPC times the previous round, equals $1/(1 - MPC)$ times the initial change. Translated, the cumulative spending equals $1/(1 - MPC)$, which, in our example, was 1/0.2, or 5, times the initial increase in spending, which was $100 billion. In short, the increase in planned investment eventually boosts real GDP demanded by 5 times $100 billion, or $500 billion.

The **simple spending multiplier** is the factor by which real GDP demanded changes for a given initial change in spending.

$$\text{Simple spending multiplier} = \frac{1}{1 - MPC}$$

The simple spending multiplier provides a shortcut to the total change in real GDP demanded. This multiplier depends on the MPC. The larger the MPC, the larger the simple spending multiplier. That makes sense—the more people spend from each dollar of fresh income, the more total spending will increase. For example, if the MPC was 0.9 instead of 0.8, the denominator of multiplier formula would equal 1.0 minus 0.9, or 0.1, so the multiplier would be 1/0.1, or 10. With an MPC of 0.9, a $0.1 trillion investment increase would boost real GDP demanded by $1.0 trillion. On the other hand, an MPC of 0.75 would yield a denominator of 0.25 and a multiplier of 4. So a $0.1 trillion investment increase would raise real GDP demanded by $0.4 trillion.

Let's return to Exhibit 3. The $0.1 trillion rise in autonomous investment raised real GDP demanded from $12.0 trillion to $12.5 trillion. Note that real GDP demanded would have increased by the same amount if consumers had decided to spend $0.1 trillion more at each income level—that is, if the consumption function, rather than the investment function, had shifted up by $0.1 trillion. Real GDP demanded likewise would have increased if government purchases or net exports increased $0.1 trillion. *The change in aggregate output demanded depends on how much the aggregate expenditure line shifts, not on which spending component causes the shift.*

In our example, planned investment increased by $0.1 trillion in the year in question. *If this greater investment is not sustained the following year, real GDP demanded will fall back.* For example, if planned investment returns to its initial level, other things constant, real GDP demanded would return to $12.0 trillion. Finally, recall from the previous chapter that the MPC and the MPS sum to 1, so 1 minus the MPC equals the MPS. With this information, we can define the simple spending multiplier in terms of the MPS as follows:

SIMPLE SPENDING MULTIPLIER

The ratio of a change in real GDP demanded to the initial change in spending that brought it about; the numerical value of the simple spending multiplier is $1/(1 - MPC)$; called "simple" because only consumption varies with income

$$\text{Simple spending multiplier} = \frac{1}{1 - MPC} = \frac{1}{MPS}$$

We can see that the smaller the MPS, the less leaks from the spending stream as saving. Because less is saved, more gets spent each round, so the spending multiplier is greater. Incidentally, this spending multiplier is called "simple" because consumption is the only spending component that varies with income.

As an example of how a decline in aggregate expenditure can ripple through the economy, consider what happened to air travel in the wake of the September 11 terrorist attacks.

Fear of Flying

© Toru Yamanaka/AFP/Getty Images

When hijacked planes hit the World Trade Center and the Pentagon, America's sense of domestic security changed. The thousands of lives lost and the billions of dollars of property destroyed were chronicled at length in the media. Let's look at the impact of the tragedy on just one industry—air travel—to see how slumping demand there had a multiplier effect on aggregate expenditure.

Once aviation regulators became aware of the hijackings, they grounded all nonmilitary aircraft immediately. This cost the airlines hundreds of millions of dollars a day during the week of the shutdown. During the days following the attack, video of the second plane crashing into the twin towers was shown again and again, freezing this image in people's minds and heightening concerns about airline safety. These worries, coupled with the airport delays from added security (passengers were told to arrive up to three hours before flights), reduced the demand for air travel. Two weeks after the attacks, airlines were operating only 75 percent of their flights, and these flights were only 30 percent full instead of the usual 75 percent full. Airlines requested federal support, saying they would go bankrupt otherwise. Congress quickly approved a $15 billion package of loans and grants.

Despite the promise of federal aid, airlines laid off 85,000 workers, or about 20 percent of their workforce. Flight reductions meant that as many as 900 aircraft would be parked indefinitely, so investment in new planes collapsed. Boeing, the major supplier of new planes, announced layoffs of 30,000 workers. This triggered layoffs among suppliers of airline parts, such as jet engine and electronic components. For example, Rockwell Collins, an electronics supplier, said 15 percent of its workforce would lose jobs. Other suppliers in the airline food chain also cut jobs. Sky Chef, a major airline caterer, laid off 4,800 of its 16,000 employees.

Airports began rethinking their investment plans. Half the major U.S. airports said they were reevaluating their capital improvement plans to see if these investments made sense in this new environment. Honolulu airport, for example, suspended plans to add extra gates and renovate its overseas terminals.

Just within the first three weeks after the attacks, job cuts announced in the industry exceeded 150,000. These were part of only the first round of reduced consumption and investment. In an expanding economy, job losses in one sector can be made up by job expansions in other sectors. But the U.S. economy was already in a recession at the time of the attack. People who lost jobs or who feared for their jobs reduced their demand for housing, clothing, entertainment, restaurant meals, and other goods and services. For example, unemployed flight attendants would be less likely to buy a new car, reducing the income of autoworkers and suppliers. People who lost jobs in this declining auto industry would reduce *their* demand for goods and services. So the reductions in airline jobs had a multiplier effect.

Airlines are only one part of the travel industry. With fewer people traveling, fewer needed hotels, rental cars, taxi rides, and restaurant meals. Each of those sectors generated a cascade of job losses. The terrorist attacks also shook consumer confidence, which in September 2001 suffered its largest monthly drop since October 1990, on the eve of the first Persian Gulf War. Within 10 days following the attacks, the number of people filing for unemployment benefits jumped to a nine-year high. Again, these early job losses could be viewed as just part of the first round of reduced aggregate expenditure. The second round would occur when people who lost jobs or who feared they would lose their jobs started spending less. The U.S. economy continued to lose jobs for nearly two more years.

Sources: Scott McCartney, "Coast-to-Coast Fares Drop to New Lows," *Wall Street Journal*, 12 May 2004; Susan Carey, "UAL Reports a Narrower Loss, But Profits Remain Elusive," *Wall Street Journal*, 29 April 2004; Will Pinkston, "Airports Reconsider Expansion Plans as Future of Air Travel Gets Murkier," *Wall Street Journal*, 27 September 2001; Luke Timmerman, "Boeing Warns Bad May Get Worse," *Seattle Times*, 21 September 2001; and the Federal Aviation Administration at http://www.faa.gov/.

The Aggregate Demand Curve

In this chapter, we have used the aggregate expenditure line to find real GDP demanded *for a given price level*. But what happens to planned spending if the price level changes? As you will see, for each price level, there is a specific aggregate expenditure line, which yields a unique real GDP demanded. By altering the price level, we can derive the aggregate demand curve.

A Higher Price Level

What is the effect of a higher price level on planned spending and, in turn, on real GDP demanded? Recall that consumers hold many assets that are fixed in dollar terms, such as currency and bank accounts. A higher price level decreases the real value of these money holdings. This cuts consumer wealth, making people less willing to spend at each income level. For reasons that will be explained in a later chapter, a higher price level also tends to increase the market interest rate, and a higher interest rate reduces investment. Finally, a higher U.S. price level means that foreign goods become cheaper for U.S. consumers, and U.S. goods become more expensive abroad. So imports rise and exports fall, decreasing net exports. Therefore, *a higher price level reduces consumption, planned investment, and net exports, which all reduce aggregate spending*. This decrease in planned spending reduces real GDP demanded.

Exhibit 5 represents two different ways of expressing the effects of a change in the price level on real GDP demanded. Panel (a) offers the income-expenditure model, and panel (b) offers the aggregate demand curve, showing the inverse relationship between the price level and real GDP demanded. The idea is to find the real GDP demanded for a given price level in panel (a) and show that price-quantity combination as a point on the aggregate demand curve in panel (b). The two panels measure real GDP on the horizontal axes. At the initial price level of 130 in panel (a), the aggregate expenditure line, now denoted simply as *AE,* intersects the 45-degree line at point *e* to yield real GDP demanded of $12.0 trillion. Panel (b) shows more directly the link between real GDP demanded and the price level. As you can see, when the price level is 130, real GDP demanded is $12.0 trillion. This combination is identified by point *e* on the aggregate demand curve.

What if the price level increases from 130 to, say, 140? As you've just learned, an increase in the price level reduces consumption, planned investment, and net exports. This reduction

EXHIBIT **5**

≡HOMEWORK≡
Xpress!≡
Graphing

The Income-Expenditure Approach and the Aggregate Demand Curve

At the initial price level of 130, the aggregate expenditure line is *AE*, which identifies real GDP demanded of $12.0 trillion. This combination of a price level of 130 and a real GDP demanded of $12.0 trillion determines one combination (point *e*) on the aggregate demand curve in panel (b).

At the higher price level of 140, the aggregate expenditure line shifts down to *AE'*, and real GDP demanded falls to $11.5 trillion. This price-quantity combination is plotted as point *e'* in panel (b).

At the lower price level of 120, the aggregate expenditure line shifts up to *AE"*, which increases real GDP demanded. This combination is plotted as point *e"* in panel (b).

Connecting points *e*, *e'*, and *e"* in panel (b) yields the downward-sloping aggregate demand curve, which shows the inverse relation between price and real GDP demanded.

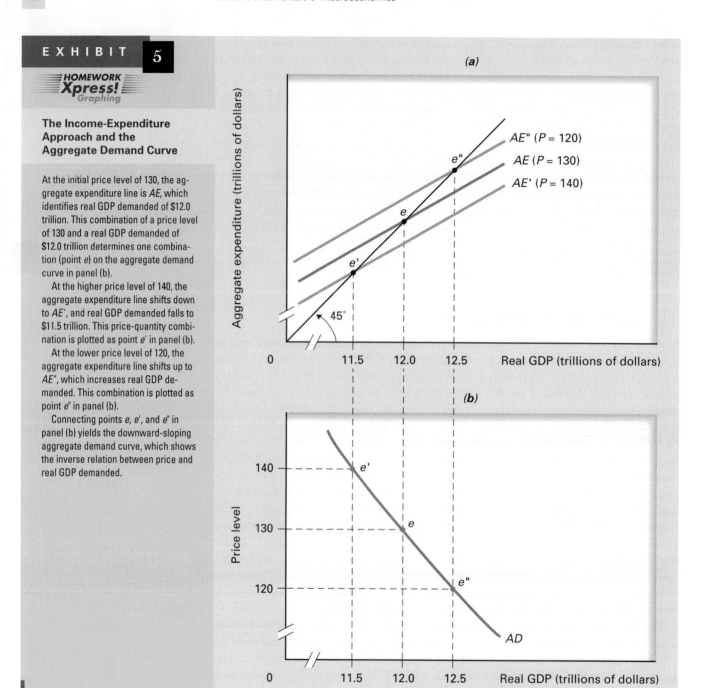

in planned spending is reflected in panel (a) by a downward shift of the aggregate expenditure line from *AE* to *AE'*. As a result, real GDP demanded declines from $12.0 trillion to $11.5 trillion. Panel (b) shows that an increase in the price level from 130 to 140 decreases real GDP demanded from $12.0 trillion to $11.5 trillion, as reflected by the movement from point *e* to point *e'*.

A Lower Price Level

The opposite occurs if the price level falls. At a lower price level, the value of bank accounts, currency, and other money holdings increases. Consumers on average are richer and thus consume more at each real GDP. A lower price level also tends to decrease the market interest rate, which increases investment. Finally, a lower U.S. price level, other things constant, makes U.S. products cheaper abroad and foreign products more expensive here, so exports increase and imports decrease. *Because of a decline in the price level, consumption, investment, and net exports increase at each real GDP.*

Refer again to Exhibit 5 and suppose the price level declines from 130 to, say, 120. This increases planned spending at each income level, as reflected by an upward shift of the spending line from *AE* to *AE"* in panel (a). An increase in planned spending increases real GDP demanded from $12.0 trillion to $12.5 trillion, as indicated by the intersection of the top aggregate expenditure line with the 45-degree line at point *e"*. This same price decrease can be viewed more directly in panel (b). As you can see, when the price level decreases to 120, real GDP demanded increases to $12.5 trillion.

The aggregate expenditure line and the aggregate demand curve present real output from different perspectives. The aggregate expenditure line shows, for a given price level, how planned spending relates to real GDP in the economy. Real GDP demanded is found where planned spending equals real GDP. The aggregate demand curve shows, for various price levels, the quantities of real GDP demanded.

The Multiplier and Shifts in Aggregate Demand

Now that you have some idea how changes in the price level shift the aggregate expenditure line to generate the aggregate demand curve, let's reverse course and return to the situation where the price level is assumed to remain constant. What we want to do now is trace through the effects of a shift of a spending component on aggregate demand, assuming the price level does not change. For example, suppose that a bounce in business confidence spurs a $0.1 trillion increase in planned investment at each real GDP level. Each panel of Exhibit 6 shows a different way of expressing the effects of an increase in planned spending on real GDP demanded, assuming the price level remains unchanged. Panel (a) presents the income-expenditure model and panel (b), the aggregate demand model. Again, the two panels measure real GDP on the horizontal axes. At a price level of 130 in panel (a), the aggregate expenditure line, $C + I + G + (X - M)$, intersects the 45-degree line at point *e* to yield $12.0 trillion in real GDP demanded. Panel (b) shows more directly the link between real GDP demanded and the price level. As you can see, when the price level is 130, real GDP demanded is $12.0 trillion, identified as point *e* on the aggregate demand curve.

Exhibit 6 shows how a shift of the aggregate expenditure line relates to a shift of the aggregate demand curve, given a constant price level. In panel (a), a $0.1 trillion increase in investment shifts the aggregate expenditure line up by $0.1 trillion. Because of the multiplier effect, real GDP demanded climbs from $12.0 trillion to $12.5 trillion. Panel (b) shows the effect of the increase in spending on the aggregate demand curve, which shifts to the right, from *AD* to *AD'*. At the prevailing price level of 130, real GDP demanded increases from $12.0 trillion to $12.5 trillion as a result of the $0.1 trillion increase in planned investment.

Our discussion of the simple spending multiplier exaggerates the actual effect we might expect. For one thing, we have assumed that the price level remains constant. As we shall see in the next chapter, incorporating aggregate supply into the analysis reduces the multiplier because of the resulting price change. Moreover, as income increases there are leakages from the circular flow in addition to saving, such as higher income taxes and greater imports; these

**A Shift of the Aggregate
Expenditure Line That
Shifts the Aggregate
Demand Curve**

A shift of the aggregate expenditure
line at a given price level shifts the aggregate demand curve. In panel (a), an
increase in investment of $0.1 trillion,
with the price level constant at 130,
causes the aggregate expenditure line
to increase from $C + I + G + (X - M)$
to $C + I' + G + (X - M)$. As a result,
real GDP demanded increases from
$12.0 trillion to $12.5 trillion. In panel (b),
the aggregate demand curve has
shifted from *AD* out to *AD'*. At the prevailing price level of 130, real GDP demanded has increased by $0.5 trillion.

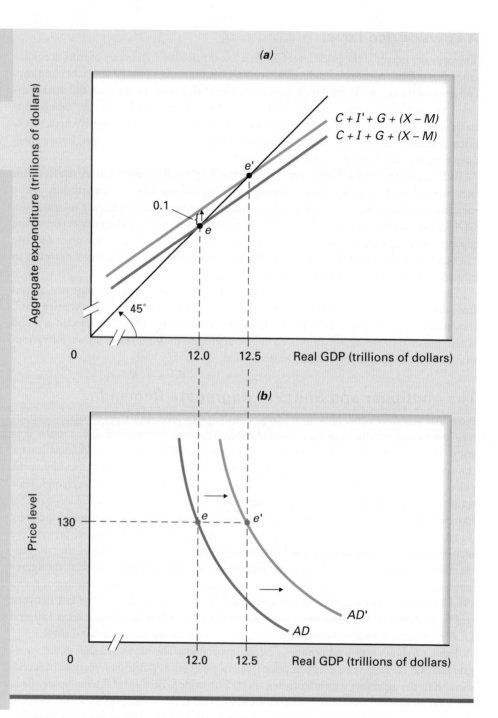

leakages reduce the multiplier. Finally, although we have presented the process in a timeless
framework, the spending multiplier takes time to work through rounds—perhaps a year
or more.

In summary: For a given price level, the aggregate expenditure line relates spending plans
to income, or real GDP. A change in the price level will shift the aggregate expenditure line,
changing real GDP demanded. Changes in the price level and consequent changes in real
GDP demanded generate points along an aggregate demand curve. But at a given price

level, changes in spending plans, such as changes in planned investment, consumption, or government purchases, will shift the aggregate demand curve.

We close with a case study that considers the problem created when Japanese consumers decided to spend less and save more.

Falling Consumption Triggers Japan's Recession

As noted already, consumer spending is the largest component of aggregate expenditure, accounting for about two-thirds of the total. Consumption depends primarily on disposable income. But at any given income level, consumption depends on several other factors, including household wealth, the interest rate, and consumer expectations. Look what happened in Japan, where by 2003 the stock market stood two-thirds below its 1990 level, taking a big bite from household wealth. A collapse in the once-booming real estate market cut household wealth even more.

This sharp reduction in household wealth, combined with an erosion of consumer confidence in the economy, prompted Japanese consumers to spend less and save more. Japan's consumption function shifted downward, and their saving function shifted upward. The drop in consumption reduced aggregate expenditure and shifted the aggregate demand curve to the left. The decline in aggregate demand resulted in Japan's longest economic downturn in 50 years, with the unemployment rate doubling between 1990 and 2003. Retail sales declined in 2003 for the seventh consecutive year. Japan, the second largest economy in the world (after the United States), is by far the largest economy in Asia. A weak economy in Japan hurts the already troubled economies across Asia because Japan is a customer for their exports. Thus, the decline in consumption in Japan had global implications. But by 2004 Japan was starting to show signs of life, with a growing real GDP.

Sources: "Japanese Retail Sales Fell Last Year, *Taipei Times*, 29 January 2004; and "Japan Is Flying Again," *The Economist*, 14 February 2004. For a survey of the Japanese economy, go to http://www.oecd.org/home/.

Case **Study**

Bringing Theory to Life

eActivity
Keep track of what is happening in the Japanese economy through a Web page from NikkeiNet at http://www. nni.nikkei.co.jp sponsored by Nikkei, "the primary source of business information for top executives and decision makers in Japan." What current policies for stimulating consumption can you find among the most current headlines? What are the latest economic indicators reported?

Conclusion

Three ideas central to this chapter are (1) certain forces determine the quantity of real GDP demanded at a given price level, (2) changes in the price level generate the aggregate demand curve, and (3) at a given price level, changes in planned spending shift the aggregate demand curve. The simple multiplier provides a crude but exaggerated idea of how a change in spending plans affects real GDP demanded.

This chapter focused on aggregate spending. A simplifying assumption used throughout was that net exports do not vary with income. Appendix A adds more realism by considering what happens when imports increase with income. Because spending on imports leak from the circular flow, this more realistic approach reduces the spending multiplier.

So far, we have derived real GDP demanded using several approaches, including intuition, tables, and graphs. With the various approaches, we find that for each price level there is a specific quantity of real GDP demanded, other things constant. Appendix B uses algebra to show the same results.

SUMMARY

1. The aggregate expenditure line indicates, for a given price level, planned spending at each income level. At a given price level, real GDP demanded is found where the amount that people plan to spend equals the amount produced.

2. The simple spending multiplier indicates the multiple by which a shift of planned spending changes real GDP demanded. The simple spending multiplier developed in this chapter is $1/(1 - MPC)$. The larger the MPC, the more will be spent and the less will be saved, so the larger the simple multiplier.

3. A higher price level causes a downward shift of the aggregate expenditure line, leading to a lower real GDP de-

manded. A lower price level causes an upward shift of the aggregate expenditure line, increasing real GDP demanded. By tracing the impact of price changes on real GDP demanded, we can derive an aggregate demand curve.

4. The aggregate expenditure line and the aggregate demand curve portray real output from different perspectives. The aggregate expenditure line shows, for a given price level, how much people plan to spend at each income level. Real GDP demanded is found where planned spending equals the amount produced. The aggregate demand curve shows, for various price levels, the quantities of real GDP demanded. At a given price level, a change in spending plans shifts the aggregate demand curve.

QUESTIONS FOR REVIEW

1. *(Aggregate Expenditure)* What are the components of aggregate expenditure? In the model developed in this chapter, which components vary with changes in the level of real GDP? What determines the slope of the aggregate expenditure line?

2. *(Real GDP Demanded)* In your own words, explain the logic of the income-expenditure model. What determines the amount of real GDP demanded?

3. *(Real GDP Demanded)* What equalities hold at the level of real GDP demanded? When determining real GDP demanded, what do we assume about the price level? What do we assume about inventories?

4. *(When Output and Spending Differ)* What role do inventories play in determining real GDP demanded? In answering this question, suppose initially that firms are either producing more than people plan to spend, or producing less than people plan to spend.

5. *(Simple Spending Multiplier)* "A rise in planned investment in an economy will lead to a rise in the amount of planned spending." Use the spending multiplier to verify this statement.

6. (*C a s e* **S t u d y** : Fear of Flying) How do events, such as the World Trade Center and Pentagon attacks described in the case study "Fear of Flying," affect the aggregate expenditure line and the aggregate demand curve? Explain fully.

7. *(The Aggregate Demand Curve)* What is the effect of a lower price level, other things constant, on the aggregate expenditure line and real GDP demanded? How does the multiplier interact with the price change to determine the new real GDP demanded?

8. (*C a s e* **S t u d y** : Falling Consumption Triggers Japan's Recession) What happened to consumption in Japan? Why did this happen? What was the impact on aggregate demand there?

PROBLEMS AND EXERCISES

9. *(Simple Spending Multiplier)* For each of the following values for the MPC, determine the size of the simple spending multiplier and the total change in real GDP demanded following a $10 billion decrease in autonomous spending:

   a. *MPC* = 0.9
   b. *MPC* = 0.75
   c. *MPC* = 0.6

10. *(Simple Spending Multiplier)* Suppose that the MPC is 0.8 and that $12 trillion of real GDP is currently being demanded. The government wants to increase real GDP demanded to $13 trillion at the given price level. By how much would it have to increase government purchases to achieve this goal?

11. *(Simple Spending Multiplier)* Suppose that the MPC is 0.8, while planned investment, government purchases, and net exports sum to $500 billion. Suppose also that the government budget is in balance.

    a. What is the sum of saving and net taxes when desired spending equals real GDP? Explain.
    b. What is the value of the multiplier?
    c. Explain why the multiplier is related to the slope of the consumption function.

12. *(Investment and the Multiplier)* This chapter assumes that investment is autonomous. What would happen to the size of the multiplier if investment increases as real GDP increases? Explain.

13. *(Shifts of Aggregate Demand)* Assume the simple spending multiplier equals 10. Determine the size and direction of any changes of the aggregate expenditure line, real GDP demanded, and the aggregate demand curve for each of the following changes in autonomous spending:

    a. Autonomous spending rises by $8 billion.
    b. Autonomous spending falls by $5 billion.
    c. Autonomous spending rises by $20 billion.

EXPERIENTIAL EXERCISES

14. (*C a s e* **S t u d y** : Falling Consumption Triggers Japan's Recession) Professor Nouriel Roubini of New York University maintains an extensive Web page at http://www.stern.nyu.edu/globalmacro/ devoted to global financial crises. Visit the page and determine what are the latest developments in Japan and around the world.

15. *(Wall Street Journal)* This chapter pointed out that net exports are an important influence on aggregate demand.

Find a story in today's *Wall Street Journal* that describes an event that will affect U.S. imports or exports. A good place to look is the "International" page in the first section of the *Journal*. Analyze the story you have chosen, and illustrate the event using both the aggregate expenditure line and the aggregate demand curve.

HOMEWORK XPRESS! EXERCISES

*These exercises require access to McEachern Homework Xpress! If Homework Xpress! did not come with your book, visit **http://homeworkxpress.swlearning.com** to purchase.*

1. Use the diagram for this exercise to draw a level of aggregate expenditures that would lead to an economy at an equilibrium, *E,* with a real GDP of $8 trillion.

2. Use the diagram for this exercise to draw a level of aggregate expenditures that would lead to an economy at an equilibrium, *E,* with a real GDP of $8 trillion. Illustrate how a change in aggregate expenditures would lead to an increase in the equilibrium level of GDP to $10 trillion.

3. Use the diagram to draw in a level of aggregate expenditures that would lead to an economy at an equilibrium, *E,* with a real GDP of $8 trillion for a price level of *P* =

100. Illustrate the effect of an increase in the price level to *P* = 120. Identify the new equilibrium.

4. In the diagram, draw a level of aggregate expenditures that would lead to an economy at an equilibrium, *E,* with a real GDP of $8 trillion for a price level of *P* = 100. Illustrate the effect of a decrease in the price level to *P* = 80. Identify the new equilibrium.

5. Draw an aggregate demand curve that shows the economy at an equilibrium level of real GDP of $8 trillion when the price level is *P* = 120.

Variable Net Exports Revisited

This chapter has assumed that net exports do not vary with income. A more realistic approach has net exports varying inversely with income. Such a model was developed in the appendix to the previous chapter. The resulting net export function, $X - M$, is presented in panel (a) of Exhibit 7. Recall that the higher the income level in the economy, the more is spent on imports, so the lower the net exports. (If this is not clear, review the appendix to the previous chapter.) Panel (b) of Exhibit 7 shows what happens when vari-

able net exports are added to consumption, government purchases, and investment. We add the variable net export function to $C + I + G$ to get $C + I + G + (X - M)$. Perhaps the easiest way to see how introducing net exports affects planned spending is to begin where real GDP equals $10.0 trillion. Because net exports equal zero when real GDP equals $10.0 trillion, the addition of net exports has no effect on planned spending. So the $C + I + G$ and $C + I + G + (X - M)$ lines intersect where real GDP equals $10.0

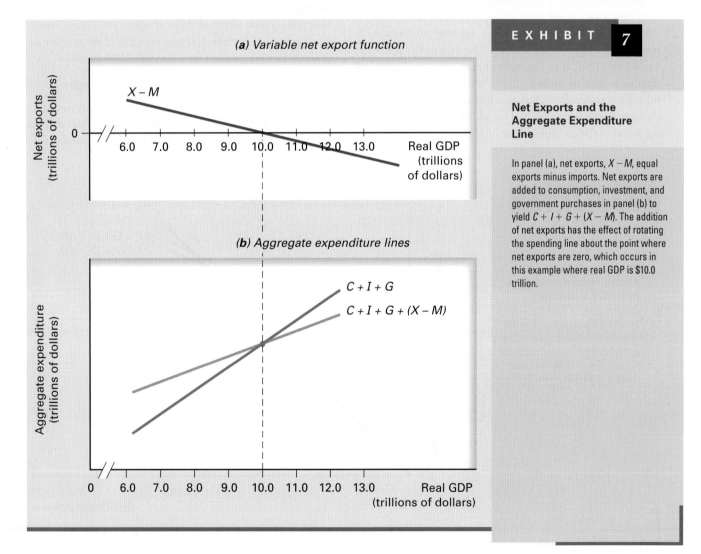

(a) Variable net export function

(b) Aggregate expenditure lines

EXHIBIT 7

Net Exports and the Aggregate Expenditure Line

In panel (a), net exports, $X - M$, equal exports minus imports. Net exports are added to consumption, investment, and government purchases in panel (b) to yield $C + I + G + (X - M)$. The addition of net exports has the effect of rotating the spending line about the point where net exports are zero, which occurs in this example where real GDP is $10.0 trillion.

trillion. At real GDP levels less than $10.0 trillion, net exports are positive, so the $C + I + G + (X - M)$ line is above the $C + I + G$ line. At real GDP levels greater than $10.0 trillion, net exports are negative, so the $C + I + G + (X - M)$ line is below the $C + I + G$ line. *Because variable net exports and real GDP are inversely related, the addition of variable net exports has the effect of flattening out, or reducing the slope of, the aggregate expenditure line.*

Net Exports and the Spending Multiplier

The inclusion of variable net exports makes the model more realistic but more complicated, and it requires a reformulation of the spending multiplier. If net exports are autonomous, or independent of income, only the marginal propensity to consume determines how much gets spent and how much gets saved as income changes. The inclusion of variable net exports means that, as income increases, U.S. residents spend more on imports. The *marginal propensity to import,* or *MPM,* is the fraction of each additional dollar of disposable income spent on imported products. Imports leak from the circular flow. Thus, two leakages now increase with income: saving and imports. This additional leakage changes the value of the multiplier from $1/MPS$ to:

$$\text{spending multiplier with variable net exports} = \frac{1}{MPS + MPM}$$

The larger the marginal propensity to import, the greater the leakage during each round of spending and the smaller the resulting spending multiplier. Suppose the MPM equals $1/10$, or 0.1. If the marginal propensity to save is 0.2 and the marginal propensity to import is 0.1, then only $0.70 of each additional dollar of disposable income gets spent on output produced in the United States. We can compute the new multiplier as follows:

$$\text{Spending multiplier with variable net exports}$$
$$= \frac{1}{MPS + MPM} = \frac{1}{0.2 + 0.1} = \frac{1}{0.3} = 3.33$$

Thus, the inclusion of net exports reduces the spending multiplier in our hypothetical example from 5 to 3.33. *Because some of each additional dollar of income goes toward imports, less is spent on U.S. products, so any given shift of the aggregate expenditure line has less of an impact on real GDP demanded.*

A Change in Autonomous Spending

Given the net export function described in the previous section, what is the real GDP demanded, and how does income change when there is a change in autonomous spending? To

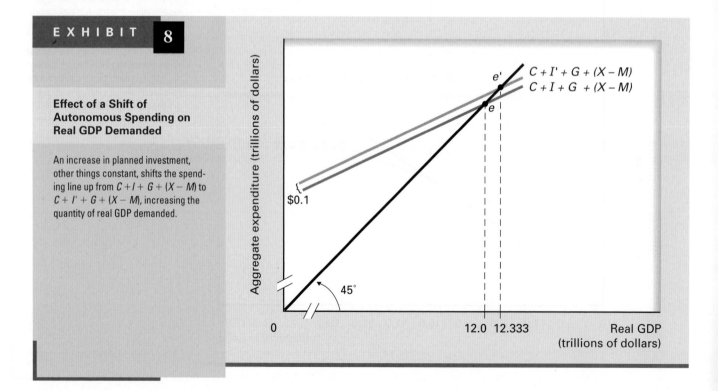

EXHIBIT 8

Effect of a Shift of Autonomous Spending on Real GDP Demanded

An increase in planned investment, other things constant, shifts the spending line up from $C + I + G + (X - M)$ to $C + I' + G + (X - M)$, increasing the quantity of real GDP demanded.

answer these questions, let's begin in Exhibit 8 with an aggregate expenditure line of $C + I + G + (X - M)$, where net exports vary inversely with income. This aggregate expenditure line intersects the 45-degree line at point *e,* determining real GDP demanded of $12.0 trillion. Suppose now that planned investment increases by $0.1 trillion at every income, with the price level unchanged. This will shift the entire aggregate expenditure line up by $0.1 trillion, from C + $I + G + (X - M)$ to $C + I' + G + (X - M)$, as shown in Exhibit 8. Output demanded increases from $12.0 trillion to $12.333 trillion, representing an increase of $0.333 trillion, or $333 billion, which is $0.1 trillion times the spending multiplier with variable exports of 3.33. The derivation of the output level and the size of the multiplier are explained in Appendix B.

APPENDIX A QUESTION

1. (*Net Exports and the Spending Multiplier*) Suppose that the marginal propensity to consume (MPC) is 0.8 and the marginal propensity to import (MPM) is 0.05.

   a. What is the value of the spending multiplier?
   b. By how much would the real GDP demanded change if planned investment increased by $100 billion?

   c. Using your answer to part (b), calculate the change in net exports caused by the change in aggregate output.

The Algebra of Income and Expenditure

This appendix explains the algebra behind real GDP demanded. You should see some similarity between this and the circular-flow explanation of national income accounts.

The Aggregate Expenditure Line

We first determine where planned spending equals output and then derive the relevant spending multipliers, assuming a given price level. Initially, let's assume net exports are autonomous. Then we'll incorporate variable net exports into the framework.

Real GDP demanded for a given price level occurs where planned spending equals income, or real GDP. Planned spending is equal to the sum of consumption, C, planned investment, I, government purchases, G, and net exports, $X - M$. Algebraically, we can write the equality as

$$Y = C + I + G + (X - M)$$

where Y equals income, or real GDP. To find where real GDP equals planned spending, we begin with the heart of the income-expenditure model: the consumption function. The consumption function used throughout this chapter is a straight line; the equation for that line can be written as

$$C = 1.4 + 0.8 \, (Y - 1.0)$$

The marginal propensity to consume is 0.8, Y is income, or real GDP, and 1.0 is autonomous net taxes in trillions of dollars. Thus $(Y - 1.0)$ is real GDP minus net taxes, which equals disposable income. The consumption function can be simplified to

$$C = 0.6 + 0.8Y$$

Consumption at each real GDP, therefore, equals $0.6 trillion (which could be called autonomous consumption—that is, consumption that does not vary with income), plus 0.8 times income, which is the marginal propensity to consume times income.

The second component of spending is investment, I, which we have assumed is autonomous and equal to $1.0 trillion. The third component of spending is autonomous government purchases, G, which we assumed to be $1.0 trillion. Net exports, $X - M$, the final spending component, we assumed to be −$0.2 trillion at all levels of income. Sub-

stituting the numerical values for each spending component in planned spending, we get

$$Y = 0.6 + 0.8Y + 1.0 + 1.0 - 0.2$$

Notice there is only one variable in this expression: Y. If we rewrite the expression as

$$Y - 0.8Y = 0.6 + 1.0 + 1.0 - 0.2$$
$$0.2Y = 2.4$$

we can solve for real GDP demanded:

$$Y = \$12.0 \text{ trillion}$$

A More General Form of Income and Expenditure

The advantage of algebra is that it allows us to derive the equilibrium quantity of real GDP demanded in a more general way. Let's begin with a consumption function of the general form

$$C = a + b \, (Y - NT)$$

where b is the marginal propensity to consume and NT is net taxes. Consumption can be rearranged as

$$C = a - bNT + bY$$

where $a - bNT$ is *autonomous* consumption (the portion of consumption that is independent of income) and bY is *induced* consumption (the portion of consumption generated by higher income in the economy). Real GDP demanded equals the sum of consumption, C, planned investment, I, government purchases, G, and net exports, $X - M$, or

$$\text{Income} = \text{Expenditure}$$
$$Y = a - bNT + bY + I + G + (X - M)$$

Again, by rearranging terms and isolating Y on the left side of the equation, we get

$$Y = \frac{1}{1 - b}(a - bNT + I + G + X - M)$$

The $(a - bNT + I + G + X - M)$ term represents autonomous spending—that is, the amount of spending that is independent of income. And $(1 - b)$ equals 1 minus the MPC. In the chapter, we showed that $1/(1 - MPC)$ equals the simple spending multiplier. One way of viewing what's going on is to keep in mind that autonomous spending is *multiplied* through the economy to arrive at real GDP demanded.

The formula that yields real GDP demanded can be used to derive the spending multiplier. We can increase autonomous spending by, say, $1, to see what happens to real GDP demanded.

$$Y' = \frac{1}{1 - b}(a - bNT + I + G + X - M + \$1)$$

The difference between this expression and the initial one (that is, between Y' and Y) is $\$1/(1 - b)$. Because b equals the MPC, the simple multiplier equals $1/(1 - b)$. Thus, the change in equilibrium income equals the change in autonomous spending times the multiplier.

Varying Net Exports

Here we explore the algebra behind variable net exports, first introduced in the appendix to the previous chapter. We begin with the equality

$$Y = C + I + G + (X - M)$$

Exports are assumed to equal $0.9 trillion at each income level. Imports increase as disposable income increases, with a marginal propensity to import of 0.1. Therefore, net exports equal

$$X - M = 0.9 - 0.1 (Y - 1.0)$$

After incorporating the values for C, I, and G presented earlier, we can express the equality as

$$Y = 0.6 + 0.8Y + 1.0 + 1.0 + 0.9 - 0.1 (Y - 1.0)$$

which reduces to $0.3Y = \$3.6$ trillion, or $Y = \$12.0$ trillion.

Algebra can be used to generalize these results. If m represents the marginal propensity to import, net exports become $X - m(Y - NT)$. Real GDP demanded can be found by solving for Y in the expression

$$Y = a + b(Y - NT) + I + G + X - m(Y - NT)$$

which yields

$$Y = \frac{1}{1 - b + m}(a - bNT + I + G + X + mNT)$$

The expression in parentheses represents autonomous spending. In the denominator, $1 - b$ is the marginal propensity to save and m is the marginal propensity to import. Appendix A demonstrated that $1/(MPS - MPM)$ equals the spending multiplier when variable net exports are included. Thus, real GDP demanded equals the spending multiplier times autonomous spending. And an increase in autonomous spending times the multiplier gives us the resulting increase in real GDP demanded.

APPENDIX B QUESTION

1. Suppose that $C = 100 + 0.75(Y - 100)$, $I = 50$, $G = 30$, and $X - M = -100$, all in billions of dollars. What is the simple spending multiplier? What is real GDP demanded? What would happen to real GDP demanded if government purchases increased to $40 billion?

Aggregate Supply

W hat is your normal capacity for academic work, and when do you exceed that effort? If the economy is already operating at full employment, how can it produce more? What valuable piece of information do employers and workers lack when they negotiate wages? Why do employers and workers fail to agree on pay cuts that might save jobs? How might a long stretch of high unemployment reduce the economy's ability to produce in the future? These and other questions are answered in this chapter, which develops the aggregate supply curve in the short run and in the long run.

Up to this point, we have focused on aggregate demand. We have not yet brought in aggregate supply, a much debated topic. The debate involves the shape of the aggregate supply curve and the reasons for that shape. This chapter develops a single, coherent framework for aggregate supply. Although the focus continues to be on

HOMEWORK Xpress!

Use Homework Xpress! for economic application, graphing, videos, and more.

economic aggregates, you should keep in mind that aggregate supply reflects billions of individual production decisions made by millions of individual resource suppliers and firms in the economy. Each firm operates in its own little world, dealing with its own suppliers and customers, and keeping a watchful eye on existing and potential competitors. Yet each firm recognizes that success also depends on the performance of the economy as a whole. The theory of aggregate supply described here must be consistent with both the microeconomic behavior of individual suppliers and the macroeconomic behavior of the economy. Topics discussed include:

- Expected price level and long-term contracts
- Potential output
- Short-run aggregate supply
- Long-run aggregate supply
- Expansionary gap
- Contractionary gap
- Changes in aggregate supply

Aggregate Supply in the Short Run

Aggregate supply is the relationship between the price level in the economy and the aggregate output firms are willing and able to supply, with other things constant. Assumed constant along a given aggregate supply curve are resource prices, the state of technology, and the set of formal and informal institutions that structure production incentives, such as the system of property rights, patent laws, tax systems, respect for the laws, and the customs and conventions of the marketplace. The greater the supply of resources, the better the technology, and the more effective the production incentives provided by the economic institutions, the greater the aggregate supply. Let's begin by looking at the key resource—labor.

Labor and Aggregate Supply

Labor is the most important resource, accounting for about 70 percent of production cost. The supply of labor in an economy depends on the size and abilities of the adult population and their preferences for work versus leisure. Along a given labor supply curve—that is, for a given adult population with given preferences for work and leisure—the quantity of labor supplied depends on the wage. The higher the wage, other things constant, the more labor supplied.

So far, so good. But things start getting complicated once we recognize that the purchasing power of any given nominal wage depends on the economy's price level. *The higher the price level, the less any given money wage will purchase, so the less attractive that wage is to workers.* Consider wages and the price level over time. Suppose a worker in 1970 was offered a job paying $20,000 per year. That salary may not impress you today, but its real purchasing power back then would exceed $75,000 in today's dollars. Because the price level matters, we must distinguish between the **nominal wage,** or money wage, which measures the wage in current dollars, and the **real wage,** which measures the wage in constant dollars— that is, dollars measured by the goods and services they will buy. A higher real wage means workers can buy more goods and services.

Both workers and employers care more about the real wage than about the nominal wage. The problem is that nobody knows for sure how the price level will change during the life of the wage agreement, so labor contracts must be negotiated in terms of nominal wages, not real wages. Some resource prices, such as wages set by long-term contracts, remain in force for extended periods, often for two or three years. Workers as well as other resource suppliers must therefore reach agreements based on the *expected* price level.

NOMINAL WAGE

The wage measured in current dollars; the dollar amount on a paycheck

REAL WAGE

The wage measured in dollars of constant purchasing power; the wage measured in terms of the quantity of goods and services it will buy

Even where there are no explicit labor contracts, there is often an implicit agreement that the wage, once negotiated, will not change for a while. For example, in many firms the standard practice is to revise wages annually. So wage agreements may be either *explicit* (based on a labor contract) or *implicit* (based on labor market practices). These explicit and implicit agreements are difficult to renegotiate while still in effect, even if the price level in the economy turns out to be higher or lower than expected.

Potential Output and the Natural Rate of Unemployment

Here's how resource owners and firms negotiate resource price agreements for a particular period, say, a year. Firms and resource suppliers expect a certain price level to prevail in the economy during the year. You could think of this as the *consensus* view for the upcoming year. Based on consensus expectations, firms and resource suppliers reach agreements on resource prices, such as wages. For example, firms and workers may expect the price level to increase 3 percent next year, so they agree on a nominal wage increase of 4 percent, which would increase the real wage by 1 percent. If these price-level expectations are realized, the agreed-on nominal wage translates into the expected real wage, so everyone is satisfied with the way things work out—after all, that's what they willingly negotiated. When the actual price level turns out as expected, we call the resulting output the economy's potential output. *The potential output is the amount produced when there are no surprises about the price level.* So, at the agreed-on real wage, workers are supplying the quantity of labor they want and firms are hiring the quantity of labor they want. Both sides are content with the outcome.

We can think of **potential output** as the economy's maximum sustainable output, given the supply of resources, the state of technology, and the formal and informal production incentives offered by the rules of the game. Potential output is also referred to by other terms, including the *natural rate of output* and the *full-employment rate of output*.

The unemployment rate that occurs when the economy is producing its potential GDP is called the **natural rate of unemployment.** That rate prevails when cyclical unemployment is zero. When the economy is producing its potential output, the number of job openings equals the number of people unemployed for frictional, structural, and seasonal reasons. Widely accepted estimates of the natural rate of unemployment range from about 4 percent to about 6 percent of the labor force.

Potential output provides a reference point, an anchor, for the analysis in this chapter. *When the price-level expectations of both workers and firms are fulfilled, the economy produces its potential output.* Complications arise, however, when the actual price level differs from expectations, as we'll see next.

Actual Price Level Higher than Expected

As you already know, each firm's goal is to maximize profit. Profit equals total revenue minus total cost. Suppose workers and firms reach a wage agreement. What if the economy's price level then turns out to be higher than they expected? What happens *in the short run* to real GDP supplied? The **short run** in macroeconomics is a period during which some resource prices remain fixed by contract. Does output in the short run exceed the economy's potential, fall short of that potential, or equal that potential?

The prices of many resources have been fixed for the duration of contracts, so firms welcome a higher than expected price level. After all, the selling prices of their products, on average, are higher than expected, while the costs of at least some of the resources they employ remain constant. *Because a price level that is higher than expected results in a higher profit per unit, firms have an incentive in the short run to increase production beyond the economy's potential level.*

POTENTIAL OUTPUT

The economy's maximum sustainable output, given the supply of resources, technology, and production incentives; the output level when there are no surprises about the price level

NATURAL RATE OF UNEMPLOYMENT

The unemployment rate when the economy produces its potential output

SHORT RUN

In macroeconomics, a period during which some resource prices, especially those for labor, are fixed by explicit or implicit agreements

At first it might appear contradictory to talk about producing beyond the economy's potential, but remember that potential output means not zero unemployment but the natural rate of unemployment. Even in an economy producing its potential output, there is some unemployed labor and some unused production capacity. If you think of potential GDP as the economy's *normal capacity,* you get a better idea of how production can temporarily exceed that capacity. For example, during World War II, the United States pulled out all the stops to win the war. Factories operated around the clock. The unemployment rate dropped below 2 percent—well under the natural rate. Overtime was common. People worked longer and harder for the war effort than they normally would have.

Think about your own study habits. During most of the term, you display your normal capacity for academic work. As the end of the term draws near, however, you may shift into high gear, finishing term papers, studying late into the night for final exams, and generally running yourself ragged trying to pull things together. During those final frenzied days of the term, you study beyond your normal capacity, beyond the schedule you would prefer to follow on a regular or sustained basis. We often observe workers exceeding their normal capacity for short bursts: fireworks technicians around the Fourth of July, accountants during tax time, farmers during harvest time, and elected officials toward the end of a campaign or legislative session. Similarly, firms and their workers are able, *in the short run,* to push output beyond the economy's potential.

Why Costs Rise When Output Exceeds Potential

The economy is flexible enough to expand output beyond potential GDP, but as output expands, the cost of additional output increases. Although many workers are bound by contracts, wage agreements may require overtime pay for extra hours or weekends. As the economy expands and the unemployment rate declines, additional workers are harder to find. Retirees, homemakers, and students may require extra pay to draw them into the labor force. Some firms may resort to hiring workers who are not prepared for the available jobs—those who had been structurally unemployed. If few additional workers are available, if workers require additional pay for overtime, or if available workers are less qualified, the nominal cost of labor will increase as output expands in the short run, even though most wages remain fixed by long-term agreements.

As production increases, the demand for nonlabor resources increases as well, so the prices of those resources in markets where prices are flexible—such as the market for oil—will increase, reflecting their greater scarcity. Also, as production increases, firms use their machines and trucks more intensively, so equipment wears out faster and is more subject to breakdown. Thus, the nominal cost per unit of output rises when production is pushed beyond the economy's potential output. But *because the prices of some resources are fixed by contracts, the price level rises faster than the per-unit production cost, so firms find it profitable to increase the quantity supplied.*

When the economy's actual price level exceeds the expected price level, the real value of an agreed-on nominal wage declines. We might ask why workers would be willing to increase the quantity of labor they supply when the price level is higher than expected. One answer is that because labor agreements require workers to offer their labor at the agreed-on nominal wage, workers are simply complying with their contracts, at least until they have a chance to renegotiate.

In summary: If the price level is higher than expected, firms have a profit incentive to increase the quantity of goods and services supplied. At higher rates of output, however, the per-unit cost of additional output increases. Firms will expand output as long as the revenue from additional production exceeds the cost of that production.

N e t Bookmark

For comprehensive coverage of the state of the United States and global economy geared to the general public, follow one of the many money Web sites, like that presented at CNN and *Money* magazine at http://money.cnn.com. If you prefer to sit and listen to a roundup of the day's economic news, tune into *Marketplace* via the show's Web site at http://marketplace.publicradio.org/. This site includes links to headline stories from *The Economist,* which you can access directly at http://www.economist.com. Much of the content is available only to subscribers, but many lead articles are accessible for free.

An Actual Price Level Lower than Expected

We have discovered that if the price level is greater than expected, firms expand output in the short run, but as they do, the per-unit cost of additional production increases. Now let's look at the effects of a price level that turns out to be lower than expected. Again, suppose that resource suppliers and firms expect a certain price level. If it turns out to be lower than expected, production is less attractive to firms. The prices they receive for their output are on average lower than they expected, yet many of their production costs, such as the nominal wage, do not fall.

Because production is less profitable when prices are lower than expected, firms reduce their quantity supplied, so the economy's output falls below its potential. As a result, some workers are laid off, those who keep their jobs may work fewer hours, and unemployment exceeds the natural rate. Not only is less labor employed, but machines go unused, delivery trucks sit idle, and entire plants may shut down—for example, automakers sometimes halt production for weeks.

Just as some costs increase in the short run when output is pushed beyond the economy's potential, some costs decline when output falls below that potential. Some resources become unemployed, so the prices of resources decline in markets where the price is flexible. Moreover, with an abundance of unemployed resources, firms can become more selective about which resources to retain, laying off the least productive first (recent hires, who typically have the least experience, are usually the first to go).

To review: If the economy's price level turns out to be higher than expected, firms maximize profit by increasing the quantity supplied beyond the economy's potential output. As output expands, the per-unit cost of additional production increases, but firms expand production as long as prices rise more than costs. If the price level turns out to be lower than expected, firms reduce output below the economy's potential output because prices fall more than costs. All of this is a long way of saying that *there is a direct relationship in the short run between the actual price level and real GDP supplied.*

The Short-Run Aggregate Supply Curve

What we have been describing so far traces out the **short-run aggregate supply (SRAS) curve,** which shows the relationship between the actual price level and real GDP supplied, other things remaining constant. Again, the *short run* in this context is the period during which some resource prices, especially those for labor, are fixed by implicit or explicit agreement. For simplicity, we can think of the short run as the duration of labor contracts, which are based on the expected price level.

Suppose the expected price level is 130. The short-run aggregate supply curve in Exhibit 1, $SRAS_{130}$, is based on that expected price level (hence the subscript 130). If the price level turns out to be 130, as expected, producers supply the economy's *potential output,* which in Exhibit 1 is $12.0 trillion. Although not shown in the exhibit, for the price level to turn out as expected, the aggregate demand curve would have to intersect the aggregate supply curve at point *a*. So, given the economy's potential output, the short-run aggregate supply curve depends on the expected price level, which depends on expectations about aggregate demand. If the economy produces its potential output, unemployment is at the *natural rate*. Nobody is surprised, and all are content with the outcome. There is no tendency to move away from point *a* even if workers and firms have a chance to renegotiate wages.

In Exhibit 1, output levels that fall short of the economy's potential are shaded red, and output levels that exceed the economy's potential are shaded blue. The slope of the short-run aggregate supply curve depends on how sharply the cost of additional production rises

SHORT-RUN AGGREGATE SUPPLY (SRAS) CURVE

A curve that shows a direct relationship between the price level and real GDP supplied in the short run, other things constant

HOMEWORK Xpress!
Ask the Instructor Video

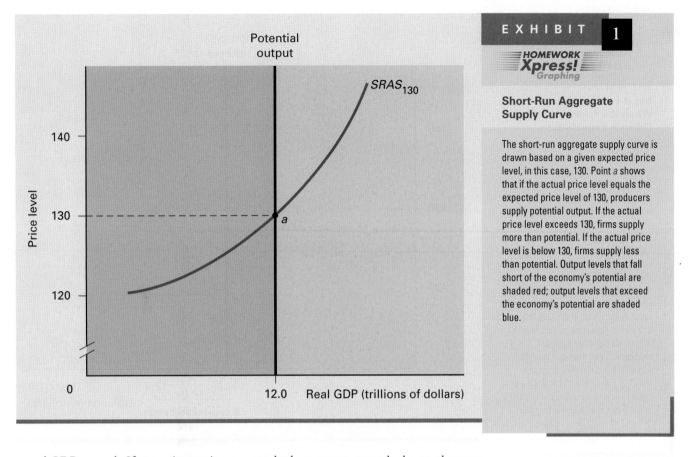

EXHIBIT 1

HOMEWORK
Xpress!
Graphing

**Short-Run Aggregate
Supply Curve**

The short-run aggregate supply curve is drawn based on a given expected price level, in this case, 130. Point *a* shows that if the actual price level equals the expected price level of 130, producers supply potential output. If the actual price level exceeds 130, firms supply more than potential. If the actual price level is below 130, firms supply less than potential. Output levels that fall short of the economy's potential are shaded red; output levels that exceed the economy's potential are shaded blue.

as real GDP expands. If per-unit costs increase modestly as output expands, the supply curve will be relatively flat. If these costs increase sharply as output expands, the supply curve will be relatively steep. Much of the controversy about the short-run aggregate supply curve involves its shape. Shapes range from flat to steep. Notice that the short-run aggregate supply curve becomes steeper as output increases, because resources become scarcer and thus more costly as output increases.

From the Short Run to the Long Run

This section begins with the price level exceeding expectations in the short run to see what happens in the long run. The long run is long enough that firms and resource suppliers can renegotiate all agreements based on knowledge of the actual price level. *So in the long run, there are no surprises about the price level.*

Closing an Expansionary Gap

Let's begin our look at the long-run adjustment in Exhibit 2 with an expected price level of 130. The short-run aggregate supply curve for that expected price level is $SRAS_{130}$. Given this short-run aggregate supply curve, the equilibrium price level and real GDP depend on the aggregate demand curve. The actual price level will equal the expected price level only if the aggregate demand curve intersects the aggregate supply curve at point *a*—that is, where the short-run quantity equals potential output. Point *a* reflects potential output of \$12.0 trillion and a price level of 130, which is the expected price level.

HOMEWORK Xpress! *Graphing*

Short-Run Equilibrium When the Price Level Exceeds Expectations

If the expected price level is 130, the short-run aggregate supply curve is $SRAS_{130}$. If the actual price level turns out as expected, the quantity supplied is the potential output of $12.0 trillion. Given the aggregate demand curve shown here, the price level ends up higher than expected, and output exceeds potential, as shown by the short-run equilibrium at point *b*. The amount by which actual output exceeds the economy's potential output is called the expansionary gap. In the long run, price-level expectations and nominal wages will be revised upward. Costs will rise and the short-run aggregate supply curve will shift leftward to $SRAS_{140}$. Eventually, the economy will move to long-run equilibrium at point *c*, thus closing the expansionary gap.

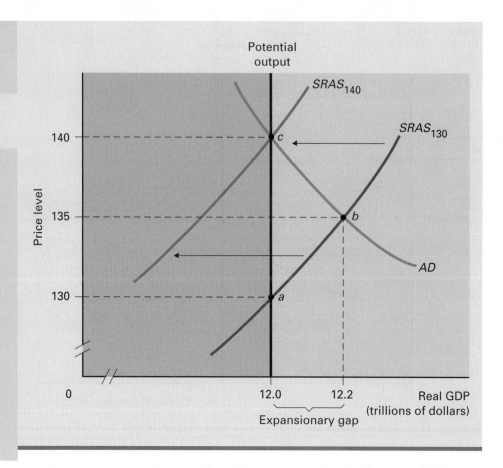

SHORT-RUN EQUILIBRIUM

The price level and real GDP that occur when the aggregate demand curve intersects the short-run aggregate supply curve

EXPANSIONARY GAP

The amount by which output in the short run exceeds the economy's potential output

LONG RUN

In macroeconomics, a period during which wage contracts and resource price agreements can be renegotiated; there are no surprises about the economy's actual price level

But what if aggregate demand turns out to be greater than expected, as shown by curve *AD*, which intersects the short-run aggregate supply curve $SRAS_{130}$ at point *b*. Point *b* is the **short-run equilibrium,** reflecting a price level of 135 and a real GDP of $12.2 trillion. The actual price level in the short run is higher than expected, and output exceeds the economy's potential of $12.0 trillion.

The amount by which short-run output exceeds the economy's potential is called an **expansionary gap.** In Exhibit 2, that gap is the short-run output of $12.2 trillion minus potential output of $12.0 trillion, or $0.2 trillion. When real GDP exceeds its potential, the unemployment rate is below its natural rate. Employees are working overtime, machines are being pushed to their limits, and farmers are sandwiching extra crops between usual plantings. Remember that the nominal wage was negotiated based on an expected price level of 130; because the actual price level is higher, that nominal wage translates into a lower-than-expected real wage. As we will see, output exceeding the economy's potential creates inflationary pressure. *The more that short-run output exceeds the economy's potential, the larger the expansionary gap and the greater the upward pressure on the price level.*

What happens in the long run? The **long run** is a period during which firms and resource suppliers know about market conditions, particularly aggregate demand and the actual price level, and have the time to renegotiate resource payments based on that knowledge. Because the higher-than-expected price level cuts the real value of the nominal wage originally agreed to, workers will try to negotiate a higher nominal wage at their earliest opportunity. Workers and other resource suppliers negotiate higher nominal payments, raising production costs for firms, so the short-run aggregate supply curve shifts leftward, resulting in cost-push inflation. In Exhibit 2, the expansionary gap causes the short-run aggregate supply curve to shift leftward to $SRAS_{140}$, which results in an expected price level of 140. Notice that the short-run aggregate supply curve shifts until the equilibrium quantity equals the economy's potential output. *Actual output can exceed the economy's potential in the short run but not in the long run.*

As shown in Exhibit 2, the expansionary gap is closed by long-run market forces that shift the short-run aggregate supply curve from $SRAS_{130}$ left to $SRAS_{140}$. Whereas $SRAS_{130}$ was based on resource contracts reflecting an expected price level of 130, $SRAS_{140}$ is based on resource contracts reflecting an expected price level of 140. At point *c* the expected price level and the actual price level are identical, so the economy is not only in short-run equilibrium but also is in **long-run equilibrium.** Consider all the equalities that hold at point *c*: (1) the expected price level equals the actual price level; (2) the quantity supplied in the short run equals potential output, which also equals the quantity supplied in the long run; and (3) the quantity supplied equals the quantity demanded. Looked at another way, *long-run equilibrium occurs where the aggregate demand curve intersects the vertical line drawn at potential output.* Point *c* will continue to be the equilibrium point unless there is some change in aggregate demand or in aggregate supply.

Note that the situation at point *c* is no different *in real terms* from what had been expected at point *a*. At both points, firms supply the economy's potential of $12.0 trillion real GDP. The same amounts of labor and other resources are employed, and although the price level, the nominal wage, and other nominal resource payments are higher at point *c*, the real wage and the real return to other resources are the same as they would have been at point *a*. For example, suppose the nominal wage averaged $13 per hour when the expected price was 130. If the expected price level increased from 130 to 140, an increase of 7.7 percent, the nominal wage would also increase by that same percentage to an average of $14 per hour, leaving the real wage unchanged. With no change in the real wage between points *a* and *c*, firms demand enough labor and workers supply enough labor to produce $12.0 trillion in real GDP.

Thus, if the price level turns out to be higher than expected, the short-run response is to increase quantity supplied. But production exceeding the economy's potential creates inflationary pressure. In the long run this causes the short-run aggregate supply curve to shift to the left, reducing output, increasing the price level, and closing the expansionary gap.

If an increase in the price level was predicted accurately year after year, firms and resource suppliers would build these expectations into their long-term agreements. The price level would move up each year by the expected amount, but the economy's output would remain at potential GDP, thereby skipping the round-trip beyond the economy's potential and back.

Closing a Contractionary Gap

Let's begin again with an expected price level of 130 as presented in Exhibit 3, where blue shading indicates output exceeding potential and red shading indicates output below potential. If the price level turned out as expected, the resulting equilibrium combination would occur at *a*, which would be both a short-run and a long-run equilibrium. Suppose this time that the aggregate demand curve intersects the short-run aggregate supply curve to the left of potential output, yielding a price level below that expected. The intersection of the aggregate demand curve, AD'', with $SRAS_{130}$ establishes the short-run equilibrium point, *d*, where the price level is below expectations and production is less than the economy's potential. The amount by which actual output falls short of potential GDP is called a

**Short-Run Equilibrium
When the Price Level Is
Below Expectations**

When the actual price level is below
expectations, as indicated by the intersection of the aggregate demand curve
AD" with the short-run aggregate supply curve *SRAS*$_{130}$, short-run equilibrium occurs at point *d.* Production below the economy's potential opens a
contractionary gap. If prices and wages
are flexible enough in the long run,
nominal wages will be renegotiated
lower. As resource costs fall, the short-
run aggregate supply curve eventually
shifts rightward to *SRAS*$_{120}$ and the
economy moves to long-run equilibrium
at point *e*, with output increasing to the
potential level of $12.0 trillion.

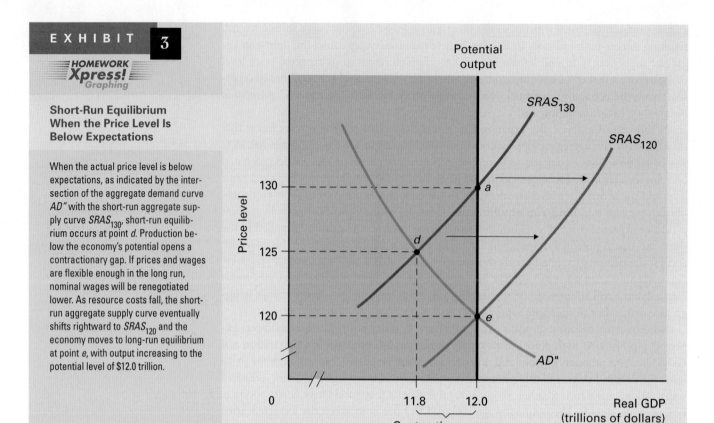

CONTRACTIONARY GAP

The amount by which actual output
in the short run falls short of the
economy's potential output

contractionary gap. In this case, the contractionary gap is $0.2 trillion, and unemploy-
ment exceeds its natural rate.

Because the price level turns out to be lower than expected, the nominal wage, which is
based on the expected price level, translates into a higher real wage in the short run. What
happens in the long run? With the price level lower than expected, employers are no longer
willing to pay as high a nominal wage. And with the unemployment rate higher than the
natural rate, more workers are competing for jobs, putting downward pressure on the nominal wage. If the price level and the nominal wage are flexible enough, the combination of a
lower price level and a pool of unemployed workers competing for jobs should make workers more willing to accept lower nominal wages when wage agreements are negotiated.

If firms and workers negotiate lower nominal wages, the cost of production decreases,
shifting the short-run aggregate supply curve rightward, leading to deflation and greater
output. The short-run supply curve will continue to shift rightward until it intersects the
aggregate demand curve where the economy produces its potential output. This increase in
supply is reflected in Exhibit 3 by a rightward shift of the short-run aggregate supply curve
from *SRAS*$_{130}$ to *SRAS*$_{120}$. *If the price level and nominal wage are flexible enough, the short-run
aggregate supply curve will move rightward until the economy produces its potential output.* The new
short-run aggregate supply curve is based on an expected price level of 120. Because the
expected price level and the actual price level are now identical, the economy is in long-
run equilibrium at point *e.*

Although the nominal wage is lower at point *e* than that originally agreed to when the expected price level was 130, the real wage is the same at point *e* as it was at point *a*. Because the real wage is the same, the amount of labor that workers supply is the same and real output is the same. All that has changed between points *a* and *e* are nominal measures—the price level, the nominal wage, and other nominal resource prices.

We conclude that when incorrect expectations cause firms and resource suppliers to overestimate the actual price level, output in the short run falls short of the economy's potential. As long as wages and prices are flexible enough, however, firms and workers should be able to renegotiate wage agreements based on a lower expected price level. The negotiated drop in the nominal wage will shift the short-run aggregate supply curve to the right until the economy once again produces its potential output. If wages and prices are not flexible, they will not adjust quickly to a contractionary gap, so shifts of the short-run aggregate supply curve may be slow to move the economy to its potential output. The economy can therefore get stuck at an output and employment level below its potential.

We are now in a position to provide an additional interpretation of the red- and blue-shaded areas of our exhibits. *If a short-run equilibrium occurs in the blue-shaded area, that is, to the right of potential output, then market forces in the long run will increase nominal resource costs, shifting the short-run aggregate supply to the left. If a short-run equilibrium occurs in the red-shaded area, then market forces in the long run will reduce nominal resource costs, shifting the short-run aggregate supply curve to the right.* Closing an expansionary gap involves inflation and closing a contractionary gap involves deflation.

Tracing Potential Output

If wages and prices are flexible enough, the economy will produce its potential output in the long run, as indicated in Exhibit 4 by the vertical line drawn at the economy's potential GDP of $12.0 trillion. This vertical line is called the economy's **long-run aggregate supply (LRAS) curve.** *The long-run aggregate supply curve depends on the supply of resources in the economy, the level of technology, and the production incentives provided by the formal and informal institutions of the economic system.*

In Exhibit 4, the initial price level of 130 is determined by the intersection of *AD* with the long-run aggregate supply curve. If the aggregate demand curve shifts out to *AD'*, then in the long run, the equilibrium price level will increase to 140 and equilibrium output will remain at $12.0 trillion, the economy's potential GDP. Conversely, a decline in aggregate demand from *AD* to *AD"* will, in the long run, lead only to a fall in the price level from 130 to 120, with no change in output. Note that these long-run movements are more like tendencies than smooth and timely adjustments. It may take a long time for resource prices to adjust, particularly when the economy faces a contractionary gap. As long as wages and prices are flexible, the economy's potential GDP is consistent with any price level. *In the long run, equilibrium output equals long-run aggregate supply, which is also potential output. The equilibrium price level depends on the aggregate demand curve.*

Wage Flexibility and Employment

What evidence is there that a vertical line drawn at the economy's potential GDP depicts the long-run aggregate supply curve? Except during the Great Depression, unemployment over the last century has varied from year to year but typically has returned to what would be viewed as a natural rate of unemployment—again, estimates range from 4 percent to 6 percent.

An *expansionary* gap creates a labor shortage that eventually results in a higher nominal wage and a higher price level. But a *contractionary* gap does not necessarily generate enough downward pressure to lower the nominal wage. Studies indicate that nominal wages are slow

LONG-RUN AGGREGATE SUPPLY (LRAS) CURVE

A vertical line at the economy's potential output; aggregate supply when there are no surprises about the price level and all resource contracts can be renegotiated

Long-Run Aggregate Supply Curve

In the long run, when the actual price level equals the expected price level, the economy produces its potential. In the long run, $12.0 trillion in real GDP will be supplied regardless of the actual price level. As long as wages and prices are flexible, the economy's potential GDP is consistent with any price level. Thus, shifts of the aggregate demand curve will, in the long run, not affect potential output. The long-run aggregate supply curve, *LRAS*, is a vertical line at potential GDP.

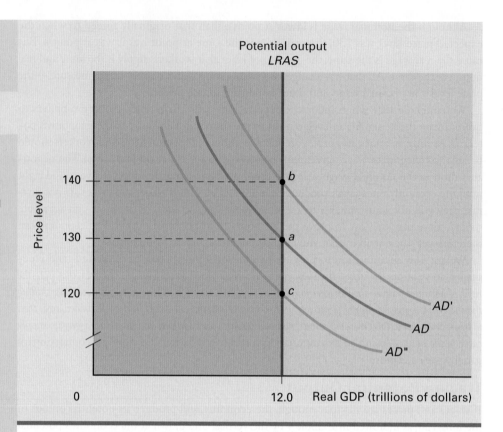

to adjust to high unemployment. Nominal wages have declined in particular industries; during the 1980s, for example, nominal wages fell in airlines, steel, and trucking. But seldom have we observed actual declines in nominal wages across the economy, especially since World War II. Nominal wages do not adjust downward as quickly or as substantially as they adjust upward, and the downward response that does occur tends to be slow and modest. Consequently, we say that nominal wages tend to be "sticky" in the downward direction. *Because nominal wages fall slowly, if at all, the supply-side adjustments needed to close a contractionary gap may take so long as to seem ineffective.* What, in fact, usually closes a contractionary gap is an increase in aggregate demand as the economy pulls out of its funk.

Although the nominal wage seldom falls, an actual decline in the nominal wage is not necessary to close a contractionary gap. All that's needed is a fall in the real wage. And *the real wage will fall as long as the price level increases more than the nominal wage*. For example, if the price level increases by 4 percent and the nominal wage increases by 2 percent, the real wage falls by 2 percent. If the real wage falls enough, firms will be willing to demand enough additional labor to produce the economy's potential output.

In the following case study, we look more at output gaps and discuss why wages are not more flexible.

U.S. Output Gaps and Wage Flexibility

Let's look at estimates of actual and potential GDP. Exhibit 5 measures actual GDP minus potential GDP as a percentage of potential GDP for the United States. When actual output exceeds potential output, the output gap is positive and the economy has an expansionary gap. For example, actual output in 2000 was 2.2 percent above potential output, amounting to an expansionary gap of about $200 billion (in 2000 dollars). When actual output falls short of potential output, the output gap is negative and the economy suffers a contractionary gap. For example, actual output in 2003 was 1.4 percent below potential output, amounting to

a contractionary gap of about $150 billion (in 2000 dollars). Note that the economy need not be in recession for actual output to fall short of potential output. For example, from 1992 to 1995, and from 2002 to 2004, the economy expanded, yet actual output fell short of potential output. As long as unemployment exceeds its natural rate, the economy will suffer a contractionary gap.

Employers and employees clearly would have been better off if these contractionary gaps had been reduced or eliminated. After all, more workers would have been employed, and more goods and services would have increased the standard of living. If workers and employers fail to reach an outcome that seems possible and that all would prefer, then they have failed to coordinate in some way. Contractionary gaps can thus be viewed as resulting from a **coordination failure.**

If employers and workers can increase output and employment by agreeing to lower nominal wages, why doesn't such an agreement occur quickly? As we have already seen,

Case **Study**

Public Policy

*e*Activity

For the latest on output gaps among the world's leading economies, go to the OECD's Web site at http://www.oecd.org/home/. From there you can access Publications & Documents, which will lead you to the latest OECD Outlook and the Annex tables. What is the current output gap in the United States? How does the U.S. gap compare to that in the other leading economies?

COORDINATION FAILURE

A situation in which workers and employers fail to achieve an outcome that all would prefer

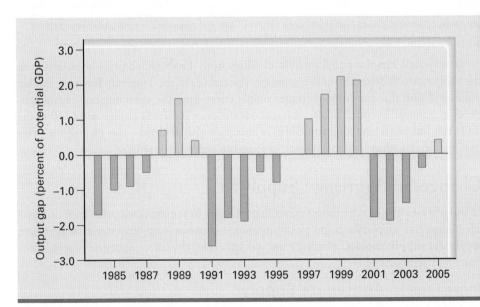

Source: Developed from estimates by the *OECD*. Figures for 2004 and 2005 are projections. OECD data can be found at http://www.oecd.org/home/.

EXHIBIT 5

U.S. Output Gap Measures Actual Output Minus Potential Output as Percentage of Potential Output

The output gap each year equals actual GDP minus potential GDP as a percentage of potential GDP. When actual output exceeds potential output, the output gap is positive and the economy has an expansionary gap, as shown by the blue bars. When actual output falls short of potential output, the output gap is negative and the economy suffers a contractionary gap, as shown by the red bars. Note that the economy need not be in recession for actual output to fall below potential output.

some workers are operating under long-term contracts, so wages are not very flexible, particularly in the downward direction. But if long-term contracts are a problem, why not negotiate shorter ones? First, negotiating contracts is costly and time-consuming (for example, airline worker contracts take an average of 1.3 years to negotiate). Longer contracts reduce the frequency, and thus the average annual cost, of negotiations. Second, long-term contracts reduce the frequency of strikes, lockouts, and other settlement disputes. Thus, both workers and employers gain from longer contracts, even though such contracts make wages more sticky and contractionary gaps more likely to linger.

When demand is slack, why do employers choose to lay off workers rather than cut nominal wages? Yale economist Truman Bewley interviewed over 300 managers, union officials, and employment recruiters and concluded that resistance to pay cuts comes, not from workers or unions, but from employers. Employers think pay cuts damage worker morale more than layoffs do. By lowering morale, pay cuts increase labor turnover and reduce productivity. In contrast, the damage from layoffs is brief and limited because laid off workers are soon gone and cannot disrupt the workplace. What's more, even during the sharpest of recessions, more than nine in ten workers still keep their jobs (or soon find other jobs), so most workers have little incentive to support a wage cut to increase employment.

Another reason workers may be reluctant to accept lower nominal wages is unemployment benefits. When a worker is laid off, the incentive to accept a lower wage is reduced by the prospect of unemployment benefits. The greater these benefits and the longer their duration, the less the pressure to accept a lower wage. For example, in the latter part of the 1920s, unemployment benefits nearly tripled in Great Britain and eligibility requirements were loosened. Despite record high unemployment, money wages remained unchanged during the period. For some people, unemployment benefits had become a viable alternative to accepting a lower wage.

Sources: Truman Bewley, *Why Wages Don't Fall During a Recession* (Cambridge, Mass.: Harvard University Press, 2000); Andrew von Nordenflycht, "Labor Contract Negotiations in the Airline Industry," *Monthly Labor Review* (July 2003): 18–28; Laurence Ball and David Romer, "Sticky Prices and Coordination Failures," *American Economic Review* 81 (June 1991): 539–552; Daniel Benjamin and Levis Kochin, "Searching for an Explanation of Unemployment in Interwar Britain," *Journal of Political Economy* 87 (June 1979): 441–470; and *Survey of Current Business* 84 (April 2004).

To review: When the actual price level differs from the expected price level, output in the short run will depart from the economy's potential. In the long run, however, market forces will shift the short-run aggregate supply curve until the economy once again produces its potential output. Thus, surprises about the price level will change real GDP in the short run but not in the long run. Shifts of the aggregate demand curve change the price level but do not affect potential output, or long-run aggregate supply.

Changes in Aggregate Supply

In this section, we consider factors other than changes in the expected price level that may affect aggregate supply. We begin by distinguishing between long-term trends in aggregate supply and **supply shocks,** which are unexpected events that affect aggregate supply, sometimes only temporarily.

Increases in Aggregate Supply

The economy's potential output is based on the willingness and ability of households to supply resources to firms, the level of technology, and the institutional underpinnings of the economic system. Any change in these factors could affect the economy's potential output. Changes in the economy's potential output over time were introduced in the earlier chapter

SUPPLY SHOCKS

Unexpected events that affect aggregate supply, sometimes only temporarily

that focused on U.S. productivity and growth. The supply of labor may change over time because of a change in the size, composition, or quality of the labor force or a change in preferences for labor versus leisure. For example, the U.S. labor force has doubled since 1948 as a result of population growth and a growing labor force participation rate, especially among women with children. At the same time, job training, education, and on-the-job experience increased the quality of labor. Increases in both the quantity and the quality of the labor force have increased the economy's potential GDP, or long-run aggregate supply.

The quantity and quality of other resources also change over time. The capital stock—machines, buildings, and trucks—increases whenever the economy's gross investment exceeds the depreciation of capital. Even the quantity and quality of land can be increased—for example, by claiming land from the sea, as is done in the Netherlands and Hong Kong, or by revitalizing soil that has lost its fertility. These increases in the quantity and quality of resources increase the economy's potential output.

Finally, institutional changes that define property rights more clearly or make contracts more enforceable, such as the introduction of clearer patent and copyright laws, will increase the incentives to undertake productive activity, thereby increasing potential output. *Changes in the labor force, in the supply of other resources, and in the institutional arrangements of the economic system tend to occur gradually.* Exhibit 6 depicts a gradual shift of the economy's potential output from $12.0 trillion to $12.5 trillion. The long-run aggregate supply curve shifts from *LRAS* out to *LRAS'*.

In contrast to the gradual, or long-term, changes that often occur in the supply of resources, *supply shocks* are unexpected events that change aggregate supply, sometimes only temporarily. **Beneficial supply shocks** increase aggregate supply; examples include (1) abundant harvests that increase the food supply, (2) discoveries of natural resources, such as oil in Alaska or the North Sea, (3) technological breakthroughs that allow firms to combine resources more efficiently, such as faster computers or the Internet, and (4) sudden changes in the economic system that promote more production, such as tax cuts that stimulate production incentives or new limits on frivolous product liability suits.

Exhibit 7 shows the effect of a beneficial supply shock from a technological breakthrough. The beneficial supply shock shown here shifts the short-run and long-run aggregate supply curves rightward. Along the aggregate demand curve, *AD,* the equilibrium

WALL STREET JOURNAL

Reading It **Right**

What's the relevance of the following statement from the Wall Street Journal: *"After a decade of fumbling, American business figured how to get more benefit than hassle from information technology, and more goods and services for each hour of work."*

BENEFICIAL SUPPLY SHOCKS

Unexpected events that increase aggregate supply, sometimes only temporarily

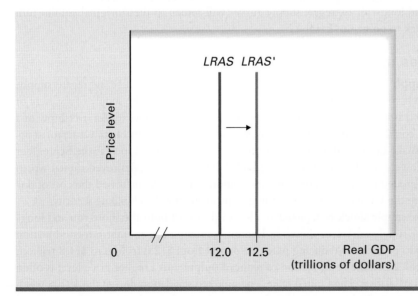

E X H I B I T 6

Effect of a Gradual Increase in Resources on Aggregate Supply

A gradual increase in the supply of resources increases the potential GDP—in this case, from $12.0 trillion to $12.5 trillion. The long-run aggregate supply curve shifts to the right.

Effects of a Beneficial Supply Shock on Aggregate Supply

Given the aggregate demand curve, a beneficial supply shock that has a lasting effect, such as a breakthrough in technology, will permanently shift both the short-run aggregate supply curve and the long-run aggregate supply curve, or potential output. A beneficial supply shock lowers the price level and increases output, as reflected by the change in equilibrium from point *a* to point *b*. A temporary beneficial supply shock, such as would result from an unusually favorable growing season, will shift the aggregate supply curves only temporarily. If the next growing season returns to normal, the aggregate supply curves will return to their original equilibrium position at point *a*.

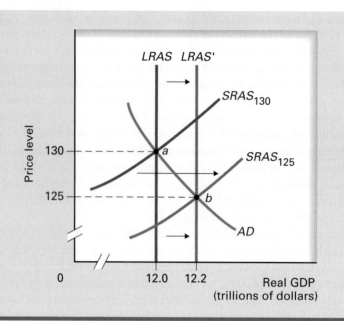

combination of price and output moves from point *a* to point *b*. *For a given aggregate demand curve, the happy outcome of a beneficial supply shock is an increase in output and a decrease in the price level.* The new equilibrium at point *b* is a short-run and a long-run equilibrium in the sense that there is no tendency to move from that point as long as whatever caused the beneficial effect continues, and a technological discovery usually has a lasting effect. Likewise, substantial new oil discoveries benefit the economy for a long time. On the other hand, an unusually favorable growing season won't last. When a normal growing season returns, the short-run and long-run aggregate supply curves will return to their original equilibrium position—back to point *a* in Exhibit 7.

Decreases in Aggregate Supply

ADVERSE SUPPLY SHOCKS

Unexpected events that reduce aggregate supply, sometimes only temporarily

Adverse supply shocks are sudden, unexpected events that reduce aggregate supply, sometimes only temporarily. For example, a drought could reduce the supply of a variety of resources, such as food, building materials, and water-powered electricity. An overthrow of a government could destabilize the economy, as occurred recently in Haiti. Or terrorist attacks could shake the institutional underpinnings of the economy, such as the September 2001 Twin Towers and Pentagon attacks, which killed thousands, destroyed capital worth billions, and eroded the civil liberties of a free nation. The attacks increased the cost of doing business in the United States—everything from airline travel to building security.

An adverse supply shock is depicted as a leftward shift of both the short-run and long-run aggregate supply curves, as shown in Exhibit 8, moving the equilibrium combination from point *a* to point *c* and reducing potential output from $12.0 trillion to $11.8 trillion. As mentioned earlier, the combination of reduced output and a higher price level is often referred to as stagflation. The United States encountered stagflation during the 1970s, when the economy was rocked by a series of adverse supply shocks, such as crop failures around

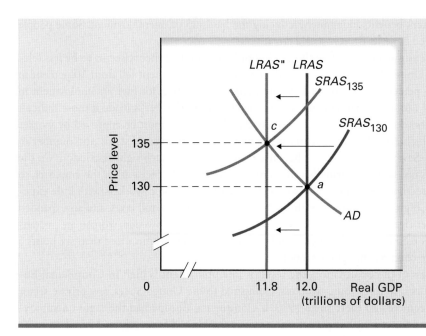

E X H I B I T **8**

≡HOMEWORK≡
Xpress!═
Graphing

**Effects of an Adverse
Supply Shock on
Aggregate Supply**

Given the aggregate demand curve, an
adverse supply shock, such as an increased threat of terrorism, shifts the
short-run and long-run aggregate supply curves to the left, increasing the
price level and reducing real GDP, a
movement called stagflation. This
change is shown by the move in equilibrium from point *a* to point *c*. If the shock
is just temporary, the shift of the aggregate supply curves will be temporary.

the globe and the oil price hikes by OPEC in 1974 and 1979. If the effect of the adverse
supply shock is temporary, such as a poor growing season, the aggregate supply curve returns to its original position once things return to normal. But some economists question
an economy's ability to bounce back, as discussed in the following case study.

Why Is Unemployment So High in Europe?

Between World War II and the mid-1970s, unemployment in Western Europe was low. From 1960 to 1974,
for example, the unemployment rate in France never
got as high as even 4 percent. The worldwide recession
of the mid-1970s, however, jacked up unemployment
rates. But unemployment continued to climb in Continental Europe long after the recession ended. Unemployment in France and Italy remained above 10 percent during most of the 1980s. After a modest decline
in the late 1980s, rates again topped 10 percent during
the 1990s. In 2004, the rates were 8 percent in Italy, 10
percent in Germany and France, 11 percent in Spain,
and 12 percent in Belgium. Some observers claim that the natural rate of unemployment
has increased in these countries.

Economists have borrowed a term from physics, **hysteresis** (pronounced *his-ter-eé-sis*), to
argue that the natural rate of unemployment depends in part on the recent history of unemployment. *The longer the actual unemployment rate remains above what had been the natural rate,
the more the natural rate itself will increase.* For example, those unemployed can lose valuable
job skills, such as the computer programmer who loses touch with the latest developments.
As weeks of unemployment turn into months and years, the shock and stigma may diminish, so the work ethic weakens. What's more, some European countries offer generous

HYSTERESIS

The theory that the natural rate of
unemployment depends in part on
the recent history of unemployment;
high unemployment rates increase
the natural rate of unemployment

C a s e **S t u d y**

Public Policy

eActivity

Learn about unemployment rates in
Europe by finding the most current
press release from Eurostat at
http://europa.eu.int/comm/eurostat/.
The OECD follows trends in market reforms in Europe designed to reduce the
structural impediments to lowering the
unemployment rate. You can access the
latest reports and analyses at http://
www.oecd.org/home/. Go to By Topic,
then to Employment, and follow the link
to Labour Markets. What changes have
been made in employment protection
and other labor laws in the European
countries to deal with high rates of unemployment? What types of liberaliza-
tion and other changes can you find
that have been made in labor and product markets to promote employment?

unemployment benefits indefinitely, reducing the hardship of unemployment. Some people have collected benefits *for more than a decade.*

No consensus exists regarding the validity of hysteresis. The theory seems to be less relevant in the United States and Great Britain, where unemployment fell from 10 percent in 1982 to 5.6 percent or less in 2004. An alternative explanation for high unemployment in Continental Europe is that legislation introduced there in the 1970s made it more difficult to lay off workers. In most European countries, job dismissals must be approved by worker councils, which consider such factors as the worker's health, marital status, and number of dependents. Severance pay has also become mandatory. With such tight restrictions on the ability to dismiss workers, hiring became almost an irreversible decision for the employer, so firms have become reluctant to add workers, particularly untested workers with little experience. Also, high minimum wages throughout Europe, high payroll taxes, and an expanded list of worker rights have increased labor costs. For example, in Sweden, women are guaranteed a year's paid leave on having a child and the right to work no more than six hours a day until the child reaches grade school.

Regardless of the explanation, the result is unemployment is high in Continental Europe, particularly among young workers. Compared to the United States, few private sector jobs have been created there since 1980. If Continental Europe had the same unemployment rate and the same labor participation rate as the United States, about 30 million more people there would be working.

Sources: Russell Smyth, "Unemployment Hysteresis in Australian States and Territories," *Australian Economic Review*, 36 (June 2003): 181–192; Horst Siebert, "Labor Market Rigidities: At the Root of Unemployment in Europe," *Journal of Economic Perspectives* 11 (Summer 1997): 37–54; "Economic and Financial Indicators," *Economist*, 15 May 2004; and *OECD Economic Outlook* 75 (June 2004).

Conclusion

This chapter explains why the aggregate supply curve slopes upward in the short run and is vertical at the economy's potential output in the long run. Firms and resource suppliers negotiate contracts based on the economy's expected price level, which depend on expectations about aggregate demand. Unexpected changes in the price level can move output in the short run away from its potential level. But as firms and resource suppliers fully adjust to price surprises, the economy in the long run moves toward its potential output. Potential output is the anchor for analyzing aggregate supply in the short run and long run.

SUMMARY

1. Short-run aggregate supply is based on resource demand and supply decisions that reflect the expected price level. If the price level turns out as expected, the economy produces its potential output. If the price level exceeds expectations, short-run output exceeds the economy's potential, creating an expansionary gap. If the price level is below expectations, short-run output falls short of the economy's potential, creating a contractionary gap.

2. Output can exceed the economy's potential in the short run, but in the long run, higher nominal wages will be negotiated at the earliest opportunity. This increases the cost of production, shifting the short-run aggregate supply curve leftward along the aggregate demand curve until the economy produces its potential output.

3. If output in the short run is less than the economy's potential, and if wages and prices are flexible enough, lower

nominal wage will reduce production costs in the long run. These lower costs shift the short-run aggregate supply curve rightward along the aggregate demand curve until the economy produces its potential output.

4. Evidence suggests that when output exceeds the economy's potential, nominal wages and the price level increase. But there is less evidence that nominal wages and the price level fall when output is below the economy's potential. Wages appear to be "sticky" in the downward direction. What usually closes a contractionary gap is an increase in aggregate demand.

5. The long-run aggregate supply curve, or the economy's potential output, depends on the amount and quality of resources available, the state of technology, and formal and informal institutions, such as patent laws and business practices, that structure production incentives. Increases in resource availability, improvements in technology, or institutional changes that provide more attractive production incentives increase aggregate supply and potential output.

6. Supply shocks are unexpected, often temporary changes in aggregate supply. Beneficial supply shocks increase output, sometimes only temporarily. Adverse supply shocks result in stagflation—reduced output and a higher price level, sometimes only temporarily.

QUESTIONS FOR REVIEW

1. *(Short-Run Aggregate Supply)* In the short run, prices may rise faster than costs do. This chapter discusses why this might happen. Suppose that labor and management agree to adjust wages continuously for any changes in the price level. How would such adjustments affect the slope of the aggregate supply curve?

2. *(Potential Output)* Define the economy's potential output. What factors help determine potential output?

3. *(Actual Price Level Higher than Expected)* Discuss some instances in your life when your actual production for short periods exceeded what you considered your potential production. Why does this occur only for brief periods?

4. *(Nominal and Real Wages)* Complete each of the following sentences:

   a. The _____ wage measures the wage rate in current dollars, while the _____ wage measures it in constant dollars.

   b. Wage agreements are based on the _____ price level and negotiated in _____ terms. Real wages are then determined by the _____ price level.

   c. The higher the actual price level, the _____ is the real wage for a given nominal wage.

   d. If nominal wages are growing at 2 percent per year while the annual inflation rate is 3 percent, then real wages change by _____.

5. *(Contractionary Gaps)* After reviewing Exhibit 3 in this chapter, explain why contractionary gaps occur only in the short run and only when the actual price level is below what was expected.

6. *(Short-Run Aggregate Supply)* In interpreting the short-run aggregate supply curve, what does the adjective *short-run* mean? Explain the role of labor contracts along the *SRAS* curve.

7. *(Contractionary Gap)* What does a contractionary gap imply about the actual rate of unemployment relative to the natural rate? What does it imply about the actual price level relative to the expected price level? What must happen to real and nominal wages in order to close a contractionary gap?

8. *(Expansionary Gap)* How does an economy that is experiencing an expansionary gap adjust in the long run?

9. *(Output Gaps and Wage Flexibility)* What are some reasons why nominal wages may not fall during a contractionary gap?

10. *(C a s e Study:* U.S. Output Gaps and Wage Flexibility) Unemployment is costly to employers, employees, and the economy as a whole. What are some explanations for the *coordination failures* that prevent workers and employers from reaching agreements?

11. *(Long-Run Adjustment)* In the long run, why does an actual price level that exceeds the expected price level lead to changes in the nominal wage? Why do these changes cause shifts of the short-run aggregate supply curve?

12. *(Long-Run Aggregate Supply)* The long-run aggregate supply curve is vertical at the economy's potential output level. Why is the long-run aggregate supply curve located at this output rather than below or above potential output?

13. *(Long-Run Aggregate Supply)* Determine whether each of the following, other things held constant, would lead to an increase, a decrease, or no change in long-run aggregate supply:

    a. An improvement in technology
    b. A permanent decrease in the size of the capital stock

    c. An increase in the actual price level
    d. An increase in the expected price level
    e. A permanent increase in the size of the labor force

14. *(Changes in Aggregate Supply)* What are supply shocks? Distinguish between beneficial and adverse supply shocks. Do such shocks affect the short-run aggregate supply curve, the long-run aggregate supply curve, or both? What is the resulting impact on potential GDP?

<hr>

PROBLEMS AND EXERCISES

15. *(Real Wages)* In Exhibit 2 in this chapter, how does the real wage rate at point *c* compare with the real wage rate at point *a*? How do nominal wage rates compare at those two points? Explain your answers.

16. *(Natural Rate of Unemployment)* What is the relationship between potential output and the natural rate of unemployment?

    a. If the economy currently has a frictional unemployment rate of 2 percent, structural unemployment of 2 percent, seasonal unemployment of 0.5 percent, and cyclical unemployment of 2 percent, what is the natural rate of unemployment? Where is the economy operating relative to its potential GDP?
    b. What happens to the natural rate of unemployment and potential GDP if cyclical unemployment rises to 3 percent with other types of unemployment unchanged from part (a)?
    c. What happens to the natural rate of unemployment and potential GDP if structural unemployment falls to 1.5 percent with other types of unemployment unchanged from part (a)?

17. *(Expansionary and Contractionary Gaps)* Answer the following questions on the basis of the following graph:

    a. If the actual price level exceeds the expected price level reflected in long-term contracts, real GDP equals _____ and the actual price level equals _____ in the short run.

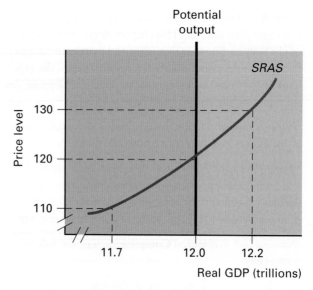

    b. The situation described in part (a) results in a(n) _____ gap equal to _____.
    c. If the actual price level is lower than the expected price level reflected in long-term contracts, real GDP equals _____ and the actual price level equals _____ in the short run.
    d. The situation described in part (c) results in a(n) _____ gap equal to _____.
    e. If the actual price level equals the expected price level reflected in long-term contracts, real GDP equals _____ and the actual price level equals _____ in the short run.

f. The situation described in part (e) results in _____ gap equal to _____.

18. *(Long-Run Adjustment)* The ability of the economy to eliminate any imbalances between actual and potential output is sometimes called self-correction. Using an aggregate supply and aggregate demand diagram, show why this self-correction process involves only temporary periods of inflation or deflation.

19. *(Changes in Aggregate Supply)* List three factors that can change the economy's potential output. What is the impact of shifts of the aggregate demand curve on potential output? Illustrate your answers with a diagram.

20. *(Supply Shocks)* Give an example of an adverse supply shock and illustrate graphically. Now do the same for a beneficial supply shock.

EXPERIENTIAL EXERCISES

21. (*C a s e* **Study**: Why Is Unemployment So High in Europe?) European unemployment is a hot topic. Use any Web browser to search for the words "European unemployment." Just by scanning the headlines, see how many possible explanations you can list. How do they compare to the explanations reviewed in the chapter case study?

22. *(Wall Street Journal)* In the short run, some workers' wages are determined by contracts, and some are not. The split between costs that change as production changes and those that do not is a key determinant of the shape of the short-run aggregate supply curve. To get a better feel for wage determination, look at the "Work Week" column in the first section of Tuesday's *Wall Street Journal*. Determine how some of the developments described there are likely to affect aggregate supply. Make sure that you distinguish between the short-run and the long-run effects. Draw a diagram to illustrate your conclusions.

HOMEWORK XPRESS! EXERCISES

These exercises require access to McEachern Homework Xpress! If Homework Xpress! did not come with your book, visit **http://homeworkxpress.swlearning.com** *to purchase.*

1. In the diagram sketch a line representing a potential output of $10 trillion. Sketch a short-run aggregate supply curve when the expected price level is 120.

2. In the diagram for this exercise, use aggregate demand and short-run aggregate supply curves to show an economy at a short-run equilibrium with an expansionary gap, when potential output is $10 trillion. Then illustrate how the gap would close in the long run.

3. In the diagram, use aggregate demand and short-run aggregate supply curves to show an economy at a short-run equilibrium with a contractionary gap, when potential output is $10 trillion. Then illustrate how the gap would close in the long run.

4. In the diagram for this exercise, sketch a line representing a long-run aggregate supply at $10 trillion. Illustrate the effect of an increase in long-run aggregate supply. Then illustrate the effect of a decrease in long-run aggregate supply.

5. In the diagram use aggregate demand and short-run and long-run aggregate supply curves to show an economy at a long-run equilibrium of $10 trillion. Then illustrate the effects of an adverse supply shock.

12 Fiscal Policy

© Vince Streano/Corbis

P resident George W. Bush pushed through tax cuts to "get the country moving again." The Japanese government cut taxes and increased spending to stimulate its troubled economy. These are examples of *fiscal policy,* which focuses on the effect of taxing and public spending on aggregate economic activity. What is the proper role of fiscal policy in the economy? Can fiscal policy reduce swings in the business cycle? Why did fiscal policy fall on hard times for nearly two decades, and what has brought it to life? Does fiscal policy affect aggregate supply? Answers to these and other questions are addressed in this chapter, which examines the theory and practice of fiscal policy.

In this chapter, we first explore the effects of fiscal policy on aggregate demand. Next, we bring aggregate supply into the picture to consider the impact of taxes and government purchases on the level of income and employment in the economy.

Then, we examine the role of fiscal policy in moving the economy to its potential output. Finally, we review fiscal policy as it has been practiced since World War II. Throughout the chapter, we use simple tax and spending programs to explain fiscal policy. A more complex treatment, along with the algebra behind it, appears in the appendix to this chapter. Topics discussed include:

- Theory of fiscal policy
- Discretionary fiscal policy
- Automatic stabilizers
- Lags in fiscal policy
- Limits of fiscal policy
- The supply-side experiment

Theory of Fiscal Policy

Our macroeconomic model so far has viewed government as passive. But government purchases and transfer payments at all levels in the United States now exceed $3 trillion a year, making government an important player in the economy. From tax cuts to highways to national defense, fiscal policy affects the economy in myriad ways. We now move fiscal policy to center stage. As introduced in Chapter 3, *fiscal policy* refers to government purchases, transfer payments, taxes, and borrowing as they affect macroeconomic variables such as real GDP, employment, the price level, and economic growth. When economists study fiscal policy, they usually focus on the federal government, although governments at all levels affect the economy.

Fiscal Policy Tools

The tools of fiscal policy sort into two broad categories: automatic stabilizers and discretionary fiscal policy. **Automatic stabilizers** are revenue and spending programs in the federal budget that automatically adjust with the ups and downs of the economy to stabilize disposable income and, consequently, consumption and real GDP. For example, the federal income tax is an automatic stabilizer because (1) once adopted, it requires no congressional action to operate year after year, so it's *automatic*, and (2) it reduces the drop in disposable income during recessions and reduces the jump in disposable income during expansions, so it's a *stabilizer*. **Discretionary fiscal policy,** on the other hand, requires the deliberate manipulation of government purchases, taxation, and transfers to promote macroeconomic goals like full employment, price stability, and economic growth. President Bush's tax cuts are examples of discretionary fiscal policy. Some discretionary policies are temporary, such as a boost in government spending to fight a recession. The Bush tax cuts were originally scheduled to expire, and thus would remain discretionary fiscal policy measures unless they are made permanent.

Using the income-expenditure framework developed earlier, we will initially focus on the demand side to consider the effect of changes in government purchases, transfer payments, and taxes on real GDP demanded. The short story is that *at any given price level, an increase in government purchases or in transfer payments increases real GDP demanded, and an increase in net taxes decreases real GDP demanded, other things constant.* Next, we see how and why.

Changes in Government Purchases

Let's begin by looking at Exhibit 1, with real GDP demanded of $12.0 trillion, as reflected at point *a,* where the aggregate expenditure line crosses the 45-degree line. This equilibrium was determined two chapters back, where government purchases and net taxes each equaled $1.0 trillion and did not vary with income. Because government purchases equal net taxes, the government budget is balanced.

AUTOMATIC STABILIZERS

Structural features of government spending and taxation that reduce fluctuations in disposable income, and thus consumption, over the business cycle

DISCRETIONARY FISCAL POLICY

The deliberate manipulation of government purchases, taxation, and transfer payments to promote macroeconomic goals, such as full employment, price stability, and economic growth

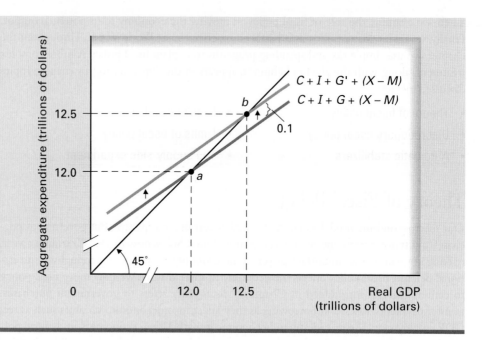

EXHIBIT 1

Effect of a $0.1 Trillion Increase in Government Purchases on Aggregate Expenditure and Real GDP Demanded

As a result of a $0.1 trillion increase in government purchases, the aggregate expenditure line shifts up by $0.1 trillion, increasing the level of real GDP demanded by $0.5 trillion. This model assumes the price level remains unchanged.

Net **Bookmark**

The Office of Management and Budget prepares *A Citizen's Guide to the Federal Budget* each year, with numerous, easy-to-read charts and graphs indicating sources of revenue and the types of spending. Access to these guides and other budget documents for the current year and previous years is available at http://www.whitehouse.gov/omb/budget/fy2002/guide.html.

Now suppose the federal policy makers, troubled by rising unemployment, decide to stimulate aggregate demand by increasing government purchases $0.1 trillion, or by $100 billion. To consider the effect on aggregate demand, let's initially assume that nothing else changes, including the price level and net taxes. This additional spending shifts the aggregate expenditure line up by $0.1 trillion to $C + I + G' + (X - M)$. At real GDP of $12.0 trillion, planned spending now exceeds output, so production will increase. This increase in production increases income, which in turn increases planned spending, and so it goes through the series of spending rounds.

The initial increase of $0.1 trillion in government purchases eventually increases real GDP demanded at the given price level from $12.0 trillion to $12.5 trillion, shown as point *b* in Exhibit 1. Because output demanded increases by $0.5 trillion as a result of an increase of $0.1 trillion in government purchases, the government purchases multiplier in our example is equal to 5. *As long as consumption is the only spending component that varies with income, the multiplier for a change in government purchases, other things constant, equals $1/(1 - MPC)$, or $1/(1 - 0.8)$ in our example.* Thus, we can say that for a given price level, and assuming that only consumption varies with income,

$$\Delta \text{Real GDP demanded} = \Delta G \times \frac{1}{1 - MPC}$$

where, again, Δ means "change in." This same multiplier appeared two chapters back, when we discussed shifts in consumption, investment, and net exports.

Changes in Net Taxes

A change in net taxes also affects real GDP demanded, but the effect is less direct. A *decrease* in net taxes, other things constant, *increases* disposable income at each level of real GDP, so consumption increases. In Exhibit 2, we begin again at equilibrium point *a,* with real GDP demanded equal to $12.0 trillion. To stimulate aggregate demand, suppose federal policy makers cut net taxes by $0.1 trillion, or by $100 billion, other things constant. We continue to assume that net taxes are autonomous—that is, that they do not vary with income. A $100 billion reduction in net taxes could result from a tax cut, an increase in transfer payments, or some combination of the two. The $100 billion decrease in net taxes increases disposable income by $100 billion at each level of real GDP. Because households now have more disposable income, they spend more and save more at each level of real GDP.

Because households save some of the tax cut, consumption increases in the first round of spending by less than the full tax cut. Specifically, *consumption spending at each level of real GDP rises by the decrease in net taxes multiplied by the marginal propensity to consume.* In our example, consumption at each level of real GDP increases by $100 billion times 0.8, or $80 billion. Decreasing net taxes by $100 billion causes the aggregate expenditure line to shift up by $80 billion, or $0.08 trillion, at all levels of income, as shown in Exhibit 2. This initial increase in spending triggers subsequent rounds of spending, following a now-familiar pattern in the income-expenditure cycle based on the marginal propensities to consume and to save. For example, the $80 billion increase in consumption increases output and income by $80 billion, which in the second round leads to $64 billion in consumption and $16 billion in saving, and so on through successive rounds. As a result, real GDP demanded eventually increases from $12.0 trillion to $12.4 trillion per year, or by $400 billion.

The effect of a change in net taxes on real GDP demanded equals the resulting shift of the aggregate expenditure line times the simple spending multiplier. Thus, we can say that the effect of a change in net taxes is

$$\Delta \text{ Real GDP demanded} = (-MPC \times \Delta NT) \times \frac{1}{1 - MPC}$$

The simple spending multiplier is applied to the shift of the aggregate expenditure line that results from the change in net taxes. This equation can be rearranged as

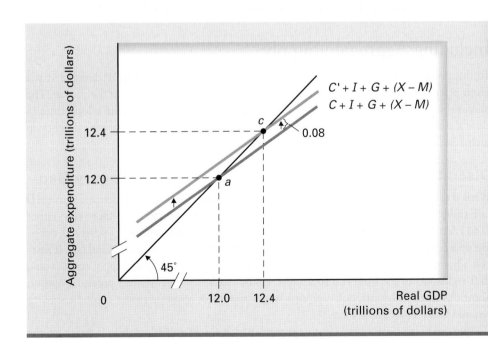

HOMEWORK
Xpress!
econ-apps debate

E X H I B I T **2**

Effect of a $0.1 Trillion Decrease in Autonomous Net Taxes on Aggregate Expenditure and Real GDP Demanded

As a result of a decrease in autonomous net taxes of $0.1 trillion, or $100 billion, consumers, who are assumed to have a marginal propensity to consume of 0.8, spend $80 billion and save $20 billion. The consumption function shifts up by $80 billion, or $0.08 trillion, as does the aggregate expenditure line. An $80 billion increase in the aggregate expenditure line eventually increases real GDP demanded by $0.4 trillion. Keep in mind that the price level is assumed to remain constant.

$$\Delta \text{ Real GDP demanded} = \Delta \text{ NT} \times \frac{-MPC}{1 - MPC}$$

SIMPLE TAX MULTIPLIER

The ratio of a change in real GDP demanded to the initial change in autonomous net taxes that brought it about; the numerical value of the simple tax multiplier is $-MPC/(1 - MPC)$

where $-MPC/(1 - MPC)$ is the **simple tax multiplier,** which can be applied directly to the change in net taxes to yield the change in real GDP demanded at a given price level. This tax multiplier is called *simple* because, by assumption, only consumption varies with income. For example, with an MPC of 0.8, the simple tax multiplier equals -4. In our example, a *decrease* of $0.1 trillion in net taxes results in an *increase* in real GDP demanded of $0.4 trillion, assuming a given price level. As another example, an *increase* in net taxes of $0.2 trillion would, other things constant, *decrease* real GDP demanded by $0.8 trillion.

Note two differences between the government purchase multiplier and the simple tax multiplier. First, the government purchase multiplier is positive, so an increase in government purchases leads to an increase in real GDP demanded. The tax multiplier is negative, so an increase in net taxes leads to a decrease in real GDP demanded. Second, the multiplier for a given change in government purchases is larger by 1 than the absolute value of the multiplier for an identical change in net taxes. In our example, the government purchase multiplier is 5, while the absolute value of the tax multiplier is 4. This holds because changes in government purchases affect aggregate spending directly—a $100 billion increase in government purchases increases spending in the first round by $100 billion. In contrast, a $100 billion decrease in net taxes increases consumption indirectly by way of a change in disposable income. Thus, each $100 billion decrease in net taxes increases disposable income by $100 billion, which, given an MPC of 0.8, increases consumption in the first round by $80 billion; people save the other $20 billion. In short, an increase in government purchases has a greater impact than does an identical tax cut because some of the tax cut gets saved, so it leaks from the spending flow.

To summarize: An increase in government purchases or a decrease in net taxes, other things constant, increases real GDP demanded. Although not shown, the combined effect of changes in government purchases and in net taxes is found by adding their individual effects.

Including Aggregate Supply

To this point in the chapter, we have focused on the amount of real GDP demanded at a given price level. We are now in a position to bring aggregate supply into the picture. The previous chapter introduced the idea that natural market forces may take a long time to close a contractionary gap. Let's consider the possible effects of discretionary fiscal policy in such a situation.

Discretionary Fiscal Policy to Close a Contractionary Gap

What if the economy produces less than its potential? Suppose aggregate demand curve *AD* in Exhibit 3 intersects the aggregate supply curve at point *e*, yielding the short-run output of $11.5 trillion and price level of 125. Output falls short of the economy's potential, opening up a contractionary gap of $0.5 trillion. Unemployment exceeds the natural rate. If markets adjusted naturally to high unemployment, the short-run aggregate supply curve would shift rightward in the long run to achieve equilibrium at the economy's potential output, point *e″*. History suggests, however, that wages and other resource prices could be slow to respond to a contractionary gap.

Suppose policy makers believe that natural market forces will take too long to return the economy to potential output. They also believe that the appropriate increase in government purchases, decrease in net taxes, or some combination of the two could increase aggregate

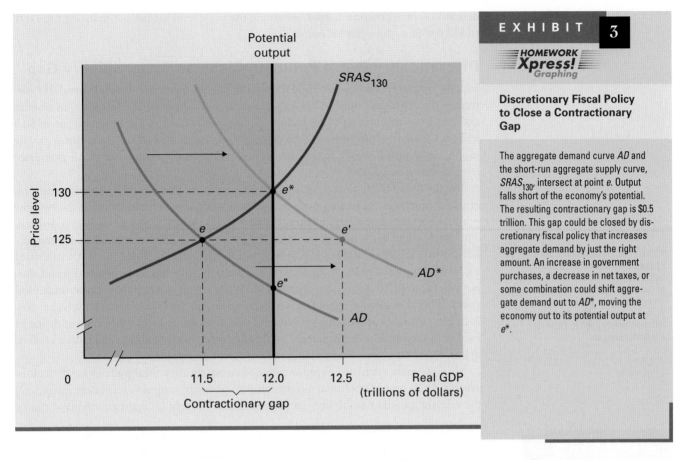

E X H I B I T **3**

HOMEWORK
Xpress!
Graphing

Discretionary Fiscal Policy to Close a Contractionary Gap

The aggregate demand curve *AD* and the short-run aggregate supply curve, *SRAS*₁₃₀, intersect at point *e*. Output falls short of the economy's potential. The resulting contractionary gap is $0.5 trillion. This gap could be closed by discretionary fiscal policy that increases aggregate demand by just the right amount. An increase in government purchases, a decrease in net taxes, or some combination could shift aggregate demand out to *AD**, moving the economy out to its potential output at *e**.

demand enough to return the economy to its potential output. A $0.2 trillion increase in government purchases reflects an **expansionary fiscal policy** that increases aggregate demand, as shown in Exhibit 3 by the rightward shift from *AD* to *AD**. If the price level remains at 125, the additional spending would increase the quantity demanded from $11.5 to $12.5 trillion. This increase of $1.0 trillion reflects the simple multiplier effect, given a constant price level.

At the original price level of 125, however, excess quantity demanded causes the price level to rise. As the price level rises, real GDP supplied increases, but real GDP demanded decreases along the new aggregate demand curve. The price level will rise until quantity demanded equals quantity supplied. In Exhibit 3, the new aggregate demand curve intersects the aggregate supply curve at *e**, where the price level is 130, the one originally expected, and output equals potential GDP of $12.0 trillion. Note that *an expansionary fiscal policy aims to close a contractionary gap.*

The intersection at point *e** is not only a short-run equilibrium but a long-run equilibrium. If fiscal policy makers are accurate enough (or lucky enough), the appropriate fiscal stimulus can close the contractionary gap and foster a long-run equilibrium at potential GDP. But the increase in output results in a higher price level. What's more, if the federal budget was in balance before the fiscal stimulus, the increase in government spending creates a budget deficit. In fact, the federal government has run deficits nearly every year since the early 1970s.

What if policy makers overshoot the mark and stimulate aggregate demand more than needed to achieve potential GDP? In the short run, real GDP will exceed potential output. In the long run, the short-run supply curve will shift back until it intersects the aggregate

EXPANSIONARY FISCAL POLICY

An increase in government purchases, decrease in net taxes, or some combination of the two aimed at increasing aggregate demand enough to return the economy to its potential output thereby reducing unemployment; policy used to close a contractionary gap

demand curve at potential output, increasing the price level further but reducing real GDP to $12.0 trillion, the potential output.

Discretionary Fiscal Policy to Close an Expansionary Gap

Suppose output exceeds potential GDP. In Exhibit 4, the aggregate demand curve, *AD'*, intersects the aggregate supply curve to yield short-run output of $12.5 trillion, an amount exceeding the potential of $12.0 trillion. The economy faces an expansionary gap of $0.5 trillion. Ordinarily, this gap would be closed by a leftward shift of the short-run aggregate supply curve, which would return the economy to potential output but at a higher price level, as shown by point *e"*.

But the use of discretionary fiscal policy introduces another possibility. By reducing government purchases, increasing net taxes, or employing some combination of the two, the government can implement a **contractionary fiscal policy** to reduce aggregate demand. This would move the economy to potential output without the resulting inflation. If the policy succeeds, aggregate demand in Exhibit 4 will shift leftward from *AD'* to *AD★*, establishing a new equilibrium at point *e★*. Again, with just the right reduction in aggregate demand, output will fall to $12.0 trillion, the potential GDP. Closing an expansionary gap through fiscal policy rather than through natural market forces results in a lower price level, not a higher one. Increasing net taxes or reducing government purchases also reduces a government deficit or increases a surplus. So a contractionary fiscal policy could reduce inflation and reduce a federal deficit. Note that *a contractionary fiscal policy aims to close an expansionary gap.*

Such precisely calculated expansionary and contractionary fiscal policies are difficult to achieve. Their proper execution assumes that (1) potential output is accurately gauged, (2) the relevant spending multiplier can be predicted accurately, (3) aggregate demand can be

CONTRACTIONARY FISCAL POLICY

A decrease in government purchases, increase in net taxes, or some combination of the two aimed at reducing aggregate demand enough to return the economy to potential output without worsening inflation; policy used to close an expansionary gap

---

EXHIBIT 4

Discretionary Fiscal Policy to Close an Expansionary Gap

The aggregate demand curve *AD'* and the short-run aggregate supply curve, *SRAS₁₃₀*, intersect at point *e'*, resulting in an expansionary gap of $0.5 trillion. Discretionary fiscal policy aimed at reducing aggregate demand by just the right amount could close this gap without inflation. An increase in net taxes, a decrease in government purchases, or some combination could shift the aggregate demand curve back to *AD** and move the economy back to potential output at point *e**.

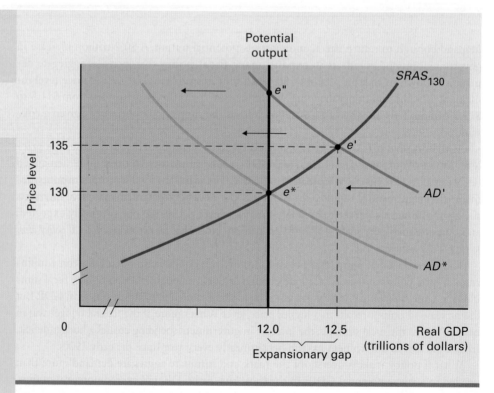

shifted by just the right amount, (4) various government entities can somehow coordinate their fiscal efforts, and (5) the shape of the short-run aggregate supply curve is known and will remain unaffected by the fiscal policy.

The Multiplier and the Time Horizon

In the short run, the aggregate supply curve slopes upward, so a shift of aggregate demand changes both the price level and the level of output. When aggregate supply gets in the act, we find that the simple multiplier overstates the amount by which output changes. The exact change of equilibrium output in the short run depends on the steepness of the aggregate supply curve, which in turn depends on how sharply production costs increase as output expands. *The steeper the short-run aggregate supply curve, the less impact a given shift of the aggregate demand curve has on real GDP and the more impact it has on the price level, so the smaller the spending multiplier.*

If the economy is already producing its potential, then in the long run, any change in fiscal policy aimed at stimulating demand will increase the price level but will not affect output. Thus, *if the economy is already producing its potential, the spending multiplier in the long run is zero.*

You now have some idea of how fiscal policy can work in theory. Let's take a look at fiscal policy in practice.

The Evolution of Fiscal Policy

Before the 1930s, discretionary fiscal policy was seldom used to influence the macroeconomy. Prior to the Great Depression, public policy was shaped by the views of **classical economists,** who advocated *laissez-faire,* the belief that free markets were the best way to achieve economic prosperity. Classical economists did not deny that depressions and high unemployment occurred from time to time, but they argued that the sources of such crises lay outside the market system, in the effects of wars, tax increases, poor growing seasons, changing tastes, and the like. Such external shocks could reduce output and employment, but classical economists believed that natural market forces, such as changes in prices, wages, and interest rates, could correct these problems.

Simply put, classical economists argued that if the economy's price level was too high to sell all that was produced, prices would fall until the quantity supplied equaled the quantity demanded. If wages were too high to employ all who wanted to work, wages would fall until the labor supplied equaled the labor demanded. And if the interest rate was too high to invest all that had been saved, interest rates would fall until the amount invested equaled the amount saved.

So the classical approach implied that natural market forces, through flexible prices, wages, and interest rates, would move the economy toward potential GDP. There appeared to be no need for government intervention. What's more, the government, like households, was expected to live within its means. The idea of government running a deficit was considered immoral. Thus, before the onset of the Great Depression, most economists believed that discretionary fiscal policy could do more harm than good. Besides, the federal government itself was a bit player in the economy. At the onset of the Great Depression, for example, federal outlays were less than 3 percent of GDP (compared to about 20 percent today).

The Great Depression and World War II

Although classical economists acknowledged that capitalistic, market-oriented economies could experience high unemployment from time to time, the prolonged depression of the 1930s strained belief in the economy's ability to mend itself. The Great Depression was marked by unemployment reaching 25 percent

CLASSICAL ECONOMISTS

A group of 18th- and 19th-century economists who believed that economic downturns were short-run phenomena that corrected themselves through natural market forces; thus, they believed the economy was self-correcting and needed no government intervention

with many factories sitting idle. With vast unemployed resources, output and income fell well short of the economy's potential.

The stark contrast between the natural market adjustments predicted by classical economists and the years of high unemployment during the Great Depression represented a collision of theory and fact. In 1936, John Maynard Keynes of Cambridge University, England, published *The General Theory of Employment, Interest, and Money*, a book that challenged the classical view and touched off what would later be called the Keynesian revolution. *Keynesian theory and policy were developed to address the problem of unemployment arising from the Great Depression.* Keynes's main quarrel with the classical economists was that prices and wages did not seem to be flexible enough to ensure the full employment of resources. According to Keynes, prices and wages were relatively inflexible in the downward direction—they were "sticky"— so natural market forces would not return the economy to full employment in a timely fashion. Keynes also believed business expectations might at times become so grim that even very low interest rates would not spur firms to invest all that consumers might save.

It is said that geologists learn more about the nature of the Earth's crust from one major upheaval, such as a huge earthquake or major volcanic eruption, than from a dozen more-common events. Likewise, economists learned more about the economy from the Great Depression than from many more-modest business cycles. Even though this depression began nearly eight decades ago, economists continue to sift through the rubble, looking for hints about how the economy really works.

Three developments in the years following the Great Depression bolstered the use of discretionary fiscal policy in the United States. The first was the influence of Keynes's *General Theory,* in which he argued that natural forces would not necessarily close a contractionary gap. Keynes thought the economy could get stuck well below its potential, requiring the government to increase aggregate demand so as to boost output and employment. The second development was the impact of World War II on output and employment. The demands of war greatly increased production and erased cyclical unemployment during the war years, pulling the U.S. economy out of its depression. The third development, largely a consequence of the first two, was the passage of the **Employment Act of 1946**, which gave the federal government responsibility for promoting full employment and price stability.

Prior to the Great Depression, the dominant fiscal policy was a balanced budget. Indeed, to head off a modest deficit in 1932, federal tax rates were raised, which only deepened the depression. In the wake of Keynes's *General Theory* and World War II, however, policy makers grew more receptive to the idea that fiscal policy could improve economic stability. The objective of fiscal policy was no longer to balance the budget but to promote full employment with price stability even if budget deficits resulted.

EMPLOYMENT ACT OF 1946

Law that assigned to the federal government the responsibility for promoting full employment and price stability

Automatic Stabilizers

This chapter has focused mostly on discretionary fiscal policy—conscious decisions to change taxes and government spending. Now let's get a clearer picture of automatic stabilizers. *Automatic stabilizers smooth out fluctuations in disposable income over the business cycle, thereby stimulating aggregate demand during recessions and dampening aggregate demand during expansions.* Consider the federal income tax. For simplicity, we assumed net taxes to be independent of income. In reality, the federal income tax system is progressive, meaning that the fraction of income paid in taxes increases as income increases. During an economic expansion, taxes claim a growing fraction of income, slowing the growth in disposable income and, hence, slowing the growth in consumption. Therefore, the progressive income tax relieves some of the inflationary pressure that might otherwise arise as output exceeds its potential during an economic expansion. Conversely, when the economy is in recession, output declines, but taxes decline faster, so disposable income does not fall as much as GDP. Thus, the progressive income tax cushions declines in disposable income, in consumption, and in aggregate demand.

Another automatic stabilizer is unemployment insurance. During economic expansions, the system automatically increases the flow of unemployment insurance taxes from the income stream into the unemployment insurance fund, thereby moderating aggregate demand. During recessions, unemployment increases and the system reverses itself. Unemployment payments automatically flow from the insurance fund to the unemployed, increasing disposable income and propping up consumption and aggregate demand. Likewise, welfare transfer payments automatically increase during hard times as more people become eligible. *Because of these automatic stabilizers, GDP fluctuates less than it otherwise would, and disposable income varies proportionately less than does GDP.* Because disposable income varies less than GDP does, consumption also fluctuates less than GDP does (as we saw in an earlier case study).

The progressive income tax, unemployment insurance, and welfare benefits were initially designed not so much as automatic stabilizers but as income redistribution programs. Their roles as automatic stabilizers were secondary effects of the legislation. Automatic stabilizers do not eliminate economic fluctuations, but they do reduce their magnitude. The stronger and more effective the automatic stabilizers are, the less need for discretionary fiscal policy. Because of the greater influence of automatic stabilizers, *the economy is more stable today than it was during the Great Depression and before.* As a measure of just how successful these automatic stabilizers have become in cushioning the impact of recessions, real consumption increased on average during the last six recession years. Without much fanfare, automatic stabilizers have been quietly doing their work, keeping the economy on a more even keel.

From the Golden Age to Stagflation

The 1960s was the Golden Age of fiscal policy. John F. Kennedy was the first president to propose a federal budget deficit to stimulate an economy experiencing a contractionary gap. Fiscal policy was also used on occasion to provide an extra kick to an expansion already under way, as in 1964, when Kennedy's successor, Lyndon B. Johnson, cut income tax rates to keep an expansion alive. *This tax cut, introduced to stimulate business investment, consumption, and employment, was perhaps the shining example of fiscal policy during the 1960s.* The tax cut seemed to work wonders, increasing disposable income and consumption. The unemployment rate dropped under 5 percent for the first time in seven years, the inflation rate dipped under 2 percent, and the federal budget deficit in 1964 equaled only about 1 percent of GDP (compared with about 4 percent in recent years).

Discretionary fiscal policy is a demand-management policy; the objective is to increase or decrease aggregate demand to smooth economic fluctuations. Demand-management policies were applied during much of the 1960s. But during the 1970s came a different problem—stagflation, the double trouble of higher inflation and higher unemployment resulting from a decrease in aggregate supply. The aggregate supply curve shifted left because of crop failures around the world, sharply higher OPEC-driven oil prices, and other adverse supply shocks. Demand-management policies were ill suited to cure stagflation because an increase of aggregate demand would worsen inflation, whereas a decrease of aggregate demand would worsen unemployment.

Other concerns also caused economists and policy makers to question the effectiveness of discretionary fiscal policy. These concerns included the difficulty of estimating the natural rate of unemployment, the time lags involved in implementing fiscal policy, the distinction between current and permanent income, and the possible feedback effects of fiscal policy on aggregate demand. We will consider each in turn.

Fiscal Policy and the Natural Rate of Unemployment

As we have seen, the unemployment that occurs when the economy is producing its potential GDP is called the *natural rate of unemployment*. Before adopting discretionary policies, public officials must correctly estimate this natural rate. Suppose the economy is producing its potential output of $12.0 trillion, as in Exhibit 5, where the natural rate of unemployment is 5.0 percent. Also suppose that public officials mistakenly believe the natural rate to be 4.0 percent, and they attempt to reduce unemployment and increase real GDP through discretionary fiscal policy. As a result of their policy, the aggregate demand curve shifts to the right, from *AD* to *AD'*. In the short run, this stimulation of aggregate demand expands output to $12.2 trillion and reduces unemployment to 4.0 percent, so the policy appears successful. But stimulating aggregate demand opens up an expansionary gap, which in the long run results in a leftward shift of the short-run aggregate supply curve. This reduction in aggregate supply pushes up prices and reduces real GDP to $12.0 trillion, the economy's potential. Thus, policy makers believe temporarily their plan worked, but pushing production beyond the economy's potential leads only to inflation in the long run.

Lags in Fiscal Policy

The time required to approve and implement fiscal legislation may hamper its effectiveness and weaken discretionary fiscal policy as a tool of macroeconomic stabilization. Even if a fiscal prescription is appropriate for the economy at the time it is proposed, the months and sometimes years required to approve and implement legislation means the medicine could do more harm than good. The policy might kick in only after the economy has already

---

EXHIBIT 5

When Discretionary Fiscal Policy Overshoots Potential Output

If public officials underestimate the natural rate of unemployment, they may attempt to stimulate aggregate demand even if the economy is already producing its potential output, as at point *a*. In the short run, this expansionary policy yields a short-run equilibrium at point *b*, where the price level and output are higher and unemployment is lower, so the policy appears to succeed. But the resulting expansionary gap will, in the long run, reduce the short-run aggregate supply curve from $SRAS_{130}$ to $SRAS_{140}$, eventually reducing output to its potential level of $12.0 trillion while increasing the price level to 140. Thus, attempts to increase production beyond potential GDP lead only to inflation in the long run.

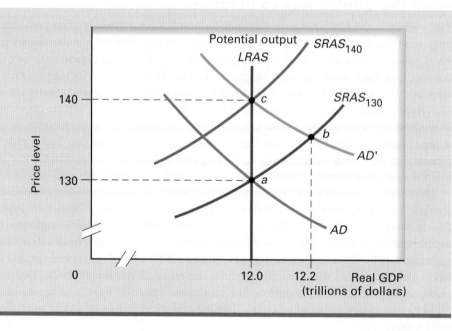

turned itself around. Because a recession is not usually identified until at least six months after it begins, and because the 10 recessions since 1945 lasted only 11 months on average, discretionary fiscal policy allows little room for error (more in a later chapter about timing problems).

Discretionary Fiscal Policy and Permanent Income

It was once believed that discretionary fiscal policy could be turned on and off like a water faucet, stimulating the economy at the right time by just the right amount. Given the marginal propensity to consume, tax changes could increase or decrease disposable income to bring about desired change in consumption. A more recent view suggests that people base their consumption decisions not merely on changes in their current income but on changes in their permanent income.

Permanent income is the income a person expects to receive on average over the long term. Changing tax rates for a year or two will not affect consumption much as long as people view the changes as only temporary. In 1967, for example, the escalating war in Vietnam increased military spending, pushing real GDP beyond its potential. The combination of a booming domestic economy and higher defense spending opened up an expansionary gap by 1968. That year, Congress approved a *temporary* tax hike, raising rates for 18 months. Higher taxes were supposed to soak up some disposable income, thereby reducing consumption to relieve inflationary pressure in the economy. But the reduction in aggregate demand turned out to be disappointingly small, and inflation was hardly affected. The *temporary* nature of the tax increase meant that consumers faced only a small cut in their permanent income. Because permanent income changed little, consumption changed little. Consumers simply saved less. As another example, in late 1997, Japanese officials introduced an income tax cut intended to stimulate Japan's flat economy. People expected the cut would be repealed after a year, so economists were skeptical that the plan would work, and it didn't. In short, *to the extent that consumers base spending decisions on their permanent income, attempts to fine-tune the economy with temporary tax changes will be less effective.*

The Feedback Effects of Fiscal Policy on Aggregate Supply

So far we have limited the discussion of fiscal policy to its effect on aggregate demand. Fiscal policy may also affect aggregate supply, although the effect is usually unintentional. For example, suppose the government increases unemployment benefits, paid with higher taxes on workers. If the marginal propensity to consume is the same for both groups, the reduced spending by workers should just offset the increased spending by beneficiaries. There should be no change in aggregate demand and thus no change in equilibrium real GDP, simply a redistribution of disposable income from the employed to the unemployed.

But could the program affect labor supply? Unemployed beneficiaries have less incentive to find work, so they may search at a more leisurely pace. A higher tax on workers reduces their opportunity cost of leisure, so they may work less. In short, the supply of labor could decrease as a result of offsetting changes in transfers and taxes. A decrease in the supply of labor would decrease aggregate supply, reducing the economy's potential GDP.

Both automatic stabilizers, such as unemployment insurance and the progressive income tax, and discretionary fiscal policies, such as changes in tax rates, may affect individual incentives to work, spend, save, and invest, although these effects are usually unintended consequences. We should keep these secondary effects in mind when we evaluate fiscal policies. It was concern about the effects of taxes on the supply of labor that motivated the tax cuts approved in 1981, as we will see next.

WALL STREET JOURNAL

Reading It **Right**

What's the relevance of the following statement from the Wall Street Journal*: "Inevitably, there is a big, long lag between the time spending is ordered by Congress and the time spending actually shows up in the economy."*

PERMANENT INCOME

Income that individuals expect to receive on average over the long term

U.S. Budget Deficits of the 1980s and 1990s

In 1981, President Reagan and Congress agreed on a 23 percent reduction in average income tax rates and a major buildup in defense programs, with no substantial offsetting reductions in domestic programs. Reagan argued that a reduction in tax rates would make people more willing to work and to invest because they could keep more of what they earned. Lower taxes would increase the supply of labor and the supply of other resources in the economy, thereby increasing the economy's potential output. In its strongest form, this supply-side theory held that output would increase enough to increase tax revenues despite the cut in tax rates. In other words, a smaller tax share of a bigger pie would exceed a larger tax share of a smaller pie. What happened as a result of the tax cut? Let's review events during the 1980s in the following case study.

The Supply-Side Experiment

Taking 1981 to 1988 as the time frame for examining the supply-side experiment, we can make some observations about the effects of the 1981 federal income tax cut, which was phased in over three years. After the tax cut was approved but before it took effect, a recession hit the economy and the unemployment rate climbed to nearly 10 percent in 1982.

Although it is difficult to untangle the growth generated by the tax cuts from the cyclical upswing following the recession of 1981–1982, we can say that between 1981 and 1988, the number employed climbed by 15 million and number unemployed fell by 2 million. Real GDP per capita, a good measure of the standard of living, increased by about 2.5 percent per year between 1981 and 1988. This rate was higher than the 1.4 percent average annual increase between 1973 and 1981 but lower than the 3.1 percent annual growth rate between 1960 and 1973.

Does the growth in employment and in real GDP mean the supply-side experiment was a success? Part of the growth in employment and output could be explained by the huge federal stimulus resulting from deficits during the period. The tax cuts, in effect, resulted in an expansionary fiscal policy. *The stimulus from the tax cut helped sustain a continued expansion during the 1980s—the longest peacetime expansion to that point in the nation's history.*

Despite the job growth, government revenues did not increase enough to offset the combination of tax cuts and increased government spending. Between 1981 and 1988, federal outlays grew an average of 7.1 percent per year, and federal revenues averaged 6.3 percent. So the tax cut failed to generate the revenue required to fund growing government spending. Before 1981, deficits had been relatively small—typically less than 1 percent compared with GDP. But deficits grew to about 4 percent compared with GDP by the middle of the decade. These were the largest peacetime deficits to that point on record. The recession of the early 1990s pushed the federal deficit up to 5 percent of GDP by 1992. These deficits accumulated into a huge national debt. *The national debt, which is the accumulation of annual deficits, nearly doubled relative to GDP from 33 percent in 1981 to 64 percent in 1992.*

Sources: *Economic Report of the President*, February 2004; *Survey of Current Business*, April 2004; and Herbert Stein, *The Fiscal Revolution in America*, 2nd ed. (Washington, D.C.: The AEI Press, 1996).

Given the effects of fiscal policy, particularly in the short run, we should not be surprised that elected officials might use it to get reelected. Let's look at how political considerations may shape fiscal policies.

Discretionary Fiscal Policy and Presidential Elections

After the recession of 1990–1991, the economy was slow to recover. At the time of the 1992 presidential election, the unemployment rate still languished at 7.5 percent, up two percentage points from when President George H. W. Bush took office in 1989. The higher unemployment rate was too much of a hurdle to overcome, and Bush lost his reelection bid to challenger Bill Clinton. Clinton's guide to the campaign was: "It's the economy, stupid."

© Michael Kleinfld/UPI/Landov

The link between economic performance and reelection success has a long history. Ray Fair of Yale University examined presidential elections dating back to 1916 and found, not surprisingly, that the state of the economy during the election year affected the outcome. Specifically, Fair found that a declining unemployment rate and strong growth rate in GDP per capita increased election prospects for the incumbent party. Another Yale economist, William Nordhaus, developed a theory of **political business cycles,** arguing that incumbent presidents use expansionary policies to stimulate the economy, often only temporarily, during an election year. For example, observers claim that President Nixon used expansionary policies to increase his chances for reelection in 1972. The evidence to support the theory of political business cycles is not entirely convincing. One problem is that the theory limits presidential motives to reelection, when in fact presidents may have other objectives. For example, President Bush passed up an opportunity in 1992 to sign a tax cut for the middle class because that measure would also have increased taxes on a much smaller group—upper-income taxpayers.

An alternative to the theory of political business cycles is that Democrats care more about unemployment and less about inflation than do Republicans. This view is supported by evidence indicating that during Democratic administrations, unemployment is more likely to fall and inflation is more likely to rise than during Republican administrations. Republican presidents tend to pursue contractionary policies soon after taking office and are more willing to endure a recession to reduce inflation. The country suffered a recession in the first term of the last six Republican presidents, including President George W. Bush. Democratic presidents tend to pursue expansionary policies to reduce unemployment and are willing to put up with higher inflation to do so. But George W. Bush pushed tax cuts early in his administration to fight a recession. Bush, like Reagan before him, seemed less concerned about the impact of tax cuts on federal deficits.

A final problem with the political business cycle is that other issues sometimes compete with the economy for voter attention. For example, in the 2004 election, President Bush's handling of the war on terrorism, especially in Iraq, became at least as much of a campaign issue as his handling of the economy.

Sources: *Economic Report of the President*, February 2004; Ray Fair, "The Effects of Economic Events on Votes for President," *Review of Economics and Statistics* (May 1978): 159–172; Ray Fair, *Predicting Presidential Elections and Other Things* (Stanford, Calif.: Stanford University Press, 2002); and William Nordhaus, "Alternative Approaches to the Political Business Cycle," *Brookings Papers on Economic Activity*, No. 2 (1989): 1–49.

Case **Study**

Public Policy

eActivity

Visit http://www.cato.org, which is the Web site for the Cato Institute, a nonprofit public policy research foundation in Washington, D.C. Read the Fiscal Policy Report Card on America's Governors: 2002. In the report, governors with the most fiscally conservative records—the tax and budget cutters—received the highest grades. Those who increased spending and taxes the most received the lowest grades. Find the grade for the governor of your state. Then check the previous report for 2000. Did your governor's grade improve or become worse? Do you know why?

POLITICAL BUSINESS CYCLES

Economic fluctuations that result when discretionary policy is manipulated for political gain

The large federal budget deficits of the 1980s and first half of the 1990s reduced the use of discretionary fiscal policy as a tool for economic stabilization. Because deficits were already large during economic expansions, it was hard to justify increasing deficits to stimulate the economy. For example, President Clinton proposed a modest stimulus package in early 1993 to help the recovery that was under way. His opponents blocked the measure, arguing that it would increase the deficit.

Balancing the Federal Budget—Temporarily

Clinton did not get his way with the stimulus package, but in 1993, he did manage to substantially increase taxes on high-income households, a group that now pays the lion's share of federal income taxes (the top 10 percent of earners pay about two-thirds of federal income taxes collected). The Republican Congress elected in 1994 imposed more discipline on federal spending as part of a plan to balance the budget. Meanwhile, the economy experienced a vigorous recovery fueled by growing consumer spending and rising business optimism based on technological innovation, market globalization, and the strongest stock market in history. The confluence of these events—tax increases on the rich, spending restraints, and a strengthening economy—changed the dynamic of the federal budget. Tax revenues gushed into Washington, growing an average of 8.3 percent per year between 1993 and 1998; meanwhile, federal outlays remained in check, growing only 3.2 percent per year. By 1998, that one-two punch knocked out the federal deficit, a deficit that only six years earlier reached a record at the time of $290 billion. The federal surplus grew from $70 billion in 1998 to $236 billion in 2000.

But by early 2001, the economy was in recession, so newly elected President George W. Bush pushed through an across-the-board $1.35 trillion, 10-year tax cut to "get the economy moving again." Then on September 11, 2001, nineteen men in four hijacked airplanes ended thousands of lives and ended chances of a strong economic recovery. Given the softening economy and uncertainty created by the terrorist attacks, consumers took a wait-and-see approach. Unemployment rose.

The president and Congress approved measures to help rebuild New York City, support the troubled airlines, beef up domestic security, and wage a worldwide war on terrorism. These programs coupled with tax cuts provided fiscal stimulus to an ailing economy. According to the President's Council of Economic Advisors, these measures "provided substantial short-term stimulus to economic activity and helped put the economy on the road to recovery."[1] Although the recession officially ended in November 2001, the recovery was slow and uneven and the unemployment rate rose until peaking in June 2003 at 6.3 percent. But the tax cuts and spending programs, including the war in Iraq, increased the federal deficit, which was projected to exceed $400 billion in 2004.

Conclusion

This chapter reviewed several factors that reduce the size of the spending and taxing multipliers. In the short run, the aggregate supply curve slopes upward, so the impact on equilibrium output of any change in aggregate demand is blunted by a change in the price level. In the long run, aggregate supply is a vertical line, so if the economy is already producing at its potential, the spending multiplier is zero. To the extent that consumers respond primarily to changes in their permanent incomes, temporary changes in taxes affect consumption less, so the tax multiplier will be smaller.

1. *Economic Report of the President,* February 2004, p. 43.

Throughout this chapter, we assumed net taxes and net exports would remain unchanged with changes in income. In reality, income taxes increase with income and net exports decrease with income. The appendix introduces these more realistic assumptions. The resulting spending multipliers and tax multipliers are smaller than those developed to this point.

Because of huge federal deficits between 1982 and 1996, discretionary fiscal policy fell out of favor in the 1980s and most of the 1990s. But fiscal policy came back into the picture during the recession of 2001. During the time when discretionary fiscal policy was dormant, monetary policy took center stage as *the* tool of economic stabilization. Monetary policy is the regulation of the money supply by the Federal Reserve. The next three chapters introduce money and financial institutions, review monetary policy, and discuss the impact of monetary and fiscal policy on economic stability and growth. Once we bring money into the picture, we will consider yet another reason why the simple spending multiplier is overstated.

SUMMARY

1. The tools of fiscal policy are automatic stabilizers and discretionary fiscal measures. Automatic stabilizers, such as the federal income tax, once implemented, operate year after year without congressional action. Discretionary fiscal policy results from specific legislation about government spending, taxation, and transfers.

2. The effect of an increase in government purchases on aggregate demand is the same as that of an increase in any other type of spending. Thus, the simple multiplier for a change in government purchases is $1/(1 - MPC)$.

3. A decrease in net taxes (taxes minus transfer payments) affects consumption by increasing disposable income. A decrease in net taxes does not increase spending as much as would an identical increase in government purchases because some of the tax cut is saved. The multiplier for a change in autonomous net taxes is $-MPC/(1 - MPC)$.

4. An expansionary fiscal policy can close a contractionary gap by increasing government purchases, reducing net taxes, or both. Because the short-run aggregate supply curve slopes upward, an increase in aggregate demand raises both output and the price level in the short run. A contractionary fiscal policy can close an expansionary gap by reducing government purchases, increasing net taxes, or both. Fiscal policy that reduces aggregate demand to close

an expansionary gap reduces both output and the price level.

5. Fiscal policy focuses primarily on the demand side, not the supply side. The problems of the 1970s, however, resulted more from a decline of aggregate supply than from a decline of aggregate demand, so demand-side remedies seemed less effective.

6. The tax cuts of the early 1980s were introduced as a way of increasing aggregate supply. But government spending grew faster than tax revenue, creating budget deficits that stimulated aggregate demand, leading to the longest peacetime expansion to that point in the nation's history. These huge deficits discouraged additional discretionary fiscal policy as a way of stimulating aggregate demand further, but success in reducing the deficit in the late 1990s spawned renewed interest in discretionary fiscal policy, as reflected by President Bush's tax cuts and spending programs beginning in 2001.

7. Tax cuts and new spending helped fight the recession of 2001 and strengthened a weak recovery. But these federal programs, combined with the recession and its aftermath, resulted in huge budget deficits in 2003 and 2004. The 2004 election became a referendum on President Bush's handling of the economy and the war on terror.

QUESTIONS FOR REVIEW

1. *(Fiscal Policy)* Define *fiscal policy*. Determine whether each of the following, other factors held constant, would lead to an increase, a decrease, or no change in the level of real GDP demanded:

   a. A decrease in government purchases
   b. An increase in net taxes
   c. A reduction in transfer payments
   d. A decrease in the marginal propensity to consume

2. *(The Multiplier and the Time Horizon)* Explain how the steepness of the short-run aggregate supply curve affects the government's ability to use fiscal policy to change real GDP.

3. *(Evolution of Fiscal Policy)* What did classical economists assume about the flexibility of prices, wages, and interest rates? What did this assumption imply about the self-correcting tendencies in an economy in recession? What disagreements did Keynes have with classical economists?

4. *(Automatic Stabilizers)* Often during recessions, the number of young people who volunteer for military service increases. Could this rise be considered a type of automatic stabilizer? Why or why not?

5. *(Permanent Income)* "If the federal government wants to stimulate consumption by means of a tax cut, it should employ a permanent tax cut. If the government wants to stimulate saving in the short run, it should employ a temporary tax cut." Evaluate this statement.

6. *(Fiscal Policy)* Explain why effective discretionary fiscal policy requires information about each of the following:

   a. The slope of the short-run aggregate supply curve
   b. The natural rate of unemployment
   c. The size of the multiplier
   d. The speed with which self-correcting forces operate

7. *(Automatic Stabilizers)* Distinguish between discretionary fiscal policy and automatic stabilizers. Provide some examples of automatic stabilizers. What is the impact of automatic stabilizers on disposable income as the economy moves through the business cycle?

8. *(Fiscal Policy Effectiveness)* Determine whether each of the following would make fiscal policy more effective or less effective:

   a. A decrease in the marginal propensity to consume
   b. Shorter lags in the effect of fiscal policy
   c. Consumers suddenly becoming more concerned about permanent income than about current income
   d. More accurate measurement of the natural rate of unemployment

9. (***Case* Study:** The Supply-Side Experiment) Explain why it is difficult to determine whether or not the supply-side experiment was a success.

10. (***Case* Study:** Discretionary Fiscal Policy and Presidential Elections) Suppose that fiscal policy changes output faster than it changes the price level. How might such timing play a role in the theory of political business cycles?

11. *(Balancing the Federal Budget)* Once the huge federal budget deficits of the 1980s and the first half of the 1990s turned into budget surpluses, why were policy makers more willing to consider discretionary fiscal policy?

PROBLEMS AND EXERCISES

12. *(Changes in Government Purchases)* Assume that government purchases decrease by $10 billion, with other factors held constant. Calculate the change in the level of real GDP demanded for each of the following values of the MPC. Then, calculate the change if the government, instead of reducing its purchases, increased autonomous net taxes by $10 billion.

    a. 0.9
    b. 0.8

    c. 0.75
    d. 0.6

13. *(Fiscal Multipliers)* Explain the difference between the government purchases multiplier and the net tax multiplier. If the MPC falls, what happens to the tax multiplier?

14. *(Changes in Net Taxes)* Using the income-expenditure model, graphically illustrate the impact of a $15 billion drop in government transfer payments on aggregate ex-

penditure if the MPC equals 0.75. Explain why it has this impact. What is the impact on the level of real GDP demanded, assuming the price level remains unchanged?

15. *(Fiscal Policy with an Expansionary Gap)* Using the aggregate demand–aggregate supply model, illustrate an economy with an expansionary gap. If the government is to close the gap by changing government purchases, should it increase or decrease those purchases? In the long run, what happens to the level of real GDP as a result of government intervention? What happens to the price level? Illustrate this on an AD–AS diagram, assuming that the government changes its purchases by exactly the amount necessary to close the gap.

16. *(Fiscal Policy)* This chapter shows that increased government purchases, with taxes held constant, can eliminate a contractionary gap. How could a tax cut achieve the same result? Would the tax cut have to be larger than the increase in government purchases? Why or why not?

17. *(Multipliers)* Suppose investment, in addition to having an autonomous component, also has a component that varies directly with the level of real GDP. How would this affect the size of the government purchase and net tax multipliers?

EXPERIENTIAL EXERCISES

18. *(Fiscal Policy)* The University of Washington's Fiscal Policy Center at http://depts.washington.edu/fpcweb/center/links.htm provides an extensive list of links about U.S. fiscal policy. Visit that site and use the links to determine what tax and spending proposals have been made in Congress during the past six months. Choose one of those proposals and use the *AD–AS* framework to explain its likely impact.

19. *(The Evolution of Fiscal Policy)* In the United States, fiscal policy is determined jointly by the president and Congress. The Congressional Budget Office at http://www.cbo.gov/ provides analysis to Congress, and the Office of

Management and Budget at http://www.whitehouse.gov/omb/index.html does the same for the executive branch. Visit these Web sites to get a sense of the kinds of analysis these groups do and how they might be used in determining fiscal policy.

20. *(Wall Street Journal)* "Washington Wire" is a column that appears on the front page of the *Wall Street Journal* each Friday. Review the latest column to determine what fiscal policy proposals are under consideration. Do the proposals deal more with discretionary fiscal policy or with automatic stabilizers? Are they designed to affect aggregate demand or aggregate supply?

HOMEWORK XPRESS! EXERCISES

*These exercises require access to McEachern Homework Xpress! If Homework Xpress! did not come with your book, visit **http://homeworkxpress.swlearning.com** to purchase.*

1. Use the diagram for this exercise with the helping line to draw a level of aggregate expenditure that would lead to an economy at an equilibrium with a real GDP of $9 trillion. Illustrate the effect of an increase in government purchases of $200 billion when the marginal propensity to consume is 0.75

2. Use the diagram with the helping line to draw a level of aggregate expenditure that would lead to an economy at an equilibrium with a real GDP of $9 trillion. Illustrate the effect of a decrease in autonomous net taxes of $200 billion when the marginal propensity to consume is 0.75

3. In the diagram use aggregate demand and short-run aggregate supply curves to show an economy at a short-run equilibrium, with a $0.5 trillion contractionary gap when

potential output is $9.5 trillion. Identify the equilibrium point and price level. Illustrate how fiscal policy can close the contractionary gap.

4. In the diagram use aggregate demand and short-run aggregate supply curves to show an economy at a short-run with a $0.5 trillion expansionary gap when potential output is $9.5 trillion. Identify the equilibrium point and price level. Illustrate how fiscal policy can close the expansionary gap.

5. In the diagram use aggregate demand and short-run aggregate supply curves to show an economy at equilibrium at its potential output of $9.5 trillion. Identify the equilibrium point and price level. Illustrate how fiscal policy can create an expansionary gap of $0.5 trillion.

The Algebra of Demand-Side Equilibrium

In this appendix, we continue to focus on aggregate demand, using algebra. In Appendix B two chapters back, we solved for real GDP demanded at a particular price level, then derived the simple multiplier for changes in spending, including government purchases. The change in real GDP demanded, here denoted as ΔY, resulting from a change in government purchases, ΔG, is

$$\Delta Y = \Delta G \times \frac{1}{1 - MPC}$$

The government spending multiplier is $1/(1 - MPC)$. In this appendix, we first derive the multiplier for net taxes that do not vary with income. Then, we incorporate proportional income taxes and variable net exports into the framework. *Note the simple multiplier assumes a shift of the aggregate demand curve at a given price level. By ignoring the effects of aggregate supply, we exaggerate the size of the multiplier.*

Net Tax Multiplier

How does a $1 increase in net taxes that do not vary with income affect real GDP demanded? We begin with Y, real GDP demanded, originally derived in Appendix B two chapters back:

$$Y = \frac{1}{1 - b}(a - bNT + I + G + X - M)$$

where b is the marginal propensity to consume and $a - bNT$ is that portion of consumption that is independent of the level of income (review Appendix B two chapters back if you need a refresher).

Now let's increase net taxes by $1 to see what happens to the level of real GDP demanded. Increasing net taxes by $1 yields

$$Y' = \frac{a - b(NT + \$1) + I + G + X - M}{1 - b}$$

The difference between Y' and Y is

$$Y - Y' = \frac{\$1(-b)}{1 - b}$$

Because b is the marginal propensity to consume, this difference can be expressed as $\$1 \times -MPC/(1 - MPC)$, which is the net tax multiplier discussed in this chapter. With the MPC equal to 0.8, the net tax multiplier equals $-0.8/0.2$, or -4, so the effect of decreasing net taxes by $1 is to increase GDP demanded by $4, with the price level assumed

constant. For any change larger than $1, we simply scale up the results. For example, the effect of decreasing net taxes by $10 billion is to increase GDP demanded by $40 billion. A different marginal propensity to consume will yield a different multiplier. For example, if the MPC equals 0.75, the net tax multiplier equals $-0.75/0.25$, or -3.

The Multiplier When Both *G* and *NT* Change

Although we did not discuss in the chapter the combined effects of changing both government purchases and net taxes, we can easily summarize these effects here. Suppose both increase by $1. We can bring together the two changes in the following equation:

$$Y'' = \frac{a - b(NT + \$1) + I + G + \$1 + X - M}{1 - b}$$

The difference between this equilibrium and Y (the income level before introducing any changes in G or NT) is

$$Y'' - Y = \frac{\$1(-b) + \$1}{1 - b}$$

which simplifies to

$$Y'' - Y = \frac{\$1(1 - b)}{1 - b} = \$1$$

Equilibrium real GDP demanded increases by $1 as a result of $1 increases in both government purchases and net taxes. This result is referred to as the *balanced budget multiplier*, which is equal to 1.

More generally, we can say that if ΔG represents the change in government purchases and ΔNT represents the change in net taxes, the resulting change in aggregate output demanded, ΔY, can be expressed as

$$\Delta Y = \frac{\Delta G - b\Delta NT}{1 - b}$$

The Multiplier with a Proportional Income Tax

A net tax of a fixed amount is easy to manipulate, but it is not realistic. Instead, suppose we introduce a *proportional income tax* rate equal to t, where t lies between 0 and 1. Incidentally, the proportional income tax is also the so-called *flat tax* discussed as an alternative to the existing progressive income tax. Tax collections under a proportional income tax equal the tax rate, t, times real GDP, Y. With tax collections of tY, disposable income equals

$$Y - tY = (1 - t)Y$$

We plug this value for disposable income into the equation for the consumption function to yield

$$C = a + b(1 - t)Y$$

To consumption, we add the other components of aggregate expenditure, I, G, and $X - M$, to get

$$Y = a + b(1 - t)Y + I + G + (X - M)$$

Moving the Y terms to the left side of the equation yields

$$Y - b(1 - t)Y = a + I + G + (X - M)$$

or

$$Y[1 - b(1 - t)] = a + I + G + (X - M)$$

By isolating Y on the left side of the equation, we get

$$Y = \frac{a + I + G + (X - M)}{1 - b(1 - t)}$$

The numerator on the right side consists of the autonomous spending components. A \$1 change in any of these components would change real GDP demanded by

$$\Delta Y = \frac{\$1}{1 - b(1 - t)}$$

Thus, the spending multiplier with a proportional income tax equals

$$\frac{1}{1 - b(1 - t)}$$

As the tax rate increases, the denominator increases, so the multiplier gets smaller. *The higher the proportional tax rate, other things constant, the smaller the multiplier.* A higher tax rate reduces consumption during each round of spending.

Including Variable Net Exports

The previous section assumed that net exports remained independent of disposable income. If you have been reading the appendixes along with the chapters, you already know how variable net exports fit into the picture. *The addition of variable net exports causes the aggregate expenditure line to flatten out because net exports decrease as real income increases.* Real GDP demanded with a proportional income tax and variable net exports is

$$Y = a + b(1 - t)Y + I + G + X - m(1 - t)Y$$

where $m(1 - t)Y$ shows that imports are an increasing function of disposable income. The above equation reduces to

$$Y = \frac{a + I + G + X}{1 - b + m + t(b - m)}$$

The higher the proportional tax rate, t, or the higher the marginal propensity to import, m, the larger the denominator, so the smaller the spending multiplier. If the marginal propensity to consume is 0.8, the marginal propensity to import is 0.1, and the proportional income tax rate is 0.2, the spending multiplier would be about 2.3, or less than half the simple spending multiplier of 5. And this still assumes the price level remains unchanged.

Since we first introduced the simple spending multiplier, we have examined several factors that reduce that multiplier: (1) a marginal propensity to consume that responds primarily to permanent changes in income, not transitory changes; (2) a marginal propensity to import; (3) a proportional income tax; and (4) the upward-sloping aggregate supply curve in the short run and a vertical aggregate supply curve in the long run. After we introduce money in the next two chapters, we will consider still other factors that reduce the size of the spending multiplier.

APPENDIX QUESTIONS

1. (*The Algebra of Demand-Side Equilibrium*) Suppose that the autonomous levels of consumption, investment, government purchases, and net exports are \$500 billion, \$300 billion, \$100 billion, and \$100 billion, respectively. Suppose further that the MPC is 0.85, that the marginal propensity to import is 0.05, and that income is taxed at a proportional rate of 0.25.

   a. What is the level of real GDP demanded?

   b. What is the size of the government deficit (or surplus) at this output level?

   c. What is the size of net exports at the level of real GDP demanded?

   d. What is the level of saving at this output?

   e. What change in autonomous spending is required to change equilibrium real GDP demanded by \$500 billion?

2. *(Spending Multiplier)* If the MPC is 0.8, the MPM is 0.1, and the proportional income tax rate is 0.2, what is the value of the spending multiplier? Determine whether each of the following would increase the value of the spending multiplier, decrease it, or leave it unchanged:

   a. An increase in the MPM
   b. An increase in the MPC
   c. An increase in the proportional tax rate
   d. An increase in autonomous net taxes

3. *(The Multiplier with a Proportional Income Tax)* Answer the following questions using the following data, all in billions. Assume an MPC of 0.8.

Disposable Income	Consumption
$ 0	$ 500
500	900
1,000	1,300
1,500	1,700

   a. Assuming that net taxes are equal to $200 billion regardless of the level of income, graph consumption against income (as opposed to disposable income).
   b. How would an increase in net taxes to $300 billion affect the consumption function?
   c. If the level of taxes were related to the level of income (i.e., income taxes were proportional to income), how would this affect the consumption function?

Money and the Financial System

W hy are you willing to exchange a piece of paper bearing Alexander Hamilton's portrait and the number 10 in each corner for a pepperoni pizza with extra cheese? If Russia can't pay its bills, why don't they simply print more rubles? Why are only a few of the world's largest banks American? Why was someone able to cash a check written on underpants? And why is there so much fascination with money? These and other questions are answered in this chapter, which introduces money and banking.

The word *money* comes from the name of the goddess (*Juno Moneta*) in whose temple Rome's money was coined. Money has come to symbolize all personal and business finance. You can read *Money* magazine and the "Money" section of *USA Today*, watch TV shows such as *Moneyline*, *Moneyweek*, and *Your Money*, and go to Web sites such as money.cnn.com, moneycentral.msn.com/home.asp, and smartmoney.com. With money, you can articulate your preferences—after all, money talks. And when it talks, it says a lot, as in, "Put your money where your mouth is" and "Show me the money." Money is the grease that lubricates the wheels of commerce (in fact, the old expression "grease the palm" means to pay someone). Just as grease makes for an easier fit among gears, money reduces the friction—the transaction costs—of market exchange. Too little can leave some parts creaking; too much can gum up the works.

This chapter is obviously about money. We begin with the evolution of money, tracing its use from primitive economies to our own. Then we turn to developments in the United States.

Topics discussed in this chapter include:

- Barter
- Functions of money
- Commodity and fiat money

- The Federal Reserve System
- Depository institutions
- Banking developments

The Evolution of Money

In the beginning, there was no money. The earliest families were largely self-sufficient. Each produced all it consumed and consumed all it produced, so there was little need for exchange. Without exchange, there was no need for money. When specialization first emerged, as some people went hunting and others took up farming, hunters and farmers had to trade. Thus, the specialization of labor resulted in exchange, but the assortment of goods traded was limited enough that people could easily exchange their products directly for other products—a system called *barter*.

Barter and the Double Coincidence of Wants

DOUBLE COINCIDENCE OF WANTS

Two traders are willing to exchange their products directly

Barter depends on a **double coincidence of wants,** which occurs when one trader is willing to exchange his or her product for something another trader offers. If a hunter was willing to exchange hides for a farmer's corn, that was a coincidence. But if the farmer was also willing to exchange corn for the hunter's hides, that was a double coincidence—a *double coincidence of wants*. As long as specialization was limited, to, say, two or three goods, mutually beneficial trades were relatively easy to realize—that is, trade wasn't much of a coincidence. As specialization increased, however, finding the particular goods that each trader wanted became more difficult.

In a barter system, traders must not only discover a double coincidence of wants, they must also agree on an exchange rate. How many hides should the farmer get for a bushel of corn? If only two goods are produced, only one exchange rate needs to be worked out. As the types of goods traded increased, however, exchange rates increased too. Specialization raised the transaction costs of barter. A huge difference in the values of the units to be exchanged can also made barter difficult. For example, a hunter who wanted a home that exchanged for 1,000 hides would be hard-pressed to find a home seller needing so many hides. High transaction costs of barter gave birth to money.

The Earliest Money and Its Functions

Nobody actually recorded the emergence of money. We can only speculate now about how it first came into use. Through experience with barter, traders may have found they could always find ready buyers for certain goods. If a trader could not find a good that he or she desired personally, some good with a ready market could be accepted instead. So traders began to accept a certain good not for immediate consumption but because that good was readily accepted by others and therefore could be retraded later. For example, corn might become accepted because traders knew that it was always in demand. As one good became generally accepted in return for all other goods, that good began to function as **money.** *Any commodity that acquires a high degree of acceptability throughout an economy becomes money.*

Money fulfills three important functions: a *medium of exchange,* a *unit of account,* and a *store of value.* Let's consider each.

Medium of Exchange

Separating the sale of one good from the purchase of another requires an item acceptable to all involved in the transactions. If a society, by luck or by design, can find a commodity that everyone will accept in exchange for whatever is sold, traders can save time, disappointment, and sheer aggravation. Suppose corn plays this role, a role that clearly goes beyond its role as food. We then call corn a medium of exchange because it is accepted in exchange by all buyers and sellers, whether or not they want corn for food. A **medium of exchange** is anything that is generally accepted in payment for goods and services. The person who accepts corn in exchange for some product believes corn can be traded later for whatever is desired.

In this example, corn is both a *commodity* and *money,* so we call it **commodity money.** The earliest money was commodity money. Gold and silver have been used as money for at least 4,000 years. Cattle served as money, first for the Greeks, then for the Romans. In fact, the word *pecuniary* (meaning "of or relating to money") comes from the Latin word for cattle, *pecus.* Salt also served as money. Roman soldiers received part of their pay in salt; the salt portion was called the *salarium,* the origin of the word *salary.* Also used as money were wampum (polished strings of shells) and tobacco in colonial America, tea pressed into small cakes in Russia, rice in Japan, and palm dates in North Africa. Note that commodity money was a good, not a service; a service is intangible and cannot be held for later exchange.

Unit of Account

A commodity such as corn that grows to be widely accepted becomes a **unit of account,** a standard on which prices are based. The price of shoes or pots or hides is measured in bushels of corn. Thus, corn serves not only as a medium of exchange; it also becomes a common denominator, a yardstick, for *measuring the value* of each product. Rather than having to determine exchange rates among all products, as with a barter economy, people can price everything using a single measure, such as corn. For example, if a pair of shoes sells for 2 bushels of corn and a 5-gallon pot sells for 1 bushel of corn, then a pair of shoes has the same value in exchange as two 5-gallon pots.

Store of Value

Because people do not want to make purchases every time they sell something, the purchasing power acquired through a sale must somehow be preserved. Money serves as a **store of value** when it retains purchasing power over time. The better it preserves purchasing power, the better money serves as a store of value, and the more willing people are to hold it. Consider again the distinction between a stock and a flow. Recall that a *stock* is an amount measured at a particular point in time, such as the amount of food in your refrigerator, or the amount of money you have with you right now. In contrast, a *flow* is an amount per unit of time, such as the calories you consume per day, or the income you earn per week. *Money* is a stock and *income* is a flow. Don't confuse money with income. The role of money as a stock is best reflected by money's role as a store of value.

MONEY

Anything that is generally accepted in exchange for goods and services

MEDIUM OF EXCHANGE

Anything that facilitates trade by being generally accepted by all parties in payment for goods or services

COMMODITY MONEY

Anything that serves both as money and as a commodity; money that has intrinsic value

UNIT OF ACCOUNT

A common unit for measuring the value of each good or service

STORE OF VALUE

Anything that retains its purchasing power over time

Desirable Qualities of Money

The introduction of commodity money reduced the transaction costs of exchange compared with barter, but commodity money also involves some transaction costs. First, if the commodity money is perishable, as is corn, it must be properly stored or its quality deteriorates; even then, it won't maintain its quality for long. Coins have a projected life of 30 years, a dollar note, only 18 months. So money should be *durable*. Second, if the commodity money is bulky, major purchases can become unwieldy. For example, many cartloads of corn would be needed to purchase a home selling for 5,000 bushels of corn. So money should be *portable*, or easily carried. Dollar notes are easier to carry than dollar coins, which may explain why dollar coins have never become popular. Third, some commodity money was not easily divisible into smaller units to offer a range of prices. For example, when cattle served as money, any price involving a fraction of a cow posed an exchange problem. So money should be *divisible*.

Fourth, if commodity money like corn is valued equally in exchange, regardless of its quality, people will keep the best corn and trade away the rest. As a result, the quality remaining in circulation will decline, reducing its acceptability. Sir Thomas Gresham wrote back in the 16th century that "bad money drives out good money"; this has come to be known as **Gresham's law.** People tend to trade away inferior money and hoard the best. Over time, the quality of money in circulation becomes less acceptable. To avoid this problem, money should be of *uniform quality*.

Fifth, commodity money usually ties up otherwise valuable resources, so it has a higher opportunity cost than, say, paper money. For example, corn that is used for money cannot at the same time be used for corn on the cob, corn flour, popcorn, or other food. So money should have *a low opportunity cost*.

If the supply or demand for money fluctuates unpredictably, so will the economy's price level, and this is the final problem with commodity money. For example, if a bumper crop increases the supply of corn, more corn is required to purchase other goods. This we call *inflation*. Likewise, any change in the demand for corn *as food* from, say, the invention of corn chips, would affect the exchange value of corn. Erratic fluctuations in the market for corn limit its usefulness as money, particularly as a unit of account and a store of value. So money *should maintain a relatively stable value*. Money supplied by a responsible issuing authority is likely to retain its value better than money whose supply depends on uncontrollable forces of nature such as good or bad growing seasons.

What all this boils down to is that *the best money is durable, portable, divisible, of uniform quality; has a low opportunity cost; and is relatively stable in value*. These qualities are offered in Exhibit 1, which also lists the rationale, good examples, and bad examples. Please spend a minute reviewing the table.

GRESHAM'S LAW

People tend to trade away inferior money and hoard the best

Coins

The division of commodity money into units was often natural, as in bushels of corn or heads of cattle. When rock salt was used as money, it was cut into uniform bricks. Because salt was usually of consistent quality, a trader had only to count the bricks to determine the total amount of money. When silver and gold were used as money, both their quantity and quality were open to question. Because precious metals could be *debased* with cheaper metals, the quantity and the quality of the metal had to be determined with each exchange.

This quality control problem was addressed by coining the metal. *Coinage determined both the amount and quality of the metal*. Coins allowed payment by count rather than by weight. A table on which this money was counted came to be called the *counter*, a term still used to-

| EXHIBIT | 1 | Six Desirable Qualities of Money | | |

Quality	Rationale	Good Examples	Bad Examples
1. Durable	Money should not wear out quickly	Coins; sea shells	Strawberries; seafood
2. Portable	Money should be easy to carry, even relatively large sums	Diamonds; paper money	Lead bars; potatoes
3. Divisible	Market exchange is easier if denominations support a range of possible prices	Honey; paper money and coins	Cattle; diamonds
4. Uniform Quality	If money is not of uniform quality, people will hoard the best and spend the rest, reducing its quality	Salt bricks; paper money; coins	Diamonds; DVDs
5. Low Opportunity Cost	The fewer resources tied up in creating money, the more available for other uses	Iron coins; paper money	Gold, silver; diamonds
6. Stable Value	People are more willing to accept and hold money if they believe it will keep its value over time	Anything whose supply can be controlled by issuing authority, such as paper money	Farm crops; gold

day. Initially, coins were stamped with an image on only one side, but before spending the coin someone could shave of the precious metal from the smooth side. To prevent this, coins came to be stamped with an image on both sides. But another problem arose because bits of metal could still be clipped from the edge. To prevent clipping, coins were bordered with a well-defined rim. If you have a dime or a quarter, notice the tiny serrations on the edge. These serrations, throwbacks from the time when coins were silver or gold rather than cheaper metals, reduced the chances of "getting clipped."

The power to issue coins, which was vested in the *seignior,* or feudal lord, was considered an act of sovereignty. Counterfeiting was considered an act of treason. If the face value of the coin exceeded the cost of coinage, minting coins was profitable. **Seigniorage** (pronounced "seen´-your-edge") refers to the profit earned by the seignior from coinage. **Token money** is money whose face value exceeds its production cost. Coins and paper money now in circulation in the United States are token money. For example, the 25-cent coin costs the U.S. Mint only about 3 cents to make. Coin production nets the federal government about $500 million a year in seigniorage. Paper money is a far greater source of seigniorage, as we'll see later.

SEIGNIORAGE

The difference between the face value of money and the cost of supplying it; the "profit" from issuing money

TOKEN MONEY

Money whose face value exceeds its cost of production

Money and Banking

The word *bank* comes from the Italian word *banca,* meaning "bench." Italian money changers originally conducted their business on benches. Banking spread from Italy to England, where London goldsmiths offered "safekeeping" for money and other valuables. The goldsmith gave depositors their money back on request, but because deposits by some people tended to offset withdrawals by others, the amount of idle cash, or gold, in the vault changed

Net **Bookmark**

Tour the American Currency Exhibit, an online money museum created by the Federal Reserve Bank of San Francisco at http://www.frbsf.org/currency/index.html. You can view pictures of the types of currency used throughout U.S. history. For an informative history of money in America, follow the "Tour Historical Context" link. Who produced money before the Federal Reserve was created? What determined the value(s) of a dollar?

little over time. Goldsmiths found that they could earn interest by making loans from this pool of idle cash.

Goldsmiths offered depositors safekeeping, but visiting the goldsmith to get money to pay for each purchase became a nuisance. For example, a farmer might visit the goldsmith to withdraw enough money to buy a horse. The farmer would then pay the horse trader, who would promptly deposit the receipts with the goldsmith. Thus, money took a round trip from goldsmith to farmer to horse trader and back to goldsmith. Because depositors soon grew tired of visiting the goldsmith every time they needed money, they began instructing the goldsmith to pay someone from their account. The payment amounted to moving gold from one stack (the farmer's) to another (the horse trader's). *These written instructions to the goldsmith were the first checks.* **Checks** have since become official-looking, but they need not be, as evidenced by the actions of a Montana man who paid a speeding fine with a check written on clean but frayed underpants. The Western Federal Savings and Loan of Missoula honored the check.

By combining the ideas of cash loans and checks, the goldsmith soon discovered how to make loans by check. Rather than lend idle cash, the goldsmith could simply create a checking balance for the borrower. *The goldsmith could extend a loan by creating an account against which the borrower could write checks. In this way goldsmiths, or banks, were able to create a medium of exchange, or to "create money."* This money, based only on an entry in the goldsmith's ledger, was accepted because of the public's confidence that these claims would be honored.

The total claims against the goldsmith consisted of claims by people who had deposited their money plus claims by borrowers for whom the goldsmith had created deposits. Because these claims exceeded the value of gold on reserve, this was the beginning of a **fractional reserve banking system,** a system in which reserves amounted to just a fraction of total deposits. The *reserve ratio* measured reserves as a percentage of total claims against the goldsmith, or total deposits. For example, if the goldsmith had reserves of $5,000 but deposits of $10,000, the reserve ratio would be 50 percent.

Paper Money

Another way a bank could create money was by issuing bank notes. **Bank notes** were pieces of paper promising the bearer specific amounts of gold or silver when the notes were presented to the issuing bank for redemption. In London, goldsmith bankers introduced bank notes about the same time they introduced checks. *Whereas checks could be redeemed only if endorsed by the payee, notes could be redeemed by anyone who presented them.* Paper money was often "as good as gold," because the bearer could redeem it for gold. In fact, paper money was more convenient than gold because it was less bulky and more portable. Bank notes that exchange for a specific commodity, such as gold, were called **representative money.** The paper money *represented* gold in the bank's vault.

The amount of paper money issued by a bank depended on that bank's estimate of the proportion of notes that would be redeemed. The greater the redemption rate, the fewer notes could be issued based on a given amount of reserves. Initially, these promises to pay were issued by private individuals or banks, but over time, governments took a larger role in printing and circulating notes. Once paper money became widely accepted, it was perhaps inevitable that governments would begin issuing **fiat money,** which derives its status as money from the power of the state, or by *fiat*. Fiat (pronounced "fee´at") money is money because the government says so. The word *fiat* is from the Latin and means "so be it." Fiat money is not redeemable for anything other than more fiat money; it is not backed by something of intrinsic value. You can think of fiat money as mere paper money. It is acceptable not because it is intrinsically useful or valuable—as is corn or gold—but because the

CHECK

A written order instructing the bank to pay someone from an amount deposited

FRACTIONAL RESERVE BANKING SYSTEM

Only a portion of bank deposits is backed by reserves

BANK NOTES

Originally, papers promising a specific amount of gold or silver to anyone who presented them to issuing banks for redemption; today, Federal Reserve notes are mere paper money

REPRESENTATIVE MONEY

Bank notes that exchange for a specific commodity, such as gold

FIAT MONEY

Money not redeemable for any commodity; its status as money is conferred initially by the government but eventually by common experience

government says it's money. Fiat money is declared **legal tender** by the government, meaning that you have made a valid and legal offer of payment of your debt when you pay with such money. *Gradually, people came to accept fiat money because they believed that others would accept it as well.* The currency issued in the United States today, and indeed paper money throughout most of the world, is fiat money.

A well-regulated system of fiat money is more efficient for an economy than commodity money. Fiat money uses only paper (a dollar note costs about 5 cents to make), but commodity money ties up something intrinsically valuable. Paper money makes up only part of the money supply. Modern money also includes checking accounts, which are electronic entries in bank computers.

LEGAL TENDER

U.S. currency that constitutes a valid and legal offer of payment of debt

The Value of Money

Economics in the Movies

Money has grown increasingly more abstract—from a physical commodity, to a piece of paper representing a claim on a physical commodity, to a piece of paper of no intrinsic value, to an electronic entry representing a claim on a piece of paper of no intrinsic value. So why does money have value? The commodity feature of early money bolstered confidence in its acceptability. Commodities such as corn, tobacco, and gold had value in use even if for some reason they became less acceptable in exchange. When paper money came into use, its acceptability was initially fostered by the promise to redeem it for gold or silver. But because most paper money throughout the world is now fiat money, there is no promise of redemption. So why can a piece of paper bearing the portrait of Alexander Hamilton and the number 10 in each corner be exchanged for a pizza or anything else selling for $10? *People accept these pieces of paper because, through experience, they have reason to believe that others will do so as well.* The acceptability of money, which we now take for granted, is based on years of experience with the stability of its value and with the willingness of others to accept it as payment. As we will soon see, when money's value becomes questionable, so does its acceptability.

The *purchasing power* of money is the rate at which it exchanges for goods and services. The higher the price level in the economy, the less can be purchased with each dollar, so the less each dollar is worth. The purchasing power of each dollar over time varies inversely with the economy's price level. As the price level increases, the purchasing power of money falls. To measure the purchasing power of the dollar in a particular year, you first compute the price index for that year and then divide 100 by that price index. For example, relative to the base period of 1982 through 1984, the consumer price index for April 2004 was 188. The purchasing power of a dollar in April 2004 was therefore 100/188, or $0.53, measured in 1982–1984 dollars. Exhibit 2 shows the steady decline in the value of the dollar since 1960, when it was worth $3.38 in 1982–1984 dollars.

When Money Performs Poorly

One way to understand the functions of money is to look at instances when money did not perform well. In an earlier chapter, we examined hyperinflation in Brazil. With prices growing by the hour, money no longer served as a reliable store of value, so people couldn't wait to exchange their money for goods or for some "hard" currency—that is, a more stable currency. If inflation gets high enough, people no longer accept the nation's money and instead resort to some other means of exchange. On the other hand, if the supply of money dries up or if the price system is not allowed to function properly, barter may be the only alternative. The following case study discusses instances when money performed poorly because of too much money, too little money, or a hobbled price system.

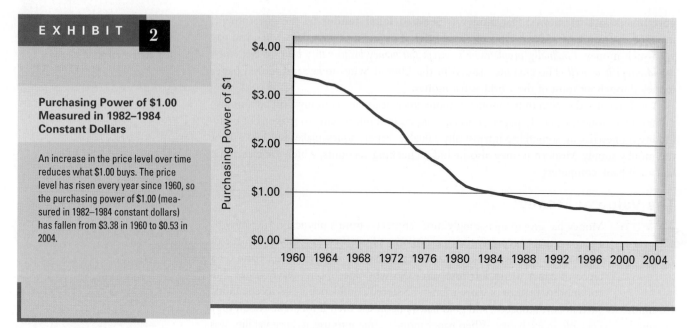

Source: Developed with CPI figures from the U.S. Bureau of Labor Statistics. For the latest CPI, go to http://bls.gov/cpi/home.htm.

EXHIBIT 2

Purchasing Power of $1.00 Measured in 1982–1984 Constant Dollars

An increase in the price level over time reduces what $1.00 buys. The price level has risen every year since 1960, so the purchasing power of $1.00 (measured in 1982–1984 constant dollars) has fallen from $3.38 in 1960 to $0.53 in 2004.

Case **Study**

Public Policy

*e*Activity

Are U.S. dollars still flowing into Russia? Find out from the Bank of Russia's statistics page at http://www.cbr.ru/eng/statistics/credit_statistics/ See how the flow of dollars has changed over time. For an Internet guide to Russian banks and finance, visit Russia on the Net at http://www.ru/

When Monetary Systems Break Down

What happens when there is too much money in circulation? We already discussed the transaction costs and distortions created by hyperinflation in Brazil. As a different example, hyperinflation in Russia following the breakup of the Soviet Union increased demand for so-called hard currencies, especially the dollar. Advertisers even quoted prices in "bucks." In keeping with Gresham's law, Russians traded rubles and hoarded dollars.

Consider the opposite problems: What if there isn't enough money to go around? Money became extremely scarce in 19th-century Brazil because a copper shortage halted minting of copper coins. People hoarded rather than traded the limited supply of coins available. In response, some merchants and tavern keepers printed vouchers redeemable for products sold by those merchants and taverns. These vouchers circulated as money until enough copper coins reappeared. Similarly, people coped with the shortage of money in the early American colonies by maintaining careful records, showing who owed what to whom.

For a more recent example of a money shortage, consider Panama, a Central American country that uses U.S. dollars as its currency. In 1988, the United States, responding to charges that Panama's leader was dealing drugs, froze Panamanian assets in the United States. This touched off a panic in Panama as bank customers tried to withdraw their dollars. Banks were forced to close for nine weeks. Dollars were hoarded, so people resorted to barter. Because barter is less efficient than a smoothly functioning monetary system, the currency shortage contributed to Panama's 30 percent GDP decline in 1988.

Finally, what happens when the price system is not allowed to operate? After Germany lost World War II, money in that country became close to useless. Despite tremendous inflationary pressure in the German economy, those who won the war imposed strict price controls. Because most price ceilings were set well below the market clearing level, sellers stopped accepting money, and this forced people to barter. Experts estimate that the lack of a viable currency cut German output in half. Germany's "economic miracle" of 1948 was due largely to the adoption of a reliable monetary system.

Thus, when the official money fails to serve as a medium of exchange because of price controls or hyperinflation or when hoarding dries up money in circulation, some other means of exchange emerges. But this diverts more resources from production to exchange. A poorly functioning monetary system increases the transaction costs of exchange. *No machine increases the economy's productivity as much as properly functioning money.* Indeed, it seems hard to overstate the value of a reliable monetary system. This is why we pay so much attention to money and banking.

Sources: Michael Casey, "Argentina Gets First Whiff of Inflation—Is It Back?" *Dow Jones Newswire*, 10 May 2004; and Michael Bryan et al., "Who Is That Guy on the $10 Bill?" *Economic Commentary: Federal Reserve Bank of Cleveland*, July 2000. Recent inflation rates around the world are available in the *World Development Report*; for the latest, go to http://econ.worldbank.org/wdr/.

Let's turn now to the development of money and banking in the United States.

Financial Institutions in the United States

You have already learned about the origin of modern banks: Goldsmiths lent money from deposits held for safekeeping. So you already have some idea of how banks work. Recall from the circular-flow model that household saving flows into financial markets where it is lent to investors. Financial institutions accumulate funds from savers and lend them to borrowers. Financial institutions, or **financial intermediaries,** earn a profit by "buying low and selling high"—that is, by paying a lower interest rate to savers than they charge borrowers.

Commercial Banks and Thrifts

A wide variety of financial intermediaries respond to the economy's demand for financial services. **Depository institutions**—such as commercial banks, savings banks, and credit unions—obtain funds primarily by accepting customer *deposits*. Depository institutions play a key role in providing the nation's money supply. Depository institutions can be classified broadly into commercial banks and thrift institutions.

Commercial banks are the oldest, largest, and most diversified of depository institutions. They are called **commercial banks** because historically they made loans primarily to *commercial* ventures, or businesses, rather than to households. Commercial banks hold about two-thirds of all deposits held by depository institutions. **Thrift institutions,** or **thrifts,** include savings banks and credit unions. Historically, savings banks specialized in making home mortgage loans. Credit unions, which are more numerous but smaller than savings banks, extend loans only to their "members" to finance homes or other major consumer purchases, such as new cars.

The Birth of the Fed

Before 1863, banks were chartered by the states in which they operated, so they were called *state banks.* These banks, like the English goldsmiths, issued bank notes. Thousands of different notes circulated and nearly all were redeemable for gold. The National Banking Act of

FINANCIAL INTERMEDIARIES

Institutions that serve as go-betweens, accepting funds from savers and lending them to borrowers

DEPOSITORY INSTITUTIONS

Commercial banks and thrift institutions; financial institutions that accept deposits from the public

COMMERCIAL BANKS

Depository institutions that historically made short-term loans primarily to businesses

THRIFT INSTITUTIONS, OR THRIFTS

Savings banks and credit unions; depository institutions that historically lent money to households

WALL STREET JOURNAL

Reading It **Right**

What's the relevance of the following statement from the Wall Street Journal: *One of Russia's biggest private banks, Alfa Bank, moved to reassure the market that it has enough money to meet obligations after lines of depositors formed outside its branches."*

FEDERAL RESERVE SYSTEM, OR THE FED

The central bank and monetary authority of the United States

RESERVES

Funds that banks use to satisfy the cash demands of their customers and the reserve requirements of the Fed; reserves consist of cash held by banks plus deposits at the Fed

1863 and later amendments created a new system of federally chartered banks called *national banks.* National banks were authorized to issue notes and were regulated by the Office of the Comptroller of the Currency, part of the U.S. Treasury. State bank notes were taxed out of existence, but state banks survived by creating checking accounts for borrowers. To this day, the United States has a *dual banking system* consisting of state banks and national banks.

During the 19th century, the economy experienced a number of panic "runs" on banks by depositors seeking to withdraw their funds. A panic was usually set off by the failure of some prominent financial institution. Following such a failure, fearful customers besieged their banks. Borrowers wanted additional loans and extensions of credit, and depositors wanted their money back. *As many depositors tried to withdraw their money, they couldn't because each bank held only a fraction of its deposits as reserves.* The failure of the Knickerbocker Trust Company in New York triggered the Panic of 1907. This banking calamity so aroused the public that Congress authorized a study that led to the creation of the **Federal Reserve System** in 1913 as the central bank and monetary authority of the United States.

Nearly all industrialized countries had formed central banks by 1900—the Bundesbank in Germany, the Bank of Japan, the Bank of England. But the American public's suspicion of such monopoly power led to the establishment of not one central bank but separate banks in 12 Federal Reserve districts around the country. The new banks were named after the cities in which they were located—the Federal Reserve Banks of Boston, New York, Chicago, San Francisco, and so on, as shown in Exhibit 3 (which district are you in?). *Throughout most of its history, the United States had what is called a decentralized banking system. The Federal Reserve Act moved the country toward a system that was partly centralized and partly decentralized.* All national banks joined the Federal Reserve System and were thus subject to new regulations issued by *the Fed,* as it came to be called (don't confuse *the Fed* with *the Feds,* shorthand for the FBI or other federal crime fighters). For state banks, membership was voluntary, and, to avoid the new regulations, most did not join.

Powers of the Federal Reserve System

The founding legislation established the Federal Reserve Board "to exercise general supervision" over the Federal Reserve System and to ensure sufficient money and credit in the banking system needed to support a growing economy. The power to issue bank notes was taken away from national banks and turned over to Federal Reserve Banks. (Take out a $1 note and notice what it says across the top: "Federal Reserve Note." On the $1 note, the seal to the left of George Washington's portrait identifies which Federal Reserve Bank issued the note.) The Federal Reserve was also given other powers: *to buy and sell government securities, to extend loans to member banks, to clear checks, and to require that member banks hold reserves equal to at least some specified fraction of their deposits.*

Federal Reserve Banks do not deal with the public directly. Each may be thought of as a bankers' bank. Reserve banks hold deposits of member banks, just as depository institutions hold deposits of the public, and they extend loans to member banks, just as depository institutions extend loans to the public. The name *reserve bank* comes from the responsibility to hold member bank *reserves* on deposit. **Reserves** are cash that banks have on hand or on deposit with the Fed to promote banking safety, to facilitate interbank transfers of funds, to satisfy the cash demands of their customers, and to comply with Federal Reserve regulations. By holding bank reserves, a reserve bank can clear a check written by a depositor at one bank and deposited at another bank, much like the goldsmith's moving of gold reserves from the farmer's account to the horse trader's account. Reserve banks were also authorized to lend to banks in need of reserves; the interest rate charged is called the *discount rate.*

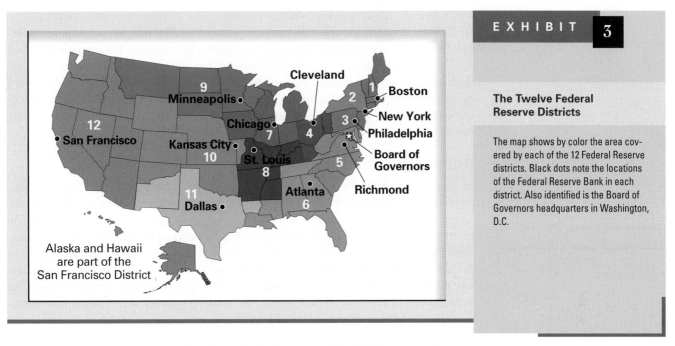

Source: Federal Reserve Board Web page at http://www.federalreserve.gov/otherfrb.htm.

A member bank is required to own stock in its district Federal Reserve Bank, and this entitles the bank to a specified dividend. Any additional profit earned by the reserve banks is turned over to the U.S. Treasury. So, technically, the reserve banks are owned by the member banks in the district.

Banking During the Great Depression

From 1913 to 1929, both the Federal Reserve System and the national economy performed relatively well. But the stock market crash of 1929 was followed by the Great Depression, creating a new set of problems for the Fed, such as bank runs caused by panicked depositors. The Fed, however, dropped the ball by failing to act as a lender of last resort—that is, the Fed did not lend banks the money they needed to satisfy deposit withdrawals in cases of runs on otherwise sound banks.

The Federal Reserve System was established precisely to prevent such panics and to add stability to the banking system. What went wrong? In a word, everything. Between 1930 and 1933, the support offered banks by the Federal Reserve System seemed to crumble in stages. As businesses failed, they were unable to repay their loans. These loan defaults led to the initial bank failures. As the crisis deepened, the public worried about the safety of their deposits, so cash withdrawals increased. To satisfy the greater demand for currency, banks were forced to sell their holdings of stocks and bonds. But with many banks trying to sell and with few buyers, securities prices collapsed, sharply reducing the market value of bank assets. Many banks did not survive. Between 1930 and 1933, about one-third of all U.S. banks failed.

Because the Fed failed to understand its role as the lender of last resort, it failed to extend loans on a large scale to banks experiencing short-run shortages of cash (in contrast, the Fed was a ready source of loans a half century later during the stock market crash of

1987). Fed officials viewed bank failures as a regrettable but inevitable result of poor management or simply as the effect of a collapsing economy. The Fed did not seem to understand that the banking system's instability was hurting the economy. For example, the stock market collapsed between 1929 and 1933 in part because many banks were trying to sell their securities at the same time. And the collapse came just when banks were badly in need of cash. Fed officials appeared concerned primarily with the solvency of the Federal Reserve Banks. These officials did not seem to realize they had unlimited money-creating power, so they could not fail.

Roosevelt's Reforms

In his first inaugural address in 1933, newly elected President Franklin D. Roosevelt said, "The only thing we have to fear is fear itself," a statement especially apt for a fractional reserve banking system. Most banks were sound as long as people had confidence in the safety of their deposits. But if many depositors, fearing the safety of their deposits, tried to withdraw their money, they could not do so because each bank held only a fraction of deposits as reserves. When he took office, Roosevelt declared a "banking holiday," closing banks for a week. This drastic measure was welcomed as a sign that something would be done. The Banking Acts of 1933 and 1935 shored up the banking system and centralized power with the Fed. Consider some important features of these acts.

Board of Governors

The Federal Reserve Board was renamed the *Board of Governors* and became responsible for setting and implementing the nation's monetary policy. *Monetary policy,* a term introduced in Chapter 3, is the regulation of the economy's money supply and interest rates to promote macroeconomic objectives. All 12 reserve banks moved under the Board of Governors, which consists of seven members appointed by the president and confirmed by the Senate. Each member serves a 14-year nonrenewable term, with one appointed every two years. *The long tenure of office was designed to insulate board members from political pressure.* A new U.S. president can be sure of appointing or reappointing only two members during a presidential term, so a new president could not change much. One governor is also appointed to chair the Board of Governors for a four-year renewable term.

Federal Open Market Committee

Originally, the power of the Federal Reserve System was vested in each of the 12 reserve banks. The Banking Acts established the **Federal Open Market Committee** (**FOMC**) to consolidate decisions about the key tool of monetary policy, **open-market operations**— the Fed's buying and selling government securities (tools of monetary policy will be examined in the next chapter). The FOMC consists of the 7 board governors plus 5 of the 12 presidents of the reserve banks; the chair of the Board of Governors heads the group. Because the New York Federal Reserve Bank carries out open-market operations, that bank's president always sits on the FOMC. The structure of the Federal Reserve System as it now stands is presented in Exhibit 4. The FOMC and, less significantly, the Federal Advisory Committee (which consists of a commercial banker from each of the 12 reserve bank districts) advise the board.

Regulating the Money Supply

Because reserves amount to just a fraction of deposits, the United States has a *fractional reserve* banking system, as already noted. The Banking Acts gave the Board of Governors more authority in setting reserve requirements, thereby giving the Fed an additional tool of

FEDERAL OPEN MARKET COMMITTEE (FOMC)

The 12-member group that makes decisions about open-market operations—purchases and sales of U.S. government securities by the Fed that affect the money supply and interest rates; consists of the 7 Board governors plus 5 of the 12 presidents of the reserve banks

OPEN-MARKET OPERATIONS

Purchases and sales of government securities by the Federal Reserve in an effort to influence the money supply

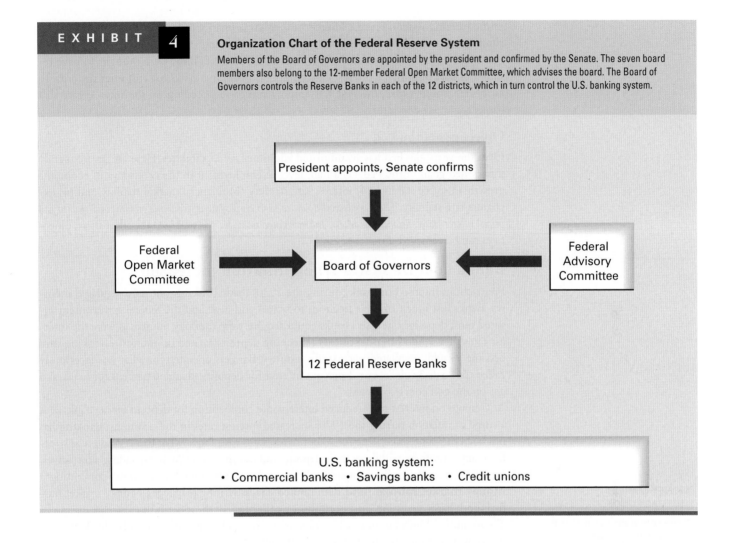

EXHIBIT 4

Organization Chart of the Federal Reserve System

Members of the Board of Governors are appointed by the president and confirmed by the Senate. The seven board members also belong to the 12-member Federal Open Market Committee, which advises the board. The Board of Governors controls the Reserve Banks in each of the 12 districts, which in turn control the U.S. banking system.

President appoints, Senate confirms

Federal Open Market Committee → Board of Governors ← Federal Advisory Committee

12 Federal Reserve Banks

U.S. banking system:
• Commercial banks • Savings banks • Credit unions

monetary policy. Thus, as of 1935, the Federal Reserve System has a variety of tools to regulate the money supply, including *(1) conducting open-market operations—buying and selling U.S. government securities; (2) setting the discount rate—the interest rate charged by reserve banks for loans to member banks; and (3) setting legal reserve requirements for member banks.* We will explore these tools in greater detail in the next chapter.

Deposit Insurance

Panic runs on banks stemmed from fears about the safety of bank deposits. The *Federal Deposit Insurance Corporation (FDIC)* was established in 1933 to insure the first $2,500 of each deposit account. Today the insurance ceiling is $100,000 per account. Banks purchase FDIC insurance. Over 90 percent of all banks now buy FDIC insurance. Other insurance programs take care of the rest. *Deposit insurance, by calming fears about the safety of bank deposits, worked wonders to reduce bank runs.*

Restricting Bank Investment Practices

As part of the Banking Act of 1933, commercial banks could no longer own corporate stocks and bonds, financial assets that fluctuate widely in value and contributed to instability of the banking system. The act limited bank assets primarily to loans and government securities—bonds issued by federal, state, and local governments. A *bond* is an IOU, so a government bond is an IOU from the government. Also, bank failures were thought to have resulted in part from fierce interest-rate competition among banks for customer deposits. To curb such competition, the Fed was empowered to set a ceiling on the interest rate that banks could pay depositors.

Objectives of the Fed

Over the years, the Fed has accumulated additional responsibilities. Here are six frequently mentioned goals of the Fed: (1) a high level of employment in the economy, (2) economic growth, (3) price stability, (4) interest rate stability, (5) financial market stability, and (6) exchange rate stability. *These goals boil down to high employment; economic growth; and stability in prices, interest rates, financial markets, and exchange rates.* As we will see, not all of these objectives can be achieved simultaneously.

Banks Lost Deposits When Inflation Increased

Restrictions imposed on banks during the 1930s made banking a heavily regulated industry. Banks lost much of their freedom to wheel and deal, and the federal government insured most deposits. The assets banks could acquire were carefully limited, as were the interest rates they could offer depositors (checking deposits earned no interest). Banking thus became a highly regulated, even stuffy, industry. Bankers operated on what was facetiously called the "3-6-3 rule"—pay 3 percent interest for deposits, charge 6 percent for loans, and get on the golf course by 3 P.M.

Ceilings on interest rates reduced interest-rate competition for deposits *among* banks. But a surge of inflation during the 1970s increased interest rates in the economy. Banking has not been the same since. When market interest rates rose above what banks could legally offer, many customers withdrew their deposits and put them into higher-yielding alternatives. In 1972, Merrill Lynch, a major brokerage house, introduced an account combining a **money market mutual fund** with limited check-writing privileges. Money market mutual fund shares are claims on a portfolio, or collection, of short-term interest-earning assets. These mutual funds became stiff competition for bank deposits, especially checkable deposits, which at the time paid no interest at banks.

Banks, like the London goldsmiths, used deposits to make loans. When people withdrew their deposits, banks had to support their loans by borrowing at prevailing interest rates, which were typically higher than the rates banks earned on their existing loans. Commercial banks, because their loans were usually for short periods, got in less trouble than savings banks did when interest rates rose. Savings banks had made loans for long-term mortgages, loans that would not be fully repaid for 30 years. Because they had to pay more interest to borrow funds than they were earning on these mortgages, savings banks were in big trouble, and many failed.

Bank Deregulation

In response to the loss of deposits and other problems, Congress tried to ease regulations, giving banks greater discretion in their operations. For example, interest-rate ceilings for deposits were eliminated, and all depository institutions were allowed to offer money market deposit accounts. Such accounts jumped from only $8 billion in 1978 to $200 billion in 1982. Some states, like California and Texas, also deregulated state-chartered savings banks. The combination of deposit insurance, unregulated interest rates, and wider latitude in the kinds of assets that savings banks could purchase gave them a green light to compete for large deposits in national markets. Once-staid financial institutions moved into the fast lane.

MONEY MARKET MUTUAL FUND

A collection of short-term interest-earning assets purchased with funds collected from many shareholders

Savings banks could wheel and deal but with the benefit of deposit insurance. The combination of deregulation and deposit insurance encouraged some on the verge of failing to take bigger risks—to "bet the bank"—because their depositors would be protected by deposit insurance. This created a *moral hazard,* which in this case was the tendency of bankers to take unwarranted risks in making loans because deposits were insured. Banks that were virtually bankrupt—so-called "zombie" banks—were able to attract additional deposits because of deposit insurance. Zombie banks, by offering higher interest rates, also drew deposits away from healthier banks. Meanwhile, because depositors were insured, most paid little attention to their banks' health. Thus, *deposit insurance, originally introduced during the Great Depression to prevent bank panics, caused depositors to become complacent about the safety of their deposits. Worse still, it caused those who ran the banks to take wild gambles to survive.*

Savings Banks on the Ropes

Many of these gambles didn't pay off, particularly loans to real estate developers, and banks lost a ton of money. The insolvency and collapse of a growing number of savings banks prompted Congress in 1989 to approve the largest financial bailout of any U.S. industry in history—a measure that would eventually cost about $250 billion. Taxpayers paid nearly two-thirds of the total, and savings banks paid the remaining third through higher deposit insurance premiums. The money was spent to shut down failing banks and to pay off insured depositors. Exhibit 5 shows the number of savings bank failures in the United States

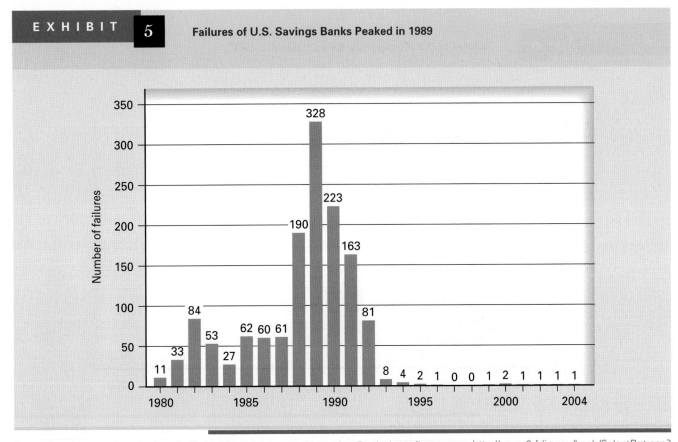

EXHIBIT **5** **Failures of U.S. Savings Banks Peaked in 1989**

Source: Based on annual reports from the Federal Deposit Insurance Corporation. For the latest figures, go to http://www2.fdic.gov/hsob/SelectRpt.asp?EntryTyp=30

by year since 1980. From their 1989 peak of 328, annual failures dropped to 2 or fewer since 1995. Because of failures and mergers the number of FDIC-insured savings banks fell from 3,418 in 1984 to 1,404 by 2004, a drop of 59 percent.

Credit unions, which make up the bulk of thrift institutions, got into less trouble than savings banks because credit unions typically lend for shorter periods. Still, because of failures and mergers, the number of federally insured credit unions declined about 25 percent from 12,596 in 1992 to 9,490 in 2004.

Commercial Banks Were Also Failing

The U.S. banking system experienced more change and upheaval during the 1980s and early 1990s than at any other time since the Great Depression. As was the case of savings banks, risky decisions based on deposit insurance coupled with a slump in real estate values hastened the demise of many commercial banks. Banks in Texas and Oklahoma failed when loans to oil drillers and farmers proved unsound. Banks in the Northeast failed because of falling real estate values, which caused borrowers to default. Hundreds of troubled banks, like Continental Illinois Bank, First Republic Bank of Dallas, and the Bank of New England, were taken over by the FDIC or forced to merge with healthier competitors. Exhibit 6 shows commercial bank failures since 1980. The rising tide during the 1980s is clear, with failures peaking at 280 in 1988. But by the mid-1990s, failures fell sharply, and have been in

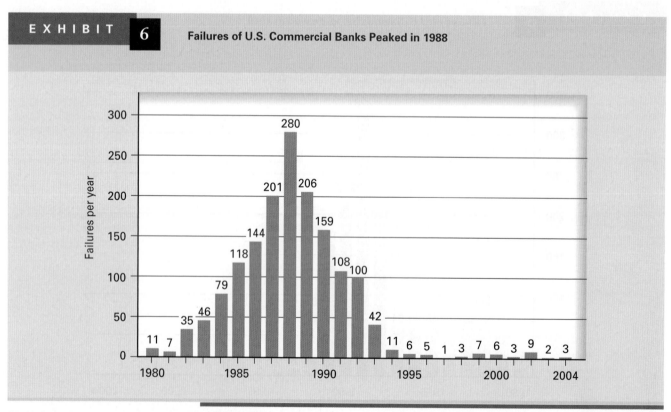

EXHIBIT 6

Failures of U.S. Commercial Banks Peaked in 1988

Source: Based on annual reports from the Federal Deposit Insurance Corporation. For the latest figures, go to http://www2.fdic.gov/hsob/SelectRpt.asp?EntryTyp=30.

single digits since 1995. Because of failures, mergers, and acquisitions, the number of FDIC-insured commercial banks fell from 14,496 in 1984 to 7,712 by 2004, a drop of 47 percent.

U.S. Banking Structure

As failed banks disappeared or merged with stronger banks, the industry got healthier. Bank profits grew fourfold during the 1990s. Although the number of commercial banks fell nearly by half over the last two decades, the United States still has more than any other country. Other major economies have fewer than 1,000 commercial banks. The large number of U.S. banks reflects past restrictions on **bank branches**, which are additional offices that carry out banking operations. Again, Americans, fearing monopoly power, did not want any one bank to become too large and too powerful. The combination of intrastate and interstate restrictions on branching spawned the many commercial banks that exist today, most of which are relatively small. For example, the largest 5 percent of commercial banks hold 86 percent of all commercial bank assets in 2004, meaning that 95 percent of commercial banks hold only 14 percent of the assets. Branching restrictions create inefficiencies, because banks cannot achieve optimal size and could not easily diversify their portfolios of loans across different regions.

In recent years, federal legislation has lifted restrictions on interstate branching and on the kinds of assets that banks can own. Two developments have allowed banks to get around branching restrictions: bank holding companies and mergers. A **bank holding company** is a corporation that may own several different banks. The *Graham-Leach-Bliley Act* of 1999 repealed some Depression-era restrictions on the kinds of assets a bank could own. A holding company can provide other services that banks are not authorized to offer, such as financial advising, leasing, insurance, credit cards, and securities trading. Thus, holding companies have blossomed in recent years. More than three-quarters of the nation's checking deposits are in banks owned by holding companies.

Another important development that allowed banks to expand their geographical reach is *bank mergers,* which have spread the presence of some banks across the country. Banks are merging because they want more customers and expect the higher volume of transactions to reduce operating costs per customer. Nationwide banking is also seen as a way of avoiding the concentration of bad loans that sometimes occur in one geographical area. The merger movement was fueled by a rising stock market during the 1990s and by federal legislation that facilitates consolidation of merged banks.

Bank holding companies and bank mergers have reduced the number of banks, but increased the number of branches. Exhibit 7 shows the number of commercial banks and bank branches in the United States since 1934. The number of banks remained relatively constant between 1934 and the mid-1980s but then declined, falling nearly in half since 1984 as a result of failures, mergers, and holding companies. The number of bank branches increased steadily, however, nearly doubling since 1984. So the number of branches per bank increased. In 1984, the average U.S. bank had about three branches; by 2003, the average bank had more than eight branches.

Exhibit 8 (a) shows the top 10 U.S. banks based on assets. The top three clearly dominate, with triple the assets of the next three. The top three banks grew mostly through mergers and acquisitions. For example, BankAmerica and NationsBank merged to form Bank of America, which then acquired FleetBoston, a major bank in the Northeast, which itself was a product of several mergers. Bank of America now stretches from coast to coast with over 6,000 branches. As another example of growth through merger, J.P Morgan

BANK BRANCHES

A bank's additional offices that carry out banking operations

BANK HOLDING COMPANY

A corporation that owns banks

EXHIBIT   7   **The Number of Commercial Banks Declined over the Last Two Decades, but the Number of Branches Continues to Grow**

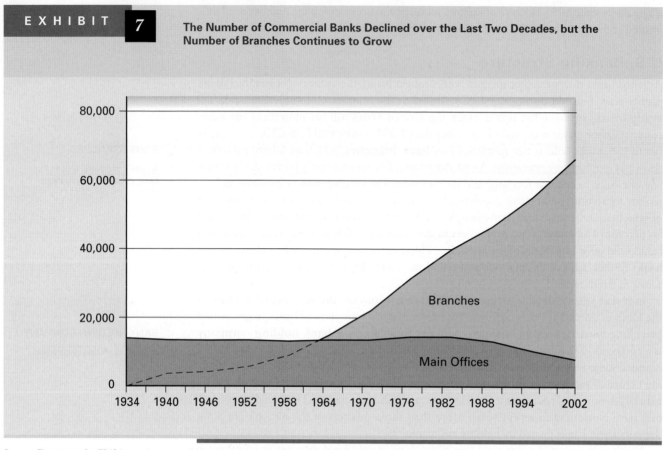

Source: Figures are for FDIC-insured commercial banks in the United States based on Federal Deposit Insurance Corporation data.

Chase in 2004 acquired Bank One, which had been the nation's sixth largest. National banks are the wave of the future.

How big are U.S. banks on the world stage? As indicated by Exhibit 8 (b), three of the largest four banks in the world are now American. Citigroup, the world's largest, had 275,000 employees as of 2004 in 100 countries on six continents. Citibank continues to expand, in 2004 acquiring over 400 branches from Washington Mutual and buying KorAm Bank of Korea. In the first quarter of 2004, Citibank earned $5.3 billion, a near record for any U.S. corporation. Although the top three U.S. banks are among the largest in the world, the next ranking U.S. bank was well down the 2004 list, ranking 35th. So there are only three world-class U.S. banks.

While U.S. banks were getting stronger and more global, Japanese banks were getting weaker. American banks have displaced Japanese banks at the top. Japan still placed three banks among the top 10, and a giant merger could soon create the largest bank in the world, but banking in Japan has suffered since 1990, as discussed in the following case study.

EXHIBIT 8

Top 10 Banks in America and the World
Among America's top 10 banks in panel (a), the top three are each more than twice the size of any other U.S. banks. Among the world's top 10 banks in panel (b), three of the top four are American.

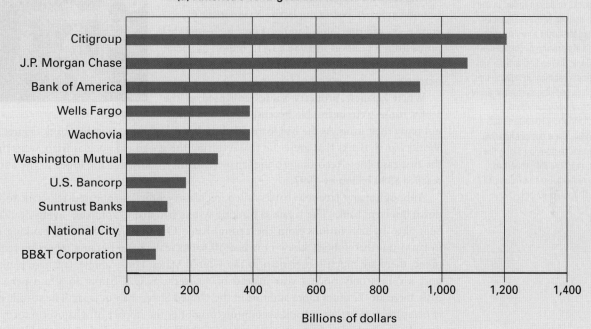

(a) America's 10 largest banks based on assets

Billions of dollars

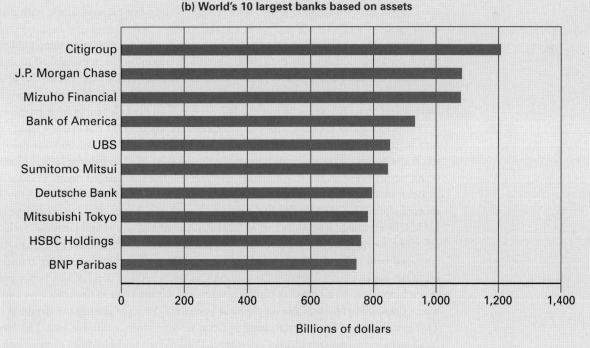

(b) World's 10 largest banks based on assets

Billions of dollars

(a) Source: SNL Financial. Figures are for 2003 but have been updated by the author to reflect mergers announced as of early 2004.
(b) Source: *The Banker*. Figures are for 2003 but have been updated by the author to reflect mergers announced as of early 2004.

C a s e **S t u d y**

Public Policy

*e*Activity

Numerous banks in Japan failed in the early 2000s, leaving Mizuho Financial Group the largest, after a restructuring that included absorption of the formerly stable Fuji Bank. To read an article and view statistical graphics on how things were in Japan's banking system in early 2004 visit http://www.die-bank.de/index.asp?channel=121010&art=305&issue=022004. For a comprehensive report of Japanese banking since the Asian crisis, read the IMF report at http://www.imf.org/External/Pubs/FT/GFSR/2003/01/pdf/chp2.pdf.

Banking Troubles in Japan

Prior to the 1980s, financial markets in Japan were heavily regulated, with restrictions on the interest rates that banks could offer. After deregulation, banks became more aggressive in attracting deposits and more willing to make riskier loans, particularly in real estate (sound familiar?). For example, the Kizu Credit Cooperative, by offering high interest rates, increased deposits from $2 billion in 1988 to $12 billion by 1995. Kizu lent these deposits to finance risky real estate purchases.

When Japanese property values collapsed in the 1990s, banks were in trouble because borrowers could not repay their loans. As the bad loans piled up, Japan experienced its first bank failures since World War II. Banks that grew the fastest during the go-go era, such as Kizu, were among the first casualties. According to the Japanese finance minister, bank losses in the country reached $350 billion by 1997.

Although many Japanese banks failed, regulatory officials appeared reluctant to close down insolvent banks. The Japanese banking system had many "zombies," living-dead banks kept alive by transfusions from the central bank. One problem with the banking crisis in Japan was that nobody knew how bad off banks really were because reporting requirements there are much looser than in the United States. For example, Japanese banks report earnings only once a year instead of quarterly, as U.S. banks do. On a per-capita basis, there are 12 times more auditors in the United States than in Japan. The so-called *lack of transparency* in Japanese bank accounting magnifies the impact of whatever information does become public. For example, when Fuji Bank reported that its problem loans were higher than it had previously disclosed, Fuji's share price plunged, along with shares of other banks.

To help resolve its banking crisis, the Japanese government in 1998 began using public funds to bail out troubled banks. By early 1999, about $75 billion had been earmarked to shore up 15 major banks. But by April 2001, Japanese banks and credit unions had as much as $1.2 trillion in problem loans, equivalent to about 30 percent of Japan's GDP. This made Japan's banking problem about five times bigger, in relative terms, than the U.S. savings bank problem.

Two major banks required bailouts by the central bank in 2003, but in 2004 Japan's economy began to brighten. Retail sales edged up, real GDP grew 3 percent, and unemployment fell. A decline in corporate bankruptcies cut the amount of *nonperforming loans*, or loans not being repaid. A rise in the stock market also dressed up bank balance sheets, because banks in Japan own much stock. The three Japanese banks ranked among the world's top 10 all showed a profit in 2004 for the first time in more than a decade. But Japan's fourth largest bank, UFJ Holdings, lost $4 billion in 2004 because of bad loans. Still Japanese banks were on course to cut their bad loans in half between 2002 and 2005. The Bank of Japan has encouraged banks to strengthen their liquidity management and become more transparent. Healthier banks are now helping the economy in Japan because they are in a better position to lend money to firms making capital investments. Japanese banks' troubles over the years were compounded by the "blanket deposit insurance" in place during the troubled times. This gave banks an incentive to gamble because depositors could not lose. The Bank of Japan plans to remove that blanket coverage in 2005. When UFJ Holdings merges with Mitsubishi Tokyo Financial Group in September 2005, the resulting bank will displace Citibank as the world's largest.

Sources: Ginny Parker, "Japan's Banks Post Profits," *Wall Street Journal*, 25 May 2004; "Economic and Financial Indicators," *Economist*, 5 June 2004; Hussain Kahn, "Ripples from a Japanese Bank Collapse," *Asia Times Online*, 15 December 2003, http://www.atimes.com; "Top 1000 World Banks," *The Banker*, 2 July 2003; Leika Kihara, "Japan Takenaka: No Comment On UFJ-MTFG Merger Talks," Dow Jones Newswires, 13 July 2004; an English-language Web site for Japan's central bank can be found at http://www.boj.or.jp/en/index.htm.

Conclusion

Money has grown increasingly more abstract over time, moving from commodity money to paper money that represented a claim on some commodity such as gold, to paper money with no intrinsic value. As you will see, paper money constitutes only a fraction of the money supply. Modern money also consists of electronic entries in the banking system's computers. So money has changed from a physical commodity to an electronic entry. Money today does not so much change hands as change computer accounts.

Money and banking have been intertwined ever since the early goldsmiths offered to hold customers' valuables for safekeeping. Banking has evolved from one of the most staid and regulated industries to one of the most competitive. Deregulation, branching innovations, and mergers have increased competition and have expanded the types of bank deposits. Reforms have given the Federal Reserve System more uniform control over depository institutions and have given the institutions greater access to the services provided by the Fed. Thus, all depository institutions can compete on more equal footing.

Deregulation provided greater freedom not only to prosper but also to fail. Failures of depository institutions create a special problem, however, because these institutions provide the financial underpinning of the nation's money supply, as you will see in the next chapter. There we will examine more closely how banks operate and supply the nation's money.

SUMMARY

1. Barter was the first means of exchange. As specialization grew, it became more difficult to discover the double coincidence of wants that barter required. The time and inconvenience of barter led even simple economies to develop money.

2. Anything that acquires a high degree of acceptability throughout an economy thereby becomes money. The first moneys were commodities, such as gold. Eventually, what changed hands were pieces of paper that could be redeemed for something of value, such as gold. As paper money became widely accepted, governments introduced fiat money—pieces of paper not redeemable for anything. Fiat money is money by law, or by fiat. Most currencies throughout the world today are fiat money. People accept

fiat money because, through experience, they believe that other people will do so as well.

3. The value of money depends on what it buys. If money fails to serve as a medium of exchange, traders find other means of exchange, such as barter, careful record keeping, some informal commodity money, or some other nation's currency. If a monetary system breaks down, more time must be devoted to exchange, leaving less time for production, so efficiency suffers.

4. The Federal Reserve System, or the Fed, was established in 1913 to regulate the banking system and issue the nation's currency. After a third of the nation's banks failed during the Great Depression, the Fed's powers were increased and centralized. After the Great Depression, the

primary powers of the Fed were to (a) conduct open-market operations (buying and selling U.S. government securities), (b) set the discount rate (the interest rate the Fed charges borrowing banks), and (c) establish reserve requirements (the share of deposits banks must hold in reserve).

5. Regulations introduced during the Great Depression turned banking into a closely regulated industry. Reforms in the 1980s gave banks more flexibility to compete for deposits with other kinds of financial intermediaries.

Some banks used this flexibility to make risky loans, but these gambles often failed, causing bank failures. In 1989, Congress approved a measure to close failing banks, pay off insured depositors, and impose tighter regulations. By the mid-1990s, U.S. banks were thriving once again, but Japanese banks remained troubled. Mergers and holding companies are creating banks that span the nation and are becoming the largest in the world.

QUESTIONS FOR REVIEW

1. *(Barter)* Define a double coincidence of wants and explain its role in a barter system.

2. *(Money Versus Barter)* "Without money, everything would be more expensive." Explain this statement. Then take a look at a Web page devoted to barter at http://www.ex.ac.uk/~RDavies/arian/barter.html. What are some current developments in barter exchange?

3. *(Functions of Money)* What are the three important functions of money? Define each of them.

4. *(Functions of Money)* "If an economy had only two goods (both *nondurable*), there would be no need for money because exchange would always be between those two goods." What important function of money does this statement disregard?

5. *(Characteristics of Money)* Why is universal acceptability such an important characteristic of money? What other characteristics can you think of that might be important to market participants?

6. *(Commodity Money)* Why do you think rice was chosen to serve as money in medieval Japan? What would happen to the price level if there was a particularly good rice harvest one year?

7. *(Commodity Money)* Early in U.S. history, tobacco was used as money. If you were a tobacco farmer and had two loads of tobacco that were of different qualities, which would you supply as money and which would you supply for smoking? Under what conditions would you use both types of tobacco for money?

PROBLEMS AND EXERCISES

8. *(Origins of Banking)* Discuss the various ways in which London goldsmiths functioned as early banks.

9. *(Types of Money)* Complete each of the following sentences:

   a. If the face value of a coin exceeds the cost of coinage, the resulting revenue to the issuer of the coin is known as _____.

   b. A product that serves both as money and as a commodity is _____.

   c. Coins and paper money circulating in the United States have face values that exceed the value of the

   materials from which they are made. Therefore, they are forms of _____.

   d. If the government declares that creditors must accept a form of money as payment for debts, the money becomes _____.

   e. A common unit for measuring the value of every good or service in the economy is known as a(n) _____.

10. *(Fiat Money)* Most economists believe that the better fiat money serves as a store of value, the more acceptable it is. What does this statement mean? How could people lose faith in money?

11. *(The Value of Money)* When the value of money was based on its gold content, new discoveries of gold were frequently followed by periods of inflation. Explain.

12. *(C a s e **Study**:* When Monetary Systems Break Down) In countries where the monetary system has broken down, what are some alternatives to which people have resorted to carry out exchange?

13. *(Depository Institutions)* What is a depository institution, and what types of depository institutions are found in the United States? How do they act as intermediaries between savers and borrowers? Why do they play this role?

14. *(Federal Reserve System)* What are the main powers and responsibilities of the Federal Reserve System?

15. *(Bank Deregulation)* Some economists argue that deregulated deposit rates combined with deposit insurance led to the insolvency of many depository institutions. On what basis do they make such an argument?

16. *(The Structure of U.S. Banking)* Discuss the impact of bank mergers on the structure of American banking. Why do banks merge?

17. *(C a s e **Study**:* Banking Troubles in Japan) Discuss problems with the banking system in Japan. In what ways are they similar to U.S. banking problems in the late 1980s and early 1990s? What is the current status of bank restructuring in Japan?

EXPERIENTIAL EXERCISES

18. *(When Money Performs Poorly)* Visit Glyn Davies's History of Money site at http://www.ex.ac.uk/~RDavies/arian/llyfr.html. Click on "A Comparative Chronology of Money" and check the years since 1939. How many hyperinflations are mentioned for those years? What does that tell you about the relationship between monetary systems and economic well-being?

19. *(U.S. Banking Structure)* The Federal Reserve Bank of Philadelphia often runs informative articles that are accessible to introductory economics students. At http://www.phil.frb.org/econ/wps/wp02.html, read the Working Paper titled "Do Bankers Sacrifice Value to Build Empires? Managerial Incentives, Industry Consolidation, and Financial Performance" by Joseph P. Hughes, William

W. Lang, Loretta J. Mester, Choon-Geol Moon, and Michael S. Pagano. Consider the numerous bank mergers of the early 2000s. Are bank mergers a good thing? What are the authors' conclusions about this?

20. *(Wall Street Journal)* The *Wall Street Journal* prints several features that track key interest rates. The daily Money Rates box lists the current prime lending rate, along with a variety of short-term rates. The weekly Key Interest Rates table reports on Treasury securities. And a weekly Consumer Savings Rates List shows the rates paid by 100 large banks. Take a look at these sources—you can find them on the Money and Credit Markets pages—and determine the extent to which all these interest rates move together.

Banking and the Money Supply

© Michael S. Yamashita/Corbis

How do banks create money? Why are banks called First Trust or Security National rather than Benny's Bank or Easy Money Bank and Trust? Why are we so interested in banks, anyway? After all, isn't banking a business like any other, such as dry cleaning, auto washing, or home remodeling? Why not devote a chapter to the home-remodeling business? Answers to these and related questions are provided in this chapter, which examines banking and the money supply.

In this chapter, we take a closer look at the unique role banks play in the economy. Banks are special in macroeconomics because, like the London goldsmith, they can convert a borrower's IOU into money, one key to a healthy economy. Because regulatory reforms have eliminated many of the distinctions between commercial banks and thrift institutions, and because thrifts represent a dwindling share of depository institutions, all depository institutions will usually be referred to more simply as *banks*.

We begin by going over the definitions of money, from the narrowest to the broadest. Then, we look at how banks work and how they create money. We also consider the Fed in more detail. As you will see, the Fed attempts to control the money supply directly by issuing currency and indirectly by regulating bank reserves. Topics discussed in this chapter include:

- Money aggregates
- Checkable deposits
- Balance sheets

- Money creation
- Money multiplier
- Tools of the Fed

Money Aggregates

When you think of money, what comes to mind is probably currency—dollar notes and coins. But as you learned in the last chapter, dollar notes and coins account for only part of the money supply. In this section, we consider three definitions of money.

The Narrow Definition of Money: M1

Suppose you have some cash with you right now—dollar notes and coins. Dollar notes and coins are part of the money supply as it's narrowly defined. If you were to deposit this cash in your checking account, you could then write checks directing your bank to pay someone from your account. **Checkable deposits,** or deposits against which checks can be written, are another part of the narrow definition of money. Checkable deposits can also be tapped with an ATM card or a debit card, usable at a growing number of retailers. Banks hold a variety of checkable deposits. In recent years, financial institutions have developed other kinds of accounts that carry check-writing privileges but also earn interest.

Money aggregates are various measures of the money supply defined by the Federal Reserve. The narrowest definition, called **M1,** consists of currency (including coins) held by the nonbanking public, checkable deposits, and traveler's checks. Note that currency sitting in bank vaults is not counted as part of the money supply because it is not being used as a medium of exchange. But checkable deposits are money because their owners can write checks or use debit cards to tap them. Checkable deposits are the liabilities of the issuing banks, which stand ready to convert them into cash. But unlike cash, checks are *not* legal tender, as signs that say "No Checks!" attest.

The primary currency circulating in the United States consists of Federal Reserve notes, which are produced by the U.S. Bureau of Engraving and Printing and are issued by and are liabilities of the 12 Federal Reserve Banks. Over 90 percent of the Fed's liabilities consist of Federal Reserve notes. The Fed spends about $750 million a year printing, storing, and distributing notes—the Fed's largest single expense. Because Federal Reserve notes are redeemable for nothing other than more Federal Reserve notes, U.S. currency is *fiat money.* The other component of currency is coins, manufactured and distributed by the U.S. Mint. Like paper money, U.S. coins are token money because their metal value is usually less than their face value (as noted in the previous chapter, a quarter costs about 3 cents to make).

About 60 percent of Federal Reserve notes now in circulation are in foreign hands. Some countries, such as Panama, Ecuador, and El Salvador, use U.S. dollars as their currency. This is actually a good deal for Americans because a $100 note that costs only about 5 cents to print can be "sold" to foreigners for $100 worth of goods and services. It's as if these countries were granting us an interest-free loan during the period the $100 note circulates abroad, usually several years. But having our currency used around the world poses special problems when it comes to counterfeiting, as discussed in the following case study.

CHECKABLE DEPOSITS

Deposits in financial institutions against which checks can be written and ATM or debit cards can be applied

MONEY AGGREGATES

Measures of the economy's money supply

M1

The narrowest measure of the money supply, consisting of currency and coins held by the non-banking public, checkable deposits, and traveler's checks

Faking It

One threat to the integrity of U.S. currency is the so-called supernote—a counterfeit $100 note of extremely high quality that began circulating around 1990. It's a remarkable forgery, including sequential serial numbers and a polymer security thread that took Crane & Company, the supplier of paper for U.S. currency since 1879, years to develop. By perfectly emulating the ferrous oxide inked in Benjamin Franklin's portrait, the supernote sometimes fools currency-scanning machines at the nation's 12 Federal Reserve Banks. Supernotes are ubiquitous abroad, especially in Europe. Up to one-fifth of the $100 notes circulating in Russia in a recent year were believed to be fake. Because of the supernote, merchants and bank tellers in Europe and the Far East grew reluctant to accept $100 notes.

© 2003, Mark Wilson/Getty Images

Expert engravers produced the supernote, but technological improvements in copy machines, computers, and printers now allow even amateurs to make passable counterfeits. About half the fake notes found in a recent year were produced with computers, copiers, and printers, up from just 1 percent in 1995. On U.S. soil, the Secret Service seizes most counterfeit money before it circulates. But foreign counterfeiting poses a problem for the U.S. Secret Service, which is primarily a domestic police force (few of the 2,000 agents work abroad). Most counterfeit money seized here is printed abroad, and seizures abroad have been growing.

To combat technological improvements in counterfeiting, U.S. currency was recently redesigned for the first time since 1929. In fact, U.S. currency had changed so little that on the back of a $10 note the car driving by the U.S. Treasury building was from the 1920s. The U.S. Treasury will redesign U.S. currency every 7 to 10 years to keep ahead of counterfeiters. In the first round of changes, the new notes remained the same size as the old ones and were printed on the same Crane paper in the same green and black ink. Changes to the $100 note included a new off-center portrait of Franklin, microprinting around the portrait that repeats the phrase "The United States of America," a watermark image of Franklin, and a "100" that shifts from green to black when viewed from different angles. A new security thread buried in the paper repeats "USA 100" in print 42-thousandths of an inch tall. This lettering is visible when the note is held up to light but is not reproducible on a photocopier, and the thread glows red under ultraviolet light. New $50, $20, $10, and $5 notes were also issued during that first round, each with its own security features, such as a security strip with a distinct color under ultraviolet light. The $1 note is not scheduled for a makeover because it is not popular with counterfeiters. Apparently, the cost of counterfeiting a $1 note and the risk of trying to pass it exceed the expected benefits.

Counterfeiters are fighting back. The watermark is faked by light printing. The security strip is faked by laboriously threading material between the two thin sheets of paper that make up the note. The hardest features to fake are microprinting, fine-line printing patterns, and details in the U.S. Treasury seal. The $20 note is most popular among domestic counterfeiters, and the $100 note most popular among foreign counterfeiters. Colombia is now the world's largest source of bogus American currency, accounting for 40 percent of the world total. Colombia borders on Ecuador, which converted to the U.S. dollar in 2000 and thus offers a ready outlet for counterfeits. In some countries, such as El Salvador, the U.S. dollar circulates alongside the native currency, which offers outlets for counterfeiters.

U.S. currency is now going through its second redesign in a decade, with a new $20 note introduced in 2003 and the $50 note in 2004. The most noticeable difference in the newly designed $20 note is the subtle background colors of peach and blue on both sides of the note. This marks the first coloring of U.S. currency other than black or green in modern American history. The $50 note adds a blue and red background to both sides of the note.

The United States has a policy of never recalling currency for fear that the world's hoarders of dollars might switch to other currencies, like euros or yen (remember, we want foreigners to hold onto their U.S. dollars). Over time, preference for the new currency and the replacement of old notes as they pass through the Fed will eventually eliminate old notes. But different designs of the same denomination will circulate side by side for some time, especially $100 notes. To give you some idea how long this could take, U.S. notes of $500 and up were last printed in 1946, and the Fed began taking them out of circulation in 1969. Yet hundreds of thousands of these big denominations are still hoarded by the public, about 60 years after they were last printed. Some big notes still show up at Federal Reserve Banks, where they are destroyed. But they remain legal tender. In fact, every U.S. note issued since 1861 remains legal tender today. That's one reason U.S. dollars are prized around the world.

Sources: Timothy O'Brien, "Lockboxes, Iraqi Loot and a Trail to the Fed," *New York Times*, 6 June 2004; "Spotting Counterfeit Currency," Federal Reserve Bank of Atlanta, http://www.frbatlanta.org; "The Use and Counterfeiting of U.S. Currency Abroad," *A Report to the Congress by the Secretary of the Treasury*, January 2000, at http://www.federalreserve.gov/boarddocs/rptcongress/counterfeit.pdf. The U.S. Treasury has a Web site providing information about new notes at http://www.moneyfactory.com/section.cfm/4.

Broader Money Aggregates

Economists regard currency and checkable deposits as money because each serves as a medium of exchange, a unit of account, and a store of value. Some other financial assets perform the store-of-value function and can be converted into currency or to checkable deposits. Because these are so close to money, they are called money under a broader definition.

Savings deposits earn interest but have no specific maturity date. Banks often allow depositors to shift funds from savings accounts to checking accounts by phone, an ATM card, or online, so distinctions between narrow and broad definitions of money have become blurred. **Time deposits** (also called *certificates of deposit,* or *CDs*) earn a fixed rate of interest if held for a specified period, ranging from several months to several years. Premature withdrawals are penalized by forfeiture of several months' interest. Neither savings deposits nor time deposits serve directly as media of exchange, so they are not included in M1, the narrowest definition of money.

Money market mutual fund accounts, mentioned in the previous chapter, are another component of money when defined more broadly. But, because of restrictions on the minimum balance, on the number of checks that can be written per month, and on the minimum amount of each check, these popular accounts are not viewed as money when narrowly defined.

Recall that M1 consists of currency (including coins) held by the nonbanking public, checkable deposits, and traveler's checks. **M2** includes M1 as well as savings deposits, small-denomination time deposits, and money market mutual fund accounts. **M3** includes M2 plus large-denomination time deposits ($100,000 or more). M3 is less liquid than M2, which is less liquid than M1. Exhibit 1 shows the size and relative importance of each aggregate. As you can see, compared to M1, M2 is nearly five times larger and M3 is nearly seven times larger. Thus, the narrowest definition of money includes only a fraction of broader aggregates. But distinctions between M1 and M2 become less meaningful as banks allow depositors to transfer funds from one account to another.

SAVINGS DEPOSITS

Deposits that earn interest but have no specific maturity date

TIME DEPOSITS

Deposits that earn a fixed rate of interest if held for the specified period, which can range from several months to several years; also called certificates of deposit

M2

A money aggregate consisting of M1 plus savings deposits, small-denomination time deposits, and money market mutual funds

M3

A money aggregate consisting of M2 plus large-denomination time deposits

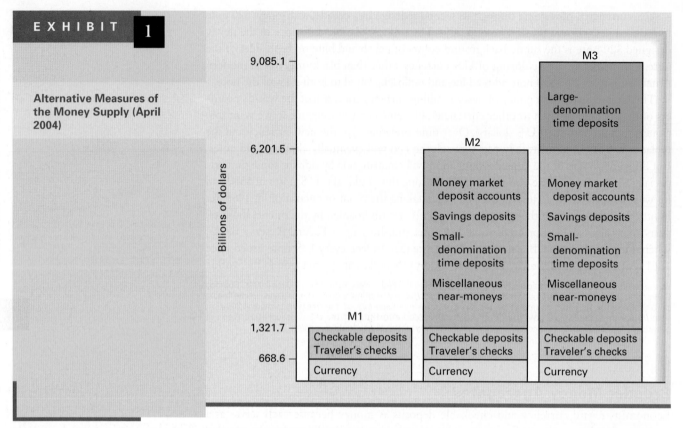

EXHIBIT 1

Alternative Measures of the Money Supply (April 2004)

Source: Based on seasonally adjusted monthly figures from the Federal Reserve Board. For the latest data, go to http://www.federalreserve.gov/releases/h6/Current/.

Credit Cards and Debit Cards: What's the Difference?

You may be curious why the definitions of money include debit cards but not credit cards. After all, most sellers accept credit cards as readily as they accept cash or checks (some, such as Internet sites, even prefer credit cards to checks), and credit cards finance more than 20 percent of all consumer purchases. Credit cards offer an easy way to get a loan from the card issuer. If you buy an airline ticket with a credit card, the card issuer lends you the money to pay for the ticket. You don't need money until you repay the credit card issuer. The credit card has not eliminated your use of money, merely delayed it. Three in four households have credit cards. About half of those with credit cards carry a balance from month to month, and that group's median balance was about $2,000 in 2003.

On the other hand, when you use your debit card at a grocery store or drugstore, you tap directly into your checking account, paying with electronic money—part of M1. Debit cards get their name because they *debit*, or reduce, your bank balance immediately. A **debit card**, also called a check card, combines the functions of an ATM card and a check. Debit cards are issued by banks, sometimes jointly with Visa, MasterCard, or other major card issuers. Even though debit cards look like credit cards, and even may bear a name such as Visa, they are not credit cards.

Many people prefer debit cards to checks because no checkbook is required and payments are made directly and immediately. Like ATM cards, debit cards usually require a personal identification number, or PIN, to use. In that regard, debit cards are safer than credit

DEBIT CARD

Cards that tap directly into the depositor's bank account to fund purchases; also called a check card, and usually doubles as an ATM card

cards, which could be more easily used by a thief. But debit cards have some disadvantages. Whereas a debit cards draws down your checking account immediately, credit cards provide a 20- to 30-day grace period between a purchase and required payment. And some people prefer to borrow beyond the grace period—that is, they carry a balance from month to month. Also, because debit cards immediately reduce your bank account, you can't dispute a bill or withhold payment as you can with a credit card and you can't stop payment as you can with a check. Still, debit cards came from nowhere a few years ago to be used by half the households surveyed in 2003.[1]

How Banks Work

Banks attract deposits from savers to lend to borrowers, earning a profit on the difference between the interest paid depositors and the interest charged borrowers. Savers need a safe place for their money, and borrowers need credit; banks try to earn a profit by serving both groups. To inspire depositor confidence, banks usually present an image of trust and assurance. For example, banks are more apt to be called Fidelity Trust, Security National, Surety Bank, or Federal Savings than Benny's Bank, Easy Money Bank and Trust, Loans 'R' Us, or Loadsamoney. In contrast, *finance companies* are financial intermediaries that do not get their funds from depositors, so they can choose names aimed at borrowers—names such as Household Finance, The Money Store, or Home Improvement Loan Online.

Banks Are Financial Intermediaries

By bringing together both sides of the money market, banks serve as financial intermediaries, or as go-betweens. They gather various amounts from savers and repackage these funds into the amounts demanded by borrowers. Some savers need their money next week, some next year, some only after retirement. Likewise, borrowers need credit for different lengths of time. Banks, as intermediaries, offer desirable durations to both groups. In short, *banks reduce the transaction costs of channeling savings to creditworthy borrowers.* Here's how.

Coping with Asymmetric Information

Banks, as lenders, try to identify borrowers who are willing to pay interest and are able to repay the loans. But borrowers have more reliable information about their own credit history and financial plans than do lenders. Thus, in the market for loans, there is **asymmetric information**—an inequality in what's known by each party to the transaction. Asymmetric information is unequal information. This wouldn't be a problem if borrowers could be trusted to report relevant details to lenders. Some borrowers, however, have an incentive to suppress important information, such as other debts outstanding, a troubled financial history, or plans to use the borrowed funds in a risky venture. Because of their experience and expertise in evaluating loan applicants, banks can better cope with asymmetric information than could an individual saver. Banks also know more about lending agreements than do individual savers. Thus, savers, rather than lending their money directly, are better off depositing their money in banks, and let banks do the lending. *The economy is more efficient because banks develop expertise in evaluating creditworthiness, structuring loans, and enforcing loan contracts.*

ASYMMETRIC INFORMATION

A situation in which one side of the market has more reliable information than the other side

Reducing Risk Through Diversification

By developing a diversified portfolio of assets rather than lending funds to a single borrower, banks reduce the risk to each individual saver. A bank, in effect, lends a tiny fraction of each

---

1. Survey results reported by C. E. Anguelov et al. "U.S. Consumers and Electronic Banking, 1995–2003," *Federal Reserve Bulletin* (Winter 2004): 1–18, also available at http://www.federalreserve.gov/pubs/bulletin/2004/winter04_ca.pdf.

saver's deposits to each of its many borrowers. If one borrower fails to repay a loan, it hardly affects a large, diversified bank. Certainly such a default does not represent the personal disaster it would if one saver's entire nest egg was loaned directly to that defaulting borrower.

Starting a Bank

We could consider the operation of any type of depository institution (commercial bank, savings bank, or credit union), but let's focus on starting a commercial bank because they are the most important in terms of total assets. What's more, the operating principles apply to other depository institutions as well. Suppose some business leaders in your hometown want to establish a commercial bank called Home Bank. To obtain a *charter*, or the right to operate, they must apply to the state banking authority in the case of a state bank or to the U.S. Comptroller of the Currency in the case of a national bank. The chartering agency reviewing the application judges the quality of management, the need for another bank in the region, and the likely success of the bank.

Suppose the founders plan to invest $500,000 in the bank, and they so indicate on their application for a national charter. If their application is approved, they incorporate, issuing themselves shares of stock—certificates of ownership. Thus, they exchange $500,000 for shares of stock in the bank. These shares are called the *owners' equity,* or the **net worth,** of the bank. Part of the $500,000, say $50,000, is used to buy shares in their district Federal Reserve Bank. So Home Bank is now a member of the Federal Reserve System. With the remaining $450,000, the owners acquire and furnish the bank building.

To focus our discussion, we will examine the bank's **balance sheet,** presented in Exhibit 2. As the name implies, a balance sheet shows a balance between the two sides of the bank's accounts. The left side lists the bank's assets. An **asset** is any physical property or financial claim owned by the bank. At this early stage, assets include the building and equipment owned by Home Bank plus its stock in the district Federal Reserve Bank. The right side lists the bank's liabilities and net worth. A **liability** is an amount the bank owes. So far the bank owes nothing, so the right side includes only the net worth of $500,000. The two sides of the ledger must always be equal, or in *balance*, which is why we call it a *balance sheet*. So assets must equal liabilities plus net worth:

$$\text{Assets} = \text{Liabilities} + \text{Net worth}$$

The bank is now ready for business. Opening day is the bank's lucky day, because the first customer carries in a briefcase full of $100 notes and deposits $1,000,000 into a new checking account. In accepting this, the bank promises to repay the depositor that amount. The

NET WORTH

Assets minus liabilities

BALANCE SHEET

A financial statement that shows assets, liabilities, and net worth at a given point in time; all these are stock measures; because assets must equal liabilities plus net worth, the statement is in balance

ASSET

Anything of value that is owned

LIABILITY

Anything that is owed to another individual or institution

EXHIBIT 2	Assets		Liabilities and Net Worth	
	Building and furniture	$450,000	Net worth	$500,000
	Stock in district Fed	50,000		
Home Bank's Balance Sheet	Total	$500,000	Total	$500,000

Assets		Liabilities and Net Worth	
Cash	$1,000,000	Checkable deposits	$1,000,000
Building and furniture	450,000	Net worth	500,000
Stock in district Fed	50,000		
Total	$1,500,000	Total	$1,500,000

EXHIBIT 3

Home Bank's Balance Sheet After $1,000,000 Deposit into Checking Account

deposit therefore is an amount the bank owes—it's a liability of the bank. As a result of this deposit, the bank's assets increase by $1,000,000 in cash and its liabilities increase by $1,000,000 in checkable deposits. Exhibit 3 shows the effects of this transaction on Home Bank's balance sheet. The right side now shows two claims on the bank's assets: claims by the owners, called net worth, and claims by nonowners, called liabilities, which at this point consist of checkable deposits.

Reserve Accounts

Where do we go from here? As mentioned in the previous chapter, banks are required by the Fed to set aside, or to hold in reserve, a percentage of their checkable deposits. The dollar amount that must be held in reserve is called **required reserves**—checkable deposits multiplied by the required reserve ratio. The **required reserve ratio** dictates the minimum proportion of deposits the bank must hold in reserve. The current reserve requirement is 10 percent on checkable deposits (other types of deposits have no reserve requirement). All depository institutions are subject to the Fed's reserve requirements. Reserves are held either as cash in the bank's vault or as deposits at the Fed, but neither earns the bank any interest. Home Bank must therefore hold $100,000 as reserves, or 10 percent times $1,000,000.

Suppose Home Bank deposits $100,000 in a reserve account with its district Federal Reserve Bank. Home Bank's reserves now consist of $100,000 in required reserves on deposit with the Fed and $900,000 in **excess reserves** held as cash in the vault. So far Home Bank has not earned a dime. Excess reserves, however, can be used to make loans or to purchase interest-bearing assets, such as government bonds. By law, the bank's interest-bearing assets are limited primarily to loans and to government securities (if a bank is owned by a holding company, the holding company has broader latitude in the kinds of assets it can hold).

Liquidity Versus Profitability

Like the early goldsmiths, modern banks must be prepared to satisfy depositors' requests for funds. A bank loses reserves whenever a depositor withdraws cash or writes a check that gets deposited in another bank. The bank must be in a position to satisfy all depositor demands, even if many depositors ask for their money at the same time. Required reserves are not meant to be used to meet depositor requests for funds; therefore, banks often hold excess reserves or other assets, such as government bonds, that can be easily converted to cash to satisfy any unexpected demand for funds. Banks may also want to hold excess reserves in case a valued customer needs immediate credit.

REQUIRED RESERVES

The dollar amount of reserves a bank is obligated by regulation to hold

REQUIRED RESERVE RATIO

The ratio of reserves to deposits that banks are obligated by regulation to hold

EXCESS RESERVES

Bank reserves exceeding required reserves

LIQUIDITY

A measure of the ease with which an asset can be converted into money without a significant loss of value

FEDERAL FUNDS MARKET

A market for overnight lending and borrowing of reserves among banks; the market for reserves on account at the Fed

FEDERAL FUNDS RATE

The interest rate charged in the federal funds market; the interest rate banks charge one another for overnight borrowing; the Fed's target interest rate

The bank manager must therefore structure the portfolio of assets with an eye toward liquidity but must not forget that survival also depends on profitability. **Liquidity** is the ease with which an asset can be converted into cash without a significant loss of value. *The objectives of liquidity and profitability are at odds.* For example, more liquid assets yield lower interest than less liquid assets do. The most liquid asset is bank reserves, either in the bank's vault as cash or on account with the Fed, but reserves earn no interest.

At one extreme, suppose a bank is completely liquid, holding all its assets as cash reserves. Such a bank would have no difficulty meeting depositors' demands for funds. This bank is playing it safe—too safe. The bank earns no interest and will fail. At the other extreme, suppose a bank uses all its excess reserves to acquire high-yielding but illiquid assets, such as long-term loans. Such a bank will run into problems whenever withdrawals exceed new deposits. There is a trade-off between liquidity and profitability. The portfolio manager's task is to strike the right balance between liquidity, or safety, and profitability.

Because reserves earn no interest, banks try to keep excess reserves to a minimum. Banks continuously "sweep" their accounts to find excess reserves that can be put to some interest-bearing use. They do not let excess reserves remain idle even overnight. The **federal funds market** provides for day-to-day lending and borrowing among banks of excess reserves on account at the Fed. These funds usually do not leave the Fed—instead, they shift among accounts. For example, suppose that at the end of the business day, Home Bank has excess reserves of $100,000 on account with the Fed and wants to lend that amount to another bank that finished the day short $100,000 in required reserves. These two banks are brought together by a broker who specializes in the market for federal funds—that is, the market for reserves at the Fed. The interest rate paid on this loan is called the **federal funds rate;** this is the rate the Fed targets as a tool of monetary policy, but more on that later.

How Banks Create Money

Let's now discuss how the Fed, Home Bank, and the banking system as a whole can create fiat money. Excess reserves are the raw material the banking system uses to create money. Again, our discussion focuses on commercial banks because they are the largest and most important depository institutions, although thrifts operate the same way.

Creating Money Through Excess Reserves

Suppose Home Bank has already used its $900,000 in excess reserves to make loans and buy government bonds and has no excess reserves left. In fact, let's assume there are no excess reserves in the banking system. With that as a point of departure, let's walk through the money creation process.

Round One

To start, suppose the Fed buys a $1,000 U.S. government bond from a securities dealer, with the transaction handled by the dealer's bank—Home Bank. The Fed pays the dealer by crediting Home Bank's reserve account with $1,000, so Home Bank can increase the dealer's checking account by $1,000. Where does the Fed get these reserves? It makes them up—creates them out of thin air, out of electronic ether! The securities dealer has exchanged one asset, a U.S. bond, for another asset, checkable deposits. A U.S. bond is not money, but checkable deposits are, so the money supply increases by $1,000 in this first round. Exhibit 4 shows changes in Home Bank's balance sheet as a result of the Fed's bond purchase. On the assets side, Home Bank's reserves at the Fed increase by $1,000. On the liabilities side, checkable deposits increase by $1,000. Of the dealer's $1,000 checkable deposit, Home Bank must set aside $100 in

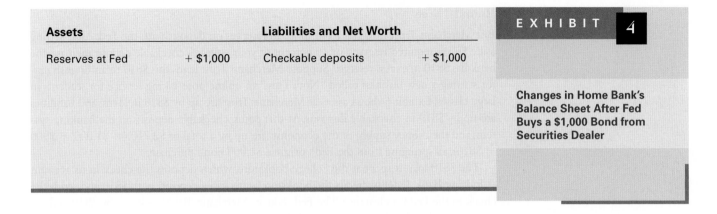

Assets		Liabilities and Net Worth	
Reserves at Fed	+ $1,000	Checkable deposits	+ $1,000

EXHIBIT 4

Changes in Home Bank's Balance Sheet After Fed Buys a $1,000 Bond from Securities Dealer

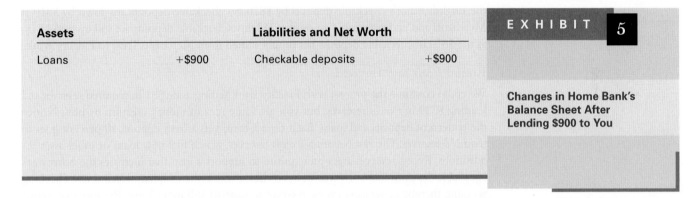

Assets		Liabilities and Net Worth	
Loans	+$900	Checkable deposits	+$900

EXHIBIT 5

Changes in Home Bank's Balance Sheet After Lending $900 to You

required reserves (based on a 10 percent required reserve ratio). The remaining $900 becomes excess reserves, which can fuel a further increase in the money supply.

Round Two

Suppose Home Bank is your regular bank, and you apply for a $900 student loan to help pay student fees. Home Bank approves your loan and increases your checking account by $900. *Home Bank has converted your promise to repay, your IOU, into a $900 checkable deposit. Because checkable deposits are money, this action increases the money supply by $900.* The money supply has increased by a total of $1,900 to this point—the $1,000 increase in the securities dealer's checkable deposits and now the $900 increase in your checkable deposits. In the process, what had been $900 in Home Bank's excess reserves now back up its loan to you (remember, a bank can lend no more than its excess reserves). As shown in Exhibit 5, Home Bank's loans increase by $900 on the assets side because your IOU becomes the bank's asset. On the bank's liabilities side, checkable deposits increase by $900 because the bank has increased your account by that amount. In short, Home Bank has created $900 in checkable deposits based on your promise to repay the loan.

When you write a $900 check for student fees, your college promptly deposits the check into its checking account at Merchants Trust, which increases the college's account by $900, and sends your check to the Fed. The Fed transfers $900 in reserves from Home Bank's account to Merchants Trust's account. The Fed then sends the check to Home Bank, which reduces your checkable deposits by $900. The Fed has thereby "cleared" your check by settling the claim that Merchants Trust had on Home Bank. The $900 in checkable deposits has simply shifted banks, so the total increase in the money supply to this point is still $1,900.

Round Three

But Merchants Trust now has $900 more in reserves on deposit with the Fed. After setting aside $90 as required reserves, or 10 percent of your college's checkable deposit increase, the bank has $810 in excess reserves. Suppose Merchants Trust lends this $810 to an English major starting a new business called "Note This," an online note-taking service for students in large classes. Exhibit 6 shows assets at Merchants Trust are up by $810 in loans, and liabilities are up by $810 in checkable deposits. At this point, checkable deposits in the banking system, and the money supply in the economy, are up by a total of $2,710 (= $1,000 + $900 + $810), all springing from the Fed's original $1,000 bond purchase.

The $810 loan is spent at the college bookstore, which deposits the check in its account at Fidelity Bank. Fidelity credits the bookstore's checkable deposits with $810 and sends the check to the Fed for clearance. The Fed reduces Merchants Bank's reserves by $810 and increases Fidelity's by the same. The Fed then sends the check to Merchants, which reduces the English major's checkable deposits by $810. So checkable deposits are down by $810 at Merchants and up by the same amount at Fidelity. Checkable deposits are still up by $2,710, as the $810 in checkable deposits has simply shifted from Merchants Trust to Fidelity Bank.

Round Four and Beyond

We could continue the process with Fidelity Bank setting aside $81 in required reserves and lending $729 in excess reserves, but you get some idea of money creation by now. Notice the pattern of deposits and loans. Each time a bank gets a fresh deposit, 10 percent goes to required reserves. The rest becomes excess reserves, which fuel new loans or other asset acquisitions. Excess reserves are a prerequisite to support a loan that increases the borrower's checkable deposits. The borrower writes a check, which the recipient deposits in a checking account, thereby generating excess reserves to support still more loans. Because this example began with the Fed, the Fed can rightfully claim, "The buck starts here"—a slogan that appears on a large plaque in the Federal Reserve chairman's office.

An individual bank can lend no more than its excess reserves. When the borrower spends those funds, reserves at one bank usually fall, but total reserves in the banking system do not. The recipient bank uses most of the new deposit to extend more loans, creating more checkable deposits. The potential expansion of checkable deposits in the banking system therefore equals some multiple of the initial increase in reserves. Note that our example assumes that banks do not allow excess reserves to sit idle, that borrowed funds do not idle in checking accounts, and that the public does not choose to hold some of the newly created money as cash. If excess reserves remained just that or if borrowed funds idled in checking

EXHIBIT 6	**Assets**		**Liabilities and Net Worth**	
	Loans	+ $810	Checkable deposits	+ $810

Changes in Merchants Trust's Balance Sheet After Lending $810 to English Major

accounts, they could not fuel an expansion of the money supply. And if people chose to hold borrowed funds in cash rather than in checking accounts, that idle cash could not add to reserves in the banking system.

A Summary of the Rounds

Let's review the money creation process: *The initial and most important step is the Fed's injection of $1,000 in fresh reserves into the banking system.* By buying the bond from the securities dealer, the Fed immediately increased the money supply by $1,000. Home Bank set aside $100 as required reserves and lent you its $900 in excess reserves. You paid your college fees, and the $900 ended up in your college's checkable account. This fueled more money creation, as shown in a series of rounds of Exhibit 7. As you can see, during each round, the increase in checkable deposits (column 1) minus the increase in required reserves (column 2) equals the potential increase in loans (column 3). Checkable deposits in this example can potentially increase by as much as $10,000.

In our example, money creation results from the Fed's $1,000 bond purchase from the securities dealer, but excess reserves would also have increased if the Fed purchased a $1,000 bond from Home Bank, lent Home Bank $1,000, or freed up $1,000 in excess reserves by lowering the reserve requirement.

What if the Fed paid the securities dealer in cash? By exchanging Federal Reserve notes, which become part of the money supply in the hands of the public, for a U.S. bond, which is not part of the money supply, the Fed would have increased the money supply by $1,000. Once the securities dealer put this cash into a checking account—or spent the cash, so the money ended up in someone else's checking account—the banking system's money creation process would have been off and running.

Reserve Requirements and Money Expansion

The banking system as a whole eliminates excess reserves by expanding the money supply. With a 10 percent reserve requirement, the Fed's initial injection of $1,000 in fresh reserves could support up to $10,000 in new checkable deposits in the banking system as a whole, *assuming no bank holds excess reserves, borrowers do not let their funds sit idle, and borrowers do not want to hold cash.*

The multiple by which the money supply increases as a result of an increase in the banking system's reserves is called the **money multiplier.** The **simple money multiplier** equals the reciprocal of the required reserve ratio, or $1/r$, where r is the reserve ratio. In our

MONEY MULTIPLIER

The multiple by which the money supply increases as a result of an increase in fresh reserves in the banking system

SIMPLE MONEY MULTIPLIER

The reciprocal of the required reserve ratio, or $1/r$, the maximum multiple of fresh reserves by which the money supply can increase

Bank	(1) Increase in Checkable Deposits	(2) Increase in Required Reserves	(3) Increase in Loans (3) = (1) − (2)
1. Home Bank	$ 1,000	$ 100	$ 900
2. Merchants Trust	900	90	810
3. Fidelity Bank	810	81	729
All remaining rounds	7,290	729	6,561
Totals	$10,000	$1,000	$9,000

EXHIBIT 7

Summary of the Money Creation Resulting from Fed's Purchase of $1,000 U.S. Government Bond

example, the reserve ratio was 10 percent, or 0.1, so the reciprocal is 1/0.1, which equals 10. The formula for the multiple expansion of money supply can be written as:

$$\text{Change in the money supply} = \text{Change in fresh reserves} \times 1/r$$

Again, the simple money multiplier assumes that banks hold no excess reserves, that borrowers do not let the funds sit idle, and that people do not want to hold cash. The higher the reserve requirement, the greater the fraction of deposits that must be held as reserves, so the smaller the money multiplier. A reserve requirement of 20 percent instead of 10 percent would require each bank to set aside twice as much in required reserves. The simple money multiplier in this case would be 1/0.2, which equals 5, and the maximum possible increase in checkable deposits resulting from an initial $1,000 increase in fresh reserves would therefore be $1,000 × 5, or $5,000. *Excess reserves fuel the deposit expansion process, and a higher reserve requirement drains this fuel from the banking system, thereby reducing the amount of new money that can be created.*

On the other hand, with a reserve requirement of only 5 percent, banks would set aside less for required reserves, leaving more excess reserves available for loans. The simple money multiplier in that case would be 1/0.05, or 20. With $1,000 in fresh reserves and a 5 percent reserve requirement, the banking system could increase the money supply by a maximum of $1,000 × 20, which equals $20,000. Thus, the change in the required reserve ratio affects the banking system's ability to create money.

In summary, money creation usually begins with the Fed injecting new reserves into the banking system. An individual bank lends an amount no greater than its excess reserves. The borrower's spending ends up in someone else's checking account, fueling additional loans. *The fractional reserve requirement is the key to the multiple expansion of checkable deposits.* If each $1 deposit had to be backed by $1 in required reserves, the money multiplier would be reduced to 1, which is no multiplier at all.

Limitations on Money Expansion

Various leakages from the multiple expansion process reduce the size of the money multiplier, which is why 1/r is called the *simple* money multiplier. You could think of "simple" as meaning maximum. To repeat, our example assumed (1) that banks do not let excess reserves sit idle, (2) that borrowers do something with the money, and (3) that people do not choose to increase their cash holdings. How realistic are these assumptions? With regard to the first, banks have a profit incentive to make loans or buy some other interest-bearing asset with excess reserves. The second assumption is also easy to defend. Why would people borrow money if they didn't plan to spend it? The third assumption is trickier. Cash may sometimes be preferable to checking accounts because cash is more versatile, so people may choose to hold some of the newly created money as cash. To the extent that people prefer to hold cash, this drains reserves from the banking system. With reduced reserves, banks are less able to make loans, reducing the money multiplier. Incidentally, for the money multiplier to operate, a particular bank need not use excess reserves in a specific way; it could use them to pay all its employees a Christmas bonus, for that matter. As long as that spending ends up as checkable deposits in the banking system, away we go with the money expansion process.

Multiple Contraction of the Money Supply

We have already outlined the money creation process, so the story of how the Federal Reserve System can reduce bank reserves, thereby reducing the money supply, can be a brief one. Again, we begin by assuming there are no excess reserves in the system and the reserve requirement is 10 percent. Suppose the Fed *sells* a $1,000 U.S. bond to a securities dealer and gets paid with a check drawn on the security dealer's account at Home Bank. So the Fed gets paid by drawing down Home Bank's reserves at the Fed by $1,000. The Fed has thereby reduced the money supply by $1,000 in this first round.

Because the dealer's checking account was reduced by $1,000, Home Bank no longer needs to hold $100 in required reserves. But Home Bank is still short $900 in required reserves (remember, when we started, there were no excess reserves in the banking system). To replenish reserves, Home Bank must recall loans (ask for repayment before the due date), sell some other asset, or borrow additional reserves. Suppose the bank calls in $900 loaned to a local business, and the loan is repaid with a check written against Merchants Bank. When the check clears, Home Bank's reserves are up by $900, just enough to satisfy its reserve requirement, but Merchants Bank's reserves and checkable deposits are down by $900. Checkable deposits are now down $1,900 as a result of the Fed's purchase of a $1,000 bond. Because there were no excess reserves at the outset, the loss of $900 in reserves leaves Merchants $810 short of its required level of reserves, forcing that bank to get more reserves.

And so it goes down the line. The Fed's sale of government bonds reduces bank reserves, forcing banks to recall loans or to somehow replenish reserves. This reduces checkable deposits each additional round. *The maximum possible effect is to reduce the money supply by the original reduction in bank reserves times the simple money multiplier, which again equals 1 divided by the reserve requirement, or 1/r.* In our example, the Fed's sale of $1,000 in U.S. bonds could reduce the money supply by as much as $10,000.

For a change of pace, let's end this section with a case study that looks at new developments in banking sparked by the revolution in personal computers and the Internet.

Banking on the Net

The Bank of Internet USA never closes. It's open 24 hours a day, 365 days a year. From anywhere in the world with Internet access, bank customers can pay bills, check balances, or apply for a loan. Virtual banks have little physical presence beyond ATMs. For example, the Bank of Internet USA has a single, 6,000-square-foot office with only 20 employees. But the bank's customers can withdraw funds and make deposits at more than 300,000 ATMs around the country and the world. They can even print out deposit slips online.

With the money saved on buildings and bank tellers, Internet banks can offer depositors higher interest rates. At a time when money market rates averaged less than 1.0 percent, most Internet banks offered interest at least twice that. The three banks offering the highest interest rates in 2004 were Internet banks: Bank of Internet USA, VirtualBank, and National InterBank.

But virtual banks remain the exception. The overwhelming share of banks now accessible via the Internet consist of physical banks that offer Internet banking for customer convenience. For example, Wells Fargo, a bank with about 3,000 branches in 23 states and 16 million customers, has invested $1 billion in online banking and claims to be the market leader. Like some other banks, Wells Fargo also offers customers the ability to verify online all account balances, *including accounts at other banks.* Many banks even offer wireless banking for customers with Web-enabled cell phones or personal digital assistants.

With such easy access, customers are increasingly shopping nationwide for the best rates for deposits, credit cards, and loans. So a customer in St. Louis can get a mortgage in Atlanta,

C a s e **Study**

The Information Economy

*e*Activity
Visit the FDIC at http://www.fdic.gov/bank/individual/online/safe.html for tips on safe Internet banking. The first tip is to confirm that an online bank is legitimate and that your deposits are insured; the FDIC has an interactive site where you can check this, at http://www2.fdic.gov/edie.

ELECTRONIC BANKING, OR E-BANKING

Conducting banking transactions over the Internet

a car loan in Phoenix, a credit card in Boston, a checking account in New York, and a savings account in Los Angeles. For example, ING Direct offers 2.1 percent interest on FDIC-insured savings accounts with no minimum balance and no fees. Customers can transfer funds online between this account and online checking accounts at other banks.

For the banks, **electronic banking**, or **e-banking,** speeds processing, lowers costs, and helps attract and keep customers. For depositors, e-banking saves time, money, and is often more convenient. Households can manage their money, pay bills, and can keep track of their credit. There has been an increase in the share of bank customers using a variety of e-banking technologies. According to a broad survey, the share of households banking by computer tripled from 10 percent in 1999 to 32 percent in 2003. These newer technologies tend to be used by higher income, higher asset, younger, and more educated households.

The Internet could become the biggest market in history, and banks want to be part of it. Over the long run, the Internet offers convenience for customers and potential cost savings for banks. The Internet reduces the need for branches and branch personnel. Citibank, for example, encourages online use by eliminating fees for those who bank online. Because e-banking reduces the search costs of shopping around for the best deal, banking will become more competitive, squeezing down interest rate differences across banks for similar products.

Sources: John Kimelman, "How Internet Banks Have Inched Ahead on Rates," *New York Times*; 28 December 2003; Bambi Francisco, "Internet Banking Surges," CBS.MarketWatch.com, 17 June 2004; and C. E. Anguelov et al. "U.S. Consumers and Electronic Banking, 1995–2003," *Federal Reserve Bulletin* (Winter 2004): 1–18, also available at http://www.federalreserve.gov/pubs/bulletin/2004/winter04_ca.pdf. The Bank of Internet USA is at http://www.bankofinternet.com/. VirtualBank is at http://www.virtualbank.com/. National InterBank is at http://www.nationalinterbank.com/nib/. Wells Fargo's is http://www.wellsfargo.com/. And ING Direct is http://home.ingdirect.com/.

N e t B o o k m a r k

For an online introduction to the Federal Reserve System and a monetary policy link to the Federal Reserve Bank of New York, go to the introduction page at http://www.ny.frb.org/introduce/. This site provides a very readable overview of the Fed's structure and operations. It includes links giving more details about particular terms. Be sure to take a peek inside the gold vault.

Now that you have some idea how fractional reserve banking works, we are in a position to summarize the Federal Reserve's role in the economy.

The Fed's Tools of Monetary Control

As mentioned in the previous chapter, in its capacity as a bankers' bank, the Fed clears checks for, extends loans to, and holds deposits of banks. The Fed, through its regulation of financial markets, also tries to prevent major disruptions and financial panics. For example, during the dark days following the terrorist attacks on America of September 11, 2001, people used their ATM cards to load up on cash. Some were hoarding cash. To provide the banking system with sufficient liquidity, the Fed bought all the government securities offered for sale, purchasing a record $150 billion worth in two days.[2] The Fed also eased some regulations to facilitate bank clearances, especially for banks hit by the attacks. Fed Chairman Alan Greenspan also worked behind the scenes to ensure that banks had sufficient liquidity to calm panics in 1987, 1989, and 1998, when financial crises threatened. The Fed also stockpiles cash in bank vaults around the country and around the world in case of emergencies.

As noted already, about half of the narrow definition of money (M1) consists of checkable deposits. The Fed's control over checkable deposits works indirectly through its control over reserves in the banking system. You are already familiar with the Fed's three tools for

---

2. Anita Rachavan, Susan Pulliam, and Jeff Opdyke, "Banks and Regulators Drew Together to Calm Rattled Markets After Attack," *Wall Street Journal,* 18 October 2001.

controlling reserves: (1) open-market operations, or the buying and selling of U.S. government bonds; (2) the discount rate, which is the interest rate the Fed charges for loans it makes to banks; and (3) the required reserve ratio, which is the minimum fraction of reserves that banks must hold against deposits. Let's examine each of these in more detail.

Open-Market Operations and the Federal Funds Rate

The Fed carries out open-market operations whenever it buys or sells U.S. government bonds in the open market. To increase the money supply, the Fed directs the New York Fed to buy U.S. bonds. This is called an **open-market purchase**. To reduce the money supply, the Fed can carry out an **open-market sale**. Policy decisions about open-market operations are made by the Federal Open Market Committee, or FOMC, which meets every six weeks and during emergencies. Open-market operations are relatively easy to carry out. They require no change in laws or regulations and can be executed in any amount—large or small—chosen by the Fed. Their simplicity and ease of use make them the tool of choice for the Fed.

Through open-market operations, the Fed influences bank reserves and the *federal funds rate,* which is the interest rate banks charge one another for borrowing excess reserves at the Fed, typically just for a day or two. Banks that need reserves can borrow excess reserves from other banks, paying the federal funds rate. The federal funds rate serves as a good indicator of the "tightness" of monetary policy. For example, suppose the Fed buys bonds in the open market and thereby increases reserves in the banking system. As a result, more banks have excess reserves. Demand for excess reserves in the federal funds market will fall and supply will increase, so the federal funds rate—the interest rate for reserves in this market—will decline. We can expect that this lower federal funds rate will spread quickly to the economy at large: The excess reserves that have created the lower federal funds rate will prompt banks to lower short-term interest rates in general and this will increase the quantity of loans demanded by the public.

The Discount Rate

The second monetary policy tool available to the Fed is the **discount rate**, which is the interest rate the Fed charges for loans it makes to banks. Banks borrow from the Fed to satisfy their reserve requirements. A lower discount rate reduces the cost of borrowing, encouraging banks to borrow reserves from the Fed. But the Fed considers itself as the "lender of last resort," and a lender during a financial crisis. The Fed does not encourage banks to borrow through the discount window. There are actually two discount rates. The *primary discount rate* is usually one percentage point above the federal funds rate. Thus, discount borrowing is less attractive than borrowing through the federal funds market. But during a financial crisis, the Fed could lower the primary discount rate to supply liquidity to the banking system. The Fed charges more interest on loans to banks considered less sound than other banks. This *secondary discount rate* is usually about one-half a percentage point higher than the primary discount rate.

The Fed uses the discount rate more as a signal to financial markets about its monetary policy than as a tool for increasing or decreasing the money supply. The discount rate might also be thought of as an emergency tool for injecting liquidity into the banking system in the event of some financial crisis, such as a stock market crash. Banks would prefer to borrow reserves from other banks in the federal funds market rather than borrow reserves directly from the Fed. The discount rate has become largely symbolic, and discount lending has declined sharply in the last two decades.

OPEN-MARKET PURCHASE

The purchase of U.S. government bonds by the Fed to increase the money supply

OPEN-MARKET SALE

The sale of U.S. government bonds by the Fed to reduce the money supply

DISCOUNT RATE

The interest rate the Fed charges banks that borrow reserves

HOMEWORK
Xpress!
Ask the Instructor
Video

Reserve Requirements

The Fed also influences the money supply through reserve requirements, which are regulations regarding the minimum amount of reserves that banks must hold to back up deposits. Reserve requirements determine how much money the banking system can create with each dollar of fresh reserves. If the Fed increases the reserve requirement, then banks have less excess reserves to lend out. This reduces the banking system's ability to create money. On the other hand, a lower reserve requirement increases the banking system's ability to create money. Reserve requirements can be changed by a simple majority vote of the Board of Governors. But changes in the reserve requirement disrupt the banking system, so the Fed seldom makes such changes. As noted already, the current reserve requirement is 10 percent on checkable deposits and zero on other deposits. Some countries such as Australia, Canada, and the United Kingdom have no reserve requirement. Banks there still hold reserves to deal with everyday cash requirements and can borrow from their central banks (at high rates) if necessary.

The Fed Is a Money Machine

One way to get a better idea of the Fed is to review its balance sheet, shown as Exhibit 8, with assets on the left and liabilities and net worth on the right. Note that U.S. government bonds account for over 90 percent of Fed assets. These IOUs from the federal government result from open-market operations, and they earn the Fed interest. On the other side of the ledger, Federal Reserve notes outstanding account for over 90 percent of Fed liabilities. These notes—U.S. currency—are IOUs from the Fed and are therefore liabilities of the Fed, but the Fed pays no interest on these notes. Thus, the Fed's primary asset—U.S. government bonds—earns interest, whereas the Fed's primary liability—Federal Reserve notes—requires no interest payments by the Fed. *The Fed is therefore both literally and figuratively a money machine. It is literally a money machine because it supplies the economy with Federal Reserve notes; it is figuratively a money machine because its main asset earns interest, but its main liability requires no interest payments.* The Fed also earns revenue from various services it provides banks. After covering its operating costs, the Fed turns over any remaining income, some years in excess of $20 billion, to the U.S. Treasury.

The asset side of Exhibit 8 also indicates how tiny the Fed's discount loans are relative to total assets. As of the end of 2003, the Fed's discount lending stood at only $62 million. On the right side of the ledger, you can see that depository institutions' reserves at the Fed totaled $23,058 million, or about $23 billion. You can also see that the Fed held deposits of the U.S. Treasury, a reminder that the Fed is the federal government's banker.

Conclusion

Banks play a unique role in the economy because they can transform someone's IOU into a checkable deposit, and a checkable deposit is money. The banking system's ability to expand the money supply depends on the amount of excess reserves in that system. In our example, it was the purchase of a $1,000 U.S. bond that started the ball rolling. The Fed can also increase reserves by lowering the discount rate enough to stimulate bank borrowing from the Fed (although the Fed uses changes in the discount rate more to signal its policy than to alter the money supply). And, by reducing the required reserve ratio, the Fed not only instantly creates excess reserves in the banking system but also increases the money multiplier. In practice, the Fed rarely changes the reserve requirement because of the disruptive effect of such a change on the banking system. *To control the money supply, the Fed relies primarily on open-market operations.*

Assets		Liabilities and Net Worth	
U.S. Treasury securities	$ 710,415	Federal Reserve notes outstanding	$ 689,754
Foreign currencies	19,868	Depository institution reserves	23,058
Bank buildings	1,630	U.S. Treasury balance	5,723
Discount loans to depository institutions	62	Other liabilities	37,665
Other assets	41,919	Net worth	17,694
Total	$ 773,894	Total	$ 773,894

EXHIBIT 8

HOMEWORK **Xpress!** *Graphing*

Federal Reserve Bank Balance Sheet as of December 31, 2003 (Millions of dollars)

Source: Developed from data in *90ᵗʰ Annual Report: 2003*, Federal Reserve Board, Table 1, p. 260. This report is available at http://www.federalreserve.gov/ boarddocs/rptcongress/annual03/default.htm. For the latest, go to http://www.federalreserve.gov/publications.htm, click on "Annual Report," then find "Statistical Tables."

Open-market operations can have a direct effect on the money supply, as when the Fed buys bonds from the public. But the Fed also affects the money supply indirectly, as when the Fed's bond purchase increases bank reserves, which then serve as fuel for the money multiplier. In the next chapter, we will consider the effects of changes in the money supply on the economy.

SUMMARY

1. The money supply is narrowly defined as M1, which consists of currency held by the nonbanking public plus checkable deposits and traveler's checks. Broader money aggregates include other kinds of bank deposits. M2 includes M1 plus savings deposits, small-denomination time deposits, and money market mutual funds. M3 includes M2 plus time deposits of $100,000 and up.

2. Banks are unlike other businesses because they can turn a borrower's IOU into money—they can create money. Banks match the different desires of savers and borrowers. Banks also evaluate loan applications and diversify portfolios of assets to reduce the risk to any one saver.

3. In acquiring portfolios of assets, banks try to maximize profit while maintaining enough liquidity to satisfy depositors' requests for money. Assets that earn the bank more interest are usually less liquid.

4. Any single bank can expand the money supply by the amount of its excess reserves. For the banking system as a whole, however, the maximum expansion of the money supply equals a multiple of fresh bank reserves. The simple money multiplier is the reciprocal of the reserve ratio. This multiplier is reduced to the extent that (a) banks allow excess reserves to remain idle, (b) borrowers sit on their proceeds, and (c) the public withdraws cash from the banking system and holds it.

5. The key to changes in the money supply is the Fed's impact on excess reserves in the banking system. To increase excess reserves and thus increase the money supply, the Fed can buy U.S. government bonds, reduce the discount rate, or lower the reserve requirement. To reduce excess reserves and thus reduce the money supply, the Fed can sell U.S. government bonds, increase the discount rate, or increase the reserve requirement. By far the most important monetary tool for the Fed is open-market operations—buying or selling U.S. bonds.

QUESTIONS FOR REVIEW

1. *(Money Aggregates)* What are the three measures of the money supply and how is each measure determined?

2. *(Money Aggregates)* What portion of U.S. Federal Reserve notes circulate outside the United States? How does this affect the United States?

3. (*C a s e* **S t u d y** : Faking It) Why did the U.S. government consider it important to redesign the $100 note in order to combat the effects of the "supernote"?

4. *(Money Aggregates)* Determine whether each of the following is included in any of the M1, M2, or M3 measures of the money supply:

   a. Currency held by the nonbanking public
   b. Available credit on credit cards held by the nonbanking public
   c. Savings deposits
   d. Large-denomination time deposits
   e. Money market mutual fund accounts

5. *(Banks Are Financial Intermediaries)* In acting as financial intermediaries, what needs and desires of savers and borrowers must banks consider?

6. *(Money Aggregates)* Suppose that $1,000 is moved from a savings account at a commercial bank to a checking account at the same bank. Which of the following statements are true and which are false?

   a. The amount of currency in circulation will fall.
   b. M1 will increase.
   c. M2 will increase.

7. *(Bank Deposits)* Explain the differences among checkable deposits, savings deposits, and time deposits. Explain whether each of these deposits represents a bank asset or a bank liability.

8. *(Reserve Accounts)* Explain why a reduction in the required reserve ratio cannot, at least initially, increase total reserves in the banking system. Is the same true of lowering the discount rate? What would happen if the Fed bought U.S. bonds from, or sold them to, the banking system?

9. *(Liquidity Versus Profitability)* Why must a bank manager strike a balance between liquidity and profitability on the bank's balance sheet?

10. *(Creating Money)* Often it is claimed that banks create money by making loans. How can commercial banks create money? Is the government the only institution that can legally create money?

11. *(Fed Tools of Monetary Control)* What three tools can the Fed use to change the money supply? Which tool is used most frequently? What are three limitations on the money expansion process?

12. *(Discount Rate)* What is the difference between the federal funds rate and the discount rate? What is the ultimate impact on the money supply of an increase in the discount rate?

13. *(Federal Funds Market)* What is the federal funds market? How does it help banks strike a balance between liquidity and profitability?

14. *(The Fed Is a Money Machine)* Why is the Fed both literally and figuratively a money machine?

15. (*C a s e* **S t u d y** : Banking on the Net) What impact is increased Internet banking likely to have on money's function as a medium of exchange?

PROBLEMS AND EXERCISES

16. *(Monetary Aggregates)* Calculate M1, M2, and M3 using the following information:

Large-denomination time deposits	$304 billion
Currency and coin held by the non-banking public	$438 billion
Checkable deposits	$509 billion
Small-denomination time deposits	$198 billion
Traveler's checks	$18 billion
Savings deposits	$326 billion
Money market mutual fund accounts	$637 billion

17. *(Money Creation)* Show how each of the following *initially* affects bank assets, liabilities, and reserves. Do *not* include the results of bank behavior resulting from the Fed's action. Assume a required reserve ratio of 0.05.

 a. The Fed purchases $10 million worth of U.S. government bonds from a bank.
 b. The Fed loans $5 million to a bank.
 c. The Fed raises the required reserve ratio to 0.10.

18. *(Money Creation)* Show how each of the following would initially affect a bank's assets and liabilities.

 a. Someone makes a $10,000 deposit into a checking account.
 b. A bank makes a loan of $1,000 by establishing a checking account for $1,000.
 c. The loan described in part (b) is spent.
 d. A bank must write off a loan because the borrower defaults.

19. *(Reserve Accounts)* Suppose that a bank's customer deposits $4,000 in her checking account. The required reserve ratio is 0.25. What are the required reserves on this new deposit? What is the largest loan that the bank can make on the basis of the new deposit? If the bank chooses to hold reserves of $3,000 on the new deposit, what are the excess reserves on the deposit?

20. *(Money Multiplier)* Suppose that the Federal Reserve lowers the required reserve ratio from 0.10 to 0.05. How does this affect the simple money multiplier, assuming that excess reserves are held to zero and there are no currency leakages? What are the money multipliers for required reserve ratios of 0.15 and 0.20?

21. *(Money Creation)* Suppose Bank A, which faces a reserve requirement of 10 percent, receives a $1,000 deposit from a customer.

 a. Assuming that it wishes to hold no excess reserves, determine how much the bank should lend. Show your answer on Bank A's balance sheet.
 b. Assuming that the loan shown in Bank A's balance sheet is redeposited in Bank B, show the changes in Bank B's balance sheet if it lends out the maximum possible.
 c. Repeat this process for three additional banks: C, D, and E.
 d. Using the simple money multiplier, calculate the total change in the money supply resulting from the $1,000 initial deposit.
 e. Assume Banks A, B, C, D, and E each wish to hold 5 percent excess reserves. How would holding this level of excess reserves affect the total change in the money supply?

22. *(Monetary Control)* Suppose the money supply is currently $500 billion and the Fed wishes to increase it by $100 billion.

 a. Given a required reserve ratio of 0.25, what should it do?
 b. If it decided to change the money supply by changing the required reserve ratio, what change should it make?

EXPERIENTIAL EXERCISES

23. *(Fed Tools of Monetary Control)* Review the Fed's online brochure on the Federal Open Market Committee (FOMC) at http://www.federalreserve.gov/pubs/ frseries/frseri2.htm, especially the sections titled "The Decisionmaking Process" and "Reports." What information does the FOMC consider as it plans open-market operations? Look at the minutes of the most recent meeting to determine what kinds of open-market operations are going on now.

24. (*C a s e* **Study:** Banking on the Net) The *Journal of Internet Banking and Commerce* at http://www.arraydev.com/ commerce/JIBC/current.asp is a Web-based magazine devoted to Internet banking and related issues. Take a look at the current edition and see whether you can determine what effect electronic banking is having on the Fed's ability to control the U.S. money supply. Also, see what you can learn about the status of Internet banking outside the United States.

25. *(Wall Street Journal)* If you have access to the Interactive Edition of the *Wall Street Journal*, you can use the Briefing Books feature to obtain data on over 10,000 public companies. Use this feature to locate the briefing book on a large commercial bank in your area. Look at some of its press releases to determine how this bank has been influenced by Federal Reserve regulations and monetary policy operations.

26. *(Wall Street Journal)* Open-market operations, in which the Federal Reserve buys and sells U.S. government bonds, are an important tool of monetary control. Look in the *Wall Street Journal* in the Money and Investing section. Find the page where bond activity is reported. Is the market for U.S. government bills and bonds an active market? What impact does the liquidity of this market have on the ability of the Federal Reserve to exert monetary control?

Monetary Theory and Policy

© James Leynse/Corbis

W hy do people maintain checking accounts and have cash in their pockets,
purses, wallets, desk drawers, coffee cans—wherever? In other words, why
do people hold money? How does the stock of money in the economy affect your
chances of finding a job, your ability to finance a new car, the interest rate you pay
on credit cards, the ease of getting a student loan, and the interest rate on that loan?
What have economic theory and the historical record taught us about the relationship between the quantity of money in the economy and other macroeconomic
variables? Answers to these and related questions are addressed in this chapter, which
examines monetary theory and policy.

The amount of money in the economy affects you in a variety of ways, but to understand these effects, we must dig a little deeper. So far, we have focused on how
banks create money. But a more fundamental question is how money affects the

economy, a topic called *monetary theory*. Monetary theory explores the effect of the money supply on the economy's price level, employment, and real GDP. The Fed's control over the money supply is called *monetary policy*. In the short run, changes in the money supply affect the economy by working through changes in the interest rate. In the long run, changes in the money supply affect the price level. In this chapter, we consider the theory behind each time frame. Topics discussed include:

- Demand and supply of money
- Money in the short run
- Federal funds rate
- Money in the long run
- Velocity of money
- Monetary policy targets

The Demand and Supply of Money

Let's begin by reviewing the important distinction between the *stock of money* and the *flow of income*. How much money do you have with you right now? That amount is a *stock*. Income, in contrast, is a *flow*, indicating how much money you earn per period. Income has no meaning unless the period is specified. You would not know whether to be impressed that a friend earned $400 unless you knew whether this was earnings per month, per week, per day, or per hour.

DEMAND FOR MONEY

The relationship between how much money people want to hold and the interest rate

The **demand for money** is a relationship between how much money people want to hold and the interest rate. Keep in mind that the quantity of money held is a stock measure. It may seem odd at first to be talking about the demand for money. You might think people would demand all the money they could get their hands on. But remember that money, the stock, is not the same as income, the flow. People express their demand for income by selling their labor and other resources. People express their demand for money by holding some of their wealth as money rather than holding other assets that earn more interest.

But we are getting ahead of ourselves. The question is: why do people demand money? Why do people have money on them, stash money around the house, and have money in checking accounts? The most obvious reason people demand money is that money is a convenient medium of exchange. *People demand money to carry out market transactions.*

The Demand for Money

Because barter represents an insignificant portion of exchange in the modern industrialized economy, households, firms, governments, and foreigners need money to conduct their daily transactions. Consumers need money to buy products, and firms need money to buy resources. *Money allows people to carry out economic transactions more easily and more efficiently.* With credit cards, the short-term loan delays the payment of money, but all accounts must eventually be settled with money.

The greater the value of transactions to be financed in a given period, the greater the demand for money. *So the more active the economy is—that is, the more goods and services exchanged, reflected by real output—the more money demanded.* Obviously an economy with a real GDP of $12 trillion will need more money than one-half that size. *Also, the higher the economy's price level, the greater the demand for money.* The more things cost on average, the more money is needed to buy them.

You demand the money needed to fund your normal spending in the course of the day or week, and you may need money for unexpected expenditures. If you plan to buy lunch tomorrow, you will carry enough money to pay for it. But you may also want to be able to pay for other possible contingencies. For example, you could have car trouble or you could come across an unexpected sale on a favorite item. You can use credit cards for some of these unexpected purchases, but you still feel safer with some extra cash. You may have a little extra money with you right now for who knows what. Even *you* don't know.

The demand for money is rooted in money's role as a medium of exchange. But as we have seen, money is more than a medium of exchange; it is also a store of value. People save for a new home, for college, for retirement. People can store their purchasing power as money or as other financial assets, such as corporate and government bonds. When people purchase bonds and other financial assets, they are lending their money and are paid interest for doing so.

The demand for any asset is based on the services it provides. The big advantage of money as a store of value is its liquidity: Money can be immediately exchanged for whatever is for sale. In contrast, other financial assets, such as corporate or government bonds, must first be *liquidated,* or exchanged for money, which can then be used to buy goods and services. Money, however, has one major disadvantage when compared to other financial assets. Money in the form of currency and traveler's checks earns no interest, and the rate earned on checkable deposits is well below that earned on other financial assets. So holding wealth as money means giving up some interest. For example, suppose a corporation could earn 3 percent more interest by holding financial assets other than money. The opportunity cost of holding $10 million as money rather than as some other financial asset would amount to $300,000 per year. *The interest forgone is the opportunity cost of holding money.*

Money Demand and Interest Rates

When the market interest rate is low, other things constant, the cost of holding money—the cost of maintaining liquidity—is low, so people hold more of their wealth in the form of money. When the interest rate is high, the cost of holding money is high, so people hold less of their wealth in money and more in other financial assets that pay higher interest. Thus, *other things constant, the quantity of money demanded varies inversely with the market interest rate.*

The money demand curve, D_m, in Exhibit 1 shows the quantity of money people demand at alternative interest rates, other things constant. Both the quantity of money and the

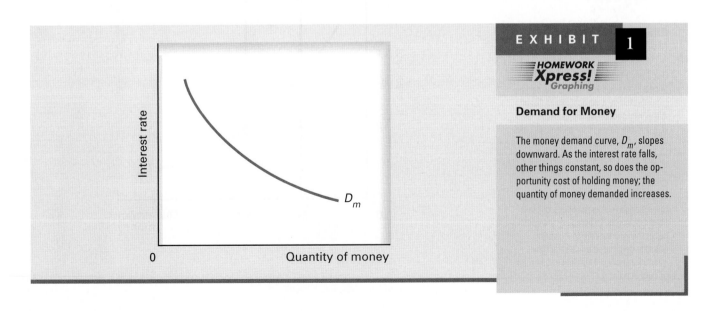

EXHIBIT 1

HOMEWORK
Xpress!
Graphing

Demand for Money

The money demand curve, D_m, slopes downward. As the interest rate falls, other things constant, so does the opportunity cost of holding money; the quantity of money demanded increases.

interest rate are in nominal terms. *The money demand curve slopes downward because the lower the interest rate, the lower the opportunity cost of holding money.* Movements along the curve reflect the effects of changes in the interest rate on the quantity of money demanded, other things assumed constant. The quantity of money demanded is inversely related to the price of holding money, which is the interest rate. *Assumed constant along the curve are the price level and real GDP. If either increases, the demand for money increases, as reflected by a rightward shift of the money demand curve.*

The Supply of Money and the Equilibrium Interest Rate

The supply of money—the stock of money available in the economy at a particular time—is determined primarily by the Fed through its control over currency and over excess reserves in the banking system. The supply of money, S_m, is depicted as a vertical line in Exhibit 2. *A vertical supply curve implies that the quantity of money supplied is independent of the interest rate.*

The intersection of the demand for money, D_m, with the supply of money, S_m, determines the equilibrium interest rate, i—the interest rate that equates the quantity of money demanded in the economy with the quantity supplied. At interest rates above the equilibrium level, the opportunity cost of holding money is higher, so the quantity of money people want to hold is less than the quantity supplied. At interest rates below the equilibrium level, the opportunity cost of holding money is lower, so the quantity of money people want to hold exceeds the quantity supplied.

If the Fed increases the money supply, the money supply curve shifts to the right, as shown by the movement from S_m to S'_m in Exhibit 2. The quantity supplied now exceeds the quantity demanded at interest rate i. Because of the increased supply of money, people are *able* to hold more money. But at interest rate i they are *unwilling* to hold that much. Because people are now holding more of their wealth as money than they would like, they

EXHIBIT   2

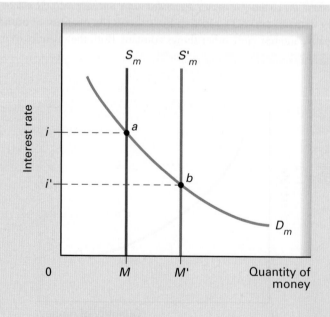

Effect of an Increase in the Money Supply

Because the supply of money is determined by the Federal Reserve, it can be represented by a vertical line. At point *a*, the intersection of supply of money, S_m, and the demand for money, D_m, determines the market interest rate, i. Following an increase in the money supply to S'_m, the quantity of money supplied exceeds the quantity demanded at the original interest rate, i. People attempt to exchange money for bonds or other financial assets. In doing so, they push down the interest rate to i', where quantity demanded equals the new quantity supplied. This new equilibrium occurs at point *b*.

exchange some money for other financial assets, such as bonds. As the demand for bonds increases, bond sellers can pay less interest yet still attract enough buyers. The interest rate falls until the quantity of money demanded just equals the quantity supplied. With the decline in the interest rate to *i'* in Exhibit 2, the opportunity cost of holding money falls enough that the public is willing to hold the now-larger stock of money. Equilibrium moves from point *a* to point *b*. *For a given money demand curve, an increase in the supply of money drives down the market interest rate, and a decrease in the supply of money drives up the market interest rate.*

Now that you have some idea how money demand and supply determine the market interest rate, you are ready to see how money fits into our model of the economy. Specifically, let's see how changes in money supply affect aggregate demand and equilibrium output.

Money and Aggregate Demand in the Short Run

In the short run, money affects the economy through changes in the interest rate. Monetary policy influences the market interest rate, which in turn affects the level of planned investment, a component of aggregate demand. Let's work through the chain of causation.

Interest Rates and Planned Investment

Suppose the Fed believes that the economy is producing less than its potential and decides to stimulate output and employment by increasing the money supply. Recall from the previous chapter that the Fed's primary tool for increasing the money supply is open-market purchases of U.S. government securities. The three panels of Exhibit 3 trace the links between changes in the money supply and changes in aggregate demand. We begin with

---

E X H I B I T   3

Effects of an Increase in the Money Supply on Interest Rates, Investment, and Aggregate Demand

In panel (a), an increase in the money supply drives the interest rate down to *i'*. With the cost of borrowing lower, the amount invested increases from *I* to *I'*, as shown in panel (b). This sets off the spending multiplier process, so the aggregate output demanded at price level *P* increases from *Y* to *Y'*. The increase is shown by the shift of the aggregate demand curve to the right in panel (c).

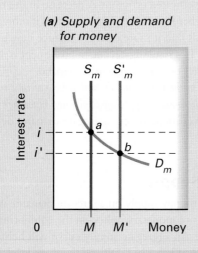
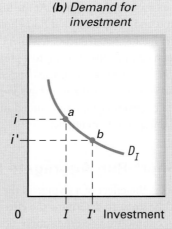
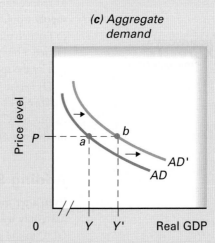

equilibrium interest rate *i*, which is determined in panel (a) by the intersection of the money demand curve D_m with the money supply curve S_m. Suppose the Fed purchases U.S. government bonds and thereby increases the money supply, as shown by a rightward shift of the money supply curve from S_m to S'_m. After the increase in the supply of money, people are holding more money than they would prefer at interest rate *i*, so they try to exchange one form of wealth, money, for other financial assets. Exchanging dollars for financial assets has no direct effect on aggregate demand, but it does reduce the market interest rate.

A decline in the interest rate to *i'*, other things constant, reduces the opportunity cost of financing new plants and equipment, thereby making new investment more profitable. Likewise, a lower interest rate reduces the cost of financing a new house. So the decline in the interest rate increases the amount of investment demanded. Panel (b) shows the demand for investment, D_I, first introduced several chapters back. When the interest rate falls from *i* to *i'*, planned investment increases from *I* to *I'*.

The spending multiplier magnifies this increase in investment, leading to a greater increase in aggregate demand, reflected in panel (c) by a rightward shift of the aggregate demand curve from *AD* to *AD'*. At the given price level *P*, real GDP increases from *Y* to *Y'*. The sequence of events can be summarized as follows:

$$M \uparrow \rightarrow i \downarrow \rightarrow I \uparrow \rightarrow AD \uparrow \rightarrow Y \uparrow$$

An increase in the money supply, *M*, reduces the interest rate, *i*. The lower interest rate stimulates investment, *I*, which increase in aggregate demand from *AD* to *AD'*. At a given price level, real GDP demanded increased from *Y* to *Y'*. The entire sequence is also traced out in each panel by the movement from point *a* to point *b*.

Note that the graphs presented here ignore any feedback effects of changes in real GDP on the demand for money. Because the demand for money depends on the level of real GDP, an increase in real GDP would shift the money demand curve to the right in panel (a). If we had shifted the money demand curve, the equilibrium interest rate would still have fallen, but not by as much, so investment and aggregate demand would not have increased by as much. Thus, Exhibit 2 is a simplified view, but it still offers the essential story of how changes in the money supply affect the economy.

Now let's consider the effect of a Fed-orchestrated *increase* in interest rates. In Exhibit 3 such a policy could be traced by moving from point *b* to point *a* in each panel, but we will dispense with a blow-by-blow discussion of the graphs. Suppose the Federal Reserve decides to reduce the money supply to cool down an overheated economy. A decrease in the money supply would increase the interest rate. At the higher interest rate, businesses find it more costly to finance plants and equipment, and households find it more costly to finance new homes. Hence, a higher interest rate reduces investment. The resulting decline in investment is magnified by the spending multiplier, leading to a greater decline in aggregate demand.

As long as the interest rate is sensitive to changes in the money supply, and as long as investment is sensitive to changes in the interest rate, changes in the money supply affect planned investment. The extent to which a given change in planned investment affects aggregate demand depends on the size of the spending multiplier.

Adding Short-Run Aggregate Supply

Even after tracing the effect of a change in the money supply on aggregate demand, we still have only half the story. To determine the effects of monetary policy on the equilibrium real GDP in the economy, we need the supply side. An aggregate supply curve will help show how a given shift of the aggregate demand curve affects real GDP and the price level. In the

short run, the aggregate supply curve slopes upward, so the quantity supplied will expand only if the price level increases. *For a given shift of the aggregate demand curve, the steeper the short-run aggregate supply curve, the smaller the increase in real GDP and the larger the increase in the price level.*

Suppose the economy is producing at point *a* in Exhibit 4, where the aggregate demand curve *AD* intersects the short-run aggregate supply curve $SRAS_{130}$, yielding a short-run equilibrium output of $11.8 trillion and a price level of 125. As you can see, the actual price level of 125 is below the expected price level of 130, and the short-run equilibrium output of $11.8 trillion is below the economy's potential of $12.0 trillion, yielding a contractionary gap of $0.2 trillion.

At point *a*, real wages are higher than had been negotiated and many people are looking for jobs. The Fed can wait to see whether the economy recovers on its own. Market forces could cause employers and workers to renegotiate lower nominal wages. This would lower production costs, pushing the short-run aggregate supply curve rightward, thus closing the contractionary gap. But if the Fed has little confidence in natural market forces or thinks this would take too long, the Fed could intervene and attempt to close the gap using an expansionary monetary policy. For example, during 2001 and 2002, the Fed aggressively cut the federal funds rate to stimulate aggregate demand. If the Fed lowers the rate by just the right amount, this stimulates investment, thus increasing the aggregate demand curve enough to achieve a new equilibrium at point *b*, where the economy produces its potential output. Given all the connections in the chain of causality between changes in the money

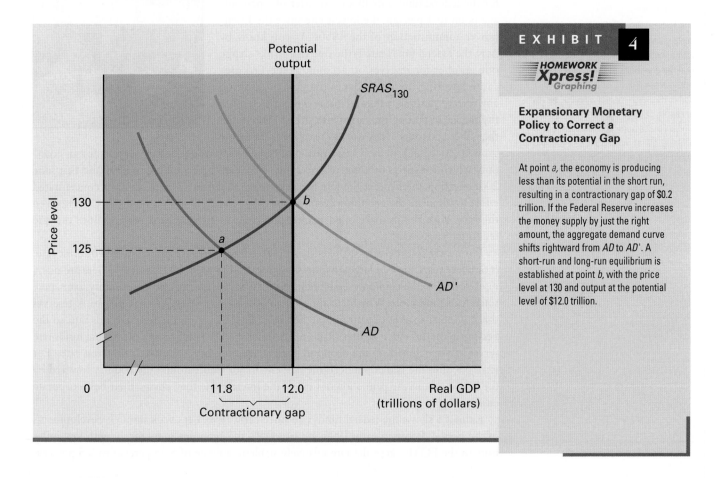

EXHIBIT 4

HOMEWORK
Xpress!
Graphing

Expansionary Monetary Policy to Correct a Contractionary Gap

At point *a*, the economy is producing less than its potential in the short run, resulting in a contractionary gap of $0.2 trillion. If the Federal Reserve increases the money supply by just the right amount, the aggregate demand curve shifts rightward from *AD* to *AD'*. A short-run and long-run equilibrium is established at point *b*, with the price level at 130 and output at the potential level of $12.0 trillion.

supply and changes in equilibrium output, however, it would actually be quite remarkable for the Fed to execute monetary policy so precisely. If the Fed overshoots the mark and stimulates aggregate demand too much, this would create an expansionary gap, thus creating inflationary pressure in the economy.

To review: As long as the demand for money slopes downward and investment demand is sensitive to changes in the interest rate, an increase in the money supply will reduce the market interest rate, increasing planned investment and consequently increasing aggregate demand. And as long as the short-run aggregate supply curve slopes upward, the short-run effect of an increase in the money supply is an increase in both real output and the price level. But one final caution: Lowering the interest rate may not always stimulate investment. Economic prospects may be so grim that lower interest rates may fail to achieve the desired increase in aggregate demand. In Japan, for example, the central bank has lowered the interest rate to nearly zero, yet that economy remained stagnant for a decade.

That's the theory of monetary policy in the short run. The following case study looks at how the Fed executes that policy.

Public Policy

*e*Activity

The Federal Reserve Banks provide reports, surveys, speeches, and other information for Fed Watchers. At the Federal Reserve Bank of Philadelphia at http://www.phil.frb.org, click on Economic Research. Select a recent survey or report, such as the Survey of Professional Forecasters, and read the latest offering. What indications can you find about the future direction of interest rates?

Targeting the Federal Funds Rate

At 2:15 P.M. on June 25, 2003, immediately following a regular meeting, the Federal Open Market Committee (FOMC) announced that it would lower its target for the federal funds rate by one-quarter of a percentage point to 1 percent, the lowest rate since the Eisenhower administration of the 1950s. As you know by now, the federal funds rate is the one that banks charge one another for reserves on account at the Fed. Because lowering the rate reduces the cost of covering any reserve shortfall, banks are more willing to lend to the public. In cutting the target rate, the FOMC noted that the economy "has yet to exhibit sustainable growth," so "a slightly more expansive monetary policy would further support for an economy which it expects to improve over time." Between the beginning of 2001 and that June 2003 meeting, the Fed cut the rate 5.5 percentage points in 13 steps, its most concentrated effort to stimulate the economy ever. To lower the federal funds rate, the FOMC authorized the New York Fed to make open-market purchases to increase bank reserves until the rate fell to the target level.

For nearly four decades, the Fed has reflected its monetary policy in this interest rate. (For a few years, the Fed targeted money aggregates, but more on that later.) There are many interest rates in the economy—for credit cards, new cars, mortgages, home equity loans, personal loans, and more. Why focus on such an obscure rate? First, by changing bank reserves through open-market operations, the Fed has a direct lever on the federal funds rate, so the Fed's grip on this rate is tighter than on any other market rate. Second, the federal funds rate serves as a benchmark in the economy for determining other short-term interest rates. For example, after the Fed announced the rate cut, major banks around the country lowered by the same amount the prime interest rate—the interest rate they charge their best corporate customers.

Exhibit 5 shows the federal funds rate since early 1996. Let's walk through developments of the period. Between early 1996 and late 1998, the economy grew nicely with low inflation, so the FOMC kept the rate relatively stable in a range of 5.25 percent to 5.5 percent.

But in late 1998, a Russian default on its bonds and the near collapse of a U.S. financial institution prompted the FOMC to drop its target rate to 4.75 percent. By the summer of 1999, those fears abated, and instead the FOMC became concerned that robust economic growth would trigger higher inflation. In a series of steps, the federal funds target rate was raised from 4.75 percent to 6.5 percent. The FOMC announced at the time that the moves "should markedly diminish the risk of rising inflation going forward." Some observers suggest that the Fed's aggressive rate hikes contributed to the subsequent recession. In early 2001, concerns about waning consumer confidence, weaker capital spending, falling manufacturing output, and a sinking stock market prompted the FOMC to reverse course, beginning the series of rate cuts discussed already. As it turned out, the economy was already in recession at the time.

In 1994, the Fed began announcing after each FOMC meeting whether the target interest rate would increase, decrease, or remain unchanged. Later, the Fed began indicating the probable "bias" of policy in the near term—that is, whether or not its current level or direction of interest rate changes would continue. For example, with its June 2003 announcement, the FOMC was worried more about "substantial fall in inflation" than in "a pickup in inflation." This signaled financial markets that the Fed would not likely raise interest rates soon. With such concrete news coming after each meeting, these FOMC meetings became media events. Some of the cuts during the recent drop in rates came between regular meetings. Such intermeeting actions have a more dramatic impact on markets, particularly the stock market, because of the surprise element. Still, in announcing target rate cuts, the FOMC must be careful not to appear too alarmed about the economy, because those doubts could harm business and consumer confidence further. Also, the Fed has to avoid overdoing rate cuts. As one member of the Board of Governors warned, the Fed must not cut the rate so much that it "ends up adding to price pressure as the growth strengthens."

Before making a decision about changes in the target interest rate, the Fed tracks a variety of indicators, including real GDP and the unemployment rate. One of Chairman

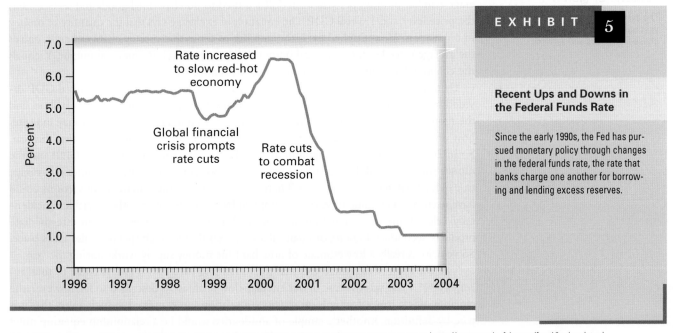

E X H I B I T **5**

Recent Ups and Downs in the Federal Funds Rate

Since the early 1990s, the Fed has pursued monetary policy through changes in the federal funds rate, the rate that banks charge one another for borrowing and lending excess reserves.

Source: Based on monthly averages from the St. Louis Federal Reserve Bank. For the latest rates, go to http://www.stls.frb.org/fred/index.html.

Greenspan's favorites is the employment cost index, which measures changes in the cost of labor. If labor costs increase more than labor productivity, this signals to Greenspan that inflationary pressure is building in the economy, suggesting that an interest rate hike might be the appropriate remedy.

Sources: Aaron Luchetti, "Fed Sharpens Rate-Cut Shears," *Wall Street Journal*, 25 June 2003; Gregory Ip, "Fed to Keep Rates at Historic Low Despite Growth," *Wall Street Journal*, 14 November 2003; "Minutes of the Federal Open Market Committee" and "FOMC Statement on Interest Rates," various meetings. Find the latest FOMC minutes and statements at http://www.federalreserve.gov/fomc/#calendars.

Money and Aggregate Demand in the Long Run

When we looked at the impact of money on the economy in the short run, we found that money influences aggregate demand and equilibrium output through its effect on the interest rate. Here we look at the long-run effects of changes in the money supply on the economy. The long-run view of money is more direct: if the central bank supplies more money to the economy, sooner or later people spend more. But because the long-run aggregate supply curve is fixed at the economy's potential output, this greater spending simply increases the price level. Here are the details.

The Equation of Exchange

EQUATION OF EXCHANGE

The quantity of money, *M*, multiplied by its velocity, *V*, equals nominal GDP, which is the product of the price level, *P*, and real GDP, *Y*

VELOCITY OF MONEY

The average number of times per year each dollar is used to purchase final goods and services

Every transaction in the economy involves a two-way swap: The buyer exchanges money for goods and the seller exchanges goods for money. One way of expressing this relationship among key variables in the economy is the **equation of exchange,** first developed by classical economists. Although this equation can be arranged in different ways, depending on the emphasis, the basic version is

$$M \times V = P \times Y$$

where M is the quantity of money in the economy; V is the **velocity of money,** or the average number of times per year each dollar is used to purchase final goods and services; P is the price level; and Y is real GDP. The equation of exchange says that the quantity of money in circulation, M, multiplied by V, the number of times that money changes hands, equals the average price level, P, times real output, Y. The price level, P, times real output, Y, equals the economy's nominal income and output, or nominal GDP.

By rearranging the equation of exchange, we find that velocity equals nominal GDP divided by the money stock. For example, nominal GDP in 2003 was about $11 trillion, and the money stock as measured by M1 averaged $1.3 trillion. The velocity of money indicates how often each dollar is used on average to pay for final goods and services during the year. So in 2003, velocity was $11 trillion divided by $1.3 trillion, or 8.5. Given GDP and the money supply, each dollar must have been spent about eight and one-half times on average to pay for final goods and services. There is no other way these market transactions could have occurred. The value of velocity is implied by the values of the other variables. Incidentally, velocity measures spending only on final goods and services—not on intermediate products, secondhand goods, or financial assets, even though such spending also takes place. So velocity is really a low estimate of how hard the money supply works during the year.

The equation of exchange says that total spending $(M \times V)$ is always equal to total receipts $(P \times Y)$, as was the case in our circular-flow analysis. As described so far, however, the equation of exchange is simply an *identity*—a relationship expressed in such a way that it is true by definition. Another example of an identity would be a relationship equating miles per gallon to the distance driven divided by the gasoline required.

The Quantity Theory of Money

If velocity is relatively stable over time, or at least predictable, the equation of exchange turns from an identity into a theory—the quantity theory of money. The **quantity theory of money** states that if the velocity of money is stable, or at least predictable, then the equation of exchange can be used to predict the effects of changes in the money supply on *nominal* GDP, $P \times Y$. For example, if M is increased by 5 percent and V remains constant, then $P \times Y$, or nominal GDP, must also increase by 5 percent. For a while, some economists believed they could use the equation of exchange to predict nominal output in the short run. Now it's used primarily as a guide in the long run.

So an increase in the money supply results in more spending in the long run, which leads to a higher nominal GDP. How is this increase in $P \times Y$ divided between changes in the price level and changes in real GDP? The answer does not lie in the quantity theory, for that theory is stated only in terms of nominal GDP. The answer lies in the shape of the aggregate supply curve.

The long-run aggregate supply curve is vertical at the economy's potential level of output. With output, Y, fixed and the velocity of money, V, relatively stable, a change in the stock of money translates directly into a change in the price level. Exhibit 6 shows the effect of an increase in the supply of money in the long run. An increase in the money supply causes a rightward shift of the aggregate demand curve, which increases the price level but leaves output unchanged at potential GDP. So the economy's potential output level is not affected by changes in the money supply. *In the long run, increases in the money supply, with velocity stable or at least not decreasing, result only in higher prices.* For example, three years of an easy money policy began to catch up on the economy in early 2004, when the inflation rate doubled to four percent.[1] And an examination of 73 inflation periods across major economies since 1960 concludes that important triggers to inflation were expansionary policies.[2]

QUANTITY THEORY OF MONEY

If the velocity of money is stable, or at least predictable, changes in the money supply have predictable effects on nominal GDP

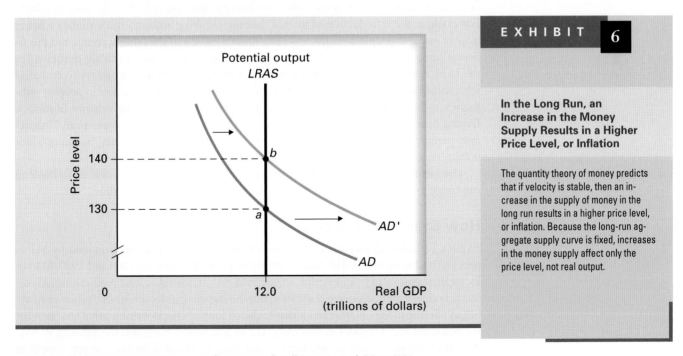

E X H I B I T   6

In the Long Run, an Increase in the Money Supply Results in a Higher Price Level, or Inflation

The quantity theory of money predicts that if velocity is stable, then an increase in the supply of money in the long run results in a higher price level, or inflation. Because the long-run aggregate supply curve is fixed, increases in the money supply affect only the price level, not real output.

1. E. S. Browning, "Investors Cross Fingers As Inflation Looms," *Wall Street Journal,* 7 June 2004.
2. John Boschen and Charles Weise, "What Starts Inflation: Evidence from OECD Countries," *Journal of Money, Credit and Banking* 35 (June 2003): 323–349.

To review: *If velocity is stable, or at least predictable, the quantity theory of money says that changes in the money supply will, in the long run, result in predictable effects on the economy's price level.* Velocity's stability and predictability are key to the quantity theory of money. Let's consider some factors that might influence velocity.

What Determines the Velocity of Money?

Velocity depends on the customs and conventions of commerce. In colonial times, money might be tied up in transit for days as a courier on horseback carried a payment from a merchant in Boston to one in Baltimore. Today, the electronic transmission of funds takes only an instant, so the same stock of money can move around much more quickly to finance many more transactions. *The velocity of money has also increased because of a variety of commercial innovations that facilitate exchange.* For example, a wider use of charge accounts and credit cards has reduced the need for shoppers to carry cash. Likewise, automatic teller machines have made cash more accessible at more times and in more places. What's more, debit cards are used at a growing number of retail outlets, such as grocery stores and drug stores, so people have reduced their "walking around" money.

Another institutional factor that determines velocity is the frequency with which workers get paid. Suppose a worker earns $26,000 per year and is paid $1,000 every two weeks. Earnings are spent evenly during the two-week period and are gone by the end of the period. In that case, a worker's average money balance during the pay period is $500. If a worker earns the same $26,000 per year but, instead, gets paid $500 weekly, the average money balance during the week falls to $250. *Thus, the more often workers get paid, other things constant, the lower their average money balances, so the more active the money supply and the greater its velocity.* Payment practices change slowly over time, and the effects of these changes on velocity are predictable.

Another factor affecting velocity depends on how stable money is as a store of value. *The better money serves as a store of value, the more money people want to hold, so the lower its velocity.* For example, the introduction of interest-bearing checking accounts made money a better store of value, so people were more willing to hold money in checking accounts and this financial innovation reduced velocity. When inflation increases unexpectedly, money turns out to be a poor store of value. People become reluctant to hold money and try to exchange it for some asset that retains its value better during inflation. This reduction in people's willingness to hold money during periods of high inflation increases the velocity of money. During hyperinflation, workers usually get paid daily, boosting velocity even more. Thus, *velocity increases with a rise in the inflation rate, other things constant.* Money becomes a hot potato—nobody wants to hold it for long.

The usefulness of the quantity theory in predicting changes in the price level in the long run hinges on how stable and predictable the velocity of money is over time.

How Stable Is Velocity?

Exhibit 7 graphs velocity since 1960, measured both as nominal GDP divided by M1 in panel (a) and as nominal GDP divided by M2 in panel (b). Between 1960 and 1980, M1 velocity increased steadily and in that sense could be considered at least predictable. M1 velocity bounced around during the 1980s. But during the last decade, more and more banks began offering money market funds that included limited check-writing privileges, or what is considered M2. Deposits shifted from M1 to M2, which increased the velocity of M1. Also in recent years, more people began using their ATM and debit cards to pay directly at grocery stores, drugstores, and a growing number of outlets, and this too increased the velocity of M1 because people had less need for walking-around money.

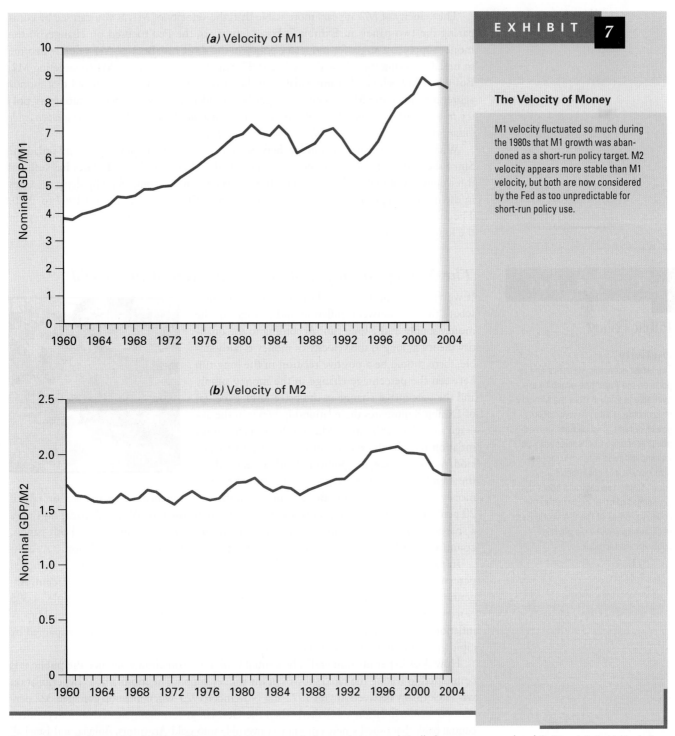

EXHIBIT 7

The Velocity of Money

M1 velocity fluctuated so much during the 1980s that M1 growth was abandoned as a short-run policy target. M2 velocity appears more stable than M1 velocity, but both are now considered by the Fed as too unpredictable for short-run policy use.

Source: *Economic Report of the President*, February 2004. To compute the latest velocity, go to http://w3.access.gpo.gov/eop/, find the statistical tables in the appendix then divide nominal GDP by M1 and by M2.

The velocity of M2 appears more stable than the velocity of M1, as you can see by comparing the two panels in Exhibit 7. For a few years, the Fed focused on changes in the money supply as a target for monetary policy in the short run. Because M1 velocity became so unstable during the 1980s, the Fed in 1987 switched from targeting M1 to targeting M2. But when M2 velocity became volatile in the early 1990s, the Fed announced that money aggregates, including M2, would no longer be considered reliable guides for monetary policy in the short run. *Since 1993, the equation of exchange has been considered more of a rough guide linking changes in the money supply to inflation in the long run.*

What is the long-run relationship between increases in the money supply and inflation? Since the Federal Reserve System was established in 1913, the United States has suffered three episodes of high inflation, and each was preceded and accompanied by sharp increases in the money supply. These occurred from 1913 to 1920, 1939 to 1948, and 1967 to 1980. The following case study examines other evidence linking money growth with inflation in the long run worldwide.

C a s e **S t u d y**

Public Policy

*e*Activity

The latest economic statistics and reports on the Argentine economy are available in English from the Ministry of Economy at http://www.mecon. gov.ar/default_english.htm. Or read about economic trends, monetary policy, and inflation rates in Israel at http://www.mof.gov.il/beinle/ie/ israe_1.htm. You can read about the economies of other countries in the country profiles at the CIA World Factbook at http://www.cia.gov/cia/ publications/factbook.

The Money Supply and Inflation Around the World

If we view economies around the world as evidence, what's the link between inflation and changes in the money supply in the long run? According to the quantity theory, as long as the velocity of money is fairly stable, there should be a positive relation in the long run between the percentage change in the money supply and the percentage change in the price level. Panel (a) of Exhibit 8 illustrates the relationship between the average annual growth rate in M2 and the average annual inflation rate for the 85 countries over a 10-year period. As you can see, the points fall rather neatly along the trend line, showing a positive relation between

© Art Zamur/Gamma

money growth and inflation. Because most countries are bunched below an inflation rate of 20 percent, let's break these points out in finer detail in panel (b). Although panel (a) shows a sharper link between money growth and inflation than does panel (b), in both panels, countries with higher rates of money growth experience higher rates of inflation.

In panel (a), Argentina, Bolivia, and Israel—countries with inflation of more than 100 percent per year—also experienced annual money growth exceeding 100 percent. Argentina, which had the highest inflation rate over the 10-year period in the sample, at 395 percent per year, also had the highest average annual money growth, at 369 percent. Hyperinflation first appeared about a century ago, and in every case it has been accompanied by rapid growth in the supply of paper money.

How does hyperinflation end? The central bank must somehow convince the public it is committed to halting the rapid growth in the money supply. The most famous hyperinflation was in Germany between August 1922 and November 1923, when inflation averaged 322 percent *per month*. Inflation was halted when the German government created an independent central bank that issued a new currency convertible into gold. Argentina, Bolivia, and Israel all managed to tame inflation, with inflation under 3 percent by 2000. Incidentally, households in all three countries, perhaps mindful of their hyperinflation, still hold a lot of U.S. currency.

Sources: *World Development Report 1997* (Oxford: Oxford University Press, 1997); Gerald Dwyer and R. W. Hafer, "Are Money Growth and Inflation Still Related?" *Federal Reserve Bank of Atlanta Economic Review* (Second Quarter 1999): 32–43; and "Emerging Market Indicators," *Economist*, 2 April 2004. Recent inflation rates around the world are available in the *World Development Report*; for the latest, go to http://econ.worldbank.org/wdr/.

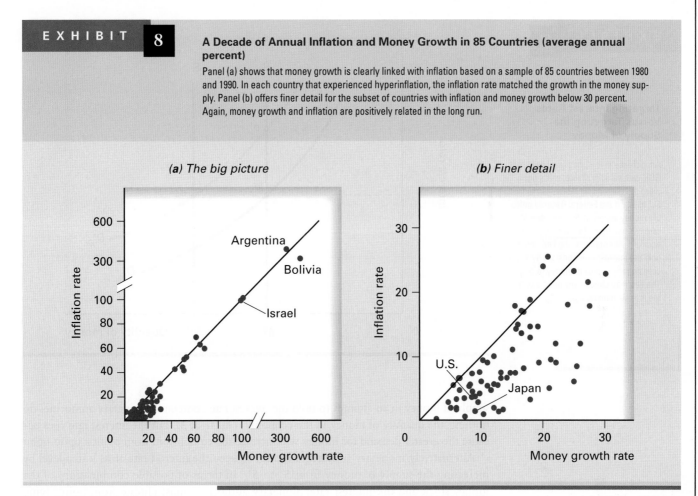

EXHIBIT **8**

A Decade of Annual Inflation and Money Growth in 85 Countries (average annual percent)

Panel (a) shows that money growth is clearly linked with inflation based on a sample of 85 countries between 1980 and 1990. In each country that experienced hyperinflation, the inflation rate matched the growth in the money supply. Panel (b) offers finer detail for the subset of countries with inflation and money growth below 30 percent. Again, money growth and inflation are positively related in the long run.

Source: The World Bank, *World Development Report 1992* (New York: Oxford University Press, 1992), Table 13. Figures are annual averages for 1980 to 1990.

Targets for Monetary Policy

In the short run, monetary policy affects the economy largely by influencing the interest rate. In the long run, changes in the money supply affect the price level, though with an uncertain lag. Should monetary authorities focus on the interest rates in the short run or the supply of money in the long run? As we will see, the Fed lacks the tools to focus on both at the same time.

Contrasting Policies

To demonstrate the effects of different policies, we begin with the money market in equilibrium at point *e* in Exhibit 9. The interest rate is *i* and the money stock is *M*, values the monetary authorities find appropriate. Suppose there is an increase in the demand for money in the economy, perhaps because of an increase in nominal GDP. The money demand curve shifts to the right, from D_m to D'_m.

When confronted with an increase in the demand for money, monetary authorities can choose to do nothing, thereby allowing the interest rate to rise, or they can increase the

Targeting Interest Rates Versus Targeting the Supply of Money

An increase in the price level or in real GDP, with velocity stable, shifts rightward the demand for money curve from D_m to D'_m. If the Federal Reserve holds the money supply at S_m, the interest rate will rise from i (at point e) to i' (at point e'). Alternatively, the Fed could hold the interest rate constant by increasing the supply of money to S'_m. The Fed may choose any point along the money demand curve D'_m.

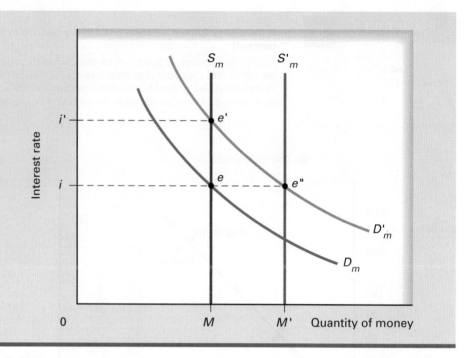

supply of money in an attempt to hold the interest rate constant. If monetary authorities do nothing, the quantity of money in the economy remains at M, but the interest rate rises because the greater demand for money will increase the equilibrium from point e up to point e'. Alternatively, monetary authorities can try to keep the interest rate at its initial level by increasing the supply of money from S_m to S'_m. In terms of possible combinations of the money stock and the interest rate, monetary authorities must choose from points lying along the new money demand curve, D'_m.

A growing economy usually needs a growing money supply to pay for the increase in aggregate output. If monetary authorities maintain a constant growth in the money supply, and if velocity remains stable, the interest rate will fluctuate unless the growth in the supply of money each period just happens to match the growth in the demand for money (as in the movement from e to e'' in Exhibit 9). Alternatively, monetary authorities could try to adjust the money supply each period by the amount needed to keep the interest rate stable. In this approach, changes in the money supply would have to offset any changes in the demand for money. This essentially is what the Fed does when it holds the federal funds target constant.

Interest rate fluctuations could be harmful if they created undesirable fluctuations in investment. For interest rates to remain stable during economic expansions, the money supply would have to grow at the same rate as the demand for money. Likewise, for interest rates to remain stable during economic contractions, the money supply would have to shrink at the same rate as the demand for money. Hence, for monetary authorities to maintain the interest rate at some specified level, the money supply must increase during economic expansions and decrease during contractions. But an increase in the money supply during an expansion would increase aggregate demand even more, and a decrease in the money supply during a contraction would reduce aggregate demand even more. *Such changes in the money supply would thus tend to worsen fluctuations in economic activity, thereby adding more instability to the economy.* With this in mind, let's examine monetary policy over the years.

Targets Before 1982

Between World War II and October 1979, the Fed attempted to stabilize interest rates. Stable interest rates were viewed as a prerequisite for an attractive investment environment and, thus, for a stable economy. Milton Friedman, the Nobel Prize winner, argued that this exclusive attention to interest rates made monetary policy a source of instability in the economy because changes in the money supply reinforced fluctuations in the economy. He said that the Fed should pay less attention to interest rates and instead should focus on a steady and predictable growth in the money supply. The debate raged during the 1970s, and Friedman won some important converts. Amid growing concern about the rising inflation rate, the Fed, under a new chairman, Paul Volcker, announced in October 1979 that it would deemphasize interest rates and would instead target specific money aggregates. Not surprisingly, interest rates became much more volatile.

But many observers believe that a sharp reduction in money growth in the latter half of 1981 caused the recession of 1982. Inflation declined rapidly, but unemployment jumped to 10 percent. People were worried. As you might expect, the Fed was widely criticized. Farmers, politicians, and businesspeople denounced Volcker. Emotions ran high. Volcker was reportedly even given Secret Service protection. In October 1982, three years after the focus on interest rates was dropped, Volcker announced that the Fed would again pay more attention to interest rates.

Targets After 1982

The Fed is always feeling its way, looking for signs about the direction of the economy. The rapid pace of financial innovations and deregulation during the 1980s made the definition and measurement of the money supply more difficult. Alan Greenspan, who became the Fed chairman in 1987, said that, in the short run, changes in the money supply "are not linked closely enough with those of nominal income to justify a single-minded focus on the money supply."[3] In 1993, he testified in Congress that the Fed would no longer target money aggregates, such as M1 and M2, as a guide to monetary policy. As we've seen, the Fed in recent years has targeted the federal funds rate. No central bank in a major economy now makes significant use of money aggregates to guide policy in the short run. Still, most policy makers also agree that in the long run, changes in the money supply influenced the price level and inflation.

Conclusion

This chapter has described two ways of viewing the effects of money on the economy's performance, but we should not overstate the differences. In the model that focuses on the short run, an increase in the money supply means that people are holding more money than they would like at the prevailing interest rate, so they exchange one form of wealth, money, for other financial assets, such as corporate or government bonds. This greater demand for other financial assets has no direct effect on aggregate demand, but it does reduce the interest rate, and this lower interest rate stimulates investment. The higher investment gets magnified by the spending multiplier, increasing aggregate demand. The effect of this increase in demand on real output and the price level depends on the shape of the short-run aggregate supply curve.

In the model that focuses on the long run, changes in the money supply act more directly on the price level. If velocity is relatively stable or at least fairly predictable, then

3. Quoted in "Greenspan Asks That Fed Be Allowed to Pay Interest," *Wall Street Journal,* 11 March 1992.

changes in the money supply will have a predictable effect on the price level in the long run. As long as velocity is not declining, an increase in the money supply means that people eventually spend more, increasing aggregate demand. But because long-run aggregate supply is fixed at the economy's potential output, increased aggregate demand leads simply to a higher price level, or to inflation.

SUMMARY

1. The opportunity cost of holding money is the higher interest forgone by not holding other financial assets instead. Along a given money demand curve, the quantity of money demanded relates inversely to the interest rate. The demand for money curve shifts rightward as a result of an increase in the price level, an increase in real GDP, or an increase in both.

2. The Fed determines the supply of money, assumed to be independent of the interest rate. The intersection of the supply and demand for money determines the equilibrium interest rate. In the short run, an increase in the supply of money reduces the interest rate, which increases investment. This boosts aggregate demand, which increases real output and the price level.

3. The long-run approach focuses on the role of money through the equation of exchange, which states that the quantity of money, M, multiplied by velocity, V, the average number of times each dollar gets spent, equals the price level, P, multiplied by real GDP, Y. So $M \times V = P \times Y$. Because the aggregate supply curve in the long run is a vertical line at the economy's potential output, a change in the money supply affects the price level but not real output.

4. Between World War II and October 1979, the Fed targeted stable interest rates as a way of promoting a stable investment environment. During the 1980s and early 1990s, the Fed paid more attention to growth in money aggregates, first M1 and then M2. But the velocity of M1 and M2 became so unstable that the Fed decided to shift focus back to interest rates, particularly the federal funds rate.

QUESTIONS FOR REVIEW

1. *(Demand for Money)* Determine whether each of the following would lead to an increase, a decrease, or no change in the quantity of money people wish to hold. Also determine whether there is a shift of the money demand curve or a movement along a given money demand curve.

    a. A decrease in the price level
    b. An increase in real output
    c. An improvement in money's ability to act as a store of value
    d. An increase in the market interest rate

2. *(Demand for Money)* If money is so versatile and can buy anything, why don't people demand all the money they can get their hands on?

3. *(Monetary Policy)* What is the impact of a decrease in the required reserve ratio on aggregate demand?

4. (*C a s e* **Study:** Targeting the Federal Funds Rate) Why has the Federal Reserve chosen to focus on the federal funds rate rather than some other interest rate as a tool of monetary policy?

5. *(Equation of Exchange)* Using the equation of exchange, show why fiscal policy alone cannot increase nominal GDP if the velocity of money is constant.

6. *(Velocity)* Why do some economists believe that higher expected inflation will lead to a rise in velocity?

7. *(Velocity of Money)* Determine whether each of the following would lead to an increase or a decrease in the velocity of money:

    a. Increasing the speed of funds transfers
    b. Decreased use of credit cards

c. Decreasing the frequency with which workers are paid

d. Increased customer use of ATM, or debit, cards at retailers

8. *(Quantity Theory of Money)* The quantity theory states that the impact of money on nominal GDP can be determined without details about the *AD* curve, so long as the velocity of money is predictable. Discuss the reasoning behind this claim.

9. *(**C a s e S t u d y**: The Money Supply and Inflation Around the World)* According to Exhibit 8 in this chapter, what is the relationship between the rate of money supply growth and the inflation rate? How does this explain the hyperinflation experienced in some economies?

10. *(How Stable Is Velocity?)* What factors have led to changes in the velocity of M1 and M2 over the past 25 years?

11. *(Money Supply Versus Interest Rate Targets)* In recent years the Fed's monetary target has been the federal funds rate. How does the Fed raise or lower that rate, and how is that rate related to other interest rates in the economy such as the prime rate?

PROBLEMS AND EXERCISES

12. *(Money Demand)* Suppose that you never carry cash. Your paycheck of $1,000 per month is deposited directly into your checking account, and you spend your money at a constant rate so that at the end of each month your checking account balance is zero.

    a. What is your average money balance during the pay period?

    b. How would each of the following changes affect your average monthly balance?
       i. You are paid $500 twice monthly rather than $1,000 each month.
       ii. You are uncertain about your total spending each month.
       iii. You spend a lot at the beginning of the month (e.g., for rent) and little at the end of the month.
       iv. Your monthly income increases.

13. *(Money and Aggregate Demand)* Would each of the following increase, decrease, or have no impact on the ability of open-market operations to affect aggregate demand? Explain your answer.

    a. Investment demand becomes less sensitive to changes in the interest rate.

    b. The marginal propensity to consume rises.

    c. The money multiplier rises.

    d. Banks decide to hold additional excess reserves.

    e. The demand for money becomes more sensitive to changes in the interest rate.

14. *(Monetary Policy and Aggregate Supply)* Assume that the economy is initially in long-run equilibrium. Using an *AD–AS* diagram, illustrate and explain the short-run and long-run impacts of an increase in the money supply.

15. *(Monetary Policy and an Expansionary Gap)* Suppose the Fed wishes to use monetary policy to close an expansionary gap.

    a. Should the Fed increase or decrease the money supply?

    b. If the Fed uses open-market operations, should it buy or sell government securities?

    c. Determine whether each of the following increases, decreases, or remains unchanged in the short run: the market interest rate, the quantity of money demanded, investment spending, aggregate demand, potential output, the price level, and equilibrium real GDP.

16. *(Equation of Exchange)* Calculate the velocity of money if real GDP is 3,000 units, the average price level is $4 per unit, and the quantity of money in the economy is $1,500. What happens to velocity if the average price level drops to $3 per unit? What happens to velocity if the average price level remains at $4 per unit but the money supply rises to $2,000? What happens to velocity if the average price level falls to $2 per unit, the money supply is $2,000, and real GDP is 4,000 units?

17. *(Quantity Theory of Money)* What basic assumption about the velocity of money transforms the equation of exchange into the quantity theory of money? Also:

    a. According to the quantity theory, what will happen to nominal GDP if the money supply increases by 5 percent and velocity does not change?

b. What will happen to nominal GDP if, instead, the money supply decreases by 8 percent and velocity does not change?

c. What will happen to nominal GDP if, instead, the money supply increases by 5 percent and velocity decreases by 5 percent?

d. What happens to the price level in the short run in each of these three situations?

18. *(Money Supply Versus Interest Rate Targets)* Assume that the economy's real GDP is growing.

a. What will happen to money demand over time?

b. If the Fed leaves the money supply unchanged, what will happen to the interest rate over time?

c. If the Fed changes the money supply to match the change in money demand, what will happen to the interest rate over time?

d. What would be the effect of the policy described in part (c) on the economy's stability over the business cycle?

EXPERIENTIAL EXERCISES

19. *(Money Supply Versus Interest Rate Targets)* A favorite activity of many macroeconomists is Fed watching. Go to the Federal Reserve Board's Web site and look for the most recent Congressional testimony of the Board Chairperson at http://www.federalreserve.gov/boarddocs/testimony/2004/. Is the Fed targeting interest rates, the money supply, or something else?

20. *(Targets After 1982)* The Federal Reserve Bank of Cleveland's monthly publication *Economic Trends* at http://www.clevelandfed.org/Research/index.htm is available online. Choose the current issue and find "Monetary Policy." What are some current developments in monetary policy? See if you can illustrate them using the *AD–AS* model.

21. *(Wall Street Journal)* The Federal Reserve Report appears in each Friday's *Wall Street Journal*. You can find it in the Money and Investing section. In addition to the weekly report, a monthly chart shows the recent performance of money supply indicators, compared with Fed targets. Does it look as if the Fed has been hitting its targets over the last year?

22. *(Wall Street Journal)* Look in the Money and Investing section of the *Wall Street Journal* for interest rate information. Find the current federal funds rate. How has it changed over the past year?

HOMEWORK XPRESS! EXERCISES

These exercises require access to McEachern Homework Xpress! If Homework Xpress! did not come with your book, visit **http://homeworkxpress.swlearning.com** *to purchase.*

1. In the Homework Xpress! graph for this problem, sketch a curve illustrating the relationship between the interest rate and the demand for money.

2. Draw a demand for money curve and a supply of money at $2 trillion. Identify the rate of interest at which people would hold this quantity of money. Illustrate the effect of an increase in the supply of money by the Fed.

3. In the diagram, sketch a line showing long-run aggregate supply at a potential output of $10 trillion. Sketch in an

aggregate demand curve and identify the price level. Illustrate the long-run effect of an increase in the money supply.

4. Sketch a demand for money curve and a supply of money at $2 trillion. Identify the rate of interest at which people would hold this quantity of money. Illustrate the effect of an increase in the demand for money. Show how the Fed could act to keep the interest rate constant.

The Policy Debate: Active or Passive?

© William Philpott/AFP/Getty Images

D oes the private sector work fairly well on its own, or does it require active government intervention? Does government intervention do more harm than good? If people expect government to intervene if the economy falters, does this expectation affect people's behavior? What is the relationship between unemployment and inflation in the short run and in the long run? Answers to these and other questions are provided in this chapter, which examines the appropriate role for government in economic stabilization.

You have studied both fiscal and monetary policy and are now in a position to consider the overall impact of public policy on the U.S. economy. This chapter distinguishes between two general approaches: the *active approach* and the *passive approach*. The active approach views the private sector as relatively unstable and unable to recover from shocks when they occur. According to the active approach,

HOMEWORK Xpress!

Use Homework Xpress! for economic application, graphing, videos, and more.

economic fluctuations arise primarily from the private sector, particularly investment, and natural market forces may not help much or may be too slow when the economy gets off track. To move the economy to its potential output, the active approach calls for government intervention and discretionary policy. The passive approach, on the other hand, considers the private sector to be relatively stable and able to recover from shocks when they do occur. When the economy derails, natural market forces nudge it back on track in a timely manner. Not only is government intervention unnecessary, but according to the passive approach, such activism may do more harm than good.

In this chapter, we consider the pros and cons of *active* intervention in the economy versus *passive* reliance on natural market forces. We also examine the role that expectations play in determining the effectiveness of stabilization policy. You will learn why unanticipated stabilization policies have more impact on employment and output than do anticipated ones. Finally, the chapter explores the trade-off between unemployment and inflation. Topics discussed include:

- Active versus passive approaches
- Self-correcting mechanisms
- Rational expectations
- Policy rules and policy credibility

- The time-inconsistency problem
- Short-run and long-run Phillips curves
- Natural rate hypothesis

Active Policy Versus Passive Policy

According to the *active approach,* discretionary fiscal or monetary policy can reduce the costs of an unstable private sector, such as higher unemployment. According to the *passive approach,* discretionary policy may contribute to the instability of the economy and is therefore part of the problem, not part of the solution. The two approaches differ in their assumptions about how well natural market forces operate and the effectiveness of government intervention.

Closing a Contractionary Gap

Perhaps the best way to describe each approach is by examining a particular macroeconomic problem. Suppose the economy is in short-run equilibrium at point *a* in panel (a) of Exhibit 1, with real GDP at $11.8 trillion, which is below the economy's potential of $12.0 trillion. The contractionary gap of $0.2 trillion drives unemployment above its natural rate (the rate when the economy produces potential GDP). This gap could have resulted from lower-than-expected aggregate demand. What should public officials do?

Those who follow the passive approach, as did their classical predecessors, have more faith in the *self-correcting forces* of the economy than do those who favor the active approach. In what sense is the economy self-correcting? According to the passive approach, wages and prices are flexible enough to adjust within a reasonable period to labor shortages or surpluses. High unemployment will cause wages to fall, which will reduce production costs, which will shift the short-run aggregate supply curve rightward in panel (a) of Exhibit 1. (Money wages need not actually fall; money wage increases need only lag behind price increases, so that real wages fall.) The short-run aggregate supply curve will, within a reasonable period, shift from $SRAS_{130}$ to $SRAS_{120}$, moving the economy to its potential output at point *b. According to the passive approach, the economy is stable enough, gravitating in a reasonable time toward potential GDP. Consequently, advocates of passive policy see little reason for discretionary policy.* The passive approach is to let natural market forces close the contractionary gap. So

EXHIBIT 1

Closing a Contractionary Gap

At point *a* in both panels, the economy is in short-run equilibrium, with unemployment exceeding its natural rate. According to the passive approach, shown in panel (a), high unemployment eventually causes wages to fall, reducing the cost of doing business. The decline in costs shifts the short-run aggregate supply curve rightward from $SRAS_{130}$ to $SRAS_{120}$, moving the economy to its potential output at point *b*. In panel (b), the government employs an active approach to shift the aggregate demand curve from *AD* to *AD'*. If the active policy works, the economy moves to its potential output at point *c*.

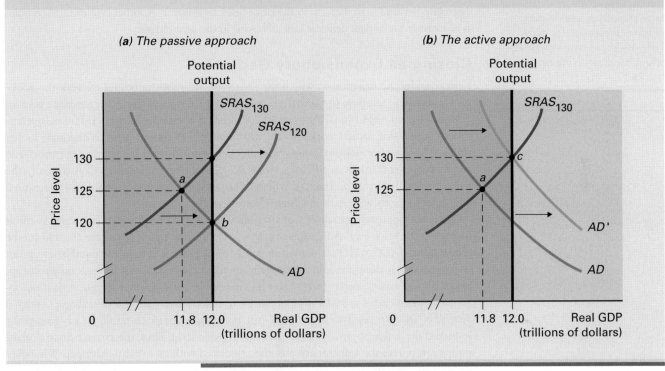

the prescription of passive policy is to do nothing beyond the automatic stabilizers already built into taxes, transfers, and government purchases.

Advocates of an active approach, on the other hand, believe that prices and wages are not very flexible, particularly in the downward direction. They think that when adverse supply shocks or sagging demand push unemployment above its natural rate, market forces are slow to respond. The longer market forces take to reduce unemployment to the natural rate, the greater the output lost and the greater the economic and psychological cost to those unemployed. *Because advocates of an active policy associate a high cost with the passive approach, they advocate an active stabilization policy to stimulate aggregate demand.*

A decision by public officials to intervene in the economy to achieve potential output—that is, a decision to use discretionary policy—reflects an active approach. In panel (b) of Exhibit 1, we begin at the same point *a* as in panel (a). At point *a,* short-run equilibrium output is below potential output, so the economy is experiencing a contractionary gap. Through discretionary monetary policy, discretionary fiscal policy, or some of both, as occurred in 2001, active policy attempts to increase aggregate demand from *AD* to *AD'*, moving equilibrium from point *a* to point *c*, thus closing the contractionary gap.

WALL STREET JOURNAL

Reading It **Right**

What's the relevance of the following statement from the Wall Street Journal: *"The U.S. could rebound quickly from its downturn because of the monetary and fiscal stimulus already in the 'pipeline' in response to early signs of a slowdown and particularly in response to the terrorist attacks."*

In 2001, policy makers tried to revive a slowing economy using both fiscal and monetary policy. George W. Bush's first tax cut, the largest in a decade, was approved by Congress in May and was aimed, in Bush's words, at "getting the country moving again." Later that year, Congress and the president also approved a multibillion dollar package of federal outlays to support greater national security in the wake of the terrorist attacks. Meanwhile, throughout 2001, as noted in the previous chapter, the Fed cut its target interest rate a record amount. This combination of fiscal and monetary policy was the most concentrated attempt to boost aggregate demand since World War II. One possible cost of using discretionary policy to stimulate aggregate demand is an increase in the price level, or inflation. Another cost of fiscal stimulus is to increase the budget deficit, a cost addressed in the next chapter.

Closing an Expansionary Gap

Let's consider the situation in which the short-run equilibrium output exceeds the economy's potential. Suppose the actual price level of 135 exceeds the expected price level of 130, causing an expansionary gap of $0.2 trillion, as shown in Exhibit 2. The passive approach argues that natural market forces will prompt workers and firms to negotiate higher wages. These higher nominal wages will increase production costs, shifting the short-run supply curve leftward, from $SRAS_{130}$ to $SRAS_{140}$, as shown in panel (a). Consequently, the price level will increase and output will decrease to the economy's potential. So the natural adjustment process will result in a higher price level, or inflation.

An active approach sees discretionary policy as a way to reach potential output without increasing the price level. Advocates of active policy believe that if aggregate demand can be reduced from AD'' to AD', as shown in panel (b) of Exhibit 2, then the equilibrium point will move down along the initial aggregate supply curve from d to c. *Whereas the passive approach relies on natural market forces to close an expansionary gap through a decrease in short-run aggregate supply, the active approach relies on just the right discretionary policy to close the gap through a decrease of aggregate demand.* In the long run, the passive approach results in a higher price level and the active approach results in a lower price level. Thus, the correct discretionary policy can relieve the inflationary pressure associated with an expansionary gap. Whenever the Fed attempts to cool down an overheated economy by increasing its target interest rate, as it did in 2000, it employs an active monetary policy to close an expansionary gap. In 2000, when the economy was flying high, with output exceeding potential, the Fed tried to orchestrate a so-called *soft landing* to gently slow the rate of growth before that growth triggered inflation. Critics say the Fed overdid it and contributed to the recession of 2001.

Problems with Active Policy

The timely adoption and implementation of an active policy is not easy. One problem is identifying the economy's potential output and the natural rate of unemployment. Suppose the natural rate of unemployment is 5 percent, but policy makers believe it's 4 percent. As they pursue their elusive goal of 4 percent, they push output beyond its potential, fueling higher prices in the long run but with no permanent reduction in unemployment. Recall that when output exceeds the economy's potential, this opens up an expansionary gap, causing a leftward shift of the short-run aggregate supply curve until the economy returns to its potential output at a higher price level.

Even if policy makers can accurately estimate the economy's potential output and the natural rate of unemployment, formulating an effective policy requires detailed knowledge of current and future economic conditions. To craft an effective strategy, policy makers must first be able to forecast aggregate demand and supply without active intervention. In other

EXHIBIT 2

Closing an Expansionary Gap

At point *d* in both panels, the economy is in short-run equilibrium, producing $12.2 trillion, which exceeds the economy's potential output. Unemployment is below its natural rate. In the passive approach reflected in panel (a), the government makes no change in policy, so natural market forces eventually bring about a higher negotiated wage, increasing firm costs and shifting the short-run supply curve leftward to $SRAS_{140}$. The new equilibrium at point *e* results in a higher price level and lower output and employment. An active policy reduces aggregate demand, shifting the equilibrium in panel (b) from point *d* to point *c*, thus closing the expansionary gap without increasing the price level.

(a) The passive approach

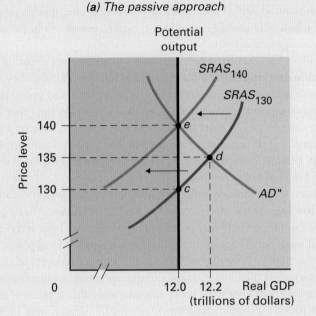

(b) The active approach

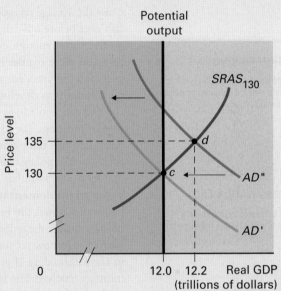

words, they must be able to predict what would happen with a passive approach. Second, they must have the tools needed to achieve the desired result relatively quickly. Third, they must be able to predict the effects of an active policy on the economy's key performance measures. Fourth, policy makers must work together, or at least not work at cross-purposes. Congress and the president pursue fiscal policy while the Fed pursues monetary policy; these groups often fail to coordinate their efforts. If an active policy requires coordination, the policy may not work as desired. In early 1995, for example, Congress was considering an expansionary tax cut while the Fed was pursuing a contractionary monetary policy. Fifth, policy makers must be able to implement the appropriate policy, even when this involves short-term political costs. For example, during inflationary times, the optimal policy may call for a tax increase or a tighter monetary policy—policies that are unpopular because they increase unemployment. Finally, policy makers must be able to deal with a variety of timing lags. As we will see next, these lags compound the problems of pursuing an active policy.

The Problem of Lags

So far, we have ignored the time required to implement policy. That is, we have assumed that the desired policy is selected and implemented instantaneously. We have also assumed

RECOGNITION LAG

The time needed to identify a macroeconomic problem and assess its seriousness

DECISION-MAKING LAG

The time needed to decide what to do once a macroeconomic problem has been identified

IMPLEMENTATION LAG

The time needed to introduce a change in monetary or fiscal policy

EFFECTIVENESS LAG

The time needed for changes in monetary or fiscal policy to affect the economy

that, once implemented, the policy works as advertised—again, in no time. Actually, there may be long, sometimes unpredictable, lags at several stages in the process. These lags reduce the effectiveness and increase the uncertainty of active policies.

First, is a **recognition lag**—the time it takes to identify a problem and determine how serious it is. For example, time is required to accumulate evidence that the economy is indeed performing below its potential. Even if initial data look troubling, data are usually revised later. For example, the government releases three estimates of quarterly GDP growth coming weeks apart—an *advanced* estimate, a *preliminary* estimate, and a *final* estimate. What's more these estimates are often revised years later or even a decade later. Therefore, policy makers sometimes wait for more proof before responding to what may turn out to be a false alarm. Because a recession is not identified until more than 6 months after it begins and because the average recession lasts only about 11 months, a typical recession will be more than half over before officially recognized as such.

Even after enough evidence accumulates, policy makers often take time deciding what to do, so there is a **decision-making lag.** In the case of discretionary fiscal policy, Congress and the president must agree on an appropriate course of action. Fiscal policy usually takes months to develop and approve; it could take more than a year. On the other hand, the Fed can implement monetary policy more quickly and does not even have to wait for regular meetings. For example, as the economy weakened in 2001, the Fed announced interest rate cuts three times between regular meetings. So the decision-making lag is shorter for monetary policy than for fiscal policy.

Once a decision has been made, the new policy must be introduced, which usually involves an **implementation lag.** Again, monetary policy has the advantage: After a policy has been adopted, the Fed can immediately buy or sell bonds to influence bank reserves and thereby change the federal funds rate. The implementation lag is longer for fiscal policy. If tax rates change, new tax forms must be printed and distributed advising employers of changes in tax withholding. If government spending changes, the appropriate government agencies must get involved. The implementation of fiscal policy can take more than a year. For example, in February 1983, the nation's unemployment rate reached 10.3 percent, with 11.5 million people unemployed. The following month, Congress passed the Emergency Jobs Appropriation Act, providing $9 billion to create what supporters claimed would be hundreds of thousands of new jobs. Fifteen months later, only $3.1 billion had been spent and only 35,000 new jobs had been created, according to a U.S. General Accounting Office study. By that time, the economy was already recovering on its own, lowering the unemployment rate from 10.3 percent to 7.1 percent and adding 6.2 million new jobs. So this public spending program was implemented only after the recession had bottomed out and recovered. Likewise, in spring 1993, President Clinton proposed a $16 billion stimulus package to boost what appeared to be a sluggish recovery. The measure was defeated because it would have increased what already was a large federal deficit, yet the economy still added 5.6 million jobs over the next two years. As a final example, in early 2001, President Bush proposed a tax cut to stimulate the economy. Although Congress passed the measure relatively quickly, tax rebate checks were not mailed until six months after Bush introduced the legislation.

Once a policy has been implemented, there is an **effectiveness lag** before the full impact of the policy registers on the economy. One problem with monetary policy is that the lag between a change in the federal funds rate and the change in aggregate demand and output can take from months to a year or more. Fiscal policy, once enacted, usually requires 3 to 6 months to take effect and between 9 and 18 months to register its full effect.

These various lags make active policy difficult to execute. The more variable the lags, the harder it is to predict when a particular policy will take hold and what the state of the economy will be at that time. To advocates of passive policy, these lags are reason enough to avoid active discretionary policy. *Advocates of a passive approach argue that an active stabilization policy imposes troubling fluctuations in the price level and real GDP because it often takes hold only after market forces have already returned the economy to its potential output level.*

Talk in the media about "jump-starting" the economy reflects the active approach, which views the economy as a sputtering machine that can be fixed by an expert mechanic. The passive approach views the economy as more like a supertanker on automatic pilot. The policy question then becomes whether to trust that automatic pilot (the self-correcting tendencies of the economy) or to try to override the mechanism with active discretionary policies.

A Review of Policy Perspectives

The active and passive approaches embody different views about the stability and resiliency of the economy and the ability of Congress or the Fed to implement appropriate discretionary policies. So the two approaches disagree about the inherent stability of the private sector and the role of public policy in the economy. As we have seen, advocates of an active approach think that the natural adjustments of wages and prices can be excruciatingly slow, particularly when unemployment is high, as it was during the Great Depression. Prolonged high unemployment means that much output must be sacrificed, and the unemployed must suffer personal hardship during the slow adjustment period. If high unemployment lasts a long time, labor skills may grow rusty, and some may drop out of the labor force. Therefore, prolonged unemployment may cause the economy's potential GDP to fall, as suggested in the case study of hysteresis several chapters back.

Thus, active policy associates a high cost with the failure to pursue a discretionary policy. And, despite the lags involved, advocates of the active approach prefer action—through discretionary fiscal policy, discretionary monetary policy, or some combination of the two—to inaction. Passive policy advocates, on the other hand, believe that uncertain lags and ignorance about how the economy works prevent policy makers from accurately determining and effectively implementing the appropriate active policy. Therefore, the passive approach, rather than pursuing a misguided activist policy, relies more on the economy's natural ability to correct itself just using automatic stabilizers.

Differences between active and passive approaches emerged during the presidential campaign of 1992, when the economy was slow to recover from a recession, as discussed in the following case study.

Active Versus Passive Presidential Candidates

During the third quarter of 1990, after what at the time had become the longest peacetime economic expansion of the century, the U.S. economy slipped into a recession, triggered by Iraq's invasion of oil-rich Kuwait. Because of large federal deficits at the time, policy makers were reluctant to adopt discretionary fiscal policy to revive the economy. That task was left to monetary policy. The recession lasted only nine months, but the recovery was sluggish—so sluggish that unemployment continued to edge up in what was derisively called a "jobless recovery."

That sluggish recovery was the economic backdrop for the presidential election of 1992 between Republican President George H. W. Bush and

© Jeff Haynes/AFP/Getty Images

C a s e **S t u d y**

Public Policy

*e*Activity
President George H. W. Bush's last State of the Union address was on January 28, 1992—a time when the country was recovering from a mild recession. The text of his speech—and the State of the Union speeches of other presidents—is available from the C-Span archives at http://www.c-span.org/executive/stateoftheunion.asp.

Read it to determine whether he was in favor of an active or passive approach to dealing with the sluggish recovery. Next compare President Clinton's last address to that of President George W. H. Bush. How activist did Clinton appear given economic conditions during his last year? What additional government programs and/or tax cuts was he proposing? Were these to stimulate the economy or for some other purpose? Also read President George W. Bush's State of the Union address for January of 2004. How does his approach compare to that of the first President Bush's approach?

Democratic challenger Bill Clinton. Because monetary policy did not seem to be providing enough kick, was additional fiscal stimulus needed? With the federal budget deficit in 1992 already approaching $300 billion, a record level to that point, would a higher deficit do more harm than good?

Bush's biggest political liabilities during the campaign were the sluggish recovery and ballooning federal deficits; these were Clinton's biggest political assets. Clinton argued that (1) Bush had not done enough to revive the economy; (2) Bush and his predecessor, Ronald Reagan, were responsible for the huge federal deficits; and (3) Bush could not be trusted because he broke his 1988 campaign pledge of "no new taxes" by signing a tax increase in 1990 to help cut federal deficits. Clinton promised to raise tax rates on the rich and cut them for the middle class. He also promised to create jobs through government spending that would "invest in America."

Bush tried to remind voters that, technically, the recession was over and the economy was on the mend. But that was a hard sell with unemployment averaging 7.6 percent during the six months leading up to the election. Bush blamed a Democratic Congress for blocking his recovery proposals, and he renewed his pledge of no new taxes. In fact, he promised to cut taxes by 1 percent, arguing that this would reallocate spending from government back to households.

Clinton saw a stronger role for government, and Bush saw a stronger role for the private sector. Clinton's approach was more *active* and Bush's more *passive*. In the end, the high unemployment rates during the campaign made people more willing to gamble on Clinton. Apparently, during troubled times, an active policy has more voter appeal than a passive one. Ironically, the economy at the time was stronger than conveyed by the media and by challenger Clinton ("It's the economy, stupid" became Clinton's rallying cry). Real GDP in 1992 grew 3.3 percent, which would turn out to be more than the 2.7 percent growth experienced during Clinton's first year in office. The unemployment rate began falling in October 1992, the month before the election (but the unemployment report came in early November—too late to help Bush). The unemployment rate then proceeded to fall *for the next eight years*. Bush's timing was awful; Clinton's, incredible.

George W. Bush was not about to make the same mistake as his father. Shortly after taking office in 2001, he proposed the first of three tax cuts to boost a lifeless economy. These cuts, along with a growth in government spending, offered the most fiscal stimulus in more than a decade. This expansionary fiscal policy combined with the Fed's interest rate cuts for the greatest stimulus of aggregate demand since World War II. Although the recession was over by the end of 2001, the unemployment rate continued to rise until its peak of 6.3 percent in June 2003. Jobs started coming back in earnest just before the 2004 presidential election.

Sources: David Wessel, "Wanted: Fiscal Stimulus Without Higher Taxes," *Wall Street Journal*, 5 October 1992; *Economic Report of the President*, February 2004; Bob Woodward, *The Agenda* (New York: Simon and Schuster, 1994); and the St. Louis Federal Reserve Bank's database at http://www.stls.frb.org/fred/index.html.

The Role of Expectations

The effectiveness of a particular government policy depends in part on what people expect. As we saw in an earlier chapter, the short-run aggregate supply curve is drawn for a given expected price level reflected in long-term wage contracts. If workers and firms expect continuing inflation, their wage agreements will reflect these inflationary expectations. One approach in macroeconomics, called **rational expectations,** argues that people form expectations on the basis of all available information, including information about the probable future actions of policy makers. Thus, aggregate supply depends on what sort of

RATIONAL EXPECTATIONS

A school of thought that argues people form expectations based on all available information, including the likely future actions of government policy makers

macroeconomic course policy makers are expected to pursue. For example, if people were to observe policy makers using discretionary policy to stimulate aggregate demand every time output falls below potential, people would come to anticipate the effects of this policy on the price level and output. Robert Lucas, of the University of Chicago, won the 1995 Nobel Prize for his studies of rational expectations.

Monetary authorities are required to testify before Congress regularly, indicating the policy they plan to pursue. The Fed also announces, after each meeting of the FOMC, any changes in its interest rate targets and the likely direction of future changes. We will consider the role of expectations in the context of monetary policy by examining the relationship between policy pronouncements and equilibrium output. We could focus on fiscal policy, but monetary policy has been calling the shots for most of the last quarter century. Only with George W. Bush's tax cuts did fiscal policy make something of a comeback.

Monetary Policy and Expectations

Suppose the economy is producing potential output so unemployment is at its natural rate. At the beginning of the year, firms and employees must negotiate wage agreements. While negotiations are under way, the Fed announces that throughout the year, its monetary policy will aim at maintaining potential output while keeping the price level stable. This seems the appropriate policy because unemployment is already at the natural rate. Workers and firms understand that the Fed's stable price policy appears optimal under the circumstances because an expansionary monetary policy would lead only to higher inflation in the long run. Until the year is under way and monetary policy is actually implemented, however, the public cannot be sure what the Fed will do.

As long as wage increases do not exceed the growth in labor productivity, the Fed's plan of a stable price level should work. Alternatively, workers could try for higher wage growth, but that option would ultimately lead to inflation. Suppose workers and firms believe the Fed's pronouncements and agree on wage settlements based on a constant price level. If the Fed follows through as promised, the price level should turn out as expected. Output will remain at the economy's potential, and unemployment will remain at the natural rate. The situation is depicted in Exhibit 3. The short-run aggregate supply curve, $SRAS_{130}$, is based on wage contracts reflecting an expected price level of 130. If the Fed follows the announced course, aggregate demand will be AD and equilibrium will be at point a, where the price level is as expected and the economy is producing $12.0 trillion, the potential output.

Suppose, however, that after workers and firms have agreed on nominal wages—that is, after the short-run aggregate supply curve has been determined—public officials become dissatisfied with the unemployment rate. Perhaps election-year concerns with unemployment, a false alarm about a recession, or overestimating potential output convince the Fed to act. An expansionary monetary policy increases aggregate demand from AD, the level anticipated by firms and employees, to AD'. This unexpected policy stimulates output and employment in the short run to equilibrium point b. Output increases to $12.2 trillion, and the price level increases to 135. This temporary boost in output and reduction in unemployment may last long enough to help public officials get reelected.

So the price level is now higher than workers expected, and their agreed-on wage buys less in real terms than workers bargained for. At their earliest opportunity, workers will negotiate higher wages. These higher wage agreements will eventually cause the short-run aggregate supply curve in Exhibit 3 to shift leftward, intersecting AD' at point c, the economy's potential output (to reduce clutter, the shifted short-run aggregate supply curve is not shown). So output once again returns to the economy's potential GDP, but in the process the price level rises to 142.

EXHIBIT 3

Short-Run Effects of an Unexpected Expansionary Monetary Policy

At point *a*, workers and firms expect a price level of 130; supply curve *SRAS*₁₃₀ reflect that expectation. If the Fed unexpectedly pursues an expansionary monetary policy, the aggregate demand curve becomes *AD'* rather than *AD*. Output in the short run (at point *b*) exceeds its potential, but in the long run costs increase, shifting *SRAS* leftward until the economy produces its potential output at point *c* (the resulting supply curve is not shown). The short-run effect of an unexpected monetary expansion is greater output, but the long-run effect is just a higher price level.

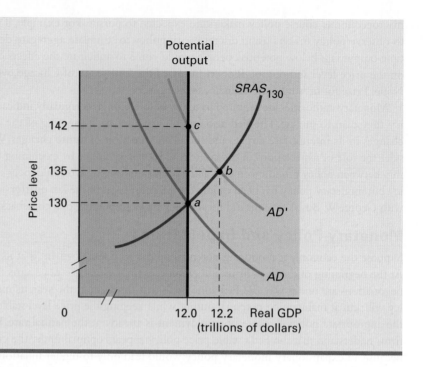

Thus, the unexpected expansionary policy causes a short-run pop in output and employment. But in the long run, the increase in the aggregate demand curve yields only inflation. The **time-inconsistency problem** arises when policy makers have an incentive to announce one policy to shape expectations but then to pursue a different policy once those expectations have been formed and acted on.

Anticipating Monetary Policy

Workers may be fooled once by the Fed's actions, but they won't be fooled again. Suppose Fed policy makers become alarmed by the high inflation. The next time around, the Fed once again announces a monetary policy aimed at producing potential output while keeping the price level stable at 142. Based on their previous experience, however, workers and firms have learned that the Fed is willing to accept higher inflation in exchange for a temporary boost in output. Consequently, people take the Fed's announcement with a grain of salt. Workers, in particular, do not want to get caught again with their real wages down should the Fed implement a stimulative monetary policy. The bottom line is that workers and firms negotiate a high wage increase.

In effect, workers and firms are betting the Fed will pursue an expansionary policy regardless of pronouncement to the contrary. The short-run aggregate supply curve reflecting these higher wage agreements is depicted by *SRAS*₁₅₂ in Exhibit 4, where 152 is the expected price level. Note that *AD'* would result if the Fed followed its announced policy; that demand curve intersects the potential output line at point *c*, where the price level is 142. But *AD"* is the aggregate demand that workers and firms expect based on an expansionary monetary policy. They have agreed to wage settlements that will produce the economy's potential output if the Fed behaves as *expected,* not as *announced.* Thus, a price level of 152 is based on rational expectations. In effect, workers and firms expect the expansionary monetary policy to shift aggregate demand from *AD'* to *AD"*.

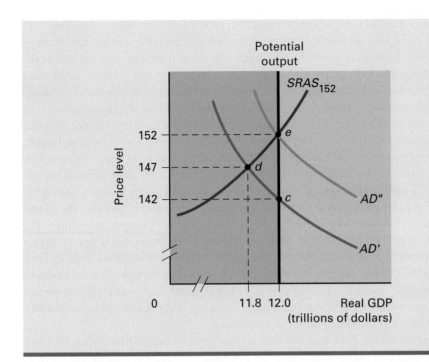

EXHIBIT 4

Short-Run Effects of the Fed Pursuing a More Expansionary Policy Than Announced

The Fed announces it plans to keep prices stable at 142. Workers and firms, however, do not believe this. Based on their experience, they expect monetary policy to be expansionary. The short-run aggregate supply curve, $SRAS_{152}$, reflects their expectations. If the Fed follows the announced stable-price policy, aggregate demand will be AD', and short-run output at point d will be less than the economy's potential output of 12.0 trillion. To keep the economy performing at its potential, the Fed must stimulate aggregate demand as much as workers and firms expect, but this is inflationary.

Monetary authorities must now decide whether to stick with their announced plan of holding the price level constant or to follow a more expansionary monetary policy. If they pursue the constant-price-level policy, aggregate demand will turn out to be AD' and short-run equilibrium will occur at point d. Short-run output will fall below the economy's potential, resulting in unemployment exceeding the natural rate. If monetary authorities want to keep output at its potential, they have only one alternative—to match public expectations. Monetary authorities must pursue an expansionary monetary policy, an action that reinforces public skepticism of policy announcements and increases inflation. This expansionary policy will result in an aggregate demand of AD'', leading to equilibrium at point e, where the price level is 152 and output equals the economy's potential.

Thus, workers and firms enter negotiations realizing that the Fed has an incentive to pursue an expansionary monetary policy. So workers and firms agree to higher wage increases, and the Fed follows with an expansionary policy, one that results in more inflation. Once workers and firms come to expect an expansionary monetary policy and the resulting inflation, such a policy does not spur even a temporary jump in output beyond the economy's potential. *Economists of the rational expectations school believe that if the economy is already producing its potential, an expansionary policy, if fully anticipated, has no effect on output or employment. Only unanticipated or incorrectly anticipated changes in policy can temporarily push output beyond its potential.*

Policy Credibility

If the economy was already producing its potential, an unexpected expansionary monetary policy would increase output and employment temporarily. The costs, however, include not only inflation in the long term but also a loss of credibility the next time around. Is there any way out of this? For the Fed to pursue a policy consistent with a constant price level, its announcements must somehow be *credible*, or believable. Worker and firms must believe that when the time comes to make a hard decision, the Fed will follow through as promised. Perhaps the Fed could offer some sort of guarantee to convince people it will stay the course—for example, the chairman of the Fed could promise to resign if the Fed does not pursue the announced policy. Ironically, policy makers are often more credible and therefore more effective if they have their discretion taken away. In this case, a hard-and-fast rule could be substituted for a policy maker's discretion. We will examine policy rules in the next section.

Consider the problems facing central banks in countries that have experienced hyperinflation. For an anti-inflation policy to succeed at the least possible cost in forgone output, the public must believe central bankers. How can central bankers in an economy ripped by hyperinflation establish credibility? Some economists believe that the most efficient anti-inflation policy is **cold turkey,** which is to announce and execute tough measures to stop inflation, such as halting the growth in the money supply. For example, in 1985, the annual rate of inflation in Bolivia was running at 20,000 percent when the new government announced a stern policy. The restrictive measures worked, and inflation was stopped within a month, with little loss in output. Around the world, credible anti-inflation policies have been successful.[1] Drastic measures sometimes involve costs. For example, some economists argue that the Fed's dramatic efforts to curb high U.S. inflation in the early 1980s triggered the worst recession since the Great Depression. Some say that the Fed's pronouncements were not credible and therefore resulted in a recession.

Much depends on the Fed's time horizon. If policy makers take the long view, they will not risk their long-run policy effectiveness for a temporary reduction in unemployment. If Fed officials realize that their credibility is hard to develop but easy to undermine, they will be reluctant to pursue policies that will ultimately just increase inflation.

Often Congress tries to pressure the Fed to stimulate the economy. By law, the Fed must "promote effectively the goals of maximum employment, stable prices, and moderate long-term interest rates." The law lets the Fed decide how best to do this. The Fed does not rely on congressional appropriations, so Congress cannot threaten to withhold funds. Thus, although the U.S. president appoints the Board of Governors, and the Senate must approve these appointments, the Fed operates somewhat independently. Consider the link around the world between central bank independence and price stability in the following case study.

COLD TURKEY

The announcement and execution of tough measures to reduce high inflation

Central Bank Independence and Price Stability

Some economists argue that the Fed would do better in the long run if it committed to the single goal of price stability. But to focus on price stability, a central bank should be insulated from political influence, because price stability may involve some painful remedies. When the Fed was established, several features insulated it from politics, such as the 14-year terms with staggered appointments of Board members. Also, the Fed has its own income source (interest on government securities and fees from bank services), so it does not rely on Congress for a budget.

Does central bank independence affect performance? When central banks for 17 advanced industrial countries were ranked from least

© Bossu Regis/Corbis Sygma

Case **Study**

Public Policy

eActivity

With a currency board, a country fixes its exchange rate and backs its money supply entirely with foreign exchange, as Argentina did in the 1990s. Read articles, readings, and debates, and find more links at http://www.stern.nyu.edu/globalmacro/exchange_rates/currency_boards.html. What are the benefits of imposing the strict rules of currency boards? How does a currency board derive its own credibility?

---

1. For a discussion about how four hyperinflations in the 1920s ended, see Thomas Sargent, "The Ends of Four Big Inflations," in *Inflation: Causes and Consequences,* edited by Robert Hall (Chicago: University of Chicago Press, 1982), pp. 41–98.

independent to most independent, inflation turned out to be the lowest in countries with the most independent central banks and highest in countries with the least independent central banks. For example, the most independent central banks in the study were in Germany and Switzerland, and their inflation rates averaged about 3 percent per year during the 15-year span examined. The least independent banks were in Spain, New Zealand, Australia, and Italy, where inflation averaged 11.5 percent. The U.S. central bank is considered relatively independent, and U.S. inflation averaged 6.5 percent—between the most independent and least independent groups.

The trend around the world is toward greater central bank independence. For example, in 1990 the Central Bank of New Zealand adopted a monetary policy of inflation rate targeting, with price stability as the primary goal. Altogether, more than a dozen central banks adopted targets of low inflation and none has abandoned the goal. Chile, Colombia, and Argentina—developing countries that suffered hyperinflation—have legislated more central bank independence. The Maastricht agreement, which defined the framework for a single European currency, the euro, identified price stability as the main objective of the new European Central Bank. That bank announced a policy rule that it would not reduce its interest rate target as long as inflation exceeded 2.0 percent. In fact, the European Central Bank came under criticism recently for not cutting interest rate targets even though a recession loomed and unemployment topped 8 percent. And in March 2004 the Coalition Provisional Authority directed the Central Bank of Iraq to "maintain domestic price stability" as its primary objective.

Sources: Alberto Alesina and Lawrence Summers, "Central Bank Independence and Macroeconomic Performance: Some Comparative Evidence," *Journal of Money, Credit and Banking* 25 (May 1993): 151–162; Ben Bernanke, "A Perspective on Inflation Targeting: Why It Seems to Work," *Business Economics* 38 (July 2003): 7–15; "New Law Governing the Central Bank of Iraq," Coalition Provisional Authority, 7 March 2004; for links to more than 80 central bank Web sites, including all those discussed in this case study, go to http://www.bis.org/cbanks.htm.

Policy Rules Versus Discretion

Again, the active approach views the economy as unstable and in need of discretionary policy to eliminate excessive unemployment when it arises. The passive approach views the economy as stable enough that discretionary policy is not only unnecessary but may actually worsen economic fluctuations. In place of discretionary policy, the passive approach often calls for predetermined rules to guide the actions of policy makers. In the context of fiscal policy, these rules take the form of automatic stabilizers, such as unemployment insurance, a progressive income tax, and transfer payments, all of which are aimed at reducing economic fluctuations. In the case of monetary policy, passive rules might be the decisions to allow the money supply to grow at a predetermined rate, to maintain interest rates at some predetermined level, and to keep inflation below a certain rate. For example, as noted in the previous case study, the European Central Bank announced a rule that it would not lower its target interest rate as long as inflation exceeded 2.0 percent a year. Most central banks have committed to achieving low **inflation targets**, usually specifying a particular rate for the next year or two. Advocates of inflation targets say this would encourage workers, firms, and investors to plan on a low and stable inflation rate. Opponents of inflation targets worry that the Fed would pay less attention to economic growth.[2] In this section, we examine the arguments for policy rules versus discretion mostly in the context of monetary policy, because that's where the action has been in recent decades.

INFLATION TARGET

Central bankers commit not to exceed a certain inflation rate for the next year or two

2. Gregory Ip, "Fed Considers Targets for Inflation," *Wall Street Journal,* 20 October 2003.

Limitations on Discretion

The rationale for the passive approach rather than the use of active discretion arises from different views of how the economy works. One view holds that *the economy is so complex and economic aggregates interact in such obscure ways and with such varied lags that policy makers cannot comprehend what is going on well enough to pursue an active monetary or fiscal policy.* For example, if the Fed adopts a discretionary policy that is based on a misreading of the current economy or a poor understanding of the lag structure, the Fed may be lowering the target interest rate when a more appropriate course would be to leave the rate unchanged or even to raise it. As a case in point, during a meeting of the FOMC, one member lamented the difficulty of figuring out what was going on with the economy, noting, "As a lesson for the future, I'd like to remind us all that as recently as two meetings ago [in September] we couldn't see the strength that was unfolding in the second half [of the year]. . . . It wasn't in our forecast; it wasn't in the other forecasts; and it wasn't in the anecdotal reports. We were standing right on top of it and we couldn't see it. That's just an important lesson to remember going forward."[3]

A comparison of economic forecasters and weather forecasters may shed light on the position of those who advocate the passive approach. Suppose you are in charge of the heating and cooling system at a major shopping mall. You realize that weather forecasts are unreliable, particularly in the early spring, when days can be either warm or cold. Each day you must guess what the temperature will be and, based on that guess, decide whether to fire up the heater, turn on the air conditioner, or leave them both off. Because the mall is so large, you must start the system long before you know for sure what the weather will be. Once it's turned on, it can't be turned off until much later in the day.

Suppose you guess the day will be cold, so you turn on the heat. If the day turns out to be cold, your policy is correct and the mall temperature will be just right. But if the day turns out to be warm, the heater will make the mall unbearable. You would have been better off with nothing. In contrast, if you turn on the air conditioner expecting a warm day but the day turns out to be cold, the mall will be freezing. The lesson is that if you are unable to predict the weather, you should use neither heat nor air conditioning. Similarly, if policy makers cannot predict the course of the economy, they should not try to fine-tune monetary or fiscal policy. Complicating the prediction problem is the fact that policy officials are not sure about the lags involved with discretionary policy. The situation is comparable to your not knowing how long the system actually takes to come on once you flip the switch.

This analogy applies only if the cost of doing nothing—using neither heat nor air conditioning—is relatively low. In the early spring, you can assume that there is little risk of weather so cold that water pipes freeze or so hot that walls sweat. A similar assumption in the passive view is that the economy is fairly stable and periods of prolonged unemployment unlikely. In such an economy, the costs of *not* intervening are relatively low. In contrast, advocates of active policy believe that wide and prolonged swings in the economy (analogous to wide and prolonged swings in temperature) make doing nothing risky.

Rules and Rational Expectations

Another group of economists also advocates the passive approach, but not because they think the economy is too complex. Proponents of the rational expectations approach, discussed earlier, claim that people have a pretty good idea about how the economy works and

3. FOMC board member Thomas Melzer, in a transcript of the 22 December 1992 meeting of the Federal Open Market Committee, p. 14. Meeting transcripts are published after a five-year lag and are available at http://www.federalreserve.gov/fomc/transcripts/.

what to expect from government policy makers. For example, people know enough about the monetary policy pursued in the past to forecast, with reasonable accuracy, future policies and their effects on the economy. Some individual forecasts will be too high and some too low, but on average, forecasts will turn out to be about right. *To the extent that monetary policy is fully anticipated by workers and firms, it has no effect on the level of output; it affects only the price level.* Thus, only unexpected changes in policy can bring about short-run changes in output.

In the long run, changes in the money supply affect only inflation, not potential output, so followers of the rational expectations theory believe that the Fed should avoid discretionary monetary policy. Instead, the Fed should follow a predictable monetary rule. A monetary rule would reduce monetary surprises and keep output near the natural rate. *Whereas some economists favor rules over discretion because of ignorance about the lag structure of the economy, rational expectations theorists advocate a predictable rule to avoid surprises, which result in unnecessary departures from the potential output.*

Despite support by some economists for explicit rules rather than discretion, central bankers appear reluctant to follow hard-and-fast rules about the course of future policy. Discretion has been used more than explicit rules since the early 1980s, though policy has become more predictable because the Fed now announces the probable trend of future target rate changes. As former Fed Chairman Paul Volcker argued two decades ago:

> The appeal of a simple rule is obvious. It would simplify our job at the Federal Reserve, make monetary policy easy to understand, and facilitate monitoring of our performance. And if the rule worked, it would reduce uncertainty. . . . But unfortunately, I know of no rule that can be relied on with sufficient consistency in our complex and constantly evolving economy.[4]

This sentiment was echoed more recently by Fed Chairman Alan Greenspan:

> The Federal Reserve, should, some conclude, attempt to be more formal in its operations by tying its actions solely to the prescriptions of a formal policy rule. That any approach along these lines would lead to an improvement in economic performance, however, is highly doubtful.[5]

So far, we have looked at active stabilization policy, which focuses on shifts of the aggregate demand curve, and passive stabilization policy, which relies more on natural shifts of the short-run aggregate supply curve. In the final section, we focus on an additional model, the Phillips curve, to shed more light on the relationship between aggregate demand and aggregate supply in the short and long runs.

The Phillips Curve

At one time, policy makers thought they faced a long-run trade-off between inflation and unemployment. This view was suggested by the research of New Zealand economist A. W. Phillips, who in 1958 published an article that examined the historical relation between inflation and unemployment in the United Kingdom.[6] Based on about 100 years of evidence, his data traced an inverse relationship between the unemployment rate and the rate of

---

4. Former Federal Reserve Chairman Paul Volcker, before the Committee on Banking, Finance, and Urban Affairs, U.S. House of Representatives, August 1983.

5. Chairman Alan Greenspan, "Monetary Policy Under Uncertainty," Remarks at a symposium sponsored by the Federal Reserve Bank of Kansas City, Jackson Hole, Wyoming, 29 August 2003, which can be found at http://www.federalreserve.gov/boarddocs/speeches/2003/20030829/default.htm.

6. A. W. Phillips, "Relation Between Unemployment and the Rate of Change in Money Wage Rates in the United Kingdom, 1861–1957," *Economica* 25 (November 1958): 283–299.

PHILLIPS CURVE

A curve showing possible combinations of the inflation rate and the unemployment rate

change in nominal wages (serving as a measure of inflation). This relationship implied that the opportunity cost of reducing unemployment was higher inflation, and the opportunity cost of reducing inflation was higher unemployment.

The possible options with respect to unemployment and inflation are illustrated by the hypothetical **Phillips curve** in Exhibit 5. The unemployment rate is measured along the horizontal axis and the inflation rate along the vertical axis. Let's begin at point *a*, which depicts one possible combination of unemployment and inflation. Fiscal or monetary policy could be used to stimulate output and thereby reduce unemployment, moving the economy from point *a* to point *b*. Notice, however, that the reduction in unemployment comes at the cost of higher inflation. A reduction in unemployment with no change in inflation would be represented by point *c*. But as you can see, this alternative is not available.

Most policy makers of the 1960s came to believe that they faced a stable, long-run trade-off between unemployment and inflation. The Phillips curve was based on an era when inflation was low and the primary disturbances in the economy were shocks to aggregate demand. The effect of changes in aggregate demand can be traced as movements along a given short-run aggregate supply curve. If aggregate demand increases, the price level increases but unemployment falls. If aggregate demand decreases, the price level decreases but unemployment increases. With appropriate demand-management policies, policy makers believed they could choose any point along the Phillips curve.

The 1970s proved this view wrong in two ways. First, some of the biggest disturbances were adverse *supply* shocks, such as those created by oil embargoes and worldwide crop failures. These shocks shifted the aggregate supply curve leftward. A reduction in aggregate supply led to both higher inflation *and* higher unemployment. Stagflation was at odds with the Phillips curve. Second, economists learned that when short-run output exceeds potential, an expansionary gap opens. As this gap closes by a leftward shift of the short-run aggregate supply curve, greater inflation *and* higher unemployment result—again, an outcome inconsistent with a Phillips curve.

EXHIBIT   5

Hypothetical Phillips Curve

The Phillips curve shows an inverse relation between unemployment and inflation. Points *a* and *b* lie on the Phillips curve and represent alternative combinations of inflation and unemployment that are attainable as long as the curve itself does not shift. Points *c* and *d* are off the curve.

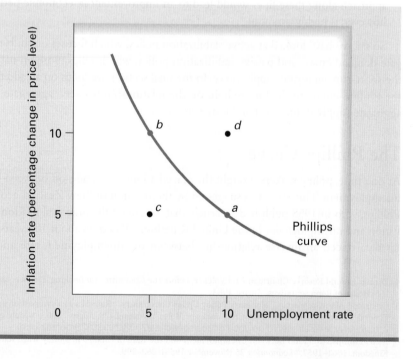

The combination of high inflation and high unemployment resulting from stagflation and the closing of expansionary gaps can be represented by an outcome such as point *d* in Exhibit 5. By the end of the 1970s, simultaneous increases in inflation and unemployment suggested either that the Phillips curve had shifted outward or that it no longer described economic reality. The situation called for a reexamination of the Phillips curve, which led to a distinction between the short-run Phillips curve and the long-run Phillips curve.

The Short-Run Phillips Curve

To discuss the underpinnings of the Phillips curve, we must return to the short-run aggregate supply curve. Suppose the price level this year is reflected by a price index of, say, 100, and that people expect prices to be about 3 percent higher next year. So the price level expected for next year is 103. Workers and firms therefore negotiate wage contracts based on an expected price level of 103. As the short-run aggregate supply curve in Exhibit 6(a) indicates, if *AD* is the aggregate demand curve and the price level is 103, as expected, output equals the economy's potential, shown here to be $12.0 trillion. Recall that when the economy produces its potential, unemployment is at the natural rate.

The short-run relationship between inflation and unemployment is presented in Exhibit 6(b) under the assumption that people expect inflation to be 3 percent. Unemployment is measured along the horizontal axis and inflation along the vertical axis. Panel (a) shows that when inflation is 3 percent, the economy produces its potential. Unemployment is at the natural rate, assumed in panel (b) to be 5 percent. The combination of 3 percent inflation and 5 percent unemployment is reflected by point *a* in panel (b), which corresponds to point *a* in panel (a).

What if aggregate demand turns out to be greater than expected, as indicated by *AD'*? In the short run, the greater demand results in point *b,* with a price level of 105 and output of $12.1 trillion. Because the price level exceeds the level reflected in wage contracts, inflation also exceeds expectations. Specifically, inflation turns out to be 5 percent, not 3 percent. Because output exceeds potential, unemployment falls below the natural rate to 4 percent. The new combination of unemployment and inflation is depicted by point *b* in panel (b), which corresponds to point *b* in panel (a).

What if aggregate demand turns out to be lower than expected, as indicated by *AD"*? In the short run, the lower demand results in point *c,* where the price level of 101 is less than expected and output of $11.9 trillion is below potential. Inflation of 1 percent is less than the expected 3 percent, and unemployment of 6 percent exceeds the natural rate. This combination is reflected by point *c* in panel (b), which corresponds to point *c* in panel (a).

Note that the short-run aggregate supply curve in panel (a) can be used to develop the inverse relationship between inflation and unemployment shown in panel (b), called a **short-run Phillips curve.** This curve is created by the intersection of alternative aggregate demand curves along a given short-run aggregate supply curve. *The short-run Phillips curve is based on labor contracts that reflect a given expected price level, which implies a given expected rate of inflation.* The short-run Phillips curve in panel (b) is based on an expected inflation of 3 percent. If inflation turns out as expected, unemployment equals the natural rate. If inflation exceeds expectations, unemployment in the short run falls below the natural rate. If inflation is less than expected, unemployment exceeds the natural rate.

The Long-Run Phillips Curve

If inflation exceeds expectations, output will exceed the economy's potential in the short run but not in the long run. Labor shortages and shrinking real wages will prompt higher

SHORT-RUN PHILLIPS CURVE

Based on an expected inflation rate, a curve that reflects an inverse relationship between the inflation rate and the unemployment rate

EXHIBIT   6

Aggregate Supply Curves and Phillips Curves in the Short Run and Long Run

If people expect a price level of 103, which is 3 percent higher than the current level, and if *AD* turns out to be the aggregate demand curve, then the price level will actually be 103 and output will be at its potential. Point *a* in both panels represents this situation. Unemployment will be the natural rate, assumed to be 5 percent in panel (b).

If aggregate demand turns out to be greater than expected (*AD′* instead of *AD*), the economy in the short run will be at point *b* in panel (a), where the price level of 105 will exceed expectations and output will exceed its potential. Higher inflation and lower unemployment are shown as point *b* in panel (b). If aggregate demand turns out to be less than expected (*AD″* instead of *AD*), short-run equilibrium will be at point *c* in panel (a), where the price level of 101 will be lower than expected and output will be short of potential. Lower inflation and higher unemployment are shown as point *c* in panel (b). In panel (b), points *a*, *b*, and *c* trace a short-run Phillips curve.

In the long run, the actual price level equals the expected price level. Output is at the potential level, $12.0 trillion, in panel (a). Unemployment is at the natural rate, 5 percent, in panel (b). Points *a*, *d*, and *e* depict long-run points in each panel. In panel (a) these points trace potential output, or long-run aggregate supply. In panel (b), these points trace a long-run Phillips curve.

(a) *Short-run aggregate supply curve*   **(b)** *Short-run and long-run Phillips curves*

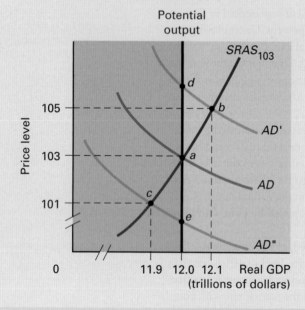

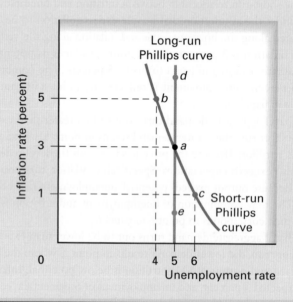

wage agreements. The short-run aggregate supply curve will shift leftward until it passes through point *d* in panel (a) of Exhibit 6, returning the economy to its potential output. The unexpectedly higher aggregate demand curve has no lasting effect on output or unemployment. Point *d* corresponds to a higher price level, and thus higher inflation. Closing the expansionary gap generates both higher unemployment and higher inflation, a combination depicted by point *d* in panel (b). Note that whereas points *a, b,* and *c* are on the same short-run Phillips curve, point *d* is not.

To trace the long-run effects of a lower-than-expected price level, let's return to point *c* in panel (a), where the actual price level is below the expected level, so output is below its potential. If workers and firms negotiate lower money wages (or if the growth in nominal wages trails inflation), the short-run aggregate supply curve will shift rightward until it passes through point *e*, where the economy returns once again to its potential output. Both inflation and unemployment will fall, as reflected by point *e* in panel (b).

Note that points *a, d,* and *e* in panel (a) depict long-run equilibrium points; the expected price level equals the actual price level. At those same points in panel (b), expected inflation equals actual inflation, so unemployment equals the natural rate. We can connect points *a, d,* and *e* in the right panel to form the **long-run Phillips curve.** *When workers and employers adjust fully to any unexpected change in aggregate demand, the long-run Phillips curve is a vertical line drawn at the economy's natural rate of unemployment.* As long as prices and wages are flexible, the rate of unemployment, in the long run, is independent of the rate of inflation. *Thus, according to proponents of this type of analysis, policy makers cannot, in the long run, choose between unemployment and inflation. They can choose only among alternative rates of inflation.*

The Natural Rate Hypothesis

The natural rate of unemployment occurs at the economy's potential output, discussed extensively already. An important idea that emerged from this reexamination of the Phillips curve is the **natural rate hypothesis,** which states that in the long run, the economy tends toward the natural rate of unemployment. This natural rate is largely independent of any *aggregate demand* stimulus provided by monetary or fiscal policy. Policy makers may be able to push output beyond its potential temporarily, but only if the policy surprises the public. The natural rate hypothesis implies that *the policy that results in low inflation is generally the optimal policy in the long run.*

Evidence of the Phillips Curve

What has been the actual relationship between unemployment and inflation in the United States? In Exhibit 7, each year since 1960 is represented by a point, with the unemployment

LONG-RUN PHILLIPS CURVE

A vertical line drawn at the economy's natural rate of unemployment that traces equilibrium points that can occur when workers and employers have the time to adjust fully to any unexpected change in aggregate demand

NATURAL RATE HYPOTHESIS

The natural rate of unemployment is largely independent of the stimulus provided by monetary or fiscal policy

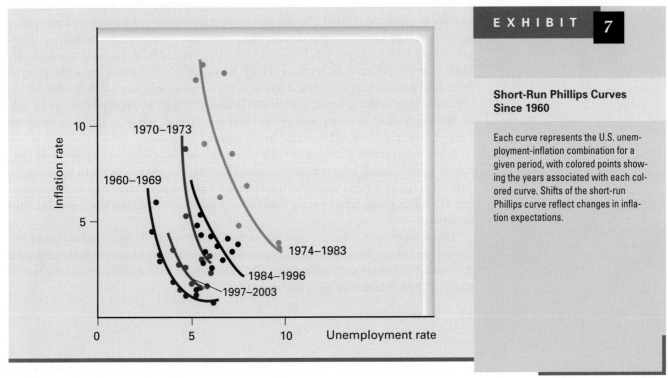

EXHIBIT 7

Short-Run Phillips Curves Since 1960

Each curve represents the U.S. unemployment-inflation combination for a given period, with colored points showing the years associated with each colored curve. Shifts of the short-run Phillips curve reflect changes in inflation expectations.

Source: Based on inflation and unemployment figures from the *Economic Report of the President*, February 2004, at http://www.gpoaccess.gov/eop/index.html.

rate measured along the horizontal axis and the inflation rate measured along the vertical axis. Superimposed on these points is a series of short-run Phillips curves showing patterns of unemployment and inflation during what turns out to be five distinct periods since 1960. Remember, each short-run Phillips curve is drawn for a given *expected inflation.* A change in inflationary expectations shifts the short-run Phillips curve.

The clearest trade-off between unemployment and inflation occurred between 1960 and 1969; the points for those years fit neatly along the curve. In the early part of the decade, inflation was low but unemployment relatively high; as the 1960s progressed, unemployment declined but actual inflation increased. Inflation during the decade averaged only 2.5 percent, and unemployment averaged 4.8 percent.

The short-run Phillips curve shifted to the right for the period from 1970 to 1973, when inflation and unemployment each climbed to an average of 5.2 percent. In 1974, sharp increases in oil prices and crop failures around the world reduced aggregate supply, which sparked another shift of the Phillips curve. During the 1974–1983 period, inflation averaged 8.2 percent and unemployment 7.5 percent. After two recessions in the early 1980s, the short-run Phillips curve shifted leftward, or inward. Average inflation for 1984–1996 fell to 3.7 percent and average unemployment fell to 6.1 percent. Finally, data for 1997 to 2003 suggest a new, lower short-run Phillips curve, with average inflation of only 2.3 percent and average unemployment of 4.9 percent. Thus, the Phillips curve shifted rightward between the 1960s and the early 1980s. Since then, the Fed has learned more about how to control inflation, thereby shifting the Phillips curve back to about where it started in the 1960s.

Conclusion

This chapter examined the implications of active and passive policy. The important question is whether the economy is essentially stable and self-correcting when it gets off track or essentially unstable and in need of active government intervention. Advocates of active policy believe that the Fed or Congress should reduce economic fluctuations by stimulating aggregate demand when output falls below its potential level and by dampening aggregate demand when output exceeds its potential level. Advocates of active policy argue that government attempts to reduce the ups and downs of the business cycle may not be perfect but are still better than nothing. Some activists also believe that high unemployment may be self-reinforcing, because some unemployed workers lose valuable job skills and grow to accept unemployment as a way of life, as may have happened in Europe.

Advocates of passive policy, on the other hand, believe that discretionary policy may contribute to the cyclical swings in the economy, leading to higher inflation in the long run with no permanent boost in potential output and no permanent reduction in the employment rate. This group favors passive rules for monetary policy and automatic stabilizers for fiscal policy.

The active-passive debate in this chapter has focused primarily on monetary policy because discretionary fiscal policy, until quite recently, had been hampered by large federal deficits that ballooned the national debt. The next chapter takes a closer look at the federal budget, federal deficits, and government debt.

SUMMARY

1. Advocates of active policy view the private sector—particularly fluctuations in investment—as the primary source of economic instability in the economy. Activists argue that achieving potential output through natural market forces can be slow and painful, so the Fed or Congress should stimulate aggregate demand when actual output falls below potential.

2. Advocates of passive policy argue that the economy has enough natural resiliency to return to potential output within a reasonable period if upset by some shock. They point to the variable and uncertain lags associated with discretionary policy as reason enough to steer clear of active intervention.

3. The effect of particular government policies on the economy depends on what people expect. The theory of rational expectations holds that people form expectations based on all available information including past behavior by public officials. According to the rational expectations school, government policies are mostly anticipated by the public, and therefore have less effect than unexpected policies.

4. The passive policy approach suggests that the government should follow clear and predictable policies and avoid discretionary intervention to stimulate or dampen aggregate demand over the business cycle. Passive policies are reflected in automatic fiscal stabilizers and in explicit monetary rules, such as maintaining a constant target interest rate or a steady growth in the money supply.

5. At one time, public officials thought they faced a stable trade-off between higher unemployment and higher inflation. More recent research suggests that if there is a trade-off, it exists only in the short run, not in the long run. Expansionary fiscal or monetary policies may stimulate output and employment in the short run. But if the economy is already at or near its potential output, these expansionary policies will, in the long run, result only in more inflation.

QUESTIONS FOR REVIEW

1. *(Active Versus Passive Policy)* Contrast the active policy view of the behavior of wages and prices during a contractionary gap to the passive policy view.

2. *(Active Policy)* Why do proponents of active policy recommend government intervention to close an expansionary gap?

3. *(Active Versus Passive Policy)* According to advocates of passive policy, what variable naturally adjusts in the labor market, shifting the short-run aggregate supply curve to restore unemployment to the natural rate? Why does the active policy approach assume that the short-run aggregate supply curve shifts leftward more easily and quickly than it shifts rightward?

4. *(Review of Policy Perspectives)* Why might an active policy approach be more politically popular than a passive approach, especially during a recession?

5. *(The Role of Expectations)* Some economists argue that only unanticipated increases in the money supply can affect real GDP. Explain why this may be the case.

6. *(Anticipating Monetary Policy)* In 1994, the Fed began announcing its interest rate targets immediately following each meeting of the FOMC. Prior to that, observers were left to draw inferences about Fed policy based on the results of that policy. What is the value of this greater openness?

7. *(Policy Credibility)* What is policy credibility and how is it relevant to the problem of reducing high inflation? How is credibility related to the time-inconsistency problem?

8. (*Case* **Study**: Central Bank Independence and Price Stability) One source of independence for the Fed is the length of term for members of the Board of Governors. In the chapter before last, we learned that the Fed is a "money machine." Does this suggest another source of Fed independence from Congress?

9. *(Rationale for Rules)* Some economists call for predetermined rules to guide the actions of government policy makers. What are two rationales that have been given for such rules?

10. *(Rational Expectations)* Suppose that people in an election year believe that public officials are going to pursue expansionary policies to enhance their reelection prospects. How could such expectations put pressure on officials to pursue expansionary policies even if they hadn't planned to?

11. *(Potential GNP)* Why is it hard for policy makers to decide if the economy is operating at its potential output level? Why is this uncertainty a problem?

12. *(Phillips Curves)* Describe the different policy trade-offs implied by the short-run Phillips curve and the long-run Phillips curve. What forces shift the long-run Phillips curve?

PROBLEMS AND EXERCISES

13. *(Active Versus Passive Policy)* Discuss the role each of the following plays in the debate between the active and passive approaches:

    a. The speed of adjustment of the nominal wage
    b. The speed of adjustment of expectations about inflation
    c. The existence of lags in policy creation and implementation
    d. Variability in the natural rate of unemployment over time

14. (*C a s e* **Study**: Active Versus Passive Presidential Candidates) What were the main differences between candidates Bush and Clinton in the 1992 presidential campaign? Illustrate their ideas using the aggregate supply and demand model.

15. *(Problems with Active Policy)* Use an *AD–AS* diagram to illustrate and explain the short-run and long-run effects on the economy of the following situation: Both the natural rate of unemployment and the actual rate of unemployment are 5 percent. However, the government believes that the natural rate of unemployment is 6 percent and that the economy is overheating. Therefore, it introduces a policy to reduce aggregate demand.

16. *(Policy Lags)* What lag in discretionary policy is described in each of the following statements? Why do long lags make discretionary policy less effective?

    a. The time from when the government determines that the economy is in recession until a tax cut is approved to reduce unemployment
    b. The time from when the money supply is increased until the resulting effect on the economy is felt
    c. The time from the start of a recession until the government identifies the existence and severity of the recession
    d. The time from when the Fed decides to reduce the money supply until the money supply actually declines

17. *(Rational Expectations)* Using an *AD–AS* diagram, illustrate the short-run effects on prices, output, and employment of an increase in the money supply that is correctly anticipated by the public. Assume that the economy is initially at potential output.

18. *(Long-Run Phillips Curve)* Suppose the economy is at point *d* on the long-run Phillips curve shown in Exhibit 6. If that inflation rate is unacceptably high, how can policy makers get the inflation rate down? Would rational expectations help or hinder their efforts?

EXPERIENTIAL EXERCISES

19. *(Active Versus Passive Policy)* The Federal Reserve Bank of Minneapolis's *The Region* at http://woodrow.mpls.frb.fed.us/pubs/region/int.cfm features an ongoing series of interviews with prominent U.S. policy makers. Choose a Fed governor or a regional Reserve Bank president and try to determine whether that person leans more toward an active or a passive policy view. What specific policy views does that person advocate?

20. (*C a s e* **S t u d y** : Central Bank Independence and Price Stability) The Bank for International Settlements maintains a list of links to central banks around the world at http://www.bis.org/cbanks.htm. Many of those banks maintain English-language Web pages. Choose one or two nations and explore their central bank Web pages. How much independence do those banks have? To what extent are their functions and goals similar to those of the U.S. Federal Reserve System?

21. *(Wall Street Journal)* A good source for the latest information regarding macroeconomic policy is the "Economy" column that appears in the daily *Wall Street Journal*. Take a look at today's issue and review the latest hot topics. Then, turn to the editorial pages, where the *Journal's* editorial board, contributors, and letter writers have their say.

HOMEWORK XPRESS! EXERCISES

These exercises require access to McEachern Homework Xpress! If Homework Xpress! did not come with your book, visit **http://homeworkxpress.swlearning.com** *to purchase.*

1. In the diagram for this exercise, use aggregate demand and short-run and long-run aggregate supply curves to show an economy at a short-run equilibrium with a contractionary gap of $0.5 trillion when potential output is $10 trillion. Then illustrate how the gap would close in the long run if the economy is self-correcting.

2. In the diagram, use aggregate demand and short-run and long-run aggregate supply curves to show an economy at a short-run equilibrium with an expansionary gap of $0.5 trillion when potential output is $10 trillion. Then illustrate how the gap would close in the long run using an activist approach.

3. In the diagram, use aggregate demand and short-run and long-run aggregate supply curves to show an economy at a short-run equilibrium at its potential output of $10 trillion. Illustrate the short-run effects if the Fed unexpectedly pursues an expansionary monetary policy. Then show the long-run effect.

4. In the diagram, use aggregate demand and long-run aggregate supply curves to show an economy at a long-run equilibrium at its potential output of $10 trillion and a price level of $P = 120$. Illustrate the effects if firms and workers do not believe that the Fed will maintain a price level of 120 but the Fed does not increase the money supply as expected.

5. In the diagram use aggregate demand and long-run aggregate supply curves to show an economy at a long-run equilibrium at its potential output of $10 trillion and a price level of $P = 120$. Illustrate the effects if firms and workers do not believe that the Fed will maintain a price level of 120 and the Fed increases the money supply as expected.

Federal Budgets and Public Policy

© AP Photo/APTN

How big is the federal budget, and where does the money go besides national defense? Why is the federal budget process such a tangled web? In what sense is the federal budgeting at odds with discretionary fiscal policy? How is a sluggish economy like an empty restaurant? Why has the federal budget been in deficit most years, and why did a surplus briefly materialize at the end of the 1990s? What is the federal debt, and who owes it to whom? Answers to these and other questions are examined in this chapter, which considers federal budgeting in theory and practice.

The word *budget* derives from the Old French word *bougette,* which means "little bag." The federal budget is now over $2,400,000,000,000—$2.4 trillion a year. That's big money! If this "little bag" held $100 notes, it would weigh more than 26,000 *tons!* These $100 notes could paper over a 14-lane highway stretching from northern Maine to southern California. This total could cover every U.S. family's mortgage and car payments for the year.

**HOMEWORK
Xpress!**

*Use Homework Xpress! for
economic application,
graphing, videos, and more.*

Government budgets have a tremendous impact on the economy. Government outlays at all levels amount to about 36 percent relative to GDP. Our focus in this chapter will be the federal budget, beginning with the budget process. We then look at the source of federal deficits and how they briefly became surpluses. We also examine the national debt and its impact on the economy. Topics discussed include:

- The budget process
- Rationale for deficit spending
- Impact of deficits

- Crowding out and crowding in
- The short-lived budget surplus
- The burden of the federal debt

The Federal Budget Process

The **federal budget** is a plan of outlays and revenues for a specified period, usually a year. Federal *outlays* include both government purchases and transfer payments. Exhibit 1 shows federal outlays by major category since 1960. As you can see, the share of outlays going to national defense dropped from over half in 1960 to only 20 percent in 2004. Social Security's share has grown every decade. Medicare, medical care for the elderly, was introduced in the 1965 and has also grown every year. In fact, Social Security and Medicare, programs aimed primarily at the elderly, now combine for 33 percent of federal outlays. For the last two decades, welfare spending, which consists of cash and in-kind transfer payments, has remained at about 15 percent of federal outlays. And, thanks to record low interest rates, 7 percent of the budget in 2004 paid interest on the national debt, down from 15 percent as recently as 1996. So 48 percent, or nearly half the federal budget in 2004, redistributed income (Social Security, Medicare, and welfare); 20 percent went toward defense; 7 percent serviced the national debt; and the remaining 25 percent paid for everything else in the federal budget—from environmental protection to federal prisons and aid to education.

FEDERAL BUDGET

A plan for federal government outlays and revenues for a specified period, usually a year

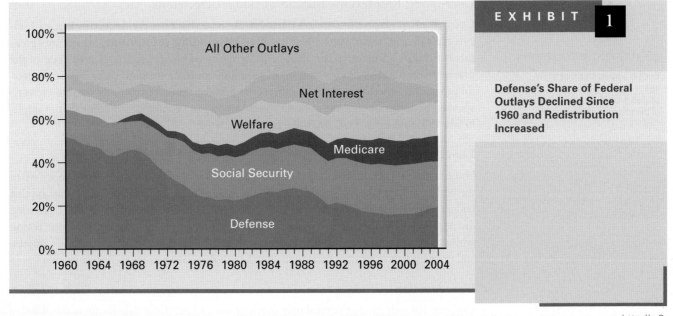

EXHIBIT 1

Defense's Share of Federal Outlays Declined Since 1960 and Redistribution Increased

Sources: *Economic Report of the President*, February 2004, Table B-80; and the Office of Management and Budget. For the most recent year, go to http://w3.access.gpo.gov/eop/.

BUDGET RESOLUTION

A congressional agreement about
total outlays, spending by major
category, and expected revenues;
it guides spending and revenue decisions by the many congressional
committees and subcommittees

CONTINUING RESOLUTIONS

Budget agreements that allow
agencies, in the absence of an approved budget, to spend at the rate
of the previous year's budget

The Presidential and Congressional Roles

The president's budget proposal begins to take shape a year before it is submitted to Congress, with each agency preparing a budget request. In late January or early February, the presidents submits to Congress *The Budget of the United States Government,* a big pile of books detailing spending and revenue proposals for the upcoming fiscal year, which begins October 1. At this stage, the president's budget is little more than detailed suggestions for congressional consider-ation. About the same time, the president's Council of Economic Advisors sends Congress the *Economic Report of the President,* which offers the president's take on the economy.

Budget committees in both the House and the Senate rework the president's budget un-til they agree on total outlays, spending by major category, and expected revenues. This agreement, called a **budget resolution,** establishes a framework to guide spending and rev-enue decisions and to guide the many congressional committees and subcommittees that authorize spending. The budget cycle is supposed to end before October 1, the start of the new fiscal year. Before that date, Congress should have approved detailed plans for outlays along with revenue projections. Thus, the federal budget has a congressional gestation pe-riod of about nine months—though, as noted, the president's budget usually begins taking shape a year before it's submitted to Congress.

The size and composition of the budget and the difference between outlays and revenues measure the budget's fiscal impact on the economy. *When outlays exceed revenues, the budget is in deficit. A deficit stimulates aggregate demand in the short run but reduces national saving, which in the long run could impede economic growth. Alternatively, when revenues exceed outlays, the federal budget is in surplus. A surplus dampens aggregate demand in the short run but enhances domestic sav-ing, which in the long run could promote economic growth.*

Problems with the Federal Budget Process

The federal budget process sounds good on paper, but it does not work that well in prac-tice. There are several problems.

Continuing Resolutions Instead of Budget Decisions

Congress often ignores the budget timetable. Because deadlines are frequently missed, bud-gets typically run from year to year based on **continuing resolutions,** which are agree-ments to allow agencies, in the absence of an approved budget, to spend at the rate of the previous year's budget. Poorly conceived programs continue through sheer inertia; success-ful programs cannot expand. On occasion, the president must temporarily shut down some agencies because not even the continuing resolution can be approved on time. For example, in late 1995 and early 1996, most federal offices closed for 27 days.

Lengthy Budget Process

You can imagine the difficulty of using the budget as a tool of discretionary fiscal policy when the budget process takes so long. Given that the average recession lasts less than a year and that budget preparations begin more than a year and a half before the budget takes effect, planning discretionary fiscal measures to smooth economic fluctuations is difficult. That's one reason why attempts to stimulate an ailing economy often seem so halfhearted; by the time Congress and the president agree on a fiscal remedy, the economy has often recovered on its own.

Uncontrollable Budget Items

Congress has only limited control over much of the budget. *About three-fourths of federal budget outlays are determined by existing laws.* For example, once Congress establishes eligibility criteria,

entitlement programs, such as Social Security and Medicare, take on lives of their own, with each annual appropriation simply reflecting the amount required to support the expected number of entitled beneficiaries. Congress has no say in such appropriations unless it chooses to change benefits or eligibility criteria. Most entitlement programs have such politically powerful constituencies that Congress is reluctant to mess with the structure.

No Separate Capital Budget

Congress approves a single budget that mixes together *capital* expenditures, like new federal buildings or aircraft carriers, with *operating* expenditures, like employee payrolls or military meals. Budgets for businesses and for state and local governments usually distinguish between a *capital budget* and an *operating budget.* The federal government, by mixing the two, offers a fuzzier picture of what's going on.

Overly Detailed Budget

The federal budget is divided into thousands of accounts and subaccounts, which is why it fills volumes. To the extent that the budget is a way of making political payoffs, such micromanagement allows elected officials to reward friends and punish enemies with great precision. For example, a recent budget included $176,000 for the Reindeer Herders Association in Alaska, $400,000 for the Southside Sportsman Club in New York, and $5 million for an insect-rearing facility in Mississippi. By budgeting in such detail, Congress may lose sight of the big picture. When economic conditions change or when the demand for certain public goods shifts, the federal government cannot easily reallocate funds. Detailed budgeting is not only time consuming, it reduces the flexibility of discretionary fiscal policy and is subject to political abuse.

Possible Budget Reforms

Some reforms might improve the budget process. First, the annual budget could become a two-year budget, or *biennial budget.* As it is, Congress spends nearly all of the year working on the budget. The executive branch is always dealing with three budgets: administering an approved budget, defending a proposed budget before congressional committees, and preparing the next budget for submission to Congress. With a two-year budget, Congress would not be continually involved with budget deliberations, and cabinet members could focus more on running their agencies (many states have adopted two-year budgets). A two-year budget, however, would require longer-term economic forecasts and would be less useful than a one-year budget as a tool of discretionary fiscal policy.

Another possible reform would be to simplify the budget document by concentrating only on major groupings and eliminating line items. Each agency head would receive a total budget, along with the discretion to allocate that budget in a manner consistent with the perceived demands for agency services. The drawback is that agency heads may have different priorities than those of elected representatives.

A final reform is to sort federal spending into a capital budget and an operating budget. A *capital budget* would include spending on physical capital such as buildings, highways, computers, military equipment, and other public infrastructure. An *operating budget* would include spending on the payroll, building maintenance, computer paper, and other ongoing expenses.

The Fiscal Impact of the Federal Budget

When government outlays—that is, government purchases plus transfer payments—exceed government revenue, the result is a *budget deficit,* a flow measure already introduced.

Although the federal budget was in surplus from 1998 to 2001, before that it had been in deficit every year but one since 1960 and in all but eight years since 1930. Since 2001 the budget has slipped back in the red. To place deficits in perspective, let's first examine the economic rationale for deficit financing.

The Rationale for Deficits

Deficit financing has been justified for outlays that increase the economy's productivity—capital outlays for investments such as highways, waterways, and dams. The cost of these capital projects should be borne in part by future taxpayers, who will also benefit from these investments. Thus, there is some justification for government borrowing to finance capital projects and for future taxpayers helping to pay for them. State and local governments issue debt to fund capital projects, such as schools. But, as noted already, the federal government does not budget capital projects separately, so there is no explicit link between capital budgets and federal deficits.

Before the Great Depression, federal deficits occurred only during wartime. Because wars involved much personal hardship, public officials were understandably reluctant to tax citizens much more to finance war-related spending. Deficits incurred during wars were largely self-correcting, however, because government spending dropped after a war, but the tax revenue did not.

The Depression led John Maynard Keynes to argue that public spending should offset any drop in private spending. As you know by now, Keynes said a federal budget deficit would stimulate aggregate demand. As a result of the Depression, automatic stabilizers were also introduced, which increased public outlays during recessions and decreased them during expansions. Deficits increase during recessions because tax revenues decline while spending programs such as unemployment benefits and welfare increase. For example, during the 1990–1991 recession, corporate tax revenue fell 10 percent but welfare spending jumped 25 percent. An economic expansion is the other side of the coin. As the economy picks up, so do personal income and corporate profits, boosting federal revenue. Unemployment compensation and welfare spending decline. Thus, federal deficits usually fall during the recovery stage of the business cycle.

Budget Philosophies and Deficits

Several budget philosophies have emerged over the years. Prior to the Great Depression, fiscal policy focused on maintaining an **annually balanced budget,** except during wartime. Because tax revenues rise during expansions and fall during recessions, an annually balanced budget means that spending increases during expansions and declines during recessions. But such a pattern magnifies fluctuations in the business cycle, overheating the economy during expansions and increasing unemployment during recessions.

A second budget philosophy calls for a **cyclically balanced budget,** meaning that budget deficits during recessions are covered by budget surpluses during expansions. Fiscal policy dampens swings in the business cycle without increasing the national debt. Nearly all states have established "rainy day" funds to build up budget surpluses during the good times for use during bad times.

A third budget philosophy is **functional finance,** which says that policy makers should be concerned less with balancing the budget annually, or even over the business cycle, and more with ensuring that the economy produces its potential output. If the budgets needed to keep the economy producing its potential involve chronic deficits, so be it. Since the Great Depression, budgets in this country have seldom balanced. *Although budget deficits have been larger during recessions than during expansions, the federal budget has been in deficit in all but a dozen years since 1930.*

ANNUALLY BALANCED BUDGET

Budget philosophy prior to the Great Depression; aimed at matching annual revenues with outlays, except during times of war

CYCLICALLY BALANCED BUDGET

A budget philosophy calling for budget deficits during recessions to be financed by budget surpluses during expansions

FUNCTIONAL FINANCE

A budget philosophy using fiscal policy to achieve the economy's potential GDP, rather than balancing budgets either annually or over the business cycle

Federal Deficits Since the Birth of the Nation

Between 1789, when the U.S. Constitution was adopted, and 1930, the first full year of the Great Depression, the federal budget was in deficit 33 percent of the years, primarily during wartime. After a war, government spending dropped more than government revenue. Thus, deficits arising during wars were largely self-correcting once the wars ended.

Since the onset of the Great Depression, however, federal budgets have been in deficit 85 percent of the time. Exhibit 2 shows federal deficits and surpluses as a percentage of GDP since 1934. Unmistakable are the huge deficits during World War II, which dwarf deficits in other years. Turning now to the last quarter century, we see that large tax cuts during the 1980s along with higher defense spending contributed to modern deficits. Supply-side economists argued that tax cuts would stimulate enough economic activity to keep tax revenues from falling. Unspecified spending cuts were supposed to erase a projected deficit, but Congress never made the promised cuts. Moreover, overly optimistic revenue projections— so-called rosy scenarios—were built into the budget. For example, the budget projected that real GDP would grow by 5.2 percent in 1982, but instead the economy fell into a recession, which cut output 2.0 percent that year. The recession triggered automatic stabilizers, reducing revenues and increasing spending still more. The deficit in 1982 amounted to 4 percent of GDP—at the time one of the largest peacetime deficits ever.

President Reagan's budget strategy during the 1980s called for defense increases but no new taxes and no cuts in Social Security. In short, the president and Congress cut tax rates but not expenditures. *Relative to GDP, federal revenues declined but federal spending increased.* The deficit climbed to 6 percent of GDP in 1983. As the economy improved during the 1990s,

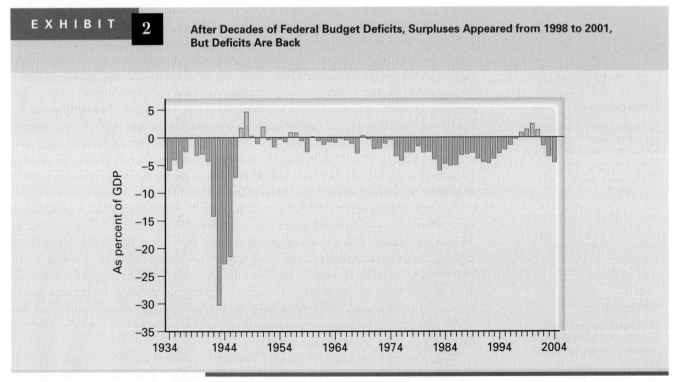

E X H I B I T   **2**   **After Decades of Federal Budget Deficits, Surpluses Appeared from 1998 to 2001, But Deficits Are Back**

Sources: *Economic Report of the President*, February 2004. Deficit for 2004 is a projection from the president and Congress. For the latest data, go to http://w3.access.gpo.gov/eop/.

the deficit decreased and then disappeared, turning into a surplus by 1998. But a recession in 2001, tax cuts, and higher federal spending turned surpluses into deficits. A weak recovery and the war against terrorism worsened the deficits in 2002, 2003, and 2004. By 2004 the deficit exceeded 4 percent of GDP, a level not seen since 1992.

That's a short history of federal deficits. Now let's consider why the federal budget has been in deficit so long.

Why Have Deficits Persisted?

As we have seen, huge deficits in the 1980s and more recently came from a combination of tax cuts and spending increases. But why has the budget been in deficit for all but 12 years since 1934? The most obvious answer is that, unlike budgeters in 49 states, federal officials are not required to balance the budget. But why deficits? One widely accepted model of the public sector assumes that elected officials try to maximize their political support, including votes and campaign contributions. Voters like public spending programs but hate paying taxes, so spending programs win support and taxes lose it. Because of this asymmetry, candidates try to maximize their chances of getting elected and reelected by offering budgets long on benefits but short on taxes. Moreover, members of Congress push their favorite programs with little concern about the overall budget. For example, a senator from Mississippi was able to include $1.5 billion in a recent budget for an amphibious assault ship to be built in his hometown of Pascagoula. The Navy never even asked for the ship.

Deficits, Surpluses, Crowding Out, and Crowding In

What effect do federal deficits and surpluses have on interest rates? Recall that interest rates affect investment, a critical component of economic growth. What's more, year-to-year fluctuations in investment are the primary source of shifts in the aggregate demand curve. Let's look at the impact of government deficits and surpluses on investment.

Suppose the federal government increases spending without raising taxes, thereby increasing the budget deficit. How will this affect national saving, interest rates, and investment? An increase in the government deficit reduces the supply of national saving, leading to higher interest rates. Higher interest rates discourage, or *crowd out,* some private investment, reducing the stimulating effect of the government's deficit. The extent of **crowding out** is a matter of debate. Some argue that although government deficits may displace some private-sector borrowing, discretionary fiscal policy will result in a net increase in aggregate demand, leading to greater output and employment in the short run. Others believe that the crowding out is more extensive, so borrowing from the public in this way will result in little or no net increase in aggregate demand and output.

CROWDING OUT

The displacement of interest-sensitive private investment that occurs when higher government deficits drive up interest rates

Although crowding out is likely to occur to some degree, there is another possibility. If the economy is operating well below its potential, the additional fiscal stimulus provided by a higher government deficit could encourage firms to invest more. Recall that an important determinant of investment is business expectations. Government stimulus of a weak economy could put a sunny face on the business outlook. As expectations grow more favorable, firms become more willing to invest. This ability of government deficits to stimulate private investment is sometimes called **crowding in,** to distinguish it from crowding out. For nearly a decade, the Japanese government pursued deficit spending as a way of getting that flat economy going, but with only recent success.

CROWDING IN

The potential for government spending to stimulate private investment in an otherwise dead economy

Were you ever unwilling to patronize a restaurant because it was too crowded? You simply did not want to put up with the hassle and long wait and were thus "crowded out." As that baseball-player-turned-philosopher Yogi Berra said, "No one goes there nowadays. It's too crowded." Similarly, large government deficits may "crowd out" some investors by driving up interest rates. On the other hand, did you ever pass up an unfamiliar restaurant because the place seemed dead—it had no customers? Perhaps you wondered why? If you had seen just a few customers, you might have stopped in—you might have been willing to "crowd in." Similarly, businesses may be reluctant to invest in a seemingly lifeless economy. The economic stimulus resulting from deficit spending could encourage some investors to "crowd in."

The Twin Deficits

To finance the huge deficits of the 1980s, the U.S. Treasury had to sell a lot of bonds, pushing up market interest rates. With U.S. interest rates relatively high, foreigners were more willing to buy dollar-denominated bonds. To buy them, foreigners had to exchange their currencies for dollars. This greater demand for dollars caused the dollar to appreciate relative to foreign currencies during the first half of the 1980s. The rising value of the dollar made foreign goods cheaper in the United States and U.S. goods more expensive abroad. Thus, U.S. imports increased and U.S. exports decreased, so the foreign trade deficit increased.

Higher trade deficits meant that foreigners were accumulating dollars. With these dollars, they purchased U.S. assets, including U.S. government bonds, and thereby helped fund federal deficits. The increase in funds from abroad is both good news and bad news for the U.S. economy. The supply of foreign saving increased investment spending in the United States over what would have occurred in the absence of these funds. Ask people what they think of foreign investment in their town; they will likely say it's great. But foreign funds to some extent simply offsets a decline in U.S. saving rates. Such a pattern could pose problems in the long run. The United States has surrendered a certain amount of control over its economy to foreign investors. And the return on foreign investments in the United States flows abroad. For example, a growing share of the federal government's debt is now owed to foreigners, as will be discussed later in this chapter.

The Short-Lived Budget Surplus

Exhibit 3 summarizes the federal budget since 1970, with outlays relative to GDP shown as the red line and revenues relative to GDP as the blue line. When outlays exceeded revenues, the federal budget was in deficit, measured each year by the vertical distance between the blue and red lines. The pink shading shows the annual deficit as a percent of GDP. In the early 1990s, outlays started to decline relative to GDP, while revenues increased. This shrank the deficit and, by 1998, created a surplus, as indicated by the blue shading. Specifically, the deficit in 1990, which amounted to 3.8 percent relative to GDP, became a surplus by 1998, which lasted until 2001. What turned a hefty deficit into a surplus, and why has the surplus turned back into a deficit?

Tax Increases

With concern about the deficit growing, Congress and President George H. W. Bush agreed in 1990 to a package of spending cuts and tax increases aimed at trimming budget deficits. Ironically, those tax increases not only may have cost President Bush reelection in 1992 (because it violated his 1988 election promise of "no new taxes"), but they also began the groundwork for erasing the budget deficit, for which President Clinton was able to take credit. For his part, President Clinton increased taxes on high-income households in 1993, boosting the top marginal tax rate from 31 percent to 40 percent. The economy also enjoyed a vigorous recovery during the 1990s, fueled by rising worker productivity, growing consumer spending, globalization of markets, and the strongest stock market in history. The combined effects of higher taxes on the rich and a strengthening economy raised federal revenue from 17.8 percent of GDP in 1990 to 20.3 percent in 2000.

Slower Growth in Federal Outlays

Because of spending discipline imposed by the 1990 legislation, growth in federal outlays slowed compared with those in the 1980s. What's more, the collapse of the Soviet Union reduced U.S. military commitments abroad. Between 1990 and 2000, military personnel dropped one-third and defense spending dropped 30 percent in real terms. An additional impetus for slower spending growth came from Republicans, who attained congressional majority in 1994. Between 1994 and 2000, domestic spending grew little in real terms. Another beneficial development was the drop in interest rates, which fell to their lowest level in 30 years, saving billions in interest charges on the national debt. In short, federal outlays dropped from 21.6 percent relative to GDP in 1990 to 17.9 percent in 2000.

A Reversal of Fortune in 2001

Thanks to the tax-rate increases and the strong economy, revenues gushed into Washington, growing an average of 8.4 percent per year between 1993 and 2000. Meanwhile, federal outlays remained in check, growing only 3.5 percent per year. By 2000, that combination created a federal budget surplus of $236 billion, quite a turnaround from a deficit that had topped $290 billion only eight years earlier. But in 2001 unemployment increased, the stock market sank, and terrorists crashed jets and spread anthrax. All this slowed federal revenues and accelerated federal spending. To counter the recession and cope with terrorism, Congress and the president cut taxes and increased federal spending. As a result, the federal bud-

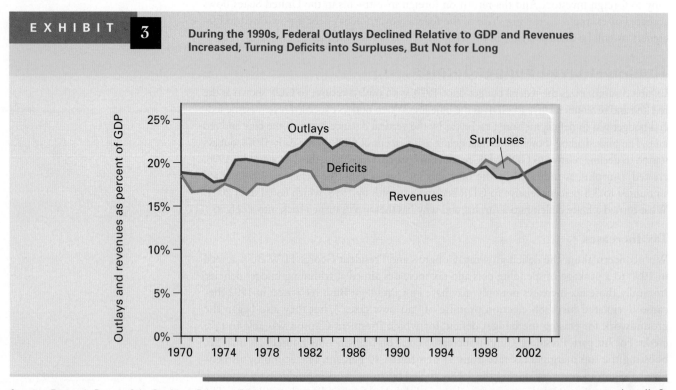

EXHIBIT 3

During the 1990s, Federal Outlays Declined Relative to GDP and Revenues Increased, Turning Deficits into Surpluses, But Not for Long

Sources: *Economic Report of the President*, February, Tables B-1 and B-78; and the Office of Management and Budget. For the latest data, go to http://w3. access.gpo.gov/eop/.

get surplus of 2001 turned into a deficit exceeding $400 billion by 2004. The era of federal budget surpluses was short-lived. Worse yet, two major federal programs spelled trouble for the budget in the long run, as discussed in the following case study.

Reforming Social Security and Medicare

Social Security is a federal redistribution program established during the Great Depression that collects payroll taxes from current workers and their employers to pay pensions to current retirees. About 40 million retirees averaged $880 per month from the program in 2004. For the first 50 years of the program, whenever tax revenues exceeded the cost of the program, Congress raised benefits, expanded eligibility, or spent the surplus. Medicare, a program established in 1965 to provide short-term medical care for the elderly, is also funded by a payroll tax. Social Security and Medicare are credited with helping reduce poverty among the elderly from more than 30 percent in 1960 to only 10 percent by 2002—a rate as low or lower than that of any other age group.

© Frank Siteman/Index Stock Imagery

In the early 1980s, policy makers recognized the tremendous impact that baby boomers would have on such a pay-as-you-go program. When 77 million baby boomers begin retiring in 2011, Social Security costs and, especially, Medicare costs are set to explode. Reforms adopted in 1983 raised the payroll tax rate, expanded the tax base by the rate of inflation, gradually increased the retirement age from 65 to 67, increased the penalty for early retirement, and offered incentives to delay retirement. These reforms ensured that revenues would exceed costs at least while baby boomers remain in the workforce. To help pay for baby boomer retirements, the 1983 reform began accumulating the resulting surplus in trust funds.

But here's the problem: Both programs are projected to go broke. Growth in beneficiaries and higher medical costs per beneficiary will bankrupt the Medicare Trust Fund by 2019. The problem is that the American population is aging and technological developments are boosting healthcare costs even as they extend lives. The Social Security Trust Fund is projected to go broke later—estimates range from 2042 to 2052. Things only get worse after that as retirees live longer and fewer new workers enter the labor force. In 1940, there were 42 workers per retiree. Today, there are 3.2 workers per retiree. By 2033 only two workers will support each retiree. Based on current benefits and payroll taxes, spending on the Social Security and Medicare, now about 7 percent of GDP, will claim 12 percent by 2030, and exceed 20 percent in 2078. The huge sucking sound will be Social Security and Medicare deficits.

What to do, what to do? These programs have been called the "third rail" of American politics: electrically charged and untouchable. Interest groups are so well organized and senior voter participation is so high that any legislator who proposes limiting benefits risks instant electrocution. Possible reforms include tax increases, delaying retirement, using a more accurate index to calculate the annual cost-of-living increase in benefits (meaning smaller annual increases), and raising the eligibility age. Federal Reserve Chairman Alan Greenspan urged Congress in 2004 to cut the growth of these programs. Lawmakers predictably distanced themselves from Greenspan's suggestions.

Recent changes in these programs will cost more money. President George W. Bush pushed through a new prescription-drug benefit expected to cost some $500 billion over the next 10 years. He also proposed offering young workers the chance to invest a small

Case **Study**

Public Policy

eActivity

The National Academy of Social Insurance is a nonpartisan research organization formed to study Social Security and Medicare. Go to its Web site, at http://www.nasi.org, to access its publications. There you will find Briefs and Fact Sheets about the current status of and issues related to both Medicare and Social Security. How much progress has been made in implementing President George W. Bush's proposals to partially privatize Social Security? Do you think the prescription-drug coverage for those on Medicare will be viable?

portion of their Social Security taxes in the stock market or some other asset, which could yield a better return than Social Security. Diverting payroll taxes to private investment could ultimately contribute to a long-term solution, but the near-term cost would be to reduce revenue supporting this pay-as-you-go plan.

In summary, Social Security and Medicare helped reduce poverty among the elderly, but the program will grow more costly as the elderly population increases and as the flow of young people into the workforce slows. Something has to give if these programs are to be available when you retire.

Sources: Laurence Kotlikoff and Scott Burns, *The Coming Generational Storm* (MIT Press, 2004); John McKinnon, "Medicare's Health to Fail, Rapidly," *Wall Street Journal*, 24 March 2004; "Status of the Social Security and Medicare Programs: A Summary of the 2004 Annual Report," Social Security and Medicare Boards of Trustees, at http://www.ssa.gov/OACT/TRSUM/trsummary.html.

The Relative Size of the Public Sector in the United States

So far, we have focused on the federal budget, but a fuller picture includes state and local governments as well. For added context, we can look at government budgets over time compared to the experience in other major economies. Exhibit 4 shows government outlays at all levels relative to GDP in 10 industrial economies in 1994 and in 2004. Government outlays in the United States in 2004 were 35.7 percent relative to GDP, the smallest share in the group. This amount is down slightly from 36.5 percent in 1994, a year when only Japan among the 10 industrial economies had a smaller government. Between 1994 and 2004, government outlays relative to GDP shrank in 9 of the 10 industrial economies; the average dropped from 46.5 percent to 43.1 percent. Why the drop? The demise of the Soviet Union in the early 1990s reduced defense spending in major economies, and the failure of the socialist experiment shifted sentiment more toward private markets, thus diminishing the role of government. The exception to the trend toward less government spending was Japan, where real estate and stock market prices crashed in 1990, crushing consumer confidence and hobbling the economy for more than a decade.

Let's now turn our attention to an unintended consequence of federal deficits—a sizable federal debt.

The National Debt

Federal deficits add up. It took 39 presidents, six wars, the Great Depression, and more than 200 years for the federal debt to reach $1 trillion, as it did in 1981. It took only 3 presidents and another 15 years for that debt to triple in real terms, as it did by 1996. Ironically, the biggest growth in debt occurred under President Reagan, who ran on a promise to balance the budget.

NATIONAL DEBT

The net accumulation of federal budget deficits

The federal deficit is a flow variable measuring the amount by which outlays exceed revenues in a particular year. The federal debt, or the **national debt,** is a stock variable measuring the net accumulation of past deficits, the amount owed by the federal government. This section puts the national debt in perspective by looking at (1) changes over time, (2) U.S. debt levels compared with those in other countries, (3) interest on the debt, and (4) the prospect of paying off the debt. Note that the national debt ignores the projected liabilities of Social Security, Medicare, or other federal retirement programs. If these liabilities were included, the national debt would triple.

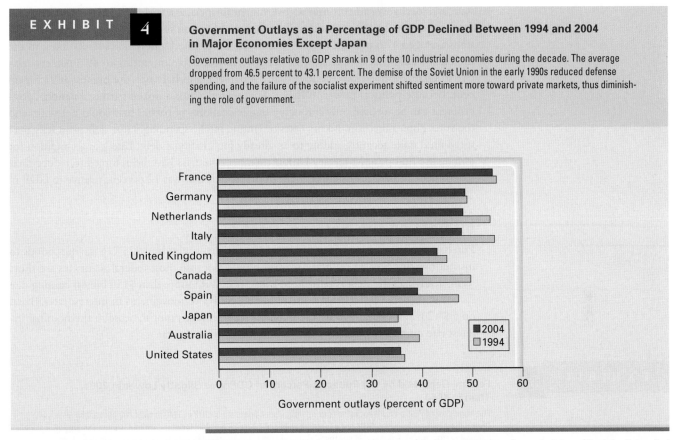

EXHIBIT 4

Government Outlays as a Percentage of GDP Declined Between 1994 and 2004 in Major Economies Except Japan

Government outlays relative to GDP shrank in 9 of the 10 industrial economies during the decade. The average dropped from 46.5 percent to 43.1 percent. The demise of the Soviet Union in the early 1990s reduced defense spending, and the failure of the socialist experiment shifted sentiment more toward private markets, thus diminishing the role of government.

Sources: *OECD Economic Outlook*, Vol. 75 (June 2004), Annex Table 28. For the latest data, go to http://www.oecd.org/home/, click on "Statistics," then find *OECD Economic Outlook*.

In talking about the national debt, we should distinguish between the gross debt and debt held by the public. The *gross debt* includes U.S. Treasury securities purchased by various federal agencies. Because the federal government owes this debt to itself, analysts often focus instead on *debt held by the public,* which includes debt held by households, firms, banks (including Federal Reserve Banks), and foreign entities. As of 2004, the gross federal debt stood at about $7.2 trillion, and the debt held by the public stood at $4.2 trillion.

One way to measure debt over time is relative to the economy's production and income, or GDP (just as a bank might compare the size of a mortgage to a borrower's income). Exhibit 5 shows federal debt held by the public relative to GDP. The cost of World War II ballooned the debt to over 100 percent relative to GDP by 1946. By 1980, it had dropped to 26 percent. But high deficits in the 1980s and early 1990s nearly doubled debt to 49 percent by 1993. Favorable developments already discussed cut debt to 33 percent relative to GDP by 2001. A recession, a stock market crash, tax cuts, and higher government spending created deficits that boosted debt to 38 percent relative to GDP by 2004, about where it was in 1940, after the Great Depression but before World War II.

International Perspective on Public Debt

Exhibit 6 compares the net government debt in the United States relative to GDP with those of nine other industrial countries. *Net debt* includes outstanding liabilities of federal, state, and local governments minus government financial assets, such as loans to students and farmers, securities, cash on hand, and foreign exchange on reserve. Net debt for the ten nations averaged 47.6 percent in 2004 relative to GDP. The United States ranks about in the middle for industrial countries, with net government debt amounting to 49.5 percent relative to GDP. Australia was the lowest at 2.4 percent, and Italy was the highest at 93.5 percent. Because political power in Italy is fragmented across a dozen parties, a national government can be formed only through a fragile coalition of parties that could not withstand the voter displeasure from hiking taxes or cutting public spending. Thus, deficits in Italy persisted until quite recently, adding to an already high national debt. Lately, as a condition for joining the European Monetary Union, member countries have been forced to reduce their federal deficits. Italy, for example, went from a deficit that was 12 percent relative to GDP in 1990 to only 3 percent by 2004.

Interest on the National Debt

Purchasers of federal securities range from individuals who buy $25 U.S. savings bonds to institutions that buy $1 million Treasury bonds. Because most federal securities are short term, nearly half the debt is refinanced every year. With more than $150 billion coming due each month, debt service payments are quite sensitive to movements in interest rates. Based on a $4.2 trillion debt held by the public, a 1 percentage point increase in the nominal interest rate ultimately increases costs by about $42 billion a year.

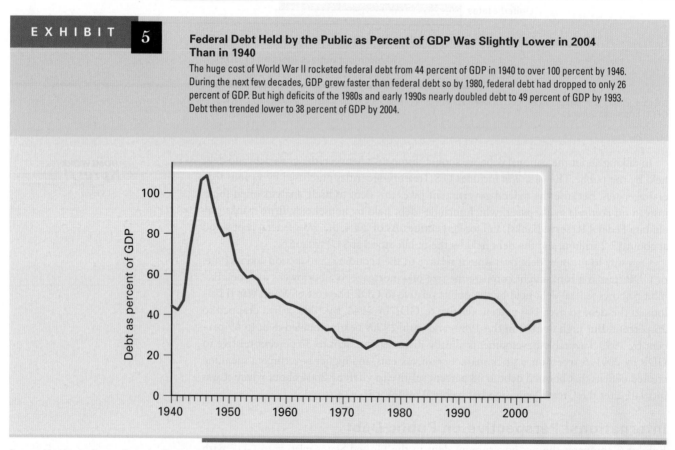

EXHIBIT   **5**

Federal Debt Held by the Public as Percent of GDP Was Slightly Lower in 2004 Than in 1940

The huge cost of World War II rocketed federal debt from 44 percent of GDP in 1940 to over 100 percent by 1946. During the next few decades, GDP grew faster than federal debt so by 1980, federal debt had dropped to only 26 percent of GDP. But high deficits of the 1980s and early 1990s nearly doubled debt to 49 percent of GDP by 1993. Debt then trended lower to 38 percent of GDP by 2004.

Source: Fiscal year figures from the *Economic Report of the President*, February 2004. Figures for 2004 are projections. For the latest data go to http://w3.access.gpo.gov/eop/.

Exhibit 7 shows interest on the federal debt held by the public as a percentage of federal outlays since 1960. After remaining relatively constant for two decades, interest climbed in the 1980s because growing deficits added to the debt and because of higher interest rates. Interest payments peaked at 15.4 percent of outlays in 1996, then began falling first because of budget surpluses and later because of falling interest rates. Thanks to the lowest interest rates in more than four decades, interest payments slipped to only 6.7 percent of the federal budget by 2004, the lowest since 1972. Interest's share of federal outlays is likely to climb as interest rates rise from their historic lows.

Who Bears the Burden of the Debt?

Deficit spending is a way of billing future taxpayers for current spending. The national debt raises moral questions about the right of one generation of taxpayers to bequeath to the next generation the burden of its borrowing. To what extent do deficits and debt shift the burden to future generations? Let's examine two arguments about the burden of the federal debt.

We Owe It to Ourselves

It is often argued that the debt is not a burden to future generations because, although future generations must service the debt, those same generations receive the payments. It's true that if U.S. citizens forgo present consumption to buy bonds, they or their heirs will be repaid, so debt service payments will stay in the country. Thus, future generations will both service the debt and receive the payments. In that sense, the debt is not a burden on future generations. It's all in the family, so to speak.

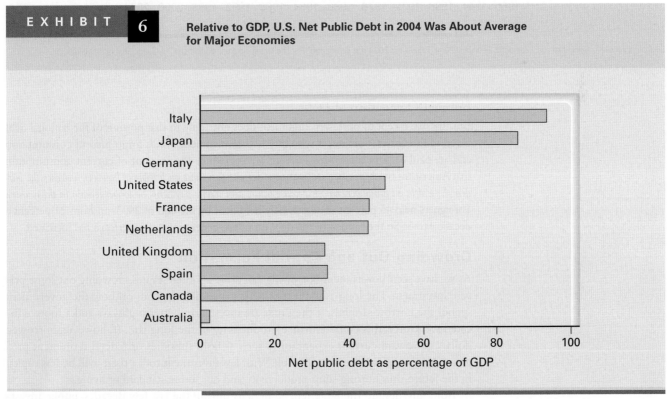

| EXHIBIT | 6 | Relative to GDP, U.S. Net Public Debt in 2004 Was About Average for Major Economies |

Net public debt as percentage of GDP

Source: *OECD Economic Outlook,* 75 (June 2004), Annex Table 35. Figures are projections for net debt at all levels of government in 2004. For the latest data, go to http://www.oecd.org/home/, click on "Statistics," then find *OECD Economic Outlook.*

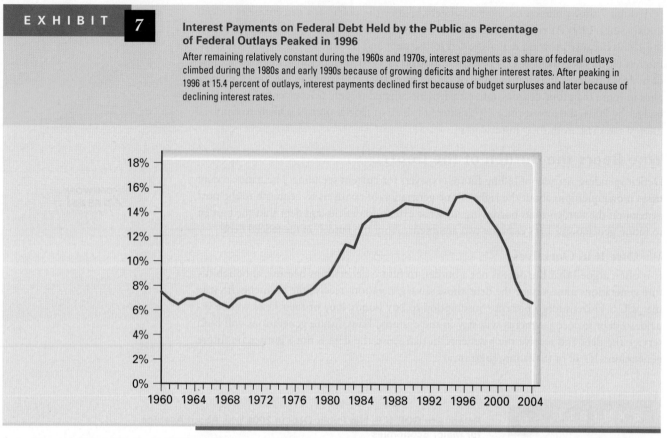

Source: *Economic Report of the President,* February 2004. Figure for 2004 is a projection. For the latest figures, go to http://w3.access.gpo.gov/eop.

Foreign Ownership of Debt

But the "we owe it to ourselves" argument does not apply to that portion of the national debt owed to foreigners. Foreigners who buy U.S. government bonds forgo present consumption and are paid back in the future. Foreign buyers reduce the amount of current consumption that Americans must sacrifice to finance a deficit. *A reliance on foreigners, however, increases the burden of the debt on future generations because future debt service payments no longer remain in the country.* Foreigners held 45 percent of all privately held debt by the end of 2003, up from 21 percent a decade earlier. So the burden of the debt on future generations of Americans has increased.

Crowding Out and Capital Formation

As we have seen, government borrowing can drive up interest rates, crowding out some private investment. The long-run effect of deficit spending depends on how the government spends the borrowed funds. If the funds are invested in better highways and a more educated workforce, this could enhance productivity in the long run. If, however, borrowed dollars go toward current expenditures such as farm subsidies or federal retirement programs, less capital formation will result. With less investment today, there will be less capital in the future, thus hurting labor productivity and our future standard of living.

Ironically, despite the large federal deficits during the last few decades, public investments in roads, bridges, and airports—so-called *public capital*—declined, perhaps because a growing share of the federal budget goes toward income redistribution, especially for the elderly. In 1970, the value of the nation's public infrastructure was about 50 percent relative to GDP; this figure has since declined to about 40 percent. Some argue that declining investment in the public infrastructure serves as a drag on productivity growth. For example, the failure to invest sufficiently in airport safety and efficiency and in the air traffic control system has led to congested airports and flight delays, a problem compounded by the terrorist attacks.

Therefore, government deficits of one generation can affect the standard of living of the next. Note again that our current measure of the national debt does not capture all burdens passed on to future generations. As mentioned earlier, if the unfunded liabilities of government retirement programs, especially Medicare, were included, this would triple the national debt. A model that considers some intergenerational issues of public budgeting is discussed in the following case study.

An Intergenerational View of Deficits and Debt

Harvard economist Robert Barro has developed a model that assumes parents are concerned about the welfare of their children who, in turn, are concerned about the welfare of *their* children, and so on for generations. Thus, the welfare of all generations is tied together. According to Barro, parents can reduce the burden of federal debt on future generations. Here's his argument. When the government runs deficits, it keeps current taxes lower than they would otherwise be, but taxes in the future must increase to service the higher

© Photodisc/Getty Images

Case **Study**

Public Policy

eActivity
Visit the Third Millennium at http://www.thirdmil.org/, an organization of nonpartisan Generation Xers proposing solutions to long-term problems facing the United States. The site also provides links to other organizations concerned with like topics.

debt. If there is no regard for the welfare of future generations, then the older people become, the more attractive debt becomes relative to current taxes. Older people can enjoy the benefits of public spending now but will not live long enough to help finance the debt through higher taxes or lower public benefits.

But parents can undo the harm that deficit financing imposes on their children by consuming less now and saving more. As governments substitute deficits for taxes, parents will consume less and save more to increase gifts and bequests to their children. If greater saving offsets federal deficits, deficit spending will not increase aggregate demand because the decline in consumption will negate the fiscal stimulus provided by deficits. According to Barro, this intergenerational transfer offsets the future burden of higher debt and neutralizes the effect of deficit spending on aggregate demand, output, and employment.

The large budget deficits caused in part by tax cuts and spending increases of the 1980s would seem to provide a natural experiment for testing Barro's theory. The evidence fails to support his theory because the large federal deficits coincided with lower, not higher, saving rates. Yet defenders of Barro's view say that maybe the saving rate was low because people were optimistic about future economic growth, an optimism reflected by the strong performance of stock markets. Or maybe the saving rate was low because people believed tax cuts would result not in higher future taxes but in lower government spending, as President Reagan promised.

But there are other reasons to question Barro's theory. First, those with no children may be less concerned about the welfare of future generations. Second, his theory assumes that people are well informed about federal spending and tax policies and about the future consequences of current policies. Most people, however, seem to know little about such matters. One survey found that few adults polled had any idea about the size of the federal deficit. In the poll, respondents were offered a range of choices, but only 1 in 10 said correctly that the deficit that year was between $100 billion and $400 billion.

Sources: Robert J. Barro, "The Ricardian Approach to Budget Deficits," *Journal of Economic Perspectives* 3 (Spring 1989); Jay Mathews, "How High Is the Deficit, the Dow? Most in Survey Didn't Know," *Hartford Courant*, 19 October 1995; and John McKinnon, "House Narrowly Passes Budget Plan," *Wall Street Journal*, 26 March 2004.

WALL STREET JOURNAL

Reading It **Right**

What's the relevance of the following statement from the Wall Street Journal: "In a recent Oval Office meeting with his top aides, President Bush sought to sum up the administration's new economic philosophy by saying, 'We are both supply-siders and Keynesian.'"

Conclusion

John Maynard Keynes introduced the idea that federal deficit spending is an appropriate fiscal policy when private aggregate demand is insufficient to achieve potential output. The federal budget has not been the same since. Beginning in 1960, the federal budget was in deficit every year but one until 1998. And beginning in the early 1980s, huge federal deficits dominated the fiscal policy debate, tripling the national debt in real terms and putting discretionary fiscal policy on hold. But after peaking at $290 billion in 1992, the deficit disappeared briefly because of higher tax rates on high-income households, lower growth in federal outlays, and a rip-roaring economy fueled by faster labor productivity growth and a dazzling stock market. The softening economy of 2001 and the terrorist attacks put discretionary fiscal policy back in the picture. A recession and weak recovery, tax cuts, and spending increases swelled the federal deficit by 2004 to rival those of the 1980s and early 1990s.

SUMMARY

1. The federal budget process suffers from a variety of problems, including overlapping committee jurisdictions, lengthy budget deliberations, continuing resolutions, budgeting in too much detail, failure to distinguish between capital costs and operating costs, and a lack of control over most of the budget. Suggested improvements include instituting a biennial budget, budgeting in less detail, and distinguishing between a capital budget and an operating budget.

2. Deficits usually increase during wars and severe recessions, but deficits remained high during the economic expansion of the 1980s. Those deficits arose from a combination of tax cuts during the early 1980s and growth in federal spending. As a percentage of GDP, the federal debt held by the public nearly doubled between 1980 and 1992.

3. To the extent that deficits crowd out private capital formation, this decline in private investment reduces the econ-

omy's ability to grow. This is one cost of deficit spending. Foreign holdings of debt also impose a burden on future generations because debt service payments go to foreigners. Thus, the deficits of one generation can reduce the standard of living of the next.

4. After peaking at $290 billion in 1992, the federal deficit turned into a surplus by 1998 because of higher tax rates, reduced outlays especially for defense, declining interest rates, and a strengthening economy fueled by growing labor productivity.

5. The recession of 2001 and terrorist attacks prompted tax cuts to "get the economy moving again." The weak recovery plus the tax cuts and federal spending increases all contributed to a growing federal deficit, which topped $400 billion in 2004. Interest payments on the national debt will likely increase as interest rates rise from their 40-year low.

QUESTIONS FOR REVIEW

1. *(The Federal Budget Process)* The federal budget passed by Congress and signed by the president shows the relationship between *budgeted* expenditures and *projected* revenues. Why does the budget require a forecast of the economy? Under what circumstances would actual government spending and tax revenue fail to match the budget as approved?

2. *(The Federal Budget Process)* In what sense is the executive branch of the U.S. government always dealing with three budgets?

3. *(The Budget Process)* In terms of the policy lags described in the previous chapter, discuss the following issues associated with the budget process:
   a. Continuing resolutions
   b. Uncontrollable budget items
   c. Overly detailed budget

4. *(Budget Philosophies)* Explain the differences among an annually balanced budget, a cyclically balanced budget, and functional finance. How does each affect economic fluctuations?

5. *(Budget Philosophies)* One alternative to balancing the budget annually or cyclically is to produce a government budget that would be balanced if the economy were at potential output. Given the cyclical nature of government tax revenues and spending, how would the resulting budget deficit or surplus vary over the business cycle?

6. *(Budget Philosophies)* The functional finance approach to budget deficits would set the federal budget to promote an economy operating at potential output. What problems would you expect if the country were to employ this kind of budgetary philosophy?

7. *(Crowding Out)* Is it possible for U.S. federal budget deficits to crowd out investment spending in other countries? How could German or British investment be hurt by large U.S. budget deficits?

8. *(Crowding Out)* How might federal deficits crowd out private domestic investment? How could this crowding out affect future living standards?

9. *(Interest on the Debt)* Why did interest payments on the national debt fall from 15.4 percent of the federal budget in 1996 to 6.7 percent in 2004. Why is this percentage expected to increase in the future?

10. *(Burden of the Debt)* Suppose that budget deficits are financed to a considerable extent by foreigners. How does this create a potential burden on future generations of Americans?

11. *(The Twin Deficits)* How is the U.S. budget deficit related to the trade deficit?

12. *(The Miraculous Budget Surplus)* Why did the federal budget go from a huge deficit in 1992 to a surplus in 1998? Explain the factors that contributed to the turnaround.

13. *(C a s e **Study**:* Reforming Social Security and Medicare) Why are the Social Security and Medicare programs headed for trouble? When will the trouble begin? What possible solutions have been proposed?

14. *(Crowding Out and Capital Formation)* In earlier chapters, we've seen that the government can increase GDP in the short run by running a budget deficit. What are some long-term effects of deficit spending?

15. (*Case***Study:** An Intergenerational View of Deficits and Debt) Explain why Robert Barro argues that if parents are concerned about the future welfare of their children, the effects of deficit spending on the economy will be neutralized.

16. *(The Private Sector)* Look at Exhibit 4. How have government outlays as a percent of GDP changed in the industrial countries depicted between 1994 and 2004? Why has Japan been an exception to the trend?

PROBLEMS AND EXERCISES

17. *(The National Debt)* Try the following exercises to better understand how the national debt is related to the government's budget deficit.

    a. Assume that the gross national debt initially is equal to $3 trillion and the federal government then runs a deficit of $300 billion:
       i. What is the new level of gross national debt?
       ii. If 100 percent of the deficit is financed by the sale of securities to federal agencies, what happens to the amount of debt held by the public? What happens to the level of gross debt?
       iii. If GDP increased by 5 percent in the same year that the deficit is run, what happens to gross debt as a percentage of GDP? What happens to the level of debt held by the public as a percentage of GDP?

    b. Now suppose that the gross national debt initially is equal to $2.5 trillion and the federal government then runs a deficit of $100 billion:
       i. What is the new level of gross national debt?
       ii. If 100 percent of this deficit is financed by the sale of securities to the public, what happens to the level of debt held by the public? What happens to the level of gross debt?
       iii. If GDP increases by 6 percent in the same year as the deficit is run, what happens to gross debt as a percentage of GDP? What happens to the level of debt held by the public as a percentage of GDP?

EXPERIENTIAL EXERCISES

18. *(Federal Budget Deficits)* Try your hand at balancing the federal budget by trying the National Budget Simulation at UC Berkeley's Center for Community Economic Research at http://www.budgetsim.org/nbs/.

    a. Develop a budget and see what happens. Were you successful in balancing the budget? If not, how much of a deficit or surplus did you end up with? What does this exercise tell you about the process of creating a balanced budget?
    b. Reexamine the budget cuts or increases you made. What problems would such changes pose for a politician facing reelection?
    c. This budget simulator allows you only to change spending and tax expenditures over a one-year period. What problems does this pose to finding a realistic economic solution for balancing the budget?

19. *(CaseStudy: Reforming Social Security and Medicare)* Visit Econ-Debates Online at http://www.swlearning.com/economics /policy_debates/econ_debates_productivity.html. Review the materials on "Will Social Security survive into the 21st century?" What are some of the macroeconomic implications of Social Security reform?

20. *(Wall Street Journal)* You learned that the government pays billions of dollars in interest each year to finance the national debt. Those debt payments are sensitive to changes in the nominal interest rate. Check the "Treasury Issues" table in the Money and Investing section of today's *Wall Street Journal*. Have interest rates on Treasury bonds and bills been increasing or decreasing lately? What are the implications of interest rate changes for bond prices and for debt finance?

21. *(National Debt)* Go to the Web site for the Bureau of the Public Debt at http://www.publicdebt.treas.gov/. The site contains information on the current public debt of the United States, holders of the debt, and historical information. What is the current value of the national debt? How has this changed over the past year?

International Finance

© Brand X Pictures/Getty Images

How can the United States export more than any other country yet still have the world's highest trade deficit? Are high trade deficits a worry? What's a "strong dollar"? Why do U.S. consumers favor a strong dollar while U.S. producers have mixed feelings? How is the foreign exchange market like an all-night diner? Why do some nations try to influence the value of their currency? And what's the big idea with the European currency, the euro? Answers to these and other questions are explored in this chapter, which focuses on international finance.

A U.S. firm shopping for a German printing press will be quoted a price in euros. Suppose that machine costs 1 million euros. How many dollars is that? The cost in dollars will depend on the exchange rate. When trade takes place across international borders, two currencies are usually involved. Supporting the flows of goods and services are flows of currencies that connect all international transactions.

The *exchange rate* between two currencies—the price of one in terms of the other—is the means by which the price of a good produced in one country translates into the price paid by a buyer in another country. The willingness of buyers and sellers to strike deals therefore depends on the exchange rate. In this chapter we examine the international transactions that determine the relative value of one currency in terms of another. Topics discussed include:

- Balance of payments
- Trade deficits and surpluses
- Foreign exchange markets
- Purchasing power parity
- Flexible exchange rates
- Fixed exchange rates
- International monetary system
- Bretton Woods agreement
- Managed float

Balance of Payments

A country's gross domestic product measures the economy's output and income during a given period. To account for dealings abroad, countries also keep track of international transactions. A country's *balance of payments,* as introduced in Chapter 3, summarizes all economic transactions during a given period between residents of that country and residents of other countries. *Residents* include people, firms, and governments.

International Economic Transactions

The balance of payments measures economic transactions between countries, whether they involve goods and services, real and financial assets, or transfer payments. As a measure reflecting the volume of transactions during a particular period, usually a year, the balance of payments measures a *flow.* Some transactions reflected in the balance of payments do not involve actual payments. For example, if *Time* magazine ships a new printing press to its Australian subsidiary, no payment is involved, yet an economic transaction involving another country occurs. Similarly, if CARE sends food to Africa or the Pentagon provides military assistance to the Middle East, these transactions must be captured in the balance of payments. So remember, although we speak of the *balance of payments,* a more descriptive phrase would be the *balance of economic transactions.*

Balance-of-payments accounts are maintained according to the principles of *double-entry bookkeeping,* in which entries on one side of the ledger are called *credits,* and entries on the other side are called *debits.* As you will see, the balance of payments consists of several individual accounts. A deficit in one or more accounts must be offset by a surplus in the other accounts. Because total credits must equal total debits, there is a *balance* of payments. During a given period, such as a year, the inflow of receipts from the rest of the world, which are entered as credits, equals the outflow of payments to the rest of the world, which are entered as debits. The next few sections describe major accounts in the balance of payments.

The Merchandise Trade Balance

The *merchandise trade balance,* a term introduced in Chapter 3, equals the value of merchandise exports minus the value of merchandise imports. The merchandise account reflects trade in goods, or tangible products (stuff you can drop on your toe), like French wine and U.S. computers, and is often referred to simply as the *trade balance.* The value of U.S. merchandise exports is a credit in the U.S. balance-of-payments account because U.S. residents get *paid* for the exported goods. The value of U.S. merchandise imports is a debit in the balance-of-payments account because U.S. residents *pay* foreigners for imported goods.

If merchandise exports exceed merchandise imports, the trade balance is in *surplus.* If merchandise imports exceed merchandise exports, the trade balance is in *deficit.* The merchandise trade balance, which is reported monthly, influences foreign exchange markets, the stock market, and other financial markets. The trade balance depends on a variety of factors, including the relative strength and competitiveness of the domestic economy compared with other economies and the relative value of the domestic currency compared with other currencies.

U.S. merchandise trade since 1960 is depicted in Exhibit 1, where exports, the blue line, and imports, the red line, are expressed as a percentage of GDP. During the 1960s, exports exceeded imports, and the resulting trade surpluses are shaded blue. Since 1976, imports have exceeded exports, and the resulting trade deficits are shaded pink. Trade deficits as a percentage of GDP increased from 1.3 percent in 1991 to 5.0 percent in 2003, when the deficit reached a record $549 billion. Notice in Exhibit 1 that exports as a percentage of GDP dipped during the 1980s, when the value of the dollar rose sharply relative to other currencies (more on this later). Despite that dip, merchandise exports since 1980 have remained in the range of about 5 percent to 8 percent of GDP with no upward trend. But merchandise imports have trended up from about 9 percent in 1980 to about 12 percent in 2003.

The United States imports more goods from each of the world's major economies than it exports to them. Exhibit 2 shows the U.S. merchandise trade deficit with major economies or regions of the world in 2003. The $124 billion trade deficit with China was by far the largest, nearly double that with Japan or Latin America. The Chinese bought $28 billion in U.S. goods in 2003, but Americans bought $152 billion in Chinese goods, including $93 billion in nonfood consumer goods. So China sells America five times more than it buys from America. Chances are, most of the utensils in your kitchen were made in China; most toys are also Chinese made. The United States does not have a trade surplus with any major economy in the world and is the world's biggest importer.

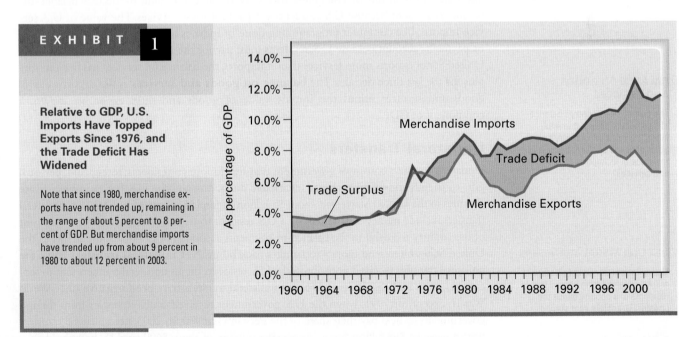

EXHIBIT 1

Relative to GDP, U.S. Imports Have Topped Exports Since 1976, and the Trade Deficit Has Widened

Note that since 1980, merchandise exports have not trended up, remaining in the range of about 5 percent to 8 percent of GDP. But merchandise imports have trended up from about 9 percent in 1980 to about 12 percent in 2003.

Source: Developed from merchandise trade data from the *Economic Report of the President*, February 2004, and *Survey of Current Business*, May 2004, U.S. Department of Commerce. For the latest data, go to http://www.bea.doc.gov/.

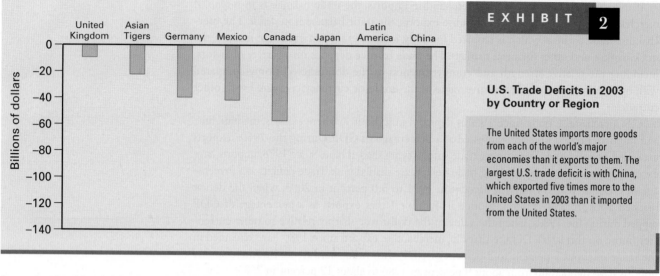

Source: Developed from data in "U.S. International Transactions, 2003," *Survey of Current Business*, April 2004, Table J. The so-called Asian Tigers are Hong Kong, Singapore, South Korea, and Taiwan.

The Balance on Goods and Services

The merchandise trade balance focuses on the flow of goods, but services are also traded internationally. *Services* are intangibles, such as transportation, insurance, banking, education, consulting, and tourism. Services also include the income earned from foreign investments less the income earned by foreigners from their investments in the U.S. economy. Services are often called "invisibles" because they are not tangible. The value of U.S. service exports, like when an Irish tourist visits New York City, is listed as a credit in the U.S. balance-of-payments account because U.S. residents get paid for these services. The value of U.S. service imports, like computer programming done in India, is listed as a debit in the balance-of-payments account because U.S. residents must pay for the imported services. Because the United States exports more services than it imports, the balance on services has been in surplus for the last three decades. The **balance on goods and services** is the export value of goods and services minus the import value of goods and services, or *net exports*, a component of GDP.

Unilateral Transfers

Unilateral transfers consist of government transfers to foreign residents, foreign aid, personal gifts to friends and relatives abroad, charitable donations, and the like. For example, private charities in the United States sent about $5 billion to foreign countries in 2003. U.S. unilateral transfers include money sent abroad by a U.S. resident to friends or relatives. Money sent out of the country is a debit in the balance-of-payments account. For example, immigrants to the United States often send money to families back home. **Net unilateral transfers** equal the unilateral transfers received from abroad by U.S. residents minus unilateral transfers sent to foreign residents by U.S. residents. U.S. net unilateral transfers have been negative since World War II, except for 1991, when the U.S. government received sizable transfers from foreign governments to help pay their share of the Persian Gulf War. In 2003, net unilateral transfers were a negative $68 billion, for an average net outflow of about $600 per U.S. household.

BALANCE ON GOODS AND SERVICES

The portion of a country's balance-of-payments account that measures the value of a country's exports of goods and services minus the value of its imports of goods and services

NET UNILATERAL TRANSFERS

The unilateral transfers (gifts and grants) received from abroad by residents of a country minus the unilateral transfers sent abroad

The United States places few restrictions on money sent out of the country. Other countries, particularly developing countries, strictly limit the amount that may be sent abroad. More generally, many developing countries, such as China, restrict the convertibility of their currency into other currencies.

When we add net unilateral transfers to the exports of goods and services minus the imports of goods and services, we get the **balance on current account,** which is reported quarterly. Thus, *the current account includes all transactions in currently produced goods and services plus net unilateral transfers.* It can be negative, reflecting a current account deficit; positive, reflecting a current account surplus; or zero.

The Capital Account

The current account records international transactions involving the flows of goods (including capital goods), services, and unilateral transfers. When economists talk about capital, they typically mean the physical goods employed to produce goods and services. But sometimes *capital* is just another word for *money*—money to acquire financial assets, such as stocks, bonds, and bank balances, and money to buy foreign land, housing, factories, and other physical assets. The **capital account** records international transactions involving foreign assets and liabilities. For example, U.S. residents purchase foreign securities to earn a higher rate of return and to diversify their portfolios. U.S. capital flows out when Americans buy foreign assets. Foreign capital flows in when foreigners buy U.S. assets.

Between 1917 and 1982, the United States ran a capital account deficit, meaning that U.S. residents purchased more foreign assets than foreigners purchased assets from the United States. The net income from these foreign assets improved our current account balance. But in 1983, for the first time in 65 years, high real interest rates in the United States (relative to those in the rest of the world) resulted in foreigners purchasing more assets in the United States than U.S. residents purchased abroad. Since 1983, foreigners have continued to buy more U.S. assets most years than the other way around, meaning there has usually been a surplus in our capital account.

Americans owe foreigners more and more each year. *The United States is now the world's largest net debtor nation.* This is not as bad as it sounds, because foreign purchases of assets in the United States add to America's productive capacity and promote employment and labor productivity. But the return on these assets flows to foreigners, not to Americans.

Deficits and Surpluses

Nations, like households, operate under a budget constraint. Spending cannot exceed income plus cash on hand and borrowed funds. We have distinguished between *current* transactions, which are the income and expenditures from exports, imports, and unilateral transfers, and *capital* transactions, which reflect international investments and borrowing. Any surplus or deficit in one account must be offset by deficits or surpluses in other balance-of-payments accounts. The current account has been in deficit since 1982, meaning that the sum of U.S. imports of goods and services plus unilateral transfers to foreigners has exceeded the sum spent by foreigners on our exports and sent as unilateral transfers to us.

Exhibit 3 presents the U.S. balance-of-payments statement for 2003. All transactions requiring payments from foreigners to U.S. residents are entered as credits, indicated by a plus sign (+), because they result in an inflow of funds from foreign residents to U.S. residents. All transactions requiring payments to foreigners from U.S. residents are entered as debits, indicated by a minus sign (−), because they result in an outflow of funds from

BALANCE ON CURRENT ACCOUNT

The portion of a country's balance-of-payments account that measures that country's balance on goods and services plus its net unilateral transfers

CAPITAL ACCOUNT

The record of a country's international transactions involving purchases or sales of financial and real assets

U.S. residents to foreign residents. As you can see, a surplus in the capital account of $579.0 billion more than offsets a current account deficit of $541.8 billion. The statistical discrepancy that *balances* payments is a negative $37.2 billion. Think of the statistical discrepancy as the official "fudge factor" that (1) measures the error in the balance-of-payments and (2) satisfies the double-entry bookkeeping requirement that total debits equal total credits.

Foreign exchange is the currency of another country needed to carry out international transactions. A country runs a deficit in its current account when the amount of foreign exchange that country gets from exporting goods and services and from receipts of unilateral transfers falls short of the amount needed to pay for its imports and to make unilateral transfers. The additional foreign exchange required must come from a net capital inflow (borrowing from abroad, foreign purchases of domestic stocks and bonds, foreigners buying a steel plant in Pittsburgh or a ski lodge in Aspen, and so forth). If a country runs a current account surplus, the foreign exchange received from selling exports and from unilateral transfers exceeds the amount required to pay for imports and to make unilateral transfers. This excess foreign exchange could be held in a bank account, converted to the domestic currency, or used to purchase foreign stocks, bonds, or other foreign assets, such as a shoe plant in Italy or a villa on the French Riviera.

When all transactions are considered, accounts must always balance, though specific accounts usually don't. A deficit in a particular account should not necessarily be viewed as a source of concern, nor should a surplus be a source of satisfaction. The deficit in the U.S. current account in recent years has been offset by a capital account surplus. As a result, foreigners are acquiring more claims on U.S. assets.

Current Account	
1. Merchandise exports	+713.8
2. Merchandise imports	−1,263.2
3. Trade balance (1 + 2)	−549.4
4. Service exports	+580.5
5. Service imports	−504.6
6. Goods and services balance (3 + 4 + 5)	−473.5
7. Net unilateral transfers	−68.3
8. Current account balance (6 + 7)	−541.8
Capital Account	
9. Outflow of U.S. capital	−277.7
10. Inflow of foreign capital	+856.7
11. Capital account balance (9 + 10)	+579.0
12. Statistical discrepancy	−37.2
TOTAL (8 + 11 + 12)	**0.0**

EXHIBIT 3

U.S. Balance of Payments for 2003 (billions of dollars)

Source: *Survey of Current Business*, May 2004, Table F-2, U.S. Department of Commerce. For the latest data, go to http://www.bea.doc.gov/.

Foreign Exchange Rates and Markets

Now that you have some idea about international flows, we can take a closer look at the forces that determine the underlying value of the currencies involved. Let's begin by looking at exchange rates and the market for foreign exchange.

Foreign Exchange

Foreign exchange, recall, is foreign money needed to carry out international transactions. The **exchange rate** is the price measured in one country's currency of buying one unit of another country's currency. Exchange rates are determined by the interaction of the households, firms, private financial institutions, governments, and central banks that buy and sell foreign exchange. The exchange rate fluctuates to equate the quantity of foreign exchange demanded with the quantity supplied. Typically, foreign exchange is made up of bank deposits denominated in the foreign currency. When foreign travel is involved, foreign exchange often consists of foreign paper money.

The foreign exchange market incorporates all the arrangements used to buy and sell foreign exchange. This market is not so much a physical place as a network of telephones and computers connecting financial centers all over the world. Perhaps you have seen pictures of foreign exchange traders in New York, Frankfurt, London, or Tokyo in front of computer screens amid a tangle of phone lines. The foreign exchange market is like an all-night diner—it never closes. A trading center is always open somewhere in the world.

We will consider the market for the euro in terms of the dollar. But first, a little background about the euro. For decades the nations of Western Europe have tried to increase their economic cooperation and trade. These countries believed they would be more productive and more competitive with the United States if they acted less like many separate economies and more like the 50 United States, with a single set of trade regulations and one currency. Imagine the hassle involved if each of the 50 states had its own currency.

In January 2002, euro notes and coins entered circulation in the 12 European countries adopting the common currency. The big advantage of a common currency is that Europeans no longer have to change money every time they cross a border or trade with another country in the group. Again, the inspiration for this is the United States, arguably the most successful economy in world history.

So the euro is now the common currency of the *euro area,* as the region is usually called. The price, or exchange rate, of the euro in terms of the dollar is the number of dollars required to purchase one euro. An increase in the number of dollars needed to purchase a euro indicates weakening, or **depreciation,** of the dollar. A decrease in the number of dollars needed to purchase a euro indicates strengthening, or **appreciation,** of the dollar. Put another way, a decrease in the number of euros needed to purchase a dollar is a depreciation of the dollar, and an increase in the number of euros needed to purchase a dollar is an appreciation of the dollar.

Because the exchange rate is a price, it is determined by demand and supply: The equilibrium price is the one that equates quantity demanded with quantity supplied. To simplify the analysis, suppose that the United States and the euro area make up the entire world, so the demand and supply for euros in international finance is the demand and supply for foreign exchange from the U.S. perspective.

EXCHANGE RATE

The price measured in one country's currency of purchasing 1 unit of another country's currency

CURRENCY DEPRECIATION

With respect to the dollar, an increase in the number of dollars needed to purchase 1 unit of foreign exchange in a flexible rate system

CURRENCY APPRECIATION

With respect to the dollar, a decrease in the number of dollars needed to purchase 1 unit of foreign exchange in a flexible rate system

The Demand for Foreign Exchange

Whenever U.S. residents need euros, they must buy them in the foreign exchange market, which could include their local bank, paying for them with dollars. Exhibit 4 depicts a market for foreign exchange—in this case, euros. The horizontal axis shows the quantity of foreign exchange, measured here in millions of euros. The vertical axis shows the price per unit of foreign exchange, measured here as the number of dollars required to purchase one euro. The demand curve *D* for foreign exchange shows the inverse relationship between the dollar price of the euro and the quantity of euros demanded, other things assumed constant. Assumed constant along the demand curve are the incomes and preferences of U.S. consumers, the expected inflation rates in the United States and the euro area, the euro price of goods in the euro area, and interest rates in the United States and the euro area. People have many reasons for demanding foreign exchange, but in the aggregate, the lower the dollar price of foreign exchange, other things constant, the greater the quantity demanded.

A drop in the dollar price of foreign exchange, in this case the euro, means that fewer dollars are needed to purchase each euro, so the dollar prices of euro area products (like German cars, Italian shoes, tickets to Euro Disney, and euro area securities), which list prices in euros, become cheaper. The cheaper it is to buy euros, the lower the dollar price of euro area products to U.S. residents, so the greater the quantity of euros demanded by U.S. residents, other things constant. For example, a cheap enough euro might persuade you to tour Rome, climb the Austrian Alps, wander the museums of Paris, or crawl the pubs of Dublin.

The Supply of Foreign Exchange

The supply of foreign exchange is generated by the desire of foreign residents to acquire dollars—that is, to exchange euros for dollars. Euro area residents want dollars to buy U.S.

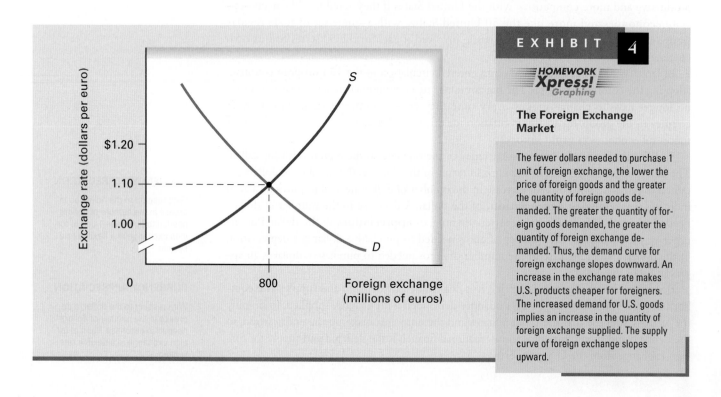

EXHIBIT 4

HOMEWORK Xpress! *Graphing*

The Foreign Exchange Market

The fewer dollars needed to purchase 1 unit of foreign exchange, the lower the price of foreign goods and the greater the quantity of foreign goods demanded. The greater the quantity of foreign goods demanded, the greater the quantity of foreign exchange demanded. Thus, the demand curve for foreign exchange slopes downward. An increase in the exchange rate makes U.S. products cheaper for foreigners. The increased demand for U.S. goods implies an increase in the quantity of foreign exchange supplied. The supply curve of foreign exchange slopes upward.

goods and services, acquire U.S. assets, make loans in dollars, or give cash gifts in dollars to their U.S. friends and relatives. Euros are supplied in the foreign exchange market to acquire the dollars people want. An increase in the dollar-per-euro exchange rate, other things constant, makes U.S. products cheaper for foreigners because foreign residents need fewer euros to get the same number of dollars. For example, suppose a Dell computer sells for $500. If the exchange rate is $1.00 per euro, that computer costs 500 euros; if the exchange rate is $1.25 per euro, it costs only 400 euros. The number of Dell computers demanded in the euro area increases as the dollar-per-euro exchange rate increases, other things constant, so more euros will be supplied on the foreign exchange market to buy dollars.

The positive relationship between the dollar-per-euro exchange rate and the quantity of euros supplied on the foreign exchange market is expressed in Exhibit 4 by the upward-sloping supply curve for foreign exchange (again, euros in our example). The supply curve assumes that other things remain constant, including euro area incomes and tastes, expectations about the rates of inflation in the euro area and the United States, and interest rates in the euro area and the United States.

Determining the Exchange Rate

Exhibit 4 brings together the demand and supply for foreign exchange to determine the exchange rate. At a rate of $1.10 per euro, the quantity of euros demanded equals the quantity supplied—in our example, 800 million euros. Once achieved, this equilibrium rate will remain constant until a change occurs in one of the factors that affect supply or demand. If the exchange rate is allowed to adjust freely, or to *float,* in response to market forces, the market will clear continually, as the quantities of foreign exchange demanded and supplied are equated.

What if the initial equilibrium is upset by a change in one of the underlying forces that affect supply or demand? For example, suppose higher U.S. incomes increase American demand for all normal goods, including those from the euro area. This shifts the U.S. demand curve for foreign exchange to the right, as Americans buy more Italian marble, Dutch chocolate, German machines, Parisian vacations, and euro securities.

This increased demand for euros is shown in Exhibit 5 by a rightward shift of the demand curve for foreign exchange. The demand increase from D to D' leads to an increase in the exchange rate per euro from $1.10 to $1.12. Thus, the euro increases in value, or appreciates, while the dollar falls in value, or depreciates. An increase in U.S. income should not affect the euro supply curve, though it does increase the *quantity of euros supplied.* The higher exchange value of the euro prompts those in the euro area to buy more American products and assets, which are now cheaper in terms of the euro.

To review: Any increase in the demand for foreign exchange or any decrease in its supply, other things constant, causes an increase in the number of dollars required to purchase one unit of foreign exchange, which is a depreciation of the dollar. On the other hand, any decrease in the demand for foreign exchange or any increase in its supply, other things constant, causes a reduction in the number of dollars required to purchase one unit of foreign exchange, which is an appreciation of the dollar.

Arbitrageurs and Speculators

Exchange rates between two currencies are nearly identical at any given time in markets around the world. For example, the dollar price of a euro is the same in New York, Frankfurt, Tokyo, London, Zurich, Hong Kong, Istanbul, and other financial centers. **Arbitrageurs**—dealers who take advantage of any difference in exchange rates between

ARBITRAGEUR

Someone who takes advantage of temporary geographic differences in the exchange rate by simultaneously purchasing a currency in one market and selling it in another market

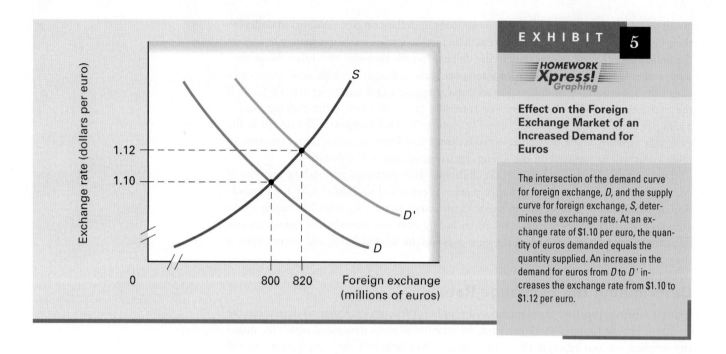

HOMEWORK
Xpress!
Graphing

Effect on the Foreign Exchange Market of an Increased Demand for Euros

The intersection of the demand curve for foreign exchange, *D*, and the supply curve for foreign exchange, *S*, determines the exchange rate. At an exchange rate of $1.10 per euro, the quantity of euros demanded equals the quantity supplied. An increase in the demand for euros from *D* to *D'* increases the exchange rate from $1.10 to $1.12 per euro.

markets by buying low and selling high—ensure this equality. Their actions help to equalize exchange rates across markets. For example, if one euro costs $1.09 in New York but $1.10 in Frankfurt, an arbitrageur could buy, say, $10,000,000 worth of euros in New York and at the same time sell them in Frankfurt for $10,091,743, thereby earning $91,743 minus the transaction costs of the trades.

Because an arbitrageur buys and sells simultaneously, relatively little risk is involved. In our example, the arbitrageur increased the demand for euros in New York and increased the supply of euros in Frankfurt. These actions increased the dollar price of euros in New York and decreased it in Frankfurt, thereby squeezing down the difference in exchange rates. Exchange rates may still change because of market forces, but they tend to change in all markets simultaneously.

The demand and supply of foreign exchange arises from many sources—from importers and exporters, investors in foreign assets, central banks, tourists, arbitrageurs, and speculators. **Speculators** buy or sell foreign exchange in hopes of profiting by trading the currency at a more favorable exchange rate later. By taking risks, speculators aim to profit from market fluctuations—they try to buy low and sell high. In contrast, arbitrageurs take less risk, because they *simultaneously* buy currency in one market and sell it in another.

SPECULATOR

Someone who buys or sells foreign exchange in hopes of profiting from fluctuations in the exchange rate over time

Finally, people in countries suffering from economic and political turmoil, such as recently occurred in Russia, Indonesia, and the Philippines, may buy *hard* currency as a hedge against the depreciation and instability of their own currencies. The dollar has long been accepted as an international medium of exchange. It is also the currency of choice in the world markets for oil and illegal drugs. But the euro eventually may challenge that dominance, in part because the largest euro denomination, the 500 euro note, is worth over five times the largest U.S. note, the $100 note. So it would be five times easier to smuggle euro notes than U.S. notes of equal value.

Purchasing Power Parity

As long as trade across borders is unrestricted and as long as exchange rates are allowed to adjust freely, the **purchasing power parity (PPP) theory** predicts that the exchange rate between two currencies will adjust in the long run to reflect price-level differences between the two currency regions. *A given basket of internationally traded goods should therefore sell for about the same around the world (except for differences reflecting transportation costs and the like).* Suppose a basket of internationally traded goods that sells for $10,000 in the United States sells for 9,000 euros in the euro area. According to the purchasing power parity theory, the equilibrium exchange rate should be $1.11 per euro. If this were not the case—if the exchange rate were, say, $1.00 per euro—then you could exchange $9,000 for 9,000 euros, with which you buy the basket of commodities in the euro area. You could then sell the basket of goods in the States for $10,000, yielding you a profit of $1,000 minus any transaction costs. Selling dollars and buying euros will drive up the dollar price of euros.

The purchasing power parity theory is more of a long-run predictor than a day-to-day indicator of the relationship between changes in the price level and the exchange rate. For example, a country's currency generally appreciates when inflation is low compared with other countries and depreciates when inflation is high. Likewise, a country's currency generally appreciates when its real interest rates are higher than those in the rest of the world, because foreigners are more willing to buy and hold investments denominated in that high-interest currency. As a case in point, the dollar appreciated during the first half of the 1980s, when real U.S. interest rates were relatively high, and depreciated in the 2002 and 2003, when real U.S. interest rates were relatively low.

Because of trade barriers, central bank intervention in exchange markets, and the fact that many products are not traded or are not comparable across countries, the purchasing power parity theory usually does not explain exchange rates at a particular point in time. For example, if you went shopping in London tomorrow, you would soon notice a dollar does not buy as much there as it does in the United States. The following case study considers the purchasing power parity theory based on the price of Big Macs around the globe.

The Big Mac Price Index

As you have already learned, the PPP theory says that in the long run the exchange rate between two currencies should move toward the one that equalizes the prices in each country of an identical basket of internationally traded goods. A lighthearted test of the theory has been developed by *The Economist* magazine, which compares prices around the world for a "market basket" consisting simply of one McDonald's Big Mac—a product that, though not internationally traded, is essentially the same in more than 100 countries. *The Economist* begins with the price of a Big Mac in the local currency and then converts that price into dollars based on the exchange rate prevailing at the time. A comparison of the dollar price of Big Macs across countries offers a crude test of the PPP theory, which predicts that these prices should move toward equality in the long run.

Exhibit 6 lists the dollar price of a Big Mac in May 2004, in each of 30 surveyed countries plus the euro area average. By comparing the price of a Big Mac in the United States (shown as a green bar) with prices in other countries, we can derive a crude measure of

© David Marshall/Index Stock Imagery

PURCHASING POWER PARITY (PPP) THEORY

The idea that the exchange rate between two countries will adjust in the long run to reflect price-level differences between the countries

C a s e **S t u d y**

Bringing Theory to Life

eActivity

The Economist has published several articles about the Big Mac Index. Go to http://www.economist.com/markets/Bigmac/Index.cfm to access the latest edition of the index. Which currencies have had the largest changes in value? Which currencies went from being overvalued to undervalued between 1989 and 2004?

whether particular currencies, relative to the dollar, are overvalued (red bars) or overvalued (blue bars). For example, because the price of a Big Mac in Switzerland, at $4.90, was 69 percent higher than the U.S. price of $2.90, the Swiss franc appears overvalued compared to the dollar. The euro was 13 percent overvalued. But Big Macs were cheaper in most of the countries surveyed. The cheapest was in Saudi Arabia, where a Big Mac price of 64 cents was 78 percent below the U.S. price.

Thus, Big Mac prices in May 2004 ranged from 69 percent above to 78 percent below the U.S. price. These prices lend little support to the PPP theory, but that theory relates only to traded goods. The Big Mac is not traded internationally. A large share of the total cost of a Big Mac is rent, which can vary substantially across countries. Taxes and trade barriers, such as tariffs and quotas on beef, may also distort local prices. And wages differ across countries, with a McDonald's worker averaging $7 an hour in the United States versus less than $1 an hour in China. So there are understandable reasons why Big Mac prices differ across countries.

Sources: "The Big Mac Index: Food for Thought," *Economist*, 27 May 2004; Michael Pakko and Patricia Pollard, "Burgernomics: A Big Mac Guide to Purchasing Power Parity," *Federal Reserve Bank of St. Louis Review*, (November/December 2003): 9–28; and the McDonald's Corporation Web site at http://www.mcdonalds.com.

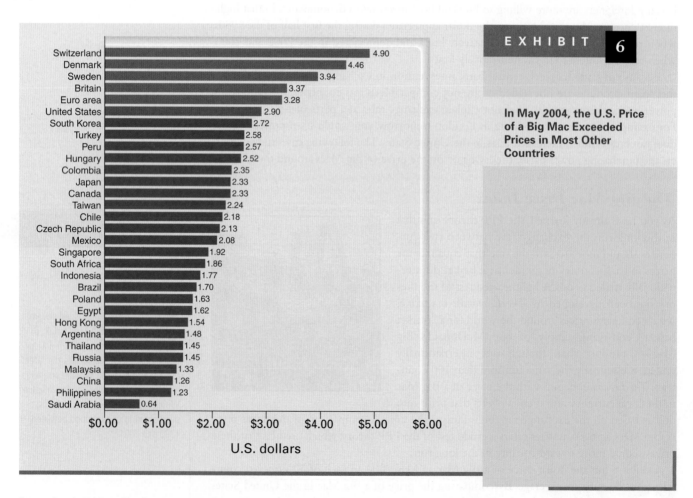

EXHIBIT 6

In May 2004, the U.S. Price of a Big Mac Exceeded Prices in Most Other Countries

Source: Developed from the price survey appearing in "The Big Mac Index: Food for Thought," *Economist*, 27 May 2004.

Flexible Exchange Rates

For the most part, we have been discussing a system of **flexible exchange rates,** with rates determined by demand and supply. Flexible, or *floating,* exchange rates adjust continually to the myriad forces that buffet the foreign exchange market. Consider how the exchange rate is linked to the balance-of-payments accounts. Debit entries in the current and capital accounts increase the demand for foreign exchange, resulting in a depreciation of the dollar. Credit entries in these accounts increase the supply of foreign exchange, resulting in an appreciation of the dollar.

Fixed Exchange Rates

When exchange rates are flexible, governments usually have little direct role in foreign exchange markets. But if governments try to set exchange rates, active and ongoing central bank intervention is necessary to establish and maintain these **fixed exchange rates.** Suppose the European Central Bank selects what it thinks is an appropriate rate of exchange between the dollar and the euro. It attempts to *fix,* or to *peg,* the exchange rate within a narrow band around the particular value selected. If the euro threatens to climb above the maximum acceptable exchange rate, monetary authorities must sell euros and buy dollars, thereby keeping the dollar price of the euro down. Conversely, if the euro threatens to drop below the minimum acceptable exchange rate, monetary authorities must sell dollars and buy euros. This increased demand for the euro will keep its value up relative to the dollar. Through such intervention in the foreign exchange market, monetary authorities try to stabilize the exchange rate, keeping it within the specified band.

If monetary officials must keep selling foreign exchange to maintain the pegged rate, they risk running out of foreign exchange reserves. Faced with this threat, the government has several options for eliminating the exchange rate disequilibrium. First, the pegged exchange rate can be increased, which is a **devaluation** of the domestic currency. (A decrease in the pegged exchange rate is called a **revaluation.**) Second, the government can reduce the domestic demand for foreign exchange directly by imposing restrictions on imports or on capital outflows. China and many other developing countries do this. Third, the government can adopt contractionary fiscal or monetary policies to reduce the country's income level, increase interest rates, or reduce inflation relative to that of the country's trading partners, thereby indirectly decreasing the demand for foreign exchange and increasing the supply of foreign exchange. Several Asian economies, such as South Korea and Indonesia, pursued such policies to stabilize their currencies in 1998. Finally, the government can allow the disequilibrium to persist and ration the available foreign reserves through some form of foreign exchange control.

This concludes our introduction to the theories of international finance. Let's examine international finance in practice.

Development of the International Monetary System

From 1879 to 1914, the international financial system operated under a **gold standard,** whereby the major currencies were convertible into gold at a fixed rate. For example, the U.S. dollar could be redeemed at the U.S. Treasury for one-twentieth of an ounce of gold. The British pound could be redeemed at the British Exchequer, or treasury, for one-fourth of an ounce of gold. Because each British pound could buy five times as much gold as each dollar, one British pound exchanged for $5.

The gold standard provided a predictable exchange rate, one that did not vary as long as currencies could be redeemed for gold at the announced rate. But the money supply in each country was determined in part by the flow of gold between countries, so each

FLEXIBLE EXCHANGE RATE

Rate determined by the forces of demand and supply without government intervention

FIXED EXCHANGE RATE

Rate of exchange between currencies pegged within a narrow range and maintained by the central bank's ongoing purchases and sales of currencies

CURRENCY DEVALUATION

An increase in the official pegged price of foreign exchange in terms of the domestic currency

CURRENCY REVALUATION

A reduction in the official pegged price of foreign exchange in terms of the domestic currency

GOLD STANDARD

An arrangement whereby the currencies of most countries are convertible into gold at a fixed rate

country's monetary policy was influenced by the supply of gold. A balance-of-payments deficit resulted in a loss of gold, which theoretically caused a country's money supply to decline. A balance-of-payments surplus resulted in an increase in gold, which theoretically caused a country's money supply to rise. The supply of money throughout the world also depended on the vagaries of gold discoveries. When gold production did not keep pace with the growth in economic activity, the price level dropped. When gold production exceeded the growth in economic activity, the price level rose. For example, gold discoveries in Alaska and South Africa in the late 1890s expanded the U.S. money supply, leading to inflation.

The Bretton Woods Agreement

During World War I, many countries could no longer convert their currencies into gold, and the gold standard eventually collapsed, disrupting international trade during the 1920s and 1930s. Once an Allied victory in World War II appeared certain, the Allies met in Bretton Woods, New Hampshire, in July 1944 to formulate a new international monetary system. Because the United States had a strong economy and was not ravaged by the war, the dollar was selected as the key reserve currency in the new international monetary system. All exchange rates were fixed in terms of the dollar, and the United States, which held most of the world's gold reserves, stood ready to convert foreign holdings of dollars into gold at a rate of $35 per ounce. Even though exchange rates were fixed by the Bretton Woods agreement, *other* countries could adjust *their* exchange rates relative to the U.S. dollar if they found a chronic disequilibrium in their balance of payments—that is, if a country faced a large and persistent deficit or surplus.

The Bretton Woods agreement also created the **International Monetary Fund (IMF)** to set rules for maintaining the international monetary system, to standardize financial reporting for international trade, and to make loans to countries with temporary balance-of-payments problems. The IMF lends a revolving fund of $300 billion to economies in need of reserves. Headquartered in Washington, D.C., the IMF has more than 180 member countries and a staff of 2,500 drawn from around the world.

The Demise of the Bretton Woods System

During the latter part of the 1960s, inflation began heating up in the United States. Higher U.S. prices meant that those exchanging foreign currencies for dollars at the official exchange rates found these dollars bought fewer U.S. goods and services. Because of U.S. inflation, the dollar had become *overvalued* at the official exchange rate, meaning that the gold value of the dollar exceeded the exchange value of the dollar. With the dollar overvalued, foreigners redeemed more dollars for gold. To halt this outflow of gold, the United States in August 1971 stopped exchanging gold for dollars. In December 1971, the world's 10 richest countries met in Washington and devalued the dollar by 8 percent. The hope at the time was that this devaluation would put the dollar on firmer footing and would save the "dollar standard." With prices rising at different rates around the world, however, an international monetary system based on fixed exchange rates was doomed.

In 1971, U.S. merchandise imports exceeded merchandise exports for the first time since World War II. When the trade deficit tripled in 1972, it became clear that the dollar was still overvalued. In early 1973, the dollar was devalued another 10 percent, but this did not quiet foreign exchange markets. The dollar, for three decades the anchor of the international monetary system, suddenly looked vulnerable, and speculators began betting the dollar would fall

HOMEWORK
Xpress!
econ-apps debate

INTERNATIONAL MONETARY FUND (IMF)

An international organization that establishes rules for maintaining the international monetary system and makes loans to countries with temporary balance-of-payments problems

even more. Dollars were exchanged for German marks because the mark appeared to be the most stable currency. Bundesbank, Germany's central bank, exchanged marks for dollars in an attempt to defend the official exchange rate and prevent an appreciation of the mark. Why didn't Germany want the mark to appreciate? Appreciation would make German goods more expensive abroad and foreign goods cheaper in Germany, thereby reducing German exports and increasing German imports. So the mark's appreciation would reduce German output and employment. But after selling $10 billion worth of marks, the Bundesbank gave up defending the dollar. As soon as the value of the dollar was allowed to float against the mark, the Bretton Woods system, already on shaky ground, collapsed.

The Current System: Managed Float

The Bretton Woods system has been replaced by a **managed float system,** which combines features of a freely floating exchange rate with sporadic intervention by central banks as a way of moderating exchange rate fluctuations among the world's major currencies. Most small countries, particularly developing countries, still peg their currencies to one of the major currencies (such as the U.S. dollar) or to a "basket" of major currencies. What's more, in developing countries, private international borrowing and lending are severely restricted; some governments allow residents to purchase foreign exchange only for certain purposes. In some countries, different exchange rates apply to different categories of transactions.

Critics of flexible exchange rates argue that they are inflationary, because they free monetary authorities to pursue expansionary policies; and they have often been volatile. This volatility creates uncertainty and risk for importers and exporters, increasing the transaction costs of international trade. Furthermore, exchange rate volatility can lead to wrenching changes in the competitiveness of a country's export sector. These changes cause swings in employment, resulting in louder calls for import restrictions. For example, the exchange rate between the Japanese yen and the U.S. dollar has been relatively unstable, particularly because of international speculation.

Policy makers are always on the lookout for a system that will perform better than the current managed float system, with its fluctuating currency values. *Their ideal is a system that will foster international trade, lower inflation, and promote a more stable world economy.* International finance ministers have acknowledged that the world must find an international standard and establish greater exchange rate stability.

The wild swings in exchange rates that sometimes occur with flexible exchange rates have triggered interventions to reduce undesirable fluctuations, as discussed in the following case study about recent financial troubles in Asia.

The Asian Contagion

The trouble started in Thailand in early 1997. Speculators began betting that the Thai currency, the baht, was in for a fall. The Thai central bank tried to defend the baht's value by buying baht and selling foreign reserves. At the time, the baht's value was pegged to the U.S. dollar. As the central bank's foreign reserves dwindled, the government decided in July 1997 to let the baht float. It lost 40 percent of its value against the dollar in a matter of weeks. With the baht worth so much less, Thai businesses and government had difficulty repaying foreign loans, most of which had to be paid back in dollars.

© Susumu Takahashi/Reuters New Media/Corbis

MANAGED FLOAT SYSTEM

An exchange rate system that combines features of freely floating rates with sporadic intervention by central banks

Case **Study**

World of Business

eActivity

The Institute for International Economics Policy Briefs, at http://www.iie.com/publications/pb/pb04.htm, presents an article, "Islam, Globalization, and Economic Performance in the Middle East" by Marcus Noland and

Howard Pack, which discusses the impact of globalization on countries in the Middle East. What explains the relative underperformance of the Middle East in the past few decades? Other economists' views and analyses are available at the Brookings Institution at http://www.brook.edu /index/papersarticles.htm.

WALL STREET JOURNAL

Reading It **Right**

What's the relevance of the following statement from the Wall Street Journal: "While Japan's direct investment around the world has fallen 36 percent in the last 10 years as it has grappled with its own economic downturn, its investment in Southeast Asia has been cut in half."

The crisis prompted a $17 billion bailout of Thailand, supervised by the International Monetary Fund (IMF) and aimed at helping Thailand pay back some foreign debt. But problems in Thailand deepened, as outside credit agencies continued to downgrade Thai debt. Falling currency values soon spread to neighboring Indonesia, Malaysia, and South Korea, as the so-called Asian Contagion ripped through the region, cutting real GDP in each of these countries more than 5 percent in 1998. Note that a plunging currency value was not so much the source of economic instability as a reflection of other problems in the economy, such as falling exports and an unstable banking sector due to bad loans. Indonesia and South Korea were forced to seek IMF assistance.

In Japan, where the economy had been on the ropes since 1990, matters worsened. In November 1997, four large financial institutions went bankrupt, the yen suffered its biggest drop against the dollar in years, and the stock market continued its eight-year slide. Japan, the second-largest economy in the world (after the United States), is by far the largest in Asia. A weakened Japan threatened the fragile economies of Asia as they tried to recover from financial chaos. A weakened Japan meant the country would buy less from its Asian neighbors, and a weakened yen meant Japanese exports would be cheaper on world markets, thus undercutting exports from elsewhere in Asia. Faced with growing problems in Asia, the U.S. government joined forces with the Japanese government to intervene in currency markets and spent $2 billion buying yen. By increasing the demand for yen, the U.S. intervention reversed the slide in the yen's value. In one day, the yen-per-dollar exchange rate appreciated 5 percent. By 2001, output in the other economies affected by the Asian Contagion was growing.

Asian economies have now recovered in large part because they used their cheap currencies to boost their exports to the United States. This strategy has generated growing trade surpluses with the United States and infused Asian central banks with billions of dollars. These banks have used these surplus dollars to buy dollar-denominated securities, primarily U.S. Treasury bonds. By 2004, Asians held about $1 trillion in U.S. bonds, or about 55 percent of the U.S. bonds held by foreigners. This is up from 40 percent in 1996, the year before the Asian Contagion started. Chinese holdings of U.S. bonds more than doubled between 2000 and 2004. This is an example of the twin deficits: the U.S. trade deficits put dollars in the hands of foreigners; they use those dollars to buy U.S. Treasury bonds, thus funding our federal deficit.

Sources: John Andrews, *Pocket Asia*, 7 ed. (The Economist Books, 2002); "Banking in South-East Asia?" 1 May 2004; "Emerging Market Indicators," *Economist*, 27 May 2004; "Stocks Stumble Across Asia as Yen Hits Lowest Since '90," *Wall Street Journal*, 11 June 1998; Craig Karmin et al., "Despite U.S. Bond Selloff, Asia Continues Buying," *Wall Street Journal*, 4 August 2003.

Conclusion

The United States is very much a part of the world economy, not only as the largest exporter but also as the largest importer. Although the dollar remains the unit of transaction in many international settlements—OPEC, for example, still states oil prices in dollars—gyrations of exchange rates have made those involved in international finance wary of putting all their eggs in one basket. The international monetary system is now going through a difficult period as it gropes for a new source of stability more than three decades after the collapse of the Bretton Woods agreement.

SUMMARY

1. The balance of payments reflects all economic transactions between one country and the rest of the world. The current account measures flows of (a) merchandise; (b) services, including investment income, military transactions, and tourism; and (c) unilateral transfers, or public and private transfer payments to and from foreign residents. The capital account measures international transactions in real and financial assets.

2. Foreign exchange funds the flow of goods and services across international borders. The interaction of the supply and demand for foreign exchange determines the equilibrium exchange rate.

3. Under a system of flexible exchange rates, the value of the dollar relative to foreign exchange varies over time. An increase in the demand for foreign exchange or a decrease in its supply, other things constant, will increase the value

of foreign exchange relative to the dollar, which is a depreciation of the dollar. Conversely, a decrease in the demand for foreign exchange or an increase in its supply will decrease the value of foreign exchange relative to the dollar, which is an appreciation of the dollar.

4. Under a system of fixed exchange rates, monetary authorities try to stabilize the exchange rate, keeping it between a specified ceiling and floor value.

5. For much of this century, the international monetary system was based on fixed exchange rates. A managed float system has been in effect for the major currencies since the demise of the Bretton Woods system in the early 1970s. Although central banks often try to stabilize exchange rates, fluctuations in rates persist. These fluctuations usually reflect market forces but they still raise the transaction costs of international trade and finance.

QUESTIONS FOR REVIEW

1. *(Balance of Payments)* Suppose the United States ran a balance-on-goods-and-services surplus by exporting goods and services while importing nothing.

   a. How would such a surplus be offset elsewhere in the balance-of-payments accounts?
   b. If the level of U.S. production does not depend on the balance on goods and services, how would running this surplus affect our *current* standard of living?
   c. What is the relationship between total debits and total credits in the balance on goods and services?
   d. When all international economic transactions are considered, what must be true about the sum of debits and credits?
   e. What is the role of the statistical discrepancy?

2. *(Foreign Exchange)* What is the difference between a depreciation of the dollar and a devaluation of the dollar?

3. *(Purchasing Power Parity)* According to the theory of purchasing power parity, what will happen to the value of the

dollar (against foreign currencies) if the U.S. price level doubles and price levels in other countries remain constant? Why is the theory more suitable to analyzing events in the long run?

4. (*Case* **Study:** The Big Mac Price Index) The Big Mac Price Index computed by *The Economist* has consistently found the U.S. dollar to be undervalued against some currencies and overvalued against others, which seems to call for a rejection of the purchasing power parity theory. Explain why this index may not be a valid test of the theory.

5. *(The Current System: Managed Float)* What is a managed float? What are the disadvantages of freely floating exchange rates that led countries to the managed float system?

6. *(Merchandise Trade Balance)* Explain why a U.S. recession that does not occur at the same time as recessions in the rest of the world will tend to reduce the U.S. trade deficit.

PROBLEMS AND EXERCISES

7. *(Balance of Payments)* The following are hypothetical data for the U.S. balance of payments. Use the data to calculate each of the following:

   a. Merchandise trade balance
   b. Balance on goods and services
   c. Balance on current account
   d. Capital account balance
   e. Statistical discrepancy

	Billions of Dollars
Merchandise exports	350.0
Merchandise imports	2,425.0
Service exports	170.0
Service imports	2,145.0
Net unilateral transfers	221.5
Outflow of U.S. capital	245.0
Inflow of foreign capital	70.0

8. *(Balance of Payments)* Explain where in the U.S. balance of payments an entry would be made for each of the following:

   a. A Hong Kong financier buys some U.S. corporate stock.
   b. A U.S. tourist in Paris buys some perfume to take home.
   c. A Japanese company sells machinery to a pineapple company in Hawaii.
   d. U.S. farmers make a gift of food to starving children in Ethiopia.
   e. The U.S. Treasury sells a bond to a Saudi Arabian prince.
   f. A U.S. tourist flies to France on Air France.
   g. A U.S. company sells insurance to a foreign firm.

9. *(Determining the Exchange Rate)* Use these data to answer the following questions about the market for British pounds:

Price of Pound (in $)	Quantity Demanded (of pounds)	Quantity Supplied (of pounds)
$4.00	50	100
3.00	75	75
2.00	100	50

   a. Draw the demand and supply curves for pounds, and determine the equilibrium exchange rate (dollars per pound).
   b. Suppose that the supply of pounds doubles. Draw the new supply curve.
   c. What is the new equilibrium exchange rate?
   d. Has the dollar appreciated or depreciated?
   e. What happens to U.S. imports of British goods?

EXPERIENTIAL EXERCISES

10. *(Foreign Exchange Rates and Markets)* Trade among European nations has been bolstered by the introduction of the euro. Visit http://www.euro.gov.uk/home.asp?f=1 to review the latest developments.

11. (*C a s e* **S t u d y** : The Asian Contagion) Visit the Business section of *Time* magazine's Asia edition at http://www.time.com/time/asia/biz/ and determine if the Asian economic situation seems to be easing or getting worse. You can also try Yahoo!, which maintains a page devoted to the Asian economy at http://dailynews.yahoo.com/fc/Business/Asian_Economy.

12. *(Wall Street Journal)* The latest data on exchange rates appear in the "Currency Trading" column in the daily *Wall Street Journal.* You can find it in the Money and Investing section. Try tracking a particular foreign currency over the course of several weeks. Has the dollar been appreciating or depreciating relative to that currency? Try to explain why it has been appreciating or depreciating.

HOMEWORK XPRESS! EXERCISES

These exercises require access to McEachern Homework Xpress! If Homework Xpress! did not come with your book, visit **http://homeworkxpress.swlearning.com** *to purchase.*

1. In the diagram for this exercise, sketch demand and supply curves to represent the market for exchanging British pounds for U.S. dollars to illustrate an equilibrium exchange rate of $1.50 per pound for a volume of exchange of 500 million pounds.

2. In the diagram, sketch demand and supply curves to represent the market for exchanging British pounds for U.S. dollars to illustrate an equilibrium exchange rate of $1.50 per pound for a volume of exchange of 500 million pounds. Then show how the exchange rate could increase to $1.80 with an increase in volume to 600 million pounds.

A

ability-to-pay tax principle Those with a greater ability to pay, such as those with a higher income or those who own more property, should pay more taxes

absolute advantage The ability to produce something using fewer resources than other producers use

actual investment The amount of investment actually undertaken; equals planned investment plus unplanned changes in inventories

adverse supply shocks Unexpected events that reduce aggregate supply, sometimes only temporarily

aggregate demand The relationship between the economy's price level and the quantity of aggregate output demanded, with other things constant

aggregate demand curve A curve representing the relationship between the economy's price level and real GDP demanded per period, with other things constant

aggregate expenditure Total spending on final goods and services during a given period, usually a year

aggregate expenditure line A relationship showing, for a given price level, planned spending at each income, or real GDP; the total of $C + I + G + (X - M)$ at each income, or real GDP

aggregate income The sum of all income earned by resource suppliers in an economy during a given period

aggregate output A composite measure of all final goods and services produced in an economy during a given period; real GDP

aggregate supply curve A curve representing the relationship between the economy's price level and real GDP supplied per period, with other things constant

alternative goods Other goods that use some or all of the same resources as the good in question

annually balanced budget Budget philosophy prior to the Great Depression; aimed at matching annual revenues with outlays, except during times of war

applied research Research that seeks answers to particular questions or to apply scientific discoveries to develop specific products

arbitrageur Someone who takes advantage of temporary geographic differences in the exchange rate by simultaneously purchasing a currency in one market and selling it in another market

asset Anything of value that is owned

association-is-causation fallacy The incorrect idea that if two variables are associated in time, one must necessarily cause the other

asymmetric information A situation in which one side of the market has more reliable information than the other side

automatic stabilizers Structural features of government spending and taxation that reduce fluctuations in disposable income, and thus consumption, over the business cycle

autonomous A term that means "independent"; for example, autonomous investment is independent of income

B

balance of payments A record of all economic transactions between residents of one country and residents of the rest of the world during a given period

balance on current account The portion of a country's balance-of-payments account that measures that country's balance on goods and services plus its net unilateral transfers

balance on goods and services The portion of a country's balance-of-payments account that measures the value of a country's exports of goods and services minus the value of its imports of goods and services

balance sheet A financial statement that shows assets, liabilities, and net worth at a given point in time; all these are stock measures; because assets must equal liabilities plus net worth, the statement is in balance

bank branches A bank's additional offices that carry out banking operations

bank holding company A corporation that owns banks

bank notes Originally, papers promising a specific amount of gold or silver to anyone who presented them to issuing banks for redemption; today, Federal Reserve notes are mere paper money

barter The direct exchange of one good for another without using money

base year The year with which other years are compared when constructing an index; the index equals 100 in the base year

basic research The search for knowledge without regard to how that knowledge will be used

behavioral assumption An assumption that describes the expected behavior of economic decision makers, what motivates them

beneficial supply shocks Unexpected events that increase aggregate supply, sometimes only temporarily

benefits-received tax principle Those who receive more benefits from the government program funded by a tax should pay more taxes

budget resolution A congressional agreement about total outlays, spending by major category, and expected revenues; it guides spending and revenue decisions by the many congressional committees and subcommittees

C

capital The buildings, equipment, and human skill used to produce goods and services

capital account The record of a country's international transactions involving purchases or sales of financial and real assets

capital deepening An increase in the amount of capital per worker; one source of rising labor productivity

chain-weighted system An index that adjusts the weights from year to year in calculating a price index, thereby getting rid of much of the bias caused by a fixed-price weighting system

check A written order instructing the bank to pay someone from an amount deposited

checkable deposits Deposits in financial institutions against which checks can be written and ATM or debit cards can be applied

circular-flow model A diagram that outlines the flow of resources, products, income, and revenue among economic decision makers

classical economists A group of 18th- and 19th-century economists who believed that economic downturns were short-run phenomena that corrected themselves through natural market forces; thus, they believed the economy was self-correcting and needed no government intervention

coincident economic indicators Variables that reflect peaks and troughs as they occur; examples include employment, personal income, and industrial production

COLA Cost-of-living adjustment; the increase in a transfer payment or wage that reflects the increase in the price level

cold turkey The announcement and execution of tough measures to reduce high inflation

commercial banks Depository institutions that historically made short-term loans primarily to businesses

commodity money Anything that serves both as money and as a commodity; money that has intrinsic value

comparative advantage The ability to produce something at a lower opportunity cost than other producers face

complements Goods, such as milk and cookies, that are related in such a way that an increase in the price of one shifts the demand for the other leftward

consumer price index, or CPI A measure of inflation based on the cost of a fixed market basket of goods and services

consumption Household purchases of final goods and services, except for new residences, which count as investments

consumption function The relationship between consumption and income, other things constant

continuing resolutions Budget agreements that allow agencies, in the absence of an approved budget, to spend at the rate of the previous year's budget

contractionary fiscal policy A decrease in government purchases, increase in net taxes, or some combination of the two aimed at reducing aggregate demand enough to return the economy to potential output without worsening inflation; policy used to close an expansionary gap

contractionary gap The amount by which actual output in the short run falls short of the economy's potential output

convergence A theory predicting that the standard of living in economies around the world will grow more similar over time, with poorer countries eventually catching up with richer ones

coordination failure A situation in which workers and employers fail to achieve an outcome that all would prefer

corporation A legal entity owned by stockholders whose liability is limited to the value of their stock

cost-push inflation A sustained rise in the price level caused by a leftward shift of the aggregate supply curve

crowding in The potential for government spending to stimulate private investment in an otherwise dead economy

crowding out The displacement of interest-sensitive private investment that occurs when higher government deficits drive up interest rates

currency appreciation With respect to the dollar, a decrease in the number of dollars needed to purchase 1 unit of foreign exchange in a flexible rate system

currency depreciation With respect to the dollar, an increase in the number of dollars needed to purchase 1 unit of foreign exchange in a flexible rate system

currency devaluation An increase in the official pegged price of foreign exchange in terms of the domestic currency

currency revaluation A reduction in the official pegged price of foreign exchange in terms of the domestic currency

cyclical unemployment Unemployment that fluctuates with the business cycle, increasing during contractions and decreasing during expansions

cyclically balanced budget A budget philosophy calling for budget deficits during recessions to be financed by budget surpluses during expansions

D

debit card Cards that tap directly into the depositor's bank account to fund purchases; also called a check card, and usually doubles as an ATM card

decision-making lag The time needed to decide what to do once a macroeconomic problem has been identified

deflation A sustained decrease in the price level

demand A relation between the price of a good and the quantity that consumers are willing and able to buy during a given period, other things constant

demand curve A curve showing the relation between the price of a good and the quantity demanded during a given period, other things constant

demand for money The relationship between how much money people want to hold and the interest rate

demand-pull inflation A sustained rise in the price level caused by a rightward shift of the aggregate demand curve

demand-side economics Macroeconomic policy that focuses on shifting the aggregate demand curve as a way of promoting full employment and price stability

dependent variable A variable whose value depends on that of the independent variable

depository institutions Commercial banks and thrift institutions; financial institutions that accept deposits from the public

depreciation The value of capital stock used up to produce GDP or that becomes obsolete during a year

depression A sharp reduction in an economy's total output accompanied by high unemployment lasting more than a year; a severe economic contraction

developing countries Countries with a low living standard because of little human and physical capital per worker

discount rate The interest rate the Fed charges banks that borrow reserves

discouraged workers Those who drop out of the labor force in frustration because they can't find work

discretionary fiscal policy The deliberate manipulation of government purchases, taxation, and transfer payments to promote macroeconomic goals, such as full employment, price stability, and economic growth

disequilibrium The condition that exists in a market when the plans of buyers do not match those of sellers; a temporary mismatch between quantity supplied and quantity demanded as the market seeks equilibrium

disinflation A reduction in the rate of inflation

disposable income (DI) The income households have available to spend or to save after paying taxes and receiving transfer payments

division of labor Organizing production of a good into its separate tasks

double coincidence of wants Two traders are willing to exchange their products directly

double counting The mistake of including the value of intermediate goods plus the value of final goods in gross domestic product; counting the same good more than once

E

economic fluctuations The rise and fall of economic activity relative to the long-term growth trend of the economy; also called business cycles

economic growth An increase in the economy's ability to produce goods and services; an outward shift of the production possibilities frontier

economic system The set of mechanisms and institutions that resolve the what, how, and for whom questions

economic theory, or economic model A simplification of reality used to make predictions about cause and effect in the real world

economics The study of how people use their scarce resources to satisfy their unlimited wants

economy The structure of economic activity in a community, a region, a country, a group of countries, or the world

effectiveness lag The time needed for changes in monetary or fiscal policy to affect the economy

efficiency The condition that exists when there is no way resources can be reallocated to increase the production of one good without decreasing the production of another

electronic banking, or e-banking Conducting banking transactions over the Internet

Employment Act of 1946 Law that assigned to the federal government the responsibility for promoting full employment and price stability

entitlement programs Guaranteed benefits for those who qualify for government transfer programs such as Social Security and Medicare

entrepreneurial ability Managerial and organizational skills needed to start a firm, combined with the willingness to take risks

equation of exchange The quantity of money, *M,* multiplied by its velocity, *V,* equals nominal GDP, which is the product of the price level, *P,* and real GDP, *Y*

equilibrium The condition that exists in a market when the plans of buyers match those of sellers, so quantity demanded equals quantity supplied and the market clears

excess reserves Bank reserves exceeding required reserves

exchange rate The price measured in one country's currency of purchasing 1 unit of another country's currency

expansion A phase of economic activity during which the economy's output increases

expansionary fiscal policy An increase in government purchases, decrease in net taxes, or some combination of the two aimed at increasing aggregate demand enough to return the economy to its potential output thereby reducing unemployment; policy used to close a contractionary gap

expansionary gap The amount by which output in the short run exceeds the economy's potential output

expenditure approach to GDP A method of calculating GDP by adding spending on all final goods and services produced in the nation during the year

externality A cost or a benefit that falls on a third party and is therefore ignored by the two parties to the market transaction

F

fallacy of composition The incorrect belief that what is true for the individual, or part, must necessarily be true for the group, or whole

federal budget A plan for federal government outlays and revenues for a specific period, usually a year

federal budget deficit A flow variable that measures the amount by which federal government outlays exceed federal government revenues in a particular period, usually a year

federal funds market A market for overnight lending and borrowing of reserves among banks; the market for reserves on account at the Fed

federal funds rate The interest rate charged in the federal funds market; the interest rate banks charge one another for overnight borrowing; the Fed's target interest rate

Federal Open Market Committee (FOMC) The 12-member group that makes decisions about open-market operations—purchases and sales of U.S. government securities by the Fed that affect the money supply and interest rates; consists of the 7 Board governors plus 5 of the 12 presidents of the reserve banks

Federal Reserve System, or the Fed The central bank and monetary authority of the United States

fiat money Money not redeemable for any commodity; its status as money is conferred initially by the government but eventually by common experience

final goods and services Goods and services sold to final, or end, users

financial intermediaries Institutions that serve as go-betweens, accepting funds from savers and lending them to borrowers

financial markets Banks and other financial institutions that facilitate the flow of funds from savers to borrowers

firms Economic units formed by profit-seeking entrepreneurs who use resources to produce goods and services for sale

fiscal policy The use of government purchases, transfer payments, taxes, and borrowing to influence economy-wide activity such as inflation, employment, and economic growth

fixed exchange rate Rate of exchange between currencies pegged within a narrow range and maintained by the central bank's ongoing purchases and sales of currencies

flexible exchange rate Rate determined by the forces of demand and supply without government intervention

flow variable A variable that measures something over an interval of time, such as your income per week

foreign exchange Foreign money needed to carry out international transactions

fractional reserve banking system Only a portion of bank deposits is backed by reserves

frictional unemployment Unemployment that occurs because job seekers and employers need time to find each other

full employment Employment level when there is no cyclical unemployment

functional finance A budget philosophy using fiscal policy to achieve the economy's potential GDP, rather than balancing budgets either annually or over the business cycle

G

GDP price index A comprehensive price index of all goods and services included in the gross domestic product

gold standard An arrangement whereby the currencies of most countries are convertible into gold at a fixed rate

good A tangible item used to satisfy human wants

government debt A stock variable that measures the net accumulation of annual budget deficits

government purchase function The relationship between government purchases and the economy's income, other things constant

government purchases Spending for goods and services by all levels of government; government outlays minus transfer payments

graph A picture showing how variables relate in two-dimensional space; one variable is measured along the horizontal axis and the other along the vertical axis

Gresham's Law People tend to trade away inferior money and hoard the best

gross domestic product (GDP) The market value of all final goods and services produced in the nation during a particular period, usually a year

H

horizontal axis Line on a graph that begins at the origin and goes to the right and left; sometimes called the x axis

hyperinflation A very high rate of inflation

hypothesis A theory about relationships among key variables

hysteresis The theory that the natural rate of unemployment depends in part on the recent history of unemployment; high unemployment rates increase the natural rate of unemployment

I

implementation lag The time needed to introduce a change in monetary or fiscal policy

income approach to GDP A method of calculating GDP by adding all payments for resources used to produce output in the nation during the year

income effect of a price change A fall in the price of a good increases consumers' real income, making consumers more able to purchase goods; for a normal good, the quantity demanded increases

income-expenditure model A relationship between aggregate income and aggregate spending that determines, for a given price level, where the amount people plan to spend equals the amount produced

independent variable A variable whose value determines that of the dependent variable

individual demand The demand of an individual consumer

individual supply The supply of an individual producer

industrial market countries Economically advanced capitalist countries of Western Europe, North America, Australia, New Zealand, and Japan, plus the newly industrized Asian economies of Taiwan, South Korea, Hong Kong, and Singapore

industrial policy The view that government—using taxes, subsidies, and regulations—should nurture the industries and technologies of the future, thereby giving these domestic industries an advantage over foreign competition

Industrial Revolution Development of large-scale factory production that began in Great Britain around 1750 and spread to the rest of Europe, North America, and Australia

inferior good A good, such as used clothes, for which demand decreases, or shifts leftward, as consumer incomes rise

inflation An increase in the economy's average price level

inflation target Central bankers commit not to exceed a certain inflation rate for the next year or two

Information Revolution Technological change spawned by the invention of the microchip and the Internet that enhanced the acquisition, analysis, and transmission of information

injection Any spending other than by households or any income other than from resource earnings; includes investment, government purchases, exports, and transfer payments

interest Payment to resource owners for the use of their capital; the dollar amount paid by borrowers to lenders

interest rate Interest per year as a percentage of the amount loaned

intermediate goods and services Goods and services purchased by firms for further reprocessing and resale

International Monetary Fund (IMF) An international organization that establishes rules for maintaining the international monetary system and makes loans to countries with temporary balance-of-payments problems

inventories Producers' stocks of finished and in-process goods

investment The purchase of new plants, new equipment, new buildings, and new residences, plus net additions to inventories

investment function The relationship between the amount businesses plan to invest and the economy's income, other things constant

L

labor The physical and mental effort used to produce goods and services

labor force Those 16 years of age and older who are either working or looking for work

labor force participation rate The labor force as a percentage of the adult population

labor productivity Output per unit of labor; measured as real GDP divided by the hours of labor employed to produce that output

lagging economic indicators Variables that follow, or trail, changes in overall economic activity; examples include the interest rate and the average duration of unemployment

law of comparative advantage The individual, firm, region, or country with the lowest opportunity cost of producing a particular good should specialize in that good

law of demand The quantity of a good demanded during a given period relates inversely to its price, other things constant

law of increasing opportunity cost To produce each additional increment of a good, a successively larger increment of an alternative good must be sacrificed if the economy's resources are already being used efficiently

law of supply The quantity of a good supplied during a given period is usually directly related to its price, other things constant

leading economic indicators Variables that predict, or *lead to,* a recession or recovery; examples include consumer confidence, stock market prices, business investment, and big-ticket purchases, such as automobiles and homes

leakage Any diversion of income from the domestic spending stream; includes saving, taxes, and imports

legal tender U.S. currency that constitutes a valid and legal offer of payment of debt

liability Anything that is owed to another individual or institution

life-cycle model of consumption and saving Young people borrow, middle agers pay off debts and save, and older people draw down their savings; on average net savings over a lifetime is small

liquidity A measure of the ease with which an asset can be converted into money without a significant loss of value

long run In macroeconomics, a period during which wage contracts and resource price agreements can be renegotiated; there are no surprises about the economy's actual price level

long-run aggregate supply (LRAS) curve A vertical line at the economy's potential output; aggregate supply when there are no surprises about the price level and all resource contracts can be renegotiated

long-run equilibrium The price level and real GDP that occurs when (1) the actual price level equals the expected price level, (2) real GDP supplied equals potential output, and (3) real GDP supplied equals real GDP demanded

long-run Phillips curve A vertical line drawn at the economy's natural rate of unemployment that traces equilibrium points that can occur when workers and employers have the time to adjust fully to any unexpected change in aggregate demand

M

M1 The narrowest measure of the money supply, consisting of currency and coins held by the nonbanking public, checkable deposits, and traveler's checks

M2 A money aggregate consisting of M1 plus savings deposits, small-denomination time deposits, and money market mutual funds

M3 A money aggregate consisting of M2 plus large-denomination time deposits

macroeconomics The study of the economic behavior of entire economies

managed float system An exchange rate system that combines features of freely floating rates with sporadic intervention by central banks

marginal Incremental, additional, or extra; used to describe a change in an economic variable

marginal propensity to consume (MPC) The fraction of a change in income that is spent on consumption; the change in consumption divided by the change in income that caused it

marginal propensity to save (MPS) The fraction of a change in income that is saved; the change in saving divided by the change in income that caused it

marginal tax rate The percentage of each additional dollar of income that goes to the tax

market A set of arrangements through which buyers and sellers carry out exchange at mutually agreeable terms

market demand Sum of the individual demands of all consumers in the market

market failure A condition that arises when the unregulated operation of markets yields socially undesirable results

market supply The sum of individual supplies of all producers in the market

medium of exchange Anything that facilitates trade by being generally accepted by all parties in payment for goods or services

mercantilism The incorrect theory that a nation's economic goal should be to accumulate precious metals in the public treasury; this theory prompted trade barriers to reduce imports, but other countries retaliated, reducing trade and the gains from specialization

merchandise trade balance The value of a country's exported goods minus the value of its imported goods during a given period

microeconomics The study of the economic behavior in particular markets, such as that for computers or unskilled labor

mixed system An economic system characterized by the private ownership of some resources and the public ownership of other resources; some markets are unregulated and others are regulated

monetary policy Regulation of the money supply to influence economy-wide activity such as inflation, employment, and economic growth

money Anything that is generally accepted in exchange for goods and services

money aggregates Measures of the economy's money supply

money income The number of dollars a person receives per period, such as $400 per week

money market mutual fund A collection of short-term interest-earning assets purchased with funds collected from many shareholders

money multiplier The multiple by which the money supply increases as a result of an increase in fresh reserves in the banking system

monopoly A sole producer of a product for which there are no close substitutes

movement along a demand curve Change in quantity demanded resulting from a change in the price of the good, other things constant

movement along a supply curve Change in quantity supplied resulting from a change in the price of the good, other things constant

N

national debt The net accumulation of federal budget deficits

national income All income earned by American-owned resources, whether located in the United States or abroad

natural monopoly One firm that can serve the entire market at a lower per-unit cost than can two or more firms

natural rate hypothesis The natural rate of unemployment is largely independent of the stimulus provided by monetary or fiscal policy

natural rate of unemployment The unemployment rate when the economy produces its potential output

natural resources So-called gifts of nature used to produce goods and services; includes renewable and exhaustible resources

negative, or inverse, relation Occurs when two variables move in opposite directions; when one increases, the other decreases

net domestic product Gross domestic product minus depreciation

net export function The relationship between net exports and the economy's income, other things constant

net exports The value of a country's exports minus the value of its imports

net taxes (NT) Taxes minus transfer payments

net unilateral transfers The unilateral transfers (gifts and grants) received from abroad by residents of a country minus the unilateral transfers sent abroad

net wealth The value of a assets minus liabilities

net worth Assets minus liabilities

nominal GDP GDP based on prices prevailing at the time of the transaction; current-dollar GDP

nominal interest rate The interest rate expressed in current dollars as a percentage of the amount loaned; the interest rate on the loan agreement

nominal wage The wage measured in current dollars; the dollar amount on a paycheck

normal good A good, such as new clothes, for which demand increases, or shifts rightward, as consumer incomes rise

normative economic statement A statement that represents an opinion, which cannot be proved or disproved

O

open-market operations Purchases and sales of government securities by the Federal Reserve in an effort to influence the money supply

open-market purchase The purchase of U.S. government bonds by the Fed to increase the money supply

open-market sale The sale of U.S. government bonds by the Fed to reduce the money supply

opportunity cost The value of the best alternative forgone when an item or activity is chosen

origin On a graph depicting two-dimensional space, the zero point; the point of departure

other-things-constant assumption The assumption, when focusing on the relation among key economic variables, that other variables remain unchanged

P

partnership A firm with multiple owners who share the firm's profits and bear unlimited liability for the firm's debts

permanent income Income that individuals expect to receive on average over the long term

per-worker production function The relationship between the amount of capital per worker in the economy and average output per worker

personal income The amount of before-tax income received by households; national income less income earned but not received plus income received but not earned

Phillips curve A curve showing possible combinations of the inflation rate and the unemployment rate

physical capital Manufactured items used to produce goods and services; includes new plants and new equipment

planned investment The amount of investment that firms plan to undertake during a year

political business cycles Economic fluctuations that result when discretionary policy is manipulated for political gain

positive economic statement A statement that can be proved or disproved by reference to facts

positive, or direct, relation Occurs when two variables increase or decrease together; the two variables move in the same direction

potential output The economy's maximum sustainable output, given the supply of resources, technology, and production incentives; the output level when there are no surprises about the price level

price ceiling A maximum legal price above which a good or service cannot be sold; to have an impact, a price ceiling must be set below the equilibrium price

price floor A minimum legal price below which a good or service cannot be sold; to have an impact, a price floor must be set above the equilibrium price

price index A number that shows the average price of goods; changes in a price index over time show changes in the economy's average price level

price level A composite measure reflecting the prices of all goods and services in the economy relative to prices in a base year

private good A good that is both rival in consumption and exclusive, such as pizza

private property rights An owner's right to use, rent, or sell resources or property

product market A market in which a good or service is bought and sold

production possibilities frontier (PPF) A curve showing alternative combinations of goods that can be produced when available resources are used fully and efficiently; a boundary between inefficient and unattainable combinations

productivity The ratio of a specific measure of output, such as real GDP, to a specific measure of input, such as labor; in this case productivity measures real GDP per hour of labor

profit The reward for entrepreneurial ability; the revenue from sales minus the cost of resources used by the entrepreneur

progressive taxation The tax as a percentage of income increases as income increases

proportional taxation The tax as a percentage of income remains constant as income increases; also called a flat tax

public good A good that, once produced, is available for all to consume, regardless of who pays and who doesn't; such a good is nonrival and nonexclusive, such as national defense

purchasing power parity (PPP) theory The idea that the exchange rate between two countries will adjust in the long run to reflect price-level differences between the countries

pure capitalism An economic system characterized by the private ownership of resources and the use of prices to coordinate economic activity in unregulated markets

pure command system An economic system characterized by the public ownership of resources and centralized planning

Q

quantity demanded The amount demanded at a particular price, as reflected by a point on a given demand curve

quantity supplied The amount offered for sale at a particular price, as reflected by a point on a given supply curve

quantity theory of money If the velocity of money is stable, or at least predictable, changes in the money supply have predictable effects on nominal GDP

quota A legal limit on the quantity of a particular product that can be imported or exported

R

rational expectations A school of thought that argues people form expectations based on all available information, including the likely future actions of government policy makers

real GDP per capita Real GDP divided by the population; the best measure of an economy's standard of living

real gross domestic product (real GDP) The economy's aggregate output measured in dollars of constant purchasing power

real income Income measured in terms of the goods and services it can buy

real interest rate The interest rate expressed in dollars of constant purchasing power as a percentage of the amount loaned; the nominal interest rate minus the inflation rate

real wage The wage measured in dollars of constant purchasing power; the wage measured in terms of the quantity of goods and services it will buy

recession A decline in the economy's total output lasting at least two consecutive quarters, or six months; an economic contraction

recognition lag The time needed to identify a macroeconomic problem and assess its seriousness

regressive taxation The tax as a percentage of income decreases as income increases

relevant resources Resources used to produce the good in question

rent Payment to resource owners for the use of their natural resources

representative money Bank notes that exchange for a specific commodity, such as gold

required reserve ratio The ratio of reserves to deposits that banks are obligated by regulation to hold

required reserves The dollar amount of reserves a bank is obligated by regulation to hold

reserves Funds that banks use to satisfy the cash demands of their customers and the reserve requirements of the Fed; reserves consist of cash held by banks plus deposits at the Fed

residential construction Building new homes or dwelling places

resource market A market in which a resource is bought and sold

resources The inputs, or factors of production, used to produce the goods and services that people want; resources consist of labor, capital, natural resources, and entrepreneurial ability

rules of the game The formal and informal institutions that promote economic activity; the laws, customs, conventions, and other institutional elements that determine transaction costs and thereby affect people's incentive to undertake production and exchange

S

saving function The relationship between saving and income, other things constant

savings deposits Deposits that earn interest but have no specific maturity date

scarcity Occurs when the amount people desire exceeds the amount available at a zero price

seasonal unemployment Unemployment caused by seasonal changes in the demand for certain kinds of labor

secondary effects Unintended consequences of economic actions that may develop slowly over time as people react to events

seigniorage The difference between the face value of money and the cost of supplying it; the "profit" from issuing money

service An activity used to satisfy human wants

shift of a demand curve Movement of a demand curve right or left resulting from a change in one of the determinants of demand other than the price of the good

shift of a supply curve Movement of a supply curve left or right resulting from a change in one of the determinants of supply other than the price of the good

short run In macroeconomics, a period during which some resource prices, especially those for labor, are fixed by explicit or implicit agreements

shortage At a given price, the amount by which quantity demanded exceeds quantity supplied; a shortage usually forces the price up

short-run aggregate supply (SRAS) curve A curve that shows a direct relationship between the price level and real GDP supplied in the short run, other things constant

short-run equilibrium The price level and real GDP that occur when the aggregate demand curve intersects the short-run aggregate supply curve

short-run Phillips curve Based on an expected inflation rate, a curve that reflects an inverse relationship between the inflation rate and the unemployment rate

simple money multiplier The reciprocal of the required reserve ratio, or $1/r$; the maximum multiple of fresh reserves by which the money supply can increase

simple spending multiplier The ratio of a change in real GDP demanded to the initial change in spending that brought it about; the numerical value of the simple spending multiplier is $1/(1 - MPC)$; called "simple" because only consumption varies with income

simple tax multiplier The ratio of a change in real GDP demanded to the initial change in autonomous net taxes that brought it about; the numerical value of the simple tax multiplier is $-MPC/(1 - MPC)$

slope of a line A measure of how much the vertical variable changes for a given increase in the horizontal variable; the vertical change between two points divided by the horizontal increase

sole proprietorship A firm with a single owner who has the right to all profits and who bears unlimited liability for the firm's debts

specialization of labor Focusing work effort on a particular product or a single task

speculator Someone who buys or sells foreign exchange in hopes of profiting from fluctuations in the exchange rate over time

stagflation A contraction, or *stag*nation, of a nation's output accompanied by in*flation* in the price level

stock variable A variable that measures something at a particular point in time, such as the amount of money you have with you right now

store of value Anything that retains its purchasing power over time

structural unemployment Unemployment because (1) the skills in demand do not match those of the unemployed, or (2) the unemployed do not live where the jobs are

substitutes Goods, such as Coke and Pepsi, that are related in such a way that an increase in the price of one shifts the demand for the other rightward

substitution effect of a price change When the price of a good falls, consumers substitute that good for other goods, which become relatively more expensive

sunk cost A cost that has already been incurred in the past, cannot be recovered, and thus is irrelevant for present and future economic decisions

supply A relation between the price of a good and the quantity that producers are willing and able to sell during a given period, other things constant

supply curve A curve showing the relation between price of a good and the quantity supplied during a given period, other things constant

supply shocks Unexpected events that affect aggregate supply, sometimes only temporarily

supply-side economics Macroeconomic policy that focuses on a rightward shift of the aggregate supply curve through tax cuts or other changes that increase production incentives

surplus At a given price, the amount by which quantity supplied exceeds quantity demanded; a surplus usually forces the price down

T

tangent A straight line that touches a curve at a point but does not cut or cross the curve; used to measure the slope of a curve at a point

tariff A tax on imports

tastes Consumer preferences; likes and dislikes in consumption; assumed to be constant along a given demand curve

tax incidence The distribution of tax burden among taxpayers; who ultimately pays the tax

thrift institutions, or thrifts Savings banks and credit unions; depository institutions that historically lent money to households

time deposits Deposits that earn a fixed rate of interest if held for the specified period, which can range from several months to several years; also called certificates of deposit

time-inconsistency problem When policy makers have an incentive to announce one policy to influence expectations but then pursue a different policy once those expectations have been formed and acted on

token money Money whose face value exceeds its cost of production

transaction costs The costs of time and information required to carry out market exchange

transfer payments Cash or in-kind benefits given to individuals as outright grants from the government

U

underemployment Workers are overqualified for their jobs or work fewer hours than they would prefer

underground economy Market exchange that goes unreported either because it is illegal or because those involved want to evade taxes

unemployment benefits Cash transfers for those who lose their jobs and actively seek employment

unemployment rate The number unemployed as a percentage of the labor force

unit of account A common unit for measuring the value of each good or service

utility The satisfaction or sense of well-being received from consumption

V

value added The difference at each stage of production between the selling price of a product and the cost of intermediate goods purchased from other firms

variable A measure, such as price or quantity, that can take on different values

velocity of money The average number of times per year each dollar is used to purchase final goods and services

vertical axis Line on a graph that begins at the origin and goes up and down; sometimes called the y axis

W

wages Payment to resource owners for their labor

A

Abadie, Albert, 115
ability to purchase, 65
ability to produce, 70
ability-to-pay tax principle, 57
absolute advantage, 31–32
Accenture database, 53
account units, money as, 263
accounts
    capital, 372
    checking, 266
    fractional reserve banking systems, 266
active policy approaches
    criticisms of, 338
    for closing gaps, 326–328
    implementation time lags, 329–330
    problems associated with, 328–329
    underlying assumptions, 331–332
actual investment, 198, 200
adult population, defined, 155
advantage
    absolute, 31–32
    comparative, 31, 32
adverse supply shocks, 234–235
advertising costs, 64
age, impact on unemployment rate, 156
agencies, federal, 56
aggregate consumption, 177
aggregate demand, 96
    aggregate demand curve, 97–98, 198
        during the Great Depression, 99–100
        equilibrium with supply curve, 98
        and Keynesian economics, 100–101
        increase in, 334
        and long-run equilibrium, 227
        and price level changes, 198–199, 207–209
        and stagflation, 102
        and supply-side economics, 103
    and aggregate expenditure, 134, 209–211
    and discretionary fiscal policies
        natural rate of unemployment, 250–251
        time lags, 250
    demand-side equilibrium calculating, 258

and proportional income taxes, 258–259
    and variable net exports, 259
efforts to boost, 328
and fiscal policy
    contractionary policies, 246
    expansionary policies, 244–245
and money policy
    long-run effects, 314
    short-run effects, 309–310
    and natural rate hypothesis, 343
    and stagflation, 249
    and short-run Phillips curves, 341
aggregate expenditure, 134
    and aggregate demand, 134, 209–211
    aggregate expenditure line, 201
    and aggregate income, 138
    autonomous spending changes, 216–217
    calculating, 134, 137
    components, 191–192
    consumption, 177, 179, 181–184
    government outlays and purchases, 189–190, 200
    household consumption and saving, 199
    investment
        factors that affect, 187
        investment demand curve, 186–187
        microeconomic perspective, 184
        planned investment, 187–188
    net exports, 200, 215–216
        and disposable income, 196
        net export function, 191
        net income function, 190, 196
        nonincome determinants, 191
    planned, 200–201
    unplanned inventory adjustments, 200
aggregate income
    defined, 134
    and disposable income, 135
    in GDP calculations, 135, 137
    relationship to aggregate expenditure, 138
aggregate output
    and aggregate supply, 221
    and price levels, 96
aggregate spending
    in GDP calculations, 137
    and national income calculations, 152

aggregate supply
    aggregate supply curve, 98
        during the Great Depression, 99–100
        under Keynesian economics, 100–101
        impact on spending multiplier, 259
        and stagflation, 102
    debates about, 220
    and discretionary fiscal policies
        tax cuts, 252
        time lags, 251
    and excess output, 223, 225–227
    and fiscal policy
        contractionary policies, 246
        expansionary policies, 244–245
        supply-side policies, 103, 252–253
    and money policy, 310–312, 314–315
    labor supplies, 221–222
    and lower-than-expected output, 227–229
    Phillips curves, 341, 343
    and price level changes, 222–224
    and resource changes
        beneficial supply shocks, 233–234
        capital stock, 233
        institutional changes, 233
        labor supplies, 232
        resource decreases, 234–235
    short-run, 221
agricultural economies, households, 47
air
    clean, scarcity of, 4
    as renewable resource, 3
Airline Deregulation Act (1978), 323
airline industry, and 9-11 terrorist attacks, 206–207
allocation of goods and services, decisions about, 39
alternative goods, defined, 72–73
American Federation of Labor (AFL), 270
amusement parks, price discrimination, 211
analysis, economic
    approaches
        assumptions, 6
        marginal analysis, 23
        scientific method, 8–10

law of comparative advantage, 31–32
marginal analysis, 7–10, 23
opportunity cost calculations
    attending college example, 28–29
    effect of circumstances, 30
    information constraints, 30
    subjectivity of, 29–30
    time constraints, 30
PPF (production possibilities frontier), 34–35
    and increased capital stock, 37
    and increased resources, 36–37
    and opportunity costs, 35–36
    and technological innovation, 37
    importance of as model, 37–38
    predicting behavior, 12
    sunk cost calculations, 30
annual earnings, 3
annually balanced budgets, 353
anticipated inflation, 167, 171–172
antitrust laws, policies, 54
applied research, 123
appreciation of currency, 374
arbitrageurs, 377
Argentina, money supply and inflation, 318
Asia
    and currency speculation, 382–383
    evidence of convergence, 125–126
    standards of living, 115
assertions, positive versus normative, 10
assets, of banks, 290–291
association-is-causation fallacy, 12
assumptions, economic
    behavioral, 9
    other-things-constant, 9
    rational self-interest, 6
asymmetric information, 289–290
Australia
    inflation, 337
    national debt, 361
auto industry and international trade (case study), 60–61
automatic stabilizers
    income taxes, 248–249
    taxes, 241
    unemployment insurance, 249
    welfare transfer payments, 249
autonomous components, 199
autonomous consumption, 218

autonomous economic activities, 187
autonomous spending, 218
average behavior, 12
axes (graph), 20

B

baht (Thai currency), speculation in, 382–383
balance of payments
balance on current account, 372
balance on goods and services, 371
defined, 59–60
double-entry bookkeeping for, 369
as flow variable, 369
foreign exchange, 373
merchandise trade balance, 369–370
statistical discrepancy account, 372–373
balance sheets, banks, 290–291
balanced budgets
balanced budget multiplier, 258
balancing options, 353
as goal of fiscal policy, 247
versus federal debt, 254
balances, trade
current account, 372
defined, 59
foreign exchange, 373
Bank of America, 277
Bank of Internet USA, 297
Bank of Japan, 280
Banking Acts of 1933 and 1935, 272, 273
banking system, banks. See also money
assets of, limiting, 274
balance sheets
assets, 290–291
liabilities, 290
liquidity versus profitability, 291–292
reserve accounts, 291
banking structure, 277
branches, 277
central bank independence, 336–337
charters, 290
checking accounts, checks, 266
commercial, 269
depository institutions, 269
and deregulation, 274–275
failures, 270–272, 274, 276–277
Federal Deposit Insurance Corporation (FDIC), 273
Federal Reserve System
Board of Governors, 272
Federal Advisory Committee, 272
Federal Open Market Committee, 272

Federal Reserve notes, 300
and the Great Depression, 271–272
objectives, 274
powers, 270–271
financial intermediary role, 283, 289
fractional reserve system, 266
holding companies, 277
and inflation, 274
inter-account transfers, 287
Internet banking, 297–298
Japanese banking system, 280
loans by
asymmetric information, 289–290
loanable funds, 288
mergers, 277
money contraction process, 296–297
money creation process, 292–296
money market mutual funds, 274
money supplies, 285, 287–288
national banks, 270
notes, 266
origin of, 265
reserves, 270
impact on money supply, 300
required reserves, 291
savings, 275–276
shares, 290
sources of profit, 289
state banks, 269
thrift institutions, 269
Barro, Robert, 363
barter, 32, 262
base year
price indexes, 142
price level, 97
basic research, 123–124
BEA (Bureau of Economic Analysis), GDP price estimates, 144–145
behavior, economic
assumptions about, 9
average, predicting, 12
Belgium, unemployment rates, 235
beneficial supply shocks, 233
benefits, in marginal analyses, 7
benefits, unemployment, 162
benefits-received tax principle, 57
Bewley, Truman, 232
biennial budgeting, 351–352
black workers, unemployment rates, 153
Board of Governors (Federal Reserve System), 272
Bolivia
hyperinflation, cold turkey remedies, 336
money supply and inflation, 318

bonds, 274
for excess reserves, 291
non-liquidity, 307
as payment for national debt, 361
purchase and sale of by Federal Reserve
and federal deficits, 355
impacts on money supply, 292, 296–297, 299
versus capital investment, 133
bookkeeping, double-entry, 132, 369
borrowing
capital, 284
in circular-flow model, 137
government
impact on interest rates, 363
impact on future generations, 362–363
and national debt, 359, 361
loanable funds market, 288
loans
and asymmetric information, 289–290
role of banks, 289
risky borrowers, 289
branches, bank, 277
Brazil, hyperinflation, 164, 267–269
Bretton Woods agreement, 381–382
budgets
balanced, as goal of fiscal policy, 247
defined, 348
federal, 349
annually balanced budgets, 353
budget philosophies, 353
budget process, 350–352
cyclically balanced budgets, 353
deficit, 101
outlays, 349
reforming entitlement programs, 357–358
budget deficits
defined, 348
economic stimulation using, 249
federal, 101
history, 353–354
impact on currency values, 355
impact on interest rates, 355
and national debt, 359
as percentage of GDP, 249
persistence, 354
rationale, 352–353
relationship to trade deficits, 383
and supply-side economics, 103
versus balanced budgets, 254

budget resolution, 350
budget surpluses
economic impacts, 364–365
reasons for, 356–357
reversal of, 357
buildings as physical capital, 2
Bundesbank, efforts to control value of the mark, 382
Bureau of Economic Analysis (U.S. Commerce Department), 139–140
GDP price estimates, 144–145
Bureau of Labor Statistics, 139–140
unemployment rate calculations, 155
bureaucracies, bureaus, federal, 56
Bush, George H. W. administration, 103, 253
economic policies, 356
and inflation, 171
public policy approaches, 331–332
Bush, George W. administration, 103, 241, 328, 330, 333
economic policies, 253–254
public policy approaches, 332
business expectations, impact on planned investment, 188
business practices, unfair, 54
business structures, 50
buyers' markets, 4

C

Canada
government outlays, 56
output per capita, 120–121
capital
in circular-flow model, 5
defined, 2
households as source of, 4
human capital, 3, 113
impact on production, 37
interest on, 3
investments, 112
labor, 113, 117–118
law of diminishing returns from capital, 113
physical capital, 2, 133
quality of, and productivity, 114–115
as substitute for labor, 152
and technological changes, 114
capital accounts (international trade), 372–374
capital budgets, 352
capital deepening, 113
capital expenditures, federal, 351
capital gains, 51
capital goods, PPF (production possibilities frontier), 35
and increased capital stock, 37
and increased resources, 36–37

and opportunity costs, 35–36
and technological innovation, 37
capital stock
  aggregate supplies, 233
  increased availability of, 37
capitalism
  modified, 40
  pure, 39–40
capture theory of regulation, 322
Cardoso, Fernando Henrique, 164
careers
  economists, 13–14
  and specialization of labor, 33–34
Carter, Jimmy, and inflation, 171
case studies, 11
  banks, Japanese banking problems, 280
  college major and career earnings, 13–14
  consumer spending and recession in Japan, 211
  consumption life-cycle model, 183–184
  demand and supply, National Basketball Association example, 80
  discretionary fiscal policy, political considerations, 253
  disequilibrium in the toy business, 83
  economic cycles, and global linkages, 94
  economic growth, industrial policy, 126
  the electronic cottage and household production, 53
  exchange rates, Big Mac price index, 378–379
  federal budgets, reforming entitlement programs, 357–358
  foreign exchange, regional impacts of currency speculation, 382–383
  free medical care, marginal value, 127–128
  GDP (gross domestic product) calculations, computer prices, 382–383
  GDP, consumption and investment, 188–189
  income and price inelasticity in agricultural markets, 105–106
  inflation
    Brazil hyperinflation example, 164
    and central bank independence, 336–337
    international trade, auto industry example, 60–61
  money supply
    Brazil hyperinflation example, 268–269

counterfeit money, 286–287
  and global inflation, 318
  Internet banking, 297–298
opportunity cost of attending college, 28–29
output gaps and wage flexibility, 231–232
productivity, and computers, 119
real GDP and price levels, 104–105
specialization of labor, 33–34
spending multiplier effect, airline industry example, 206–207
unemployment, McDowell County, WV example, 159–160
unemployment levels and hysteresis, 235–236
vending machines in Japan, 11–12
cash transfers, 49
  unemployment benefits, 162
cash. See money
cattle, as money, 263
causal relationships, 21
CDs (certificates of deposit), 287
ceilings, price, 81–82
Census Bureau, U.S. economic statistics, 139–140
Central Bank of Iraq, 337
central banks
  exchange rates, 378
  intervention in international trade, 382
centrally planned economic systems, 40–41
certificates of deposit (CDs), 287
ceteris paribus (other-things-constant) assumption, 9
chain-weighted index system, 144
chain-weighted price estimates, 144–146
change, technological, and unemployment, 123
charities, international spending by, 371–372
charters for banks, 290
checkable deposits, 285
checking accounts, checks, 266
China
  market for automobiles, 61
  national economy, 91
  per-capita production, 41
  restrictions on money exports, 372
  U.S. trade deficits with, 370
chip technology, impact on production, 53
choice
  economic, 2
    comparative versus absolute advantage, 31–32

costs and benefits, 37
  and scarcity on, 2
  individual, time allocation, 262
  law of comparative advantage, 32
  opportunity costs, calculating, 28–30
  primary versus secondary effects, 13
  and scarcity of goods and services, 3
  and specialization of labor, 33–34
  sunk cost calculations, 30
  marginal, 7
  rational, 6–7
circular-flow model, 132
  aggregate demand curve, 199
  aggregate expenditures, 199–200
  assumptions, 199
  defined, 4
  expenditure component, 137
  flow variables, 91
  households and firms in, 4
  income component, 135, 137
  injections and leakages, 138
  money, 5
  in national economies, 91
  planned spending, 205–209
circumstances and opportunity cost calculations, 30
Citigroup, Citibank, 278
  online banking, 298
classical economics, laissez-faire policies, 247
Clayton Act (1914), 270, 325
Clean Air Act, 368–369
Clinton, William, administration, 103, 253, 330
  economic policies, 254
  and inflation, 171
  public policy approaches, 332
clustering, 126
coal industry
  coal as exhaustible resource, 3
  unemployment rates, 159–160
coercion in political markets, 56
coincident economic indicators, 96
coins, 264–265
COLA (cost-of-living adjustment), 172
cold turkey monetary policies, 336
collaboration, and chip technology on, 53
college
  drop-outs, famous, 29
  impact on career earnings, 13–14
  opportunity costs, 28–29
collusion, 54

command systems
  modified, 41
  pure, 40–41
  versus market systems, 41
command-and-control environmental regulations, 368
commercial banks, 269
  failures among, 276–277
commodities
  measuring value of, units of account, 263
  and representative money, 266
commodity money, 263–264
communism, 40–41
comparative advantage
  defined, 31–32
  and the development of the firm, 49
  and efficient resource use, 32
  and market exchange, 301
  and need for money, 32
  versus absolute advantage, 31–32
compensation, unemployment, 162
competition
  and bank failures, 274
  promoting, government role, 54
competitive markets. See markets
complements, defined, 69
computers
  impact on productivity growth, 119
  prices for, 145–146
  and virtual offices, 53
conglomerate mergers, 328
Congress, role in budget process, 350–352
consensus expectations, 222
consequences, unintended, 13
conserving resources, 12
constant long-run average cost, 153
constraints, opportunity cost calculations
  availability of information, 30
  availability of time, 30
  specific circumstances, 30
construction, residential, 133
construction workers, unemployment rates, 157
consumer goods, PPF (production possibilities frontier), 35–37
consumer price index (CPI), 142
  biases and limitations, 143–144
  calculating, 142–143
  cost-of-living adjustments, 172
  and inflation, 164, 166–167
consumer surplus, 124, 185–187
  free medical care example, 127–128
  market demand curves, 125–126
  monopolies, 206–207
  perfectly competitive markets, 206

perfectly discriminating monopolists, 211–212
consumers
  demand, demand curves, 65–69, 306–307
  spending by, and discretionary fiscal policies, 251
  targeting, 217
  tastes, changes in, 70
consumption
  autonomous versus induced, 218
  defined, 133
  in GDP calculations, 137
  government, 133
  and income
    aggregate measures, 177
    disposable income, 199
  life-cycle model, 183–184
  marginal propensity to consume (MPC), 179–180
  marginal propensity to save (MPS), 179, 181
  nonincome determinants, 181–183
  private versus public goods, 54
  per capita, in poorest economies, 125
  personal expenditures, 133
  versus investment, historic trends, 188–189
consumption function, 179–180
continuing resolutions, 350
contraction of money supply, 196–297
contractionary fiscal policy, 246
contractionary gap, 227–229
  closing
    active versus passive policy approaches, 326–328
    and fiscal policy, 244–245, 249
  impact on wages, 229, 231–232
contract enforcement, government role, 54
convergence theory, 125–126
coordination failure, 231
corporations
  defined, 50
  dividends and retained earnings, 51
  overview, 50
  percent of U.S. business sales, 51
  power of large, 329
  profits
    as deferred personal income, 150
    in national income calculations, 151
  S corporations, 51
  taxes, 57
  versus government bureaus, 351
cost-of-living adjustment (COLA), 172

cost-push inflation, 165
costs
  of computers, and GDP calculations, 145–146
  currency-production, 285
  and excess output, 223
  "free" goods and services, 4
  and inflation, 165, 167
  of labor versus labor productivity, 314
  marginal, 7
  of pollution, 55
  of production, 71–72
    negative externalities, 140–141
    output shortfalls, 224
  of resources, as component of profit, 3
  oligopolistic markets, 228–229
  opportunity cost calculations, 28–30, 35–36
  perfectly competitive markets, 222
  sunk cost calculations, 30
  transaction costs, 49
    effects of markets on, 74
cottage industry system, 49
Council of Economic Advisers, 101, 350
counters, 264
counterfeit money, 286–287
counting, double, 133
countries. See foreign entities
CPI (consumer price index), 142
  biases and limitations, 143–144
  calculating, 142–143
  and COLAs (cost-of-living adjustments), 172
  and inflation, 164, 166–167
credit cards, and money supply, 288
credit unions, 269, 276
credit-worthy borrowers, identifying, 289–290
credits, 369
crowding in, crowding out, 355
cultural differences
  attitudes towards saving, 184
  impact on marketplace, 12
currency, currencies. See also money
  appreciation and depreciation, 374
  counterfeiting, 286–287
  depreciation, 374
  devaluation of, 380
  euros, 60, 374
  foreign exchange, exchange rates
    Bretton Woods agreement, 381–382
    exchange rates, 374–380
    flexible versus fixed, 380
    gold standard, 380–381

managed float system, 382–383
    markets for, 374
    sources, 373
  hard currency, as investment, 377
  international, exchange rates, 60
  legal tender, 267
  in M1 money aggregate, 281
  revaluation of, 380
  role in national economies, 91
  United States, 285
  value of
    and export expenditures, 191, 196
    impact of federal deficits on, 355
current accounts (international trade)
  balance on, 372
  offsets for deficits in, 373–374
curved lines, curves
  slope
    formula for, 22
    marginal analysis using, 23
    measurement units, 22–23
    tangents, 24–25
  straight lines, 22
curves
  aggregate demand, 199
  cost, short-run, 150
  demand (Dx), 66–67
    applicability of, 68
    and consumer expectations, 69
    and consumer income, 68
    and consumer taste, 70
    defined, 66–67
    and equilibrium price, 76–77
    and prices of related goods, 68–69
    shifts in, 76–77
  supply (Sx), 71
    and number of producers, 73
    and prices of alternative goods, 72
    and prices of relevant resources, 72
    and producer expectations, 73
    shifts in, impacts, 77–79
    and technological change, 72
customs
  impact on economic systems, 41
  impact on marketplace, 12
cycles, economic, 93–94
cyclical unemployment, 161
cyclically balanced budgets, 353

D

deadlines, budget, 350
debased metals, 264

debit cards, 288
debits, 369
debt, national, 103, 359
  debt held by public, 360
  gross debt, 360
  impact on future generations, 362–364
  impacts of paying off, 364–365
  interest payments, 361–362
  net debt, 361
  relative to GDP, 360
  and supply-side fiscal policies, 252
  versus federal deficits, 359–360
decision makers, 4, 34
decision-making
  for allocating goods and services, 39
  for allocating resources and products, 39
  comparative versus absolute advantage, 31–32
  decision-making lag, 330
  by foreign entities, 59–60
  investment decisions, 187
  law of comparative advantage, 32
  opportunity costs
    attending college example, 28–29
    effect of circumstances, 30
    information constraints, 30
    subjectivity of, 29–30
    time constraints, 30
  for producing goods and services, 39
  sunk costs, 30
deepening, capital, 113
defense industry
  defense spending by U.S. government, 56, 349
  and industrial policy, 126
deficit spending, 247
  trade balances, 370
deficits
  federal budget
    budget balancing philosophies, 353
    history, 353–354
    impact on currency values, 355
    impact of eliminating, 364–365
    impact on future generations, 362–364
    impact on interest rates, 355
    and national debt, 361
    persistence, 354
    rationale for, 352–353
    relationship to trade deficits, 384
    and supply-side fiscal policies, 103, 252–253
    versus balanced budgets, 254

versus national debt, 359–360
trade, 196, 368, 370
  association with federal budget deficit, 333, 383
deflating nominal GDP, 141
deflation, 164
delta symbol, 180
demand
  aggregate
    boosting using public policy, 328
    curves for, 97–98
    demand-side equilibrium calculations, 258–259
    and discretionary fiscal policy, 251
    and money policy, 309–310, 314
    and natural rate hypothesis, 343
    and short-run Phillips curves, 341
  defined, 65
  equilibrium price and quantity, 75–77
  greater than expected, long-run impact, 225–227, 229
  individual versus market demand, 68
  for investment, 184
  for labor, 247–249, 274–278
  law of demand, 65
  lower than expected, long-run impacts, 227–229
  and price, 65–66
  and quantity, 67
  and real GDP, 241–244
  and scarcity, 65–66
  and shortages, 74
  and surpluses, 74
demand curves (Dx)
  aggregate, 97
    during the Great Depression, 99–100
    and Keynesian economics, 100–101
    and price level changes, 207–209
    and stagflation, 102
    and supply-side economics, 103
  applicability of, 68
  and consumer expectations, 69
  and consumer income, 68
  and consumer tastes, 70
  defined, 66–67
  downward-sloping, 318
  and expenditure line, 209–211
  foreign exchange, 375
  for investment, 186–187
  loanable funds market, 170
  and output, 201
  shifts in, 68–70, 79

demand for money
  defined, 306
  and interest rates, 307–310, 314
  reasons, 306–307
demand multiplier effect, 207
demand schedule, 66–67
demand-management fiscal policy, 249. See also discretionary fiscal policy
demand-pull inflation, 165
demand-side economics, 101
democracies
  bureaucracy and, 351–353
  public choices, 342–345, 348, 350
  rent seeking in, 348–349
  special interests, 343–344
Democrats, economic policies, 253
demographics, impact on demand curve, 70
Department of Health and Human Services, 398
dependency and income assistance, 395–399
dependent variables, 20, 179
depository institutions, 269
deposits
  checkable, 285
  fractional reserve banking systems, 266
  insurance for, 273
  savings, 287
  time, 287
depreciation, 140
  of currency, 374
  and net domestic product, 140
depression, economic, 92
deregulation of banks, 274–276, 280
detail, in federal budget, 351
devaluation of currency, 380
developed countries, 115
developing countries, 115–116
DI (disposable income), 135, 150
  calculating, 151
  spending of, 137
direct (positive) variable relationships, 22
disability payments, 49
discount rate, 299
discouraged workers, 155
  and unemployment rates, 163
discretionary fiscal policy, 241, 249
  and aggregate supply, 244–246, 251
  and federal elections, 1990 example, 253
  and natural rate of unemployment, 250
  and permanent income, 251
  tax cuts, 241, 252
  and time lags, 250
disequilibrium, 81–83
disinflation, 164

displaced workers, 123
disposable income (DI), 135, 150, 177, 199
  calculating, 151
  and consumption
    aggregate measures, 177
    consumption function, 179
    and income changes, 180, 182
    marginal propensity to consume, 179–180
    marginal propensity to save, 179, 181
  and investment decisions, 187
  and net exports, 196
  and net taxes, 190
  spending of, 137
distribution of income, government role, 55
diversification, as tool for reducing risk, 290
dividends, 51, 271
divisibility of money, 264
division of labor, 33–34
dollars. See also currency; money
  current, valuing GDP output using, 141
  interrelationship with euros, 374–277
  value of, and federal deficit, 355
domestic chores, 52
domestic investment
  demand for, 184
    factors that affect, 187
    macroeconomic perspective, 186–187
  gross private, 133
domestic product, net, 140
double coincidence of wants, 262
double counting, 133–134
double-entry bookkeeping, 132
  for balance of payments transactions, 369
drop-outs, famous, 29
dual banking systems, 270
durability of money, 264
durable goods, 133

E

earnings
  in circular-flow model, 5
  and college education, 13–14
  money income, 66
  profits, 3
  real income, 66
  resource payments, 3
e-banking, 297–298
economic analyses. See also curves; equilibrium; marginal analysis
  consumption
    income-related determinants, 177, 179, 181
    life-cycle model of consumption and saving, 183–184

nonincome determinants, 181–183
  fallacies, 12
  Kuznets' analysis of economic growth, 114
  macroeconomist theory-testing, 91
  models, 8
  predicting behavior, 12
  Stigler search model, 307
  versus normative assertions, 10
economic choice, 6–7
economic cycles, 93–94
economic decision-making, 187–188
economic depression, 92
economic efficiency approach, 368
economic fluctuations
  cycles, 93–94
  depression, 92
  expansion, 93
  inflation, 92
  recession, 92, 96
economic growth
  automatic stabilizers
    income taxes, 248–249
    unemployment insurance, 249
    welfare transfer payments, 249
  and availability of capital stock, 37
  and availability of resources, 36–37
  and budget deficits, rationale for, 249, 352–353
  and capital investment, 112
  and capital resources, 113
  and computers, 119
  convergence, 125–126
  defined, 36
  and federal budget deficits, 352
  and federal funds rate targets, 312–314
  full employment, 161–162
  GDP growth figures, 330
  government role, 55
  human capital, 116–117
  and industrial policy, 126
  during late 1990's, 254
  market versus command systems, 41
  and productivity, production, 37, 111–113
  productivity growth fluctuations, 118
  recessions, 120
  research and development, 123–124
  rules of the game, 115
  and short-run versus long-run monetary policies, 319–321
  spending multiplier, factors that reduce, 259

and technological change, 37,
  111–112, 114–115, 123
  threats to
    inflation, 164–172
    unemployment, 154–157,
    160–163
economic indicators, 96
economic models, 8
economic performance, measuring
  circular flow approach, 132
  expenditure-based GDP,
    133–134
  expenditure-based GNP, 137
  GDP (gross domestic product),
    132
  income-based GNP, 134–135,
    137
  national income accounting
    system, 132–135, 137–139
  net domestic product, 140
  precious metal stocks, 132
  U.S. government statistics,
    139–140
Economic Report of the President, 350
economic statements, 10
economic systems
  allocation of goods and services, 39
  centrally planned, 40–41
  defined, 39
  and custom and religion, 41
  market systems, 40
  mixed systems, 41
  modified capitalism, 40
  modified command system, 41
  production of goods and services, 39
  pure capitalism, 39–40
  pure command system, 40–41
economic theory
  defined, 8
  Keynesian economics, 248
  laissez-faire, 247
  oligopolies, 227
  role in analysis, 8
economic welfare, and limitations
  of GDP, 141
economics, defined, 2
economics majors, 13–14
economies. See also economic
  growth; markets; United
  States economy
  aggregate demand, 96
    aggregate demand curve,
    97–98
  aggregate supply curves, 98
  aggregate output, 96
  body analogy, 91, 132
  circular flow, 91
  currency, 91
  defined, 90
  equilibrium real GDP, 98
  fluctuations, 92

coincident indicators, 96
  depression, 92
  economic cycles, 93–94
  expansion, 93
  inflation, 92
  lagging indicators, 96
  leading indicators, 96
  recession, 92, 96
  investment demand curves,
    186–188
  measuring gross domestic
    product (GDP), 90
  money, fiat money, 267
  national income, 150–152
  national versus local, 90
  net exports, 190–191, 196
  output
    gaps and wage flexibility,
    231–232
    potential output, 222
  public policy
    active intervention, 326,
    331–332
    active approaches, 326,
    328–329, 331–332
    active versus passive approaches, 325
    closing contractionary gaps,
    326–328
    closing expansionary gaps,
    328
    implementation time lags,
    329–330
    passive approaches, 331–332,
    337–339
    role of anticipation, 334–335
    role of credibility, 335
    role of expectations,
    332–334
    U.S. versus Mexico, 90
    underground, 138
Economist, The, Big Mac price index, 378
economists
  classical, 247
  earnings, 13–14
  jobs held by, 14
  Keynesian, 248
education and training
  and labor force participation
    rate, 156
  as positive externality, 55
  and worker productivity,
    116–117
effectiveness lag, 330
efficiency
  defined, 35
  and division of labor, 33
  importance of, 37
  in production, 35, 185, 302
electronic banking, 297–298
electronic cottage case study, 53
Emergency Jobs Appropriation
  Act, 1983, 330

employee compensation, in national income calculations,
  151
employees, telecommuting, 53
employers, wage agreements, 221
employment. See also unemployment
  affirmative action programs,
    393–394
  full, 161–162, 222, 248
  government role, 55
  long-run aggregate supply
    curve, 229
  natural rate of unemployment,
    hysteresis, 235–236
  and supply-side fiscal policies,
    252–253
  wages
    and production, 225–229
    and short-run aggregate supply curve, 224
    wage flexibility, 229, 231–232
Employment Act of 1946, 101,
  248, 350
employment cost index, 314
entitlement programs
  impact on budget process, 351
  reforming, 357–358
entrepreneurial ability
  in circular-flow model, 5
  defined, 3
  households as source of, 4
entrepreneurs, 294
  cottage industry system, 49
  firms, 50
  profits earned by, 3, 50,
  and transaction costs, 49
equation of exchange, 314–315
  velocity of money determinants, 316
  velocity of money stability, 316
equilibrium
  defined, 75
  market
    of price and quantity, 75–79
    short-run, 2267
equilibrium interest rate, 308–309
equipment as physical capital, 2
Ernst & Young, use of mobile
  technologies, 53
ethical issues
  federal deficits and national
    debt, 362–364
  zombie banks, 275
ethnic discrimination, and unemployment rate, 156
euro, 60, 374–277, 380
European Central Bank, 337, 380
European Monetary Union, federal deficit reduction requirements, 361
excess capacity, 222
excess quantity supplied. See
  surplus

excess reserves, 291
exchange
  barter, 32
  foreign, 60
  money, 32, 262–263
    commodity money, 263
    equation of exchange, 314
    as medium of exchange, 91,
    263, 307
    quantity theory of money,
    315
    as store of value, 263, 267
    as unit of account, 263
  of services, law of comparative
    advantages, 31–32
  and specialization of labor, 262
exchange rates, 60, 374
  demand curves, 375
  determinants of, 376
    arbitrageurs, speculators,
    377
  equilibrium price, 375
  and finance systems
    Bretton Woods agreement,
    381–382
    gold standard, 380–381
    managed float system,
    382–383
  fixed, 380
  flexible, 380
  purchasing power parity (PPP)
    theory, 378–379
  supply curves, 376
exchange, equation of, 314
exchange, foreign, 60
excise (sales) taxes, 57
exclusive goods, 54
executive branch, agencies and
  bureaus, 56
exhaustible resources, 3
expansion of money supply, 93
  limits on, 296
  money multiplier, 295–296
  role of excess reserves, 292–295
expansionary fiscal policy, 101,
  244–245
expansionary gap, 226–227
  closing
    active versus passive policy
    approaches, 328
    impacts of fiscal policy, 246
  impact on wages, 229
expectations
  business, and impact on
    planned investment, 188
  of consumers impact on demand curves, 69
  and consumption, 183
  and policy effectiveness, 332
    monetary policy, 333–335
    rational expectations,
    332–333
    time-inconsistency problem,
    334

of producers, impact on supply
curve, 73
rational, 332
of voters, 354
expected marginal benefit and
cost, 7
expected unemployment rate, 333
expenditure-based GDP (gross
domestic product), 132–134
calculating, 137
expenditures
aggregate
aggregate expenditure line,
201
below GDP, 202
components, 191–192
consumption, 177, 179,
181–184
decreases in, 205–207
and demand, 201, 209–211,
216–217
and disposable income, 199
in excess of GDP, 202
government outlays, 189–190
government spending, 200
increases in, 203–205
investment, 184, 186–188
net exports, 190–191, 196,
200, 215–216
planned investment, 200
and price level changes,
207–209
unplanned inventory adjustments, 200
by households, breakdown of,
49
consumption versus investment, trends, 188–189
exports
net export function, 134,
190–191, 196
nonincome determinants,
191
government
capital expenditures, 351
consumption and gross in-
vestment, 133
federal outlays, 349
operating expenditures, 351
and real GDP, 241–242
impact of reductions in, 357
personal consumption expenditures, 133
experience and worker productivity, 116–117
explicit wage agreements, 222
exports
in circular-flow model, 138
net, 134
and aggregate expenditures,
200
in GDP (gross domestic
product), 134
income effects, 215–216

spending multiplier effects,
216
variable, 259
spending on, 190–191, 196
U.S. trading partners, 59
externalities, 55

F

factors of production, 2–3
failures
coordination failures, 231
market, 54
fallacies
association-is-causation, 12
fallacy of composition, 12–13
FDIC (Federal Deposit Insurance
Corporation)...273
Federal Advisory Committee, 272
federal budget
balancing, 254, 353
budget deficits, 437
and currency values, 355
economic stimulation using,
249
eliminating, impacts of,
364–365
history, 353–354
and interest rates, 355
long-term effects, 362–364
and national debt, 361
as percentage of GDP, 249
persistence, 354
rationales for, 352–353
and standards of living, 363
supply-side fiscal policies,
103, 252–253
and trade deficits, 383
budget process, 350–351
budget surpluses
economic impacts, 364–365
and reduced government
spending, 357
reversal of, 357
and tax increases, 356
entitlement programs, 357–358
federal funds market, rate
as target of monetary policy,
321
impact on economy, 312–314
impact on monetary supply,
299
outlays, 349
role in money creation,
292–295
suggested process reforms,
351–352
federal government (U.S.), 55
agencies and bureaus, 56
expenditures relative to GDP,
358–359
number of jurisdictions in, 56
federal income tax
as automatic stabilizer, 241,
248-249

and tax cuts, 241
federal market funds, 292
rate targets, 312–314
Federal Open Market Committee
(FOMC, Federal Reserve
System), 272
Federal Reserve System (the Fed)
Board of Governors, 272
creation of, 270–272
currency and notes produced
by, 285–287
profits from, 300
discount rate, 299
Federal Advisory Committee,
272
Federal Open Market Com-
mittee, 272
federal funds market, 292–295
interest rate stabilization efforts,
321
member banks, 290–291
monetary control tools,
298–300
monetary policy
and credibility, 335
federal funds rate targets,
312–314
money supply
contracting, 296–297
M1, 285, 288
M2, 287
M3, 287
regulation of, 272
objectives, 274
open-market purchases and
sales, 299
and price stability, 336–337
powers, 270–271
reserve requirements, 300
federal surplus, 254
fiat money, 266–267
Federal Reserve notes, 300
U.S. currency, 285
final goods and services, 133
finance companies, 289
financial assets, liquid versus
nonliquid, 307
financial intermediaries. *See also*
Federal Reserve System
banks
asymmetric information,
289–290
balance sheets, 290–291
banking structure, 277
charters, 290
commercial banks, 276–277
deregulation, 274–275
inflation effects, 274
Japanese banking problems,
280
liquidity versus profitability,
291–292
money creation process,
292–296

money supply contraction,
296–297
profit sources, 289
reserve accounts, 291
role, 283, 289
savings and loan institutions,
275–276
shares, 290
depository institutions, 269
Federal Deposit Insurance Corporation (FDIC), 273
finance companies, sources of
profit, 289
national banks, 270
state banks, 269
financial markets, 137
firms
in circular-flow model, 4
clustering, 126
corporations, 50
defined, 50
demand for money, 306–307
development of, 49
expenditures
investment, 184
planned investments, 187–188
investment, 203–207
marginal choice, 7
maximizing profit, 50
partnerships, 50
price changes, 207–209
resource use, 4
revenue, 5
role in economic decision
making, 4
sole proprietorships, 50
specialization of labor, 33
telecommuting, 53
transaction costs, 49
virtual offices, 53
fiscal policy, 55
and aggregate supply
contractionary policies, 246
expansionary policies,
244–245
automatic stabilizers
income taxes, 248–249
taxes, 241
unemployment insurance,
249
welfare transfer payments,
249
contractionary, 246
defined, 55, 240
discretionary, 241, 249–253,
351
evolution of, 247–248
expansionary, 101, 245
functional finance, 353
government purchases,
241–242
secondary effects, 251
tax policies, 241–242
tools, 241

fixed costs (FC)
  minimizing short-run losses, 171–172
  and total cost, 146–147
fixed exchange rates, 380
fixed-price weighting systems, 145
flat taxes, 258
flexible exchange rates, 380, 382–383
floating exchange rates, 376
  managed float system, 382–383
floors, for prices, 81
flow, 132
  circular, in economics, 91
  income versus money stock, 306
flow variables, 91
  balance of payments, 369
  budget deficits, 101
  consumption and income, 181
  defined, 263
fluctuations, economic
  coincident indicators, 96
  cycles, 93
  depression, 92
  expansion, 93
  and global linkages, 94
  inflation, 92
  lagging indicators, 96
  leading indicators, 96
  recession, 92, 96
FOMC (Federal Open Market Committee), 272
  federal funds rate targets, 312–314
food stamps, 49
Ford Motor Company, markets outside the U.S., 61
Ford, Gerald administration, inflation during, 171
Ford, Henry, 135
foreign entities, economies See also foreign exchange; international trade
  role in economic decision making, 4
  specialization of labor, 33
  as users of resources, 4
foreign exchange. See also currencies
  exchange rates, 374
  demand curves, 375
  determinants of, 376
  equilibrium price, 375
  flexible, 380
  purchasing power parity (PPP) theory, 378–379
  role of arbitrageurs, 377
  role of speculators, 377
  supply curves, 376
  international finance systems
    Bretton Woods agreement, 381–382

gold standard, 380–381
  managed float system, 382–383
  markets, 374
  sources, 373
foreign investment
  foreign-owned national debt, 363
  and U.S. federal budget deficit, 355
foreign trade. See international trade
formulas
  aggregate expenditure, 137
  bank balance sheets, 290
  demand-side equilibrium, 258
  disposable income (DI) expenditures, 137
  equation of exchange, 314
  expenditure-based gross domestic product (GDP), 134
  GDP price index, 144
  government purchases and real GDP, 242
  identity relationships, 314
  income-based GDP, 137
  money multiplier, 295–296
  net tax changes and real GDP, 243
  net tax multiplier, 258
  profit, 50
  real GDP demanded, 218–219, 298–299
  equilibirium, 258
  net tax multiplier, 258
  with net taxes and variable government purchases, 258
  with proportional income tax and variable net exports, 259
  with proportional taxes, 258–259
  real interest rate, 170
  simple spending multiplier, 205, 291
  slopes, 22
forward looking decisions, 187
fractional reserve banking system, 266
France
  government outlays, 56
  unemployment rates, 235
free goods and services, 3–4
frictional unemployment, 160
Friedman, Milton, 321
full employment, 161–162
  full-employment rate of output, 222
  as goal of fiscal policy, 248
functional finance, 353
functional relationships, 20
funds rate, 292. See also federal market funds

G

game, rules of the, 115
gaps, contractionary, 227–229
  closing
    and budget deficits, 249
    and fiscal policy, 244–245
  impact on wages, 229, 231–232
gaps, expansionary, 226–227
  closing, and fiscal policy, 246
  impact on wages, 229
GDP (gross domestic product)
  and aggregate demand curve, 199
  calculating
  calculating
    expenditure approach, 132–134, 137
    final goods and services, 133
    income approach, 132, 134–135, 137
  defined, 56, 132
  and depreciation, 140
  government outlays relative to, 358–359
  government purchases, 189
  inflation indices, 141–144
  limitations, 138–139
  and national debt, 360
  and national income, 150
  negative externalities, effects of, 140
  and net exports, 215–216, 371
  nominal, 141, 315
  output valuations, 141
  potential
    and contractionary fiscal policy, 246
    and expansionary fiscal policy, 244–245
    long-run aggregate supply curve, 229, 231–235
    and lower than expected output, 227–229
  price estimates for, 144–146
  ratio to government outlays, 56
  real
    and aggregate demand curves, 98, 224
    and aggregate supply curves, 98
    at equilibrium, 98, 258–259
    and government purchases, 241–242
    and greater than expected output, 225–227
    and net taxes, 242–244
    and output per capita, 120
    per capita, 105
    and price levels, 104–105
    relationship of output and spending, 201
    relationship of spending plans and production, 202

    short-run impacts of higher than expected prices, 222–223
    short-run impacts of lower than expected prices, 224
    and simple spending multiplier calculations, 205
    and supply-side economics, 103
    U.S. government statistics, 139–140
  real GDP demanded
    and autonomous spending changes, 216–217
    underlying algebra, 218–219
  versus consumption and investment, historic trends, 188–189
General Electric, electronic inventory maintenance, 119
General Theory of Employment, Interest and Money (Keynes), 100, 248
geography and wage differences, 270
Germany
  Bundesbank, control of value of mark, 382
  central bank independence and inflation, 337
  government outlays, 56
  money supplies following World War II, 268
  unemployment rates, 235
global economies
  and business cycles, 94
  and computers, 119
  levels of net debt, 361
  relative size of public sector, 358–359
GNP (gross national product), 132
  real, as measure of aggregate output, 96
gold standard, 380–381
goldsmiths, banking services, 265–266
Gompers, Samuel, 270
goods, consumer, 2
  allocation decisions, 39
  alternative, impact on supply curve, 72
  complements, 69
  consuming, and utility maximization, 260
  defined, 3
  demand for, 306–307
  free, 3–4
  household expenditures for, 49
  in GDP calculations, 138
  income elasticity, 104
  inferior, demand for, 68
  intermediate, 133
  in international trade balances, 59

inventories, 133
leisure time and product improvements, 138
markets for, 4
net exports, 134
nondurable, 133
normal, demand for, 68
open-access, 358
opportunity costs, 35–36
per capita, and standard of living, 110
producing, 35, 39
public
   government provision of, 54–55
   production incentives, 40
purchases, and demand, 65
scarce
   and maximizing utility, 119
   and prices, 3–4
substitutes, 69
transaction costs, 49
unrelated, 69
versus services, 3
government subsidies, 346–347
governments. *See also* fiscal policy; monetary policy
   borrowing by, 103, 361–363
   federal system, 55–56
   fiat money, 266–267
   fixed exchange rates, 380
   industrial policy, 126
   intervention in markets, 81–82
   and market disequilibrium, 81
   minimum wage, living-wage laws, 253–254
   purchases, spending by
      and aggregate expenditures, 200
      and budget deficits, 254
      in circular-flow model, 137–138
      government purchase function, 189–190
      government purchase multiplier, 242
      and gross investment, 133
      long-term impacts, 362–364
      and national debt, 359
      national debt interest payments, 361–362
      rationale for, 352–354
      relationship to GDP, 358–359
      transfer payments, 190
      variable, in aggregate demand-side equilibrium calculations, 258
   resource use, 4
   revenue sources, 57
   role in market system, 4, 54–55, 81–82
   role in mixed economic systems, 41

role in modified capitalism, 40
role in pure command systems, 40–41
size of, 56
transfer payments, 150
as users of resources, 4
Graham-Leach-Bliley Act of 1999, 277
Grapes of Wrath, The (Steinbeck), 154
graphs
   components, 20
   defined, 20
   demand curves, demand schedules, 66–67
   drawing, 21
   function, 20, 22
   line shifts, 25
   slope
      defined, 22
      formula for, 22
      marginal analysis using, 23
      measurement units, 22–23
   supply curves, supply schedules, 71
   total utility, 118
   variables
      independent (unrelated) relationships, 22
      negative (inverse) relationships, 22
      positive (direct) relationships, 22
Great Britain, Industrial Revolution
Great Depression
   behavior of Federal Reserve System during, 271–272
   employment-related legislation following, 162
   federal deficits following, 353
   federal deficits prior to, 352
   and government spending, 56, 247
   and tax increase, 92
   unemployment during, 154, 156
Greenspan, Alan,
   appointment, 298
   monetary policies, 313, 321, 339
   on paying off national debt, 364
   on Social Security/Medicare reform, 358
Gresham's Law, 264
gross debt, 360
gross domestic product. *See GDP*
gross investment, 140
   government, 133
   private domestic, 133
gross national product (GNP), 132
   real, as measure of aggregate output, 96

gross private domestic investment, 184
gross state product, 90
growth, economic, 90
   and capital investment, 112
   and capital resources, 113
   convergence, 125–126
   computers and technological change, 111–112, 114–115, 119, 123
   full employment, 161–162
   and industrial policies, 126
   and labor productivity, 112–113
   productivity growth fluctuations...118
   recessions and labor productivity growth...120
   role of human capital...116–117
   role of research and development, 123–124
   rules of the game, 115
   threats to
      inflation, 164–172
      unemployment, 154–157, 160–163

H

Haiti, use of labor capital, 113
hard currency, as investment, 377
health care benefits, as in-kind transfer payment, 49
helping others, costs of, 6
high-school drop-outs, famous, 29
hill-shaped curve, slope, 25
Hispanic households, unemployment rates, 157
history, economic
   fiscal policy
      classical economists, 247
      Keynesian economists, 248
   United States economy
      the Great Depression, 99–100
      Keynesian eocnmics, 100–101
      labor productivity, 117–118
      real GDP and price levels, 104–105
      stagflation, 102
      supply-side economics, 103
holding companies, 277, 291
Hoover, Herbert, 92
horizontal axis (graph), defined, 20
hourly earnings, 3
households
   in circular-flow model, 4
   demand for money, 306–307
   expenditures by, 49
   income, 5
      high, income tax rates, 254
   maximizing utility, 47
   production by

the electronic cottage, 53
exclusion from GDP calculations, 138
factors that influence, 52
and real GDP, 98
as resource owners, 4
labor, 48–49
role in agricultural economy, 47
role in market economy, 47
housing
   government assistance, 49
   price ceilings, 82
human capital, 3
   defined, 113
   and productivity, 116–117
hyperinflation, 164
   cold turkey monetary policies, 336
   and money supply, 318
   performance of money during, Brazil example, 267–269
hypotheses, 10

I

identity relationships, 314
IMF (International Monetary Fund), 381
implementing public policy, time lags, 329–330
implicit costs, 141–142
implicit wage agreements, 222
imports
   in circular-flow model, 138
   marginal propensity to import, 216
   quotas, 60
   taxes (tariffs) on, 60
imputed income, 139
incentives, 39
   from free-market activity, 41
   and vote maximization, 56
inclusive unions, wage negotiations, 271–272
income
   aggregate, 134
      and aggregate consumption, 177
      and aggregate expenditure, 138
      in GDP calculations, 135, 137
   in circular-flow model, 4–5
   and consumption, 177
   consumer
      impact on demand curves, 68
      sources of, 48–49
   of corporations, dividends and retailed earnings, 295
   disposable, 135, 199
      and net exports, 196, 215–216
      and net taxes, 190
   distribution, 381

as flow variable, 263, 306
and government purchases, 190
government role in equalizing, 55
imputed, 139
and investment decisions, 187
median income, 384
median wage, 382–383
money income, 66
national, 150–152
of non-profit institutions, 52
per capita, market versus command systems, 41
permanent, 251
personal, 150
and taxation, 57
and transfer payments, 190
income approach to GDP, 132, 134–135, 137
income effect of a price change, 66
income expectations, 69
income-expenditure model, 201
and investment decreases, 205–207
and price level changes, 207–209
spending multiplier, 203–205
increased prices, impacts of, 66
independence of central bank, 336
independent (unrelated) variables, 20, 22
index number (price level), 96
indexes, price, 141–142
base year, 142
chain-weighted system, 144
constructing, 142
consumer price index (CPI), 142–144
GDP price index, 144
GPI price index, 144
price estimates, chain-weighted systems, 144–145
India, market for automobiles, 61
indicators, economic, 96
individual demand, 68
individual supply, 72
induced consumption, 218
industrial market countries, 115
industrial policy, 126
Industrial Revolution, 49–50
inferior goods, 68
inflation
anticipated versus unanticipated, 167
and central bank independence, 336–337
cold turkey policies, 67
cost-push inflation, 165
demand-pull inflation, 165
disinflation, 164
and excessive short-run output, 226–227
historical trends, 166–167-

hyperinflation, Brazil example, 164
impacts of, 141, 171–172, 274
inflation indexes
annual rate, 164
base year, 142
constructing, 142
consumer price index (CPI), 142–144
GDP price index, 144
price estimates...144–145
inflation target, 337
and interest rates, 169–170
measuring, 164
and money supply, 264, 318
passive policy approaches, inflation targets, 337
rise of during 1960's, 102
stagflation, 249
unpopularity of, 171
variable, 167–168
versus unemployment, 339–341, 343–344
information
asymmetric, 289–290
and opportunity cost calculations, 30
and rational choice, 6
Information Revolution, 53
infrastructure, and economic convergence, 126
injections (circular-flow model), 138
in-kind transfer programs, 49
in-kind wages, 139
inputs, 2. See also resources
capital, 2
entrepreneurial ability, 3
labor, 2
natural resources, 3
resources, 3
institutional changes, impacts on aggregate supplies, 233
institutions, financial. See banks, banking system; Federal Reserve System
institutions, non-profit, 52
insurance for bank deposits, 273
insurance, social, 249
intangibles in U.S. trade surpluses, 371
integration, vertical
constraints, 302
market purchases versus internal production, 301–302
interest, on money
defined, 3, 169
on national debt, 361–364
net, in national income calculations, 151
interest rates
annuities, present value, 292–294
banks, effects on, 274, 282

bridging time using, 285
and consumption, 183
defined, 169
equilibrium interest rate, 308–309
and federal deficits, 355
federal funds rate, 292, 312–314
and government borrowing, 363
and inflation, 169–171
and investment, 185–186, 188
and money demand curve, 307–308
and monetary policy, 309–310, 314, 319–321
and national debt payments, 361–362
and net export expenditure, 191
nominal, 170
real, 170
intergenerational transfer of debt burdens, 363–364
intermediate goods and services, 133
international finance system
Bretton Woods agreement, 381–382
gold standard, 830–381
managed float system, 382–383
International Monetary Fund (IMF), 381
international trade, 59
auto industry example, 60–61
balance of payments, 59, 369
balance on goods and services, 371
double-entry bookkeeping for, 369
as flow variable, 369
merchandise trade balance, 369–370
statistical discrepancy account, 372–373
capital accounts, 372
currency and exchange rates, 60
current accounts, 372
finance systems, 380–383
foreign exchange, 373–380
foreign investment, 355
merchandise trade balance, 59
trade restrictions, 60
unilateral transfers, 371–372
use of Federal Reserve notes, 285
Internet
impact on transaction costs, 53
online banking, 297–298
inventories, 133
unplanned adjustments, 200, 202
inverse (negative) variable relationships, 22
investing in college, opportunity costs, 28–29

investment
actual, 200, 203–205
aggregate versus planned, 200
capital, 112
in circular flow model, 138
defined, 133, 312
demand for, 184, 186–187
government, 133
gross private domestic, 133, 184
gross versus net, 140
hard currency, 377
in infrastructure, 363
marginal rate of return, 285–286
planned
and business expectations, 188
decreases in, 205–207
and market interest rates, 188
nonincome determinants, 187
and price changes, 207–209
versus consumption, historic trends, 188–189
investment function, 187
invisibles, 134. See also services
Israel, money supply and inflation, 318
Italy
government outlays, 56
inflation, 337
national debt, 361
R&D expenditures, 124–125
unemployment rates, 235

J

J. P. Morgan Chase, 277
Japan
banking system problems, 280
government outlays, 56
inflation in, 168
popularity of vending machines in, 11–12
quotas on car imports from, 61
R&D expenditures, 124–125
recession in, 211
relative size of government outlays, 358–359
saving in, 184
unemployment rates, 162–163
jobs, and population growth, 104
Johnson, Lyndon B., discretionary fiscal policy, 249

K

Kennedy, John F., discretionary fiscal policy, 249
Keynes, John Maynard, 100, 248, 352
Kizu bank (Japan), 280
knowledge as human capital, 3
Kuznets, Simon, 114, 132

L

labor. *See also* work
  capital deepening, 113–117
  capital as substitute for, 152
  in circular-flow model, 5
  costs of, 12, 249–251
    versus labor productivity, 314
    Western Europe example,
      236572
  defined, 2
  demand for
    architects example, 252–253
    and costs of other resources,
      251
    costs versus revenues, 240
    and marginal revenue prod-
      uct, 248–249
    and output demand, 252
    and technological innova-
      tion, 252
    total and marginal product,
      247–248
  division of, 33
  full employment, 161–162
  households as source of, 4,
    48–49
  as human capital, 113
  labor force participation,
    155–156
  productivity, 112, 117–121
  specialization, 262–263
    effects of, 34
    opportunity costs, 31–32
  supplies
    and discretionary fiscal poli-
      cies, 251
    long-run aggregate supplies,
      225–232
    and money policy, 310–312
    short-run aggregate supplies,
      222–224
    and supply-side fiscal poli-
      cies, 252-253
    and utility maximization,
      260
    work time and leisure, 260
  and technological change, 123
  temporal factors, 2
  underemployment, 163
  unemployment
    economic costs, 154
    international comparisons,
      162–163
    measuring, 154–157
    natural rate, 222
    personal costs, 154
    sources, 123, 160–161
    unemployment benefits, 162
  wages, 3, 221–222
lagging economic indicators, 96
laissez-faire, 40, 100, 247. *See also*
    capitalism, pure
land prices, 244, 253

Latin America, market for auto-
    mobiles, 61
law of comparative advantage
  defined, 31
  and division of labor, 33
  and efficient resource use, 32
  versus absolute advantage,
    31–32
law of demand, 65, 67
  applicability of, 68
  how it works, 65–66
law of diminishing marginal re-
    turns from capital, 1134
law of increasing opportunity
    cost, 36
law of supply, 70
lay-offs, in Western Europe, 236
leading economic indicators, 96
leakages (circular-flow model),
    138
legal restrictions. as entry barriers,
    194
legislation, economic
  Social Security Act (1935), 162
  in U.S., following World War II,
    101
leisure time, exclusion from GDP,
    139
liability
  banks, 290
  corporations, 51
  limited, 50–51
  partnerships, 50
  sole proprietorships, 50
Liechtenstein, national economy,
    90
life-cycle model of consumption
    and saving, 183–184
limits, production, visualizing, 35
line items in federal budgets, 352
line shifts (graphs), 25
lines (graphs), 22–23
liquidation, 304
liquidity, 287, 292
  of banks, versus profitability,
    291–292
loans
  credit cards as, 288
  interest rates, and inflation, 170
  nonperforming, 280
  transaction costs, 289–290
local governments (U.S.), respon-
    sibilities, 55
localized inflation, regional vari-
    ability, 168
long-run
  aggregate supply curve
    and wage flexibility, 229,
      231–232
    calculating, 229
  defined, 226
  equilibrium, 227
  monetary policy, 319–321
  Phillips curves, 341, 343–344

lower prices
  impact on demand, 66
  impact on real income, 66
  impact on supply curves, 72
  LRAS. *See* long-run aggregate
    supply curve

M

M1 money aggregate, 285, 288
M2 money aggregate, 287
  volatility in velocity of, 318
M3 money aggregate, 287
Maastricht agreement, 337
macroeconomic policy
  active policy approaches
    active versus passive ap-
      proaches, 326
    and central bank indepen-
      dence, 336–337
    closing contractionary gaps,
      326–328
    closing expansionary gaps,
      328
    effectiveness of, 334–335
    and expectations, 332–333
    and policy credibility,
      335–336
    and presidential elections,
      331–332
    and time lags, 329–330
  decision-making lag, 330
  demand-side economics, 101
  effectiveness of, 332–335
  fiscal policy, 240
    automatic stabilizers,
      248–249
    discretionary fiscal policy,
      249–253
    evolution of, 247–248
    impact on aggregate supply,
      244–246
    impact on real GDP de-
      manded, 241–244
    tools, 241
  implementation lag, 330
  industrial policy, 126
  Keynesian economics, 100
  laissez-faire, 100
  mercantilism, 92, 132
  monetary policy
    open-market operations,
      272
    responsibility of Federal Re-
      serve for, 272
    short-run versus long-run
      focus, 319–321
  monetary theory, 306
  passive policy approaches
    dependence on rules, 337
    and rational expectations,
      338–339
    rationale for, 338
  recognition lag, 330
  supply-side economics, 103

macroeconomic theory
  circular flow model, 199
  convergence, 125–126
  defined, 7
  examination of fiscal and mon-
    etary policy, 55
  focus, 89–90
  hysteresis, 235
  industrial policy, 126
  natural rate hypothesis, 343
  Phillips curves, 339–344
  political business cycle, 253
  purchasing power parity (PPP)
    theory, 378
  productivity and growth, 110
  quantity theory of money, 315
  theory-testing, 91
major, college, impact on career
    earnings, 13–14
managed float system, 382–383
managing renewable resources, 3
maps, indifference, 134–135
marginal analysis
  defined, 7, 23
  marginal production costs, 71
marginal propensity to consume
    (MPC), 179–180
  and reduction of spending mul-
    tiplier, 259
  and simple spending multiplier
    calculations, 205
marginal propensity to import,
    216
  and reduction of spending mul-
    tiplier, 259
marginal propensity to save
    (MPS), 179, 181
  and simple spending multiplier
    calculations, 205
marginal returns, from capital, 113
marginal tax rate, defined, 58
mark (German currency), 388
  impacts of asymmetric infor-
    mation, 308
market system, markets. *See also*
    demand; supply
  adjustment process, long-run,
    182–183
  agricultural, and income and
    price elasticity, 105–106
  capital, 284
  cultural factors, 12
  defined, 4, 74
  demand, demand curves, 64,
    68–70, 74–80
  disequilibrium, 81–83
  failures, 54
  federal funds market, 292
  financial, 137
  firms, 50–51
  foreign exchange markets, 60,
    374
  government role, 54–55
  households, 47

incentives of, 41
interest rates, 185–186, 188
international trade, 59–60
labor markets, supply curves, 48–49, 71
market price, versus opportunity cost, 52
and money, 263, 267, 306–307, 314–315
nonprofit institutions, 52
political markets, 55–56
product markets, 4
resource markets, 4
role in modified command systems, 41
supplies, supply curves, 71–73
transaction costs, 74
underpricing of public output, 56
versus command systems, 41
maximizing profit, 50, 222–224
maximizing utility, 47
McDowell County, WV, unemployment in, 159–160
measurement units, slope, 22–23
Medicare
funding for, 57
impact on federal budgets, 351
origins, 357
reforming, 358
spending on, 56–57, 349
mediums of exchange, 91, 263. *See also* currency; money
and demand for money, 307
men, labor force participation rate, 156
mercantilism, 92, 132
merchandise trade balance, 59, 369–370
merchandise traded, 134
mergers, among banks, 277
metals
as money, quality control issues, 264
precious, and mercantilism, 92
Mexico, national economy, 90
microchip technology, impact on production, 53
microeconomics
defined, 7
relationship between income and consumption, 177
microprinting, 286
milk, price floors for, 81
mining industry, unemployment rates, 159–160
Mitchell, Wesley C., 92
mixed economic systems, 41
mobile technologies and virtual offices, 53
models, economic
circular-flow model, 4
defined, 8

PPF (production possibilities frontier), 34–38
role in analysis, 8
modified capitalism, 40
modified command systems, 41
monetary policy, 55
anticipating, economic impacts, 334–335
defined, 55
effectiveness of, 333–335
and federal funds rate, 312–314
open-market operations, 272
and Phillips curves, 339–340
and price stability, 336–337
responsibility of Federal Reserve for, 272
short-run versus long-run focus, 319–321
supply regulation, 272
and velocity of money supply, 318
versus monetary theory, 306
money. *See also* banks; currency; Federal Reserve System
aggregates, 285
cash transfer payments, 49
in circular-flow model, 5
coins, 264–265
commodity money, 263
currency and exchange rates, 60
demand for, 306–308
desirable features, 264
evolution of, 262–263
exporting, restrictions on, 372
fiat money, 266–267
financial intermediaries for, 269–277
foreign exchange, 373–383
functions, 32, 263, 267, 314
holding, opportunity costs, 307
hyperinflation of, 267–269
income and revenue, 5, 66
international trade in, 272
liquidity of, 307
loanable funds market, 288
in national economies...91
in opportunity cost calculations, 30
quantity theory of, 315–316
real value and consumption, 182–183
representative money, 266
as stock variable, 263
token money, 265–266
value of, and export expenditures, 191, 196
velocity of, 314–316
money market mutual funds, 274
money multiplier, 295–296
money policy
focus on supply, 319–321

impact on aggregate demand, 309–310, 314
impact on aggregate supply, 310–312, 314–315
money supply. *See also* income; monetary policy
counterfeit money, 286–287
and credit cards, 288
checkable deposits, 285
components, 267
contraction of, 296–297
effects on economy, 306
excessive, and hyperinflation, 268–269
Federal Reserve monetary control tools, 298–300
government regulation of, 55
increases in, impact on inflation, 318
money aggregates, 285–287
money creation, role of excess reserves, 292–295
money multiplier, 295–296
predicting, 315–316
versus demand, and equilibrium interest rates, 308–309
monopolies, 54
monthly earnings, 3
moral hazards, bank loans, 275
mortgage loans and bank failures, 274
movement along a demand curve, 70
movement along a supply curve, 74
MPC. *See* marginal propensity to consume)
MPS. *See* marginal propensity to save
MR (marginal revenue)
multipliers, multiplier effects
autonomous spending, 218
balanced budget, 258
government purchase multiplier, 242
money multipliers, 295–296
net tax multiplier, 298
planned spending changes
airline industry example, 206–207
decreased spending, 205
effects on aggregate demand, 209–211
increased spending, 203–205
spending increases, 205
price level changes, 207–209
simple tax multiplier, 244
spending
factors that reduce, 259
and fiscal policy, 244
and net exports, 216
mutual funds, money market, 274

N

National Banking Act of 1863, 269
national banks, 270, 290
National Basketball Association (NBA) case study, 80
National Bureau of Economic Research (NBER), 92
national debt
debt held by public, 360
foreign-owned, 363
gross debt, 360
interest payments, 361–362
long-term impacts, 362–364
net debt, 361
paying off, 364–365
relative to GDP, 360
and supply-side fiscal policies, 252
versus federal deficits, 359–360
national defense, spending on, 349
national economies
aggregate demand, 96–97
aggregate output, 96
aggregate supply, 98
balance-of-payments accounts, 371–372
body analogy, 91, 132
capital accounts, 372
circular flow, 91
currency, 91
defined 90
economic cycles, 93–94
fluctuations, 92–93, 96
fully employment, defined, 161–162
inflation, 164–172
international trade, 369–372
investment demand curves, 186–188
measuring, gross domestic product (GDP), 90
national income, 150–152
net exports, 190–191, 196
performance measurements, 132–140
unemployment, 154–157, 160–163
United States economy, history, 99–105
variability in size of, 90
national income accounting system, 132–135, 137–139
national income calculations, 150–152
National InterBank, 297
natural abilities, and specialization of labor, 33
natural market forces, 326–329
natural monopolies, 54
natural rate hypotheses, 343
natural rate of output, 222

natural rate of unemployment, 222
  challenges of identifying, 328–329
  and discretionary fiscal policies, 250
  hysteresis, 235–236
  and short-run aggregate supply curve, 224
natural resources, 3–5
  productivity of, 112
NBA (National Basketball Association) case study, 80
NBER (National Bureau of Economic Research), 92
needs
  and scarcity of resources, 2
  versus demand and wants, 65
negative (inverse) variable relations, 22
negative externalities, 55, 140
net debt, 361
net domestic product, 140, 150–151
net export function, 190–191, 196
net exports, 134, 371
  and aggregate expenditures, 200
  in circular-flow model, 137
  income effects, 215–216
  spending multiplier effects, 216
  variable, 259
net imports, and real GDP demanded, 219
net interest in national income calculations, 151
net investment, 140
net taxes (NT)
  and aggregate demand-side equilibrium calculations, 258
  and aggregate expenditures, 199
  in circular flow model, 138
  defined, 190
  and disposable income, 190
  and government transfer payments, 190
  multiplier effect, calculating, 258
  and real GDP demanded, 242–244
net unilateral transfers, 371–372
net wealth, 181–182
net worth, 290–291
New Zealand, inflation in, 337
Nigeria, economic challenges, 126
Nixon, Richard, administration, 102
nominal GDP (gross domestic product)
  and changes in money supply, 315
  deflating, 141
  in GDP price index, 144

nominal interest rate, 170
nominal wages
  and inflation, 171
  versus real wages, 221
  wage flexibility, 229, 231–232
nondurable goods, 49, 133
nonexclusive goods, 54
nonperforming loans, 280
non-profit institutions, 52
nonrenewable resources, 3
nonrival goods, 54
Nordhaus, William, 253
normal goods, 68
normative economic statements, 10
North Korea, 41
notes, Federal Reserve, 285–287
NT (net taxes), 137–138
number of producers, impact on supply curve, 73

O

occupation, impact on unemployment rate, 157
offices, virtual, 53
officials, government, spending decisions, 56
oil, 3
online banking, 297–298
OPEC (Organization of Petroleum Exporting Countries), 102
open-market activities, 272, 298–299
operating budgets, 352
operating expenditures, 351
opportunity costs
  calculating, 28–30
  defined, 281
  of holding money, 307
  impact on production, 35–37
  and international trade, 59
  law of comparative advantage, 31–32
  of money, 264
  versus market price, 52
Organization of Petroleum Exporting Countries (OPEC), 102
organizations, tax-exempt, 52
origin (graphs), 20
other-things-constant assumption, 9
outlays, government, 189, 349. *See also* government; national debt
  in circular-flow model, 137
  government purchase function, 190
  ratio to GDP, 56
  transfer payments, 190

output
  aggregate, 96, 211, 229–235
  allocation decisions, 39
  below potential, long-run impacts, 227–228
  as component of productivity, 112
  demand for, impact on resources, 252–253
  excess, costs of, 223, 225–227
  and labor supplies, 222
  long-run costs
    average cost curves, 151–152
    diseconomies of scale, 153, 155
    economies of scale, 152–154
  long-run market adjustments
    constant-cost industries, 182
    handling decreases in demand, 181–182
    handling increases in demand, 179–181
    increasing-cost industries, 183
  loss-minimizing
    marginal analysis for, 172, 174
    producing at a loss, 171–172
    shutting down production, 174–175
  and marginal cost, 147
  minimum efficient scale, 154
  modeling production, 34
  per worker production function, 113
  potential, 222, 224, 244–246
    challenges of identifying, 328–329
  and price level changes, 222–224
  production decisions, 35, 39
  public, pricing of, 56
  recessions, and labor productivity, 120
  and specialization on, 32
  U.S. economy, 92
  versus spending plans, 201
output gaps and wage flexibility, 229, 231–232
owners
  of corporations, 50
  property rights, 39–40
  of resources, 3

P

palm dates, as money, 263
Panic of 1907, 270
paper money, 265–267
partnerships, 50
passive policy approaches
  closing contractionary gaps, 326–328
  closing expansionary gaps, 328

dependence on rules, 337
effectiveness of, 338–339
impact on economies, 326
rationale for, 338
underlying assumptions, 331–332
payments
  transfer, personal income from, 48–49
  use of money for, 267
payroll taxes, 57–58
payscales, and demand and supply, 80
pegged exchange rates, 380
pension payments, including in personal income, 150
per capita output, and standard of living, 120
per-worker production function, 113–114
performance (national economies), measuring
  circular flow approach, 132
  GDP (gross domestic product), 132
    expenditure-based GDP, 133–134, 137
    income-based GDP, 134–135, 137
  national income accounting system, 132–135, 137–139
  net domestic product, 140
  precious metal stocks, 132
  U.S. government statistics, 139–140
permanent income, 251
personal consumption expenditures, 133
personal income, 150–151
  sources of, 48–49
personal preferences, and specialization of labor, 33
Phillips, A.W., 339
  Phillips curves, 339–344
physical capital, 2, 113, 133
physical differentiation (products), 217
pirating, 287
planned aggregate expenditure
  below GDP, 202
  decreases in, impacts on economy, 205–207
  in excess of real GDP, 202
  increases in, 203–205
  and price level changes, 207–209
  and real GDP demanded, 201
planned investment
  and aggregate expenditures, 200
  decreases in. impact on economy, 205–207

and price level changes, 207–209
nonincome determinants, 187—188
versus actual investment, 200
planned spending
  changes in, 209–216
  and net exports, 215–216
  and prices, 207–209
policies, public
  fiscal policy, 55, 248–253
  industrial, 126
  laissez-faire, 247
  monetary, 55, 272
political business cycle, 253
political markets (U.S.), 55–56
politics, politicians
  and discretionary fiscal policy, 253
  and federal budgeting process, 351
  and persistence of federal deficits, 253
pollution
  impacts on GDP, 141
  as negative externality, 55
population changes
  impact on demand, 70
  and job creation, 104
portability of money, 264
positive (direct) variable relations, 22
positive economic statements, 10
positive externalities, 55
positive statements, 10
potential GDP
  and fiscal policy, 244–246
  and long-run aggregate supply, 227–235
potential output, 222–224, 328–329
PPF (production possibilities frontier)
  defined, 35
  and economic growth, 110–111
  and capital investments, 112
  importance of, as model, 37–38
PPP (purchasing power parity) theory, 378–379
precious metals, accumulation of, 92, 132
predetermined rules, and passive approaches to public policy, 337
prediction, as goal of theory, 12
president, U.S., role in budget process, 350
presidential elections, influence of fiscal policies, 253
price indexes, 141–145
price levels, 96–97
  and aggregate supply, 98
  and labor supplies, 221

impacts of fiscal policy, 245–246]
short-run, 224
long-run, 229, 231–232
base year, 96
and consumption, 182–183
at equilibrium, 98
expectations for
  and demand, 69
  and effectiveness of monetary policy, 333
  higher than expected price, 222–223
  natural rate of unemployment, 222
  lower than expected prices, 224
  and supply, 222
foreign exchange rates, 378–379
greater than expected output, 225–227
index number, 97
and lower than expected output, 227–229
and planned spending, 207–209
and purchasing power, 221, 267
and real GDP, 98, 104–105
and wage agreements, 222
prices
  alternative goods, 72
  base year for...144
  deflation...164
  disequilibrium effects, 83
  and demand, 65, 67
  equilibrium price, 75–79
  inflation, 165–168
  maximum settings for (price ceilings), 81–82
  minimum settings for (price floors), 81
  prevailing, and nominal GDP, 141
  and real income, 66
  relative, and demand, 68–69
  and scarcity of goods and services, 4
  substitution effect, 66, 115, 137–139
  and shortages, 74–75, 81
  stability of, 55, 336–337
  and supply, supply curves, 71
  tariffs and quotas, 60–61
  in GDP calculations, 141, 145–146
private goods, 54
private investment
  demand curve, 186–187
  domestic investment, gross, 133
  gross domestic investment, 184
private property rights, 39–40
privatization and growth in output per capita, 121

producers, impacts on supply, 71, 73
product markets, 4
production
  and aggregate income, 138
  aggregate supply, 98, 232–235
  below potential, long-run impacts, 227–229
  costs, 71–72
    negative, 140–144
    transaction costs, 49
  cottage industry system, 49
  decentralized, 53
  decisions about, 39
  defined, 113
  and excess output, 223, 225–227, 229
  of goods and services, decisions about, 39
  household, 52–53, 138
  modeling, 34
  PPF (production possibilities frontier), 35–37, 110–112
  and price level changes, 222–224
  production factors, 2–3
  specialization of, 32
  substitution in, 242
  and supplies, 229, 231–231
  total product, 143
  and unplanned inventory changes, 202
  versus spending, 201
production function, 113–114
production possibilities frontier (PPF), 35–37, 110–112
productivity
  and computers, 119
  defined, 112
  and division of labor, 33
  growth in
    fluctuations, 118
    during recessions, 120
  household, 52
  human capital, 116–117
  labor
    labor capital, 112–113
    and output per capita, 120
    versus labor costs, 314
  market versus command systems, 41
  measuring, 112
  rules of the game, 114
  and standards of living, 115–116
  U.S. productivity history, 117–118
products
  in circular-flow model, 4
  improvements in, exclusion from GDP calculations, 139
  new, and market disequilibrium, 83
  and production, 112

professional workers, 13–14, 157
profit
  banks, 278, 291–292
  defined, 3
  Federal Reserve notes, 300
  finance companies, 289
  formula for, 3, 50
  and investment decisions, 186
  maximizing, 50, 222–224
  seigniorage, 265
progressive taxation, 58, 248–249
property rights, 39–40
proportional taxation
  and aggregate demand-side equilibrium calculations, 258–259
  defined, 57
  and spending multiplier, 259
proprietor's income, in national income calculations, 151
pubic debt, 360
public assistance, welfare-to-work programs, 163
public capital, 363
public debt, 360–361
public goods, 40, 54–55
public policy
  active approaches, 325–326, 328–329, 331–332
  effectiveness of, 332–335
  impact on U.S. economy, 326–328
  implementation time lags, 329–330
  mergers and, 326–327
  passive approaches, 325, 331–332, 337–339
  Phillips curves, 339–344
public sector, expenditures, 358–359
purchases, market
  demand, 65
  by government, 133, 189–190, 241–242
  intermediate goods and services, 133
  open-market, impacts on money supply, 299
  role of money, 263, 267
  and specialization of products, 33–34
purchasing power
  and inflation, 171
  and price levels, 221
  purchasing power parity (PPP) theory, 378–379
  role of money, 263, 267
pure capitalism, 39–40
pure command systems, 40–41

Q

quality
  of capital, 114–115
  uniform, of money, 264–265

quantity (Q)
quantity demanded, 67
of money, 308
quantity produced, 98
quantity supplied, 72
relationship to price (demand curve), 67
Quesnay, François, 132
quotas, 60–61

R

R&D (research and development), 123–124
rates
inflation, 164
interest
and consumption, 183
and demand for investment, 185–186
and of inflation, 169–171
and net export expenditure, 191
nominal, 170
and planned investment, 188
real, 170
of labor force participation, 156
of return, and demand for investment, 184
of unemployment, 154–157, 162–163
taxes, marginal tax rate, 58
rational choice, 6–7
rational expectations
and passive policy approaches, 338–339
and policy effectiveness, 332–333
ratios, required reserves, 291
raw materials, accumulation of, 92
Reagan, Ronald, administration, 353
and inflation, 171
public policy approaches, 332
tax cut, 252
real GDP (gross domestic product), 92, 97, 199
and aggregate demand curves, 98
and aggregate supply curves, 98
at equilibrium, 98
in excess of spending plans, 202
in GDP price index, 144
and net exports, 215–216
and output per capita, 120
per capita, 105
and price levels, 104–105
relationship of output and spending, 201
relationship of spending plans and production, 202
and simple spending multiplier calculations, 205
and supply-side economics, 103

real GDP demanded
and autonomous spending changes, 216–217
and decreased planned spending, 205–207
equilibrium calculations, 258–259
and price level changes, 207–209
relationship with aggregate expenditure, 201
underlying algebra, 218–219
real GDP supplied
long-run aggregate supply, 225–227
short-run aggregate supply curve, 224
short-run impacts of excess output, 223
short-run impacts of price level changes. 222–224
real GNP (gross national product), 96
real income, 66
real interest rate, 170
real wages, 221–222
wage flexibility, 229, 231–232
realized capital gain, 51
rebounds, economic, 118
recalling currency, 287
receipts, relationship to spending, 314
recession, 92
and cyclical unemployment, 161
and decrease in money supply, 321
during the early 1990s, 252
indicators of, 96
regional impacts, 93
recognition lags, 330
relationship to spending, Japan example, 211
redistribution of income, 55
regions
specialization of labor, 33
variable and economic fluctuations, 93
regressive taxation, 58
regulation
government, of natural monopolies, 54
industrial policy, 126
in mixed economic systems, 41
relative price, 66, 68–69
relevant resources, 72
religion, impact on economic systems, 41
renewable resources, 3
rent, economic, 3
rental income, 139, 152
representative money, 266
Republicans, economic policies, 253
research, applied and basic, 123

research and development (R&D), 123–124
reserve accounts (banks)
excess reserves, 291–297
fractional reserve banking systems, 266
liquidity versus profitability, 291–292
required ratio, 266, 291, 299–300
residential construction, 133
residents, 369
residual accounts, trade balances, 372–373
resolutions, congressional, 350
resource markets, resources, 4
allocation of
under modified capitalism, 40
under pure capitalism, 39–40
under pure command system, 40–41
alternative goods, 72
buying and selling, 4
capital, 2
in circular-flow model, 4
combining, 12
complements, 251
complexity of, and input costs, 300–301
controlling, 195–197
coordinating, 152
costs of, and profit, 3
defined, 2, 4
demand for, 306–307
economic rent, 244–245
entrepreneurial ability, 3
exhaustible, 358
explicit costs, 141
fixed resources, 143
implicit costs, 141
labor, 2
and complexity of resource markets, 301–302
demand and supply, 240, 260
and discretionary fiscal policies, 251
full employment, 161–162
human capital, 113
labor force participation rate, 156
output, per capita, 120
output, potential, 222
productivity of, 112, 117–120, 225–229
supplies of, 98, 221–224, 229
and supply-side fiscal policies, 252–253
underemployment, 163
unemployment, 154–157, 160–16, 222
utility maximization, 260
versus physical capital, 113
wage agreements, 222

wage flexibility, 229, 231–232
wages, 241, 266–267
wages, real, 221
natural resources, 3
outsourcing, 304
ownership of, 3–4, 39, 48–49
permanent versus temporary price differences, 244
physical capital, 113
and production, 36–37, 112
relevant, impact on supply curves, 72
supplies
aggregate supply, 36–37, 221, 233–235
and monetary policy, 310–312
scarcity of, 2–3
time, 2
using
and absolute advantage, 32
decisions about, 39
law of comparative advantage, 32
restrictions, trade, 60
return on investments, 184
revaluation of currency, 380
revenue, 3–5. *See also* income; profits
government, from taxes, 57
rice as money, 263
rights, property, 39
risks, bank loans, 290
rival goods, 54
Roosevelt, Franklin D., 272
rules, economic
predetermined, and passive approaches to public policy, 337
and rational expectations, 338–339
rules of the game, 93, 110, 111
rules of the marketplace, 54

S

S corporations, 51
salaries. *See* income; wages
sales
and business type, 51
open-market, 299
salt as money, 263
savings, savings function
and capital investments, 112
channeling to borrowers, 289–290
in circular-flow model, 138
and disposable income, 199
formula for, 177
in GDP calculations, 137
household
expenditures for, 49
flow to financial markets, 137
life-cycle model, 183–184

marginal propensity to save, 179, 181
  slope, 181
savings banks, 269
  deposits, 287
  failures among, 275–276
scarcity
  defined, 2–3
  and demand, 65–66
  of goods and services, 3
  impact on choices, 2
scientific method, 8–10
seasonal unemployment, 160
seawater, clean, scarcity of, 4
secondary effects, 13
securities exchanges, 295–296
security concerns
  adverse supply shocks from, 234–235
  impacts on economic growth, 115
seigniorage, 265
self-correcting forces
  for closing contractionary gaps, 326–328
  for closing expansionary gaps, 328
self-employed individuals
  Social Security taxes, 58
  sole proprietorships, 50
self-interest, rational, 6
sellers, markets for, 4
serrations on coins, 265
services, 2
  allocation decisions, 39
  defined, 3
  demand for, 306–307
  final, 133
  free, 3–4
  household expenditures for, 49
  intermediate, 133
  as invisibles, 134
  markets for, 4
  per capita, and standard of living, 110
  prices, 4
  producing
    choosing production methods, 39
    choosing what to produce, 39
    transaction costs, 49
  scarcity of, 3
  in U.S. trade surpluses, 371
  versus goods, 3, 59
severance pay, 236
shares, bank, 290
shift of a demand curve, 70
shift of a supply curve, 74
short-run
  defined, 222
  equilibrium, 226
  as focus of monetary policy, 319–321

Phillips curves, 341, 343–344
supply curves, 175
  aggregate supply, 221, 224
  for firms and industries, 175
shortages, 74–75, 81
simple money multiplier, 295–296
simple spending multiplier, 205–209
simple tax multiplier, 244
size, of U.S. government, measuring, 56
skills
  as human capital, 3
  and structural unemployment, 161
  and underemployment, 163
slope of a line
  curved lines, 22–25
  demand curves, 67
  straight lines, 24
slowdowns, economic, 118
Smith, Adam, 40, 74, 100
Social Security, 387
  as cash transfer payment, 49
  cost-of-living adjustments, 172
  federal spending for, 56, 349, 351
  and income, 190
  origins of, 357
  reforming, 358
  spending on, by U.S. government, 56
  taxes for, 57–58, 150
Social Security Act (1935), 162
soft landings, 328
soil productivity, 112
sole proprietorships, 48, 50
solid waste disposal, 372–373
South Korea, per-capita production, 41
Spain
  inflation, 337
  unemployment rates, 235
specialization
  division of labor, 33–34
  and international trade, 59–60
  and need for money, 32, 49, 262–263
  opportunity costs, 31–32
speculation, in Thai currency, 382–383
speculators, 377
spending
  aggregate, 134
    and national income, 152
  autonomous
    in circular-flow model, 5
    impact on real GDP demanded, 216–217
    multiplier effects, 218
  consumer, 251
  and demand for money, 306–307

government, 349
  as fiscal policy, 55
  history of, 247–248
  and national debt, 359, 361–364
  and reductions in, 357
  and real GDP, 5, 137, 241–242; 358–359
  rationales for, 352–353
  and income distribution, 384
  and money supply, 314–315
  net exports, 134
  relationship to receipts, 314
  planned, 209–216
spending multiplier, 203–205
  airline industry example, 206–207
  factors that reduce, 259
  and fiscal policy, 247
  and net exports, 216
spending plans and programs, 201–202, 240
SRAS (short-run aggregate supply) curve, 224
SSI (Supplemental Security Income), 388
stabilizers, automatic
  income taxes, 241, 248–249
  unemployment insurance, 249
  welfare transfer payments, 249
stagflation, 102, 249, 340
standard of living
  developing countries, 116
  and government deficits, 363
  industrial market countries, 115
  measuring, 105, 110
  output per capita, 120
  variability in, 90, 115
state banks, 269
  charters, 290
states (U.S.), variability in unemployment rates, 157
statistical discrepancy account, 372–373
Steinbeck, John, 154
stock
  bank shares, 290
  money, versus income flow, 306
stock variables, 91
  defined, 263
  government debt, 103
  net wealth, 181
stocks, stockpiles
  of goods, 133
  of precious metals, 132
structural unemployment, 161
subjective factors, and demand, 65
subsidies, as industrial policy, 126
substitute resource, 69
  substitution effect of a price change, 69
sunk cost, 30–31
Super Bowl advertising costs, 64
Superfund, 371–372

supplies
  control over by monopolists, 196
  defined, 70
  equilibrium price and quantity, 75–79
  individual, 72
  loanable funds, 288
  maintaining quantities of, 304
  market, 72
  money
    checkable deposits, 285
    components, 267
    contraction of, 296–297
    counterfeit money, 286–287
    credit cards, 288
    and equilibrium interest rate, 308–309
    expansion limits, 296
    Federal Reserve regulatory tools, 272, 298–300
    M1 aggregate, 285, 288
    M2 aggregate, 287
    M3 aggregate, 287
    money multiplier, 295–296
    policy effects, 310–312, 318–321
    predicting, 315–216
  and shortages, 74
  and surpluses, 74
  versus quantity supplied, 72
supply curves (Sx)
  aggregate, 98
    the Great Depression, 99–100
    Keynesian economics, 100–101
    and stagflation, 102
    and supply-side economics, 103
  defined, 71
  foreign exchange, 376
  for labor, 221, 231–232
  for money, 314–315
  movement along versus shifts in, 74
  and output, 225–227
  perfectly competitive markets, 205
  and prices, 71
  shifts in, 72–73, 77–79
  spending multiplier effects, 259
supply schedule, 71
supply shocks, 232–235
supply-side economics, 103, 353
supply-side fiscal policies, 252–253
surpluses
  budget, 254, 356–357
  causes, 74
  economic impacts, 364–365
  defined, 74
  in foreign exchange, 373
  price effects, 75, 81
  trade, 370–371

Switzerland, inflation, 337
systems, economic
  allocation of goods and ser-
    vices, 39
  centrally planned, 40–41
  and custom and religion, 41
  defined, 39
  market systems, 40
  mixed systems, 41
  modified capitalism, 40
  modified command system, 41
  production of goods and ser-
    vices, 39
  pure capitalism, 39–40
  pure command system, 40–41

T

Taiwan, productivity, 41
tangent
  defined, 24–25
  measuring, 24
tariffs, 60
tastes, consumer, 70
taxable income, 142
  earned-income tax credit,
    388
taxes, taxation
  ability-to-pay principle, 57
  benefits-received tax principle,
    57
  on corporate income, 51
  as fiscal policy, 55, 240
    automatic stabilizers,
      248–249
    permanent income effects,
      251
    tax cuts, 241, 243, 252, 328
    tax increases, 356
  flat taxes, 258
  government revenue from, 57
  household expenditures for, 49
  and household production, 52
  on imports, 60
  on income, 248–249, 254
  increases in, effects of, 356
  as industrial policy, 126
  marginal tax rate, 58
  net (NT), 137, 199
    in aggregate demand-side
      equilibrium calculations, 258
    impact on disposable income,
      190
    impact on real GDP de-
      manded, 242–244
    multiplier effect, 258
  payroll taxes, 57
  on public goods, 55
  progressive systems, 248–249
  proportional systems, 258–259
  regressive taxation, 58
  S corporations, 51
  and supply-side economics, 103
  tax incidence, defined, 57
  tax-exempt organizations, 52

in Western Europe, 236
technical workers, unemployment
  rates, 157
technological innovation, change
  and capital, 114–115
  and growth, 111–112
  and industrial policy, 126
  and productivity, 52, 119
  research and development,
    123–124
  and structural unemployment,
    161
  and unemployment, 123
teenagers, nemployment rates,
  156–157
telecommuting, 53
terrorism
  adverse supply shocks, 234–235
  impact on economic growth,
    254
  impact on global economies,
    951
  impact on money supply, 298
  impacts on rules of the game,
    115
  spending multiplier effects,
    206–207
Thailand, currency speculation,
  382–383
Thatcher, Margaret, 120
theory, economic
  defined, 8
  goal of, 12
  role in analysis, 8
  verification or refutation of, 10
thrift institutions, thrifts, 265
timber as renewable resource, 3
time, temporal factors, *See also*
    long-run; short-run
  discretionary fiscal policy, 250
  and opportunity costs, 30
  policy-related lags, 329–330
  and rational choice, 6
  as resource, 2
time deposits, 287
time-inconsistency problem, 334
time-series graph, 20
tobacco as money, 263
token money, 265–266
trade
  and barter, 262
  role of money, 262–263, 267
trade, international, 59
  auto industry example, 60–61
  balance of payments, 59
    balance on goods and ser-
      vices, 371
    double-entry bookkeeping
      for, 369
    as flow variable, 369
    merchandise trade balance,
      369–370
    statistical discrepancy ac-
      count, 372–373

balances
  current account, 372
  factors that affect, 370
  and foreign exchange, 373
  surpluses and debits, 370
barriers, and exchange rates,.
  378
capital account, 372
currency and exchange rates,
  60
current account, 372
deficits, 196, 368, 370
  and federal budget deficits,
    355, 383
exports
  foreign exchange, 373
  merchandise trade balance, 59
  restrictions on, 60
  surpluses, 370–371, 373
  unilateral transfers, 371–372
tradition, impact on economic
  systems, 41
transaction costs, 49
  bank loans, 289–290
  barter, 262
  commodity money, 264
  defined, 74
  effects of markets on, 74
  and household production on,
    52
  and Internet on, 53
  unanticipated inflation, 167
transfer payments, 190
  as automatic stabilizer, 249
  and income redistribution, 55
  defined, 49
  personal income from, 48–49
transfers, unilateral, 371
travel industry, 207
traveler's checks, 285
Truman, Harry, on unemployment, 154

U

unanticipated inflation, 167, 172
uncertainty, 284
underemployment, 163
underground economy, 138, 163
underpricing of public output, 56
undifferentiated oligopoly, 224
unemployment
  combined with inflation, 249
  economic costs, 154
  expected, 333
  and labor supplies, 229
  measuring, 154–157
  natural rate, 222, 343
    challenges of identifying,
      328–329
    and discretionary fiscal poli-
      cies, 250
    hysteresis, 235–236
    and output, 222
  personal costs, 154

reasons for, 160–161
  and supply-side fiscal policies,
    252–253
  and technological change, 123
  unemployment benefits, 142
  versus inflation, 339–341,
    343–344
  and wage flexibility, 229,
    231–232
unemployment compensation, 49,
  162, 190
unemployment insurance, 249
unemployment rate, 387
  and age and ethnicity, 157
  changes over time, 156
  defined, 155
  international comparisons,
    162–163
  limitations, 163
  measuring, 154–156
  and occupation, 157
  regional variability, 157
unfair business practices, 54
uniform quality of money,
  264–265
unilateral transfers, 371–372
unintended consequences, 13
unit of account, 263
United Kingdom (UK)
  government outlays, 56
  interrelationship with US
    economy, 94
  output per capita, 120
United States economy. *See also*
    Federal Reserve System;
    gross domestic product
    (GDP); trade, international
  active public policy, 329–330
  body analogy, 91
  budget deficits, 352–355
  budget philosophies, 353
  budget surpluses, 356–357,
    364–365
  currency, 285–287, 300
  federal budget, 349–352,
    357–359
  federal system of government,
    55
  financial intermediaries
    banks, banking, 224–227
    depository institutions, 269
    Federal Deposit Insurance
      Corporation (FDIC), 273
    state banks, 269
  fluctuations, 92–93, 96
  foreign ownership of assets, 372
  history, 99–105
  inflation, 168, 337
  interrelationship with UK
    economy, 94
  labor productivity, 117–118
  mixed economic system, 41
  money supply control mecha-
    nisms, 298–300

output
  gaps in, 231–232
  per capita, comparisons with
    other countries, 120–121
  passive policy approaches,
    337–339
  performance statistics, 139–140
  productivity, 118–120
  public policy impacts, 325–335
  R&D expenditures, 124–125
  regional variability in unem-
    ployment rates, 157
  unemployment rates, 161–162
units of exchange, commodity
  money, 263
units of measurement, for slopes,
  22–23
unlimited liability, 50
unplanned inventory adjustments,
  200, 202
unrelated (independent) variables,
  22
unrelated goods, 69
U.S. Bureau of Engraving and
  Printing, 285
U.S. Census Bureau statistics,
  139–140
U-shaped curve, 25
utility, 47

V

value, 263, 267
value added, 134–135
value judgments, 10
variable inflation, 167–168
variables
  defined, 8
  dependent, 20, 179

economic indicators, 96
federal budget deficit, 101
flow, 91
  budget deficits, 101
  consumption and income,
    181
  functional relationships, 20
  in graphs, 20–21
  independent (unrelated), 20, 22
  line shifts, 25
  negative (inverse), 22
  positive (direct), 22
  stock variables, 91
  government debt, 103
  net wealth, 181
velocity of money, 314–316
vending machines, in Japan, 11–12
virtual offices, 53
VirtualBank, 297
Volcker, Paul, 321, 339
vote maximization and political
  spending, 56

W

wages. *See also* labor
  and aggregate supplies, 98, 224,
    229–232
  defined, 3
  increases in
    backward-bending labor sup-
      ply curves, 263
    income effect, 263
    substitution effect, 263
  and inflation, 171
  in-kind wages, 139
  international differences, 379
  and monetary policy, 310–312
  nominal, 221

personal income from, 48
price impacts, 244
and production, 225–229
real, 221
and resource supply, 240, 242
and total costs, 162
wage agreements, 221–222
Walton, Sam, Wal-Mart, 65
wants
  and scarcity of resources, 2
  versus demand and needs, 65
Wealth of Nations, The (Smith), 100
wealth, net
  impact on consumption, 181-
    182
  and real GDP, 98
welfare programs
  as automatic stabilizer, 249
  as cash transfer payment, 49,
    190
  spending on, by U.S. govern-
    ment, 56, 349
  welfare-to-work program, 163
Wells Fargo online banking services, 297
West Virginia unemployment
  rates, 159–160
Western Europe
  euro, 374
  inflation in, 168
  standards of living, 115
  unemployment rates, 162–163,
    235–236
willingness to produce, 70–71
willingness to purchase, 65
women, labor force participation
  rate, 156

work. *See* labor; resources; unemployment rates; workers
work participation programs (welfare-to-work), 396–399
workers
  discouraged, 155
  education, 116–117
  employment levels, 222
    full employment, 161–162
    participation rates, 156
  output per capita, 120
  and technological change, 123
  underemployed, 163
  unemployed, 154–163, 222
  wages, 221–222, 232
world economies, 90. *See also*
  trade, international
  money supply and inflation,
    318
World War II
  and government outlays, 56
  impact on U.S. economy, 101
  production levels, 223
  unemployment during, 156

XYZ

Zimbabwe, hyperinflation, 164
zombie banks, 275, 280